Oracle 10g Grid & Real Application Clusters

Oracle10g Grid Computing with RAC

Mike Ault
Madhu Tumma

I dedicate this book to the greater glory of God and to my wife, Susan. I also wish to dedicate this to my daughters Marie and Michelle and to Michael Bojczyk, Michelle's husband and my son-in-law.
- Mike Ault

I dedicate this book to my family and friends
- Madhu Tumma.

Oracle 10g Grid & Real Application Clusters

Oracle10g Grid Computing with RAC

By Mike Ault, Madhu Tumma

Printed in the United States of America.

Published by Rampant TechPress, Kittrell, North Carolina, USA

Oracle In-Focus Series: Book 18

Series Editor: Don Burleson

Production Manager: Linda Webb

Production Editor: Teri Wade

Cover Design: Bryan Hoff

Printing History: July 2004 for First Edition

ISBN: 0-9744355-4-6

Library of Congress Control Number: 2004101910

Table of Contents

Using the Online Code Depot

Purchase of this book provides complete access to the online code depot.

The scripts in this book are available in zip format and located at the following URL:

www.rampant.cc/grid.htm

Throughout the text, scripts in the code depot are named and called-out in a box like this:

myscript.sql

Once the code has been downloaded, it should be easy to locate and run the scripts. If technical assistance is needed in downloading or accessing the scripts, please contact Rampant TechPress at info@rampant.cc.

Get the Advanced Oracle Monitoring and Tuning Script Collection

The complete collection from Mike Ault, the world's best DBA. Packed with 590 ready-to-use Oracle scripts, this is the definitive collection for every Oracle professional DBA.

It would take many years to develop these scripts from scratch, making this download the best value in the Oracle industry.

It's only $39.95 (less than 7 cents per script!)

To buy for immediate download, go to www.rampant.cc/aultcode.htm

Conventions Used in This Book

It is critical for any technical publication to follow rigorous standards and employ consistent punctuation conventions to make the text easy to read.

However, this is not an easy task. Within Oracle, there are many types of notations that can confuse a reader. Some Oracle utilities such as STATSPACK and TKPROF are always spelled with CAPITAL letters, while Oracle parameters and procedures have varying naming conventions in the Oracle documentation.

It is also important to remember that many Oracle commands are case sensitive, and are always left in their original executable form, and never altered with italics or capitalization.

Hence, all Rampant TechPress books follow these conventions:

Parameters - All Oracle parameters will be *lowercase italics.* Exceptions to this rule are parameter arguments that are commonly capitalized (KEEP pool, TKPROF), these will be left in ALL CAPS.

Variables – All PL/SQL program variables and arguments will also remain in lowercase italics (*dbms_job, dbms_utility*).

Tables & dictionary objects – All data dictionary objects are referenced in lowercase italics (*dba_indexes, v$sql*). This includes all *v$* and *x$* views (*x$kcbcbh, v$parameter*) and dictionary views (*dba_tables, user_indexes*).

SQL – All SQL is formatted for easy use in the code depot, and all SQL is displayed in lowercase. The main SQL terms (select, from, where, group by, order by, having) will always appear on a separate line.

Program names – Programs and code depot script names are always in *lowercase italics.*

Products – All products that are known to the author are capitalized according to the vendor specifications (IBM, DBXray, etc). All names known by Rampant TechPress to be trademark names appear in this text as initial caps. References to UNIX are always made in uppercase.

Acknowledgements

I want to thank my co-author Madhu Tumma for all of his hard work on this book. It truly could not have been finished without his contributions and hard work. I would also like to acknowledge the hard work that the folks at Rampant Tech Press have put into getting this book ready. My thanks go out to Linda, John and all of the other folks who have worked hard to bring this book to light.

Mike Ault

First, I would like to thank Don Burleson for providing me the opportunity to join Mike Ault in writing this book. It was very enjoyable to work with him. He helped in reviewing and by making constructive suggestions.

I would like to thank the folks at Rampant TechPress, especially Janet Burleson, John Lavender, Andy Liles and Linda Webb. They were always there when I needed help and support.

I want to thank Kevin Closson for providing me installation details. His suggestions on the subject matter were very helpful.

I learned many things from my co-workers at Credit Suisse First Boston. Many of them directly and indirectly helped me in this indeavor. Thanks to all of them.

Finally, thanks to my family; my wife Hema and kids Sandi and Sudeep for understanding and providing me with enough time to get through this writing venture.

Madhu Tumma

Grid Computing

CHAPTER 1

"Ms. Jones, we need Oracle Grid computing to remain competitive. Please find-out what Grid computing is."

Introduction

In this chapter, some key concepts of Grid Computing and the enabling technologies being introduced by Oracle, the leading Database vendor, will be introduced.

Today, Information Technology plays a vital role in shaping and conducting businesses all over the globe. With the explosive growth of computer dependent operations for its core and competitive advantage, commercial government and non-profit organizations are quite sensitive to the changes occurring in technology and as well the economics of its use.

In the last two decades, there has been a steady growth of server technology and, at the same time, many changes in its form and architecture. Mainframes, Minis and powerful work-stations gave way to Server Clusters. Networking of computers is now reaching a new echelon with the advent of Grid Computing.

Parallel to the changes occurring in server technology space, business data accumulation has reached a new high. Structured business data stored in relational databases is the single most important asset for many enterprises. Most of the critical and non-critical operations depend on and make use of the information kept in databases. Databases have grown in size and complexity. To support large and scalable databases, the server platform and the associated storage and network technology have had to keep pace with these growing databases.

In research oriented projects, computer technology is now put to maximum use. Many varied applications such as drug discovery, operations research, electronic CAD, ecological modeling and Monte Carlo simulations are now driven by powerfully distributed computers.

Different architectures, centralized and de-centralized collaborative forms of computer infrastructure, are actively used.

Grid Computing is an emerging infrastructure that aims to provide a mechanism for sharing and coordinating the use of diverse computing resources. The word 'Grid' is used as an analogy with the electric power grid, which provides pervasive access to electricity. As Grid Computing makes long strides and impacts many organizations in the IT world with its utility-like access to computational resources, the question remains; can Grid Computing become something like the Electric Grid of the 20th century. While the state of Grid Computing is still in its infancy, there are definite signs of comparison, argues Rajkumar Buyya and Madhu Chetty.

Grid Computing is very well positioned to change the computing landscape in terms of the economics of computing. It can dramatically lower the cost of computing and extend the availability of computing resources.

As the time passes, Grid Computing, which was earlier mostly confined to research organizations and specific projects, is gradually making in-roads into commercial and business organizations. More and more IT vendors are formulating their Grid strategy and offering new solutions aimed at participating in this emerging computing era. Large IT vendors such as IBM, HP, Intel, Oracle, Sun and Dell have contributed to the growth of grid computing standards and to the realization of Grid goals and vision.

As such, this book is not about Grid Technology and Grid Concepts per se. The focus is more on Oracle's Presence in Grid Space. There are good textbooks that deal more eloquently on the vision and concept of Grid Computing. In this book, Grid Concepts and detailed accounts of Oracle provided grid-enabling technologies will be presented. Oracle's flagship grid-enabling product, Oracle Real Application Cluster (RAC), will be covered in detail. Oracle RAC is a Parallel Database server which is based on the shared disk model. Shared Disk is accessed by multiple nodes in the cluster configuration.

Oracle RAC database is an aggregation of Oracle Database Instances, thereby enhancing database computing power. This architecture provides a truly scalable and highly available framework to meet and support complex and large databases needed for the critical business and scientific operations. Oracle database instance is an accumulation of memory structures.

CPU cycles, or more appropriately the idle CPU cycles, are in demand. In addition, the CPU cycles are available in the servers, which are under-utilized. For processing a large problem in a fairly small amount of time, more CPU cycles are needed. The availability of such resources concurrently (in parallel mode) helps to compute much faster than a single server and its built-in processors.

The next important component is the availability of the data. Where is the data to process and then provide the results? The data is stored in organized and structured databases. While storage systems physically store the data blocks on media devices such as disk drives in the storage arrays, provided mostly notably by, EMC, Hitachi and IBM, the servers fetch and process in the name of relational databases.

The two important resources processing power and storage systems are the main areas of attention for grid planners and grid users.

What is Grid?

Back in 1998, Carl Kesselman and Ian Foster in the book *"The Grid: Blueprint for a New Computing Infrastructure,"* while attempting to give a broader vision of Grid, wrote:

> "A computational grid is a hardware and software infrastructure that provides dependable, consistent, pervasive, and inexpensive access to high-end computational capabilities."

Subsequently, Ian Foster with Steve Tuecke, redefined the definition stating that Grid Computing is concerned with *"coordinated source sharing and problem solving in dynamic, multi-institutional virtual organizations."* They further noted:

> "The sharing that we are concerned with is not primarily file exchange but rather direct access to computers, software, data, and other resources, as is required by a range of collaborative problem solving and resource-brokering strategies emerging in industry, science, and engineering. This sharing is, necessarily, highly controlled, with resource providers and consumers defining clearly and carefully just what is shared, who is allowed to share, and the conditions under which sharing occurs. A set of individuals and/or institutions defined by such sharing rules form what we call a virtual organization."

However, from the client, user, or consumer point of view, Grid computing is seen more of a utility of computing. Users do not care where their problem is computed or analyzed and where the data comes from. They are merely interested in getting the results, and getting it done faster and cheaper. From the server side, grid is all about the pooling resources, virtualization, and provisioning.

Simply put, Grid Computing is the pool of computers actively glued into a "virtual computer" by the other related components such as middleware software, interconnects, networking devices and storage units. It is distributed computing taken to a higher evolutionary level. With standards being worked out for the effective sharing of resources from the Grid Pool and with the proper security access levels; Grid is a new class of infrastructure.

Based on the technological changes occurring in the contemporary period, Ian Foster gives an interesting justification for developing and implementing Grid Computing. In his words:

"The annual doubling of data storage capacity, as measured in bits per unit area, has already reduced the cost of a terabyte disk farm to less than $10 000. Anticipating that the trend will continue, the designers of major physics experiments are planning petabyte data archives. Scientists who create sequences of high-resolution simulations are also planning petabyte archives.

Such large data volumes demand more from our analysis capabilities. Dramatic improvements in microprocessor performance mean that the lowly desktop or laptop is now a powerful computational engine. Nevertheless, computer power is falling behind storage. By doubling "only" every 18 months or so, computer power takes five years to increase by a single order of magnitude. Assembling the computational resources needed for large-scale analysis at a single location is becoming infeasible. The solution to these problems lies in dramatic changes taking place in networking"

Evolution of Grid

Over the last decade, Grid technologies have emerged out of research and development institutions in both academia and industry. In the early 1990's, work in meta-computing and related fields involved the development of custom solutions to Grid Computing problems. From 1997 onward, the open source Global Toolkit Version 2 (GT2) emerged as the de-facto standard for Grid Computing. GT2 initiative defined protocols, APIs and services used in grid deployments worldwide. GT2 creation was a remarkable event, as it pioneered the creation of interoperable grid systems and helped to develop many grid programming tools. Many standards evolved in due course, notably the GridFTP data transfer protocol and elements of Grid Security Infrastructure. However, these standards were neither formal nor subject to public review.

In 2002, Open Grid Services Architecture (OGSA) standard emerged as a consensus standard. This became a true community standard with multiple implementations, including OGSA based Global Tool Kit 3.0. OGSA now provides a foundation and framework wherein one can define a wide range of interoperable, portable services.

Figure 1.1 represents the gradual growth of grid technology over the years.

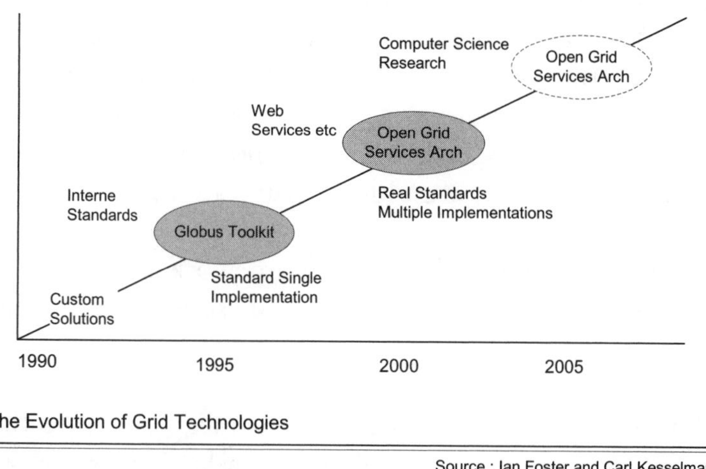

Figure 1.1: *Evolution of Grid*

Now, many researchers and industry supporters believe that the formation of OGSA technical specifications will give enough impetus for the formation of expanding the set of interoperable services and systems that address scalability issues, increased degree of virtualization, extensive sharing and increased quality services. With participation of key IT industry leaders, the grid concept is being applied toward solving more and more projects, and also there will be more sharing and virtualization in the future.

Grid and Cluster

The Grid is not a Cluster. The key distinction between clusters and grids lies mainly in the way the resources are managed. In the case of clusters, the resource allocation is performed by a centralized resource manager and all nodes cooperatively work together as a single unified resource. The result of such aggregation is to present a single system image (SSI). Clusters are generally built for a specific purpose, for instance to host a parallel database server, or for hosting an application server. In the case of Grids, each node has its own resource manager and does not aim for providing a single system view. They, in turn, provide a pool of resources for a variety of users and applications. We also notice that the autonomous resources in Grid can span across single or multiple organizations.

In a way, Grid encompasses a bigger framework and provides wider and loosely coupled aggregation of servers and other related resources.

Grid's architecture employs specialized scheduling software that identifies available resources and allocates tasks for processing accordingly. Requests for resources are processed wherever it is most efficient or wherever a specific function resides. Computers or nodes located in the grid are able to act independently without centralized control, handling requests as they are made and scheduling others. If one set of resources isn't available, they will simply use another.

Grid Goals and Objectives

Where can the Grid be used or what are the main objectives of the Grid? They can be summarized as follows:

Exploiting Under-Utilized Resources

The main attraction for using the Grid paradigm is to run an existing application on a different machine or group of machines. The machine on which the application is normally run might be unusually busy due to an unusual peak in activity. The job could be run on an idle machine elsewhere on the grid. In order for this to occur, the application must be executable remotely and without undue overhead. The remote machine must meet any special hardware, software, or resource requirements imposed by the application.

Code Depot Username = grid, Password = reader

If the applications are grid-enabled, they can be moved to under-utilized machines during such peaks. Some grid implementations can migrate the partially completed jobs. In general, a grid can provide a consistent way to balance the loads on a wider federation of resources.

Utilization of Parallel CPU Activity

Many of the modern applications are written with algorithms to exploit the CPU power across many hosts or servers. Grids with networks of multiple servers provide a very good opportunity for these parallel applications to exploit the multiple processors. A CPU intensive grid application can be thought of as a collection of many smaller sub-jobs, each executing on a different machine in the grid. To the extent that these sub-jobs do not need to communicate with each other, the more scalable the application becomes.

Virtual Computing System

Grid extends the existing distributed computing resources further into a more unified and collaborative structure. Grid also enables the heterogeneous systems to work together to form the image of a large virtual computing system offering a variety of virtual resources. The users of the grid can be organized dynamically into a number of virtual organizations, each with different policy requirements. These virtual organizations can share their resources collectively as a larger grid.

The participants and users of the grid can be members of several real and virtual organizations. The grid can help in enforcing security rules among them and implement policies, which can resolve priorities for both resources and users.

Additional Resources and Resource Balancing

In addition to CPU and Storage resources, a grid can also provide access to increased quantities of other resources and to special equipment, software, licenses, and other services. For applications that are grid enabled, the grid can offer a resource balancing effect by scheduling grid jobs on machines with low utilization as well.

This re-balance feature is quite significant for handling occasional peak loads of activity in parts of larger organizations. This can happen in two ways:

- An unexpected peak can be routed to relatively idle machines in the grid.
- If the grid is already fully utilized, the lowest priority work being performed on the grid can be temporarily suspended or even cancelled and performed again later to make room for the higher priority work.

Without a grid infrastructure, such balancing decisions are difficult to prioritize and execute. Therefore, processing the batch jobs can be achieved more quickly by spreading them across more resources.

Secure and Federated Data Access

In a large-scale distributed environment, there are many heterogeneous data sources, files, databases, XML documents and so on. Users often end up coding very complex applications to access them. The collaborative work requires that all the data is available in some uniform way. Grid can be a solution in this area as well.

There are several forces driving the progression toward the Grid Computing paradigm. Umong them are the relentless increase in microprocessor performance, and the availability, reliability, and bandwidth of global networking. New scientific experiments are producing a data explosion and the need for sharing such community data.

Grid Types

In a way, Grid Architecture is still in the evolving stage. There are many variations and types of Grids. They are often based on one's own needs and their own understanding.

There is no standard in categorization of grids. Many Research Analysts, IT vendors, and Computer scientists began classifying the grid and grid variations based their own understanding and vision. Some base it on the functionality and some base it on the architecture and some on the built-in components. Many organizations have different focuses, thus resulting in different classifications. Grid computing can be used in a variety of ways to address various kinds of application requirements. Often, grids are categorized by the type of solutions that they best address.

Again, there are no hard and fast rules or boundaries between these grid types and often grids may be a combination of two or more of these.

For example, Clubby Analytics, a research analysis organization, categorizes the Grids into four types:

Compute Grids – These are the grids designed for exploiting unused computing power or the CPU cycles. They have been in use for scientific, engineering and space research for a long time.

Information Grids – These grids are more like peer-to peer services, primarily for the purpose of collaborative computing, file sharing. These are also sometimes called "data grids", which provide standards based federated data sharing for business applications.

Service Grids – These types of Grids combine the physical elements of grid interconnection (high speed, fabric-like network interconnect) with web services program to program architecture to deliver an environment that allows different applications, running on varied operating environments, to run and interoperate.

Intelligent Grids – These grids will consist of basic grid network interconnect elements combined with systems/storage/network management hardware/software enhancements (and maybe even applications and database management capabilities) that will enable grid devices to automatically manage themselves or other devices on the network.

Looking at another example, Sun Microsystems has a different vision for Grids. They classify grids into Cluster Grids, Campus

Grids, and Global Grids. This classification is based on the geographical dispersion of the servers.

Cluster Grids - Cluster Grids consist of one or more systems working together to provide a single point of access to users. Typically owned and used by a small number of users, such as a project or department, Cluster Grids support both high-throughput and high-performance jobs. Resources in the grid can be focused on a narrow set of repetitive tasks, or made to work in true parallel fashion to execute a complex job.

Campus Grids - As capacity needs and demands for greater economy increase, organizations can combine their Cluster Grids into Campus Grids. Campus Grids enable multiple projects or departments to share computing resources in a cooperative way.

Global Grids - When application needs exceed the capacity of a Campus Grid, organizations can tap partner resources through a Global Grid. Designed to support and address the needs of multiple sites and organizations sharing resources, Global Grids provide the power of distributed resources to users anywhere in the world.

The following is IBM's spin on Grids. They define three types of Grids. The three primary types of grids are summarized below.

Computational Grid - A computational grid is focused on setting aside resources specifically for computing power. In this type of grid, most of the machines are high-performance servers.

Scavenging Grid - A scavenging grid is most commonly used with large numbers of desktop machines. Machines are scavenged for available CPU cycles and other resources. Owners of the desktop machines are usually given control over when their resources are available to participate in the grid.

Data Grid - A data grid is responsible for housing and providing access to data across multiple organizations. Users are not concerned with where this data is located as long as they have access to the data. For example, there may be two universities doing life science research, each with unique data. A data grid would allow them to share their data, manage the data, and manage security issues such as who has access to what data.

However, most researchers seem to prefer to define Girds loosely into two types: Computational Grids and Data Grids. The Computational grids are mainly focusing on the utilization of CPU cycles the so-called processing power from the under-utilized computers. There are many community projects that have been launched, and they are soliciting unused processing power from community members. In the commercial world, within the secured walls of the enterprise, there is good scope for similar exercises to pool unused resources. They all aim at harnessing and executing the jobs in parallel, and achieving higher throughput and better response times.

At the same time, another major requirement is to process, analyze and summarize huge chunks of data located in different locations and different forms. That is where the concept of Data Grid is making strides. Data Grids focus on discovering, collecting and aggregating various forms of data and presenting the data seamlessly to the users for effective processing.

There is a definite case for data and computational grids as these are the key resources, which are in high usage and demand.

Where Are We on Grid Implementation?

With the recent economic lull and with many enterprises cutting budgets, everyone is taking a serious look at the management of computing resources and looking for alternate ways to mange them more efficiently. Some enterprises are blessed with more capacity than needed; and these enterprises are evaluating their usage patterns. This is where Grid Computing is definitely becoming a relevant technology.

Many IT industry experts believe that the existing computing resource utilization requires a serious look in terms of use and availability.

It has always been a challenge for many of the enterprises to do accurate capacity planning. Capacity Planning is an elusive target, and always falls short. Grid computing direction gives them new hope and allows them to utilize all the sources as a single pool.

With the widespread availability of the commodity Intel-based servers and growth of blade servers, Grid Computing concept of virtualization is becoming an attractive proposition. Moreover, other factors like availability of storage area networks (SAN), high speed networks, such as Infiniband and Gigabit Ethernet, are able to provide a realistic and cheaper means of building a grid computing environment. Software options like Web Services and adoption of Linux and other open source technologies are helping this movement towards the virtualization of resources.

The 451 Group in its recently released report, Grids 2004: From Rocket Sciences to Business Services writes:

> ".....the grid computing developments will result commercially viable, mainframe like performance and manageability across distributed systems with in next 12 months"

The 451 group believes there is enough interest and initiative by the leading IT vendors to move Grid Computing into the commercial and business world. Commenting on the growth of the Grid environment and the role of various IT products, their report classifies the Grid related products and services vendors in broader groups. They are as follows:

Tier One Grid vendors - This is a group, which includes vendors like HP, IBM, Microsoft and Sun. These companies have strong momentum and potential to capture Grid Market Share.

Tier Two Grid Vendors - This group contains the IT companies with strong emerging strategies and technologies in Grid Computing. Vendors in this category include Computer Associates, Intel, Oracle, Platform Computing, SGI and Veritas.

Pure-play Grid Vendors - These are emerging vendors with strong presence in specific areas. These companies are further categorized by functionality - grid enablement, file systems, provisioning, application decomposition, CPU scavengers and those offering enhancements to Globus. Vendors in this category include Altair, Avaki, Axceleon, DataSynapse, Ejasent, Enigmatec, Entropia, GridFrastructure, GridIron, GridSystems, GridXpert, Powerllel, Tsunami Research, The Mind Electric and United Devices.

The last category is an interesting group of vendors, which are heavily investing in developing various software solutions that support Grid Computing and its realization. This group of vendors is also undergoing changes with active merger and acquisition activity. Bigger vendors are acquiring these smaller entities to enrich their own Grid offerings.

At the same time, there are some researchers who are very cautious. Despite the attention Grid Computing has received over the last year, according to a recent Nucleus Research survey report,

> "only 20 percent of the IT managers said that they had plans to evaluate grid computing technologies over the next six months, with most saying that more research needs to be conducted before they'll consider it. Even then, only 11 percent of the interviewees knew what problems they'd use grid computing to solve."

Therefore, it would be fair to say that while the buzz of Grid Computing is heard by many, they also feel that we are not prepared to implement readily, though we are moving steadily forward.

In a significant move, Oracle is actively getting involved and is gearing up the products, services and solutions to fit into the emerging Grid Computing arena. Oracle's addition of grid support to its application server, database, and development tools plays into the company's strategy of paving the way for the enterprise Grid Computing architecture.

Grid Today

Grid Computing is emerging as an enabling technology that helps businesses to consolidate, share, and manage IT infrastructure resources. Grid employs or follows the service oriented approach, which unifies the heterogeneous and distributed resources into a single usable resource pool. The consumers of these resources view them more as service without going into background details.

Grid Computing has already made in-roads into many key industries such as manufacturing, pharmaceuticals, financial services, analysis, seismic studies, etc. Grid solutions are being increasingly perceived as the answers for challenging computing problems.

Grid Enabling Middleware and Solutions

There are many software vendors that are actively producing software tools which enable a typical user or application to make use of the grid computing resources. IT software companies such as United Devices, Platform Computing, DataSynapse, Avaki, GridIron, Ejasent, Enigmatec and IBM have released commercial products and services to realize the dream of Grid Computing.

GridIron provides a software development kit for developers to modify code and recompile applications so they can run in Grid environments without having to use complex protocols for message passing such as MPI, PVM.

Ejasent specializes in software to solve the operations problems in server management. Ejasent (now acquired by Veritas software) offers products and solutions, which have the ability to move an application from one server to another without disrupting or terminating the application, preserving all its current settings and data, and transferring it to a different server in near real time.

United Devices provides Grid MP Enterprise, a product which is a software-based Grid Computing solution. The Grid MP product aggregates under-utilized resources -- including servers, clusters, desktops and laptops -- across a corporate enterprise. Companies can build enterprise grids that coordinate and share computing resources across departments or organizations within their firewalls to maximize the efficiency of their computing infrastructure. It also provides a single interface for management and users from anywhere within the enterprise. Application binaries for various OS platforms and data are centralized to simplify access control, versioning, and updates.

Did you know?

United Devices provides a small program called the UD Agent, which you can download from:

http://www.grid.org/download/gold/download.htm.

This allows you to become a Member of the United Devices Community. The UD Agent can recycle your PC's unused resources and use them to perform valuable scientific and medical research without disturbing your usual computer use.

Avaki specializes in providing Data Grid software. Avaki Data Grid is enterprise information integration software that simplifies provisioning, access, and integration of data from multiple, heterogeneous, distributed sources. Avaki Data Grid software creates a data service layer, which virtualizes the multiple data sources. This service layer sits between the applications and the data sources. Applications can access data via Web Services (SOAP), ODBC, JDBC, or standard file I/O.

DataSynapse offers a product called GridServer. GridServer virtualizes an enterprise's computing resources, which can be underused or intermittently available, mainframes, clusters, servers and desktops. This solution effectively decouples the applications from dedicated resources and dynamically and adaptively distributes applications over the pool of computing resources. GridServer sits between an organization's application(s) and its computing resources, managing the "demand" from applications on resources, and the "supply" of resources to the applications.

Platform Computing provides the grid-enabling software product called Platform LSF. Platform LSF is software product for managing and executing the batch workload processing for compute and data-intensive applications. With Platform LSF, the batch workload can be intelligently scheduled and completed across a distributed, virtualized IT environment. Platform LSF fully utilizes all IT resources regardless of operating system, including desktops, servers and mainframes to ensure policy-driven, prioritized service levels for always-on access to resources.

IBM is a major IT vendor who has forged many alliances with the grid software companies in providing the true Grid solutions for various commercial users. IBM's Blades Center was integrated with many grid-enabling middleware software products in providing the virtualized server platform.

Hewlett-Packard has been in the Grid forefront by providing the UDC (Utility Data Center) that simplifies the infrastructure management by virtualization of servers, storage, networks, and applications in the data center. Resources need only be physically wired into the HP UDC once; thereafter, the HP UDC logically assigns the resources to different services as needed.

Grid - Is It Disruptive Technology?

Many believe Grid Computing has the potential to disrupt technology and is capable of dramatically changing the computing landscape. Grid Computing represents a paradigm shift that will provide the next big boost in corporate productivity since the internet and web.

A report, by Grid Technology Partners, says

> "Grid computing also passes the three-point Christensen Disruptive Technology test - being inexpensive, technologically simple and a technology that doesn't require replacement of

existing systems. Disruptive technologies have the potential to substantially change the competitive landscape"

Oracle and Grid Computing

Oracle, a premier provider of database management systems, should be a natural leader to provide some kind of Data Grid. When 'Data Grid' is heard, it is normally understood as the provision of grid focusing and unifying various data sources. At present, some pure play vendors such as Avaki and DataSynapse are in the forefront, providing grid middleware that unifies various data sources.

While the leading hardware vendors like IBM, HP and Sun etc., are working with pure play grid solution providers through active partnership, Oracle is gearing up and transforming its entire product line to make them grid-ready or grid-enabled. It is trying to position itself as the leading software player for grid technology. It is worth noting what Tabb Group says about Oracle in Grid Space:

> "......while naturally starting in the data grid space, Oracle is actively enhancing their product suite to be grid compliant and has recently re-branded their whole product line with a 'g' representing grid enabled. This is the first significant re-branding of its technology since embrace of the Internet when it added an 'I' to its suite"

Similar comments were conveyed when Bob Evans, editor of *Information Week*, wrote last year,

> "Oracle itself is remarkably bullish on the technology--so much so that it's shifting the letter used in the names of its database products from "i" (e.g., Oracle 8i, 9i, etc.) to "g" in the forthcoming

release of 10g. That naming convention shouldn't be taken to mean more than it's supposed to; on the other hand, Oracle didn't make this decision lightly."

Frederick Limp, a professor in the Geosciences and Environmental Dynamics department at the University of Arkansas, added this enthusiastic perspective:

"When Oracle got behind grid, I thought it was like the move from Mosaic to Netscape." And the result, he said, is that grid computing has reached a "tipping point of acceptance" among large organizations whose databases must handle huge files from disparate sources and whose underlying architectures must be secure, scalable, and increasingly cost-effective."

Oracle's commitment to actively support Grid Computing is a solid one. The decision by Oracle to add grid-enabling components to its latest database release has definitely given a new sense and support for Grid campaign in the IT industry.

Oracle's Approach to Grid

Even though the idea of Grid is something that encompasses many organizations, technologies, resources and locations, many IT vendors tend to define and make it more practical for implementation. As the concept of Grid is somewhat broad and amorphous, many organizations tend to define according their vision and needs. In the same way, Oracle would like to confine Grid Computing within an enterprise. At present, they seem to be more focused on unified management of a variety of computer resources.

According to Chuck Phillips, Executive Vice President of Oracle Corporation:

> "Grid Computing is coordinated use of many small servers acting as one large computer."

The following is a look at Oracle's vision of the scope and sizing of Grid.

Oracle's approach seems to be limited to organization. They are not referring to a multi-organization, multi-location approach. It probably boils down to aggregation of smaller servers into a Large Computing Resource; in other words, it is more like Oracle Clusters. In turn, these large flexible clusters become the building blocks for an organization's Grid Environment. Oracle's key technologies such Oracle Real Application Clusters, Oracle Streams, Automatic Storage Management, Grid Control Utility and Oracle Transportable Tablespace are being positioned for building the Grid Infrastructure.

What Is Data Grid?

Can Oracle Database 10g fit the definition of Data Grid?

In general, the term Data Grid represents a bigger scope and broader definition. Data Grid usually refers to the access and management of all the data needs for all the applications and users. Typically, any organization has any number of data stores, which may be in relational databases, files, XML and other related sources, and often embedded in different departments and sections. Data Grid, as understood by many researchers and industry experts, is something that deals with aggregation of multiple data sources and provides a uniform view of various data sources.

As noted earlier, good examples of such vendors would be those such as Avaki and DataSynapse. These IT vendors have offered the middleware that unifies various data sources. Data grids focus on providing seamless access to data. Typically called Data Virtualization, data grid providers create a layer of abstraction between firms' databases and their users and applications.

Now the question arises, can the Oracle Database be viewed as a Data Grid? Oracle database is only providing one of such resources; no doubt, there are heterogeneous gateways to make transparent access to non-Oracle databases, and even then it can be construed as uniform data source.

What Oracle is trying to do here in the Grid Environment is not the projection of a Data Grid, but the attempt to leverage the Grid Computing infrastructure to host and manage the Oracle Database system.

Many of the well-known and minor features of Oracle's database products are enhanced with a view to participate actively in the Grid Architecture. For example, easier data transfers using data pump, oracle data files transfers among different operating systems, quicker and easier software installation, new replication and messaging methods using the streams technology, and so on, are the new features Oracle has emphasized. Oracle Streams-based replication and messaging, which was offered first in 9i database release, is improved with the new features in 10g database release. Interoperability with other relational databases, with appropriate heterogonous gateways, and significant support for XML and active support for commodity Linux operating system, etc., are aimed to integrate better with Grid Computing era.

Enhancements in Application Server and Real Application Cluster product are particularly aimed at providing power components for enterprise Grid infrastructure. Moreover, Oracle is the only database vendor to release a true and practical, and grid compliant utility called Grid Control. Grid Control is well designed to manage besides the databases, the web applications, the application servers and hosts of different operating systems. Grid control provides a bird's eye view of all resources.

There are many believers in *10g Grid Vision* as can be surmised from the remark made by Jamie Shiers, Database Group Leader CERN,

> "With Oracle Database 10g's focus on grid computing, we hope to ease deployment, management and clustering of data for our world-wide computing grid project."

Oracle's Vision of Grid Computing revolves around three basic components. They are as follows:

- **Application Server Grid** - Oracle Application Server 10g has been specifically designed to run enterprise applications on computing grids. Application Server can easily run on pools of low cost servers and storage with very high performance, scalability, and availability.
- **Database Server Grid** – The 10g Database product has been enhanced to support and to run on large-scale, low cost commodity clusters. The database product has been enriched with many features that directly and indirectly help achieve accumulation of large structured data volumes and run smoothly on the grid environment. It takes advantage of the virtualized resources such as processors and storage components. The provisioning methodology that comes with virtualized hardware setup is very well aligned with the Real Application Cluster Database. The policy-based use of the

nodes (blades or servers) is built into the Oracle 10g RAC database.

- **Storage Management Grid** – With 10g database, now it becomes possible to manage the storage units in a more efficient way. In addition to the SAN and NAS technologies that provide the cost effective storage resources for the use of the databases, Oracle 10g has the capability to manage all the allocated storage disks as a single pool for the use of stand alone or clustered databases. It views the entire storage disks as a virtualized pool of disks and uses it appropriately for various purposes. This method of storage management is termed as Oracle ASM (automatic storage management)

Oracle 10g – The Database for the Grid

Oracle 10g Database, 10g Application Server, Automatic Storage Management capability and 10g Grid Control Utility together provide an integrated environment for building Grid Architecture.

The Oracle Database is a consumer of grid resources, such as the computing resources (aka. servers), storage units and provider of the data resources for the application users. It is capable of managing and provisioning the cluster and storage resources to different databases running in the grid environment.

Oracle 10g database has many new and innovative features facilitating for the setting up of multiple databases in a clustered environment and non-clustered grid environment. It has the advantage of leveraging the underlying grid infrastructure components and manages them efficiently. The grid components, such as low cost servers or blades, powerful interconnect and storage arrays are very well utilized by the Oracle 10g database.

Grid Enabling Components

Oracle 10g Database comes equipped with many grid-enabling technologies and they are examined in the following sections.

Automatic Storage Management (ASM)

ASM simplifies the storage requirements needed to support the database. It provides data provisioning methods. As the demand for data arises, new disk devices can be added dynamically. Within a specific disk group, Oracle automatically allocates the storage, creates, and deletes the data files as needed. The detection of hot spots and I/O balancing functions are managed by the ASM methodology, thereby lessening the manual intervention by DBA and SA. ASM also offers the benefit of the RAID and logical volume functionality.

Oracle is capable of reassigning disks from one node to another and from one cluster to another. Oracle can also balance the I/O activity from multiple databases across all of the devices in disk group. It can also implement striping and mirroring methodology to improve the I/O performance.

The capacity to manage the storage supporting the database enables optimum utilization of the storage resources. Storage can be assigned when needed and can be removed when it is not needed. This gives a true Grid-Friendly functionality.

Portable Clusterware

Cluster software is the software stack that defines, configures, and manages the cluster members or the cluster nodes. Cluster software, sometimes called the cluster manager, keeps track of the health of the nodes and communicates with cluster database system. In order to provide a uniform cluster software stack across many operating systems and platforms, Oracle has introduced portable clusterware to support the Oracle Real Application Cluster. This avoids purchase, install, and configuration of third-party cluster vendor.

By supplying uniform, standard, and integrated cluster software, cluster vendor imposed limitations such as the number of nodes and using a particular type of interconnect technology, are avoided. Now Oracle RAC implementations will have a common look and feel even if they are implemented on different operating systems and different server hardware.

Support for Infiniband Interconnect

Any large scale implementation of Oracle RAC involving a large set of nodes has to depend on a reliable, low latency and high bandwidth interconnect. The architecture also requires having redundant switches to support large interconnect connections.

With the support for Infiniband interconnect and I/O connectivity technology, Oracle 10g is able to get better performance and scalability. With the support and availability of Infiniband for Oracle database and Oracle RAC Clusters, client to server, server to server, and server to storage communication achieve higher throughput and reduced bottlenecks.

Oracle Real Application Cluster

Oracle Real Application Cluster utilizes the commodity style servers or blades to provide a scalable and high performing database computing resource. Highly available and scalable Oracle RAC database becomes the main building blocks for large Data Grids for consolidating and processing large volume of the corporate data. With its shared storage model, and with multiple instances, RAC database can scale well and meet the challenge of uneven database processing loads. Oracle RAC is well suited for the provisioning of blades or servers as the need arises.

Oracle RAC also offers automatic workload management for services within a RAC a database. RAC can automatically load-balance connections as they are made across instances hosting a service. It is relatively easy to add and subtract instances or blade servers into the cluster.

The bulk of the material in this book is focused on Oracle RAC.

Oracle Database Resonance

Resources are dynamically expanded when needed and shrunk when not needed or when priority tasks are in need of those resources. Database Resonance is the provisioning utility for the Oracle RAC.

Through the database resonance utility, it becomes possible for the administrators to define and configure the policy-based CPU provisioning (in terms of nodes) and capacity on demand with automatic load balancing. DBA(s) can define the services-level policies based on CPU utilization or service response times and also set up priority of each database. Oracle automatically starts and stops the additional instances to meet service-level policies

Oracle Job Scheduler

This new tool allows the creation of jobs and schedules. Then you can assign the jobs with appropriate schedules. Oracle scheduler provides many advanced capabilities to schedule and perform business and IT tasks in the enterprise grid.

Jobs can be grouped in job classes, and suitable priority can be assigned to these groups, which affect all the jobs under a group.

Using the Oracle Resource Manager, resource plans can be designed and assigned to the job classes.

Oracle Database Resource Manager

Resource Manager provisions resources to database users, or services within an Oracle database. It allows the database administrators to limit the database resources allocated to Grid Users, Applications, or Services. By using resource manager wisely, you can ensure that each grid user, grid application, or service gets its fair share of the available computing resources.

Data Provisioning

In a multiple database scenario in the grid architecture, data may need to be moved from one database to another. In the case where all the database or data resources cannot be consolidated or pooled, active data sharing can be utilized by moving data from over-utilized databases to under-utilized databases. Sometimes the target database may be put to use for a particular purpose or particular department.

In order for the most optimum and efficient data transfers to occur, Oracle provides many new features like Oracle Streams, Transportable Tablespaces, Oracle data pump, distributed SQL support, distributed transactions, and gateways.

Transportable Tablespace

When database resources cannot be consolidated, database systems will tend to grow in different geographical locations and in different departments and often different operating systems or platforms. In such cases, Oracle Transportable Tablespaces offers an efficient way of sharing large subsets of data and then sharing the processing on this data on different hardware resources. This is a key requirement for effective grid-enable architecture.

Transportable Tablespaces give the grid users a very fast and efficient mechanism to move large data from one database system to another. Another feature that is particularly useful for large enterprises is the facility of mounting read-only tablespace by two or more databases.

Oracle Streams

In a Grid environment, different sets of user applications access a variety of databases, sometime located locally and sometimes situated at a remote location. Instead of going for remote database access, processing of the same data at a locally situated database server makes much more sense in terms of logistics and performance. Instead of accessing or sharing a remote database, maintenance of a local data copy becomes more desirable. Oracle Streams help to replicate or to duplicate the databases to different locations.

Oracle Streams provide a comprehensive and integrated framework for data and information sharing. It combines the replication of data, messaging queues, event management, data loading and notification mechanism into one integrated product and methodology. Oracle Streams help in setting up and synchronizing multiple data sources within the grid environment very efficiently. The data movements can be real-time or can be scheduled as needed. The changes are captured by way of redo log hot mining and propagated to the destination database. Oracle Streams is a key component in creating and maintaining multiple data sources within the grid.

Oracle Data Pump

Oracle Data pump provides an integrated tool to move the data among the database systems. Data pump is a high speed, parallel infrastructure that enables data and metadata to be quickly moved to another database. Data pump export and data pump imports are the enhanced versions of the original export and import tools.

Managing Grid Using Grid Control (OEM)

Grid Control is a utility that manages and monitors many diverse resources within the enterprise grid. Such resources include, Database Systems, Hosts (blades/servers), application servers, web applications, and storage devices. It is also extendible so that extra components that are not supported out of the box can be added. From a single place, Grid control allows the comparison of performance levels of various comparable resources.

Grid Control can do the day-to-day management or administration on all these controlled resources. As the performance metrics are analyzed in certain time frames, the inter-relations between the related resources can be easily understood, which leads to better problem solutions. Grid administration is covered in more detail in Chapter 11, *Grid Administration using the Grid-Control Utility*. Chapter 17 covers Grid-Enabling technologies such as Transportable Tablespaces, Oracle Streams, Scheduler and Data pump.

Oracle Globus Tool Kit

Oracle is also actively participating in open source community efforts, working with Global Grid Forum to help define grid standards. Oracle has developed Globus extensions and they are available as the Oracle Globus Toolkit. The Globus Toolkit is a set of useful components that can be used to build Grid applications. The Globus Toolkit is the de facto standard for doing Grid computing among early Grid adopters. Oracle GDK (OGDK) includes the Globus Toolkit and additional Oracle components to deliver an integrated product ready to use. The first version of Oracle GDK implements an open source, or reference version, of the APIs of the Globus Toolkit mapped to Oracle APIs. Grid application developers can use these components using their C APIs or command-line tools. Some key components of the Globus toolkit include:

Globus Resource Allocation Manager (GRAM) - GRAM provides resource allocation and process creation, monitoring, and management services. GRAM implementations map requests expressed in a Resource Specification Language (RSL) into commands understood by local schedulers and computers.

Grid Security Infrastructure (GSI): GSI provides a single-sign-on, run-anywhere authentication service, with support for local control of access rights and mappings from global to local user identities.

Monitoring and Discovery Service (MDS): This service provides a uniform framework for providing and accessing system configuration and status information, such as compute server configuration, network status, or the locations of replicated datasets. MDS is an extensible Grid information service that combines data discovery mechanisms with the Lightweight Directory Access Protocol (LDAP). MDS has two components: Grid Index Information Service (GIIS) and Grid resource information service (GRIS). GIIS provides aggregate information about a set of resources. GRIS provides information about an individual resource.

Global Access to Secondary Storage (GASS): GASS implements a variety of automatic and programmer-managed data movement and data access strategies, enabling programs running at remote locations to read and write local data.

Oracle Real Application Cluster

Oracle has been a leading relational database vendor for over two decades. They have been very responsive in meeting the ever-rising data needs of enterprises. Oracle has implemented many innovative, practical and useful features in their database systems. Oracle Database has been the leading choice for many large database systems. Oracle's Parallel Database systems are particularly suitable for complex database processing, and for providing high availability and scalability needs.

The Explosive Growth of Business Data

The need for high quality business data is exploding. In the mid-eighties databases much larger than a couple of gigabytes were rare and qualified as very large databases (VLDB). Now, normal databases are in the multi-gigabyte range and the VLDB domain doesn't start until the terabyte range, with petabyte databases on the horizon.

In traditional sectors of the business market, new needs drive the requirement for more data. Data warehouses provide access to historical sales, production, and cost information allowing detailed analysis of trends and more accurate predictions of future growth and sales. New business sectors such as wireless data are experiencing explosive growth, with the number of wireless data users predicted to grow to at least 24 million by the end of 2003 (Source: VB.NET Advisor Zone, Enterprise Business to Drive Wireless Data Market Growth). The tracking of usage data in telephone, cell phone, and wireless industries creates millions of new records in a day's time. In traditional business sectors such as the paper industry, the product is tracked from manufacture - how many board feet of lumber or how many tons of pulp are obtained from each tree, to endpoint – which truck delivered which order at what time, to sales – how profitable was the wallboard segment in relationship to manufacturing plant "A". All of this is business data and it is growing at an explosive rate in all business segments.

Business Data = Corporate Asset

The events of September 11, 2001 underscored the importance of treating corporate data as a critical company asset. Many companies experienced set backs to business operations because they lost not just personnel, but all of their corporate data when the World Trade Center was destroyed. Protecting business data and ensuring that it is always available has become a paramount issue in the modern world.

In too many companies corporate data resides in data islands or, if you prefer, stovepipes. These isolated data segments serve the needs of a limited number of personnel and may have the most up-to-date information or contain information that is woefully out-of-date. Other companies may have a consolidated database system, but they are poorly designed, inadequately maintained, and difficult to use.

In order to provide value to a business, data must be both available and timely. To be available, the database must be properly designed and maintained. For data to be timely, it must be clean, consistent, and well organized.

Modern database systems offer the means to provide both availability and timeliness for business data. Oracle offers the Real Application Clustering Technology (RAC) that will ensure that business data can be placed in its most accessible form, maintained in its most timely state, and provide nearly 100% availability.

Online and Real-Time Access to Corporate Data

In order to achieve online and real-time access, the data must be available on high-speed access devices. High-speed access devices translate into multiple fast-access disk drives (10,000 to 15,000 RPM low latency disk drives), connected by high-speed bus technology to computers capable of handling complex operations.

Today's high-speed disks and computers more than match these requirements. With CPU speeds nearing 4 gigahertz and internal bus speeds of 400 megahertz, the limiting factor in many systems is the design of the database and its queries, not the underlying technology.

In order to provide online and real-time access to corporate data, companies must eliminate single points of failure in their computer architecture and in their computer support staffing. Companies should ask themselves if there is anyone in the support staff who is irreplaceable. If so, they need to begin training their replacement as soon as possible.

Oracle RAC technology provides a scalable answer to real-time and online access to data, by increasing the amount of resources, which can be applied to a problem, and eliminating single points of failure in corporate databases. This book will reveal how, with proper planning and resource utilization, there should never be a problem with online and real-time access to a database again.

Oracle's Cluster Technology

Oracle has had the ability to run in parallel server mode since version 6.2. In Oracle parallel server mode, two or more Oracle instances share a single set of database files. An instance of Oracle is comprised of the executable image, background processes, control files, instance-specific initialization files, redo log threads, and a set of either shared or private rollback or undo segments. A shared database consists of the data files that make up all tablespaces in the database.

Until later versions of Oracle8i, a shared Oracle database system had to use a laborious process of copying blocks into and out of memory, and to and from disks, in order to share information in a single block between the multiple instances. This complex sharing mechanism resulted in performance issues if the database didn't utilize some kind of application partitioning, data partitioning, and localized use. Oracle 9i Real Application Clusters (RAC) relieved DBA(s) and designers from these limitations and problems. Now the 10g RAC extends the benefits of the RAC system and integrates well with enterprise grid enterprises. 10g RAC database focuses more on the service-oriented approach towards the client usage. Workload management has been streamlined for efficient use of the RAC database.

Using the Oracle Cache Fusion architecture, the RAC architecture provides two critical functions:

- True scalability
- Enhanced reliability

RAC allows the DBA true transparent scalability. In order to increase the number of servers in most architecture, including Oracle's previous OPS, data and application changes were required, in many cases, to prevent performance from actually deteriorating. With RAC, the following advantages exist:

- All Applications Scale – No tuning is required
- No Physical Data Partitioning is required
- ISV Applications Scale out of the box

This automatic, transparent scaling is due almost entirely to RAC's cache fusion and the unique parallel architecture of RAC implementation on Oracle9i. Since the processing of requests is spread across the RAC instances evenly, and all instances access a single database image instead of multiple images, the addition of a server or servers requires no architecture changes, no re-mapping of data, and no recoding. In addition, the failure of a single node results only in the loss of scalability.

What Is RAC Database?

Oracle RAC database system involves a configuration of multiple hosts or servers joined together with clustering software and accessing the shared disk storage structures. On each of the hosts in the cluster, an Oracle Database instance is launched that uses the shared storage structures to provide the logical database objects. Thus, the multiple database instances provide a common database access for the users. Users can access the same database from any of the instances. Table 1.1 summarizes the main features of the single instance stand-alone database and the multi-instances parallel data which is also called the RAC database.

SINGLE INSTANCE DATABASE	MULTI-INSTANCE RAC DATABASE
Only one instance to access and process database requests	Multiple Instances accessing same database.
One set of data files, redo files, undo and control files etc.	One set of Data Files and Control Files, but separate Redo Log files and undo for each instance
Locking and Concurrency Maintenance is confined to one instance	Locking and Concurrency Maintenance is extended to multiple instances
Dedicated Storage Structures for the instance	Multiple instances access the same shared storage structures
Weak on High Availability and Scalability	Provides HA and Scalability Solution

Table 1.1: *Stand alone single Instance v/s Multi-Instance RAC Database*

A RAC System, by providing multiple instances (i.e., hosts and its associated resources) access the same database, creates multiple database computing centers and extends high availability and scalability.

A RAC Cluster database uses a SAN or other network storage device as a Shared System Disk. A RAC system must use a cluster file system or a raw partition, where any server can read or write to any disk in the shared disk subsystem. This allows access to all data files, control files, and redo and rollback (undo) areas by any instance. This ability to access all disks, allows instance recovery after an instance failure has occurred. All surviving nodes automatically absorb the failed instance's tasks until the failed instance is brought back online, at which time it is fully synchronized and restored to service automatically.

A RAC cluster provides for automatic shared execution of Oracle applications. This means that for any Oracle instance application, all queries and other processing are automatically shared among all of the servers in the RAC cluster.

The sharing of application processing by all servers in the RAC cluster leads to automatic load balancing across all cluster members. The ability of a RAC cluster to provide shared application execution and automatic load balancing, leads to the true scalability of applications without code or data changes.

Before RAC

Even though Oracle introduced Oracle Parallel Server (OPS) option with version 6.2, the real usage began with version 7. The Version 7.34 OPS was generally a stable product, but needed lots of application planning and partitioned usage.

The biggest performance robber in the OPS architecture was the DB block ping. A DB block ping would occur when an instance participating in an OPS database had a block in its cache that another participating instance required. In OPS, if another instance required the block in the cache of a second instance, the block would have to be written out to disk, the locks transferred, and then the block re-read into the requesting instance.

With OPS, scalability was always an issue. OPS implementations used to suffer from tedious application design and coding, database management issues. There were many performance issues reported. OPS lacked good tools for management, which caused frustration among DBAs and application users.

Oracle 8i OPS implementation brought in many significant changes. The significant new feature was the introduction of Cache Fusion technology. Cache Fusion is a concept where Cache (or SGA) from the multiple instances coordinate the buffers (or cache) and manage the database access.

Oracle 8i (OPS) introduced the initial phase of cache fusion. The data blocks were transferred from the SGA of one instance to the SGA of another instance without the need to write the blocks to disk. This was aimed at reducing the *ping* overhead of data blocks. However, the partial implementation of cache fusion in Oracle 8i could help only in certain conditions.

With 9i RAC

With full implementation of Cache Fusion technology, the Oracle 9i RAC achieved scalable and reliable parallel database status. RAC has removed many management issues and simplified installation procedures. Support for the cluster file system, in addition to the raw devices for the shared disk structures have simplified the physical storage administration. Oracle Enterprise

Manager has been made cluster-aware, and thus helps to better administer the RAC database.

Oracle 9i RAC has revamped the Oracle Parallel Server product and the OPS were aptly renamed as Real Application Cluster, hinting at the true parallel cluster. Table 1.2 summarizes the changes that occurred and new terminology used for RAC system.

ORACLE PARALLEL SERVER	RAC DATABASE SYSTEM
Block Pinging for synchronization	Uses Cache transfers using the private interconnect
Uses the PCM locking technology	New Methodology using the Global Cache Services (GCS)
Uses Non PCM Locking	New Methodology using the Global Enqueue Service (GES)
Lock Mastering	Resource Mastering – Locks are treated as resources
Lock Database	Global Resource Directory
OPFS – Oracle Parallel Fail Safe	RAC Guard product
Fixed, Hashed Locks	Obsolete (mutually exclusive with Cache Fusion)
Parallel Cache management	GCS Block requests
Block Server Process (BSP)	GCS process (LMSn)
Manage by OPSCTL	Manage by SRVCTL
OPS Daemon	G.S.D
DLM (distributed lock manager)	Functionality is bundled under GCS and GES

Table 1.2 *Oracle Parallel Server and RAC terminology compared*

Oracle 10g RAC Database

The 10g Oracle version has brought in many new and innovative features. The most significant improvements in the 10g Oracle RAC are as follows:

- New concept of Service Registration aiming at helping high availability from the application point of view.
- Cluster Ready Service (CRS) – This is the portable clusterware Oracle had been promising for a long time. Then there is Oracle Cluster Registry (OCR) for maintaining the configuration information.
- Enhancements regarding tools supporting RAC administration – DBCA, SRVCTL, DBUA and Enterprise Manager.
- Virtual IP Configuration for a better high availability configuration for the application access.
- Limited Rolling upgrade with *opatch* tool.
- Better Workload Management and alignment with Oracle Database Resonance Utility with dynamic provision of the nodes in the cluster
- Web-based Enterprise Manager Database Control with which you can manage a RAC database and Enterprise Manager Grid Control for administering multiple RAC databases.
- The Automatic Workload Repository (AWR) to track the performance metrics and provide advice and alerts.

RAC database architecture, installation and configuration, internals of cache fusion, RAC Tuning, backup and recovery etc. will be covered in subsequent chapters.

Conclusion

In this chapter, the concept of Grid Computing and where the grid is heading has been examined. Grid Computing Technology, once confined to scientific and research institutions, is gradually moving into commercial organizations. Many IT vendors are designing Grid Solutions, even though they are at different levels and market segments.

Oracle, the premier database and business applications vendor, released the grid-ready 10g database. Besides offering many features that help to participate in grid architecture, the Oracle RAC product is being positioned as the one main grid resource.

RAC and OPS product evolution and features have also been introduced.

In the next chapter, more details about Grid, Utility Computing, and Clustering Technology will be explored.

Utility Computing and Clusters

CHAPTER 2

"Oops … Am I in Grid now?"

Understanding Grid

There is always a lingering doubt in everyone's mind as to what Grid is exactly and how it differs from other well known architectures such as Cluster and P2P architectures. In this chapter, the true nature of Grid and Clustering architectures will be highlighted.

There is a somewhat hazy notion and understanding of Grid and the types of Grids among many IT technologists. Sometimes they do not find a clear demarcation between grids and other related technologies like clusters. Those differences between the Clusters and Grid will be examined.

Another thing that often needs explanation is the concept of On-Demand and Utility Computing Model, which is often termed as Grid Computing. The *on-demand* and *utility* computing buzzwords will be explored as well.

The Clustering of Servers has been around for about two decades and it is one of the most widely understood, being deployed in scientific, research and commercial worlds. DBAs are well versed with the concept of aggregating the servers, and view them as the single system image (SSI). Now, with the gradual adoption of grid technologies, one often wonders if grid works with clusters or if it replaces the clustering. How does grid change the whole perspective of the sharing of the servers?

The Nature of Grid

Grid Computing is an emerging infrastructure that aims at providing a mechanism for sharing and coordinating the use of diverse computing resources. The word Grid is often used as an analogy with the electric power grid, which provides access to electricity.

As Grid Computing makes long strides and impacts many organizations in the IT world with its utility-like access to computational resources, a question remains in everyone's mind if Grid Computing can become similar to the Electric Power Grid of the 20th century. While the state of Grid Computing is still in its infancy, there are definite signs of similarities according to Rajkumar Buyya and Madhu Chetty, the researchers from University of Melbourne, Australia.

As seen in Table 2.1, there are many apparent similarities in the electric power grid infrastructure and computational grid structure. However, the computational grid is more varied and more complex than an electric grid. The existence of hardware components and user specific software components and applications make all the difference. Nevertheless, the comparison is worth noting.

PARAMETER	ELECTRICAL POWER GRID	COMPUTATIONAL POWER GRID
Resources	Heterogeneous: thermal, hydro, wind, solar, nuclear, others	PCs, workstations, clusters, and others; driven by different operating and management systems
Network	Transmission lines, underground cables. Various sophisticated schemes for line protection.	Internet is the carrier for connecting distributed resources, load, and so on.
Analogous quantities	Bus Energy transmission Voltage	Node Computational transmission Bandwidth
Power source	Power station (turbo generators, hydro generators), windmill	Grid resource (computers, data sources, Web services, databases)
Load type	Heterogeneous application devices: for example, mechanical energy for fans electricity for TVs, heat for irons	Heterogeneous applications: for example, graphics for multimedia applications, problem solving for scientific or engineering applications
Security / safety	Fuses, circuit breakers, and so on	Firewalls, public-key infrastructure, and PKI-based grid security
Storage	Only storage for low-power DC using batteries.	No storage of computational power is possible.
Automated accounting	Advanced metering and accounting mechanisms are in place	Local resource management systems support accounting. Resource brokers can meter resource consumption

PARAMETER	ELECTRICAL POWER GRID	COMPUTATIONAL POWER GRID
Standards body	Many standardization bodies exist for various components, devices, system operation, and so on. (For example, the IEEE publishes standards on transformers, harmonics, and so on.)	Forums such as Global Grid Forum and the P2P Working Group promote community practices. The IETF and W3C handle Internet and Web standardization issues.

Source: Rajkumar Buyya and Madhu Chetty

Table 2.1 *Electrical and computational Power grids: A comparison.*

With sudden interest in the grid and grid-related technology, many IT vendors and analysts are creating their own vision, definition, and solutions in the grid space. Grids have moved from the obscurely academic to the highly popular. We read about Compute Grids, Data Grids, Science Grids, Access Grids, Knowledge Grids, Bio Grids, Sensor Grids, Cluster Grids, Campus Grids, Tera Grids, and Commodity Grids as proposed by various IT companies and researchers. There are so many flavors and variations, based on the functionality and sometimes based on the understanding. Many IT vendors freely term their solutions as Grid technologies and try to fit them into some category.

The following is a quote from Ian Foster:

> "Ultimately the Grid must be evaluated in terms of the applications, business value, and scientific results that it delivers, not its architecture. Nevertheless, the questions above must be answered if Grid computing is to obtain the credibility and focus that it needs to grow and prosper."

Here is Ian Foster's 3-point checklist for a grid computer:

Coordination of Distributed Resources - Grid controls and integrates different resources and users within different control domains – for example desktops versus large computers, different units of the same enterprise, and different enterprises. It also addresses the issues of security, policy, membership, and payment.

Using Standard Pen, General Purpose Protocols, and Interfaces - Grid Computing is based on various protocols and interfaces. These protocols and interfaces control the authentication, resource discovery, and resource access.

Quality of Service - Grid aims at delivering at non-trivial quality services in terms of response time, throughput, availability and security. This is the motivation for the community to move towards the grid-computing era and meet the ever-increasing user core application demands. Grid computing becomes more of a utility from the user's perspective.

Ian Foster's 3-point checklist provides a broad guideline. With these definitions in mind, many IT vendors are coming up with varied Grid Architecture solutions. At the same time, some vendors are pitching their cluster solutions. This happens because the clustering or sharing servers concept and clustering solutions loosely fit into the broader sense of grid architecture.

Grid Architecture

At a very high level, Grid Architecture can be best represented in component layers. This layered architecture is by no means a rigid dictation of the components, but it is extensible and follows the open architectural framework.

As shown in the Figure 2.1, the Layered Grid Architecture, Grid Architecture follows the hourglass model, where the narrow neck of hourglass defines a small set of core abstractions and protocols such as TCP and HTTP.

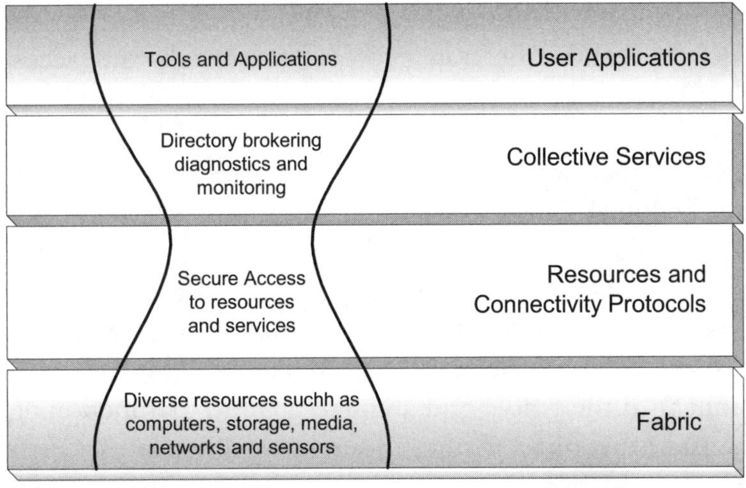

Figure 2.1: *The Layered Grid Architecture*

While the base of the model conveys the different underlying technologies, the top of model shows high-level behaviors that translate into services and user applications.

The *fabric* layer provides the resources to which the shared access is controlled by the grid protocols. The resources normally include physical and logical entities. Physical entities are resources like storage systems, catalogs, servers, and network resources. The resource may be a logical entity like distributed file system, computer cluster or distributed computer pool, and database systems to store structured data. The Grid mechanism normally permits the capability for the resource management, which involves discovery and control.

The *connectivity* layer defines core communications and authentication protocols required for Grid specific network transactions. These protocols enable the exchange of data between fabric layer resources. The *resource* layer, based on the connectivity and authentication protocols, controls the access resources.

The *collective services* layer deals with the directory brokering services, scheduling services, data replications services, and diagnostics/monitoring services. These services are not associated with any one specific resource but focus on interactions across resources. The programming models and tools define and invoke the collective layer functions. This layer is a key component in the whole grid architecture and its functioning. This is the layer that glues all the resources together in expedient exchange.

The top layer, *User Applications*, comprises the user applications that operate within a virtual organization (VO) environment.

The components in each layer share common characteristics but can build on new capabilities and behaviors provided by the lower layer. This model demonstrates the flexibility with which Grid Architecture can be extended and evolved. This is the precise reason why grid architecture is taking shape and form based on the guidelines developed by the visionaries and grid standard forums.

While looking at vision and broad framework the Grid Architecture provides, many of the IT vendors are steadily designing their own strategy and services. Many leading vendors such as IBM, SUN, Oracle, Dell, and HP offer various and diversified solutions that enable grid computing. In addition, there are many smaller companies, which focus on an innovative and specific resource or issue and they are able to design many solutions. Such groups include companies like Avaki, Axceleon, DataSynapse, Ejasent, Enigmatec, Entropia, GridFrastructure, GridIron, GridSystems, GridXpert, Powerllel, Tsunami Research, The Mind Electric and United Devices.

With Grid Technology being a new and unexplored arena for many, the tendency is to associate the technology with variations of what has been seen and what is comfortable. One such confusion is the perception of a large cluster to be synonymous with the grid framework. Clusters have been around a good number of years and their architecture and functionality are understood very well. Clusters focus on a single objective and are a collection of servers with homogenous nature.

Later sections of this chapter will cover a more detailed examination of cluster and its architecture.

Grid Concepts and Components

Grid is a collection of machines, nodes, resources, members, donors, clients, hosts, engines, and many other such items. Grid architecture provides the necessary opportunity for executing applications with optimum exploitation of grid resources. These resources are explored next. Figure 2.2 shows the key components in the grid environment.

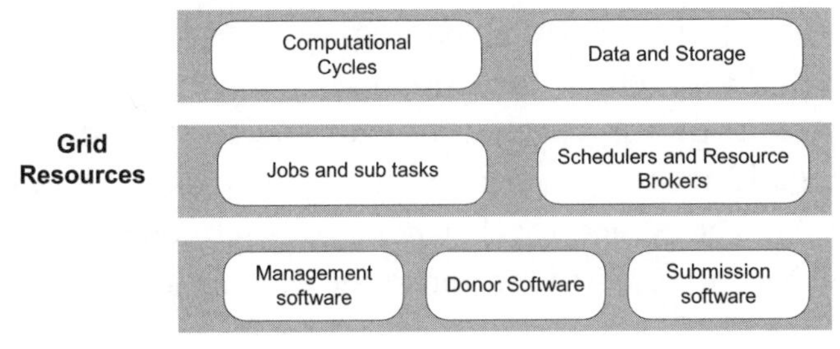

Figure 2.2: *Grid Components*

Computational Power

Processors are the main components that provide the computing cycles. Processors come in different architecture, speed, and instructional set design. The computing cycles are the main target for exploitation in a typical grid environment. There are three ways in which the applications utilize the computing cycles.

- First, the processing power can be harnessed by running an application on available machines in the grid rather than locally.
- Second, the user application can be designed to split its computation tasks or work and execute them in parallel running on different machines or processors.
- The third, involves running an application many times on many different machines in the grid. Grid architecture provides a suitable software and framework to make this work.

Data and Storage

The next significant resource that an application would like to utilize is the data or storage resource. The data is available in a variety of forms such as structured databases, data files, XML documents and others. Storage is attached to various machines or servers in the form of directly attached file systems, or network attached file systems (NFS). By providing a robust storage array attached to multiple servers in the grid environment and creating a unified file system that is attached to multiple servers, the data or files can be made accessible to many servers and thereby to the user applications. Users get local access to such data. It also becomes easier for the users to reference the data in the grid.

In the case of structured database systems, the data can be made available in two forms: the Clustered Database and the

Federation of Databases. In a clustered solution, the same data can be accessed by referring to any server in the cluster configuration. Federation of database is more like an association of data to form a comprehensive database. In a single query, a user application is able to access multiple database resources. At the same time, many grid software solution vendors are designing some kind of unifying software, which controls multiple data sources, and project a single data view for the application or user access.

Communication

In the recent past there has been a rapid growth in server-to-server and server-to-storage communication capability. 10GbEthernet and Inifniband technologies are becoming very common. With the availability of these high bandwidth and low latency communication channels, huge amounts of data are moved across the servers in the grid environment. Communication within the grid for the purpose of sending jobs and data required for those jobs is now faster. This facilitates the transfer of job execution to other machines in the grid. Bandwidth is a critical resource for effective communication and optimum functioning of grid.

Jobs and Applications

Even with all the reference to applications and transactions, ultimately the application is executed in terms of jobs and sub-jobs. As the application execution is split into multiple jobs, those jobs can effectively be moved to different processing centers in the grid. In the grid environment, processing centers are the servers or processors. Thus, a grid application that is designed or organized as a collection of jobs is quite suitable for the grid environment. These jobs can suitably be scheduled and executed within the grid and take advantage of multiple processing resources.

Schedulers/Resource Brokers

Schedulers are other key components in the grid environment. They are also sometimes called resource brokers.

The user may select a machine suitable for running his/her job and then execute a grid command that sends the job to the selected machine. More advanced grid systems would include a job scheduler of some kind that automatically finds the most appropriate machine on which to run any given job that is waiting to be executed. Schedulers react to current availability of resources on the grid. These schedulers, besides carrying the job to other machines in the grid environment, have the capability to understand the resource availability on the idle machines.

In the grid system, any machine that becomes idle would typically report its idle status to the grid management node. This management node would assign the idle machine the next job that is satisfied by the machine's resources. Scavenging of CPU cycles is usually implemented in a way that is unobtrusive to the normal machine user. If the machine becomes busy with local non-grid work, the grid job is usually suspended or delayed. This situation creates somewhat unpredictable completion times for grid jobs, although it is not disruptive to those machines donating resources to the grid.

Grid Software Components

It is important to understand that it is the software that makes the realization of Grid Computing. Even though there are many suitable hardware components lined up in the grid environment, it is the software component that glues all of these hardware resources into one usable grid framework. There are various software components which run the basic functioning of the grid system. The important software components include management software, donor software, and submission software.

A typical application when executed functions on a server and uses the resources such as memory processes and storage attached to the server. When the same application intends to utilize the resources from other servers in the grid, it needs to interact with the middleware and its API's in order to extend its reach to utilize the resources.

Management Software

The Management component keeps track of resources available to the grid and also keeps track of the users or applications that can use them. This component decides the computing locations, which are available for the job's execution, decides the assignment pattern and keeps track of utilization levels of the servers.

This information is used to schedule jobs in the grid. Such information is also used to determine the health of the grid by alerting personnel to problems such as outages, congestion, or over commitment.

Donor Software

Each of the Grid machines participating in the grid framework typically contributes the resources. It needs to have some kind of agent grid software that manages the grid's use of its resources. That software also manages the authentication procedures. The participating machine is a donor machine and it will have donor software.

Submission Software

Usually any member machine of a grid can be used to submit jobs to the grid and initiate grid queries. However, in some grid systems, this function is implemented as a separate component installed on submission nodes or submission clients. When a grid is built using dedicated resources rather than scavenged resources, separate submission software is usually installed on the user's desktop or workstation.

Open Grid Services Architecture

The Grid software is a crucial piece in combining multiple and varied resources into a homogenous and usable computing platform. Since there are many different operating systems and hardware components involved, standards and suitable API for the applications to interact are essential.

Over the years, many standards for grid computing have evolved and many leading researchers and IT vendors have contributed common specifications. The Open Grid Services Architecture (OGSA) represents an evolution towards a Grid system architecture based on Web services concepts and technologies. With the release of Globus Tool Kit 3.0 (GT3), the Globus Project now offers an open source implementation of version 1 of the OGSI (Open Grid Services Infrastructure) Specification is a key building block in the OGSA framework.

GT3 includes standards and software that provides Grid Security (GSI), remote job submission and control (GRAM), high-performance secure data transfer (GridFTP), and consistent interfaces to system and service information (MDS). All of the components provided by the Globus Tool Kit Version-2 for building Grid infrastructures and for developing Grid applications remain available in GT3. GT3 has strong support from vendors.

The OGSA effort provides basic services and the grid community is developing integrated services. OGSA describes a set of implementation and platform independent protocols and services. These classify technology and infrastructure of the next generation of Grids defined in terms of Grid Services, closely allied to Web Services, which supports the sharing and coordinated use of diverse resources in dynamic distributed virtual organizations.

What is WebService?

A Web Service is an interface that describes a collection of operations that are network accessible. They are built on XML based technologies and messaging. They use XML schemas to mark-up and describe services and their operations. Web Services commonly use the Simple Object Access Protocol (SOAP) as a communication protocol over HTTP- when this is not appropriate for performance reasons, a different protocol may be used.

It is the GSA that pulls together Open Grid Architecture and Web Services to form Grid Services. Grid Services are dynamic, transient, and have state, in other words have a finite lifetime, and are defined by a well-defined set of interfaces and behaviors. OGSA interfaces and behaviors describing Grid Services can be written in an XML schema based WSDL document – other implementations are possible.

Perception of Grid

Since the Grid Architecture involves interoperability and sharing of resources within enterprise and across enterprises, it is often pondered if the Grid is synonymous with Internet or if the grid is an alternative to the Internet. Actually, the Grid is a set of additional protocols and services that build on Internet protocols and services to support the creation and use of computation and data-enriched environments. In addition, it should be noted that any resource that is on the Grid is also, by definition, on the Net.

The Grid is perceived as a source of free CPU cycles. However, Grid computing does not imply unrestricted access to resources; rather it is about controlled sharing. The CPU cycles are normally used and controlled by resource policies defined. Usage of such resources depends on group membership, ability to pay, and so forth.

Grid experts believe that the Grid makes high-performance computers superfluous. The thousands of processors that may be accessible within a Virtual Organization represent a significant source of computational power. This does not imply, however, that traditional high-performance computers are obsolete.

Where Are We on the Grid?

As the Grid is gradually moving into the commercial world, many of the standards are finalized and many of niche software players are churning out software components needed for grid integration.

There are many IT vendors, in every aspect of the grid technology, who have released various strategies and solutions. Figure 2.3 gives an idea of various players in the grid technology.

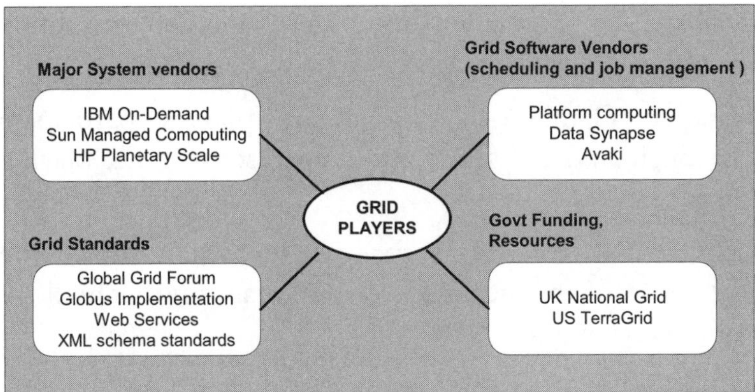

Figure 2.3: *Grid Universe and the Key Players.*

For the success and wide adoption of any new technology or new orientation, commercialization efforts are very important. For the Grid to become a widespread technology, in the same way the Internet became a mainstream technology and communication media, it needs to enter or penetrate into the commercial world. Commercialization provides necessary impetus for growth and funding.

There are many signs of Grid commercialization, even though they are at early stages. Some of examples of major business areas where Grid computing is seen as a good fit:

- Life Sciences – Grid is used for analyzing strings of biological and chemical information.
- Financial Services – For processing long running, complex financial models and arriving at decisions that are more accurate.
- Higher Education – For enabling advanced, data and computing intensive research.
- Engineering Services – In the automotive and aerospace industry, for collaborative design and data intensive testing.

- Government – For enabling multi-departmental computing projects in both civil and military agencies.
- Collaborative Games – where many players participate simultaneously and use the computing resources for playing online games.

The following is an interesting case study, which shows the gradual adaptation of this new and revolutionary grid technology into the commercial world.

Compute Backbone - JP Morgan Chase's Grid Story

Grid Computing is extending its reach beyond scientific and technical users towards large-scale commercial enterprise, as evident from the recent adoption of grid technologies at JP Morgan Chase. JP Morgan is one of the largest financial services companies in the US. With technology partners, Platform Computing and Egenera, JP Morgan has been working on what it calls 'Compute Backbone' initiative, service based architecture intended to support its capital market business.

JP Morgan and Platform Computing has collaborated and developed Platform Symphony product, which is a policy driven, real-time application execution layer, including the workload orchestration and service provisioning capabilities. It is used for grid enabling, testing and deploying the applications, and then managing them over a virtualized production environment, or 'service layer' as JP Morgan terms it. While the Platform computing contributed to the grid software layer, the other two significant contributors are the Egenera Blade servers and Linux operating system. Introduction of Linux operating system helped JP Morgan to standardize its software builds. The adoption of blade server technology provided JP Morgan a modular approach to grow its server hardware farm. With the blades platform, they are able to add blade-by-blade as the computing power need grows.

The grid set up is run as a service for internal users, and is charged for by usage. Users can buy CPU time on an hour-by-hour basis rather than having to own the CPU's for 24 hours a day, 365 days a year. It has opted for electricity-style pricing model – pay only for what you use. There are currently 500 Intel processors running the Computer Backbone, divided between New York and London. The Platform Symphony product gathers the utilization and allocation in the grid and the helps in decision to manage and extend the grid resources.

Source : Grids 2004: From Rocket Science to Business Service – The 451 Group

Armed with a fair idea of what Grid computing is about, it is time to look at the buzzwords or technologies that often go hand in hand with grid. They include utility computing and on-demand computing and they often fit into the grid framework too.

Utility and On-Demand Computing

Many pundits in the IT industry agree that the computing trend is moving away from compute-inside-the-box to compute-outside-the-box, which is also called service-oriented computing. Computing is seen as more of a service and accordingly it needs to be changed. This kind of trend is very much seen in the current business policies at leading firms like IBM, HP, Sun and EMC. The so-called On-Demand Computing is seen as a perfect alignment for the business needs and current stressed conditions.

Where's Tiger Woods right now?

Steve Evans, VP of information services for the PGA Tour, is tapping hundreds of volunteers to follow every golf pro around with Palm Pilots and survey-grade range finders. The resulting pgatour.com service offers real-time coverage of every player -- not just the front-runners. So how do you handle 100,000 subscribers during the golf season without buying boxes that sit idle most of the year? Outsource it to IBM's Virtual Linux Services, of course. If you can't tell the difference between a virtual server and a real server, then you might as well rent the server capacity on demand.

Source: Forester Research, 2003

Utility Computing is another buzzword that is often used. It is seen in the press, magazines, and IT vendor-marketing brochures. The phrase Utility Computing and Grid are often used synonymously. Either there is haziness in understanding and/or there is belief that one technology leads to another.

Although there is considerable overlap in what grids do and what utility computing can enable an enterprise to do, grid computing and utility computing are not synonymous.

It is understandable why many view them as the same. Both of these technologies deal with using computing resources. Both can be deployed internally or can make use of external resources. Both provide enterprises with opportunities to reduce computing costs. In addition, utility computing can make use of grids to provide computing power to users and applications.

However, the differences lie in the architecture and the purpose or objective.

- A Grid is a network infrastructure that exploits computing resources and storage; it is based on the idea of sharing resources. Grid finds and exploits unused computing and storage resources that reside within a distributed computing environment.
- It is the utility computing model or approach that enables computing resources and storage to be purchased or acquired on an as-needed basis. When a computer is in need of additional resources, it acquires them from another source. This usually works on a pay-as-you-go basis.

Thus, utility computing is about availability of infrastructure or switching resources in a dynamic manner. In the utility computing model, there are many ways the resource acquisition process works. Additional computing, memory, or storage resources are usually acquired using one or many of the following approaches:

- Activation of existing resources
- Reconfiguration of existing resources - to provide power/ storage to prioritized applications
- Being a part of the Grid and exploiting the extra resources
- By purchasing computing power and storage on an as needed basis from another source

Activating Existing Resources

In this approach, users activate the existing or embedded capacity that may already be available on the enterprise machines. A good example would be HP Superdome computer system. HP often ships such built-in capacity with its Superdome computer systems and makes it possible for users to activate that capacity when needed to acquire additional computing power. Using this approach, HP charges its customers on the basis of CPU utilization.

In IBM's case, additional CPU power is shipped with certain IBM servers and that CPU power can be activated or turned-on using a software key. IBM's approach packages what it calls CUoD (capacity upgrade on demand) on many of the servers.

Reconfiguration of Existing Resources

In this approach, the applications can be prioritized — and when an application requires additional computing power, storage, or memory it can acquire those resources by dynamically reconfiguring other systems to support its computing requirements. A good example is seen in blade servers. They can be re-configured with the required system image on the fly.

Using Grid Resources

When used in the context of utility computing, an application would demand and receive additional computing power from a grid network.

Service Provisioning

The final way that utility services can be obtained is to purchase the services from an external source, called utility service provisioning.

IBM has been spearheading the On-Demand vision for quite some time. It follows a new approach to system management, leveraging its WebSphere enterprise services bus and supported by techniques inherited from grid computing, involving virtualization and dynamic configurable systems. Grid computing techniques such as virtualization, dynamic provisioning, self-discovery and service isolation are the key elements in delivery of on-demand solutions.

There are many companies that are designing and marketing utility computing solutions. IT vendors such as Veritas, Sun, and HP etc., are quite active in this space. Many research analysts believe On-demand computing is on the rise.

A recent survey by Saugatuck Technology indicates that the use of on-demand or pay-as-you-go (PAYG) IT services has grown tremendously in the past year, to the point where more than 20 percent of firms recently surveyed report using one or more such services. An additional 45 percent of firms are considering using

PAYG services, with the majority of those expecting to use pay as you go IT and business services within 24 months.

Grid Enablers

So far, many aspects of the grid and grid requirements have been covered. In the next section, some significant grid enabling technologies that are making a big difference will be examined. Particularly, the growth of low cost blade servers as Infiniband communication infrastructure and commodity operating such as Linux are very significant. The helping factors can be briefly summarized as follows:

- Availability of inexpensive, commodity blade servers
- Inexpensive OS optimized for 1 to 4 CPUs such as Linux
- Storage no longer tied to a single server: NAS and SANs
- Fast interconnect technologies such as Gigabit Ethernet and Infiniband

Blade Servers

Buying the large SMP servers involves substantial capital costs. Many organizations over time have ended up buying resources and not using them to their fullest extent. With blade servers, purchases can be made incrementally blade-by-blade or frame by frame. Blades are also replaceable because they can be added and removed on an individual basis without having to shutdown the whole blade system or blade frame, thereby providing the online server management. Blades within a unified chassis are easier to manage.

A Blade Server is a thin board containing one or more microprocessors. Blades offer power and memory similar to that available in typical 1U (1.75 inch high) servers, but squeeze vertically or horizontally into a chassis which includes cabling, fans, and power supplies typically found on individual servers.

InfiniBand

The InfiniBand architecture provides an industry-standard technology for scaling out computer platforms and is an ideal interconnect for developing high performance Itanium 2 processor-based compute grid clusters.

Low cost InfiniBand silicon that supports 10 Gb/sec RDMA transfers is shipping today providing eight times the bandwidth of Ethernet and three times the bandwidth of proprietary clustering interconnects. With an approved specification for 30 Gb/sec, InfiniBand is at least a generation ahead of competing fabric technologies today and in the foreseeable future.

Leveraging the 10 Gb/sec throughput and low latency capabilities of the InfiniBand technology, the InfiniBand enabled clusters are increasingly built in research and commercial institutions. They are showing a significant improvement in rendering speed (3x to 4x) over the Gigabit Ethernet enabled grid cluster.

The Role of Linux

Linux operating system, which became quite popular for hosting web servers and firewalls is now increasingly picked up or selected for mission critical servers such as the application clusters and databases.

"Linux is able to provide the UNIX reliability at Intel prices," says a recent report by Forester Research Inc. For example, Linux based 2-way Dell machines can handle the same work load as the Solaris 4-way Sun servers and at a fraction of the cost.

Linux has achieved other technological advances such as 4-way CPU support and sophisticated threading model and enterprise class security. Linux based Intel servers and clusters are now being increasingly used for IBM WebSphere servers, BEA Web Logic Servers and for Oracle Real Application Clusters.

Figure 2.4 shows the gradual growth of Linux and its footing into the corporate IT data centers. As the Linux operating system is gaining ground and maturing as a commodity operating system, it is becoming a key resource for Grid infrastructure.

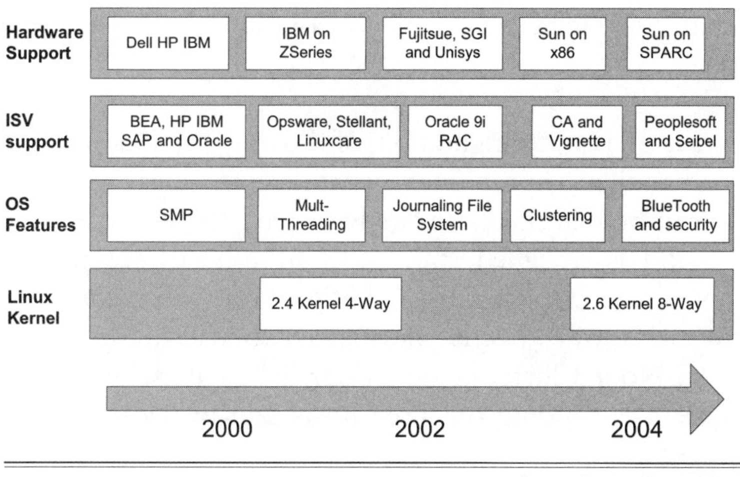

Source : Forester Research Inc

Figure 2.4: *Linux Adoption and Growth*

Clusters

When the IT technologists began examining grid computing, many mistakenly viewed the clusters as the grid environments. Adding to this confusion, vendors such as Sun Microsystems began calling their cluster offerings Grid Clusters. However, the clusters have different architecture, objective and purpose. Next, the true nature of the clustering technology will be examined.

What Is Cluster?

According to Greg Pfister, the guru of clustering,

> "A cluster is a type of parallel system that consists of interconnected whole computers and is used as a single, unified computing resource".

The whole computer is a normal combination of parts that comprise a stand-alone, usable computer. The components include one or more processors (including SMP and NUMA), memory, and I/O facilities. The whole computer is also referred to as a Node.

Thus, the cluster is a configuration of a group of independent servers, so that they appear on a network as a single machine. This group can be managed as a single system, shares a common namespace, and is designed specifically to tolerate component failures and to support the addition or subtraction of components in a way that is transparent to users. Figure 2.5 represents a 3-Node Cluster hosting a parallel database with three database instances residing on three hosts and providing jointly the database service.

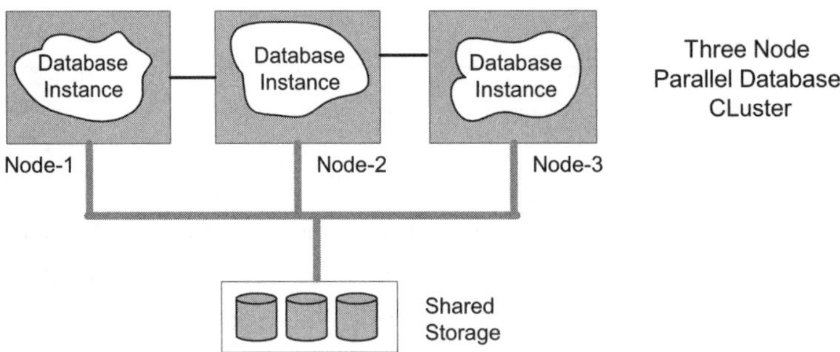

Figure 2.5: *A typical Cluster with 3-Nodes supporting Database Service*

Why Clusters?

Symmetric multiprocessors (SMP) and non-uniform memory access (NUMA) systems have grown in size and power. It is very common to see SMP or NUMA systems equipped with 8 to 64 processors. They represent an alternative to cluster systems, but clusters have remained competitive and have made inroads into commercial application environments. There are obvious reasons for the survival of clusters: [Pfister]

- **Performance** - Throughput, response time, and turn around time is improved by using several machines at the same time. Clusters generate higher levels of performance.
- **Availability** - Clusters provide uninterrupted service by redistributing work, or through shifting the application services to surviving nodes by way of a failover process.
- **Price/Performance** - Clusters or other forms of computer aggregations are typically collections of machines that individually have very good performance for their price.
- **Incremental Growth** - It is easier to justify adding to a cluster than to buy a whole new computing facility.
- **Scaling** - Clusters have the ability to add capacity as needed.
- **Manageability** - Clusters have the ability to be managed as a single system.

Cluster Objectives

Traditionally, the term cluster was used to represent Server Clusters. Clustered systems are synonymous with a group of servers. The server, being the main layer or platform where the database or application service resides, is the most important component in providing availability and high performance.

Clusters, with multiple nodes, primarily aim at protecting server availability. Any failure in a server is transparent to end-users and is hidden by the failover of the application or database to a surviving node. End users or clients have access to the surviving node, thus allowing processing to continue. In another situation, a group of nodes are joined together to provide database services, as in a parallel database. Failure of a single node does not interrupt access to the database since the secondary nodes are still active in providing database access.

Thus, the cluster technology focuses on providing an alternative to a failed server. However, we have to realize that there are many other layers or components, each of which is significant in maintaining overall availability of the database or application service. Although the server (node) is a very crucial component and plays the key role in running the database or application, there are other components, such as the disk storage units and networking equipment for which alternatives or backups need to be provided to meet the failure conditions. The traditional concept of clustering revolves around server clustering only.

With this in mind, administrators and managers should provide adequate redundancy for other components in order to have an effective high availability environment.

Clusters vs. Grids

There are many differences between Grid and Clusters. The following table shows comparison of Grid and Clusters.

CHARACTERISTIC	CLUSTER	GRID
Population	Commodity Computers	Commodity and High-end computers
Ownership	Single	Multiple

CHARACTERISTIC	CLUSTER	GRID
Discovery	Membership Services	Centralized Index and Decentralized Info
User Management	Centralized	Decentralized
Resource management	Centralized	Distributed
Allocation/ Scheduling	Centralized	Decentralized
Inter-Operability	VIA and Proprietary	No standards being developed
Single System Image	Yes	No
Scalability	100s	1000?
Capacity	Guaranteed	Varies, but high
Throughput	Medium	High
Speed(Lat. Bandwidth)	Low, high	High, Low

Table 2.2: *Comparison between Clusters and Grid*

Grid represents a bigger framework and architecture, and focuses on the broader scope or objective. Grid incorporates many varied computing resources and the clusters often become one of the many components. A Grid enables the sharing, selection, and aggregation of a wide variety of geographically distributed resources including supercomputers, storage systems, data sources, and specialized devices owned by different organizations for solving large-scale resource intensive problems in science, engineering, and commerce. Clusters, on the other hand, focus on a specific objective and purpose, such as a database service or a web logic application server. These clusters fit into grid architecture very well for ultimate sharing of resources at a higher level of aggregation.

With technological advances it may not be long before a large number of nodes (say, 50 to 100 nodes) form a database cluster incorporating a variety of data stores consolidated into a huge data source. That may lead to a true Data Grid of different stores supported in a single large cluster.

Conclusion

In this chapter, the differences between the aggregation of servers by way of clustering and by way of setting up of a Grid framework have been examined.

Clustering technology has been around for many years and it focuses on a specific objective. It is usually an aggregation of a small number of servers supporting an application or a database.

Grid Technology focuses on wider scale issues and is usually the aggregation of many varied computing resources, in which even the clusters become one of the many critical components. Grid enables the aggregation of a wide variety of geographically distributed resources including supercomputers, smaller computers, storage systems and many data sources.

The difference between Grid and Utility Computing has also been explored. Utility computing is more of a perception from the client or consumer of the grid resources.

In the next chapter, a detailed account of Database Clusters and how they fit into the high performance computing arena will be examined. Additional topics will include the types of clusters, simple fail-over clusters, and complex parallel database clusters.

Performance and Availability

CHAPTER 3

"I think we need a faster processor for my database"

High Performance and Availability

Highly available and scalable server-based computer systems and applications are an essential part of today's internet based business environment. This is achieved by cluster technology and fault tolerant systems. The clustering technology that supports both high performance computing and high availability has been widely used by many commercial and research institutions.

High Performance computing has been with us for several years. Research, scientific, and educational communities have always been in the forefront in using the high performance computers for research applications. Analysis of large data and complex algorithms in almost real-time needed high performance computing platforms.

In this chapter, high performance computing trends and high availability needs for the database systems will be examined. The main topics of this chapter include examination of growth of relational database systems, high performance computing features, and highly available database concepts and features. The role of clusters in supporting the database systems will be covered and the types of clusters will be examined.

High Performance Computing

Modern business operations depend on structured data. At all levels of the organization, there is heavy dependence on database for performing business tasks. With e-business applications and globalization of business operations, on-line database systems are essential for day-to-day operations. The internet, with its potential to connect virtually every computer in the world, has made database technology more crucial than ever. With increasing numbers of users connecting concurrently to databases to query and update data, high performing servers are essential. Uneven workload patterns and long running complex data warehousing applications require high performing database technology. Database software must be able to cope with increased demands and complexity.

Applications involving multimedia, medicine, statistical analysis, securities related modeling and projections, insurance and retail industries, to name a few, are data hungry and utilize very large databases. They all store and analyze high volumes of data. Data mining is one of the key techniques used by many enterprises to extract information diamonds. These data intensive and resource consuming applications suffer from performance problems and bottlenecks caused by using a single source of data. However, data distribution and parallel processing help to overcome these resource and performance problems and achieve guaranteed throughput, quality of service, and system availability.

Databases are growing in size and complexity. To optimize the data storage and retrieval, parallel execution or parallel processing is one of the most effective methods. Parallel Execution focuses on achieving faster response times and better utilization of multiple CPU resources on the database server. The swift growth of databases and accumulation of large amounts of data necessarily depend on parallel processing. Many of the RDBM systems, including Oracle, leverage the availability of faster and multi-CPU computers to process and retrieve data by utilizing parallel processing methodology.

Growth of Powerful Processors

The power of processors has increased exponentially in the last two decades. Widely used processors like Intel's Xeon/Itanium and Sun's UltraSparc have revolutionized the server market. Dual processor and Multi-processor based SMP servers make up the bulk of the data centers today. Theoretically, the Intel Xeon processor technology delivers about 6 to 8 gigaflops per two-processor node, and the Itanium processors promise even better performance.

Why Parallel Processing?

Parallel Processing, a part of the high performance-computing model, involves utilization of large amounts of computing resources to complete a complex task or problem. Originally confined to scientific applications, Parallel Processing has made gradual in-roads into commercial and business applications that need high performance computing facilities like data mining, decision support and risk management applications. Today, Database Applications process huge amounts of data, in terms of loading and updating, and extracting information from very large databases (VLDB) to perform sophisticated analysis.

Parallel Execution or Processing involves dividing a task into several smaller tasks, and working on each of those smaller tasks in parallel. In simple words, if multiple processors engage a computing task, it can be executed faster thereby achieving better response time and increasing throughput. Parallel execution helps systems scale in performance by making optimal use of hardware resources. In a parallel processing system, multiple processes may reside on a single computer or they may be spread across separate computers or nodes as in a cluster.

Awareness and utility of clusters have gone up tremendously in recent times. In clustered architecture, two or more nodes (hosts) are interconnected and share common storage resources. Each node has its own set of processors. A cluster is usually an aggregation of multiple SMP nodes. Scalability is better achieved in a cluster on a modular basis. As the need arises, additional servers can be added to a cluster.

Opportunities for Parallelism

By employing more resources in terms of processors, large memories and high-speed internal bus technology, many tasks are sped up. Many of the system operations or tasks occur in parallel by utilizing the multiple processors on the server.

Scalability

Scalability is the ability to maintain higher performance levels as the workload increases by incrementally adding more system capacity in terms of more processors and memory. On a single processor system, it becomes difficult to achieve scalability beyond a certain point. Parallelization, by using multi-processor servers, provides better scalability than single processor systems.

Scalability can be understood from two different perspectives: a *speed-up* of tasks within the system; and an increase in concurrency in the system, sometime referred to as *scale-up*.

There are two ways to achieve *speed-up* of tasks:

- Increasing the execution capacity of the existing hardware components of a server through multiple CPUs.
- Breaking the job into multiple sub-tasks and assigning these components to multiple processors to execute them concurrently.

By using faster components like processors, large memory, low latency messaging mechanism and efficient I/O sub-systems, generally job executions are sped up. However, this is an expensive option. Using the technique of parallelization by utilizing multiple processors helps to achieve speed-up of the jobs.

Scalability is also understood and defined as achieving maximum useful concurrency. In multi-user systems, users share all of the resources. Systems providing concurrency to a large number users should focus on better response times and better synchronization of access mechanisms.

In database applications, scale-up can be either transactional or batch. In batch situations, the user should be able to execute large and complex batch processing without affecting the response time. In transactional environment, there is usually a minimum contention for the same resources and a large number of transactions should be supported without a loss of response time. In both of these cases, response time is usually maintained by the addition of more processors either in a single SMP server or in multi-node cluster.

Parallel Databases

Modern relational database systems are typically architected with parallel capable software that is well suited to take advantage of the parallel architecture of SMP systems. The Oracle database system is a multi-process application in UNIX systems, and is a multi-threaded application under the Windows architecture.

In general, Databases are accessed by a large number of simultaneous users or connections. Many users with their own data and instructions take advantage of the multi-processor server availability to perform database processing. Moreover, a single user task, such as a SQL query, can be *parallelized* to achieve higher speed and throughput by using multiple processors.

The relational model involves the utilization of structured tables with rows and columns. Usually the SQL query aims at extracting or updating some target data, which is again a set of rows and columns based on a condition. Typically, any SQL database operation gets divided into multiple database sub-operations such as *selection*, *join*, *group*, *sort*, *projection*, etc. Thus, the sub-operations become excellent candidates for simultaneous or parallel execution, making the RDBMS system ideal parallel processing software.

Databases have a component called the *query optimizer* which selects a sequence of inputs, joins, and scans to produce the desired output table or data set. The query optimizer is aware of the underlying hardware architecture to utilize the suitable path for invoking parallel execution. Thus, from the Database point-of-view, parallel execution is useful for all types of operations that access significant amounts of data.

Generally, parallel execution improves performance for:

- Queries
- Creation of large indexes
- Bulk inserts, updates, and deletes
- Aggregations and copying

Parallel Processing involves the use of multiple processors to reduce the time needed to complete a given task. Instead of one processor executing an entire task, several processors work on separate tasks that are subordinate to the main task. There are several architectural approaches for multiple processor systems, they are:

- Symmetric Multi-Processors (SMP)
- Clustered Systems
- NUMA (or DSM - Distributed Share Model) servers
- MPP (Massively Parallel Processing)

Types of Parallelism

There are two types of parallelism that database users can utilize. They are *inter-query parallelism* and *intra-query parallelism*. The differences between these two types of parallelism will be covered next.

Inter-Query Parallelism - Individual transactions are independent, and no transaction requires the output of another transaction to complete. Many CPUs can be kept busy by assigning each task or query to a separate CPU. This type of parallelism, many separate independent queries active at the same time, is called inter-query parallelism. In OLTP environment, each query is fairly small, small enough to complete on a single process utilizing a single CPU.

Intra-Query Parallelism - To speed up execution of a large, complex query it must first be decomposed into smaller problems and these smaller problems execute concurrently (in parallel) by assigning each sub-problem concurrently to its CPUs. This is called *intra-query parallelism.* Decision support systems (DSS) need this kind of facility. Data warehousing applications often deal with huge data sets, involving data capture, analysis and summaries, so these operations also require this capability.

More details about parallel execution in oracle are covered in the chapter on *Parallel Execution.*

Highly Available Databases

One of the most significant developments of recent years in IT technology is the requirement to keep the systems, especially relational database systems, online 24/7 with as close to 100% availability as possible. This is important because most of the business operations need to access some form of data.

Many business tasks, even though simple in nature and occurring for a short duration, require dealing with persistent data. They may need to capture some data or update some data. The same data may need to be retrieved by another user located at some other business unit. For example, scheduling a visit by an external visitor, arranging a meeting, handling a student application and admission to a university, verification of zip code and last name before allowing a web site visitor access, they all need to retrieve, insert, or capture data.

These seemingly trivial examples bring out another significant point in regards to the nature of databases. Databases need to be available all the time, in other words 24/7. Non-availability of a database that provide crucial data for a business decision process has the potential effect of halting the same business task, however small or large the task may be.

The Need for Highly Available Data

The forces of globalization, 24/7 business operations, and the need for an always-on computing infrastructure means that downtime does not exist in business-critical and mission critical applications. Unplanned downtime and planned downtime are costly, in terms of lost revenue and lost time. In today's global and internet economy, planned downtime in one time zone has a direct impact on the business hours of another time zone. So if the down time is planned in the New York corporate headquarters, it will affect corporate end users located in, say, London or Sydney.

In the case of internet based business operations, data or system availability becomes much more important than ever before. It is never known which end user, sitting in their family room, would like to make online flight reservation for their next vacation or make an online purchase of a popular DVD or check status of the stock positions. Factors like 24/7 uptime, 7 seconds response, and short or zero maintenance windows bring a lot of challenges for the database administrator and managers.

However, it does not mean that every single database in a business or company is required to be kept on-line. There is always some crucial, must-be-online type data, and at the same time, there is some tolerance for other data. It is necessary, however, for high availability planning for mission-critical databases.

It is important to understand certain key terms and concepts before examining HA systems and databases.

Failure

Failure is defined as a departure from expected behavior on an individual computer system or a network system of associated computers and applications. Software, hardware, operator and procedural errors, along with environmental factors can each cause a system failure. Failure of a single component or single computer can directly influence reliability of the overall system. Component failures are unavoidable.

Availability

Availability is a measure of the amount of time a system or component performs its specified function. Availability is related to, but different than reliability. Reliability measures how frequently the system fails; availability measures the percentage of time the system is in its operational state.

To calculate availability, both the Mean Time To Failure (MTTF) and the Mean Time To Recovery (MTTR) need to be known. The MTTR is a measure of how long, on average, it takes to restore the system to its operational state after a failure. If both the MTTF and the MTTR are known, availability can be calculated using the following formula:

- Availability = MTTF / (MTTF + MTTR)

For example, if the data center takes an average of six months to fail (MTTF = six months) and it takes 20 minutes, on average, to return the data center to its operational state (MTTR = 20 minutes), then the data center availability is:

- Availability = 6 months / (6 months + 20 minutes) = 99.992 percent.

Therefore, there are two ways to improve the availability of the system; increase MTTF or reduce MTTR. Having realized that system failures do occur or are unavoidable, system and database administrators need to focus on designing a reliable system with redundant components as well as setting up reliable recovery methodology for when system failures happen.

Availability is actually the probability that an application service is available for use. Availability is usually expressed as a percentage of hours per week, month, or year during which an application service can be used for normal business.

To a large extent, reliability and serviceability influence availability. The more failure reduction built into a system, the more available it is likely to be. Features and technologies that reduce failure recovery time, or that speed up diagnosis and repair, increase a system's overall availability. The acronym RAS, which stands for reliability, availability, and serviceability, is often used in describing availability features of a system.

Reliability

Reliability is the starting point for building increasingly available systems, since a measure of system reliability is how long it has been up and/or how long it typically stays up between failures. The nature of the failure is not important — any failure affects the system's overall availability. As presented in the previous section, mean time between failures (MTBF) is often considered an important metric with respect to measuring system reliability.

There are two primary means of achieving greater reliability:

- Building high MTBF components into the system.
- Adding MTBF components in redundant (N+1) configurations.

Including technology that maintains data integrity, reducing the probability that bad data will flow undetected through the system.

Serviceability

Serviceability defines the time it takes to isolate and repair a fault or, more succinctly, the time it takes to restore a system to service following a failure. Mean Time to Repair, or MTTR, is considered an important metric when discussing the serviceability of a system or some component of the system. MTTR, however, is a unit of time and does not factor into the cost of service.

Fault-Tolerant systems

Another important distinction that needs to be made is between a high availability (HA) system and a fault tolerant (FT) system. Fault tolerant systems offer higher level of resilience and recovery. They use a high degree of hardware redundancy and specialized software to provide near-instantaneous recovery from any single hardware or software unit failure. This technology is relatively expensive and requires allocation of higher budgets. Fault Tolerant servers are primarily used for applications that support high-value, high-rate transactions such as check clearinghouses, automated teller machines, or stock exchanges. Whereas, clustered systems are more often characterized as high availability and scalable solutions. HA Clusters may not guarantee non-stop operation, but they provide availability sufficient for most mission critical business applications.

Database Availability

When referring to the availability of databases, the total environment and infrastructure in which a typical database is located need to be examined. Typically, a database is an application hosted on a server. The database application has its own availability features that are unique from the system availability point of view.

There are three situations that need to be considered:

- Database Availability is a function of the system availability, or more appropriately the server availability. If the server is inoperable for any reason, the database is not available or usable.
- The server is up and running and at the same time the database is functioning as expected, but end users or applications are unable to access the database on account of failures in the networking path. In this case, even though the system and/or database are highly available, the data service in not reachable.
- The database is a logical structure for the physical data store that resides on the physical disks, also known as the storage device. If for some reason, the storage unit fails or the server is unable to reach or connect to the storage unit, the database cannot be brought up. As a result, database service is not available for use.

As an application, the database is more viewed as a service. Factors like end-user database path failures, system failures or storage failures equally affect the ability to provide the database access to application users. As a result, all of these factors need to be taken into consideration to design a better database system. System Availability and Database Availability may not be always the same.

Another important issue relevant for the database is the need to maintain the database consistency. Unlike application servers or other application instances, multiple database instances or copies of database cannot exist. As the database contents change in real-time, multiple copies cannot be maintained in a timely manner.

The real solution is a Parallel Database that has a single copy of the database files, but can be accessed by multiple nodes concurrently through database instances.

Clustered Systems

HA systems are almost synonymous with clustered systems. In order to minimize downtime, two or more servers, called nodes, are linked to form a high-availability cluster system. At the same time, Parallel Databases are another type of the clustered systems, which offers multiple instances or database processing locations.

Types of Clusters

Clusters offer a cost-effective, high-performance, and highly available architecture for cluster-aware applications. There are many types of clusters. Generally, clusters are classified based on their functionality. The types of clusters are:

- Fail-Over Clusters
- Scalable High Performance Clusters
- Application Clusters
- Network Load balancing clusters
- Other types of clusters

Each class of clusters will be examined next to compare how they are the same and how they differ.

Fail-over Clusters

This class of clusters is most widely used in today's computing environment. Sometimes they are called HA clusters or segregated clusters. In this type, the emphasis is on complete avoidance of unplanned downtime and achieving higher availability.

If one of the nodes in a cluster becomes unavailable either due to planned downtime for maintenance or unplanned downtime due to failure, another node takes over to provide the service to the end-user—a process known as failover. When failover occurs, users who are accessing the cluster service continue to access the service, and are unaware that it is now being provided from a different server (node). This architecture emphasizes the availability of the database or application service rather than performance or load-balancing feature.

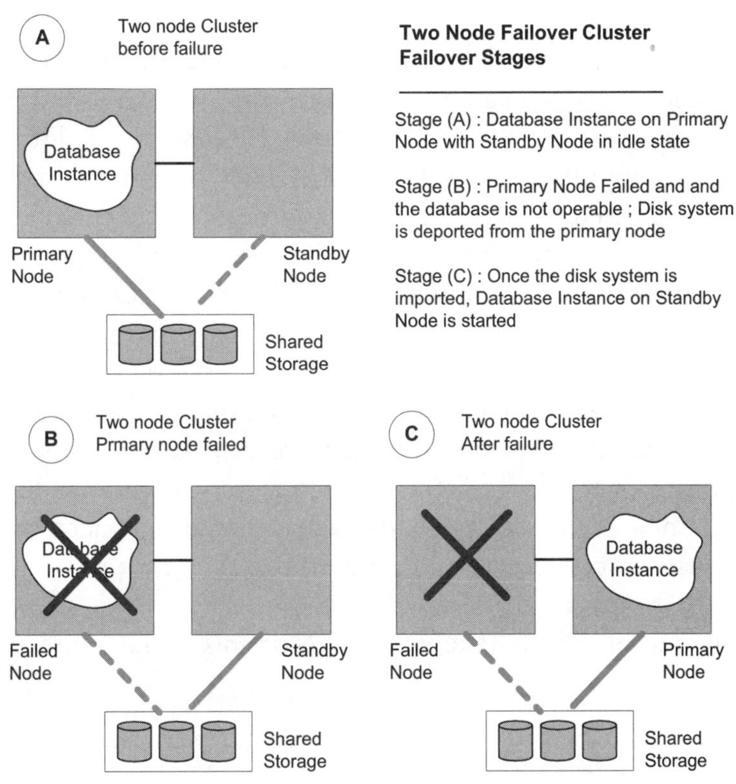

Figure 3.1: *Failover Cluster*

High-availability clusters allow multiple servers, in conjunction with shared disk storage units, to quickly recover from failures. Hardware or software failures, affecting either a critical component or an entire system, trigger a fail over from one system in the cluster to another as shown in Figure 3.1. Application processing and access to disk-based data is typically restored within minutes, although recovery times vary depending upon specific characteristics of the application and system configuration.

Scalable High Performance Clusters

This class of clusters provides scalability, high performance, load balancing, and high availability through the use of parallel middleware. These are also called Parallel Clusters or High Performance Computing Clusters (HPCC). They provide a single system image, in other words, the application can be executed on any of the servers within the cluster. They are used to execute compute-intensive and data-intensive problems by running the job on multiple nodes simultaneously.

These clusters utilize parallel-aware software that breaks down the problem into smaller chunks, which are dispatched across a network of interconnected systems that concurrently process the chunks and then communicate with each other using message-passing libraries to coordinate and synchronize their results.

Cluster aware applications take advantage of this architecture in three ways:

- Parallel Computing Multi-Threading and Modularization
- Load Balancing
- Automatic Failure

Parallel Database Clusters, like Oracle Real Application Clusters, IBM Sysplex Database Cluster, IBM's UDB EEE, and Beowulf

Computers fit into this group of clusters. Beowulf Clusters are of particular interest to the scientific and educational communities. Beowulf clusters are built by using commodity systems – PCs, Workstations or Servers running software such as Linux. It features a parallel computing system consisting of multiple nodes interconnected and aiming at executing parallel jobs.

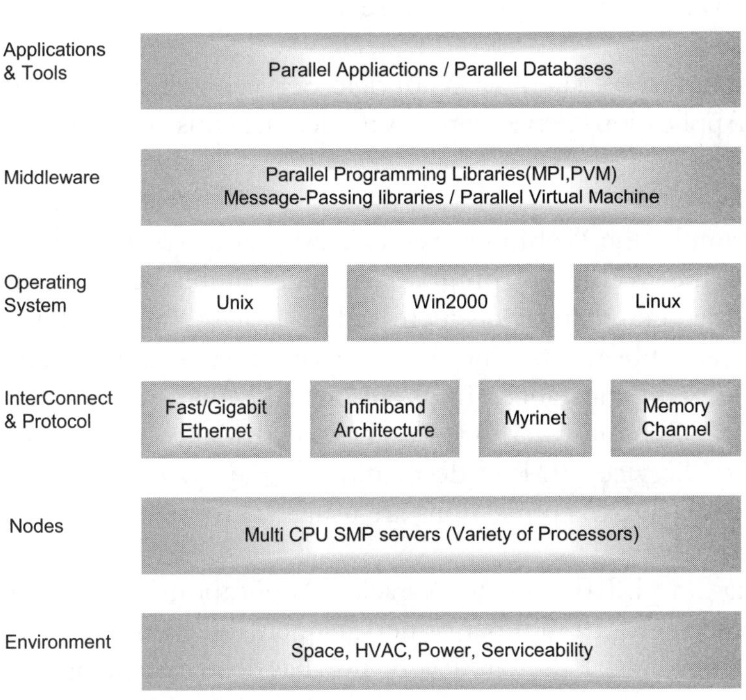

Figure 3.2: *Typical Cluster Components*

Through Message Passing, nodes synchronize data and share results. Oracle RAC uses message passing to process request and update data on each node, resulting in fast data requests and consistent databases. Figure 3.2 shows typical components in a parallel cluster.

Application Server Clusters

Nodes running application servers are connected to provide availability and scalability. In this type of cluster, each node runs an instance of an application server. They run the application server independent of each other's instance. There is no concept of failover. When clustered in this way, the state of certain objects is maintained synchronously. Web server clients can connect to either of the application server instances.

Application servers such as WebLogic Server, Websphere, and Oracle Application server are examples of this category of clusters.

As an example, the WebLogic Server cluster consists of multiple copies of the WebLogic program running simultaneously and working together to provide increased scalability and reliability. The cluster appears to the web server clients as a single WebLogic Server instance. In WebLogic deployment, Servlets, JSPs, EJB, Remote Method Invocation (RMI) objects, Java Messaging Service (JMS) destinations, and Java Database Connectivity (JDBC) connections are usually clustered.

Clustering in J2EE, as in Oracle Applications server, is implemented across a number of tiers, namely the client tier, Web tier, EJB tier, and EIS tier. Every tier has load balancing and failover.

Other Types of Clusters

The term cluster is loosely used to specify a condition when two pieces of networking equipment or two storage units are joined to provide backup and failover facility. In another usage, two clusters located at remote locations are linked to form a global cluster. We will look into some of the widely known clusters of this type.

NetApp Filer Clusters - A NetApp Filer Cluster is a pair of interconnected storage Filer units. Two NetApp storage appliances are connected through an interconnect adapter and configured as a cluster to provide increased protection against hardware failures. Both storage appliances share access to the same set of Fibre Channel disks. Each appliance uses the NetApp cluster-interconnect to continually monitor the availability of the partner storage appliance.

Each storage appliance has primary responsibility for a subset of the disks and both can operate independently. The NetApp cluster architecture is an active/active configuration. During normal operation, both storage appliances are operating and serving data from their individual disk arrays. When a failure occurs in one appliance in a cluster, the clustered partner appliance will perform a takeover of the failed appliance functions and provide clients access to the data on the failed appliance's disk arrays.

Network Load Balancing Clusters - A Network Load Balancing Cluster, sometimes called an IP Load balancing cluster, provides high availability and scalability for TCP/IP-based services, including Web servers, FTP servers, other mission-critical servers, and COM+ applications. In a Network Load Balancing scenario, multiple servers run independently, and do not share any resources. Client requests are distributed among the servers, and in the event of a server failure, a Network Load Balancing cluster detects the problem and the load is distributed to another server. From the remote users' point of view, the network requests can be serviced continuously, even in the face of server failure.

Examples include the Microsoft Network Load Balancing Cluster for Windows and the RedHat IP Load balancing Cluster (Piranha).

Global Clusters - Global Clustering is a mechanism for coordinating multiple individual clusters and resources to provide high availability services among them. It enables monitoring of systems and application services for an entire site, and the restarting of services at a different site when system resources at the main site become unavailable.

When it involves database clusters, data replication at the disk storage unit level is usually needed. The disk storage unit attached to a local cluster replicates data, almost instantaneously, to the remote storage unit by methods such as EMCs SRDF (Symmetrix Remote Data Facility). When the primary site fails due to site-specific disasters such as fire or sustained power outages the global or geo cluster framework activates the remote cluster. Veritas Global cluster and EMC Geospan cluster are good examples of this category of clusters.

Components of a Cluster

Cluster configuration is usually comprised of two or more servers or nodes and an external SCSI or Fibre Channel array. The cluster nodes are interconnected by high-speed interconnect and controlled by some cluster software or a cluster manager application. The cluster functions as a single computing resource, but it is comprised of a logical stack of integrated components.

The following section examines characteristic features of the important cluster components.

Cluster Nodes

A node in the cluster can be as simple as a computer with a single processor or it can have a symmetric multiprocessor (SMP) or NUMA architecture. Each cluster node is usually characterized by an independent copy of the Operating Environment. However, some may share a single boot image from the central shared disk storage unit. This could be, for example, an independent physical server such as the Sun Enterprise™ 6800, or a single domain within a Sun Enterprise 15000 or low cost Dell workstation running a Linux operating system.

There are two main architectural approaches for multiple processor systems: Symmetric Multi-Processors (SMP) and NUMA (or DSM - Distributed Share Model). These architectures will be reviewed next.

SMP Systems

In the SMP architecture, the computers utilize internal, multiple, processors (CPU/s) and they all share the same system memory and I/O resources. See Figure. 3.3. Sharing is achieved through the use of a high-speed systems bus. One multi-CPU aware copy of the O/S runs on the computer and controls all of the processors. Thus, the SMP architecture is also called the Shared Memory Architecture. In an SMP environment, each processor executes processes independently. A database application like Oracle, which has the ability to spawn multiple processes, is quite suitable for the SMP architecture and takes advantage of the SMP architecture in performing many parallel operations simultaneously.

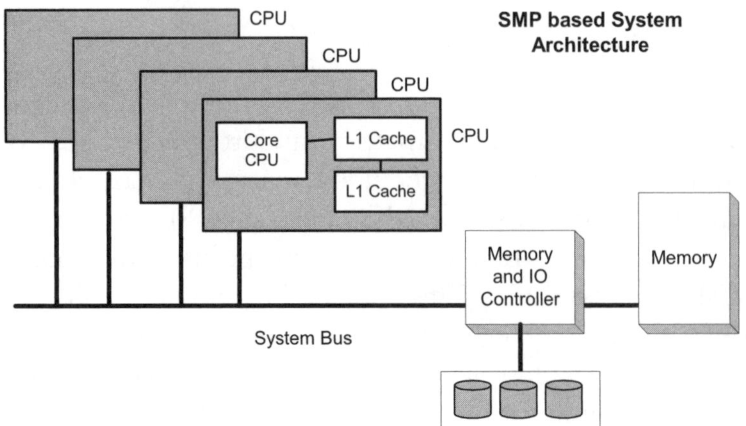

Figure 3.3: *SMP Based Node*

With current technology advances, present SMP machines are able to house up to 100 CPUs in a single SMP computer system. Advantages of utilizing SMP based servers include:

- Provides incremental paths to improve performance by adding extra processors as needed.
- Many Applications designed for a single processor do work seamlessly for SMP and take advantage of the existence of additional processors.
- SMP technology is mature and widely used.
- Administrative overhead from the operating system point-of-view is minimal.

Traditionally, scalability has been a problem in the case of SMP, although many SMP based systems from Sun and IBM support 64 to 128 processors. To scale an SMP it is not just enough to add a few sockets to plug in processors, the entire machine needs to be upgraded to achieve higher computing power. A high-speed bus and additional memory are needed. Another issue with SMP is the lack of high-availability. If one of the components of an SMP machine goes down, the entire machine can become unusable, whatever the number or processors present. In addition, the SMP servers with large numbers of processors are prohibitively expensive. For example, it may cost over one-hundred thousand dollars to simply add two processors and their companion memory boards to an existing system.

However, when several individual SMP nodes are aggregated to form a cluster, they provide a relatively inexpensive way to achieve scalability. Smaller SMP nodes, such as those provided by DELL and HP-Compaq, are relatively cheap and the aggregation of such SMP systems would result in a powerful computing cluster.

NUMA Architecture

In NUMA architecture, or non-uniform memory access, multiple processors in a computer system are grouped. They are usually called Quads, or Node Cards as in SGI servers, and the quads have their own memory and I/O controller. Quads are connected by high-speed interconnects. Unlike a cluster, all these quads are part of a single node. Thus, a NUMA system can be thought of as a large SMP system. However, the memory is non-uniformly distributed to the processors, each quad has its own localized memory, but the memory is accessible to other quads. To the processors, all of the memory in a NUMA machine appears same, but the only difference is in access time. NUMA is also called Distributed shared memory (DSM) architecture.

Good examples for NUMA systems include the Sequent (now IBM) servers and Silicon Graphics (SGI) 2000 / 3000 series.

Emerging Server Cluster Architectures

Any server requires power, connectivity to storage and to an IP network. When the servers are clustered, it usually requires a redundant heartbeat and cluster-management connection, and potentially redundant connections to dual ported storage. As a cluster begins to grow and have many nodes, with cables and connectors of the physical environment, it becomes very complex and messy. Having cluster architecture may result in many points of failure. It can be a real nightmare situation for data center managers.

The concept of the Bladed Server or Blade Server is gaining wider acceptance as it helps to solve the complexities of cluster management and also provides a modular solution to the growth of servers.

The BladeFrame architecture provides hot insertion and removal of servers, which are also called blades, and cable consolidation. Process Area Network (PAN) manager software handles the external storage mapping and virtualization, and the control of I/O and network traffic to and from individual servers. The Blade Server provides a specially designed rack into which the blades fit - the idea is to save space and power, reduce cabling, and simplify maintenance and expansion.

Thus, the main features of the Blade Technology include:

- BladeFrame is a collection of Blades
- Infrastructure of Networking and Storage Connectivity is built-in
- Infrastructure of Networking and Storage Connectivity is common to all the blades in the frame
- Power Supply is common but preferably from multiple sources
- Each blade can act as a database or application server or as a client host

- Each server can have its own flavor of operating system such as Linux or Windows
- Each server can be put to use for any number of things including Load Balancer, FireWall, App. Server, DB server, etc.
- All the components are housed in a rack.

The Blade technology based server farm is available from Egenera, IBM, HP, Dell etc. As an example, the BladeFrame system from Egenera allows for a pool of up to 96 high-end Intel® processors deployable entirely through software and without the physical intervention of a system manager. The product consists of a 24x30x84-inch chassis containing 24 two-way and/or four-way SMP processing resources, redundant central controllers, redundant integrated switches, redundant high-speed interconnects and Egenera PAN Manager software. Figure 3.4 shows an example of the Egenera blade server architecture.

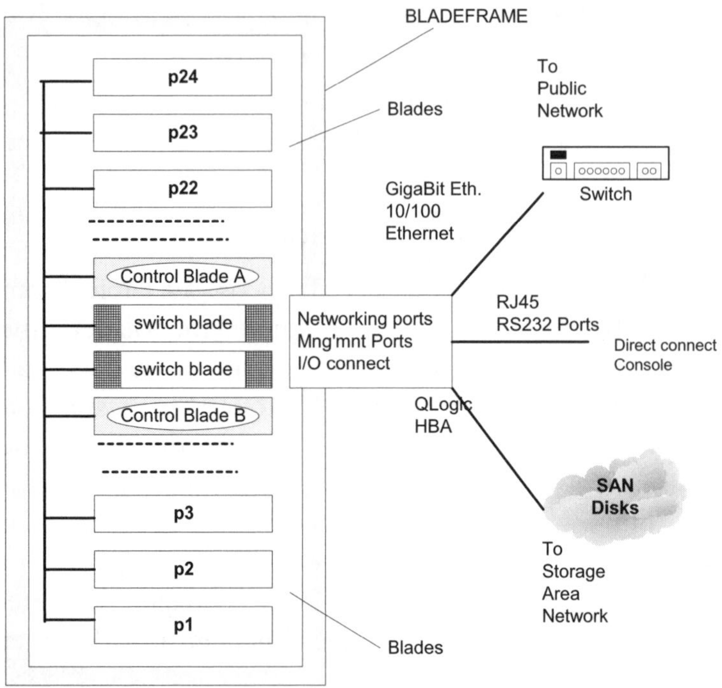

Figure 3.4: *Architecture of Egenera BladeFrame*

In another development, Switch Computing Architecture, as popularized by TopSpin Communications, provides unified switched fabric for IPC, Fibre Channel, and Ethernet for interconnecting computing elements into server area networks. This would enable the creation of virtual computers from pools of industry-standard processors, storage, and I/O building blocks. It improves performance in three parts of the network, namely host-to-host interconnect communications, host-to-LAN/WAN communications, and host-to-storage communications. Terabits of aggregate bandwidth in a single chassis, and Sub-10 microsecond latencies within the switches help in setting up high performance clusters as shown in Figure 3.5.

The new and evolving architectures, specifically Process Area Networks (PAN) and Server Area Networks, are helping to create and manage powerful clusters.

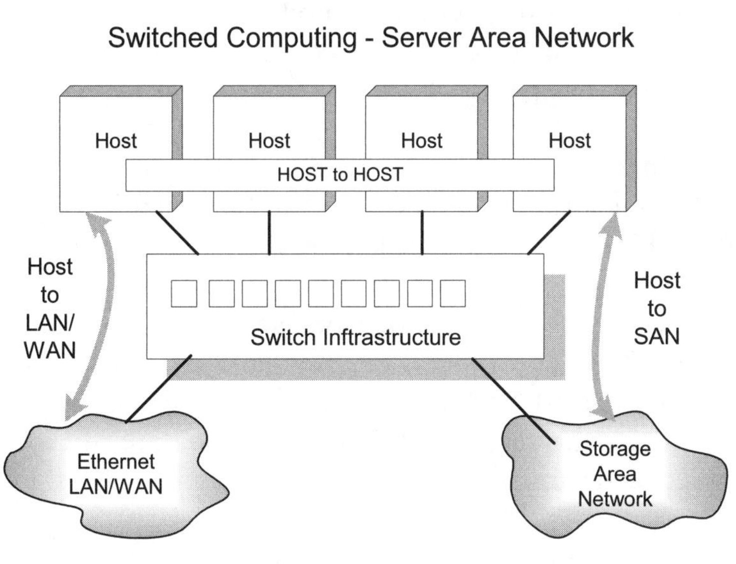

Figure 3.5: *Switched Computing Environment*

Cluster Interconnect

The cluster interconnect is a high bandwidth, low latency communication facility that connects each node to other nodes in the cluster, and routes messages and data among the nodes.

In general, the cluster-interconnect is used for the following high-level functions:

- Monitor Health, Status, and Synchronize messages
- Transport Distributed lock manager (DLM) messages
- Accessing remote file systems
- Move application-specific traffic

- Provide cluster alias routing

High performance computing involves distribution of the processing across an array of nodes in the clusters, and requires that the cluster interconnect provide high-data rate and low-latency communication between node processes. Also interconnects need to be capable of detecting and isolating faults, and of using alternative paths.

With the significant growth in the power of the processors or SMP servers, for a cluster to be successful and competitive over a large SMP machine, it should be able to move messages and data among the nodes at near the speed of the computational power of the SMP servers. Traditional network systems, using FDDI based on the TCP/IP protocol, are not able to achieve this satisfactorily. This situation has led to many vendors developing their own specialized interconnect products, which are usually a specialized set of devices in terms of switches, hubs, cables and software.

At a moderate performance level requirement, conventional networks such as Ethernet can be used as the cluster-interconnect to build clusters. However, in view of the heavy movement of the data across the nodes through the cluster interconnect; it is always desirable to utilize the specialized high-speed interconnect products as supplied by many vendors.

Essentials for Parallel Database Clusters

Parallel Clusters, much more than the HA clusters, rely on Passing Messages among the multiple processors located in the cluster nodes. Processors running parallel programs call for data and instructions, and then perform calculations. Each processor checks periodically with the other nodes or a master node to plan its next move or to synchronize the delivery of results. These activities rely on message-passing software, such as industry-standard MPI. However, in case of Failover Clusters, message traffic is usually confined to heart-beat messages and the volume of such messages is small.

In Parallel Databases, there is a great deal of message passing and data blocks or page transfers between the local cache from one node to another node. Much of the functionality and performance depends on the efficiency of the transport medium or methodology. It becomes very critical for overall performance of the cluster and usage of the parallel application that messages and blocks be transferred in as expeditious a time as possible between cluster nodes.

Key Measurements for Scalability

Low Latency: Provides fast (microsecond) passage of small (<512 bytes) lock messages between the nodes in the cluster.

High Bandwidth: Enable high throughput (Tens of GB per second) for larger Cache to Cache transfers (>4Kbytes) between nodes and between nodes and backend storage.

Low CPU Utilization: Minimum CPU and Memory Bus cycles devoted to communications to free up CPU cycles for additional database computing

---

As the Parallel Databases do not impose any constraints on the node to which users can connect and access, users have a choice to connect to any node in the cluster. Irrespective of the nature of application, OLTP or Data Warehousing databases, the movement of the data blocks from one node to another using the interconnect is widely practiced. The most significant role of the cluster interconnect and vendor provided interconnect software is to provide some kind of extended cache encompassing the data caches from all the nodes participating in the parallel database cluster.

The usual implementation of a message-passing system is based on the interconnect communication protocol. For example, a Fast Ethernet or Gigabit Ethernet interconnect runs on a TCP/IP or UDP/IP protocol based system. Systems based on the Grand Message (GM) or the Virtual Interface Architecture (VIA) use Myrinet and Emulex (formerly Giganet) interconnects, respectively. A lightweight communication protocol, such as GM or VIA, is more efficient than the conventional TCP/IP protocol. It allows user programs to communicate with the network interface card (NIC) directly, which reduces the message-passing overhead and avoids unnecessary data copies in the operating system. As a result, these protocols enable lower communication latency and higher throughput.

Cluster Interconnect Products

Many of the Cluster vendors have designed very competitive technology. Many of the interconnect products come close to the latency levels of the SMP bus. Technologies like Memory Channel, SCI and Myrinet support virtual shared memory space by means of inter-nodal memory address space mapping. Connections between nodes are established by mapping part of the nodes virtual address space interconnect interface. Because of the memory mapped nature of the interface, transmitting or receiving overhead is similar to an access to local main memory. This mechanism is the fundamental reason for the low latency levels as seen in Memory Channel, SCI and Myrinet.

Table 3.1 summarizes the various interconnect capabilities

Measurement	SMP Bus	Memory channel	Myrinet	Sun SCI	Gigabit Ethernet	Infiniband
Latency (µs)	0.5	3	7 to 9	10	100	< 10
CPU overhead (µs)	< 1	< 1	< 1		~100	
Messages/ sec (million)	> 10	> 2			< 0.1	
Bandwidth MB/sec	> 500	> 100	~ 250	~70	~ 50	10 to 30 Gb

Table 3.1: *Various Interconnect Capabilities*

Some of the popular interconnect products and technologies will be examined next.

Memory Channel - The memory channel interconnect is a high-speed network interconnect and provides applications with a cluster-wide address space. Applications map portions of this address space into their own virtual address space as 8 Kbytes pages and then read from and write into this address space just like normal memory. This is available for Alpha-based HP (now Compaq) clusters.

Myrinet - Myrinet is a cost effective, high performance, packet communication and switching technology. It is widely used in Linux Clusters. Myrinet software supports most common hosts and operating systems. The software is supplied open source. Myrinet implements host interfaces that execute a control program to interact directly with host processes (OS bypass) for low latency communication, and directly with network to send, receive, and buffer packets.

Scalable Coherent Interconnect - SCI is Sun's best performing cluster interconnect because of its high data rate and low latency. Applications that stress the interconnect will scale better using SCI compared to using lower performing alternatives. Sun SCI implements Remote Shared Memory (RSM), a feature that bypasses the TCP/IP communication overhead of Solaris. This improves cluster performance. The SCI is Sun's highest performing cluster interconnect for Sun Cluster hardware/software. It is available for the Sun Fire 4800 and 6800 servers.

Veritas - Database Edition/Advanced Cluster communications consists of Low Level Transport (LLT) and Group Membership Services (GAB). LLT provides kernel-to-kernel communications and functions as a high performance replacement for the IP stack. Use of LLT rather than IP reduces the latency and overhead associated with the IP stack.

HP Hyper Fabric (HMP): HP Hyper-Fabric supports standard TCP/UDP over IP and HP's proprietary Hyper Message Protocol. Hyper Fabric extends the scalability and reliability of TCP/UDP by providing transparent load balancing of connection traffic across multiple network interface cards. HMP coupled with OS bypass capability and the hardware support for protocol offload provides low latency and extremely low CPU utilization.

Infiniband Interconnect

Infiniband is an emerging standard that will help businesses build an ideal cluster database platform. This standard specifies channels that are created by attaching Host Channel Adapters (HCA) between servers for inter-process communication.

Some of the significant features of Infiniband include:

- Infiniband allows HCA to transfer data directly into or out of application buffers.

- Data transfers are initiated directly from user mode, thus eliminating a costly context-switch to kernels. As a result, there is no system buffer involved.
- Supports up to 3.0 Gbits/Sec bandwidth. Because it allows bundling of multiple channels, effective bandwidth can grow appreciably.
- Memory Windows provides a way for the application to grant remote read/write to a specified buffer at a byte level granularity. RDMA write and read allow a clustered application, such as Oracle RAC, to transfer data blocks directly from the cache in one instance to the cache in another instance in cluster.
- Reliability built into hardware eliminates the need for implementing additional checking in the application and thus saves CPU cycles at process level.

For building a high performance Oracle Real Application Cluster, the selection of the right interconnect is important. Care should be taken to select the highest speed, most appropriate technology that is suitable to one's environment.

ClusterWare

Clustering software is usually equipped with the functionality of monitoring, detection of failures, and managing the cluster components, which include the servers and server connections. Cluster software specializes in failure detection by use of software probes, fault isolation, and fault containment wherever applicable.

Cluster software is usually referred to as Cluster Manager or Operating system dependent layer (OSD) as in the case of Oracle Real Application clusters. Cluster Software is generally provided by the Cluster hardware manufacturer. However, in the case of

OSD layer for Oracle RAC system for Windows 2000 cluster and Linux, Oracle provides the cluster software. For building the 10g RAC database system, Oracle provides an integrated and portable ClusterWare called Cluster Ready Services (CRS).

The failure detection process involves the determination of a fault condition and the application of a proper response. A failure could result in a switch-over to a secondary component or may result in the total shutdown of the failing component, in which case some kind of reconfiguration takes place. As an example, if two interconnects are configured, fault or loss of one would not cripple the cluster but merely result in shutting it off. Whereas when one of the nodes hangs, cluster manager evicts the failed node and informs other members so that the application (database instance) can take necessary reconfiguration action.

The Cluster Manager is also responsible for node monitoring, which includes the polling of status of various resources like inter-connect hardware/software, shared disks, Oracle instances and public networks. In Oracle RAC, Cluster Manager interacts with the Global Cache Service of RAC to reconfigure the failed instance resources. The Cluster manager interacts with RAC modules and helps to reconfigure the system resources as required.

Cluster software protects against the conditions of Split-Brain and Amnesia. The Split-Brain Condition occurs when all communication between nodes is lost and the cluster becomes partitioned into sub-clusters, each believing that it is the only partition. Amnesia occurs when the cluster restarts after a shutdown with cluster configuration data older than at the time of the shutdown. Changes in cluster membership drive the cluster reconfiguration sequence that may, in turn, result in services being migrated from failed or faulty nodes to healthy ones. More details about the Split-Brain condition are covered in later sections.

In Failover Clusters, along with cluster software, cluster vendors usually supply agents or bundled scripts to control and manage the failover process. Agents are available for most of the widely used databases such as Oracle, Sybase and DB2. Agents follow preconfigured and deterministic tested procedure to initiate resources and start the database on the surviving node.

Concurrent Database Access

Before beginning a detailed evaluation of the features of failover database clusters and high performance parallel database clusters, how the database maintains consistent data in a multi-user environment will be highlighted.

While dealing with the setup of a database in a clustered environment, guaranteed data integrity and provision of consistent data results are most crucial.

Relational Database systems allow concurrent access to the database content such as rows and tables. The same data is retrieved and updated by many users. This concurrent access requires a meaningful control of access and should provide consistent results. There are two major concepts for database access. They are Data concurrency and Data Consistency. Data concurrency allows unhindered access by any number of users to the same data at the same time. Data consistency means that each user sees a consistent view of data, including visible changes made by the user's own transactions and transactions of other users. To provide consistent transaction behavior, database systems follow appropriate transaction isolation models. For example, Oracle automatically provides read consistency to queries so that all the data a query sees comes from a single point in time, also called statement level read consistency. It can also provide transaction-level read consistency as an option. Oracle makes use of rollback segments to provide these consistent views. The local cache of the instance has all the relevant data blocks to satisfy consistent results for database operations. Figure 3.6 shows the simultaneous access of data blocks by many users through same and different instances.

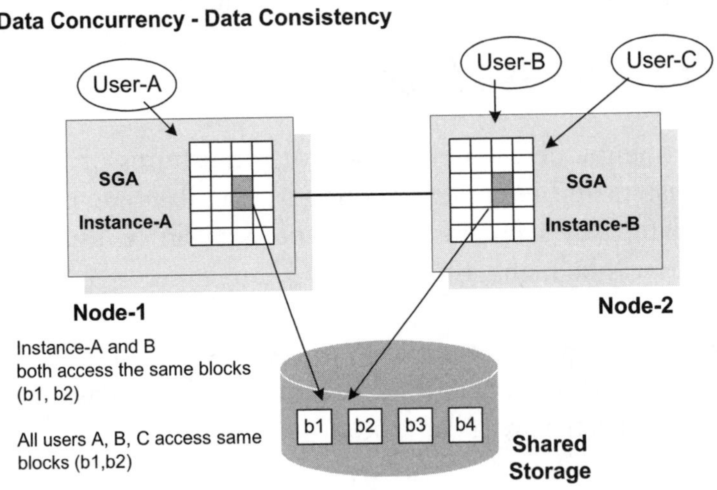

Figure 3.6: *Data Concurrency and Data Consistency*

In a failover database cluster environment, all nodes actively access the disk storage unit that provides data volumes or file systems. The active node is where the database instance is running. The database instance, with memory structures and processes, is nothing but a front end for physical data blocks or data pages. The database instance's local cache on the active node is the place where blocks are fetched into, modified and flushed back to physical storage unit. The local cache is where active buffers are handled for processing by SQL statements. Since this process deals with a single instance and only one set of cache buffers, the consistency mechanism is confined to this local cache.

However, in a parallel database clustered environment where there are multiple instances located on multiple nodes, data consistency mechanisms go beyond one instance and cover the database caches of all the nodes. Multiple caches are joined virtually to provide a single cache image and used to process SQL operations. When a user modifies a set of data blocks on one node, another user accessing the same set of blocks on a second node still gets read consistent blocks. The caches from both these nodes act as if they are one single entity. For instance, Oracle Real Application Cluster uses cache-to-cache block transfer, known as Cache Fusion, to move read-consistent images of data blocks from one instance cache to another instance cache. To support such an activity, there has to be some form of data locking.

Cache Fusion and locking mechanism will be explored in more detail in Chapter 7, *Cache Fusion and Inter-Instance Coordination*.

Failover Database Clusters

As noted earlier, fail-over (FO) database clusters are implemented by many enterprises to meet their high availability requirement. In this method, when there is a failure on the primary node, the database instance running on the failed node fails over to a backup node, in other words, it restarts the database instance on the surviving node. However, the behavior of a typical Parallel database cluster such as Oracle RAC is much different. An Oracle RAC instance is not failed over, but causes the reconfiguration of resources from the failed instance to the non-failed instance(s) to take place.

This section will explore the fail over database cluster functionality and various components such as resources, resource groups and failover mechanisms.

Resources, Resource Types

Resources are hardware or software entities, such as disks, network interface cards (NIC), IP addresses, applications and database instances controlled by cluster software. Controlling a resource means bringing it online (starting), taking it offline (stopping) as well as monitoring the health or status of the resource.

Depending on the type of resource, the clustering software, through a script or an agent, controls the status by starting and stopping activities. For example, mounting involves starting a file system resource. Starting IP resource involves configuration of the IP address on a network interface card. Monitoring a resource means testing it to determine if it is online or offline. How Cluster Software monitors a resource is also specific to the resource type. For example, a file system resource tests as online if mounted, and an IP address tests as online if configured.

Resource Groups

A resource group is a set of resources working together to provide application services to clients. A resource group is sometimes called a service group or a package. Different cluster vendors call this by different names.

For example, as shown in Figure 3.7, a database resource group might consist of:

- Disk groups on which the physical storage data volumes are located.

- Volumes built in the disk group storage.
- A file system using the volume.
- Network interface card or cards used.
- One or more IP addresses associated with the network card(s).
- A Listener Process.
- Database Instance.

A cluster software script or agent executes operations on resources, including starting, stopping, restarting and monitoring at the resource group level. Resource group operations initiate administrative operations for all resources within the group. For example, when a Resource group is brought online, all the resources within the group are brought online. When failover occurs, resources never fail-over individually rather the entire resource group fails. Thus, the resource is the unit of failover. If there is more than one group defined on a server, one group may fail-over without affecting the other group(s) on the server.

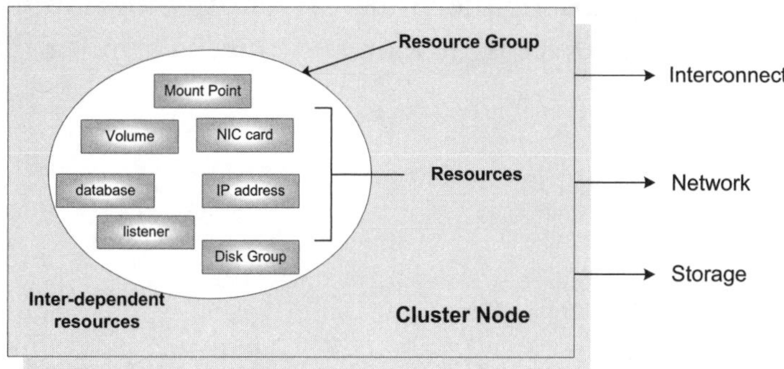

Figure 3.7: *Cluster Resource Group and Resources*

From a cluster standpoint, there are two significant aspects to this view of an application resource group as a collection of resources:

- If a Resource group is to run on a particular server, all of the resources it requires must be available to the server.
- The resources comprising a resource group have interdependencies; that is, some resources (e.g., volumes) must be operational before other resources (e.g., the file system) can be made operational.

The Concept of a Virtual Server

The concept of a virtual server is a very significant feature in a failover cluster that allows smooth and seamless connectivity to clustered computing resources or services by client applications.

To users and clients, connecting to a database or service running as a clustered virtual server appears to be the same as connecting to a single, physical server. In fact, any node in the cluster, but usually the primary or surviving node, can host the connection to a virtual server. The user or client application will not know which node is actually hosting the virtual server. As shown in the Figure 3.8, the Virtual Server is an addressing mechanism for the client connections.

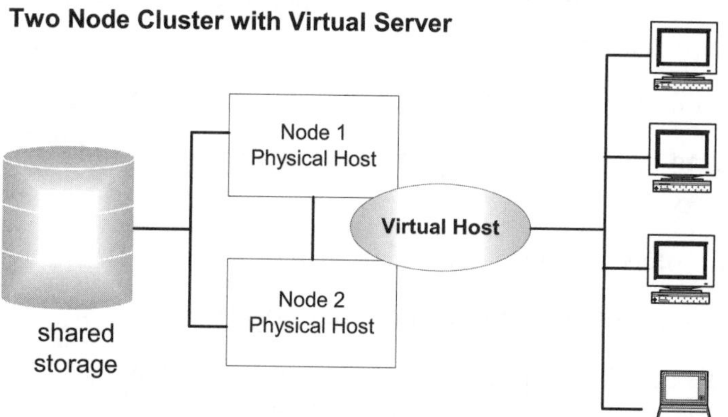

Figure 3.8: *Cluster Access by using Virtual Server*

Server clusters manage the virtual server as a resource that is mapped to the IP address or network name. Application client connections to a virtual server are made by a client session that knows only the IP address that the cluster service publishes as the address of the virtual server. The client view is simply a view of individual network names and IP addresses.

For example, in a typical database cluster having two physical nodes, each with distinct IP addresses, the cluster server configures an additional IP address, usually termed as virtual server or host. This virtual host always maps to the active node in the cluster where database service is provided.

Failover Process

Whenever there is a failure in the primary node, and the application or database is in disabled function, the failover process begins as initiated by a script or agent. Fail-over in host-based database system usually includes the following steps in sequential order.

- Detecting failure by monitoring the heartbeat and checking the status of resources.
- Reorganizing cluster membership in the Cluster Manager.
- Transferring disk ownership from the primary node to a secondary node.
- Mount the file system on secondary node.
- Starting database instance on secondary node.
- Recover the database and rollback uncommitted data.
- Reestablishing client connections to the fail over node (database)

The following are examples of how a typical resource group is configured in a Veritas Cluster server and Microsoft Cluster service.

Examples:

Veritas Cluster Server (VCS), Service Group is the basic unit of fail over. Service group fails over to backup node when failure occurs at the primary node. Service groups consist of related resources that work together to deliver database service to clients. Service Groups allow the monitoring and controlling of service availability as a whole, as opposed to the individual items (servers, disks, software, etc.) The failure of one critical item in the service group will cause the entire group to fail over to another system.

In Oracle database implementation within the framework of Microsoft Cluster Service (MSC), the Cluster Group includes the following resources:

One or more virtual addresses, each of which consists of an IP address and network name:

- The Oracle database server

- All disks used by the Oracle database
- A Net8 (or SQL*Net) network listener that listens on the virtual address (or addresses) of the group for connection requests to the databases in the group
- An Oracle Intelligent Agent configured to use one of the group's virtual addresses (if Oracle Enterprise Manager will be used to manage the database)

The Cluster group is the basic failover unit in case of MSC. Oracle provides failsafe manager tools to configure and manage Oracle database service failover with in MSC framework.

The above examples demonstrate that the database instance has been freshly started after required resources are online. It is a mutually exclusive condition in which the database instance resides on a primary node or on a backup node.

Failover Cluster Architecture

Normally the Failover cluster is implemented in two types of architectures. They are Active/Passive architecture and Active/Active architecture.

Active/Passive Clusters – This type comprises two near identical infrastructures, logically sitting side-by-side. One node hosts the database service or application, while the other rests idly waiting in case the primary system goes down. They share a storage component, and the primary server gracefully turns over control of the storage to the other server or node when it fails. On failure of the primary node, the inactive node becomes the primary and hosts the database or application.

Active/Active Clusters – In this type, one node acts as primary to a database instance and another one acts as a secondary node for failover purpose. At the same time, the secondary node acts as primary for another instance and the primary node act as the backup/secondary node.

Figure 3.9 shows an example of active/active architecture.

Active / Active Architecture

Cluster Node-1	Cluster Node-2
DATABASE Instance-A, Resource Group-A	DATABASE Instance-B, Resource Group-B
Disk Group-A	Disk Group-B

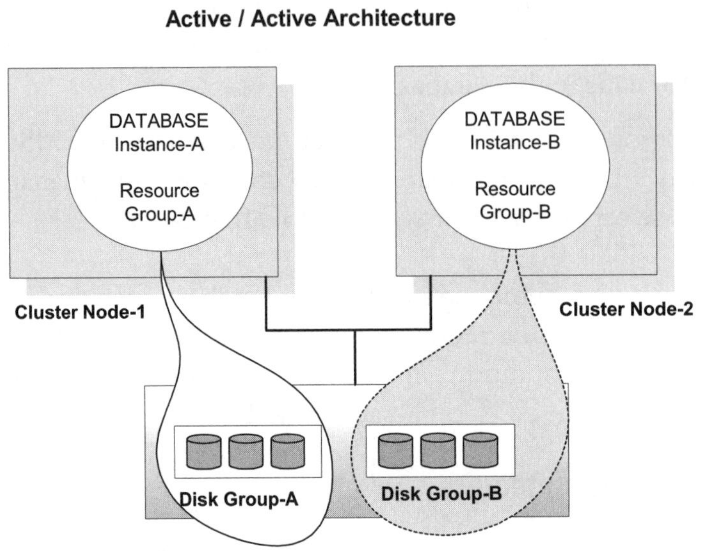

Figure 3.9: *Two Node Cluster with Active / Active Resource groups*

The Active/Passive architecture is the most widely used. Unfortunately, this option is usually capital intensive and an expensive option. For simplicity and manageability reasons many administrators prefer to implement this way. Active/Active looks attractive and is a more cost-benefit solution as the backup server is put to use. However, it can result in performance problems when both the database services (or applications) failover to single node. As the surviving node picks up the load from the failed node, performance issues may arise.

Oracle Database Service in HA Cluster

The Oracle database is a widely used database system. Large numbers of critical applications and business operations depend on the availability of the database. Most of the cluster products provide agents to support database fail over processes.

The implementation of Oracle Database service with failover in a HA cluster has the following general features.

- A single instance of Oracle runs on one of the nodes in the cluster. The Oracle instance and listener has dependencies on other resources such as file systems, mount points and IP address. etc.
- It has exclusive access to the set of database disk groups on a storage array that is shared among the nodes.
- Optionally, an Active/Active architecture of Oracle databases can be established. One node acts as the primary node to an Oracle instance and another node acts as a secondary node for failover purposes. At the same time, the secondary node acts as primary for another database instance and the primary node acts as the backup/secondary node.
- When the primary node suffers a failure, the Oracle instance is restarted on the surviving or backup node in the cluster.
- The failover process involves moving IP address, volumes, and file systems containing the Oracle data files. In other words, on the backup node, IP address is configured, disk group is imported, volumes are started and file systems are mounted.
- The restart of the database automatically performs crash recovery returning the database to a transactional consistent state.

There are some issues connected with Oracle Database failover one needs to be aware of:

- On restart of the database, there is a fresh database cache (SGA) established and it loses all the previous instance's SGA contents. All the frequently used packages and statements parsed images are lost.
- Once the new instance is created and made available on the backup node, all the client connections seeking the database service attempts to connect at the same time. This could result in a lengthy waiting period.
- The impact of the outage may be felt for an extended duration during the failover process. When there is a failure at the primary node, all the relevant resources such as mount points, disk group, listener, database instance have to be logically off-lined or shutdown. This process may take considerable time depending on failure situation.

However, when the Oracle Database Cluster is implemented in Parallel, Scalable cluster such as Oracle RAC, there are many advantages and it provides a transparent failover for the clients. The main high availability features include:

- Multiple Instances exist at the same time accessing a single database. Data files are common to the multiple instances.
- Multiple nodes have read/write access to the shared storage at the same time. Data blocks are read and updated by multiple nodes.
- Should a failure occur in a node and the Oracle instance is not usable or has crashed, the surviving node performs recovery for the crashed instance. There is no need to restart the instance on the surviving node since a parallel instance is already running there.
- All the client connections continue to access the database through the surviving node/instance. With the help of the

Transparent Application Failover (TAF) facility, clients will be able to move over to the surviving instance near instantaneously.

- There is no such thing as the moving of Volumes and File system to the surviving node.

Issues with FO Clusters – Hidden Risks

No doubt, there is wide acceptance of failover (FO) clusters, and in most situations, FO clusters provide an excellent failover mechanism, but there are some hidden risks with the nature and implementation of FO clusters.

The hidden risks with FO clusters are as follows:

- Database Failover is a time consuming process. It is usually a cold fail-over (Active/passive). A fresh database instance starts on the surviving node. For example, the un-mounting of a file system may hang and as a result off-line activity may take longer time.
- The entire process of monitoring and failover depends on scripts. Scripts can become problematic with bugs and sometimes they may not take care of all situations.
- Cluster technology cannot protect against software corruption and human-induced failures. If the server operating system crashes in such a manner that it corrupts the file system, recovery by the other member of a cluster may not be possible.
- If the owner of a file accidentally deletes it from the file system, the cluster will be unable to recover the file. Even after failing over to the second node, the same problem of file loss exists.
- Maintenance and backup is a challenge. In the case of active/active architecture for a database cluster, the

executables and other related files that you store on local storage have to be kept synchronized. Any mismatch of executables or patches might have an effect on the start up of the standby database during the fail over process.

- Configuration of the critical resources that make up the resource or service group is very significant and careful thought has to be given to the design configuration. Dependencies have to be accurately reflected, for example, in a service group, MQ Series, the database instance and Listener are defined as critical resources. In this situation, even if MQ-series fails for any reason, the database instance and listener are brought down or failover unnecessarily.

So far, many details about the FO Clusters and Database deployment and failure process have been covered. Now it is time to move on to basic features of parallel scalable clusters.

Parallel Database Clusters

The Parallel Clustered Database (PDB) is a complex application, which provides access to the same database, or group of data tables, indexes and other objects, from any server in the cluster concurrently without compromising data integrity. Well known examples include Oracle Real Application Cluster (Oracle RAC), the subject matter of this book, IBM UDB DB2 Enterprise Extended Edition (EEE), and IBM S/390 Parallel Sysplex Clusters.

Parallel Databases typically contain multiple nodes or servers accessing the same physical storage or data concurrently. PDB Architecture allows multi-server data sharing technology, allowing direct concurrent read/write access to shared data from all the processing nodes in the parallel configuration. However, this necessitates complex lock management to maintain the data integrity and resource coordination.

In terms of storage access type, a Parallel Clustered System is implemented in two ways, the Shared Nothing Model and the Shared Disk Model.

Shared Nothing Model

In the Shared Nothing model, also referred to as the Data Partitioning Model, each system owns a portion of the database and each partition can only be read or modified by the owning system as shown in Figure 3.10. Data Partitioning enables each system to locally cache its portion of the database in processor memory without requiring cross-system communication to provide data access concurrency and coherency controls.

Each server in the cluster has its own independent subset of the data called a partition it can work on independently without encountering resource contention from other servers. The clustered nodes communicate by passing messages through a network that interconnects the servers. Client requests are automatically routed to the system that owns the particular resource, memory or disk for example. Only one of the clustered systems can own and access a particular resource at a time. In the event of a failure, resource ownership can be dynamically transferred to another system in the cluster.

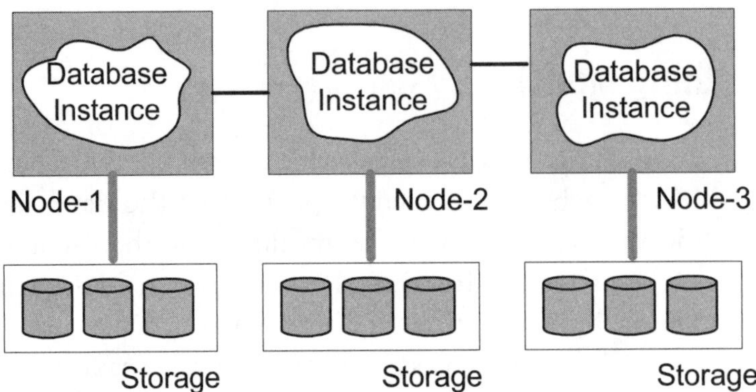

Figure 3.10: *Shared Nothing Mode – Three Node database cluster*

This architecture has several advantages:

- Shared nothing systems provide for incremental growth.
- Good for read-only databases and decision support applications.
- Failure is local - if one node fails, the other nodes stay up. However, disk system of failed node moves over to the surviving node.

It does suffer from some drawbacks as well:

- More coordination is required.
- More overhead is required in terms of processing or function shipping for a SQL operation working on a data/disk belonging to another node.
- Data skew is a potential problem. As data is added to the database and access patterns change, data re-partition is needed to balance IO.

Shared-Disk model

In the Shared-Disk model, all the disks containing data are accessible by all nodes of the cluster. Disk sharing architecture requires suitable lock management techniques to control the update concurrency control. Each of the nodes in the cluster has direct access to all disks on which shared data is placed. Figure 3.11 shows a typical three node parallel database cluster. Each node has local database buffer cache. IBM Parallel Sysplex and Oracle RAC systems follow this approach of shared-disk.

Advantages of shared-disk systems are as follows:

- Shared-disk systems permit high availability. All data is accessible even if one node fails.
- These systems have the concept of One Database and multiple access points. In other words, one can say it is multi-instance and single database. There is no issue such as data skew as the data is located and accessed at a common location.
- It provides for incremental growth of nodes and thus adds to processing power.

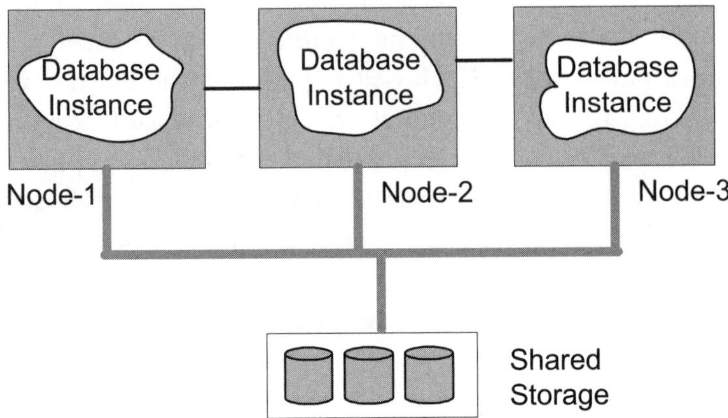

Figure 3.11: *Shared Disk Parallel Database Cluster*

Disadvantages of shared disk systems are these:

- Inter-node synchronization is required and involves complex lock management and greater dependency on high-speed interconnect.
- If the workload is not partitioned well among the processing nodes, there may be high synchronization overhead.
- There is operating system overhead of running shared disk software.

Other Architectures

There is another interesting architecture as provided by Microsoft SQL-Server Federated Database. SQL Server 2000 shares the database processing load across a group of servers by horizontally partitioning the SQL Server data. These SQL servers are configured and managed independently, but co-operate to process the database requests. Such a cooperative group of SQL Servers is called a federated database.

Federated database tiers can achieve high levels of performance only if the application sends each SQL statement to the member server that has most of the data required by the statement. This is called co-locating the SQL statement with the data required by the statement. Thus, federation of servers presents to the applications as a single database server. However, it requires careful planning and designing for a set of distributed partitioned views that spread the data across the different servers.

This configuration means significantly higher administration costs, since each individual server requires its own separate maintenance operations and prevents access to any data if any server fails. Additionally, the performance of the complete federated database is dependent on how much of the data requested is on a local server and how much is on other servers. This demands carefull partitioning of data across the multiple servers to gain performance advantages.

Table 3.2 shows differences between Single Databases and Federated databases

SINGLE SERVER	FEDERATED SERVER
There is one instance of SQL Server on the production server.	There is one instance of SQL Server on each member server.
The production data is stored in one database	Each member server has a member database. The data is spread through the member databases.
Each table is typically a single entity	The tables from the original database are horizontally partitioned into member tables. There is one member table per member database, and distributed partitioned views are used

SINGLE SERVER	FEDERATED SERVER
All connections are made to the single server, and all SQL statements are processed by the same instance of SQL Server.	The application layer must be able to collocate SQL statements on the member server containing most of the data referenced by the statement

Table 3.2: *Differences between Single Databases and Federated databases*

IBM Offered Parallel Database Systems

IBM offers DB2 databases both for a shared-nothing (for Unix, Linux, and Windows) and a shared-disk (on the mainframe only) approach. At a very high level view, architecture of IBM Parallel Sysplex and Oracle RAC look very much similar. However, they differ heavily in their implementation methodology. Both of these products follow the Shared Architecture. Oracle implementation provides an open system approach and it is possible to implement it by utilizing commodity-style components. Parallel Sysplex implantation depends on the special hardware components provided by IBM. Again looking at the UNIX based UDB EEE parallel database, it is more of a Partitioned Database than Parallel Database It is parallel to the extent that it doesn't matter where a query or access is performed. However, the processing is done by function shipping method when a query needs to access data attached to another node.

IBM Parallel SysPlex Architecture

The S/390 Parallel Sysplex follows the Shared Disk model approach with all nodes, or MVS systems, accessing the disks concurrently. The cluster is built in with coupling facility, which addresses the global concurrency issues involved in the shared-data scheme. The Coupling Facility is a special hardware component with proprietary microcode.

To share data with in the parallel cluster, DB2 subsystems must belong to a predefined data-sharing group. All members of a data-sharing group use the same shared DB2 catalog and directory.

DB2 data sharing implementation in a Parallel Sysplex environment, as shown in Figure 3.12, usually consists of:

- At least one coupling facility — a component that manages the shared resources of the connected central processor complexes (CPCs).
- At least one Sysplex Timer, which keeps the processor timestamps synchronized in the data-sharing group.
- A connection to shared DASD (Direct access storage device), where user data, system catalog and directory data, and MVS catalog data all reside.
- One or more CPCs, consisting of main storage, central processors, timers, and channels, that can attach to a coupling facility.

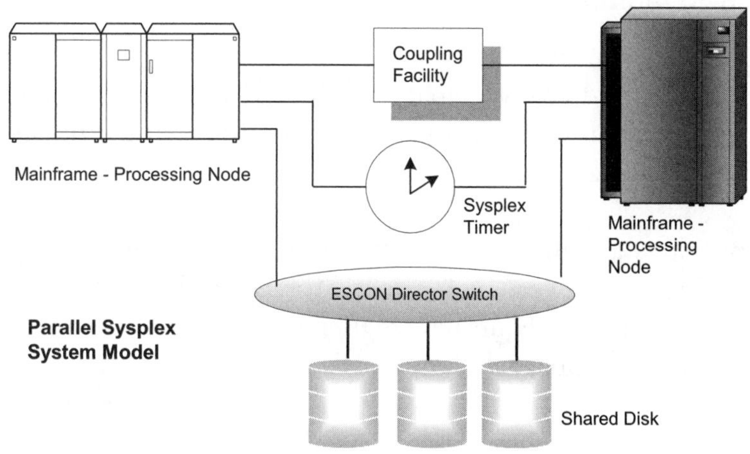

Figure 3.12: *IBM Parallel SysPlex System*

The Coupling facility is a microprocessor unit. High bandwidth fiber optic links, called channels, provides connectivity between CF and nodes/systems. DB2 uses the coupling facility to provide for inter-node communications. The coupling facility ensures data availability while maintaining data integrity across the connected DB2 subsystems. Coupling facility provides core services such as data locking, data consistency and buffering.

The coupling facility uses three structures to synchronize the activities of the data-sharing group members:

Cache structure - Supplies a mechanism called buffer invalidation to ensure consistency of cached data. The cache structure can also be used as a high-speed buffer for storing shared data with common read/write access.

List structure - Enables authorized applications to share data that is organized in a set of lists, for implementing function such as shared work queues and shared status information.

Lock structure - Supplies shared and exclusive locking capability for serialization of shared resources down to a very small unit of data.

Thus, the Coupling Facility manages all locking, contention, and concurrency issues. It does liaison with local buffers of the nodes. It is the heart of data sharing system.

While it provides a high performance parallel cluster for database support, it comes with very high price. Moreover, this system is a proprietary solution requiring higher costs in terms of administration and manageability.

UDB EEE Architecture

Another competing Parallel Database that follows the Shared Nothing Architecture is DB2 UDB Enterprise-Extended Edition (EEE). This product follows the shared nothing model with each node having its own set of disks. Each instance or node has ownership of a distinct subset of the data and all access to this data is performed by this owning instance. Thus, it is a partition database as shown in Figure 3.13. However, the disks are physically attached to more than one node. In case of a node failure, ownership of disk subsystem moves over to another node.

The basic method UDB (EEE) follows is the distribution of the data and database functions to multiple hosts. It uses a hashing algorithm that enables it to manage the distribution and redistribution of data as required. A database partition is a part of the database that has its own portion of the user data, indexes, configuration files, and transaction logs.

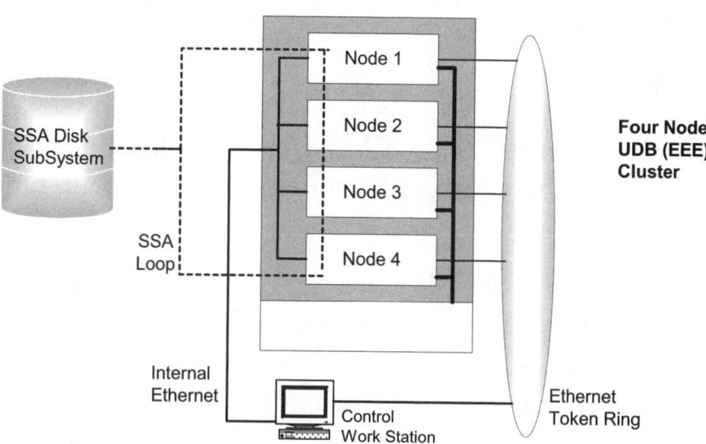

Figure 3.13: *UDB (EEE) Three Node Cluster*

The Shared nothing architecture allows parallel queries to be processed with the minimum of contention for resources between the hosts in the DB2 cluster. Because the number of data partitions has little impact on traffic between hosts, performance scales better in an almost linear manner as more machines are added to the DB2 cluster.

UDB (EEE) uses the concept of function shipping. Function shipping helps in the reduction of network traffic because functions, such as SQL queries, are shipped instead of data. Function shipping means that relational operators are executed on the node or processor containing the data whenever possible. So, the operation or the SQL is moved to where the data resides. Function shipping is well suited to the shared nothing architecture model.

In case of the failure of one node, a pre-configured node takes over the disk system and makes the data available through that node. A Cluster script starts DB2 UDB EEE database partitions on the take-over node. Once this script completes, all the database partitions in the DB2 UDB EEE database are available and processing goes on as usual.

As an example, When RS/6000 SP cluster is implemented with HACMP to support the UDB EEE, nodes are usually configured in three ways:

- **Idle Standby** - A standby SP node can be provided which will take over the work of a failed SP node. The standby SP node has access to all resources required for the provision of the essential services such as disks, networks, and so on. When the failed SP node is fixed and reintegrated into the cluster, it will reclaim its resources.
- **Rotating Standby** - A standby SP node is provided to take over the work of a failed SP node, as in the idle standby

scenario. However, when the failed SP node is reintroduced, it does not reclaim its resources, but becomes the new standby machine.

- **Mutual Takeover** - There are no standby SP nodes. All SP nodes are utilized in a normal state. After an SP node failure, the failed SP nodes resources and essential services are taken over by one of the surviving SP nodes in addition to its normal services.

DB2 UDB EEE supports a diverse set of hardware options including SMP, MPP, NUMA, and RISC servers, and clustered configurations with a range of interconnect options. DB2 exploits high-availability solutions on each platform. DB2 UDB EEE can run on multiple operating systems including IBM AIX, Linux, HP-UX, Sun Solaris, and Windows NT.

General Requirements for Parallel Database Clusters

In this section, the following critical issues pertaining to the scalable cluster and the parallel database will be examined:

- Avoiding Split Brain
- I/O Fencing
- Arbitration through Quorum Disks
- Cache Coherency and Lock Management

Avoiding Split Brain

It is reasonable to expect that server components are prone to failures. It is the responsibility of the cluster to detect and monitor and stabilize the application running on the cluster. Clusters Systems are geared to handle peculiar situations like Amnesia and Split Brain conditions.

Amnesia occurs when the cluster restarts after a shutdown with cluster data older than at the time of the shutdown. This can happen if multiple versions of the framework data are stored on disk and a new incarnation of the cluster is started when the latest version is not available.

Split Brain Condition occurs when a single cluster has a failure that results in reconfiguration of cluster into multiple partitions, with each partition forming its own sub-cluster without the knowledge of the existence of other. This would lead to collision and corruption of shared data as each sub-cluster assumes ownership of shared data.

As an example, when two systems have access to the shared storage, integrity of the data depends on the systems communication through heartbeats using the private interconnects. When the private links are lost and failed or if one of the systems is hung or too busy to send/receive heartbeats, each system thinks the other system has exited the cluster, then it tries to become the master or form a sub-cluster and claim exclusive access to the shared storage. This condition leads to Split Brain.

There are definite methods, also known as fencing, to avoid such a tricky and undesirable situation. The two basic approaches to fencing are resource based fencing and system reset or STOMITH or STONITH fencing.

Resource-based fencing includes I/O fencing and the maintenance of Quorum disks. In resource-based fencing, a hardware mechanism is employed, which immediately disables or disallows access to shared resources. If the shared resource is a SCSI disk or disk array, one can use SCSI reserve/release or better yet persistent reserve/release operations. If the shared resource is a fiber channel disk or disk array, then one can instruct a fiber channel switch to deny the problem node access to shared resources. In general, the errant node itself is left undisturbed, and its resources are instructed to deny access to it. If the node is able to later become part of a cluster with quorum, it will then go through the normal channels to reacquire its resources.

STOMITH stands for Shoot the Other Machine in the Head. STOMITH fencing takes a completely different approach. In STOMITH systems, the errant cluster node is simply reset and forced to reboot. When it rejoins the cluster it acquires resources in the normal way. In many cases, STOMITH operations are performed via smart power switches, which simply remove power from the errant node for a brief period of time.

However, implementation of processes to avoid split brain varies from vendor to vendor, and also depends on the type of shared storage in use for the cluster. For example, Sun Cluster avoids split brain by using the majority vote principle coupled with quorum disks and Linux cluster using Polyserve Matrix Server employs fabric fencing. The next section examines these techniques in detail.

I/O Fencing – exclusion strategy

There will be some situations where the leftover write operations from failed database instances reach the storage system after the recovery process starts, such as when the cluster function failed on the nodes, but the nodes are still running at OS level. Since these write operations are no longer in the proper serial order, they can damage the consistency of the stored data. Therefore, when a cluster node fails, the failed node needs to be *fenced off* from all the shared disk devices or disk groups. This methodology is called I/O Fencing, sometimes called Disk Fencing or failure fencing.

The main function of the I/O fencing includes preventing updates by failed instances, and detecting failure and preventing split brain in cluster. Cluster Volume Manager, in association with the shared storage unit, and Cluster File System play a significant role in preventing the failed nodes accessing shared devices.

For example, in Sun Cluster, disk fencing is done through SCSI-2 reservation for dual hosted SCSI devices and for multi-hosted environment through SCSI-3 PR. Veritas Advance Cluster uses the SCSI-3 persistent reservation to perform I/O fencing. In the case of Linux clusters, CFS like Polyserve and Sistina GFS are able to perform I/O fencing by using different methods like fabric fencing that uses SAN access control mechanism.

SCSI-3 PR

SCSI-3 PR, which stands for Persistent Reservation, supports multiple nodes accessing a device while at the same time blocking access to other nodes. SCSI-3 PR reservations are persistent across SCSI bus resets or node reboots and also support multiple paths from host to disk. For SCSI-2 disks, reservations are not persistent which means they do not survive node reboots.

SCSI-3 PR uses a concept of registration and reservation. Systems that participate, register a key with SCSI-3 device. Each system registers its own key. Then registered systems can establish a reservation. With this method, blocking write access is as simple as removing registration from a device. A system wishing to eject another system issues a pre-empt and abort command and that ejects another node. Once a node is ejected, it has no key registered so that it cannot eject others. This method effectively avoids the split-brain condition.

Another benefit of the SCSI-3 PR method is that since a node registers the same key down each path, ejecting a single key blocks all I/O paths from that node. For example, SCSI-3 PR is implemented by EMC Symmetrix, Sun T3, and Hitachi Storage systems. In case of SCSI-2 reservation, it works only with one path with one host.

Arbitration through Quorum Disks

In case of SCSI-2 reservation, the Clusterware seeks to reserve a quorum disk to break the tie in cases of split cluster. A quorum disk is a nominated device in the shared storage connected to the relevant nodes. The reservation is enacted as a SCSI-2 *ioctl*. The node that is granted the reservation causes the second attempt to fail. The SCSI-2 reservation *ioctl* used is part of the SCSI-2 command set. This is commonly implemented in most modern disk firmware. However, the reservation call is neither persistent, or capable of surviving reboots, nor able to cope with multiple paths to the same device.

A quorum disk must be defined for a two-node cluster. This arrangement enables any single node that obtains the vote of the quorum disk to maintain majority and continue as a viable cluster. Clusterware forces the loosing node out of the cluster.

Fabric Fencing

Polyserve Matrix Server (Cluster File System), which is widely used on Linux clusters, implements node exclusion strategy by following the Fabric-Fencing approach. The Polyserve matrix server includes a Storage Control Layer that uses SAN access control mechanism to arbitrate which servers have access to which storage resources. This is achieved by turning off the Fibre-Channel ports to which the offending node is attached.

Advantages of this approach:

- Isolates the SAN access only
- Permits non-SAN applications to continue to run
- No extra hardware is required

Exclusion with STOMITH approach

This method uses a network controlled power switch to cut off a server's power supply when it is no longer deemed to be a reliable member of the cluster. Some of the characteristics of this approach:

- It is highly disruptive to the problem node.
- It is universal - it operates on all resource types equally well, and simultaneously.
- It is very simple in concept and in practice.
- There are virtually no support problems or version interactions to complicate development, testing, and maintenance.
- Overall system availability is often helped by the reboot.

This method was adopted by Linux clusters in the earlier period of their growth and when the Linux SCSI reserve/release support was immature and not consistently implemented.

However, there are certain issues with method:

- Potential data integrity issues on account of forceful shutdown of node.
- Nodes can shoot each other and shutdown the entire cluster.
- Shot down server cannot be accessed to diagnose issues.

Sistina GFS supports multiple cascading I/O fencing methods including manual, network power control, and fibre channel switch zone control.

Cache Coherency and Lock Management

One of the most critical features for a parallel database is its ability to control global concurrency of the data (pages or blocks) located in the individual node's cache. As each of the nodes has its own local cache that has current data blocks, their status and access need to be controlled globally. Other node's cache might need to access concurrently. Blocks are moved frequently across the nodes when needed. In addition, there should be effective and accurate monitoring of the status of the blocks in cache. Lock acquisition, lock release, and lock conversions should be performed at rapid speeds. Low latency and High-speed communication between the nodes is an essential requirement.

Since a data block can be present in the database buffers of more than one node when an update occurs, all other buffered copies become obsolete. The global cache control mechanism invalidates the obsolete data blocks. Another important feature is the way in which the reconfiguration of cache occurs when a node fails. To maintain integrity of data blocks, failed instance's resources need to be taken over or re-mastered by another node's instance.

Conclusion

In this chapter, details about high performance and high available database systems have been presented as well as an overview of cluster technology and various types of clusters. There was particular emphasis on database clusters and its requirements for data consistency and concurrency.

Failover clusters are widely used for deploying high available databases. Many cluster vendors provide cluster software or agents, which support relational database failover process. Parallel Database Clusters, which allow concurrent access to data blocks form multiple nodes or instances, have to deal with more complicated issues like cache coherency and lock management. This review has also covered different architectures of parallel database clusters, and focused on the requirements for a stable parallel database cluster product.

The next chapter will cover concepts and general features of Real Application Clusters (RAC), including architectural details and all the components.

RAC Architecture

CHAPTER 4

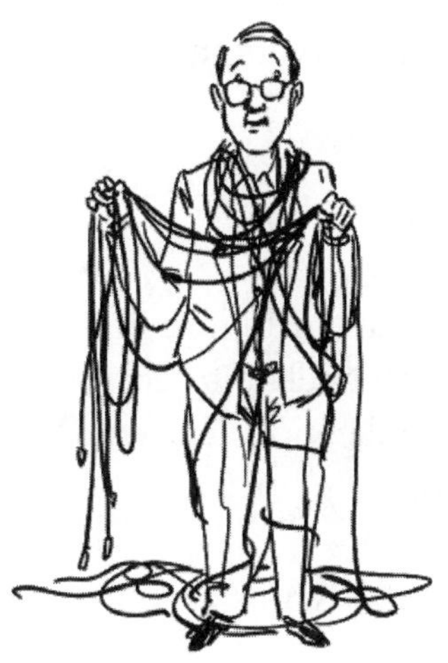

The Architecture of RAC

In this chapter, the architecture of the RAC database system is examined. RAC database is a multi-instance single database. All the components that make up total architecture will be reviewed and the inter-relations for these components will be covered.

RAC is the principal component for the Oracle Grid Architecture. Oracle's Grid vision represents a pool of database servers, storage, and networks in an inter-related resource platform. Effective Management of workload within the grid database computing arena is a key feature. RAC Database and clustering technology helps to set up and manage the overall

Oracle Grid strategy. Database processing and capability can be easily and dynamically added with the RAC technology.

Keep in mind that Clusters and Grids have different vision and objectives. Clusters have static resources for a specific application. Grids, which can consist of multiple clusters and stand alone servers, are dynamic resource pools and they are shareable among many different applications and users. A grid does not assume that all servers in the grid are running the same set of applications.

RAC Components

The Component Diagram in Figure 4.1 shows a collection of all the components that inter-relate to each other and together make up the Oracle Real Application Cluster. This diagram provides a roadmap for discussion.

At a very high level, RAC architecture consists of these components:

- Physical Nodes or Hosts
- Physical Interconnects and interconnect protocols
- Cluster Manager Software and Cluster Ready Services
- Oracle Instances and Cache Fusion
- Shared Disk System
- Clustered File System, Raw Devices, Automatic Storage Management
- Network Services
- Workload Management Services – Virtual IP configuration

The overall structure of an Oracle Single-instance database is fairly complex. A complete Oracle instance consists of disk files, shared memory structures, and background processes. The shared memory area is further subdivided into numerous caches and pools that are used to transfer data, programs, and instructions from processes to and from the disks and users.

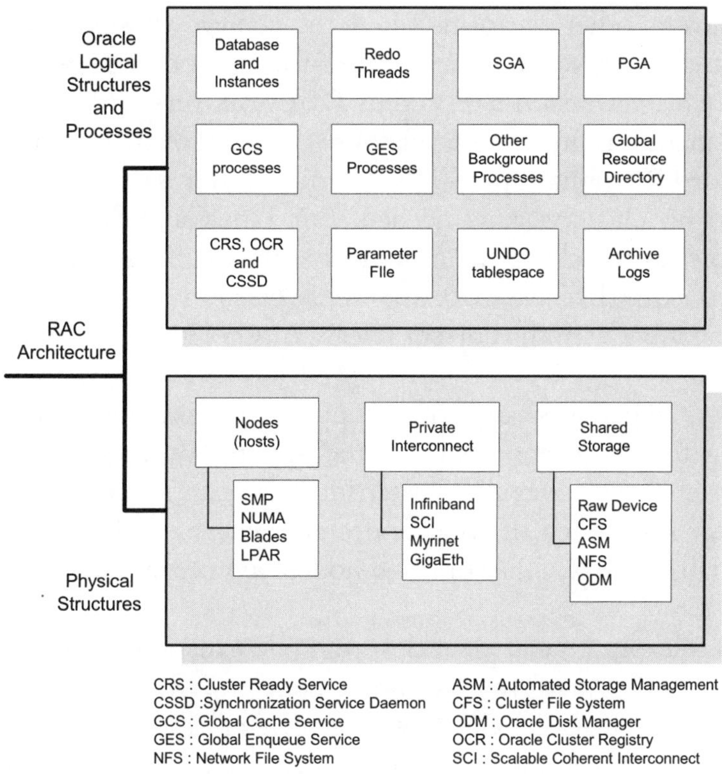

Figure 4.1: *All the Logical and Physical Components of RAC*

Each of the instances in the cluster configuration communicates with other instances by using the cluster manager or clusterware. Clusterware is the middleware that glues all the clustered instances and projects a single database system image.

Cluster platforms depend on the cluster management program to track the cluster node status, whether or not nodes in the cluster are available for work. Essentially the two types of cluster managers are vendor supplied and Oracle supplied.

HP supplies TruUnix TruCluster and HP-UX MC/Service Guard, IBM supplies HACMP/ESCRM for AIX platform and there are several other platforms where the vendor will supply the cluster manager. RAC is also certified for use on Sun Solaris using Sun Cluster version 3.0, Veritas DBE/AC version 3.5, and Fujitsu-Siemens Prime Cluster versions 4.1 and 4.0. RAC is also available for HP Alpha OpenVMS. VMS is cluster aware out-of-the-box so no clusterware is needed. For Linux and Windows, Oracle provides the cluster management software. To implement Oracle RAC on IBM-OS/390, the XCF clusterware is needed that is compatible with the current release of OS/390.

Clusterware, regardless of who supplies it, provides node monitoring for the other nodes in the system. By means of a heartbeat signal sent over the cluster interconnect, all nodes in a RAC cluster keep track of what nodes are available, which ones are unavailable, and whether or not a node becomes available.

With 10g release, Oracle provides portable clusterware which works on all the platforms to implement the RAC database solution. Oracle provided clusterware can be used independently or on top of the vendor provided cluster software. In case of Windows and Linux, the Oracle provided clusterware is the only choice, in other platforms such as Solaris, HP-UX and TruUnix, one has the choice of the vendor supplied cluster software. Oracle provided portable clusterware is named and packaged under the title Cluster Ready Service (CRS). In fact, CRS is much more than the cluster software. It provides a method to configure High Availability (HA) services and Oracle Notification Services (ONS). CRS will be examined in more detail later in this Chapter.

The shared storage provides concurrent access by all the cluster nodes to the storage array. The storage array is presented in the form of logical units (LUNS) to the cluster host or node and the file system is mounted on all nodes. Thus, when the same file system is mounted and used on all nodes in the cluster, it is called a cluster file system. There are many flavors of approved cluster file systems such as HP's CFS, Veritas CFS, PolyServe CFS, and Oracle CFS (OCFS). At the same, the option still exists to use the raw devices for many of the RAC database requirements.

With 10g release, Oracle provides a very flexible and high performing shared storage methodology which is known as Automatic Storage Management (ASM). ASM can be used in lieu of the cluster file system. More details of the shared storage and its presentation to the cluster nodes will be presented in later parts of this chapter and also in Chapter 5, *Preparing Shared Storage.*

The next section will help define the difference between Database and Database Instance? Understanding of the difference is very important in order to appreciate the RAC option.

Database and Database Instance

Oracle Database Server represents a collection of physical files, logical database objects such as tables and indexes and the host level memory structures and processes. The physical host level files are actually residing on the storage arrays, directly attached, network attached, and storage area networks (SAN). The combination of background processes and memory buffers is called the database instance. Oracle Database Instance, which resides on a host, is the actual database processing area that allows access to the physical and logical structures.

RAC Database has multiple database instances to access and manage a single database system. With the shared disk architecture, the Database consists of a single set of physical data files for data that can be accessed by multiple database instances. As shown in the Figure 4.2, each of the instances resides on a separate host and forms its own set of background processes and memory buffers. Thus, RAC enables access to a single database via multiple database instances.

When the database is not a RAC system, it has one instance and one database. Sometimes the instance and database are construed to be the same. In that case, it is called a stand-alone database system.

As an example,

```
Database Name       : NYDB50

Instance-1 Name     : NYDB51
Instance-2 Name     : NYDB52
Instance-3 Name     : NYDB53
```

The parameter *db_name* will have the value of NYDB50 and this represents the name of the database. And the parameter *instance_name* will be one of the names listed above. All these instances provide access to the same database named NYDB50.

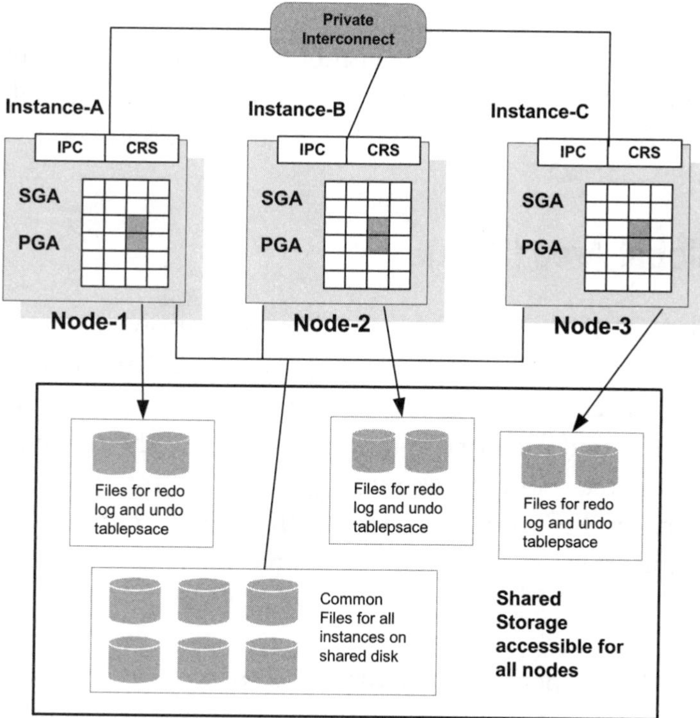

Figure 4.2: *Multi-Instance RAC Database System – At a Glance*

The examination of the Oracle Architecture will start by reviewing the memory pools and the back ground processes in a single-instance database. Then the study will extend to review the extra processes and structures that are formed in case of a RAC configuration.

Database Instance

A typical RAC database instance is very much like a stand alone database system. It has all frills and bells of a typical database instance. But it has some extra processes, memory structures, and logical structures. Since the RAC database system has to maintain concurrency of data across multiple instances, it creates additional structures to manage and coordinate the resources.

The Oracle Instance has various components to support the database processing. The memory components are broadly categorized as System Global Area (SGA) and Program Global Area (PGA).

System Global Area (SGA)

The System Global Area (SGA) consists of various memory components. A component represents a pool of memory used to satisfy a particular class of memory allocation requests. The most commonly configured memory components include the database buffer cache, shared pool, java pool, large pool, streams pool, data dictionary cache, and redo log buffer. PGA consists of session specific information that contains data and control structures.

The SGA and PGA memory structures are shown in the Figure 4.3. The SGA resources are formed at the time of database instance launch based on the instance initialization parameters. However, many of the parameters can dynamically be altered to suit the database processing needs.

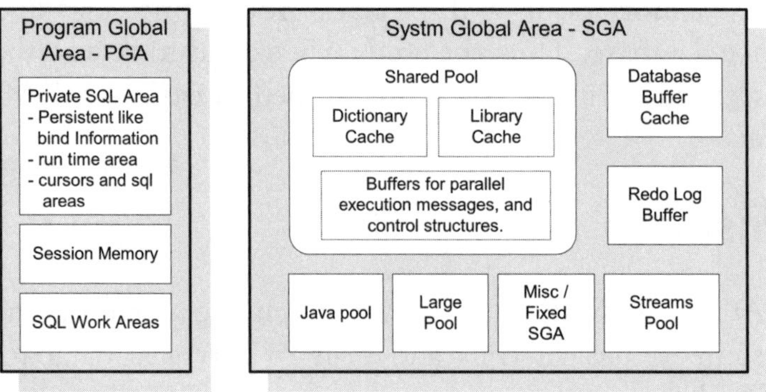

Figure 4.3: *SGA and PGA Components of a typical instance*

The size of the SGA is determined by several initialization parameters. The following Table 4.1 shows the parameters that influence the SGA size. However, when the initialization parameter *sga_target* is set to a value greater than zero, the automatic SGA configuration kicks in. This will be covered in more detail in a later part of this chapter.

PARAMETER	REMARK/DESCRIPTION
db_cache_size	Shows the size of the cache of standard blocks
log_buffer	The number of bytes allocated for the redo log buffer
shared_pool_size	Shows the size of the area allocated to shared SQL and PL/SQL statements.
large_pool_size	Size of the large pool; the default is 0.
java_pool_size	The size of the Java pool

Table 4.1: *Initialization Parameters that affect SGA size*

Database Block Buffers

The database buffer cache holds copies of the data blocks read from the data files. The term data block is used to describe a block containing table data, index data, clustered data, and so on. Basically it is a block that contains data. All user processes concurrently connected to the instance share access to the database buffer cache. The database buffer cache is logically segmented into multiple sets which reduces contention on multiprocessor systems.

This area of the SGA contains only the buffers themselves and not their control structures. For each buffer there is a corresponding buffer header in the variable area of the SGA.

From Oracle8 release onwards the buffer cache contains three buffer pools for different type of data usage. They are DEFAULT, KEEP, and RECYCLE. These three buffer pools have separate allocations of buffers and LRU lists that manage buffers.

- The RECYCLE buffer pool is used to store blocks that are virtually never used after the initial read. This pool eliminates the data blocks from the memory when no longer needed. This is more like a work area for the blocks.
- The KEEP pool is for the allocation of buffers for the objects that are accessed with medium frequency or those for which a consistent response time is desirable. This buffer pool retains the schema objects data block in memory.
- The DEFAULT buffer pool contains data blocks from schema objects that are not assigned to any buffer pool as well as for the schema objects that are explicitly assigned to the DEFAULT pool.

The database block buffers act as the holding area for data used by the user and DBWR processes. Any data that gets to the user from the database files, or data that goes into the database files from the user or other processes, passes through the database block buffers unless direct insert or direct read is used for data loading, sorting, or hashing operations.

The database block buffers in releases prior to Oracle9i had to be of uniform size, 2, 4, 8, 16, or for 64 bit OS, the 32 kilobytes in size. From Oracle9i, the database has a default database cache block size, but other sizes (2K, 4K, 8K, 16K, or 32K) can also be specified. Based on the tablespace size, appropriate Cache is employed to retrieve and manage the buffers in the SGA.

In the RAC database system, the database block buffers from each of the participating instance, through the process of cache fusion, are merged to form a logical database block buffer area that becomes many times larger than could be supported in a single instance.

Cache Fusion and Inter-Instance database buffer transfers are fully covered in Chapter 9, *Cache Fusion and Inter-Instance Coordination.*

Multiple Block Sizes in RAC environment

In RAC systems, each instance can have its own type of buffer pools. Each instance can have its own set of non-standard block size buffers. The buffer pools can be of different sizes or not at all defined. It is recommended to design and tune each instance buffer according to the requirements placed by the application on that instance.

Supporting multiple block sizes in the buffer cache is an SGA feature with the setting of the *db_nk_cache_size* parameter. Up to four block sizes can be specified in addition to a standard block size. The sizes and numbers of non-standard block size buffers are specified by the following parameters:

```
db_2k_cache_size
db_4k_cache_size
db_8k_cache_size
db_16k_cache_size
db_32k_cache_size
```

The following is an example of Setting Block and Cache Sizes

```
db_block_size=4096
db_cache_size=1024M
db_2k_cache_size=256M
db_8k_cache_size=512M
```

In the above example, the parameter *db_block_size* sets the standard block size of the database to 4k. The size of the cache of standard block size buffers will be 1024M. Additionally, 2k and 8k caches are also configured, with sizes of 256M and 512M, respectively.

In the initialization file, sub-caches can be configured within the buffer cache for each of these block sizes. Sub-caches can also be configured while an instance is running. To support this feature, *db_*n*k_cache_size* is a dynamic initialization parameter.

In a RAC system, it is possible to set up different non-standard block size buffers in different instances. But that would lead to problems during runtime. This issue is examined more in the next section.

When a tablespace is created with a *blocksize* clause, Oracle checks for the cache availability of that particular block size at the instance where it is being created. For example, assume that a tablespace is created in node-2 where the non-standard *db_2k_cache_size* is set. Since a 2k sized cache is available, the create statement goes through.

```
SQL> create tablespace TBS_2K blocksize 2K;

Tablespace created.
```

Next, assume that after creating the above tablespace with 2k block size, the instance is restarted without the 2k cache. The instance comes up without any issue, however the first time Oracle attempts access an object from the tablespace and tries to place blocks into the cache, the following error will be received:

```
ORA-00379: no free buffers available in buffer pool DEFAULT for
block size x
```

As another example, switch to Node-3 which does not have *db_2k_cache_size* set. When an attempt is made to access that tablespace, Oracle produces an error.

```
SQL> create table mytable (col1 varchar(16))
TABLESPACE TBS_2K ;
create table mytable (col1 varchar(16)) TABLESPACE TBS_2K
*
ERROR at line 1:
```

```
ORA-00379: no free buffers available in buffer pool DEFAULT for
block size 2K
```

Therefore, it is recommended that all instances start with the same set of non-standard block size buffers (sub-cache) with the *db_nk_cache_size* parameter. Note that Oracle is not enforcing the existence of the same set of sub-caches when the instance joins the cluster. It is better to create the sub-cache with all possible caches (2K, 4K, 8K, 16K, 32K etc) to avoid run time errors.

Redo Log Buffers

Redo log buffers are used to hold the redo records generated by each data changing transaction. It is a circular buffer. Redo entries contain the information necessary to reconstruct, or redo, changes made to the database by INSERT, UPDATE, DELETE, CREATE, ALTER, and DROP operations.

A redo log buffer is written out to the online redo log by the log writer process when:

- The buffer becomes one third full.
- Three seconds have elapsed.
- When a DBWn process writes modified buffers to disk.
- On commit record - when a user process commits a transaction.

While it is acceptable to have different sized redo log buffers and redo logs on each instance in a RAC database, this is not a suggested configuration. It can lead to confusion and misunderstandings during recovery operations. Each instance in a RAC database must have its own thread of redo logs.

JAVA Pool

The JAVA Pool holds the JAVA execution code in a similar manner to the PL/SQL cache in the shared pool. The JAVA pool is used by many internal routines, such as import and export, and should be sized at approximately 60 megabytes if no other JAVA will be utilized in the user applications.

Shared Pool

The shared pool holds the library cache, dictionary cache, message queues, latch and lock areas, buffers for parallel execution messages, and control structures. The shared pool also contains the RAC lock areas known as the Global Resource Directory. The total size of the shared pool is determined by the initialization parameter *shared_pool_size*.

The library cache includes the shared SQL areas, private SQL areas (in the case of a shared server configuration), PL/SQL procedures and packages, and control structures such as locks and library cache handles. Shared SQL areas are accessible to all users so the library cache is contained in the shared pool within the SGA.

The data dictionary is accessed very often by various Oracle processes. Dictionary Cache is the memory areas designated to hold dictionary data. It is also known as the row cache because it holds data as rows instead of buffers which hold entire blocks of data.

Large Pool

This area is only used if shared server architecture, also called multi-threaded server (MTS), is used, or if parallel query is utilized. The large pool holds the user global areas when MTS is used and holds the parallel query execution message queues for parallel query.

In general, large pool provides memory allocations for:

- Session memory for the shared server and the Oracle XA interface which is used where transactions interact with more than one database.
- I/O server processes.
- Oracle backup and restore operations.

Streams Pool

This is a new area in Oracle Database 10g that is used to provide buffer areas for the streams components of Oracle. To configure the Streams pool explicitly, specify the size of the pool in bytes using the *streams_pool_size* initialization parameter. If the size of the Streams pool is greater than zero, then any SGA memory used by Streams is allocated from the Streams pool. If the size of the Streams Pool is zero or not specified, then the memory used by Streams is allocated from the shared pool and may use up to 10% of the shared pool.

Fixed SGA

A portion of the SGA contains general information about the state of the database and the instance, which the background processes need to access. This is called the Fixed SGA. No user data is stored here. The SGA also includes information communicated between processes, such as locking information.

Automatic Shared Memory Management

Oracle 10g, with its emphasis on self-management and self-tuning, introduces many features that operate automatically, as well as in an advisory role. Since the values for the SGA components are fixed at instance start time, they must be used as they are during the instance runtime, with some exceptions.

Often it happens that a certain component's memory pool is never used and it is not available for another component, which is in need of extra memory. Under-sizing can lead to poor performance and out-of memory errors (ORA-4031), while over-sizing can waste memory.

With the Database 10g, the Automatic Shared Memory Management feature can be employed. This feature enables the Oracle database to automatically determine the size of each of these memory components within the limits of the total SGA size. This solves the allocation issues that are normally faced in a manual method.

This feature enables the specification of a total memory amount to be used for all SGA components. The Oracle Database periodically redistributes memory between the components according to workload requirements.

Use of the *sga_target* initialization parameter configures automatic Shared Memory Management. If a non-zero value is specified for *sga_target*, the following four memory pools are automatically sized by Oracle.

- Database Buffer cache (Only the Default pool)
- Shared Pool
- Large Pool
- Java Pool

If *sga_target* is set to the default value of 0, Automatic Shared Memory Management is disabled. When *sga_target* is not set, or equal to the default value of 0, auto-tuned SGA parameters behave as in previous releases of the Oracle database. In Oracle 10g, the initialization parameters such as *db_cache_size, shared_pool_size, large_pool_size*, and *java_pool_size* are referred to as auto-tuned SGA parameters.

Figure 4.4 shows an example of auto tuned SGA components.

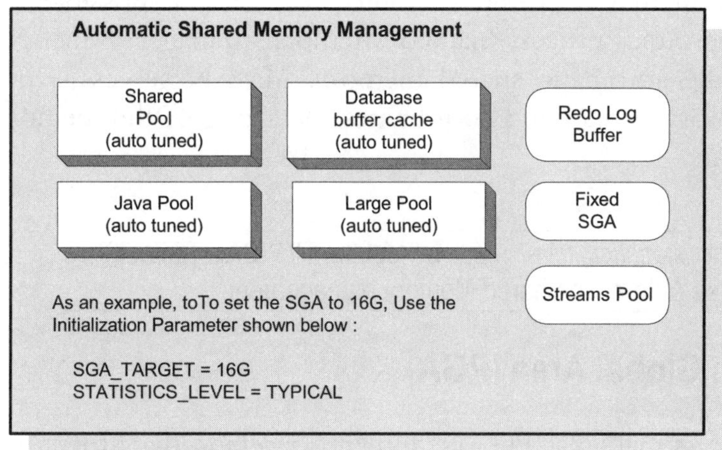

Figure 4.4: *SGA Memory Buffers managed dynamically*

Configuration of the following buffers still remains manual and they are now referred to as manually-sized components:

- Log Buffer
- Other Buffer Caches (KEEP/RECYCLE, other block sizes)
- Streams Pool (Newly introduced in Oracle Database 10g)
- Fixed SGA and other internal allocations

The user specifies manual SGA parameters, and parameter sizes precisely control the size of their corresponding components. When *sga_target* is set, the total size of manual SGA parameters are subtracted from the *sga_target* value and the balance is given to the auto-tuned SGA components.

sga_target is also a dynamic parameter and can be changed through Enterprise Manager or with the ALTER SYSTEM command. However, the *sga_target* can be increased only up to the value of *sga_max_size*.

The question may arise, how is auto management possible? A new background process named Memory Manager (MMAN) manages the automatic shared memory. MMAN serves as the SGA Memory Broker and coordinates the sizing of the memory components.

Important: *statistics_level* must be set to TYPICAL (default) or ALL to use Automatic Shared Memory Management.

Program Global Area (PGA)

A program global area (PGA) is a memory region that stores the data and control information for the server processes. Each Server process has a non-shared memory region created by Oracle when a server process is started. Access to the PGA is exclusive to that server process and it is read and written only by Oracle code. Broadly speaking, PGA contains a private SQL area and a Session memory area.

A private SQL area contains data such as bind information and runtime memory structures. Each session that issues an SQL statement has a private SQL area.

Note that the Location of a private SQL area depends on the type of connection established for a session. If a session is connected through a dedicated server, private SQL areas are located in the server process' PGA. However, if a session is connected through a shared server, part of the private SQL area is kept in the SGA.

Session memory is the memory allocated to hold a session's variables (logon information) and other information related to the session. For a shared server, the session memory is shared and not private.

With the initialization parameter *pga_aggregate_target*, sizing of work areas for all dedicated sessions is made automatic and all **_area_size* parameters are ignored for these sessions. At any given time, the total amount of PGA memory available to active work areas on the instance is automatically derived from the *pga_aggregate_target* parameter.

RAC Additional SGA Areas

RAC Database System has two important services. They are Global Cache Service (GCS) and Global Enqueue Service (GES). These are basically collections of background processes. These two processes together cover and manage the total Cache Fusion process, resource transfers, and resource escalations among the instances.

Global Resource Directory

GES and GCS together maintain a Global Resource Directory (GRD) to record the information about the resources and the enqueues. GRD remains in the memory and is stored on all the instances. Each instance manages a portion of the directory. This distributed nature is a key point for fault tolerance of the RAC.

Global Resource Directory (GRD) is the internal database that records and stores the current status of the data blocks. Whenever a block is transferred out of a local cache to another instance's cache the GRD is updated. The following resources information is available in GRD.

- Data Block Identifiers (DBA)
- Location of most current version
- Modes of the data blocks: (N)Null, (S)Shared, (X)Exclusive
- The Roles of the data blocks (local or global) held by each instance
- Buffer caches on multiple nodes in the cluster

GRD is akin to the previous version of Lock Directory in the functionality perspective but has been expanded with more components. It has accurate measure of inventory of resources and their status and location.

The Background Processes

This next section is going to cover the processes. Figure 4.5 shows various background processes that are spawned to execute the database processing.

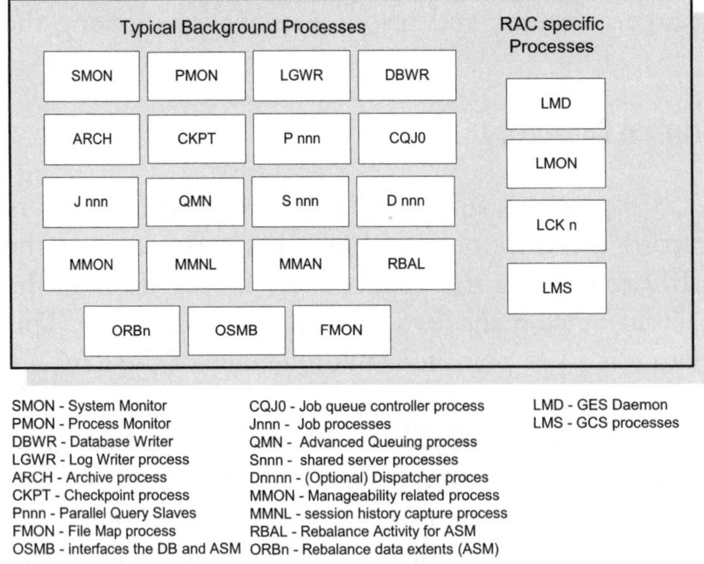

Figure 4.5: *The Background Processes*

The following is a description of each of the processes:

SMON - System Monitor process recovers after instance failure and monitors temporary segments and extents. SMON in a non-failed instance can also perform failed instance recovery for other failed RAC instances.

PMON - Process Monitor process recovers failed process resources. If MTS, also called Shared Server Architecture, is being utilized, PMON monitors and restarts any failed dispatcher or server processes. In RAC, PMON's role as service registration agent is particularly important.

DBWR - Database Writer or Dirty Buffer Writer process is responsible for writing dirty buffers from the database block cache to the database data files. Generally, DBWR only writes blocks back to the data files on commit, or when the cache is full and space has to be made for more blocks. The possible multiple DBWR processes in RAC must be coordinated through the locking and global cache processes to ensure efficient processing is accomplished.

LGWR - Log Writer process is responsible for writing the log buffers out to the redo logs. In RAC, each RAC instance has its own LGWR process that maintains that instance's thread of redo logs.

ARCH - (Optional) Archive process writes filled redo logs to the archive log location(s). In RAC, the various ARCH processes can be utilized to ensure that copies of the archived redo logs for each instance are available to the other instances in the RAC setup should they be needed for recovery.

CKPT - Checkpoint process writes checkpoint information to control files and data file headers.

Pnnn - (Optional) Parallel Query Slaves are started and stopped as needed to participate in parallel query operations.

CQJ0 - Job queue controller process wakes up periodically and checks the job log. If a job is due, it spawns Jnnnn processes to handle jobs.

Jnnn - (Optional) Job processes used by the Oracle9i job queues to process internal Oracle9i jobs. The CQJ0 process controls it automatically.

QMN - (Optional) Advanced Queuing process is used to control the advanced queuing jobs.

Snnn - (Optional) Pre-spawned shared server processes are used by the multi-threaded server (MTS) process to handle connection requests from users, and act as connection pools for user processes. These user processes also handle disk reads from database datafiles into the database block buffers.

Dnnnn - (Optional) Dispatcher process for shared server (MTS). It accepts connection requests and portions them out to the pre-spawned server processes.

MMON – This process performs various manageability-related background tasks, for example:

- Issuing alerts whenever a given metric violates its threshold value
- Capturing statistics values for SQL objects which have been recently modified

MMNL – This process performs frequent and light-weight manageability related tasks, such as session history capture and metrics computation.

MMAN - is used for internal database tasks that manage the automatic shared memory. MMAN serves as the SGA Memory Broker and coordinates the sizing of the memory components.

RBAL – This process coordinates rebalance activity for disk groups in an Automatic Storage Management instance.

ORBn performs the actual rebalance data extent movements in an Automatic Storage Management instance. There can be many of these at a time, called ORB0, ORB1, and so forth.

OSMB is present in a database instance using an Automatic Storage Management disk group. It communicates with the Automatic Storage Management instance.

FMON – The database communicates with the mapping libraries provided by storage vendors through an external non-Oracle Database process that is spawned by a background process called FMON. FMON is responsible for managing the mapping information. When the *file_mapping* initialization parameter is specified for mapping data files to physical devices on a storage subsystem, then the FMON process is spawned.

Typically, the RAC database has the same processes as that of a single-instance Oracle database. However, there are many additional RAC specific processes. Those processes will be examined in the next section.

RAC Specific Processes

The following are the additional processes spawned for supporting the multi-instance coordination:

LMON - The Global Enqueue Service Monitor (LMON) monitors the entire cluster to manage the global enqueues and the resources. LMON manages instance and process failures and the associated recovery for the Global Cache Service (GCS) and Global Enqueue Service (GES). In particular, LMON handles the part of recovery associated with global resources.

LMON-provided services are also known as cluster group services (CGS)

LMDx - The Global Enqueue Service Daemon (LMD) is the lock agent process that manages enqueue manager service requests for Global Cache Service enqueues to control access to global enqueues and resources. The LMD process also handles deadlock detection and remote enqueue requests. Remote resource requests are the requests originating from another instance.

LMSx - The Global Cache Service Processes (LMSx) are the processes that handle remote Global Cache Service (GCS) messages. Real Application Clusters software provides for up to 10 Global Cache Service Processes. The number of LMSx varies depending on the amount of messaging traffic among nodes in the cluster.

The LMSx handles the acquisition interrupt and blocking interrupt requests from the remote instances for Global Cache Service resources. For cross-instance consistent read requests, the LMSx will create a consistent read version of the block and send it to the requesting instance. The LMSx also controls the flow of messages to remote instances.

LMSn - The LMSn processes handle the blocking interrupts from the remote instance for the Global Cache Service resources by:

- Managing the resource requests and cross-instance call operations for the shared resources.
- Building a list of invalid lock elements and validating the lock elements during recovery
- Handling the global lock deadlock detection and Monitoring for the lock conversion timeouts

LCKx - This process manages the global enqueue requests and the cross-instance broadcast. Workload is automatically shared and balanced when there are multiple Global Cache Service Processes (LMSx).

DIAG – The Diagnosability Daemon monitors the health of the instance and captures the data for instance process failures.

The following shows typical background processes of the RAC instance named NYDB1.

```
$ rac-1a:NYDB1:/app/home/oracle >ps -ef | grep ora_
oracle   31136     1  0 08:45 ?        00:00:00 ora_pmon_NYDB1
oracle   31138     1  0 08:45 ?        00:00:00 ora_diag_NYDB1
oracle   31141     1  0 08:45 ?        00:00:00 ora_lmon_NYDB1
oracle   31143     1  0 08:45 ?        00:00:04 ora_lmd0_NYDB1
oracle   31145     1  0 08:45 ?        00:00:03 ora_lms0_NYDB1
oracle   31147     1  0 08:45 ?        00:00:03 ora_lms1_NYDB1
oracle   31149     1  0 08:45 ?        00:00:00 ora_mman_NYDB1
oracle   31151     1  0 08:45 ?        00:00:01 ora_dbw0_NYDB1
oracle   31153     1  0 08:45 ?        00:00:01 ora_lgwr_NYDB1
oracle   31155     1  0 08:45 ?        00:00:05 ora_ckpt_NYDB1
oracle   31157     1  0 08:45 ?        00:00:05 ora_smon_NYDB1
oracle   31159     1  0 08:45 ?        00:00:00 ora_reco_NYDB1
oracle   31161     1  0 08:45 ?        00:00:00 ora_cjq0_NYDB1
oracle   31163     1  0 08:45 ?        00:00:00 ora_d000_NYDB1
oracle   31165     1  0 08:45 ?        00:00:00 ora_s000_NYDB1
oracle   31168     1  0 08:45 ?        00:00:02 ora_lck0_NYDB1
oracle   31190     1  0 08:46 ?        00:00:00 ora_arc0_NYDB1
oracle   31193     1  0 08:46 ?        00:00:02 ora_arc1_NYDB1
oracle   31207     1  0 08:46 ?        00:00:00 ora_qmnc_NYDB1
oracle   31210     1  0 08:46 ?        00:00:07 ora_mmon_NYDB1
oracle   31213     1  0 08:46 ?        00:00:00 ora_mmnl_NYDB1
oracle   31286     1  0 08:46 ?        00:00:00 ora_q000_NYDB1
oracle   31288     1  0 08:46 ?        00:00:00 ora_q001_NYDB1
oracle   31290     1  0 08:46 ?        00:00:00 ora_q002_NYDB1
oracle   18041     1  0 20:41 ?        00:00:06 ora_j000_NYDB1
oracle   25579     1  0 23:19 ?        00:00:00 ora_pz99_NYDB1
oracle   25581     1  0 23:19 ?        00:00:00 ora_pz98_NYDB1
oracle   26703 19731  0 23:23 pts/5    00:00:00 grep ora_
$ rac-1a:NYDB1:/app/home/oracle >
```

Global Cache Service

GCS is the main controlling process that implements Cache Fusion. GCS tracks the location and the status (mode and role) of the data blocks, as well as the access privileges of various instances. GCS is the mechanism which guarantees the data integrity by employing global access levels. GCS maintains the block modes for data blocks in the global role. It is also responsible for block transfers between the instances. Upon a request from an Instance GCS organizes the block shipping and appropriate lock mode conversions. The Global Cache Service is implemented by various background processes, such as the Global Cache Service Processes (LMSn) and Global Enqueue Service Daemon (LMD).

Global Enqueue Service

The Global Enqueue Service (GES) manages or tracks the status of all the Oracle enqueuing mechanism. This involves all non Cache fusion intra-instance operations. GES performs concurrency control on dictionary cache locks, library cache locks, and the transactions. GES does this operation for resources that are accessed by more than one instance.

GES/GCS Areas

GES and GCS have the memory structures associated with global resources. It is distributed across all instances in a cluster. This area is located in the variable or shared pool section of the SGA. As an example, below list shows the additions.

```
POOL         NAME                           BYTES
------------ -------------------------- ----------
shared pool  gcs shadows                  12143272
shared pool  gcs resources                17402792
shared pool  ges enqueues                  4079516
shared pool  ges resources                 2624824
shared pool  ges big msg buffers           3839044
```

So far all the memory structures and background processes have been surveyed. Now attention will be turned to the physical database structures of the database which includes the data files, redo log files and control files among other type of files.

Database Related Files

Oracle Database is a collection of physical files. These are basically the operating system files used by the database and database instance. Oracle RAC needs shared storage to store the files. RAC follows the shared disk model, where all the cluster nodes share the same disk or storage volumes.

The files included in the RAC architecture are shown in Figure 4.6. Most of them must be available simultaneously and be updateable by all the nodes, and hence, by all the instances in the cluster. Additionally, there are some files which can remain on local file system.

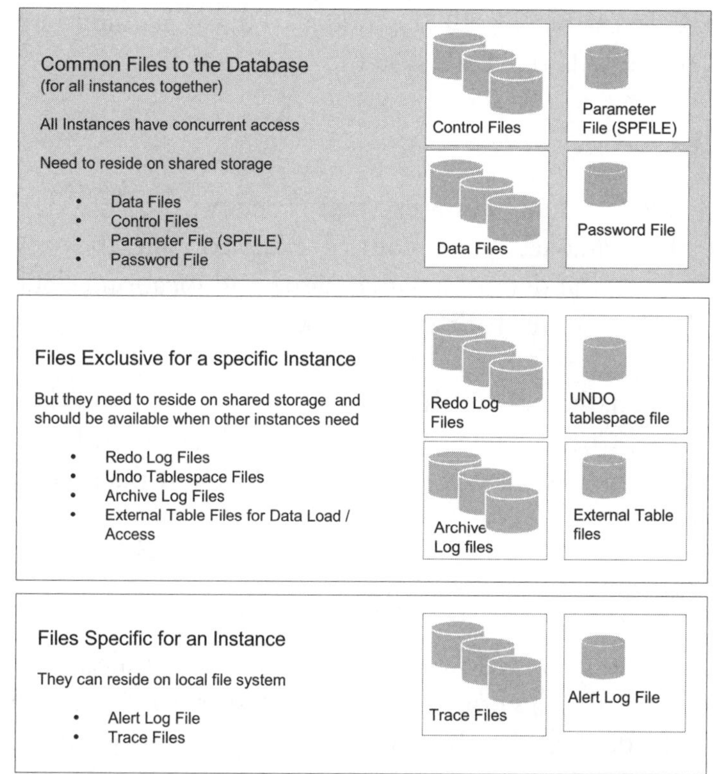

Figure 4.6: *Database related files*

The following is a description of each of the categories of files.

Data Files

These are the main files of the database. The data files contain the actual data. The logical database structures like tables and indexes are physically stored in the data files. These files are located on shared storage and are accessible by all the nodes in the cluster. One or more data files form a logical unit of database storage which is called the *tablespace*.

Data Files can be associated with only one database. By locating the data files either on a clustered file system or raw partition they are made accessible by all the nodes. This is a minimum requirement in the RAC database system.

Control Files

The control files contain entries that specify the physical structure of the database. The control files contain the key information such as the database name, name and location of the data files, and redo log files for the database.

When an instance is launched, the control files identify the data and redo log files. Control Files are usually multiplexed and they are located on the shared storage either on a clustered file system or raw partition

Redo Log Files

A redo log is made up of redo entries which are also called redo records. The primary function of the redo log is to record all changes made to data. Every database has a set of redo log files. The information in the redo log files are used to recover the database from a system or media failure. There are generally two or more redo log files. They are used by the database in a circular fashion. Once a redo log file is filled up, then the next redo log file is picked up for writing. Meanwhile, the filled redo log file is saved as an archived log file.

Redo Log files are stored as a group called Redo Log File groups. Each group can have one or more redo log files. Multiplexing the redo files within a group provides a higher level of resiliency.

Redo Log files are instance specific. In the RAC database architecture, each instance has its own set of redo log file groups. Even though they are specific to an individual instance, the redo log files need to be located on shared storage. This is because the redo files have to be accessed by other instances during the media or system recovery. Another important use is the hot-mining of redo log files for the use of Oracle streams where redo log files are scanned by the capture process in order to propagate the changes to other Oracle database systems.

Archive Log Files

Archive Log files are actually the saved redo log files. When a redo log file is filled up and the next redo log file is put to use, the filled redo log file is saved or archived. The saved files are known as archive log files.

Automatic archiving can be enabled on the redo log. Oracle automatically archives redo log files when the database in is in ARCHIVELOG mode.

A separate set of Archive Log files are created by each instance. Since each RAC instance has its own redo log files, the corresponding archive log files are produced when the log switch takes place. The archive log files can be written to either a local file system or to a cluster file system. Oracle does not insist upon a particular type of file system. Writing to a clustered file system has added the advantage of being available to archive all the nodes in the cluster, which becomes important in case of media recovery.

Parameter File (SPFILE)

The attributes of the instance depend on the initialization parameters used for starting up the instance. Initialization parameters control the configuration of the database system. They are the key directives to start and manage any instance in the database. While launching the database instance, parameters are specified and they remain until the instance is shutdown. Optionally, certain parameters can be modified during the instance run time by the ALTER SYSTEM SET method, provided the instance has been started with the SPFILE method.

The SPFILE feature allows the change of parameter values dynamically. It also allows them to be set either permanently or in memory only. For Oracle Real Application Clusters (RAC), one server parameter file can be used and shared among instances. The usage of a single copy of the SPFILE for the entire database provides administrative convenience and simplification. The SPFILE has to be located on a clustered file system.

Password File

The password file is another important file which is shared by all the instances of the RAC database system. This file, which is stored in binary format, records all the authentication privileges granted to the users. Privileges such as SYSDBA or SYSOPER are recorded in this file. The password file is required for remote authentication for the users with SYSDBA or SYSOPER privileges. This file is located on the cluster file system and is accessible to all the nodes in the cluster.

Alert Log File and Trace Files

Each instance in the RAC database keeps writing to the alert log file and also produces trace files periodically. The Alert Log file contains all the messages the Oracle database kernel generates. Trace Files contain detailed information about a specific event or issue. These log and trace files help the administrators keep track of the database activity and also assist in troubleshooting.

The Alter Log File and Trace Files can be written either to a directory within a local file system or within the cluster file system.

Files for loading into External Tables

External Tables allow direct access of data located in the operating system level files by using the SQL interface within the database. It is a new way of reading and writing files into and out of the database. Data stored in operating system level files (ASCII filer) can be accessed as if they are some kind of table with rows and columns. The usual SQL interface can be used and even the joins can be constructed with data in the O/S file and logical database tables.

For all practical purposes, external tables act the same as the usual tables; however, the data is not stored with the Oracle Data Files. External Tables are a great way to load the data into a database and do data processing.

There is no restriction as to where the external table data file has to be located. In a RAC database system, it can be located on the local file system or on a cluster file system. For the sake of concurrent access, it becomes more meaningful to keep the external table file on a shared storage or cluster file system. This allows for transparent access to the external table so any instance in the RAC database should be able to read and write to it at the operating system level (ASCII). This is possible only if the external table file is located on a clustered file system.

Oracle Cluster Registry (OCR)

The OCR contains cluster and database configuration information for RAC and Cluster Ready Services (CRS) such as the cluster node list, cluster database instances to node mapping, and CRS application resource profiles.

The OCR is a shared file located in a cluster file system. When the Cluster File System is not in use, the OCR file can be located on a shared raw device in UNIX-based systems, or a shared logical partition in Windows environments. During the installation of Cluster Ready Services software, the Oracle Universal Installer (OUI) automatically initializes the OCR file by executing the *srvconfig -init* command.

If more than one database is created on the cluster, they all share the same Oracle cluster registry. If upgrading from Oracle9i Release 2, then the raw device that was used for the SRVM configuration repository can be used instead of creating this new logical volume.

Voting Disk

The Voting Disk File is a file on the shared cluster system or a shared raw device file. Voting disk is akin to the quorum disk which helps to avoid the split brain syndrome.

ORACLE_HOME Files (Oracle Binaries)

Typically every instance in the RAC database system will have its own ORACLE HOME and a set of exclusive binaries. However, the Oracle Binaries are located either on a local file system or on a clustered file system. Locating the Oracle Home (Binaries) on a clustered file system provides easier management by keeping a single copy of Oracle Home supporting all the instances.

Common Oracle Home for multiple instances is an attractive proposition as it helps to easily expand the nodes and shrink the nodes as needed. It helps the dynamic addition and expansion of nodes without bothering with a fresh install of the Oracle binaries for the new instance. This feature is particularly useful for large clusters and it fits into the Grid strategy of easier addition and reduction of computing resources.

UNDO Tablespace Files

UNDO tablespace are special tablespaces that have system undo segments. They contain before images of blocks involved in uncommitted transactions. As such, they are the primary support structure allowing a transaction to rollback if the decision is made to not commit the transaction. These tablespaces also support the Oracle functionality known as Multi-block Read Consistency. If configured to use System Managed Undo, there must be one UNDO tablespace available for each instance in the RAC setup. With 10g, this is the only method. The earlier system of public or private rollback segments is discontinued.

RAW Partitions, Cluster File System and Automatic Storage Management (ASM)

Each of the above mentioned structures are either on raw partitions or on a cluster file system. Raw partitions are a set of unformatted devices on a shared disk sub-system. The RAC shared storage files can be stored on the cluster file system wherever it is available.

Oracle RAC database files are located on the shared storage units. Shared storage disks are physically connected to all the nodes. All the nodes need to have read and write access concurrently to the data devices. The presentation of the data devices to the operating systems can be achieved by either raw partitions or through the cluster file system. A raw partition is a disk drive device that does not have a file system set up. The raw partition is a portion of the physical disk that is accessed at the lowest possible level. The actual application that uses a raw device is responsible for managing its own I/O to the raw device with no operating system buffering.

Traditionally, they were required for Oracle Parallel Server (OPS) and provided high performance by bypassing the file system overhead. Raw partitions were used in setting up databases for performance gains and for the purpose of concurrent access by multiple nodes in the cluster without system-level buffering. Oracle9i RAC and 10g now support both the cluster file systems and the raw devices to store shared data. In addition, 10g RAC supports shared storage resources from Automatic Storage Management (ASM) instance. The data files can be created out of the disk resources located in the ASM instance. The ASM resources are sharable and accessed by all the nodes in the RAC system.

Storage occupies an important place in the overall architecture of the RAC system. It is crucial to plan and design carefully to get the right storage array in a compatible environment. More details and how to prepare the file structures are covered in Chapter 5, *Preparing Shared Storage*.

Concept of Redo Thread

In the RAC system, each instance has to have its own redo log groups. The redo log file groups of an instance are collectively called a thread, or more appropriately, a redo log thread. Each instance has its own redo thread. The redo log groups function in a true circular fashion; as one fills up, another redo log records the redo entries. In a stand-alone instance, there is only one thread. In a RAC system, typically there are as many threads as instances. The thread number identifies each thread. The threads may have different numbers of redo groups, but each group must have at least two members, as shown in Figure 4.7.

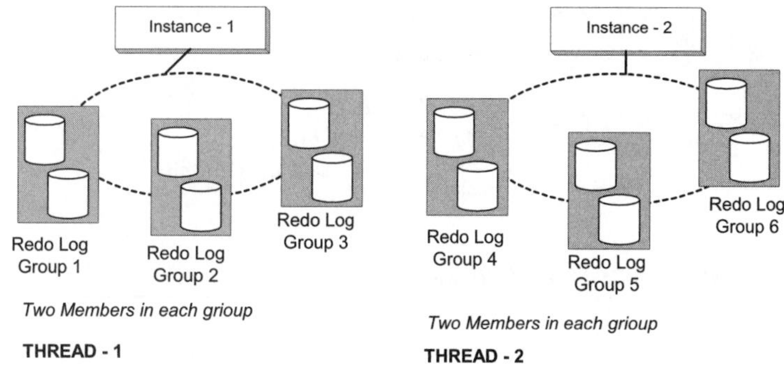

Figure 4.7: *Redo Threads in a 2 Node RAC database*

Online redo logs record the redo entries as transactions commit and rollback. Redo groups may optionally have additional members to provide mirroring of the redo groups.

Thread Features

Each instance must have a minimum of two redo groups, with each group having at least one member in the group. Every redo group has a group number, which is a unique number in the database. All the redo log files supporting the redo groups reside on shared storage so that every instance in the cluster can access all the redo groups during the recovery process. As shown in Figure 4.8, all the redo groups are located on a shared storage unit.

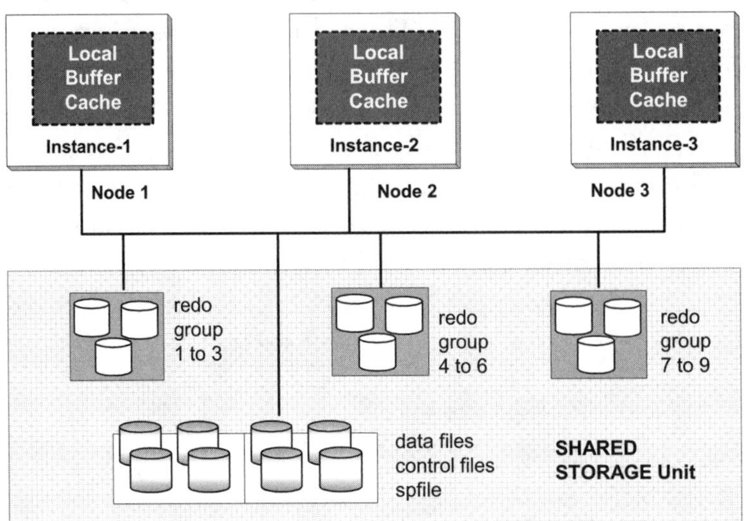

Figure 4.8: *Redo Groups on a shared storage*

Use a minimum of three redo groups in a thread. Keep at least two redo members for each redo group for multiplexing and protection. Multiplexing the redo members is optional but is highly recommended. Different degrees of mirroring are permitted in different threads. The redo log thread can be public or private. When the redo thread is enabled, it can be specified as a private thread. This means it is associated with a specific instance as defined in the initialization parameter thread of the instance. Alternatively, it can be specified as public and any instance can acquire it.

Database Logical Objects

The logical storage structures include, at the lowest level, the data blocks and next level the extents. A group of extents set aside for a specific object are grouped into a segment. At the highest level, a tablespace which consist of extents will be found.

Data Blocks

The Oracle data rows are stored in Data Blocks. The standard size of the data block is specified by the *db_block_size* initialization parameter. In addition up to five other block sizes can be specified. A Data Block is the smallest or most granular basic logical structure that is brought into the buffer cache from disk storage in order to do SQL processing.

Extents

The next level of logical database structure is an extent. An extent is a specific number of contiguous data blocks, which are obtained in a single allocation unit. It is an allocation unit.

Segments

A Segment is a set of extents allocated for a certain logical structure. There are many types of segments namely, data segment, index segments, temporary segments, and undo segments.

Tablespaces

At the highest level of the logical structure chain, there is the tablespace. It is a logical administrative unit and is composed of many Oracle Data Files. Within the tablespace area, the extents are created which are assigned to the segments. Structures like Tables and Index are created out of the tablespace.

The traditional tablespace is referred to as a small-file tablespace (SFT). A small-file tablespace contains multiple, relatively small files. However with 10g release, a new concept of bigfile tablespace (BFT) was introduced. A BFT tablespace contains a single file that can have a very large size.

The big-file tablespace has the following characteristics:

- An Oracle database can contain both big file and small file tablespaces.
- System default is to create the traditional small-file tablespace.
- The SYSTEM and SYSAUX tablespaces are always created using the system default type.
- Bigfile tablespaces are supported only for locally managed tablespaces with automatic segment-space management.

There are two exceptions when bigfile tablespace segments are managed manually:

- Locally managed undo tablespace
- Temporary tablespace

Bigfile tablespaces are intended to be used with Automated Storage Management (ASM) or other logical volume managers that support RAID. However, they can also be used without ASM.

Bigfile Tablespace Benefits are as follows:

- It simplifies large database tablespace management by reducing the number of data files needed.
- It simplifies data file management with Oracle-managed files and Automated Storage Management (ASM) by eliminating the need for adding new data files and dealing with multiple files.
- It allows the creation of a big file tablespace of up to eight exabytes (eight million terabytes) in size, and significantly increases the storage capacity of an Oracle database.

- It follows the concept that a tablespace and a data file are logically equivalent.
- Provides the Maximum Database Size

The maximum number of data files in Oracle9i and Oracle 10g Database is 65,536. However, the maximum number of blocks in a data file increase from 4,194,304 (4 million) blocks to 4,294,967,296 (4 billion) blocks.

The maximum amount of data for a 32K block size database is eight petabytes (8,192 Terabytes) in Oracle9i.

BLOCK SIZE	MAXIMUM DATA FILE SIZE	MAXIMUM DATABASE SIZE
32 K	128 GB	8,388,608 GB
16 K	64 GB	4,194,304 GB
8 K	32 GB	2,097,152 GB
4 K	16 GB	1,048,579 GB
2 K	8 GB	524,288 GB

Table 4.2: *Maximum Database Size in Oracle9i*

The maximum amount of data for a 32K block size database is eight exabytes (8,388,608 Terabytes) in Oracle 10g.

BLOCK SIZE	MAXIMUM DATA FILE SIZE	MAXIMUM DATABASE SIZE
32 K	131,072 GB	8,589,934,592 GB
16 K	65,536 GB	4,294,967,296 GB
8 K	32,768 GB	2,147,483,648 GB
4 K	16,384 GB	1,073,741,824 GB
2 K	8,192 GB	536,870,912 GB

Table 4.3: *Maximum Database Size in Oracle 10g*

With the new BFT addressing scheme, Oracle 10g can contain astronomical amounts of data within a single database.

Cluster Ready Services - CRS

Oracle10g introduces Cluster Ready Services (CRS), which provides many system management services and interacts with the vendor clusterware to coordinate cluster membership information.

The Oracle Universal Installer (OUI) installs CRS on each node on which the OUI detects that vendor clusterware is running. In addition, the CRS home is distinct from the RAC-enabled Oracle home. The CRS home can either be shared by one or more nodes, or private to each node, depending on the settings when the OUI is run. When vendor clusterware is present, CRS interacts with the vendor clusterware to coordinate cluster membership information.

For Oracle10g on Linux and Windows-based platforms, CRS co-exists with but does not inter-operate with vendor clusterware. Vendor clusterware may be used for all UNIX-based operating systems except Linux.

The Oracle Cluster Registry (OCR) contains cluster and database configuration information for RAC Cluster Ready Services (CRS), including the list of nodes in the cluster database, the CRS application, resource profiles, and the authorizations for the Event Manager (EVM). The OCR can reside in a file on a cluster file system or on a shared raw device. When Real Application Clusters is installed, the location of the OCR is specified.

CRS helps to package a set of application that work under CRS control and access the RAC database. The application resource profile defines the resources with which RAC is managed.

Prior to the 10g release, the cluster manager implementations on some platforms were referred to as Cluster Manager. In

Oracle10g, Cluster Synchronization Services (CSS) is the cluster manager on all platforms. The Oracle Cluster Synchronization Service Daemon (OCSSD) performs this function on UNIX-based platforms. On Windows-based platforms, the OracleCSService, OracleCRService, and OracleEVMService provide the cluster manager functionality.

CRS Features

CRS is required for installing the Oracle 10g RAC system. CRS can be run on top of vendor provided Cluster Software. The vendor supplied clusterware is however optional.

The CRS software is installed in the cluster with its own set of binaries. The CRS Home and Oracle Home are in different locations. CRS software installation uses the two shared disk locations or files which are the Voting Disk and OCR file. Installation of CRS configures the Virtual IP interface. Virtual IP is associated with defined Workload Service. CRS resources can also be managed by the *srvctl* utility.

CRS has many daemon processes. They are as follows:

CRDS – The CRS Daemon is the main background process for managing the HA operation of the service. Basically it manages the application resources defined within the cluster. It also maintains the configuration profiles stored in the Oracle Configuration Repository.

OCSSD – This process is associated with the Automatic Storage Management (ASM) instance. This daemon is spawned to manage shared access of the disk devices to the clustered nodes. It manages the basic cluster locking and understands the nodes and its membership status.

EVMD – This is event management logger. It monitors the message flow between the nodes and logs the relevant event information to the log files.

Cluster Private Interconnect

The cluster interconnect is a high bandwidth, low latency communication facility that connects each node to other nodes in the cluster and routes messages among the nodes. It is a key component in building the RAC system.

In case of RAC database, the cluster interconnect is used for the following high-level functions:

- Monitoring Health, Status, and Synchronize messages
- Transporting lock management or resource coordination messages
- Moving the Cache Buffers (data blocks) from node to node.

High performance database computing involves distributing the processing across an array of cluster nodes. It requires that the cluster interconnect provide high-data rates and low-latency communication between node processes.

Innterconnect technology that is employed connecting RAC Nodes should be scalable to handle the amount of traffic generated by the cache synchronization mechanism. This is directly related to the amount of contention created by the application. The more inter-instance updates and inter-instance transfers, the more message traffic it generates. It is advisable to implement the highest bandwidth, lowest latency interconnect that is available for a given platform.

The volume of synchronization traffic directly impacts the bandwidth requirement, and messaging delays are highly dependant on the IPC protocol. The interconnect is not something that should be under configured, assuming scalability is a key objective.

Oracle recommends that for Linux environments with interconnect bandwidth is 1GB Ethernet, use the UDP as IPC protocol in preference to TCP. 10g has extended support for emerging technologies like Infiniband which will greatly improve interconnect scalability and standardization for large numbers of nodes, as well as provide a choice of interconnects under Linux.

RAC Database Nodes

The next main component is the host or node where the database instance resides. This is the place where the actual database processing takes place. RAC Database system provides scalability and high availability. In order to provide large database computing power and maintain large work load, the number of nodes needs to be extended. Most cluster frameworks today differ in terms of the maximum number of nodes they can handle. Most can support a minimum of 4 nodes today, and some can support hundreds. This will also be driven by scalability objectives and capacity requirements.

The nodes themselves may or may not need to be scalable to provide additional capacity in terms of CPU or memory. Unless one uses an expensive SMP server, scalability will be an issue. The ability to scale both within a machine as well as across machines is often desirable.

Oracle RAC can be implemented on a wide range of servers from a clustered group of single CPU Windows boxes to a cluster of 32-CPU SUN E10000 boxes. One of the more promising architectures for RAC is the blade architecture.

In blade architecture, the servers are inserted into a pre-configured RAC similar to Nuclear Instrumentation Modules (NIM) in a NIM bin. Rather than a horizontal orientation they have a vertical one. Blade servers are essentially self-contained servers that rest on a single backplane. The backplane in a blade array provides power, network, and management connections, reducing cabling and overall component expense. Many blade architectures are hot-plugable, allowing online addition and removal of servers from the cluster.

Linux machines are now able to scale up to 8 CPUs, but the majority of systems are 2 or 4 CPU nodes. SMP scalability in Linux beyond 4 CPU's is not well proven, so the current Oracle recommendation is to stick with 4-CPU machines. The Blade Servers provide low cost 4-way or 2-way servers for building the large cluster environment.

At the same time, Oracle RAC can also run on platforms that allow sub-setting of CPUs, such as the SUN E10000, E15000, and the HP Superdome. In the case of CPU sub-setting the single server is divided into multiple nodes, each running an instance of Oracle9i RAC.

Server Redundancy

The database resides within a server. The server or host is an important component in the provision of the data service. Any failure in the host system causes the database to go down.

Clustered servers utilize two or more nodes, essentially keeping the extra nodes as standby or sometimes as extra computing power, as in the case of the RAC system. With the help of the additional nodes, the standby node can provide the same database service to the user community. However, when in standby, it loses the performance and scalability level for which it is intended.

Clustering servers assures the administrators and the application users that at least one node is alive. A cluster, in its most general form, comprises two or more interconnected computers that are viewed and used as a single, unified computing resource. By using multiple systems, the impact of the failure of any individual system is kept low by passing the failed system's workload to the remaining members of the cluster.

The standby node becomes functional, or becomes the primary host, when the failed host is unable to provide any host services. When some of the internal components fail and the failure is non-recoverable without intervention, the server is declared not available or simply *failed*. This indicates that there is a lot of scope for keeping the internal components safe or redundant.

Before losing the server and resorting to the use of the clustered backup node, there are many things that can be done to keep the components from failing. These methods, which act as the first level of redundancy, will be explored next. Some people call it high availability without clustering. In contrast to clustering, system availability can be improved without adding additional servers.

Redundancy Features

There are many features or options that add value to the redundancy at the server level. Taking advantage of such features helps avoid failures, and avoids degraded cluster performance in systems like the RAC system. These features address different subsystems of the server, such as the memory and processors. Redundant components such as fans, power supplies, and adapters can also provide higher availability, particularly when used with software that provides monitoring and alerting capability to the system administrators.

To make the servers more reliable, high-reliability components and best-system practices should be used. The following section examines some features of the redundancy that administrators need to focus on.

Dynamic Reorganization (DR) with in a server

DR is an operating environment feature that provides the ability to replace and reconfigure system hardware while the system is running. This feature is optional and can be implemented at the discretion of the system administrator. The main benefit of DR is that an administrator can add or replace hardware resources, such as CPUs, memory, and I/O interfaces, with little interruption of normal system operations. The DR process helps to increase the overall uptime and availability of servers.

For example, the DR method is available for Sun system architectures that contain multiple system boards and use board slots that support hot plugging. The DR facility is very well implemented for Sun Fire server series 3800-6800. By using the DR methodology, hardware components can be added or removed from a system with minimal interruption. The DR is performed at attachment points. DR allows connect or disconnect attachment points. The Sun Fire series supports the following attachment points for dynamic reorganization.

- I/O Assembly (PCI / ePCI assemblies)
- CPU/Memory Boards
- CPCI cards
- System Memory
- CPU/s

Predictive Failure analysis

Many server vendors provide a mechanism to anticipate system failures. It is called Predictive Failure Analysis (PFA). Servers keep running until they don't run anymore. Often, there are not clear signs that the servers will go down. If zero downtime is necessary, consider using predictive failure analysis technology. This technology warns a DBA up to 48 hours in advance of an imminent server failure. That's plenty of time to prevent disaster. The analysis method and terminology may differ, but most of the leading vendors provide PFA for the servers.

ECC Memory

Error Correcting and Checking (ECC) memory detects and corrects all single bit errors without impacting the operation of the system. It also detects all, and corrects some, double-bit errors. All error correction events are logged by the system.

IBM Chipkill memory is a good example. Chipkill ECC memory and automatic server restart features work to minimize server downtime. With the latest Chipkill memory technology available in select IBM xSeries and Netfinity servers, they are protected from any single memory chip that fails and any number of multi-bit errors, from any portion of a single memory chip.

To give another example, in Sun systems, memory error correction code has been adopted on all servers to minimize system downtime caused by faulty single inline memory modules (SIMMs) and dual inline memory modules (DIMMs).

Redundant Networking Components

To avoid network I/O channel failures, provide redundant physical elements in the path between the server and the network backbone, which includes network interface cards, cables, and patch panels.

Hot Swap Power

In its simplest form, two power supplies, each capable of providing power for the whole system, should be built into the server to share the load. When one of the supplies fails, the surviving supply keeps the server running. The facility of UPS is another most essential requirement.

Hot Swap Fans

A cooling fan failure will not bring a system down if it can be hot-swapped transparently. Most cooling-related issues are external to the system, such as keeping the computer room temperature stable below the required levels. High temperatures and temperature fluctuations are a form of stress to electronic components.

Partitions with in the Server

As an example, the Sun Enterprise 10K Server includes Dynamic System Domains, which allow a single machine to be divided into logical partitions, with each partition totally electrically isolated from the others.

The features mentioned above, as well as others, help maintain redundancy levels, which indirectly avoids server down time and service disruption to the application user.

Network Services and Accessing RAC

The next topic is the accessing the RAC database. The SQL*Net process controls the RAC instance access. Access to any Oracle instance can be through either a dedicated server connection or through a shared server connection. If access is through a shared server connection, then the instance is set up for shared server (multi-threaded server - MTS). If the connection is a dedicated server, then either the user process required a dedicated connection or the instance is not using MTS. The configuration of SQL*Net for RAC can be quite simple. Essentially only two files need to be configured for basic access, the SQL*Net listener control file, *listener.ora*, and the instance names file, *tnsnames.ora.* In a basic configuration, each server has a *listener.ora* and a *tnsnames.ora* file, and each client has a *tnsnames.ora* file. A third file, *sqlnet.ora*, is also present on both server and client which control the access behavior.

listener.ora File

The *listener.ora* file contains the information needed by the SQL*Net listener file to identify the instances for which connection requests are being serviced. If no instances are listed in the *listener.ora*, the listener process will wait for the instances to self-register since instances have been capable of self-registering since Oracle8i. Shown below is a basic *listener.ora* file for use with RAC.

```
LISTENER=
(DESCRIPTION=
(ADDRESS=
(PROTOCOL=tcp)
(HOST=aultlinux1)
(PORT=1521)))
```

If advanced features such as load balancing and automatic failover are desired, there are optional sections of the *listener.ora* file that must be present. For example, to configure load balancing, the *listener.ora* file shown below would be appropriate. The listener file must be the same on the servers that are participating in the load balancing for RAC. The second listener,

listener_test1 allows use of Oracle Enterprise Manager with the instance.

Another example is that the *global_dbname* parameter should not be configured if Oracle RAC connect time failover or transparent application failover are going to be used. Setting this parameter will disable these capabilities.

Chapter 10 covers the setup for automatic failover. For the second server, the second listener would be called *listener_test2*, and all instance specific references would be changed to *test2*, while all server specific references would be changed to *testlinux2*.

```
Listener_Test=
(description=
(load_balance=on)
(address=(protocol=tcp)(host=testlinux1)(port=1521)
(address=(protocol=tcp)(host=testlinux2)(port=1521)
(connect_data=
(service_name=test)))
listener_test1=
(description=
(address=(protocol=tcp)(host=testlinux1)(port=1521)
sid_list_listener_test1=
(sid_list=
(sid_desc=
(oracle-home=/u01/app/oracle/product/9.2.0.2)
(sid_name=test1)))
```

If a port other than 1521 is utilized, then the *local_listener* parameter in that instances local *init.ora* file must be set to the same port value. For example, if port 1525 was used instead of 1521, all references to port 1521 in the *listener.ora* would be changed to 1525 in and the following entry would have to be added to the local *init.ora*:

```
local_listener="(address=(port=1525)(protocol=tcp)(host=testlinux1))
"
```

More examples of *listener.ora* files for various RAC failover scenarios are included in Chapter 10, *Transparent Application Failover.*

tnsnames.ora File

Unless Oracle Names or LDAP is used, each client and server that participates in the RAC environment must have a *tnsnames.ora* file. The *tnsnames.ora* file provides the local SQL*Net process a map to all available instances. The *tnsnames.ora* file also provides failover and load balance information. Failover is automatically set if a list of addresses is placed in the *tnsnames.ora* file. However, the failover method should be explicitly set using the *failover_mode tnsnames.ora* parameter. More detail about the tnsnames.ora file will be provided in Chapter 10, *Transparent Application Failover.*

A basic *tnsnames.ora* file for a load-balancing RAC setup is shown below:

```
TEST =
(DESCRIPTION =
(LOAD_BALANCE = ON)
(ADDRESS_LIST =
(ADDRESS = (PROTOCOL = TCP)(HOST = testlinux1)(PORT = 1521))
(ADDRESS = (PROTOCOL = TCP)(HOST = testlinux2)(PORT = 1521)))
(CONNECT_DATA =
(SERVICE_NAME = TEST))))
TEST1 =
(DESCRIPTION =
(ADDRESS_LIST =
(LOAD_BALANCE = ON)
(ADDRESS = (PROTOCOL = TCP)(HOST = testlinux1)(PORT = 1521)))
(CONNECT_DATA =
(SERVICE_NAME = TEST)(INSTANCE_NAME = TEST1)))
TEST2 =
(DESCRIPTION =
(ADDRESS_LIST =
(LOAD_BALANCE = ON)
(ADDRESS = (PROTOCOL = TCP)(HOST = testlinux2)(PORT = 1521)))
(CONNECT_DATA =
(SERVICE_NAME = TEST)(INSTANCE_NAME = TEST2)))
EXTPROC_CONNECTION_DATA =
(DESCRIPTION =
(ADDRESS_LIST =
(ADDRESS = (PROTOCOL = IPC)(KEY = EXTPROC)))
(CONNECT_DATA =
(SID=PLSExtProc)(PRESENTATION = RO)))

LISTENERS_TEST =
(ADDRESS = (PROTOCOL = TCP)(HOST = testlinux1)(PORT = 1521))
(ADDRESS = (PROTOCOL = TCP)(HOST = testlinux2)(PORT = 1521))
```

If a list of listener addresses is provided in the *tnsnames.ora* file, load balancing will be done automatically and there is no need to specify the *load_balance* parameters. They are shown here for example purposes only. The *tnsnames.ora* file provides the information needed to register the service names and instance-level information with the listener process. In addition, it specifies whether load balancing and application failover are desired, and specifies the method of failover if desired. This is a very important file for RAC.

More examples of RAC *tnsnames.ora* files for various failover scenarios are included in Chapter 10, *Transparent Application Failover.*

In addition to access to the database and also to the specific instance, now users can access to the Service directly by using the Virtual IP or Virtual IP host name. Virtual IP Configuration Assistant (VIPCA) helps to create services and associate the Virtual IP. Virtual IP is the public address through which a specific RAC database service can be accessed. More details on the Service Configuration and VIP configuration are covered in the Chapter 6 and Chapter 20.

Shared Server Configuration

Oracle RAC Instance can be configured either as shared server and dedicated server. In shared server architecture, the listener assigns each new client session to one of the dispatchers. As the user makes requests, the dispatcher sends the request to the shared server. It is also possible that a different set of shared servers are utilized for a given user session. The dispatchers act as the coordinating agents between the user sessions and the shared servers.

A dispatcher is capable of supporting multiple client connections concurrently. Each client connection is bound to a virtual circuit. A virtual circuit is a piece of shared memory used by the dispatcher for the client connection requests and replies.

An idle shared server process picks up the virtual circuit from the common queue, services the request, and relinquishes the virtual circuit before attempting to retrieve another virtual circuit from the common queue. In this way, a small number of server processes are able to service a large number of clients or users. This method also supports an increased number of users with less system resources.

Note that not all applications are certified to use shared servers, but that server-side load balancing in RAC may benefit from using shared servers.

As seen in Figure 4.9, the listener communicates with the dispatchers on behalf of the user or client sessions. Once the user sessions establish connectivity with dispatchers, the shared servers service them.

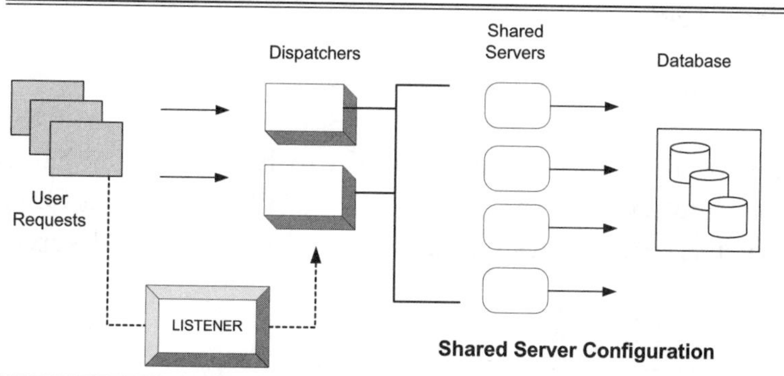

Figure 4.9: *Shared Server Architecture*

Prior to the release of Oracle Database 10g, at least one dispatcher needs to be setup for the shared server configuration to be enabled. Normally the dispatcher's initialization parameter needed to set to configure the information about dispatchers.

With Oracle Database 10g, even without specifying a dispatcher with the dispatcher's parameter, shared server can be enabled by setting *shared_servers* to a nonzero value. The default behavior is that Oracle creates one dispatcher for the TCP protocol automatically. This way, it is easier to configure a shared server environment. The equivalent dispatcher's initialization parameter for this configuration would be:

```
DISPATCHERS="(PROTOCOL=tcp)"
```

The dynamic *shared_servers* initialization parameter needs to be set to a value greater than zero with an ALTER SYSTEM command in order to use shared servers while the system is running

As with other parameters, this command can be used to change the current instance. If an SPFILE is in use, the parameter can be changed for future instances as well. For example, to activate three shared servers in the current instance and the SPFILE, enter this command:

```
SQL> ALTER SYSTEM SET SHARED_SERVERS=3 SCOPE=BOTH;
```

There are several other parameters that can be set in the shared server environment, but they are not required. Once shared_serversis set, the system will be running in shared server mode.

When needing to configure another protocol other than TCP/IP, configure a protocol address with one of the following attributes: ADDRESS, DESCRIPTION, or PROTOCOL.

Parameters with the prefix MTS are now obsolete. This means if these parameters are used to start an instance, the following error will be received: "ORA-25138: <parameter> initialization parameter has been made obsolete." This occurs even if trying to set *mts_servers* during the runtime of an instance:

```
SQL> ALTER SYSTEM SET MTS_SERVERS = 2;
ALTER SYSTEM SET MTS_SERVERS = 2
*
ERROR at line 1:
ORA-25138: MTS_SERVERS initialization parameter has been made
obsolete
```

All the replacement parameters listed in the table are dynamic, meaning that the values can be changed while the instance is running. Table 4.4 shows the replaced parameters.

OBSOLETE PARAMETER	REPLACED BY PARAMETER
mts_servers	*shared_servers*
mts_max_servers	*max_shared_servers*
mts_dispatchers	*dispatchers*
mts_max-dispatchers	*max_dispatchers*
mts_circuits	*circuits*
mts_sessions	*shared_server_sessions*
mts_listener_address *mts_multiple_listeners*	*local_listener*

Table 4.4: *Oracle 10g Replacement Parameters*

In the case of the dispatchers parameter, the results of the change will depend on which attributes are modified. Since several of the attributes affect the network session layer when a dispatcher is started, they cannot be changed for dispatchers already started. These attributes are: protocol, address, description, presentation, connections, sessions, ticks, and multiplex.

Other attributes, such as listener and service, can be dynamically modified consequently affecting existing as well as new dispatchers of the same configuration.

There is a new view, *v$dispatcher_config*, that shows more information about existing dispatchers. This view displays information about the dispatcher configurations, including attributes that were not specified and were given a default value. The column CONF_INDX in *v$dispatcher_config* can be joined to the CONF_INDX column in *v$dispatcher* to see all of the detailed information about a given dispatcher. This information helps the DBA make more informed decisions on what attributes need to be modified and helps determine if dispatchers need to be added or removed.

For example, to get service and other details about dispatchers, use the following query:

```
SQL> select name, dispatchers, substr(service,1,20) service, idle,
busy
from v$dispatcher,v$dispatcher_config
where v$dispatcher.conf_indx =
      v$dispatcher_config.conf_indx ;

NAME DISPATCHERS SERVICE                IDLE     BUSY
---- ----------- ------------- ---------- --------
D000           1 LONDBXDB          1641097        8
```

Conclusion

In this Chapter, topics concerning Oracle RAC Architecture have been covered. All the components that make up the RAC database system were reviewed. Memory Structures, background processes, cluster ready services, physical and logical structures of the database dispatchers have been examined. The differences between the database instance and database have been identified. The concept of thread was explored and how it is extended in case of RAC database system.

This chapter also covered basic SQL*Net configurations of the *listener.ora* and *tnsnames.ora* files for RAC and configuration of shared server.

Preparing Shared Storage

CHAPTER 5

"I think we may need to share the storage".

Shared Storage

In this chapter and next chapter, preparing shared storage structures, installation of Oracle software with RAC option, and creation of RAC database will be covered. Shared storage is the main and critical requirement for building and managing the RAC database.

Regardless of the number of nodes and database instances that may exist in the RAC cluster, all of them will have shared access to the underlying storage. Setting up shared storage, creating the hardware level structures, provision of the adequate storage redundancy, and preparation of host level storage logical storage units are very important. For setting up the needed shared storage structures at the host level for the RAC database, there is more than one option. These options use shared storage in terms of cluster file system, raw devices, and Oracle's Automated Storage Management (ASM)

This chapter will cover these topics. RAC system being a shared architecture and the shared storage being the crucial component overall design and well being,

The relational database system is basically a logical entity that stores and retrieves organized data. The database resides in the storage structures and provides a front end for the data's use. Thus, the database enjoys a very close connection with the storage units. Channels or paths connect the storage units with the servers and server components. The server, being the main abode of the database system, has to have many robust features to provide continuous service. As shown in Figure 5.1, there are multiple layers in the infrastructure. At the core are the storage units. The storage logical units (LUNS) are presented to the server layer and are usually available for use as raw volumes, as mounted (cluster) file systems and as the ASM (automatic storage management) resources.

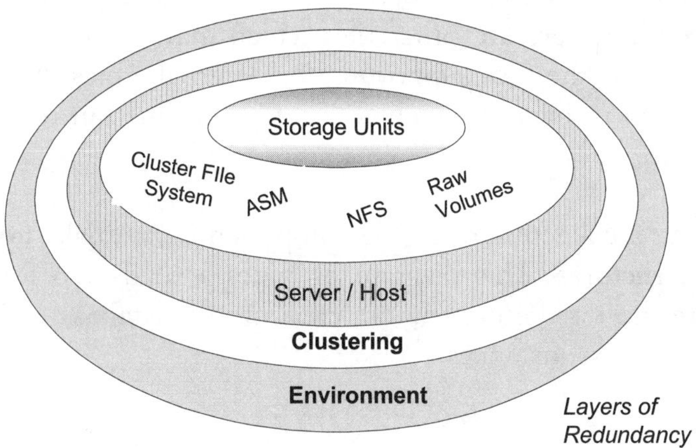

Figure 5.1: *Storage Units and other system layers*

The next layer consists of the server. Even without clustering, the server has to be designed with robust components. There should be a sense of local resiliency. When one of the components falters, there should be a backup or standby component to provide the desired functionality. The cluster layer lies outside the server layer and deals with the loss of the server by failing over to a backup or standby server. Finally, the outside layer is subject to environmental problems such as client connectivity and network failures, which cause bottlenecks between the client and the database.

Overview of the files and directories required

Bottom line is all the participating instances of an Oracle RAC database require access to the shared data files, redo log files, and control files. At the same time, the physical host level cluster consisting of physical nodes needs to have shared access to the quorum disk, voting disk, and OCR file. The use of a vendor provided cluster manager may still require the appropriate quorum disk as prescribed the cluster manager software. The Oracle provided Cluster Ready Services (CRS) need the voting disk and OCR file. There are other files which may need to be shared. They include the files supporting the external tables. It is also recommended to have the archive log files destination on a shared file system.

Figure 5.2 shows a collection of all the components that make up the RAC file structures. This diagram provides a road-map for how to prepare these structures before creating the database and launching the database instances.

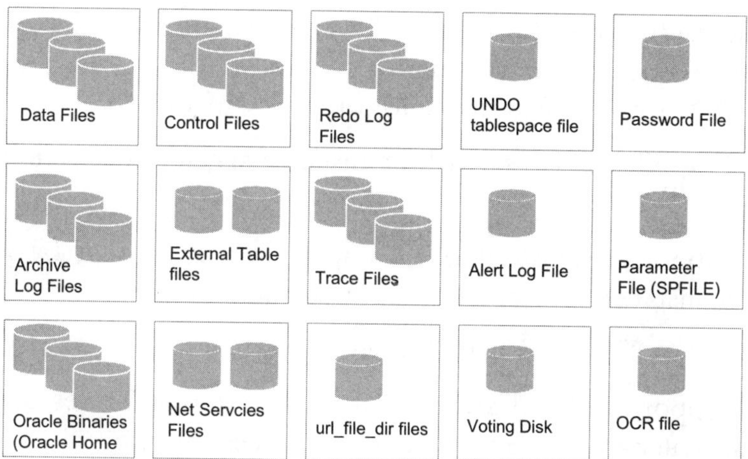

Figure 5.2: *All the Physical File Structures of the RAC Database*

Of the all files that are shown above, most of them need to be on shared storage. There are some files that can be on a local file system, but it is recommended that they are placed on shared file system. And there are some file structures which can very well reside on a local file system. These three combinations are reviewed next.

The following files reside on Shared Storage and are accessible by all RAC instances at the same time.

- Data Files, which make up the main data storage file structures
- Control Files
- Parameter File (SPFILE) – Maintain a common *spfile* located on shared file system which is accessible to all the instances of the RAC database.
- Password File which maintains the authentication privileges
- Voting Disk File and OCR files which are used by the cluster ready services.

The following files reside on Shared Storage and are accessible by a specific instance. However, under certain conditions such as recovery they need to be available for other instances also.

- Redo Log Files which record the instance specific transaction changes.
- Files supporting the Undo Tablespace which is used by a specific instance to maintain the read consistency
- Archive Log Files which are the saved redo log files
- Files supporting the External Tables – External Tables are logical database objects which are accessible to all the instances.

The following are file structures are created, accessed, and managed by a specific instance.

- Alert Log File which keeps a running log of database changes and events
- Trace Files that provide detailed information about the database events.
- Oracle Executables (Oracle Home Files)
- Oracle Cluster Ready Services (CRS) Home which has all the binaries supporting the CRS.

However, with the use of the cluster file system it is possible to use a Shared Oracle Home and shared CRS Home. When using the cluster file system such as HP's Tru64 CFS, Veritas CFS, Polyserve Matrix Server, a single Oracle Home can be maintained and shared among all the nodes of the cluster.

There are four combinations when using shared file structures as shown in Figure 5.3.

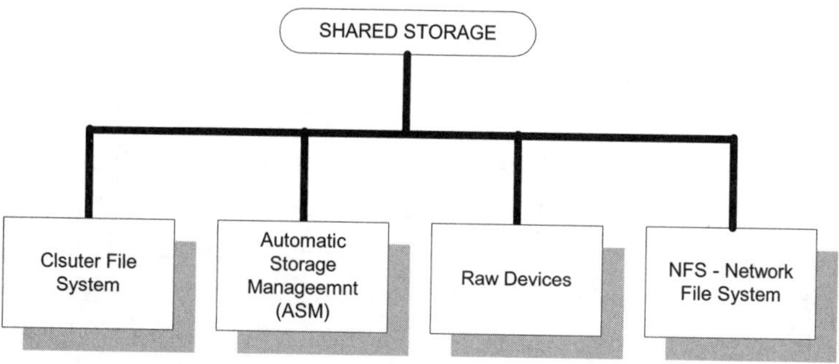

Figure 5.3: *Shared Storage Inputs*

- They can be on raw devices
- They can be on a Cluster File System (CFS). CFS is concurrently mounted on all the participating nodes of the cluster.
- They can be on accessed via the Automatic Storage Management (ASM) instance
- They can be located Network File System

Even though only three types of shared storage structures have been reviewed here, it is also possible to mix them where some shared files can be on raw devices, some can be located on CFS, and some can come out of ASM.

Raw Devices

Raw Devices have been in use for a very log time. They were the primary storage structures for data files of the Oracle Parallel Server. They remain in use even in the RAC versions 9i and 10g. Raw Devices are difficult to manage and administer but provide high performing shared storage structures. When using the raw devices for data files, redo log files, and control files, it may be necessary to use the local file systems or some sort of network attached file system for writing the archive log files, handling the *utl_file_dir* files and files supporting the external tables.

The following is an example where raw devices are still in use. When a RAC database is implemented on Solaris platform with Sun Cluster software, raw devices will have to be used as the shared storage for database files. Of course, if using the Veritas DB edition for Cluster on Solaris platform, the Veritas Cluster File system can be used and this provides more options.

Figure 5.4 shows the various types of Oracle related files located on raw devices and non-raw devices.

On Raw Devices	On Local File System
Data files	Archive Log Files
Redo files	Oracle Home Files
Control Files	CRS Home Files
Voting Disk	Alert Log, Trace Files
OCR File	Files for External Tables
	utl_file_dir location
	backup outputs (sets)

Figure 5.4: *Using raw devices for shared storage structures*

A raw device, also known as a raw partition, is a disk partition that is not formatted. Applications issue I/O calls to transfer data directly from buffers in the user virtual address space to disk. There is no operating system buffering (e.g., page cache), nor is write-order locking imposed. The I/O transfers are conducted through the character-special device driver. As such, I/O transfers generally must adhere to strict requirements imposed by the device driver such as alignment and I/O size and file offsets.

Advantages

Raw partitions have several advantages:

- They are not subject to any operating system locking.
- The operating system buffer or cache is bypassed, giving performance gains and reduced memory consumption.
- Multiple systems can be easily shared.
- The application or database system has full control to manipulate the internals of access.
- Historically, the support for asynchronous I/O on UNIX systems was generally limited to raw partitions.

The creation and usage of raw partitions should be carefully planned, even if the creation and administration of the raw volumes is relatively simple with the use of the logical volume manager.

Issues and Difficulties

There are many administrative inconveniences and drawbacks such as:

- The unit of allocation to the database is the entire raw partition. A raw partition cannot be used for multiple tablespaces. A raw partition is not the same as a file system where many files can be created.
- Administrators have to create them with specific sizes. When the databases grow in size, raw partitions cannot be extended. Partitions need to be added to support growing tablespaces. Sometimes there may be limitations on the total number of raw partitions that can be used in the system. Furthermore, there are no database operations that can occur on an individual data file. There is, therefore, no logical benefit from having a tablespace consist of many data files except for those tablespaces that are larger than the maximum Oracle can support in a single file.

- The standard file manipulation commands cannot be used on raw partitions, and therefore on the data files. Commands such as *cpio* or *tar* cannot be used for backup purposes. Backup strategy will become more complicated.
- Raw partitions cannot be used for writing the archive logs.
- Administrators need to keep track of the raw volumes with their cryptic naming conventions. However, by using symbolic links, the DBA can reduce the hassles associated with names.

  For example, a cryptic name like /dev/rdsk/c8t4d5s4 or a name like /dev/sd/sd001 is an administrative challenge. To alleviate this, administrators often rely on symbolic links to provide logical names that make sense. This, however, substitutes one complexity for another.

  In a clustered environment like Linux clusters, it is not guaranteed that the physical devices will have the same device names on different nodes or across reboots of a single node. To solve this problem, manual intervention is needed that increases administration overhead.

Cluster File System

Cluster File System (CFS) offers a very good shared storage facility for building the RAC database. CFS provides a shared file system which is mounted on all the cluster nodes simultaneously. When implementing RAC database with commercial CFS products such as the Veritas CFS or PolyServe Matrix Server, many different kinds of databases files will be able to be stored including the shared Oracle Home and CRS Home.

However the capabilities of the CFS products are not the same. For example, Oracle CFS (OCFS) used in Linux RAC implementations has limitations. It is not a general purpose file system. It cannot be used for shared Oracle Home. Figure 5.5 shows the files locatable on a Cluster File System.

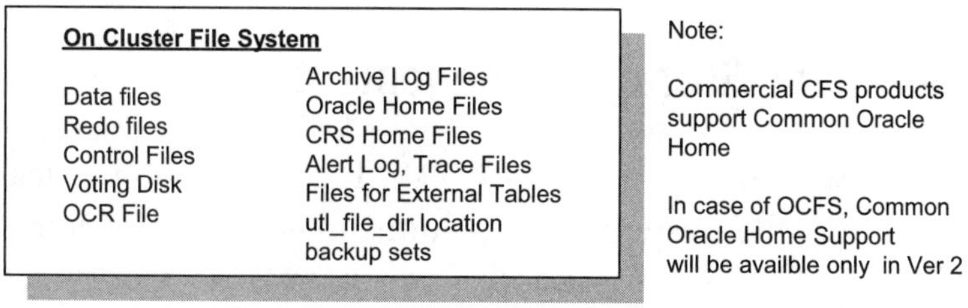

On Cluster File System

Data files	Archive Log Files
Redo files	Oracle Home Files
Control Files	CRS Home Files
Voting Disk	Alert Log, Trace Files
OCR File	Files for External Tables
	utl_file_dir location
	backup sets

Note:

Commercial CFS products support Common Oracle Home

In case of OCFS, Common Oracle Home Support will be availble only in Ver 2

Figure 5.5: *Using cluster file system for shared storage structures*

A cluster file system (CFS) is a file system that may be accessed by all the members in the cluster at the same time. This implies that all the members of the cluster have the same view. Some of the popular and widely used cluster file system products for Oracle RAC include: HP Tru64 CFS, Veritas CFS, IBM GPFS, Polyserve Matrix Server, and Oracle Cluster File system. The cluster file system offers:

- Simple management.
- The use of Oracle Managed Files with RAC.
- A Single Oracle Software Installation.
- Auto-extend Enabled on Oracle Data Files.
- Uniform accessibility of Archive Logs.
- ODM compliant File systems.

In these author's opinions, when the cluster file system is available for a given platform, it is preferable to use the CFS rather that the raw partitions. With the availability of the ODM-compliant cluster file systems, using the CFS makes much more sense. ODM-based CFS offer similar or even better performance over raw partitions, and far superior administrative convenience. The cluster file system set of features is rapidly advancing. A detailed explanation of the cluster file system, as well as advances in usage and functionality, will be offered in later sections of the chapter.

ASM – Automatic Storage Management

ASM is the new star on the block. ASM provides a vertical integration of the file system and volume manager for Oracle database files. ASM has the capability to spreads database files across all available storage for optimal performance and resource utilization. It enables simple and non-intrusive resource allocation and provides automatic rebalancing

Using ASM for building shared files would get almost the same performance as that of raw partitions. The ASM controlled disk devices will be part of ASM instance which can be shared by the RAC database instance. It is similar to the situation where raw devices supporting the RAC database had to be shared by multiple nodes. The shared devices need to be presented to multiple nodes on the cluster and those devices will be input to the ASM instance. There will be an ASM instance supporting each RAC instance on the respective node.

Figure 5.6 shows the files locatable on the ASM instance and files that have to come out of file system.

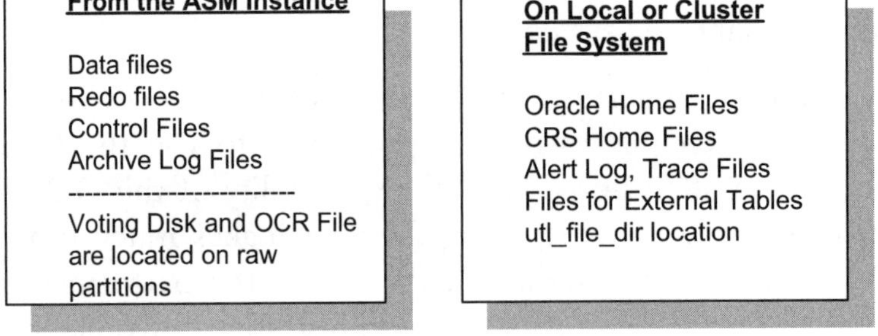

Figure 5.6: *Using ASM instance resources for shared storage structures*

As shown in the above diagram, ASM can not provide the generalized storage resources. ASM is for more Oracle specific data, redo log files, and archived log files. More detailed explanation of the ASM and its implementation method is covered in a later part of this chapter.

NFS - Network File System

NFS provides another shared storage option. Network Appliance Filers offer CFS-like functionality via NFS to the server machines. These file systems are mounted using special mount options. RAC database shared data files can be located on NFS mounts also.

And who is the winner?

From the management and maturity point, Cluster File System provides an ideal shared storage platform for all kinds of Oracle related files. Especially with the provision of Common Oracle Home, the addition of a RAC node and instance becomes relatively easy. A Large RAC cluster can be built very easily as Oracle Binaries do not need to be installed for each of the RAC instance separately. Since a single copy is maintained, it becomes easy to administer and maintain.

CFS is widely used and many stable products are available. Such examples include, HP's Tru64 CFS, Veritas CFS and PolyServe Matrix Server. The open source product such as the OCFS (oracle cluster file system) is also widely used in Linux platforms.

The cluster file system is the most reliable and proven method of setting up the storage volumes into shareable files systems. The ease of use and flexibility of administration provided by the cluster file system has brought new interest to the RAC system.

The concept, implementation, and various CFS products available for the RAC database will be examined later in this chapter.

Using the ASM based shared storage for RAC database is a recommended method by Oracle. ASM is a significant new feature in 10g release. ASM removes the management hassles of raw devices, and provides the performance advantage of the raw devices. ASM also eliminates the need for cluster file system. However, ASM is relatively new technology and it does not provide a general purpose storage platform. ASM offers better management and tuning of I/O activity. ASM also eliminates the need for any volume management.

Next, how the physical storage array is managed and presented to the host will be examined. Hardware redundancy and design issues will also be explored.

Storage Design and Redundancy

Oracle related files and directories mentioned in earlier sections reside on raw partitions or on a cluster file system or in the ASM instance. Raw partitions are a set of unformatted devices on a shared disk sub-system. The RAC shared storage files can be stored on the cluster file system wherever it is available. Disk Devices can also be placed under the control of ASM instance and make it available for the use of RAC database.

There are other file systems such as Oracle Home for the Oracle executables, the file system where the archive logs are written, and the file system where Oracle log files and trace files are written. These file systems are usually mounted on the storage volumes from either the local storage or cluster file system.

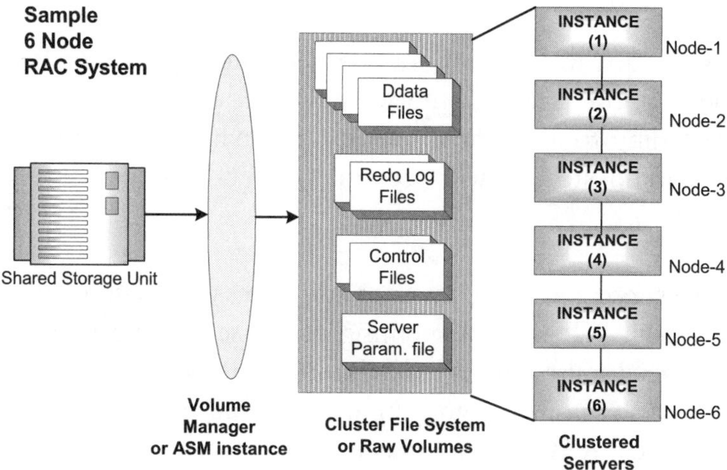

Figure 5.7: *Shared Storage supporting multiple instances*

As shown in Figure 5.7, the storage system is the key component for both the survival of the database system and for its high availability. For example, this diagram shows a 6-node cluster with a very reliable architecture comprised of powerful processors, a large memory in each server, and all 6-nodes sharing the storage system. The 6 nodes jointly provide both the parallel computing environment and high availability. Imagine a storage unit was lost and all 6-nodes are still functioning, but cannot provide the database service. The storage unit is the Achilles Heel. Thus the storage occupies an important place in the overall architecture of the RAC system. It is crucial to plan and design carefully to get the right storage array in a compatible environment.

There are a number of methods used to access the information on the storage systems in the information infrastructure. They include Direct Attached Storage (DAS), Network Attached Storage (NAS), and the Storage Area Networks (SAN). These technologies are not mutually exclusive. Instead, they are complementary.

The inherent advantages of networked storage have been responsible for the gradual replacement of the DAS storage model. According to a recent report by International Data Corp. (IDC), networked storage will account for 67% of disk storage systems by 2005.

The database servers are able to store and access the data from all of these models. When implementing database servers with the clustered server architecture it is advisable to use a storage model that provides a very reliable and highly available platform. In the case of the Oracle RAC system, clustering protects the servers (or hosts) but the shared storage system still requires a suitable protection method.

Storage Disk System

The past decade has seen many changes in disk subsystem technology. The power and intelligence of the storage system has improved considerably. These are no longer dumb disk drives. They are now equipped with intelligent RAID controllers, large cache buffers, and smart switches to control the multiple servers' access, to name just a few. Much of the RAID functionality is confined within the storage unit, thus saving CPU server cycles for other uses as well as eliminating the complexity of software RAID administration.

Some of the storage models and components will be reviewed next.

Just a Bunch of Disks

Just a Bunch of Disks (JBOD) is a simple disk subsystem that provides disk media and I/O connectivity for multiple disk drives located in an external cabinet. JBOD disk drives are individually accessed by the host system and are mirrored/striped and formed into usable volumes at the host level, usually with the help of the logical volume manager (software RAID).

Thus, the host-controlled RAID is used to provide the redundancy. There are many server systems that employ this kind of architecture, but they are becoming less frequent with the wide availability of more intelligent storage arrays. Moreover, the historical disparity in cost between JBOD and intelligent storage is decreasing.

Direct Attached Storage (DAS)

DAS is a simple method of connecting a storage device, such as a hard disk, RAID array, or tape system to the host system directly by means of a cable and switch/hub. I/O requests, also known as protocols or commands, access devices directly. DAS is commonly implemented as a SCSI connection, but other methods may also be used. DAS storage may be a disk drive, a RAID subsystem, or another storage device. The server typically communicates with the storage subsystem using a block-level interface.

Network Attached Storage (NAS)

A NAS device or appliance is usually an integrated processor plus a disk system. With the NAS server architecture, a storage array with its own file system is directly connected to a network that responds to industry standard network file system interfaces such as NFS (UNIX) and SMB/CIFS (Windows). The file requests are sent directly from clients using remote procedure calls (RPCs) to the NAS file system.

Storage Area Networks (SAN)

A SAN is a dedicated storage network designed specifically to connect storage, backup devices, and servers. Commonly used to describe fiber channel fabric switched networks, SANs have been implemented for some time. Today, most of the SANs use a fiber channel media providing any-to-any connection for servers and storage on that network.

SANs have become a popular and efficient method of providing storage consolidation for DAS systems due to some of the features fiber channel presents, such as the number of storage nodes, the ease of connectivity, and extended distance from host servers. SAN storage generally offers remarkably higher throughput capable storage than other alternatives.

What is a LUN?

A Logical Unit Number (LUN) is an indivisible unit presented by a storage device to its host. LUNs are assigned to each disk drive in an array so the host can address and access the data on those devices. This is a very important concept in understanding the relationship between storage devices and the piece of the storage device that can be used by a typical host.

Understanding I/O Path

When an application such as a RDBMS system interacts with the data stored in the physical drives, it has to travel through many layers. These hardware and software layers constitute the I/O path as shown in Figure 5.8. Though this figure is an oversimplification of the components involved, it shows the basic concept. In order to provide a reliable, robust storage path and uninterrupted I/O activity, which is a vital piece in the design of the Oracle9i RAC system, special attention must be given to setting up the redundant storage infrastructure.

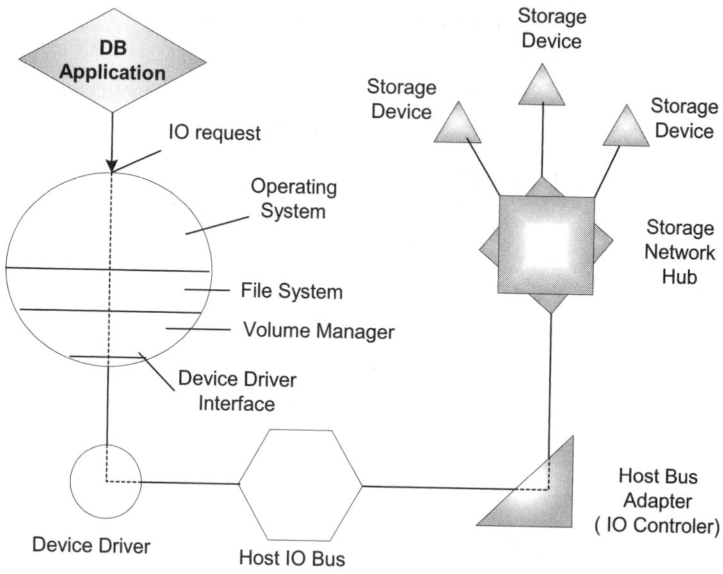

Figure 5.8: *The I/O Path from Application to Disk Media*

Figure 5.8 shows the I/O path, which presents some of the most common storage and storage-related components within the server and within the storage system. Every component has a definite life and therefore MTTF (Mean Time To Failure). In order to protect the total I/O path, there needs to be redundant features to these components. There is every possibility that any of the components like disk devices, storage switches, and HBA(s) may fail.

Host Bus Adapter (HBA)

The HBA, also known as a host I/O controller or SCSI Card, is one of the critical components that needs protection. The HBA is usually a SCSI-2 adapter that plugs into a host and lets the host communicate with a device or a storage system. The HBA usually performs the lower level of the SCSI protocol and normally operates in the initiator role. The initiator is a server or host.

The FC HBA is the fiber channel inter-connect between the server and the SAN. Dual or redundant HBA(s) help to keep an active path. The server-based software can be used for controlling and monitoring HBA failure. Such software detects and fails over the HBA's workload to the active one.

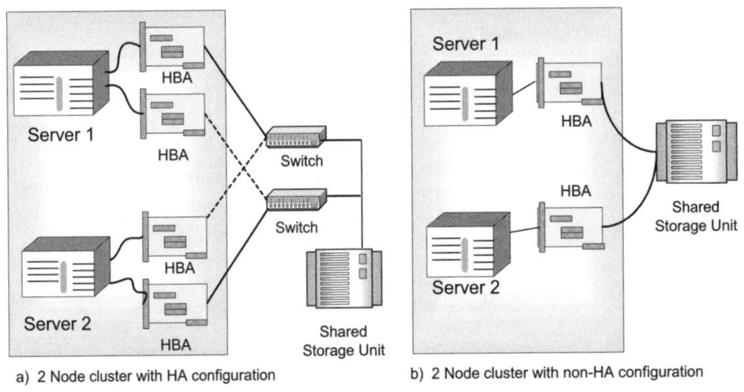

Figure 5.9: *Redundant HBA configuration*

Examples of such a software solution include HP's Secure Path, the Veritas Dynamic Multi-Path, EMC Power Path, and PolyServe Matrix Server Multi-Path I/O. These all help to continue the flow of traffic despite the path failure. When configured with dual HBAs as shown in Figure 5.9, the single point of failure can be avoided. In Figure 5.9(b) there is only one HBA fitted to each server, which can become a point of failure. In Figure 5.9(a), a pair of HBA units for each server and a pair of switches in the I/O path provides redundancy.

Storage Redundancy Components

There are many other components that help keep the storage system secure and reliable. Some of these include:

Hot Spares

A hot spare drive is a drive that contains no data and acts as a standby in case a drive fails. The hot spare drive adds another level of redundancy in the RAID Module. If a drive of similar or a smaller capacity fails, the hot spare automatically takes over on behalf of the failed drive until the failed drive can be replaced with another drive. Once the failed drive is replaced, the hot spare automatically returns to a spare-standby status. Depending on how many hot spares are configured, a LUN (logical unit) could remain optimal and still have several failed drives with each one being covered by a hot spare. This method helps to keep the RAID 1, 3, or 5 LUNs functional.

Hot Plug

A hot-plug component means that it is electrically safe to remove or add the component while the machine is still running. Typically, the system must be rebooted before the hot-plug component is configured into the system.

Hot Swapping

A hot-swap component can be installed or removed by simply pulling the component out and putting in the new one. The system will either automatically recognize the component change and reconfigure itself as necessary or will require user interaction to configure the system. In both cases a reboot is not required. All hot-swappable components are also hot pluggable, although not all hot-pluggable components are hot-swappable. The device being removed or reinstalled is the only device that is not operational during this process.

Multiple RAID Controllers and Storage Processors

RAID Controllers are the units in a storage array that control the RAID operations. They present one or more virtual devices or LUNS to the host system and distribute the I/O operations to the member disks. With the help of a RAID utility, the physical disks are grouped and formed into Logical Units (LUNS). The LUN is the basic storage unit presented to the host system for its use.

It is also responsible for maintaining the mapping between the virtual device and individual disks in the array. The existence of a RAID controller makes a JBOD array into a RAID Storage Array. RAID Controllers are also used in parallel access arrays for improving the I/O performance. Any failure in the RAID controller cripples the total functionality of the storage array.

Many of the storage arrays offer intelligent storage processors, which control the RAID activity on the array. The storage processor is the RAID controller for the storage array. In many arrays, there is a local cache to handle the data movement along with storage processors. Dual caches or battery-backed caches help with protection and provide additional redundancy.

Power Management

One of the most important and unanticipated threats is the loss of power to the entire storage unit. After providing many levels of redundancy such as multiple paths, multiple controllers, and adequate RAID levels for disk drives, if adequate power supply redundancy is neglected, the whole storage unit is still at risk of losing its functionality.

Therefore, it must be equipped with redundant power supplies. Each power supply needs to have the required connections and wattage to supply power to the entire storage system. Where possible, use different power circuits for different power supplies. This way the risk of losing storage unit functionality in the entire cluster would be minimized.

High Availability with SAN

SAN-based storage systems focus on high availability and high performance. Storage switches are the main building blocks for the implementation of the SAN infrastructure. SAN incorporates many redundant hardware components to avoid disruption to I/O activity. Even though the storage system is part of the SAN infrastructure, it can still have multiple connections to the host system, thus providing extra redundancy. These storage-to-host connections can be active or on standby with the capability of automatic failover to an alternate path.

Mirroring is another technique used in achieving high availability. SAN enables the efficient method of mirroring the data on a peer-to-peer basis across the fabric. Mirroring is commonly used to deploy remote sites within a SAN environment.

Use of FC switches provides an extremely reliable infrastructure. Many of the switches have hot-pluggable components, such as optic modules, which can do single port replacements, dual CPUs, and redundant power supplies. The dual fabric nature of the SAN provides the application with an alternate path to the data and also contributes to high availability. The dual fabric nature also eliminates the failure point in the data path.

RAID and RAID Administration

Redundant Array of Independent Disks (RAID) refers to multiple independent hard drives combined to form a single large logical array. Data is stored on the array of disks with additional redundancy information. The redundancy information can be either the data itself (mirroring), or the parity information calculated from several data blocks (RAID 4, or RAID 5). When RAID is in place, the operating system no longer deals with the individual drives, but instead with a set of virtual disks. RAID is used for the dual purpose of increasing performance and redundancy, with different RAID levels offering different solutions. RAID prevents downtime in the event of a hard disk failure, however, it cannot recover data that has been deleted by a user or destroyed by a major event such as a fire.

Where exactly is the RAID process executed? RAID can reside in several places in the I/O path such as:

- **Host I/O Controller based on special device drivers** - In this type of system, the driver is integrated into the operating system. In this case, the performance of the RAID system is completely dependent on the processing load placed on the host CPU, which can potentially become a problem during the array reconstruction phase following a disk failure.
- **Disk System based RAID** – This method involves a hardware RAID controller or storage processor that executes the RAID operations. With this kind of system installed, RAID is offloaded from the host computer and is controlled entirely within the disk system.
- **Host with the help of volume manager** – In this method, the volume manager software manages the RAID operations. It uses the host system resources to perform the RAID operations.

Each level of RAID spreads the data across the drives of the array in a different way and is optimized for specific situations. The following is an examination of the most common RAID levels.

RAID-0

Striping maps data so that the data is interleaved among two or more physical disks of the array. A striped disk contains two or more sub-disks. In this way, portions of two or more hard drives are combined and the read/write performance is improved. However, no redundancy information is stored in a RAID 0 array, which means that if one hard drive fails, all data is lost. RAID 0 is thus usually not used in servers where availability is a concern.

RAID-1

In a RAID 1 system, identical data is stored on two hard disks and is 100 percent redundant. When one disk drive fails, all data is immediately available on the other without any impact on performance or data integrity. Disk mirroring is when two disk drives are mirrored on one SCSI channel. If each disk drive is connected to a separate SCSI channel, it is referred to as disk duplexing and provides additional security. RAID 1 represents an easy and highly efficient solution for data security and system availability.

This RAID level provides redundancy and high availability. One disk may fail but the logical drive with the data is still available. However, this level requires 2 disks, but only one counts as a volume for storage. In some advanced controllers, reads and writes can be made to the disks in a mirror or duplex.

RAID-4

RAID 4 is very similar to RAID 0. Data is striped across the disk drives. However, the RAID 4 controller calculates redundancy (parity information) and stores the information on a separate disk drive (P1, P2). Even when one disk drive fails, all data is still fully available. The missing data is derived from the data that remains available and from the parity information. Unlike RAID 1, only the capacity of one disk drive is needed for the redundancy. For example, using a RAID 4 disk array with 5 disk drives, 80 percent of the installed disk drive capacity is available as user capacity and only 20 percent is used for redundancy. In situations with many small data blocks, the parity disk drive becomes a throughput bottleneck. With large data blocks, RAID 4 shows significant performance gains.

RAID 4 provides high availability since one disk may fail, but the logical drive with the data is still available. This makes good use of disk capacity (array of n disks, n-1 is used for data storage). However, this method involves the complex calculation of redundancy information, which limits the write performance.

RAID-5

Unlike RAID 4, the parity data in a RAID 5 disk array is striped across all disk drives. The RAID 5 disk array delivers a more balanced throughput. The response time is excellent even with small data blocks, which are very common in multitasking and multi-user environments. RAID 5 offers the same level of security as RAID 4 - when one disk drive fails, all data is still fully available. The missing data is recalculated from the data that remains available and from the parity information.

RAID 5 offers the advantage of high availability since one disk may fail, but the logical drive with the data is still available. This method also provides very good use of disk capacity (array of n disks, n-1 is used for data storage). However, calculation of redundancy information limits the write performance.

RAID 10 and RAID 0+1

RAID 10 or RAID 0+1 is a combination of RAID 0 (Performance) and RAID 1 (Data Security). Unlike RAID 4 and RAID 5, there is no need to calculate parity information. RAID 10 (or 0+1) disk arrays offer good performance and data security. Similar to RAID 0, optimum performance is achieved in highly sequential load situations. Like RAID 1, 50 percent of the installed capacity is lost for redundancy. However, I/O throughput may be increased with advanced RAID controllers.

This level provides high availability since one disk may fail, but the logical drive with the data is still available. It also provides good write performance. However, it requires an even number of disks with a minimum of 4. Only half of the disk volume capacity is used but most of the I/O capacity is usually available. This level is often recommended and is the most popular for database systems.

Mirrored Stripes or Striped Mirrors

This RAID level is often misunderstood. Which should be used, RAID 10 or RAID 0+1? Examine Figure 5.10 and see exactly how they work. In the case of RAID 0+1, also called mirrored stripe, striping is implemented in the lowest position, meaning from a group of drives. A stripe is formed and then two such stripes are mirrored resulting in a logical drive. With this method, the loss of any drive makes the entire stripe invalid and the stripe is detached from the mirror pair. When the failed disk is replaced, the entire stripe must be brought up to date. Recovering the entire stripe can take a substantial amount of time as all the stripe members need to update the data.

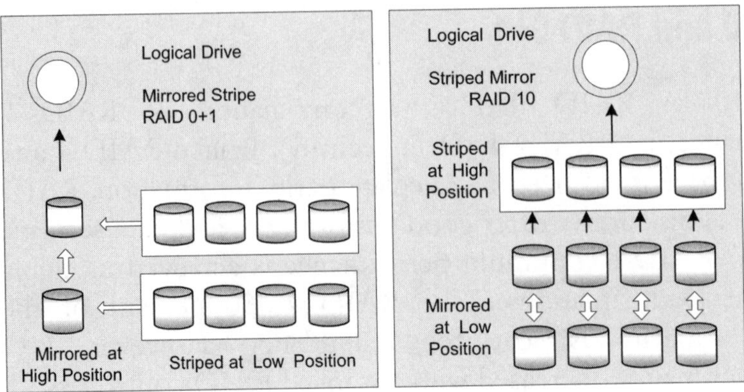

Figure 5.10: *Mirrored Stripe and Striped Mirror RAID architecture*

With RAID 1+0 (or 10), mirroring is implemented at the lowest position. A group of mirrored drives are used to create a stripe. RAID 10, also called a striped mirror, is the superior method. If a disk fails in a striped mirror layout, only the failing disk is detached, and only that portion of the volume loses redundancy. When the disk is replaced, only a portion of the volume needs to be recovered. As shown in Figure 5.10, mirrored drives are independent units. When a disk is lost, it affects only one mirrored pair. Thus, compared to a mirrored-stripe, a striped-mirror offers more tolerance to disk failure. If a disk failure occurs, the recovery time is shorter for a striped-mirror layout.

A short summary of the RAID levels is presented in Table 5.1.

RAID LEVEL	STRENGTHS	WEAKNESS
RAID 0	Performance	No redundancy
RAID 1	Redundancy without Parity	Cost (double the disks)
RAID 3	Minimal Write penalty	No Overlapping
RAID 4	Overlapped small I/Os	Parity Disk bottleneck
RAID 5	Overlapped small I/Os	Write Penalty
RAID 0+1/10	Redundancy and Performance	Cost is very high

Table: 5.1: *Strengths and Weaknesses of Various RAID Levels*

One thing to remember when calculating the number of disks required for a particular RAID configuration is not just the storage capacity required, but to also take into account the needed I/O requirements. On some configurations the added parity writes and other overhead associated with RAID5 for example, can reduce the I/O capacity of the drive set by up to 50%. Disks are limited to around 110-120 I/Os per second maximum I/O capacity for linear read/write activity. For random read/write activity this can drop to 90 I/Os per second or less. Taking I/O capacity into account, RAID10 or 01 becomes less costly with the modern RAID controllers since it essentially doubles I/O capacity even if it halves storage capacity.

Software RAID and Hardware RAID

As previously stated, the RAID operations can be performed either in the host or within the disk sub-system. When RAID is done within a host, usually with the help of volume manager software or by means of a device drive, it is referred to as software RAID. When it is implemented within the storage system it is said to be hardware RAID.

Some of the issues surrounding the software RAID implementation are:

- **Issue of Portability** – Since the RAID software implementation has some O/S specific components, these components have to be RAID operations, share the kernel mode components, and may add to the system CPU load. Software RAID uses more system resources, as more disk ports and channels are required, and it is subject to additional loads during write and copy operations.
- Software RAID is relatively complex. Creating several dozen redundant performance volumes across several dozen hard

drives results in several hundred configuration records that describe the layout.

The following advantages may be seen with hardware RAID.

- The RAID firmware is executed on a dedicated processor within the disk subsystem, and therefore does not share the system's CPU.
- It is portable across all the operating systems. In the event of a malfunction in the RAID firmware, the host system continues to operate and gives a suitable report on the RAID issue. At the same time, if the crash occurs at the system level the storage system functioning is unaffected.
- Many of the RAID solutions are equipped with battery backup modules that allow them to maintain cache coherency and complete outstanding operations without loss of data integrity.
- RAID controllers or storage processors are specialized for enhancing performance. Auxiliary processors are dedicated to calculating the parity of the data blocks that are being written to disk, while the main embedded processor concurrently fetches and executes RAID code.

However, there is one situation where software RAID becomes very useful. To mirror the drives from two different storage units, only software mirroring at the host level can do it. For example, after drives from two storage units are placed under the control of the Veritas volume manager at host level, a volume can be created by using the RAID-1 level to mirror two disks originating from two different disk systems. By this means, even if access to one of the storage units is lost, the volume can still continue to function.

Multiple Access Paths to Host

Multipathing generally allows two or more data paths to be used simultaneously for read/write operations. This enhances performance by automatically and equally dispersing data access across all the available paths. Many storage and storage software vendors offer this kind of reliability.

Some of the widely used solutions such as EMC's Power Path, HP's Secure Path, and Veritas's Dynamic Multipathing solution will be examined next.

Power Path (Dell / EMC)

EMC's Power Path helps to improve the high availability of the data or I/O path and manages the heavy storage load. It automatically detects host failures and recovers storage. Power Path is host-based software that runs on UNIX, Windows, and Linux servers. It can manage the protocols in both SCSI and fiber physical interconnects. Power Path creates a virtual power device that provides failure resistance and a load balanced path. Power devices are virtual objects that contain file systems or raw partitions. They are managed by a volume manager or host system. Each power device represents a LUN at the host level but remains available through multiple I/O paths. The detailed path is shown in Figure 5.11.

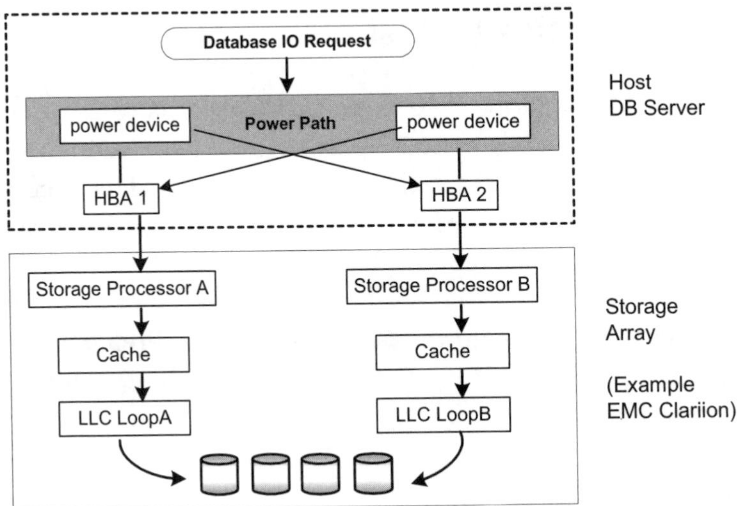

Figure 5.11: *Power Path as implemented in EMC Clariion storage array*

Secure Path

HP's Secure Path is multipath, high availability software that manages and maintains continuous data access to HP storage systems. There is no single point of failure from the server to the storage. Secure Path is host resident software that monitors the data paths between the server and the storage to increase the availability of the information. In the event a path failure is detected, Secure Path fails over the data path to an alternative path. When the original path becomes available, Secure Path can automatically fall back to the original path. Secure Path can also balance the workload among available paths to optimize system performance.

Dynamic MultiPathing

Dynamic Multipathing (DMP) is a feature of the Veritas Volume Manager. It offers greater reliability by providing a path failover mechanism. In the event a connection to a disk is lost, the system continues to access the critical data over the remaining sound connections to the disk. DMP also provides greater I/O throughput by balancing the I/O load uniformly across multiple I/O paths to the disk device.

MxMPIO

PolyServe Matrix Server supports multipath I/O in its driver stack. MxMPIO offers solid redundancy in the event of an HBA failure. Additionally, MxMPIO offers I/O load balancing by multiplexing I/O for varying LUNs between the different HBAs in the system. Bringing this feature to the Intel-based server-clustering arena makes commodity-based datacenter solutions one step closer to reality.

Volume Management

The database is constructed and maintained on file system files or raw partitions, which are entities at the operating system level. They are directly attached to storage devices, NAS devices, or SAN volumes. There are several different layers of abstraction between the physical disks and the objects that the database uses. The physical drive is at the lowest level, next comes the LUNS (logical unit numbers) of manageable sizes employing an appropriate RAID level. LUNS are presented to the host system as physical objects.

The Logical Volume Manager (LVM) is a software module running at the host level and manages the physical objects and presents them as logical units that the application can use. The volume manager hides the physical attributes of the disks or LUNs by introducing virtualization. The volume manager can also execute the RAID operations if needed. Within the volume manager, storage devices are grouped into disk groups (e.g. Veritas disk group).

Within a disk group, a logical volume can be created with an optional or desired RAID level. Finally, the logical volume is either presented as a file system after mounting, or presented as a raw partition for application use. The VM tool provides a very flexible way of managing the volumes and file systems. Without a volume manager, LUNS are physical disks with partitions.

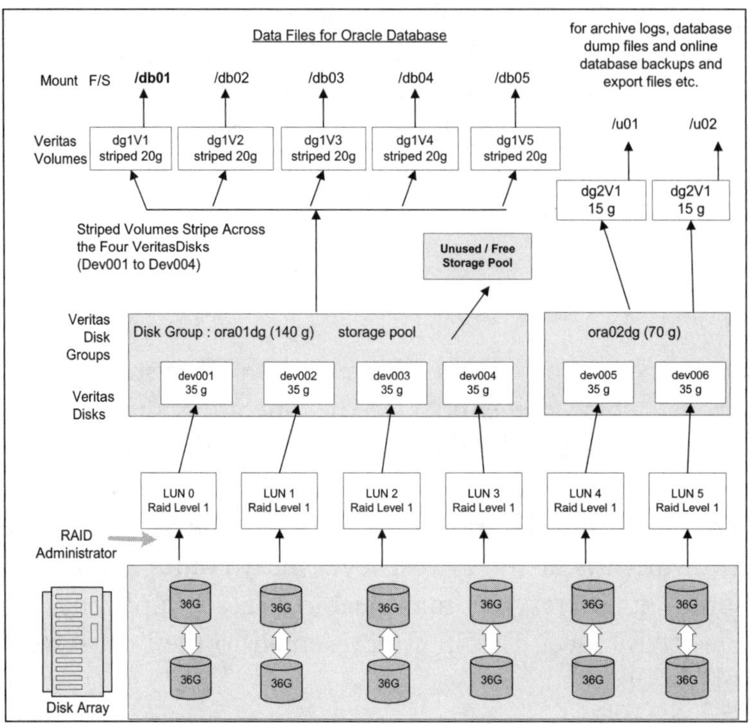

Figure 5.12: *Volume Configuration using Veritas Volume Manager*

Thus the volume manager hides the details about where data is stored in the hardware from the entire system. Volume management allows the editing of the storage configuration, for example, setting up a software RAID or extending volume size, etc., without actually changing anything on the hardware side. Some volume manager tools allow snapshot copies to be taken of volumes to move or backup. Thus, for either creating the raw partitions (or volumes) or setting up of file systems, the volume manager is a handy tool.

Figure 5.12 above shows how the LVM provides volumes and file systems to a host. LVM hides all the complexity in the backend of the disk drives or the storage units. The database system will just interact with the volumes presented by the LVM.

The Veritas volume manager has been in use on many platforms like Solaris, HP, and AIX. Now, Veritas even has the Volume Manager to support Windows systems. On the Linux side, SuSE LVM has been in use for a long time.

However it is important to note that cluster volume management is different from the normal volume management. Cluster Volume management provides the volumes for all the nodes in the cluster infrastructure.

Cluster File System

A cluster file system provides an alternative to raw devices. A file system presents a familiar environment to the user for creating and managing the files required for a RAC database. The cluster file system provides a view of the database files and makes it easy to expand, add, and copy existing files. With a shared file system, multiple instances can share archive logs.

This makes media recovery much more convenient because every node has access to every archived log file as needed. The general features include:

- For applications, the CFS functionality is just like a regular file system. The RDBMS system is easily integrated with the CFS and requires no special modifications.

- Most of the CFS solutions are based on a master-server design, where one of the nodes acts as a server and the others act as clients. The master node performs all the file system metadata manipulations, with other nodes forwarding the tasks to the server node (e.g., Veritas CFS).
- A File System like Polyserve Matrix Server is based on symmetric architecture with a distributed lock manager. This means that all the nodes in the cluster collectively undertake the metadata and lock management operations. No bottleneck and no single point of failure.
- When using a CFS, Oracle RAC requires Direct I/O. Direct I/O is generally enabled for a file by opening the file with the *o_direct* flag in the open(2) system call. Read and write requests for the file are then executed to and from disk storage through direct memory access thus bypassing CFS caching. This improves I/O performance for database applications that perform their own caching and file region synchronization. This is, however, a compile-time requirement. To that end, PolyServe Matrix Server features a mount-time Direct I/O that enables any application that is capable of using raw partitions to benefit from Direct I/O without recompiling.
- Without the Direct I/O feature (or the ODM interface), maintenance and synchronization of the local file system cache becomes complicated. A typical CFS provides an internal locking mechanism to control the concurrent use and protect the integrity of the file system (metadata). A locking mechanism, usually called the lock manager, is used for metadata integrity and cache coherency across the multiple nodes. The lock manager provides a way to ensure all nodes have a consistent view of the file system. The lock manager can be of distributed or master-slave architecture.

- One of the advantages that accrue from using the cluster file system is the combination of OMF with the ODM interface. The cluster file systems that are compliant with the ODM interface are able to provide much better I/O performance with relative ease of administration. Oracle managed files can be created and deleted directly at the operating system level. More details about OMF and ODM will be presented later.

There are two main purposes for which CFS can be used in the Oracle RAC environment.

First, CFS makes it possible to set up all the shared data files, control files, server parameter files, redo log files, voting disk file and the OCR file in the file system. These are the files that would otherwise need to be located in raw partitions. The archive log files can also be located in the CFS directory to make them accessible for all nodes, as needed.

Secondly, other relevant files and directories associated with the RAC database environment can be placed on the CFS providing administrative ease. Such files and directories include:

- Oracle External Tables (a new feature in Oracle9i).
- Oracle Home directory, including all the Oracle executables.
- Export Files generated from the database objects which is useful for all the nodes.
- Report Files and output of the *utl_file* function from other files.
- File Systems with user files.
- Files/Data Feed for loading into the database.

The cluster file system allows an administrator to install the Oracle product in a shared Oracle Home. Because Oracle Home is made available on the shared disk, all instances of Oracle will run from the same disk executables. The amount of disk space required will significantly be reduced as well as the installation time. Only one copy of the Oracle executables needs to be maintained.

A shared Oracle home also permits trace files and configuration files to be shared so that system administrators can work from any single node and access the whole system. Furthermore, patches need be applied only once. Oracle9i has a new feature called External Tables. The external table feature allows data in simple flat files to be treated as an Oracle table. It also allows the select command to be used on External Tables. Furthermore, External Tables can be accessed with Intra-node Parallel Query, taking advantage of the full processing power of the cluster. Without the CFS, the facility of External Tables becomes very limited. An External Table can be created in a non-clustered file system but the access to it will be limited to one node.

What is Context Dependent Symbolic Link?

When using the shared cluster file system, there is just one copy of the entire directory structure. Just one set of directories exists where the data files, control files, redo log files, and archive log files are located. This is advantageous in many respects. However, sometimes there may be a desire for the relationship between a set of files or a directory and the shared CFS directory to be unique for each node/host within the cluster. For example, the DBA may want to keep a local *tnsnames.ora* file or a local *listener.ora* file.

For the purpose of setting up Intelligent Agent, the DBA may want to separate the $ORACLE_HOME/network directory from the shared Oracle home installation without having to physically install the Intelligent Agent on each node in the cluster. In such situations, setting up a context dependent symbolic link (CDSL) creates a node-dependent copy of the file or directory.

There are many cluster file system products that can be used for building the RAC system. They include: Tru64 CFS for HP/Compaq Cluster servers, Veritas CFS for Solaris based RAC Clusters, PolyServe Matrix Server for Linux and Windows based RAC Clusters, and Oracle cluster files systems for Linux and Windows RAC clusters. Some of the important features of these products will be examined next. Only some of these, however, support CDSL.

Veritas CFS

The VERITAS Database Edition/Advanced Cluster for Oracle RAC enables Oracle to use the CFS. The Veritas CFS is an extension of the VERITAS File System (VxFS). The Veritas CFS allows the same file system to be simultaneously mounted on multiple nodes. Veritas CFS is designed with master/slave architecture. Any node can initiate a metadata operation (create, delete, or resize data) and the master node carries out the actual operation. All other (non metadata) I/O goes directly to the disk.

A distributed locking mechanism, called the global lock manager (GLM) is used for metadata and cache coherency across the multiple nodes. GLM provides a way to ensure that all the nodes will have a consistent view of the file system. When any node wishes to read data, it requests a shared lock. If another node wishes to write to the same area of the file system, it must request an exclusive lock. The GLM revokes all shared locks before granting the exclusive lock and informs reading nodes that their data is no longer valid.

CFS is used in DBE/AC to manage a file system in a large database environment. When used in DBE/AC for Oracle-RAC, Oracle accesses data files stored on CFS file systems with the ODM interface. This essentially bypasses the file system buffer and file system locking. This means that only Oracle handles the tasks of buffering data and coordinating writes to files and not the GLM, which is minimally used with the ODM interface.

Using this out-of-band fencing is a significant benefit in large clustered environments where the alternative fencing approach known as STOMITH (shoot the other machine in the head) is neither sufficiently reliable nor acceptable.

HP Tru64 CFS

Tru64 CFS is a layer on top of the Advfs file system. When direct I/O is enabled for a file by opening the file with the *o_directio* flag, read and write requests on it are executed to and from disk storage through direct memory access, bypassing AdvFS and CFS caching. This improves I/O performance for database applications that do their own caching and file region synchronization.

Oracle uses the direct I/O feature available in CFS. Direct I/O enables Oracle to bypass the buffer cache (no caching at file system level). Oracle manages the concurrent access to the file itself as it does on raw devices. Direct I/O does not go through the CFS server. File creation and resizing is seen as a metadata operation by Advfs and this has to be done by the CFS server. Consequently, file creations and resizes must be run on the node where the CFS server is located. File operations might take longer when the CFS server is remote.

In a TruCluster server, the device request dispatcher subsystem controls all I/O to physical devices. All cluster I/O passes through this subsystem, which enforces single-system open semantics so only one program can open a device at any one time.

The following are some general features of a Tru64 CFS:

- The Cluster File System (CFS) makes all files, including the root (/), /usr, and /var file systems, visible to and accessible by all cluster members. There is a single copy or image for all cluster members.
- A single cluster member serves each file system. Other members access that file system as CFS clients, with significant optimization for shared access.
- Oracle RAC automatically does direct I/O on Tru64 UNIX file system storage. This can significantly improve I/O performance for the database since Oracle9i does its own caching and file region synchronization.

Context Dependent Symbolic Link (CDSL)

Since Tru64 CFS provides a single namespace, there is a single copy of most configuration files. With a few exceptions, the directory structure of a cluster is identical to that of a stand-alone system. However, wherever files are not to be shared (like /etc/passwd, /etcsysconfigtab), the context dependent symbolic link (CDSL) manages the copies for cluster members.

Node-specific Oracle files like *tnsnames.ora*, *listener.ora*, and *sqlnet.ora* can also be created using the CDSL system. CDSL(s) contain a variable whose value is determined only during pathname resolution. The {memb} variable is used to access member-specific files in a cluster.

The following example shows the CDSL for /etc/rc.config:

```
/etc/rc.config -> ../cluster/members/{memb} /etc/rc.config
```

When resolving a CDSL pathname, the kernel replaces the {memb} variable with the string *membern*, where n is the member ID of the current member.

CDSL(s) are useful when running multiple instances of an application on different cluster members, where each member operates on a different set of data. The *mkcdsl* command lets system administrators create CDSL(s) and update a CDSL inventory file. The *cdslinvchk* command verifies the current CDSL inventory.

Oracle Cluster File System (OCFS)

Oracle Cluster File System (OCFS) is a shared file system designed specifically for Oracle Real Application Clusters. OCFS eliminates the requirement for Oracle database files to be located on the raw devices in Linux RAC cluster and Windows RAC cluster.

OCFS is released under the GNU General Public License (GPL). The source code for the binaries shipped with the RPM's are directly available in the source RPMS (.src.rpm) for reference and compliance. Oracle will only formally support the binary RPM's compiled by Oracle and downloadable for Red Hat Advanced Server or United Linux. Oracle provides OCFS product support to customers that already have an Oracle support license.

For Linux and Windows

With active support from open source community, Oracle has developed the cluster file system (OCFS) for use in Red Hat Linux and United Linux, and released it as an open source. It is available in the form of RPM packages. Users can download it for free. OCFS only supports Oracle data files, redo log files, and control files. It is not a general-purpose file system. It does not support a shared Oracle Home at least not until Version 2 is released.

OCFS requires the use of the operating system's *o_direct* compile-time flag to get direct I/O. I/O must be performed through aligned buffers with 512 byte (or multiples thereof) buffer offsets. These are details the Oracle server takes care of. The Oracle RAC database manages all the difficult concurrency issues and maintains the data integrity of the application just as it does when using raw partitions.

The OCFS version for Windows NT/2000 does support a shared Oracle Home.

OCFS2 is the latest version of the Oracle Cluster File System software. While OCFS Version 1 was designed specifically for Oracle Database files, OCFS Ver 2 supports a shared ORACLE_HOME installation also.

New features of the OCFS Version 2 include:

- Shared ORACLE_HOME
- Improved performance of metadata operations (space allocation, locking, etc).
- Improved metadata caching.
- Improved data caching (for files such as oracle binaries, libraries, etc)
- Network based DLM is used by default.
- Improved journaling / node recovery - we now use the Linux Kernel JBD subsystem
- Keep the same performance for Oracle data files as OCFS1.
- CDSL for node specific files

PolyServe Matrix Server (MxS)

MxS is a general-purpose cluster file system that runs on a Linux or Windows cluster. It is used for Oracle RAC and other HA solutions. MxS supports all Oracle data files and redo logs. It further supports advanced Oracle functionality including external tables, export/import from text files, and archived redo log compression. MxS also supports a shared Oracle Home, which simplifies installation, configuration, and maintenance.

Other CFS solutions:

Network Appliance Filers offers CFS-like functionality via NFS to the server machines. These file systems are mounted using special mount options.

IBM's General Parallel File System (GPFS) allows users shared access to files that may span multiple disk drives on multiple nodes. GPFS provides access to all data from all nodes of the cluster. GPFS is only supported with HACMP/ES in a RAC configuration.

Oracle Disk Manager

Oracle Disk Manager (ODM) is Oracle's innovative I/O and file management infrastructure. Oracle Disk Manager is a very significant development in the way Oracle manages and interfaces with I/O activity. The ODM interface is a set of API calls that Oracle co-developed with Veritas for incorporating underlying volume managers and file systems. Implementation of the ODM interface in a file system or a logical volume manager provides many benefits, including simplified file administration, improved file integrity, and reduced system overhead.

ODM is completely transparent from an application/DBA perspective. It is an improvement over standard Unix I/O. The ODM interface allows the Oracle kernel to allocate/release disk space, manage tablespaces, and read/write disk blocks directly. Oracle encourages customers to use file system or volume managers that are ODM compliant.

Oracle automatically takes advantage of the ODM interface when the underlying file system or logical volume manager becomes ODM-enabled. A file is considered an ODM file if it is in a file system that supports an ODM interface. ODM is also compatible with Oracle9i and 10g. Many of the leading file system and volume manager providers have incorporated the ODM interface into their products. Well known examples include Veritas Database Edition (Advanced Cluster for Oracle) and Polyserve Matrix Server. Several ODM semantics have been included in the DAFS v1.0 protocol specifications offered by Network Appliance Filers.

The following is an examination of some of the ODM features:

- Without ODM, Oracle must resort to many different sets of calls to manage the wide variety of I/O types. For example, Oracle uses calls such as *pwrite()*, *pread()*, *async_write()*, *readv()*, *read()*, *write()*, *lio_listio()*, and *kaio()*. With ODM, Oracle needs only the single call *odm_io()*. *odm_io()* supports all Oracle file I/O types on ALL files (Raw or VxFS).
- Normally, asynchronous DBWR page flushing requires two calls, one to issue the I/O and another to poll for completed I/O. With ODM, gathered writes (DBWR) and LGWR asynchronous writes occur with a single call to *odm_io()* without regard for file type (VxFS or RAW) or number of target files. Checking for completed I/O requests is conducted while issuing new requests.

- ODM includes features that enable more effective Oracle file creation. Without ODM, failed attempts to add files to a database can result in an unused file that must be cleaned up from outside Oracle. With ODM, files are no longer created with traditional *open()* or *create()* calls.
- Files are created with *odm_create()* and then initialized or filled. If the file creation is a success, it then calls *odm_commit()*. If there is failure, Oracle calls *odm_abort()*. The file will be completely cleaned up from within ODM.
- With ODM, Oracle no longer uses file descriptors. Instead, ODM identifiers are used. ODM identifiers are shareable from process to process within the node. Oracle caches ODM identifiers in the SGA at instance startup. ODM identifier usage reduces kernel overhead.

Veritas and Oracle studies indicate that the ODM files perform equal or better than the raw partitions. ODM yields roughly 8% reduction in kernel mode CPU utilization on certain platforms under certain workloads.

Configuration of Automated Storage Management

One of the most significant new features in Oracle 10g release is the introduction of Automated Storage Management (ASM). In order to use the ASM in a shared mode for the use of RAC database, an ASM instance needs to be created for each node of the RAC database involving the same disk devices as input. Each ASM instance has either an SPFILE or PFILE type parameter file. To use ASM in the RAC environment, select ASM as the storage option when creating the database with the Database Configuration Assistant (DBCA).

What is Automated Storage Management?

Automated Storage Management (ASM) was designed to simplify database administration. ASM eliminates the need for the DBA to directly manage the thousands of Oracle database files that could be present in a modern Oracle instance. ASM does this by enabling ASM disk groups, which are logical units comprised of disks and the files that reside on them. Using ASM, the management of thousands of Oracle files is reduced to managing a small number of disk groups.

The SQL statements used for creating database structures, such as tablespaces, redo logs, archive log files, and control files, must specify file location in terms of ASM disk groups in order to use ASM. ASM will then create and manage the associated underlying files.

ASM is the logical extension of the power of Oracle-managed files (OMF). In previous releases of OMF, files were created and managed automatically, but with ASM there are the additional benefits of features such as ASM disk group mirroring and striping. ASM was developed by the same group that developed Oracle Disk Manager (ODM) within Oracle Corporation.

ASM was designed to preserve all existing database functionality. Existing databases will operate as they always have. Existing databases using file systems or with storage on raw devices will operate as they always have. However, even in existing Oracle 10g Databases, new files can be created as ASM files while old ones are administered in the old way. This means that databases can have a mixture of ASM files, Oracle-Managed files, and manually managed files simultaneously.

Why ASM?

Before examining the role and position of ASM in the storage stack of the database files, a review of some of the storage management features that are often used in varying degree of the usage is warranted. They include:

- Direct I/O
- Asynchronous I/O
- Striping
- Mirroring
- SAME and Load Balancing

Direct I/O

Buffered I/O uses precious resources like memory and CPU cycles because the Oracle blocks are cached both in the SGA and in the file system buffer cache. By adopting the Direct I/O, a much higher cache hit ratio can be achieved. Oracle can handle cache much more efficiently than a file system. Oracle has a sophisticated touch count based cache replacement algorithm that is sensitive to both the frequency of usage and how recent the data blocks are.

Buffered I/O fills up the file system cache with Oracle Data, where as using the Direct I/O allows non-Oracle data to be cached in the file system much more efficiently. Also, the buffered I/O generally involves large physical writes, such as temp file writes. These writes are performed and waited for in series, and therefore they cannot be merged in the device driver or lower layers of the stack, unless a write-back disk cache is in use. This means that a full rotational latency of the physical disk is sustained between every pair of component writes.

Redo Log file writes also suffer from another severe inefficiency if buffered I/O is used. Because redo writes address an arbitrary number of log blocks, and log blocks are small relative to the size of file system buffers, it is normal that the last log block of a redo write does not align with the end of a file system buffer. Therefore, unless the target file system block is already in cache, the operating system must first read that block from disk before the new redo can be copied into part of its file system buffer.

To solve all these problems, direct I/O is highly desired. The way in which direct I/O is enabled varies from one system to another and also depends on the type of file system type. In some cases it is sufficient to set the *filesystemio_options* parameter. In other situations a file system mount option is required and direct I/O can also be configured on a file-by-file basis using special operating system commands. The use of ASM eliminates need for direct I/O configuration.

Asynchronous I/O

When a system process attempts to read or write using the normal synchronous *read()* or *write()* system calls, then it must wait until the physical I/O is completed. Once the success or failure of the read/write operation is known, the process finishes the task. During this time, the execution of the process is blocked while it waits for the results of the system call. This is synchronous or blocking I/O.

However, the desired method is Asynchronous I/O which indicates that it is a Non-blocking I/O. If the process instead uses the asynchronous *aio_read()* or *aio_write()* system calls, then the system call will return immediately once the I/O request has been passed down to the hardware or queued in the operating system, typically before the physical I/O operation has even begun. It can continue executing and then receive the results of the I/O operation later, once they are available. Thus it is asynchronous or non-blocking I/O.

Asynchronous I/O enables write intensive processes like Oracle's DBWn to make full use of the I/O bandwidth of the hardware, by queuing I/O requests to distinct devices in quick succession so that they can be processed largely in parallel. Asynchronous I/O also allows processes performing compute intensive operations like sorts to pre-fetch data from disk before it is required so that the I/O and computation can occur in parallel.

The performance of asynchronous I/O is depends much on if the kernelized asynchronous I/O or threaded asynchronous I/O is used.

- For kernelized asynchronous I/O, the kernel allocates an asynchronous I/O request data structure and calls an entry point in the device driver to set up the asynchronous I/O request. The device driver then queues the physical I/O operation and returns control to the calling process. When the physical I/O operation has completed, the hardware generates an interrupt to a CPU. The CPU switches into interrupt service context and calls the device driver's interrupt service routine to update the asynchronous I/O request data structure and possibly to signal the calling process with SIGIO.
- The threaded implementation of asynchronous I/O uses the kernel's light-weight process functionality to simulate asynchronous I/O by performing multiple synchronous I/O requests in distinct threads. This achieves I/O parallelism at the expense of additional CPU usage associated with thread creation and extra context switching overheads. If threaded asynchronous I/O is used very intensively, these costs can add as much as 5% to system CPU usage. For this reason using kernelized asynchronous I/O is a preferred method.

Kernelized Asynchronous I/O, popularly known as KIO, is only available if the underlying file system uses Oracle Disk Manager (ODM) API, Veritas Quick I/O, or a similar product that routes the I/O via a pseudo device driver that can serve as the locus for asynchronous I/O request completion. Also KIO is available if using raw partitions. Many operating systems also require special configuration of device files, device drivers and kernel parameters to enable and tune kernelized asynchronous I/O. It is definitely a complex configuration to achieve Asynchronous I/O. The best news is that the KIO is available with the ASM files automatically.

Striping

In the layout of database files, the DBA can often see many hot spots where same disk or set of blocks are accessed more often than others. Often it results in large queues and does not take advantage of the concurrent disk I/Os.

Striping Oracle database files across multiple physical disk spindles improves the concurrency of access to hot spots, and generally improves the transfer rate for large reads and writes, and spreads the I/O load evenly across the available disks. Striping spreads the I/O load evenly across all the disks in the stripe. This makes it possible for the full I/O bandwidth of the storage hardware to be used to service any I/O workload. The trend towards using fewer, larger capacity disks makes it increasingly important to be able to use the full I/O bandwidth in this way.

When striping is implemented at storage array or hardware level, Oracle Database files inherently gets the striping benefit. Striping can also be implemented using an appropriate volume manager tool.

ASM provides the facility of generic volume management type software for striping at host level. This will avoid any use of expensive striping software.

Mirroring

Storage Array or Hardware provides mirroring of disks or disk partitions and protects against the possible loss of disks and disruption to storage availability. With hardware mirroring, the operating system sees only one device and performs only one write to it. The hardware is responsible for ensuring that the write is directed to all mirrors and is logically atomic.

Mirroring can also be implemented at host level by using the volume management software. When implemented at the host level, with software mirroring, there is the possibility of a system failure occurring after a write has completed on one side of the mirror, but before it has reached the other(s). Therefore, to ensure that mirror consistency can be re-established reasonably quickly after a crash, software mirroring maintains a dirty region log on disk. This identifies the mirror regions that have been written to recently, and thus might be inconsistent in the event of a system failure. The maintenance of a dirty region log adds a major performance overhead to software mirroring. In the past, Oracle has worked with some LVM vendors to eliminate the need for dirty region logs on mirrored Oracle Database files, but this facility is only available on some platforms and introduces extra complexity.

When hardware mirroring is not available, ASM provides the best possible mirroring. No dirty region logs are needed, as Oracle manages to restore consistency between the mirrors using its own redo log data.

Load balancing (SAME)

Oracle has been promoting the concept of SAME – Stripe and Mirror Everything which aimed at using the full I/O capacity of the all disks. Many database users have implemented SAME sets, each of about 4 mirrored disk pairs. However the SAME functionality does not completely eliminate the disk imbalances. There are different types of files where I/O activity is not uniform, and the configuration of SAME is not the cure for all I/O ills.

ASM takes an additional step in balancing I/O activity. Rebalancing distributes file data evenly across all the disks of the ASM Disk Group. ASM automatically rebalances a disk group whenever disks are added or dropped. ASM ensures that a file is evenly spread across all disks in a disk group when the file is allocated, so rebalancing is not required except when the storage configuration changes. With the I/O balanced whenever files are allocated and whenever the storage configuration changes, there is no need to search for hot spots in a disk group and manually move data to restore a balanced I/O load. It also allows the addition of disks online. There are extra background processes that conduct the rebalancing activity in a non-intrusive way. Thus, ASM makes manual load balancing unnecessary because the dynamic rebalancing overcomes the major drawback of SAME. When new disks are added to a disk group, rebalancing happens automatically without an outage.

ASM is the new best practice for Storage Management

The use of ASM files provides all above mentioned features without any cost and administrative inconvenience. Above mentioned characteristics are derived from the ASM methodology inherently.

Another important benefit that accrues is the use of ASM for RAC database. ASM can very well avoid the use of Cluster File System as the ASM resources (disks and files) are sharable among the RAC instances and fits into the shared storage architecture.

Besides above advantages, there are other benefits that include:

- Ease of administration -- ASM removes the need to specify and manage filenames since ASM knows to place specific data files into specific disk groups. In ASM, every new file automatically gets a new unique name, which eliminates the concern about possibly using the same filename in two different databases.
- ASM replaces external volume managers and file systems. ASM includes storage reliability features, such as mirroring. The storage reliability policy is applied on a file basis, rather than on a volume basis. Hence, the same disk group can contain a combination of files protected by mirroring, parity, or not protected at all.
- ASM provides the performance of raw disk I/O without the problems of managing raw disks. Unlike logical volume managers, ASM maintenance operations do not require that the database be shut down.

Automated Storage Management Configuration

To turn on ASM facility, the DBA must create a separate ASM instance before starting the database instances. An ASM instance does not require that a DB instance be running as might be the case when initially configuring the components managed by the ASM instance. But to use Automated Storage Management for managing Oracle database files, both a database instance and an ASM instance must be running. Automated Storage Management is integrated into the database server so there is no need to install it as a separate product. The Oracle binaries for a normal 10g

Oracle installation are used for the ASM instance. Thus, there is no separate Oracle Home for ASM. However, to use ASM files, there must be at least one ASM instance configured and started prior to starting a database instance that uses ASM files.

The Database Configuration Assistant (DBCA) or Server Control Utility (SRVCTL) or Oracle Enterprise Manager (OEM) is used in Oracle Database 10*g* to configure the Automated Storage Management (ASM) features for conventional and Real Application Clusters (RAC) environments.

ASM is used to automate and simplify the optimal layout of data files, control files, and log files. ASM automatically distributes database files across all available disks, and whenever the storage configuration changes, the database storage is rebalanced. ASM can also be used to provide redundancy, through the mirroring of database files.

ASM essentially eliminates the management overhead involved with the use of a conventional file system. There is no need to manually place data on disks when using ASM. Also, by allowing the administrator to manage just a few disk groups, the administrator is relieved from managing hundreds or thousands of files. Using ASM, the DBA will use disk groups for setting up a database. After setup, the DBA need only be concerned with disk groups when monitoring and changing disk allocations within the disk groups.

ASM uses the process of breaking each file into multiple extents and spreading the extents evenly across all of the disks in a disk group. Once ASM disk groups are established, the Oracle database automatically allocates storage space from these disk groups for creating and deleting files.

Data files that are not needed are automatically deleted with ASM rather than requiring a manually issued command, as in previous versions. Automated Storage Management enhances database integrity for databases operating on disks that are not extremely reliable.

ASM Concepts

ASM employs several basic concepts. ASM operates on disk groups which is a collection of disks. Within the groups, it creates ASM files. Therefore the main building blocks are:

- ASM Disks
- ASM Disk Groups
- ASM Files
- ASM Templates

The next sections explore these concepts in detail. Figure 5.13 is a diagram of the components in an ASM instance and its relationship with a database instance.

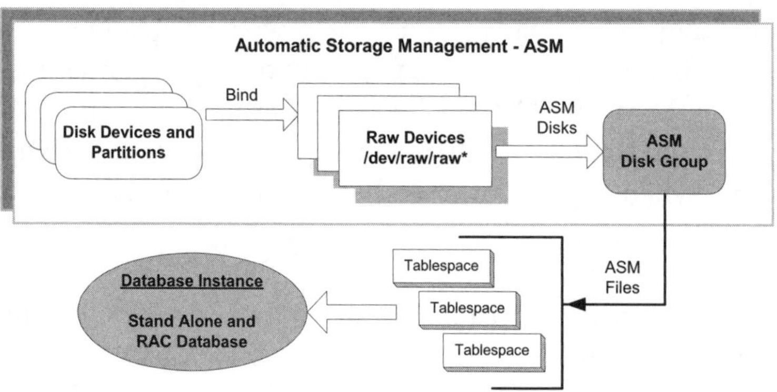

Figure 5.13: *The Components of the ASM Instance*

ASM Disk Groups

A disk group is basically one or more ASM disks that are managed as a single logical unit. Any data-structure stored in an ASM disk group is totally contained within that disk group, or self-contained. A database using ASM disks doesn't have to be shutdown in order for a disk to be added or dropped. ASM rebalances the spread of data to ensure an even I/O load to all disks in a disk group when the disk group configuration changes.

A single ASM file is self-contained in a single ASM disk group. However, an ASM disk group can contain files belonging to several databases, and a single database can use storage from multiple ASM disk groups. A disk group can be specified as the default disk group for files created in a database by specifying the disk group in file destination initialization parameters.

ASM divides files into 1MB extents and spreads the extents for each file evenly across all of the disks in a disk group. ASM uses pointers to record extent location instead of using a mathematical function to track the placement of each extent. When the disk group configuration changes, ASM moves individual extents of a file rather than having to move all extents to adhere to a formula based on the number of disks.

For files, such as log files, that require low latency, ASM provides fine-grained (128k) striping to allow larger I/Os to be split and processed in parallel by multiple disks. At file creation time, the DBA can decide whether or not to use fine-grained striping. File type specific templates in the disk group determine the default behavior.

Most installations will probably have two or more disk groups. The reasons for having multiple different disk groups include the following:

- To group disks of different manufacturers, different sizes or performance characteristics.
- To group disks with different external redundancy together; for example, JBOD (just a bunch of disks) would generally not be in the same disk group with disks from a RAID 1+0 or RAID5 configuration, but this is possible using ASM.
- To separate work and recovery areas for a given database.

Note: In any installation, non-ASM managed operating system storage repositories are required, and are used for swap files, execution libraries, and user file systems. The Oracle database and ASM executable files and libraries must reside on the server's operating system file system and cannot reside in an ASM files.

In case of RAC database environment, files for loading into externals tables are still located on non-ASM file system which can be a cluster file system or local file system.

Types of Disk Groups

There are three types of ASM disk groups:

- Normal redundancy
- High redundancy
- External redundancy

With normal and high redundancy, the disk group template specifies the ASM redundancy attributes for all files in the disk group.

Configuration of ASM high redundancy provides a greater degree of protection. With external redundancy, ASM does not provide any redundancy for the disk group.

In external redundancy, the underlying disks in the disk group must provide redundancy, for example, using a RAID storage array. The redundancy level or type is specified at the time of creating the disk groups.

ASM Files

As the database requests, ASM will create the required files. ASM assigns each file a fully qualified name ending in a dotted pair of numbers. More user-friendly alias names can be created for the Automated Storage Management filenames by using ASM aliases.

Query the *v$osm_alias* data dictionary view to see assigned alias names for ASM files. During normal operations, users do not need to be aware of ASM file names. The contents of the *v$osm_alias* view are shown in Table 5.2.

COLUMN NAME	NULL?	TYPE
NAME		VARCHAR2(48)
GROUP_NUMBER		NUMBER
FILE_NUMBER		NUMBER
FILE_INCARNATION		NUMBER
ALIAS_INDEX		NUMBER
ALIAS_INCARNATION		NUMBER
PARENT_INDEX		NUMBER
REFERENCE_INDEX		NUMBER
ALIAS_DIRECTORY		VARCHAR2(1)
SYSTEM_CREATED		VARCHAR2(1)

Table 5.2: *Contents of the v$osm_alias View*

Whenever a filename is required from an ASM disk, a mechanism for recognizing ASM file naming syntax is provided. At file creation, certain file attributes are permanently set, such as its protection policy (mirroring) and its striping policy. ASM files are not visible from the operating system or its utilities, but they are visible to database instances, RMAN, and other Oracle-supplied tools.

ASM Templates

Collections of attributes used by ASM during file creation are known as templates. Templates are used to simplify ASM file creation by mapping complex file attribute specifications into a single named object (template). Each Oracle file type has its own default template. Each disk group contains its own set of definition templates. Template names only have to be unique within a single ASM disk group, a template of the same name can exist in different disk groups with each separate template having their own unique properties.

Administrators can change the attributes of the default templates or add their own templates. This lets an administrator specify the appropriate file creation attributes as a template. However, if a DBA needs to change an ASM file attribute after a file has been created, then the file must be copied using RMAN into a new file created with a different template that contains the new attributes.

ASM Disks

The unit of storage for ASM disk groups is ASM Disks. ASM disks can be entire physical disks, LUN(s) from a storage array, partition of a LUN or pre-created files in a NAS filer. An ASM disk name is common to all nodes of the cluster. The administrator can specify the disk name, or it will be automatically generated by ASM when a disk is added to a disk group. Since different hosts can use different operating system names to refer to the same ASM disk, the ASM disk name abstraction is required.

To reduce the chances of losing data in case of single disk failure, ASM provides mirroring. If disk mirroring weren't provided, the loss of the unduplicated data from a single ASM disk would possibly damage every file in the disk group.

Failure Groups

Failure groups are manually defined groups of disks sharing a common resource. Failure group definitions determine which ASM disks are used for storing mirror copies of data. Failure groups ensure that data and its redundant copy do not both reside on disks that are likely to fail together.

Each set of failure groups is site-specific. This is because failure group decisions are based on how the system tolerates the failure of specific components. For example, suppose the system has ten disks and one SCSI controller. The failure of the one SCSI controller makes all ten disks unavailable. In this scenario, each SCSI disk should be put in its own failure group.

Each disk is assigned to its one failure group in ASM by default. However this assignment of failure groups can be over-ridden by the administrator when creating a disk group or adding a disk to a disk group. The layout of data is then optimized by ASM to reduce the unavailability of data due to failures.

A failure group is maintained in a disk group, and multiple failure groups can exist within any given disk group. However, changing a disk's failure group requires dropping the disk from the disk group and then adding the disk back to the disk group under the new failure group name.

ASM Instances

Oracle Database 10*g* introduces the ASM instance, a special Oracle instance that manages the disks in disk groups. The ASM instance must be configured and running for the database instance to access Automated Storage Management files.

ASM instances are not used to mount databases, they are simply used to coordinate data layout for database instances. However, the database instances do direct I/O to disks in disk groups. I/O doesn't go through the ASM instance.

ASM instances cannot mount a database; they mount disk groups. An ASM instance must be started before a database instance can access files in disk groups. Multiple and separate database instances can share disk groups for their files. On a single node, a single ASM instance typically manages all disk groups. In a Real Application Cluster environment, each node typically has one ASM instance that manages all disk groups for that node in a coordinated manner with the rest of the cluster.

All ASM management commands are directed through the ASM instance, no ASM commands are issued to any regular Oracle database instance using the ASM files.

ASM Instance Background Processes

There are at least two new background processes added for an ASM instance:

- RBAL - coordinates rebalance activity for disk groups
- ORB0, ORB1... - These perform the actual rebalance data extent movements. There can be many of these at a time

Any database instance that is using an ASM disk group will contain a background process called OSMB. The OSMB process is responsible for communicating with the ASM instance. The RBAL background process within a database instance, called RBAL just like in the ASM Instance, performs a global open on ASM disks. A global open means that more than one database instance can be accessing the ASM disks at a time.

Installation of ASM

In Oracle Database 10*g*, the Oracle Universal Installer (OUI) will always install ASM when the database software is installed. The Database Configuration Assistant (DBCA) determines if an ASM instance already exists, and if not, then the DBA will be given the option of creating and configuring an ASM instance as part of the installation. If an ASM instance already exists, then it will be used by default. DBCA automatically configures your ASM instance parameter file and password file.

DBCA eases the configuring and creation of the database, while EM provides an integrated approach for managing both the ASM instance and database instance.

Oracle's Enterprise Manager (EM) product or the Database Configuration Assistant (DBCA) should be used for a GUI interface to ASM that replaces the use of SQL or SQL*Plus for configuring and altering disk groups and their metadata.

Viewing Information about ASM

There are seven new *v$* views provided in Oracle Database 10*g* used to monitor ASM structures. These views are shown in Table 5.3.

VIEW	ASM INSTANCE	DB INSTANCE
v$osm_diskgroup	Shows disk group details such as number, name, state, and redundancy type	Contains one row for every open ASM disk in the DB instance.

VIEW	ASM INSTANCE	DB INSTANCE
v$osm_client	Shows databases using disk groups managed by the ASM instance.	Contains no rows.
v$osm_disk	Shows every disk discovered by the ASM instance, including disks that are not part of any disk group.	Contains rows only for disks in the disk groups in use by that DB instance.
v$osm_file	Shows the files (data, redo, control, archive logs etc) in the ASM disk groups	Contains rows only for files that are currently open in the DB instance.
v$osm_template	Shows the templates available in every disk group	Contains no rows
v$osm_alias	Shows the alias for every disk group mounted	Contains no rows.
v$osm_operation	Long operations executing the rebalance activity are shown in this view	Contains no rows.

Table 5.3: *ASM v$ Views*

Example of ASM configuration

To explain the ASM methodology, the following example will be used. There are four disk devices or partitions as shown below. For demonstration purposes, a single LUN of 9G was used and 4 partitions were created. In reality, actual environments may have many more devices and partitions. The Command FDISK manages the disk partitions.

```
[root@host-0002b /]# /sbin/fdisk /dev/sdl

The number of cylinders for this disk is set to 1110.
There is nothing wrong with that, but this is larger than 1024,
and could in certain setups cause problems with:
1) software that runs at boot time (e.g., old versions of LILO)
2) booting and partitioning software from other OSs
   (e.g., DOS FDISK, OS/2 FDISK)

Command (m for help): p

Disk /dev/sdl: 255 heads, 63 sectors, 1110 cylinders
```

```
Units = cylinders of 16065 * 512 bytes

   Device Boot    Start       End     Blocks   Id  System
/dev/sdl1             1        13     104391   83  Linux
/dev/sdl2            14        39     208845   83  Linux
/dev/sdl3            40       549    4096575   83  Linux
/dev/sdl4           550      1059    4096575   83  Linux
```

As shown above, there are four partitions, *sd1*, *sd2*, *sd3* and *sd4*. The next step is to bind them as raw and change the ownership to oracle. This will be done with two disk partitions, *sdl3* and *sdl4,* each of which is 4 GB in size.

```
[root@host-0002a dev]# raw /dev/raw/raw1 /dev/sdl3
/dev/raw/raw1:  bound to major 8, minor 179

[root@host-0002a dev]# raw /dev/raw/raw2 /dev/sdl4
/dev/raw/raw2:  bound to major 8, minor 180

> chown oracle:dba /dev/raw/raw1
> chown oracle:dba /dev/raw/raw2
```

The next step will focus on starting or creating an ASM instance. First, the ORACLE_HOME and ORACLE_SID variables are set. Next, the *initASM1.ora* file is prepared. In this example, the SID of the ASM instance is ASM1.

Shown below are the contents of the *initASM1.ora* file.

```
# created by TM 8/Apr/2004
*.ASM_DISKGROUPS=dgroup1
*.ASM_DISKSTRING='/dev/raw/raw*'
*.instance_type='ASM'
*.large_pool_size=12M
*.remote_login_passwordfile='NONE'
*.background_dump_dest= '/app/oracle/admin/ASM1/bdump'
*.core_dump_dest=       '/app/oracle/admin/ASM1/cdump'
*.user_dump_dest=       '/app/oracle/admin/ASM1/udump'
```

Ensure that the CSSD daemon is up and running. CSSD is the daemon which controls the communication between the database instance and ASM instance. To start the CSSD daemon, follow these commands:

```
[root@host-0002b init.d]# pwd
/etc/init.d
[root@host-0002b init.d]# ./init.cssd start
(Oracle CSSD will be run out of init)
```

Then start the ASM instance as follows:

```
become-2.05$ sqlplus "/ as sysdba"

SQL*Plus: Release 10.1.0.2.0 - Production on Fri Apr 9 14:34:38 2004
Copyright (c) 1982, 2004, Oracle.  All rights reserved.

Connected to an idle instance.

SQL> startup nomount
ASM instance started

Total System Global Area  100663296 bytes
Fixed Size                   777616 bytes
Variable Size              99885680 bytes
Database Buffers                  0 bytes
Redo Buffers                      0 bytes

SQL> create diskgroup TEST_DG external redundancy
disk '/dev/raw/raw1' ;

Diskgroup created.

SQL> alter diskgroup TEST_DG add disk '/dev/raw/raw2';

Diskgroup altered.
```

Now that there are two ASM disks with the disk group TEST_DG, the next step is to use the resources to create a tablespace by the Database Instance NYREP10.

```
SQL> create tablespace  ASM_TBS1 DATAFILE '+TEST_DG' size 200M ;

Tablespace created.

SQL> select BYTES, NAME,  TS# from v$datafile ;

BYTES    NAME                                                    TS#
----------  ----------------------------------------------  ----
 471859200  /u01/NYREP10//datafile/o1_mf_system_021swyso_.dbf      0
  36700160  /u01/NYREP10/datafile/o1_mf_undotbs1_021swz0t_.dbf     1
 367001600  /u01/NYREP10/datafile/o1_mf_sysaux_021swywy_.dbf       2
  20971520  /u01/NYREP10/datafile/o1_mf_users_021swz3t_.dbf        4
 157286400  /u01/NYREP10/datafile/o1_mf_example_021szorq_.dbf      6
 209715200  +TEST_DG/nyrep10/datafile/asm_tbs1.256.1               7

6 rows selected.
```

```
col GROUP_NUMBER heading GRP# format 99
col DISK_NUMBER heading Disk# format 999
col MOUNT_STATUS heading "Mount|Status" format A8

SQL> select GROUP_NUMBER, DISK_NUMBER, MOUNT_STATUS,
STATE,REDUNDANCY,
     TOTAL_MB, FREE_MB, NAME, path  from  v$asm_disk ;

           Mount
GRP# Disk# Status STATE  TOTAL_MB FREE_MB NAME         PATH
---- ----- ------ ------ -------- ------- ------------ -------------
   1     1 CACHED NORMAL   4000      3878  TEST_DG_0001 /dev/raw/raw2
   1     0 CACHED NORMAL   4000      3869  TEST_DG_0000 /dev/raw/raw1
```

The above illustration shows that the ASM file is created out of two ASM disks.

Note in case of Linux Platform, use the Oracle provided ASMLibrary (Install ASM Libraries which are available in the form of RPM/s) – Details of the installation is explained in a later part of this chapter

Limitations of ASM for RAC Database Use

No ASM Support for:

- External Tables (yet 10g offers much improved External Table Support)
- Transportable Tablespaces capability is somewhat restrictive. It can be used with RMAN only.
- Reports, Export/Import output cannot go onto ASM resources.
- SQL*Loader Files can not be located in ASM
- Oracle Home Files – Oracle need either local file system or fully functional cluster file system

Supported File Types

The following table shows the types of files ASM Supports. The default template specifications assign fixed attributes like level of redundancy and level of striping.

FILE TYPE	SUPPORTED BY ORACLE ASM	DEFAULT TEMPLATE
Control Files	Yes	CONTROLFILE
Data Files	Yes	DATAFILE
Redo Log Files	Yes	ONLINELOG
Archived Log Files	Yes	ARCHIVELOG
Trace Files	No	--
Database Temporary Files	Yes	TEMPFILE
Data File Backup pieces	Yes	BACKUPSET
Archive Log Backup Pieces	Yes	BACKUPSET
Parameter Files	Yes	PARAMTERFILE
Operating System Files	No	--
Alter Log Files	No	--
Flashback Logs	Yes	FLASHBACK
Data Punp Sets	Yes	DUMPSET

Table 5.4: *The types of files ASM Supports*

ASMLib

For the Linux platform, Oracle provides ASMLib which is a library add-on for the ASM. ASMLib is the kernel driver for generic Linux implementation. ASMLib allows an Oracle Database using ASM more efficient and capable access to the disk groups it is using.

At the time of the writing of this chapter, the Oracle ASMLib 1.0.0 was available for free download at http://otn.oracle.com/tech/linux/asmlib/index.html. This library is available for the following Linux flavors.

- Red Hat Advanced Server 2.1 (x86)
- Red Hat Enterprise Linux 3 AS
- United Linux 1.0 SP3 / SLES 8 SP3 (x86)
- United Linux 1.0 SP3 / SLES 8 SP3 (ia64)
- United Linux 1.0 SP3 / SLES 8 SP3 (amd64)

The ASM Library Files are available as rpm(s). Install the packages by using the following command:

```
rpm -Uvh oracleasm-support-1.0.0-1.i386.rpm \
     oracleasm-lib-1.0.0-1.i386.rpm \
     oracleasm-2.4.9-e-enterprise-1.0.0-1.i686.rpm
```

Once the ASMLib software is installed, the ASM driver needs to be loaded, and the driver filesystem needs to be mounted. This is achieved by the initialization script, /etc/init.d/oracleasm.

By root privilege, execute the /etc/init.d/oracleasm script with the *configure* option. It will ask for the user and group that default to owning the ASM driver access point. If the database was running as the *oracle* user and the *dba* group, the output would look like this:

```
[root@ca-test1 /]# /etc/init.d/oracleasm configure
  Configuring the Oracle ASM library driver.
```

Configuration of CFS or Raw Devices

In the previous sections, the creation and usage of the ASM instance resources was examined. In this section, how to configure raw devices and Cluster File Systems will be covered. For studying the creation of raw partitions, a typical Linux environment and raw device configuration will be used. For CFS, three products will be examined; PolyServe Matrix Server; OCFS; and Veritas CFS

Once the decision has been made to use either raw devices or cluster file system files, a plan needs to be made for setting up the necessary storage volumes and file systems. The RAC system requires a minimum set of files/raw devices for creating default tablespaces and setting the redo log files etc.

If the DBCA utility will be used to create the initial database, there are certain requirements that need to be met concerning the default schemas. Raw devices need to be provided or file systems to store them. Then the user-defined or business application-related schemas and tablespaces are created.

In the case of UNIX and Linux-oriented cluster platforms, most of the vendors provide some kind of volume manager or tool, which helps to create volumes of manageable size and layout at the host level. These volumes can be used by the RAC database as raw partitions. Optionally, when using the cluster file system, the file system can be made and mounted. When planning to use the volumes as the raw partitions, it may be necessary to plan and pre-create a large number of partitions with appropriate sizes. Figure 5.14 shows the relationship between the storage volumes and how they are presented for the use of the RAC database.

A LUN is the concept of the usable disk. LUN stands for Logical Unit Number. It is a physical disk, as seen by the node or host. They are also called RAID logical drives. Once they are introduced into a disk group at the volume manager level, they become the basis for logical volume creation. Volumes are usable pieces carved out of the storage pool. When they are used by the database application, they are the raw partitions. When a file system is created on the volumes, they become mountable at the operating system level. Figure 5.14 shows the connection between the storage structures.

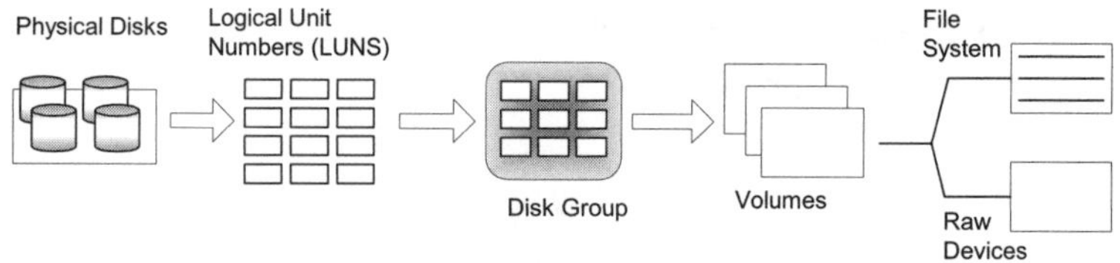

Figure 5.14: *Storage Volume Relations*

In the case of a Windows platform, the Windows disk manager provides a facility to create raw partitions. When using the OCFS (Oracle Cluster File System) module, Veritas CFS or PolyServe, appropriate cluster file system mount points can be created.

Raw Devices in Linux

Shared disks are visible to all nodes in the cluster. RAC database requires the use of raw devices or cluster file system files or ASM resources.

Raw Device binding information is available in the file /etc/sysconfig/rawdevices.

For example, usually they are specified as:

```
# format:
<rawdev> <major> <minor>
or
<rawdev> <blockdev>

For example:
/dev/raw/raw1 /dev/emcpowera5
/dev/raw/raw2 /dev/emcpowera6
/dev/raw/raw1 /dev/sda1
/dev/raw/raw2 8 5
```

In the above, the emcpowera5 is bound with /dev/raw/rwa1 and /dev/raw/raw2 is bound with /dev/emcpowera6. These are SAN (EMC symmetrix) power-devices.

Size of such raw devices can be viewed in the file /proc/partitions. For example,

```
$ cat /proc/partitions | more
 232     0     8923200 emcpowera 268 0 536 190 0 0 0 0 0 190 140
 232     1           1 emcpowera1 4 0 8 0 0 0 0 0 0 0 0
 232     5     1028097 emcpowera5 18 0 36 20 0 0 0 0 0 20 20
 232     6     1028128 emcpowera6 22 0 44 10 0 0 0 0 0 10 10
 232     7     1028128 emcpowera7 22 0 44 10 0 0 0 0 0 10 0
```

The third field/column shows the Size of the device in KB. Column(1) represents the major number and column(2) shows the minor number.

The actual size of partitions and the state of raw device bindings can also be determined using the following commands, respectively:

```
#fdisk -l
and
#raw -qa
```

In some systems, the logical volume manager is available to create the necessary disk partitions. When using raw devices, carefully partition the disks to insure partitions are sized adequately. The LVM (Logical Volume Manager) is very useful and makes the management of raw devices more flexible.

Use *pvcreate* to create a physical volume for use by the logical volume manager.

```
$ pvcreate -d /dev/sda
```

For a single partition on a multi-partition drive, use the partition designator such as /dev/sda1.

Use *vgcreate* from a root session to create a volume group for the drive or for the partition that will be used for the raw.

```
$ vgcreate -l 256 -p 256 -s 128k /dev/sda
```

The above command allows 256 logical partitions and 256 physical partitions, with a 128K extent size.

Use *lvcreate* to create the logical volumes inside the volume group. An example script is shown below.

```
pvcreate -d /dev/sda
vgcreate -l 256 -p 256 -s 128k /dev/pv1 /dev/sda
lvcreate -L 500m /dev/pv1
lvcreate -L 500m /dev/pv1
lvcreate -L 300m /dev/pv1
lvcreate -L 100m /dev/pv1
….

The above commands create /dev/pv1/lvol1 to lvoln.
```

Next, bind the volumes to the raw devices. This is accomplished through the /usr/bin/raw command.

```
vgchange -a y /dev/pv1
/usr/bin/raw /dev/raw/raw1 /dev/pv1/lvol1
/usr/bin/raw /dev/raw/raw2 /dev/pv1/lvol2
/usr/bin/raw /dev/raw/raw3 /dev/pv1/lvol3
/usr/bin/raw /dev/raw/raw4 /dev/pv1/lvol4
/usr/bin/raw /dev/raw/raw5 /dev/pv1/lvol5
/usr/bin/raw /dev/raw/raw6 /dev/pv1/lvol6
/usr/bin/raw /dev/raw/raw7 /dev/pv1/lvol7
/usr/bin/raw /dev/raw/raw8 /dev/pv1/lvol8
/usr/bin/raw /dev/raw/raw9 /dev/pv1/lvol9
```

Soft links can be created from the raw volumes to make file recognition easy.

Configure OCFS for Linux

In this section, how to create OCFS on the Linux platform will be covered. To verify disks/partitions use the command *fdisk*:

```
/sbin/fdisk /dev/sdd

Verify Partition Information

Command (m for help): p
```

```
Disk /dev/sdd: 255 heads, 63 sectors, 4443 cylinders
Units = cylinders of 16065 * 512 bytes

   Device Boot    Start       End    Blocks   Id  System
/dev/sdd1             1      1530  12289693+  83  Linux
/dev/sdd2          1531      4443  23398672+   5  Extended
/dev/sdd5          1531      1913   3076416   83  Linux
/dev/sdd6          1914      2168   2048256   83  Linux
/dev/sdd7          2169      2806   5124703+  83  Linux
```

What is shown above is a relatively simple storage scenario. One disk device /dev/sdd, is divided into multiple partitions. Based on the above plan the OCFS mount points can be created as follows:

```
/dev/sdd1  --> /data/oracle/NYREP/u02       12289693+ (i.e. 12 gb)
/dev/sdd5  --> /data/oracle/NYREP/u01        3076416  (i.e.  3 gb)
/dev/sdd6  --> /data/oracle/NYREP/r01        2048256  (i.e.  2 gb)
/dev/sdd7  --> /data/oracle/NYREP/archive    5124703+ (i.e.  5 gb)
```

Download OCFS modules for the Linux platform (for the SMP kernel or Enterprise Kernel) and Linux Version, from the website http://oss.oracle.com/projects/ocfs/files/. Always look for the latest and recommended release of the OCFS packages.

Then install the RPM(s) by root.

```
[root@host-0001 software]# pwd
/db_dumps/oracle/NYREP1/software

[root@host-0001 software]# ls -lt
total 688
-rw-r--r--    1 oracle   dba        295535 Nov  5 03:56 ocfs-
support-1.0.9-9.i686.rpm
-rw-r--r--    1 oracle   dba         80423 Nov  5 03:56 ocfs-tools-
1.0.9-9.i686.rpm
-rw-r--r--    1 oracle   dba        300863 Nov  5 03:56 ocfs-2.4.9-
e-enterprise-1.0.9-9.i686.rpm
drwxr-x---    2 oracle   dba          4096 Nov  3 03:38 9204_32P
drwxr-x---    3 oracle   dba          4096 Nov  3 03:29 9201_32


[root@host-0001 software]# rpm -Uvh ocfs-support-1.0.9-9.i686.rpm
Preparing...
########################################### [100%]
   1:ocfs-support
########################################### [100%]
```

```
[root@host-0001 software]# rpm -Uvh ocfs-2.4.9-e-enterprise-1.0.9-
9.i686.rpm
Preparing...
########################################### [100%]
   1:ocfs-2.4.9-e-
enterprise########################################### [100%]
Linking OCFS module into the module path [  OK  ]

[root@host-0001 software]# rpm -Uvh ocfs-tools-1.0.9-9.i686.rpm
Preparing...
########################################### [100%]
   1:ocfs-tools
########################################### [100%]
[root@host-0001 software]#

Then copy the rpm(s) to second node and repeat the RPM installation
```

THEN verify the installed modules on both the nodes.

```
[root@host-0002 software]# rpm -qa | grep -i ocfs
ocfs-support-1.0.9-9
ocfs-tools-1.0.9-9
ocfs-2.4.9-e-enterprise-1.0.9-9
[root@host-0002 software]#
```

To find out all the libraries, execute the following:

```
[root@host-0002 /]# find . -name '*ocfs*' -print
./etc/rc.d/init.d/ocfs
./etc/rc.d/rc3.d/S24ocfs
./etc/rc.d/rc4.d/S24ocfs
./etc/rc.d/rc5.d/S24ocfs
./lib/modules/2.4.9-e.27enterprise/kernel/drivers/addon/ocfs
./lib/modules/2.4.9-e.27enterprise/kernel/drivers/addon/ocfs/ocfs.o
./lib/modules/2.4.9-e-enterprise-ABI/ocfs
./lib/modules/2.4.9-e-enterprise-ABI/ocfs/ocfs.o
./lib/modules/2.4.9-e-enterprise-ABI/ocfs-noaio
./lib/modules/2.4.9-e-enterprise-ABI/ocfs-noaio/ocfs.o
./sbin/mounted.ocfs
./sbin/fsck.ocfs
./sbin/load_ocfs
./sbin/mkfs.ocfs
./sbin/ocfs_uid_gen
./usr/bin/debugocfs
./usr/bin/ocfstool
./usr/include/sys/procfs.h
./usr/share/man/man1/ocfstool.1.gz
./db_dumps/oracle/NYREP2/software/ocfs-support-1.0.9-9.i686.rpm
./db_dumps/oracle/NYREP2/software/ocfs-tools-1.0.9-9.i686.rpm
./db_dumps/oracle/NYREP2/software/ocfs-2.4.9-e-enterprise-1.0.9-
9.i686.rpm
[root@host-0002 /]#
```

Then, using the utility *ocfstool*, generate the file /etc/ocfs.conf. *ocfstool* is a GUI front-end for managing and debugging OCFS volumes on the system; and also the preferred method for managing OCFS. One can mount and unmount volumes, format partitions, view information and individual files, see the current node map, and block bitmap.

Now it is time to create the file systems by using the *mkfs* command:

```
e.g
mkfs.ocfs -F -b 128 -L /u01  -m /data/oracle/NYREP/u01     -u 23444
-g 252 -p 0775 /dev/sdd1
mkfs.ocfs -F -b 128 -L /u02  -m /data/oracle/NYREP/u02     -u 23444
-g 252 -p 0775 /dev/sdd5
mkfs.ocfs -F -b 128 -L /r01  -m /data/oracle/NYREP/r01     -u 23444
-g 252 -p 0775 /dev/sdd6
mkfs.ocfs -F -b 128 -L /arch -m /data/oracle/NYREP/archive -u 23444
-g 252 -p 0775 /dev/sdd7

**********  NOTES on the Format of the Command **********
# mkfs.ocfs -F -b 128 -L /u04 -m /u04 -u 1001 -g 1001 -p 0775
/dev/sde1
where the syntax for ocfstool is:
mkfs.ocfs -b block-size [-C] [-F] [-g gid] -L volume-label
-m mount-path [-n] [-p permissions] [-u uid] [-v] [-V] device
with the following options:
 -b Block size in kilo bytes
 -C Clear all data blocks
 -F Force format existing OCFS volume
 -g GID for the root directory
 -L Volume label
 -m Path where this device will be mounted
 -n Query only
 -p Permissions for the root directory
 -q quiet execution

For example, mkfs command creates file system:

[root@host-0001 ]# mkfs.ocfs -F -b 128 -L /u02  -m
/data/oracle/NYREP/u02  -u 23444 -g 252 -p 0775 /dev/sdd5
Cleared volume header sectors
Cleared node config sectors
Cleared publish sectors
Cleared vote sectors
Cleared bitmap sectors
Cleared data block
Wrote volume header
```

Configure PolyServe Cluster File System for Linux

The PolyServe Matrix Server software provides a comprehensive infrastructure that allows users to build database clusters with Oracle RAC on a Linux platform. The PolyServe SAN File System (PSFS) is part of the Matrix Server, and it provides the shared file system for the use of Oracle RAC. For building RAC on Linux clusters, the PolyServe matrix server (MxS) offers an alternative to the OCFS as well as the ASM facility.

MxS consists of two main products. The first one is the Matrix HA component, which provides manageability and high availability for applications running on groups of servers. The product supports virtual hosts, standard IP service and device monitoring, custom service and device monitoring, data replication, and administrative event notification. The second component is the PolyServe SAN File System (PSFS). The PolyServe SAN File System (PSFS) provides a flexible and easy way to manage the RAC database. PSFS is designed to complement the Oracle RAC architecture and to scale out with Oracle9i RAC running on top of it. PSFS supports the Oracle Disk Manager (ODM) and is tightly coupled with Oracle9i RAC. PSFS supports shared block access with full data integrity and cache coherency. It offers direct I/O and normal page-cache buffered I/O. PSFS allows Oracle RAC to perform direct I/O against the disk and do distributed lock management at the database level where system-wide performance can best be optimized.

The Matrix Server has an important component that deals with SAN management. It is called SCL or Storage Control Layer. It operates as a daemon running on each member of the cluster. It helps perform the I/O fencing.

The PolyServe Matrix Server complements Oracle Cluster Management Services in such a way that nodes will never have to be fenced via the default Linux RAC behavior of powering off a node (STOMITH). PolyServe Matrix Server provides fencing via the SCL.

MxS software is installed on each of the servers in the cluster or matrix. It has many components dealing with different functionalities. Some of them are:

ClusterPulse daemon – monitors the matrix, controls the virtual hosts and devices, handles communication with administrative console, and manages device monitors and event notification.

DLM daemon – provides a locking mechanism to coordinate server access to shared resources in the matrix.

SANPulse daemon – provides matrix infrastructure for managing the SAN. It coordinates file system mounts, un-mounts, and file recovery operations.

SCL daemon – helps to manage the storage devices. It assigns device names to shared disks when they are imported into the matrix and enables cluster use. It also disables the server's access to shared disks during the split-brain condition.

Psd drivers – provides matrix-wide consistent device names among all the servers.

HBA drivers – includes drives for the supported FibreChannel host bus adapters.

PanPulse daemon – monitors the network and detects any communication problems.

Figure 15.15 shows the various components of the Matrix Server.

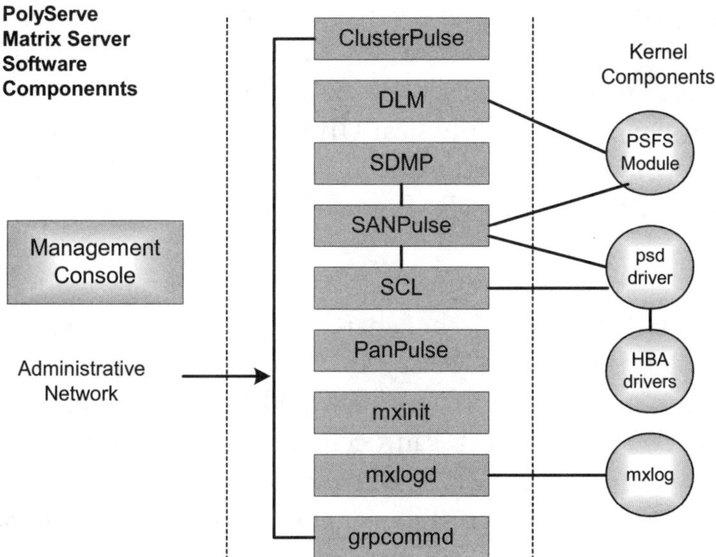

Figure 5.15: *Storage Volume Relations*

Storage Control Layer (SCL) Role

One of the main objectives of the SCL module is to physically disable SAN storage whenever the server drops out of the matrix or cluster membership. Thus, it can perform I/O fencing. I/O fencing ensures integrity within the cluster by excluding rogue nodes from accessing critical data.

MxS features true I/O fencing, for example port disabling at the FC switch, which allows an administrator to log in to the ejected node, diagnose, and repair the problem before restarting. Thereby, allowing an ejected server to rejoin the cluster.

Matrix Server provides each disk with a globally unique device name that all servers in the Matrix can use to access the device. When a SAN disk is imported into the matrix, a name prefixed by *psd* is assigned, e.g. *psd1*, *psd2*, *psd12*. Individual disk partitions also have a global device name. It has the name and partition number.

For example, partition 5 of disk *psd14* is represented as *psd14p5*. On each server, Matrix Server creates device node entries in the directory /dev/psd for every partition on the disk. The SCL stores the device name and physical UID for each imported disk device in an internal database. This database resides on a membership partition that is assigned at the time of MxS installation.

For importing SAN disks, the shared disks need to have a partition table on them before they are imported into the matrix. Once they are imported, they are managed by Matrix controls. That is, no access to the disk can occur unless it is through the cluster file system. Matrix Server is managed via a graphical user interface however; all functionality can also be carried out at the command line through the CLI. Some useful commands are:

To import the disk:

```
# mx disk import <UUID>
```

To deport the disk:

```
# mx disk deport <UUID>
```

To display the disk information:

```
# sandiskinfo
```

MxS uses multi-path I/O to eliminate single points of failure and to perform I/O load balancing. The matrix can include multiple FC switches, multiple HBAs per server, and multi-ported SAN disks. When MxS is started, it automatically configures all paths. It uses the first discovered path on each server for I/O with the SAN devices. When the first path fails, MxS automatically fails over the I/O to another path. Use the command *mxmpio* to display and manage.

```
# mxmpio enableall | disableall
```

PSFS File System

PSFS is a general-purpose cluster file system. It is an enterprise-grade symmetric file system. The general features include:

- PSFS allows Oracle Managed Files (OMF) to be used in an Oracle RAC cluster. Oracle OMF provides the ability to manage files and file systems that reduces the complexity of creating, configuring, and managing the storage for an Oracle database. Oracle9i RAC with a shared raw device cannot use OMF functionality.
- All matrix server members have access to the file system and can perform concurrent read/write operations.
- Supports Direct I/O facility, which increases the I/O performance by avoiding the file system buffering
- The Oracle Disk Manager (ODM). ODM is an API specification for I/O designed by Oracle. PolyServe's ODM offering, MxODM, is a plug-in module for PolyServe's cluster file system. MxODM comes bundled with either the Oracle RAC Option or Oracle Option for Matrix Server.
- Device Naming and Utilities – Cluster-wide device naming and file system utilities simplify administration and maintenance of the cluster. MxS provides a pseudo device layer that ensures consistent device naming across the cluster, and provides various tools for file system maintenance, including *fsck*, file system suspend, and resume and file system growth.
- PSFS also supports context dependant symbolic links that allow administrators to configure node-specific files.
- MxS supports all Oracle data files and logs and further supports advanced Oracle9i functionality, including external

tables, export/import from text files, and archived redo log compression.

- MxS also supports a shared Oracle Home, which simplifies installation, configuration, and maintenance.
- It is a standard Linux File system that supports file system operations such as *mkfs*, mount and unmount and byte-range locking with complete cache coherency.

PolyServe MxS uses a registry to control server access to the PSFS file system on the SAN disks imported into the matrix. It supports journaling and online crash recovery.

PSFS supports context dependent symbolic links (CDSL). CDSL are used to manage node-specific files and directories. CDSL(s) enable database administrators to easily create an Oracle Home directory that can be shared by all nodes in the matrix.

CDSL contains a keyword that identifies a particular location. When the operating system resolves the symbolic link, it translates the keyword into the appropriate pathname. For example, a CDSL could contain the keyword HOSTNAME, which resolves the hostname of the server where it has been logged in.

Configure and Create PSFS

The PSFS file system is created on a storage extent located on imported disks. Storage extents are disk partitions. The maximum file system is 1 TB. PSFS uses 4KB as the block size.

A file system can be created using either the management console or the command line. Then, the file system can be mounted on all the nodes or servers in the matrix. Since the disk partition is the unit on which the file system is created, plan the size of the partition carefully.

To create a file system using the CLI, use the PolyServe command:

```
# mx fs create [--size <kb>] <filesystem> <StorageExtent>
Or
# mkpsfs <device> [<size_in_blks>]
```

Where the global device name is specified as /dev/psd/psdXXXpYY where XXX is the disk number and YY is the partition number. Then, mount the PSFS file system on any server in the matrix. Use the Polyserve MxS command:

```
# mx fs mount [--persist] [--activate] [--options] <path>
<filesystem>
<server>
```

Or use the usual Linux command with option –t:

```
# mount -t psfs -o options <device> <mountpoint>
```

When using the PolyServe mount command, the *persist* option can be used for the file system to mount automatically whenever the server is rebooted. To see the status of the file system, use the PolyServe command:

```
# mx fs status [--mounted] [--persistent] [--verbose]
```

DB Optimized Option

One important mount option that is useful for setting up the file systems for an Oracle database is DB Optimized. PolyServe specially provides the DB Optimized option for the use of database files. This option bypasses file system I/O buffering allowing disk transfers to occur directly in application buffers. This allows a database system, such as RAC, to manage its own data coherency and integrity.

To take advantage of the performance optimization, the read or write system call buffer must be aligned on a page boundary and the I/O must be 512 bytes or a multiple offset. The size of the I/O must also be 512 bytes or a multiple thereof. Oracle I/O is sized as a *db_block_size* operation and will always be a 512 byte multiple.

In such a case, the files in the DB Optimized file system are treated as direct I/O files, and the I/O is completely un-buffered and not serialized through any OS locking. Any access to files in a DB Optimized mounted file system that do not fit the alignment requirements do succeed – through the buffered I/O path. Regular file system commands can be used against these files such as *cp*, *rm*, *compress*, etc.

DB Optimized file systems are used to store all Oracle data files, redo logs, control files, SPFILE, OCR file, and CRS voting disk.

Configure Veritas CFS for Solaris and HP platforms

Another option available for Solaris and HP platform is the use of Veritas Advance Cluster solution, which provides comprehensive cluster software and shared storage solutions. In this section, the shared storage solution will be examined in terms of the Veritas cluster file system (CFS).

Setting up volumes and making sure the cluster file system is accessible by all nodes configures the shared storage. In sum the volumes and the CFS depend on the physical storage. The cluster volume manager manages all related objects such as physical disks (LUNS), disk groups, volumes, and file systems. Oracle uses the ODM (Oracle disk manager) interface to communicate with Veritas volumes and CFS files.

Cluster Volume Manager (CVM)

CVM is basically an extension of the widely used Veritas Volume Manager. CVM extends the functionality of the VxVM to all the nodes in the cluster. Each node sees the same state of all volume resources. It follows master/slave architecture. One node usually acts as master and others as slaves. There is only one master in a given cluster. The volume manager daemon (*vxconfigd*) maintains the configuration of the logical volumes. Each node in the node has the *vxconfigd* daemon. Changes to a volume are propagated first to the master daemon and then the master passes it on to slave daemons. These changes happen at the kernel level.

CVM does not attempt to do any locking between the nodes. That is the responsibility of the application, as in the RAC database. CVM also follows the uniform shared storage model. This means that all systems must be connected to the same disk sets for a given disk group. If a node loses contact with a specific disk, it is excluded from using the disk.

Cluster File System (CFS)

Veritas CFS has evolved from the Veritas File System (VxFS). CFS allows the same file system to be simultaneously mounted on multiple nodes in the cluster. Once again, the CFS is designed with master/slave architecture. Though any node can initiate an operation to create, delete, or resize data, the master node carries out the actual operation. CFS caches the metadata in memory, typically in the memory buffer cache or the *vnode* cache. A distributed locking mechanism, called GLM, is used for metadata and cache coherency among the multiple nodes. However, with implementation of the ODM interface, Oracle RAC accesses data files stored on CFS, bypassing the file system buffer and file system locking processes. Oracle manages its own consistency mechanism. The ODM facility is automatically invoked with RAC.

Cluster Volume Management

The cluster volume manager is a software module that virtualizes the physical storage and presents the usable entities for the applications, such as the database at the operating system level. It is a storage administrator layer at the host level.

The Veritas cluster volume manager (CVM) uses objects for storage management. The two types of objects used by Volume Manager are physical objects and virtual objects.

- Physical objects – Volume Manager uses two physical objects: physical disks and partitions. Partitions are created on the physical disks (on systems that use partitions).
- Virtual objects - Volume Manager creates virtual objects, called volumes. Each volume records and retrieves data from one or more physical disks. A volume is a virtual disk device that appears to applications, databases, and file systems as a physical disk. Volumes are also composed of other virtual objects such as sub-disks and plexes. These are used to change volume configuration features such as concatenation, mirroring, and striping. Volumes and their virtual components are called virtual objects.

Volume management involves using physical disks or LUNS to create disk groups. These disks are combined to create volumes with a layout or configuration appropriate to their purpose, for example, mirroring or striping etc. The volumes are flexible objects that can easily be extended or modified. The volume management operations include:

- Placing the shared disks or LUNS from the shared storage array into the Volume Manager control. When the LUNS are placed under the VM control, they are known as VM disks.

- Creating the Disk Groups – the disk groups that contain the database application must be available to all nodes in the cluster. A disk group allows disks, volumes, and file systems that are relevant to a single database to be arranged into a logical collection for easy administration.
- Creating volumes with the appropriate layout (mirror, stripe. etc.) and size from the disk group storage pool. Volumes are flexible objects that can be extended or modified.
- Making file systems from the volumes and mounting them for database use. Volumes can also be used for database applications, in which case they are referred to as raw devices.

It is important to understand that volumes are the basic storage components that an Oracle database utilizes. The volumes, as created by the CVM, are accessible by all members or nodes of the cluster. This is an important distinction in the RAC environment. A volume can be accessed either directly by the RAC database as a raw partition, or through mounted file systems such as a CFS, as shown in Figure 15.16.

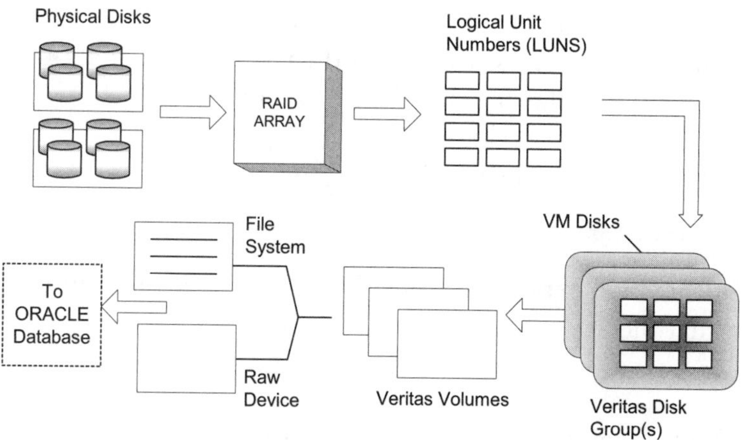

Figure 5.16: *Veritas Cluster Volume Management*

Configure NFS file system

Using NFS mount for the shared storage for the RAC database system, provides yet another option. In this section, the usage of NFS type shared storage structures will be covered by looking at the Filer System supplied by Network Appliance System.

Storage Infrastructure

- One Network Appliance F2XX/F7XX/F8XX/F9XX filer with Data ONTAP™ 6.1.3R2 or later
- One Gigabit switch with at least four ports
- One Gigabit NIC in the filer
- One or more disk shelves, based on the disk space requirements

Once the hardware connection is made to the nodes in the Linux Cluster, install Data ONTAP 6.1.3 R2 and give it a name, such as FDATA1, and an IP Address for the filer storage unit.

Create a volume on the FDATA1 filer for storing Oracle Database files. This volume will be used to store all the data files, control files, and log files for the Oracle Database.

Use the at the filer console:

```
FDATA1> vol create oradata 14
```

Then Edit the /etc/exports file on FData1 and add the following entries to that file:

```
/vol/racdata -anon=0
```

Execute the following command at the filer console:

```
FData1> exportfs -a
```

Now create mount points and mount volumes. Update the /etc/fstab file on all the server nodes and add the following entries:

```
FData1:/vol/racdata  -  /oradb nfs - Yes rw , bg , hard , nointr ,
rsize=32768,wsize=32768,tcp,noac,vers=3,timeo=600
```

Where:

- FData1 is the name of the filer.
- *oradb* is the mount point on the cluster nodes.
- The mount options that are required for the Oracle RAC are:
  - noac: This mount option disables caching on the client side.
  - tcp: Mount the file system using the tcp option.

Conclusion

So far, various options available for setting up shared storage required for building Oracle RAC Solutions have been covered. There are four basic choices for shared storage:

- raw partitions
- cluster file system
- NFS facility
- ASM.

There is quite a lot of variation in availability of these technologies. In other words, some platforms have specific requirements. Storage redundancy issues and other relevant technologies have also been examined.

Having covered the necessary shared storage preparation in this chapter, the next chapter will be devoted to the preparation of the cluster environment and creating the RAC database.

Install, Configure and Create

CHAPTER 6

"Ms. Jones, schedule a meeting with our database and system administrators."

Introduction

In this chapter, the main aspects of the Oracle RAC software installation and the RAC Database creation will be covered. Oracle RAC runs on multiple platforms and interacts with many flavors of the clustering software. With Oracle 10g release, Oracle provides portable clusterware, which can function independently or on top of the vendors provided cluster software.

The main features of the configuration process will be covered. Irrespective of the platform chosen, database creation is common to all. However, preparation of the physical hosts, installation of the operating system, clustering software, and associated system administration tasks differ.

Project coordination between the database administrators and system administrators is essential for smooth installation and configuration. There are many additional tasks, such as installing cluster software and creating the required storage volumes, which require the super user privilege. Good teamwork and understanding combined with proper planning helps achieve superior results.

With the introduction of the Automatic Storage Management (ASM) methodology for stand-alone and RAC database systems, storage management is very much simplified. In the previous chapter, many topics on preparing shared storage structures for the use of RAC database were covered. This chapter will focus on setting up the host environment, cluster platform, cluster ready services installation, and database creation.

The RAC System

The RAC system consists of multiple nodes accessing a single database. Typically, this architecture includes multiple servers or hosts connected by a private high bandwidth and low latency interconnect.

Installation and configuration of the RAC system on multiple nodes involves many steps. Unlike a stand-alone Oracle database installation, a RAC installation is highly integrated with the cluster environment at the server level. The RAC database software installation process is cluster aware; in other words, the Oracle software detects the existence of the cluster infrastructure as it begins to install.

Installation Components

From the point of view of the installation, the main architecture of the RAC environment includes the following:

- Nodes or Servers
- Private Interconnect
- Vendor Supplied Cluster Manager or Cluster Software (Optional)
- Oracle provided Cluster Ready Services
- Shared Storage Subsystem
- Raw Partitions or Cluster File System or Network Attached Storage (NAS) or Automatic Storage Management (ASM)
- Public Network Connection
- Oracle Database software with RAC option

Nodes or Hosts

The nodes or servers are the main platforms on which the Oracle RAC database is installed. The Cluster nodes range from a high-end powerful Sun Fire 15K to a low-end Linux server. They can also range from a mainframe grade IBM zSeries server to the emerging blade-server technologies such as IBM BladeCenter or Egenera. First, the appropriate operating system needs to be installed on the nodes. It is also important to choose the appropriate number of nodes while setting up the node operating environment.

Private Interconnect

The private interconnect is the physical construct that allows inter-node communication. It can be a simple crossover cable with UDP or it can be a proprietary interconnect with specialized proprietary communications protocol. When setting up more than 2- nodes, a switch is usually needed. This provides the maximum performance for RAC, which relies on inter-process communication between the instances for cache-fusion implementation.

Clusterware

Creating clusters involves installation of the cluster software on all nodes in the proposed cluster, as well as checking the configuration. The necessary tests need to be performed to verify the validity of the cluster. At the same time, the necessary software that controls the private interconnect is also installed and configured. With the availability of Oracle provided Cluster Ready Services (CRS), one can achieve a uniform and standard cluster platform. CRS is more than just cluster software, but it extends the high availability services in the cluster.

Shared Storage

The storage system provides an external common disk system accessible by all nodes of the cluster. The connection from the nodes to the disk sub-system is usually through a fiber switch or a SCSI connection. Once the storage volumes are presented to the hosts in the cluster, usually with the help of the logical volume manager, one can create volumes of suitable size for use in the RAC database. With the introduction of ASM methodology, the shared storage structures can be managed very easily. Once the disk groups are created with input of the disk devices, the ASM instances on each of the node in the cluster provide the shared storage resources to create the Database Files. The preparation of storage structures has been covered extensively in Chapter 5, *Preparing Shared Storage.*

Public Network

The clustered servers or hosts need to have public network connectivity so that client machines in the network can access the resources on the RAC system.

Virtual IP Address for CRS

Oracle 10g release supports the concept of Service, which can be assigned the Virtual IP address, and which float among the specified nodes. By creating the Virtual IP address and Virtual Host names, the applications get a sense of transparency in their connection to the RAC database service. This will be examined further in later sections of this chapter.

Oracle Database software with RAC option

Oracle Enterprise Edition contains the RAC database installation software and the Cluster Ready Services software. The Database software and Oracle CRS software need to be installed in separate Oracle Homes.

A valid license should be obtained to use the RAC option. The Oracle Configuration assistant's tools are user-friendly with a graphical interface. Typically, the tools start automatically after installation depending on the selection made when starting the installer. The configuration assistant can also be started manually as a standalone tool. The options include:

- Oracle Database Configuration Assistant (DBCA) – helps in the database creation. This is a cluster-aware utility.
- VIPCA – Virtual IP Configuration Assistant - configures the HA services and manage them.
- Oracle Database Upgrade/Migration Assistant - helps the migration process from 9i to 10g version.

- Oracle Enterprise Manager Configuration Assistant.

Servers and Operating Systems

The first critical task is the selection of the right server, or node, and operating system to host the Oracle RAC database. Oracle maintains a certification matrix for supported servers and platforms. The certification is issued only after Oracle and other vendors conduct rigorous tests. Oracle will only support RAC on certified combinations of hardware and operating system. These authors strongly recommend checking with the server vendor for Oracle Certification Matrix even if they certify and market the cluster platform for other applications.

Oracle Certification Matrix is available at Oracle Metalink through the following simple steps:

1. Connect and login to http://metalink.oracle.com
2. Click on the Certify and Availability button on the menu frame.
3. Click on View Certifications by Product hyperlink.
4. Choose Real Application Clusters.
5. Choose the correct platform.

There are many factors to be taken into consideration when deciding the number of nodes for the proposed cluster or deciding whether the cluster file system can be used: What kind of shared storage system will be chosen? What kind of cluster software and which version will be used?

Here are some examples that illustrate application of the above factors:

- Sun Solaris Servers, combined with Sun Cluster 3.x, only support raw partitions for database files.

- Using Sun Solaris Cluster with more than two nodes requires SCSI-3 Persistent Group Reservation (PGR) supporting storage such as Sun StoreEdge T3, Hitachi 9990, or EMC Symmetrix.
- However, when implementing Sun Cluster with Veritas DBE/AC, one can choose to use the cluster file system. Veritas DBE/AC also requires storage with SCSI-3 PGR. DBE/AC stands for Database Edition/Advance Cluster.
- For the IBM AIX pSeries (RS/6000) Cluster, the maximum number of nodes is 8 if SSA disks are used. If VSD(s) are used, the maximum number of nodes is 128. Again, if the disks are shared through Cluster Logical Volume Manager (CLVM), the maximum number of nodes is 16. VSD stands for virtual shared disk.
- When using the O/S version of AIX 4.3 with cluster software of HACMP/ES (CRM) 4.4.X, use the raw partitions for RAC database. However, when using AIX 5.1, one can use the cluster file system (GPFS).

These authors strongly recommend that the readers verify with the Oracle Certification matrix, as well as the server vendor suppliers, in order to choose the right combination of RAC system components. Since these specifications are frequently updated, please check for the latest edition.

Oracle certifies the combination of UNIX and Clusterware for RAC implementation. The vendor is responsible for the hardware certification. Some of these features are presented next, based on the information available at the time of writing.

For Linux

In case of Linux operating system, both the RedHat and United Linux flavors are certified for 10g RAC. As shown in Figure 6.1, for RedHat both 2.1 and 3.0 versions are certified. The products supported by Oracle, as part of the United Linux, include Conectiva, Turbo Linux and Suse SLES8.

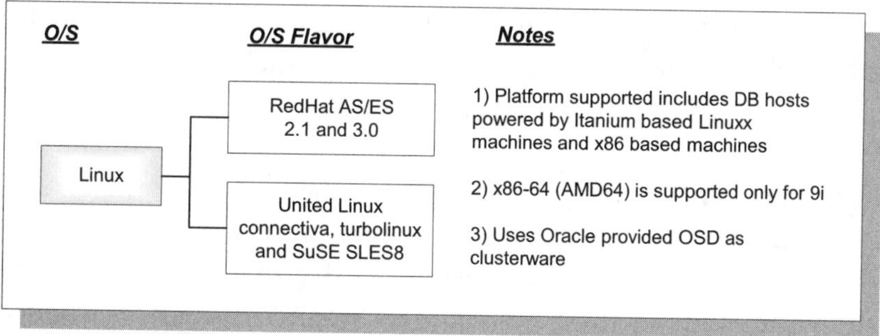

Figure 6.1: *Supported Linux Platform*

Windows

In case of Windows based RAC database systems, both the Windows 2000 and Windows 2003 are supported. Windows 2003 refers to enterprise, data center, and standard edition. Windows 2000 refers to Advanced Server and Datacenter Edition. Clusterware is supplied by Oracle.

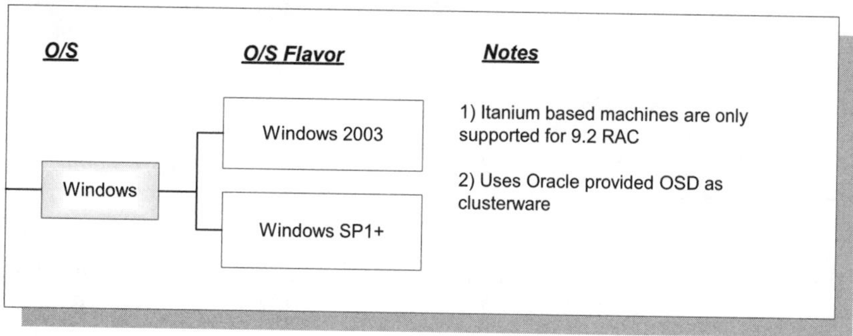

Figure 6.2: *Supported Windows Platform*

On UNIX

Oracle 10g RAC is available for all the widely used Unix Flavors as shown Figure 6.3. A variety of Clusterware is supported for building RAC Clusters. In addition to Oracle provided CRS, vendor provided Clusterware can be used.

In the case of Solaris platform, RAC database system can be built with one of these Clusterwares: Sun Cluster software, Fujitsu-Siemens Prime Cluster software, Veritas DB Edition/Advance Cluster (DBE/AC) and Oracle provided clusterware.

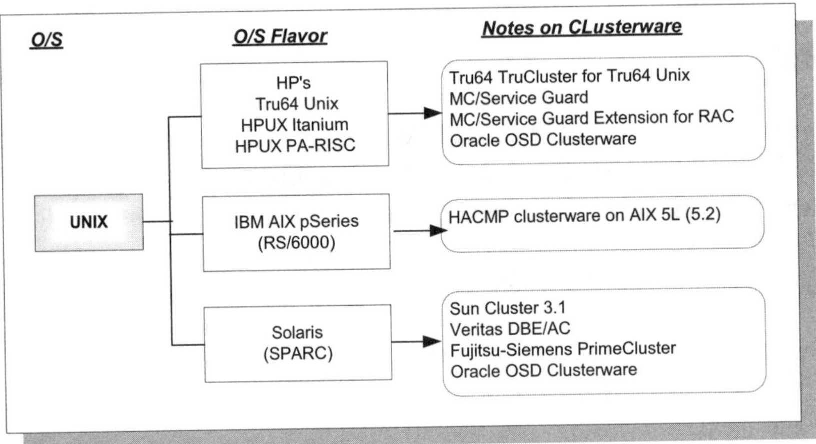

Figure 6.3: *Supported UNIX Platform and the cluster software modules*

In the case of HP's Tru64 Unix, TruCluster software is needed. However, when implemented on HPUX platform, one of these can be used: MC/Service Guard, MC/Service Guard Extension for RAC and Oracle OSD Clusterware.

HACMP cluster framework is needed when building the Oracle RAC database on IBM's AIX pSeries RS/6000 servers. However,

HACMP is not required when Oracle Files are placed on ASM or GPFS. HACMP is only required when data files are placed on concurrent raw logical volumes (CLVM). More details on the options available on RS/6000 AIX platform are provided in later sections.

Please note that as of this writing, Oracle has certified Oracle 10g RAC database mostly for the 64-bit Oracle version. It looks like Oracle is encouraging the use of 64-bit Oracle in preference over 32-bit version.

Interconnect

The cluster interconnect is a private network which is used to transfer cluster traffic, Oracle Resource directory information, and blocks for satisfying queries. There are two components involved in setting up and configuring the cluster interconnect, the physical hardware and the interconnect software. The physical connection between the nodes may be through a simple crossover cable or via a switch or hub.

There is a wide variety of technology. Fast Ethernet and Gigabit Ethernet connectivity provide high bandwidth and are widely used. However, such general purpose interconnect technology may not offer acceptable latency. To that end, special interconnect products like Memory Channel for HP Tru64 (TruCuster), Hyper Fabric Interconnect for HP-UX clusters, and SCI adapters for SunPlex Clusters should be preferred wherever possible.

In addition, there is Infiniband interconnect architecture for Linux based systems, which is being provided by vendors such as Mellanox and TopSpin. TopSpin Clustering kit provides Infiniband switch multiple ports, Fiber Channel Gateway for

SAN storage or Ethernet gateway for NAS storage, 10 Gbps Infiniband Host Channel Bus Adapters.

In another example, SunPlex Cluster systems offers support for Remote Shared Memory technology (RSM), which enhances the performance of distributed applications by allowing for fast messaging between instances of a distributed application. RSM improves bandwidth and reduces the latency many-fold, allowing a SunPlex/Oracle RAC deployment to deliver superior performance.

The RSM API provides mechanisms upon which user applications, such as Oracle Real Application Clusters, can build low-latency, high bandwidth messaging to directly access interconnect hardware, bypassing the operating system. Utilizing this feature requires SCI-PCI interconnect in the Sun Cluster 3.0 environment. The following Table 6.1 shows the protocols used and the throughput achieved.

INTERCONNECT	LATENCY (µs)	PROTOCOL	THROUGHPUT
Memory Channel	3	3 RDG	100 MB/sec
Fast Ethernet	100	UDP	10 MB/sec
Gigabit Ethernet	100	UDP	UDP 100 MB/sec
Hyper Fabric	20	HMP	400 MB/sec
SCI	10	UDP	70 MB/sec

Table 6.1: *Interconnect Types*

If more than two nodes are interconnected in a cluster, they must be linked with a switch. Wherever possible, redundant interconnects must be provided by using dual switches. The following commands show which interconnect is used for UDP or TCP:

```
sqlplus> connect / as sysdba
oradebug setmypid
```

```
oradebug ipc
exit
```

The corresponding trace can be found in the *user_dump_dest* directory, and contains the following information in the last couple of lines:

```
SKGXPCTX: 0x32911a8 ctx
admno 0x12f7150d admport:
SSKGXPT 0x3291db8 flags SSKGXPT_READPENDING
    info for network 0
  socket no 9 IP 172.16.193.1 UDP 43307
  sflags SSKGXPT_WRITESSKGXPT_UP
  info for network 1
  socket no 0 IP 0.0.0.0 UDP 0
  sflags SSKGXPT_DOWN
context timestamp 0x1ca5
  no ports
```

When other protocols such as HMP or RDG are used, the trace file will not reveal the IP address.

Another method of finding the protocol is to look into the alert log file of the Oracle instance. During startup, a message is posted showing the IPC details. For example,

```
Wed Oct 30 05:28:55 2002
cluster interconnect IPC version: Oracle UDP/IP with Sun RSM
disabled
IPC Vendor 1 proto 2 Version 1.0
```

Message Size

The message size is platform dependent. In Oracle9i Release 2 (9.2.0.1), message size was limited to 32K. Before 9.2.0.1, the Operating System UDP settings are overwritten and a 32k buffer is used.

Oracle9i allows larger message sizes, depending on the platform. To increase throughput on an interconnect, the UDP kernel parameters must be adjusted.

Oracle opens the UDP receive ports with a receive buffer size of 128k, but it also honors O/S settings and can even adjust the size based on the maximum block size seen, up to the O/S maximum. The operating system maximum for the UDP receive buffer size is:

```
Linux:                    256k
Solaris / Tru64 5.1:      1MB
HP:                       2GB
```

When implementing the Sun Cluster with the clusterware provided by Veritas, the LMX message size is up to 64K, with a default of 32K.

Cluster Software

Once the nodes are physically interconnected, with either a cable or switch, plan to install the necessary cluster software on all the nodes. The clusterware installation method differs from vendor to vendor and from platform to platform.

Cluster software is usually referred to as cluster manager or operating system dependent layer (OSD) and is provided by the hardware vendor. The notable exceptions are Linux and Windows. For example, the following Table 6.2 shows the cluster software products that are available for setting up a RAC system.

PLATFORM	CLUSTERWARE
Solaris	Sun Cluster 3.1
Solaris	Veritas Storage Foundation DBE/AC
Solaris	Fujitsu-Siemens PrimeCluster
HP UX	MC Service Guard and Veritas Storage Foundation
HP Tru64	Tru64 TruCluster
Linux	Oracle Supplied Clusterware (CRS)
Windows	Oracle Supplied Clusterware (CRS)
AIX pSeries	HACMP

Table 6.2: *Cluster Software (OSD)*

As noted in Table 6.2, Oracle provides the clusterware for Windows 2000 and Linux clusters. Please note that throughout the book, when referring to OSD, it means the cluster related operating dependent system layer. The HA framework supplied by the vendors is not needed for a RAC environment. Instead of using the HA software, Oracle uses its own cluster software or an OSD supplied by the vendor to control the cluster lock management. Clustering software monitors and manages the cluster components that include the servers and the server connections. The cluster software specializes in detecting failures through software probes, fault isolation, and fault containment, wherever applicable.

Usually the failure detection process involves determining the fault and applying the response. It could result in either switching over to a secondary component or the total shutdown of that component, in which case some kind of reconfiguration takes place. As an example, if two interconnects are configured, the fault or loss of one would not cripple the cluster, but would merely result in shutting it off. Whereas, when one of the nodes hangs, the cluster manager evicts the failed node and informs other members so that the application or database instance can take the necessary reconfiguration action.

The cluster manager is also responsible for node monitoring, which includes polling the status of various resources like interconnect hardware/software, shared disks, Oracle instances, and public networks. The cluster manager interacts with the global cache service in RAC to reconfigure the failed instance resources.

Cluster software protects against the conditions of split-brain and amnesia. Split-brain condition occurs when communication between nodes is lost and the cluster becomes partitioned into sub-clusters, each believing that it is the only partition. Amnesia occurs when the cluster restarts after a shutdown using cluster configuration data older than at the time of the shutdown. The changes in cluster membership drive the cluster reconfiguration sequence that may, in turn, result in services being migrated from failed or faulty nodes to healthy ones.

CRS – Cluster Ready Services

Oracle10g introduces Cluster Ready Services (CRS), which provides many system management services and interacts with the vendor clusterware to coordinate cluster membership information. It provides the cluster software, sometimes it is called the Oracle OSD Clusterware.

The OUI installs CRS on each node on which the OUI detects that vendor clusterware is running. In addition, the CRS home is distinct from the RAC-enabled Oracle Home. The CRS home can be shared either by one or more nodes, or privately to each node, depending on the settings used when running the OUI. When vendor clusterware is present, CRS interacts with the vendor clusterware to coordinate cluster membership information.

For Oracle10g on Linux and Windows-based platforms, CRS co-exists with but does not inter-operate with vendor clusterware. Vendor clusterware may be used for all UNIX-based operating systems except for Linux. Even though, many of the UNIX platforms have their own clusterware products, use the CRS software to provide the HA support services. CRS supports services and workload management and helps to maintain the continuous availability of the services. CRS also manages resources such as virtual IP (VIP) address for the node and the global services daemon.

The Oracle Cluster Registry (OCR) contains cluster and database configuration information for Real Application Clusters Cluster Ready Services (CRS), including the list of nodes in the cluster database, the CRS application, resource profiles, and the authorizations for the Event Manager (EVM). The OCR can reside in a file on a cluster file system or on a shared raw device. When installing Real Application Clusters, specify the location of the OCR.

CRS helps to package a set of application that work under CRS control and access the RAC database. The application resource profile defines the resources with which you manage the RAC. Prior to the 10g release, the cluster manager implementations on some platforms were referred to as Cluster Manager. In Oracle10g, Cluster Synchronization Services (CSS) is the cluster manager on all platforms. The Oracle Cluster Synchronization Service Daemon (OCSSD) performs this function on UNIX-based platforms.

On Windows-based platforms, the OracleCSService, OracleCRService, and OracleEVMService provides the cluster manager functionality. The installation of CRS is covered in later sections.

A Note on SKGXP, SKGXN Libraries

Oracle has defined APIs for inter-process communication and node membership. These are the APIs that facilitate integration with vendor clusterware or Oracle provided clusterware. Oracle communicates between processes on instances and does not have to know how the data is moved between systems. The Oracle API for IPC is referred to as system kernel generic interface inter-process communications (*skgxp*).

The OSD or clusterware normally provides a kernel module that receives communications from the *skgxp* library and passes it to the correct process on the correct instance on other nodes. It is the responsibility of the implementer to design the communication package in the form of a kernel module in compliance with the specification.

For example, Veritas DBE/AC provides a module to implement the *skgxp* functionality. This is available in the form of a library (*libskgxp9.so*), which is dynamically linked by Oracle at execute time. This *skgxp* interface utilizes the LLT multiplexer (LMX) via *ioctl()* calls. The LMX module is a kernel module designed to receive communications from the *skgxp* module and pass them to the correct process on the correct instance on other nodes. The module multiplexes communications between multiple related processes into a single multi threaded LLT port between systems.

Oracle has provided another set of APIs to provide the membership information to the RAC system. This is known as system kernel generic interface node membership (*skgxn*). Oracle RAC makes specific *skgxn* calls and gets the required membership information. The *skgxn* library, in turn, makes *ioctl()* calls to a kernel module for membership information. This kernel module is known as VCSMM (VCS membership module) and is implemented in library *libskgxn2.so.* Oracle uses the linked *skgxn* library to communicate with VCSMM, which obtains membership information from GAB.

General Installation Steps

Figure 6.4 shows the basic flow of the cluster configuration, shared storage structures preparation and installation of the Oracle software, and creation of the database. This involves a sequential process of tasks.

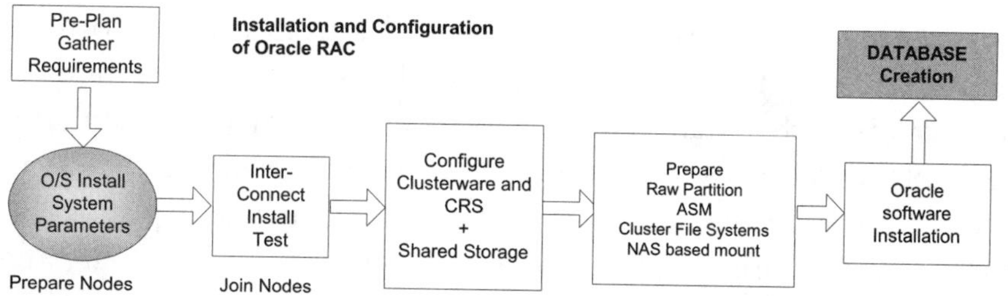

Figure 6.4: *Basic Installation Steps in creating RAC Database*

As shown in the above figure, successful setting up of a RAC environment and creating the database involves many phases. The initial phase includes the selection of the server platform and operating system. Subsequently, the DBA needs to decide how many nodes to have initially and what kind of interconnect products to use for the node communication. Pre-planning and gathering the relevant information is an important step.

Phase - 1

The first and foremost activity is to review all the platform-specific documentation. This involves all of the personnel connected with the project such as system administrators, database administrators, and vendor support personnel. A project plan and strategy for effective coordination across all involved groups needs to be developed.

The next step involves preparing the server platform.

- Configure Kernel Parameters (For example, /etc/system)
- Create Administrative UNIX groups as OSDBA, typically named *dba*,
- Create the user account *oracle* to manage and own the installation

The setting up of kernel parameters varies from one platform to another. Though the semantics are the same, the method of setting up such parameters differs from system to system. For example, in a Sun Solaris Server, specify the kernel parameters in the /etc/system file, and in a Tru64 system, they are specified in the /etc/sysconfigtab file. Though the basic commands are the same across the different UNIX flavors, the system administrative methods differ. For example, creating a user account such as *oracle* in Sun Solaris and TruUNIX, requires the command *useradd*. In the case of AIX you need *smit mkuser*.

Phase – 2

The next step will be to set up the physical interconnect and install the appropriate cluster software components. This is very specific to the physical environment. Please follow the instructions specified in the vendor documentation.

The next step is the cluster creation at the operating system level. Once the clusterware or OSD is successfully installed and tested, configure the shared storage structures. In certain situations, the configuration of shared storage volumes may precede the OSD installation. The necessary disks for the purpose of setting up a quorum have to be made available before installing the OSD. As a new feature of 10g, it is necessary to install the Cluster Ready Services.

The configuration of shared storage structures normally follows the steps outlined below.

- Configure the shared storage devices.
- Use volume manager and create volumes. Optionally create the ASM instance (Automatic Storage Method).
- Wherever the cluster file system is supported, create file systems and mount them. Otherwise, prepare raw partitions

as needed. Make a plan for the required number of raw devices.

- Also plan for the quorum devices or coordination disks required for cluster framework. For the purpose of CRS, the DBA will need to provide the Voting Disk and OCR file.

Phase – 3

This phase involves installation of Cluster Ready Services and installation of the Oracle database software and other allied functions, such as enabling the RAC option, as it is done in the case of the different Linux flavors. Subsequently, the creation of the database follows, which may be done by using DBCA GUI or by the manual method.

In the following sections, how to set up the cluster environment for Linux environment using the installation of Cluster Ready Services will be covered. CRS is the only required clusterware for the Linux and Windows environment. In case of other UNIX platforms like Solaris, HP-UX, HP Tru64 and AIX, vendor provided clusterware can also be used, but that would be optional.

Oracle software installation and database creation will also be covered. The phase involving the Oracle installation and the subsequent creation of the RAC database and configuration is mostly the same on all platforms.

Before beginning the description of the installation of CRS and Database Software and DB creation, a recap will be provided of all the storage options available for CRS Files and Database Files. Table 6.3 provides a summary of the storage options available.

O/S PLATFORM	STORAGE CHOICE FOR DB FILES	STORAGE CHOICE FOR CRS FILES
AIX	- Cluster file system using GPFS for AIX - Automatic Storage Management - Raw logical volumes using HACMP	- Cluster file system using GPFS - Raw logical volumes using HACMP (NOTE: If you are not using HACMP, you must use a GPFS file system to store the Oracle CRS files)
HP-UX	- Automatic Storage Management - Shared logical volumes using HP ServiceGuard Ext for RAC and LVM - Raw partitions (You must use either your own startup script or a Serviceguard package to activate new or existing volume groups that contain only database files)	- Shared logical volumes using HP Serviceguard Extensions for RAC and Logical Volume Manager (LVM) - Raw partitions (You do not need to create a Serviceguard package to activate the volume group that contains the Oracle CRS files)
HP Tru64 UNIX	- Cluster File System with TruCluster V5.1B - Automatic Storage Management - Logical Storage Manager with TruCluster V5.1B - Raw partitions	- Cluster File System with TruCluster V5.1B - Logical Storage Manager with TruCluster V5.1B - Raw partitions
Linux	- Automatic Storage Management - Raw Devices - Cluster file system using OCFS - Automatic Storage Management - NFS file system on a certified NAS device	- Raw Devices - Cluster file system using OCFS - Automatic Storage Management - NFS file system on a certified NAS device

O/S PLATFORM	STORAGE CHOICE FOR DB FILES	STORAGE CHOICE FOR CRS FILES
SPARC Solaris	- Certified cluster file system - Automatic Storage Management - NFS file system with Fujitsu PRIMECLUSTER and a certified NAS device - Shared logical volumes - Raw partitions	- Certified cluster file system - NFS file system with Fujitsu PRIMECLUSTER and a certified NAS device - Shared logical volumes - Raw partitions
Windows	- Cluster file system (OCFS) - Automatic Storage Management - Raw Devices	- Cluster file system (OCFS) - Raw Devices

Table 6.3: *Storage Options for Database Files and CRS Files*

Cluster Ready Services

In order to install the CRS, ensure that the nodes have user equivalence. Use *rsh* or *rlogin* to test the user equivalence for the account used to install. Usually *oracle* is the UNIX user account that is used for installation.

In addition to the host machine's public internet protocol (IP) address, obtain two or more IP addresses for each node that is going to be part of the installation for the purpose of VIP. One of the IP addresses must be a public IP address and another for the node's virtual IP address (VIP). Oracle uses VIPs for client-to-database connections. Therefore, the VIP address must be publicly accessible. The other address must be a private IP address for inter node, or instance-to-instance Cache Fusion traffic. Using public interfaces for Cache Fusion can cause performance problems.

In case of Sun Clusters, install the Oracle-provided UDLM patch onto each node. Install the UDLM patch before installing Cluster Ready Services. Even with a pre-Oracle Database 10g UDLM, install the Oracle Database 10g UDLM.

CRS Installation

To explain the CRS installation process, the following example will be used. A 3 Node Linux Cluster will be referenced that is fitted with polyserve cluster file system.

If installing CRS on a node that already has a single-instance Oracle Database 10g installation, and the ASM instance is running, stop the ASM and CSS daemon by running the $ORACLE_HOME/bin/localconfig delete in the home that is running Cluster Synchronization Services (CSS) to reset the OCR configuration information.

After CRS is installed, then start up the ASM instances again and the ASM instances will use the cluster CSS daemon instead of the earlier daemon of the single-instance Oracle database. The following steps describe the CRS installation process.

1. Launch the Oracle Universal Installer by using runInstaller command from the /crs subdirectory on the Oracle Cluster Ready Services Release 1 (10.1.0.2) CDROM. A welcome page is displayed as shown below:

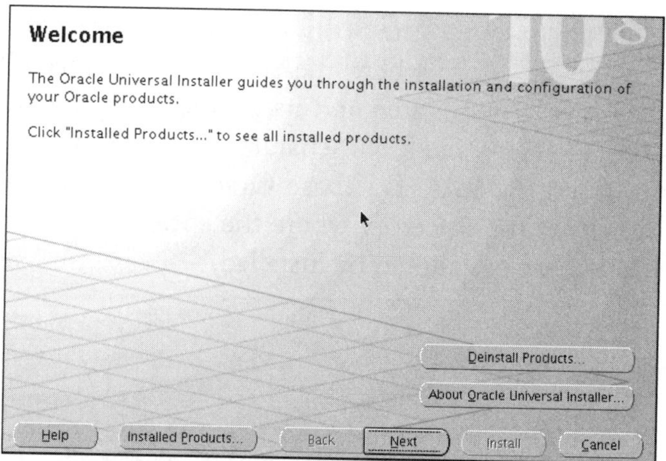

Figure 6.5: *Oracle Universal Installer Welcome Page*

2. Next, Select the inventory directory and specify the operating system group name, which is usually the *dba.* Then execute the *orainstRoot.sh* script with root privilege as shown in Figure 6.6

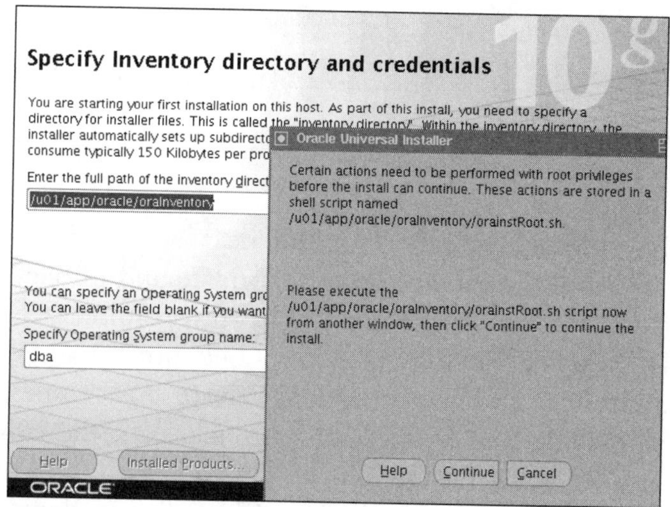

Figure 6.6: *Inventory Selection Page*

3. Next, the Specify Location Page, as shown in Figure 6.7, will be shown. Ensure that the source points to the software

location, which is either the software CD directory or the location of the directory where the software is copied. Also specify the CRS Home Name and its location. Cluster Ready Services should be installed in a separate Oracle Home, which is different from the RAC Database Oracle Home. The CRS home directory is the directory where the software for Oracle Cluster Ready Services should be installed.

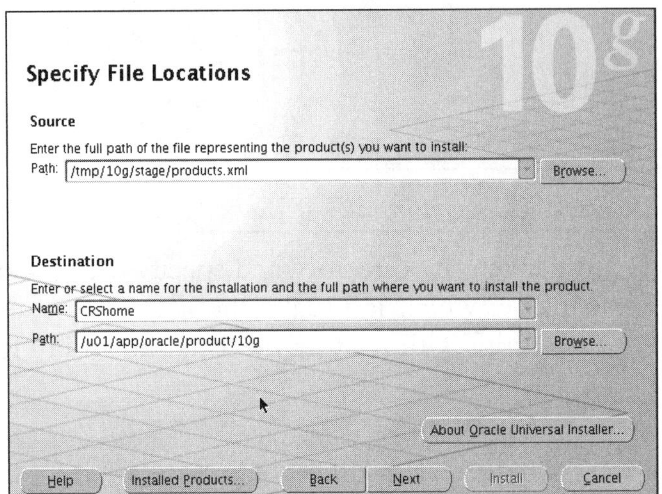

Figure 6.7: *CRS Home Location*

4. Make the language selection in the next step. After that, provide a Cluster Name and also the private and public host names for the nodes in the cluster. In this example, Cluster Name is specified as PROD and public node names are shown as node1, node2 and node3. Private host names are shown as rac1-2, rac2-2 and rac3-2. Oracle uses the private Network for Cache Fusion block transfers and inter-node messages. Also note that the Cluster Configuration Information page, shown in Figure 6.8, contains pre-defined node information if the OUI detects that the system has vendor clusterware.

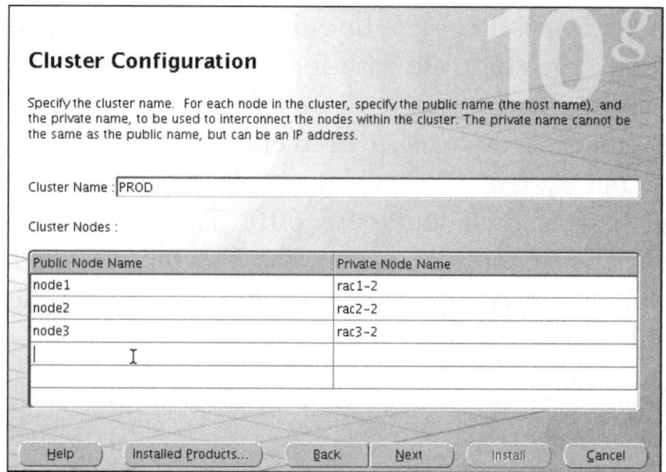

Figure 6.8: *Cluster Configuration Page*

5. On the next page, identify the interfaces to use as private interconnect. In this example, *eth2* has been provided as the private interconnect interface.

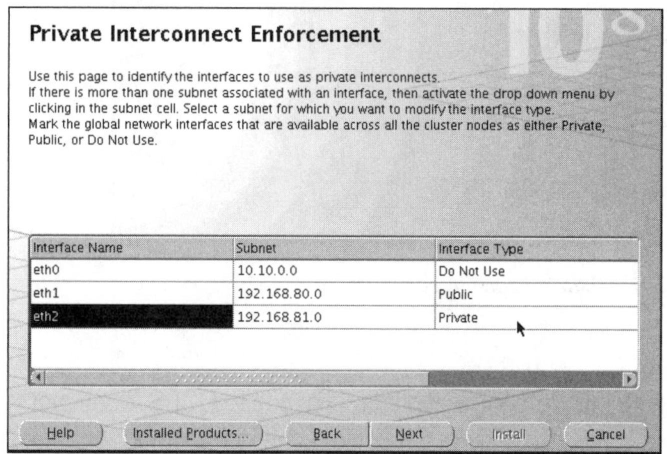

Figure 6.9: *Private Interconnect Enforcement*

6. Next, the Cluster Registry Location Information page is shown. Enter the complete path for the raw device or shared file system file for the Oracle Cluster Registry (OCR). In this example, /mnt/ps/db/ocr has been entered and is located on a cluster file system. The OCR stores the cluster nodes information as shown in Figure 6.10. This file should be about 100MB. In this installation, the Polyserve Cluster file system has been used and the OCR file has been pre-created as shown below.

```
$  mount | grep dboptimize
/dev/psd/psd1p2 on /mnt/ps/db type psfs (rw,shared,data=unordered,dboptimize)
$ cd /mnt/ps/db
$ dd if=/dev/zero of=ocr bs=1024k count=125
125+0 records in
125+0 records out
$ for NODE in 1 2 3
> do
> rsh node${NODE} ls -li /mnt/ps/db/ocr
> done
1441793 -rw-r--r--    1 oracle   dba      131072000 Mar 31 09:53 /mnt/ps/db/ocr
1441793 -rw-r--r--    1 oracle   dba      131072000 Mar 31 09:53 /mnt/ps/db/ocr
1441793 -rw-r--r--    1 oracle   dba      131072000 Mar 31 09:53 /mnt/ps/db/ocr
$ 
```

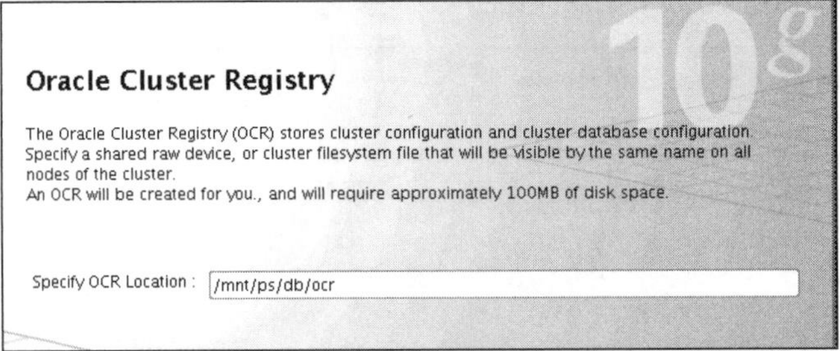
Oracle Cluster Registry
The Oracle Cluster Registry (OCR) stores cluster configuration and cluster database configuration.
Specify a shared raw device, or cluster filesystem file that will be visible by the same name on all nodes of the cluster.
An OCR will be created for you., and will require approximately 100MB of disk space.
Specify OCR Location :
/mnt/ps/db/ocr

Figure 6.10: *Oracle Cluster Registry Page*

Note that at the time of writing of this book, OCFS does not support the CRS files. The CRS files can be located on the following: 1) RAW device. 2) Any Cluster File system other than OCFS. 3) NFS file system on a certified NAS device. However, this situation may change with OCFS Rel 2.0

7. Next, the Voting Disk Information page appears as shown in Figure 6.11. CSS Voting Disk is used to arbitrate the ownership of the cluster nodes in the event of split-brain syndrome. Voting disk is same as the quorum disk, a more familiar term. Voting Disk needs to reside either on a cluster file system or on a shared raw disk. In this installation, a voting disk file *css_voting_disk* has been pre-created and specified in the voting disk page.

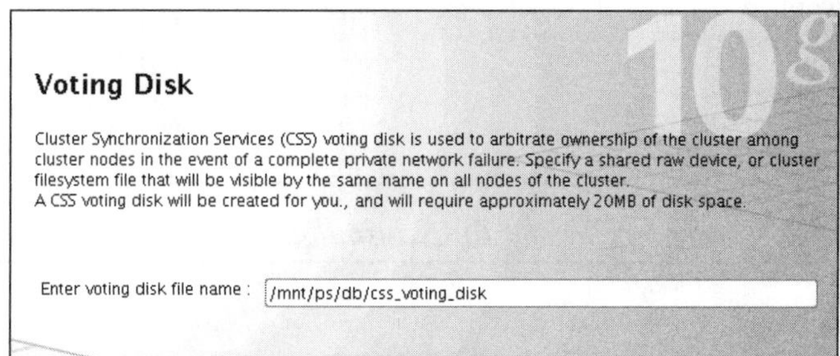

Voting Disk
Cluster Synchronization Services (CSS) voting disk is used to arbitrate ownership of the cluster among cluster nodes in the event of a complete private network failure. Specify a shared raw device, or cluster filesystem file that will be visible by the same name on all nodes of the cluster.
A CSS voting disk will be created for you., and will require approximately 20MB of disk space.
Enter voting disk file name :
/mnt/ps/db/css_voting_disk

Figure 6.11: *Select the CSS Voting Disk*

Note that the storage size for the OCR should be at least 100MB and the storage size for the voting disk should be at least 20MB.

8. Next, the OUI displays a dialog asking that the *orainstRoot.sh* script be run on all of the nodes. After the *orainstRoot.sh* script processing completes, the OUI displays a Summary page as shown in Figure 6.12.

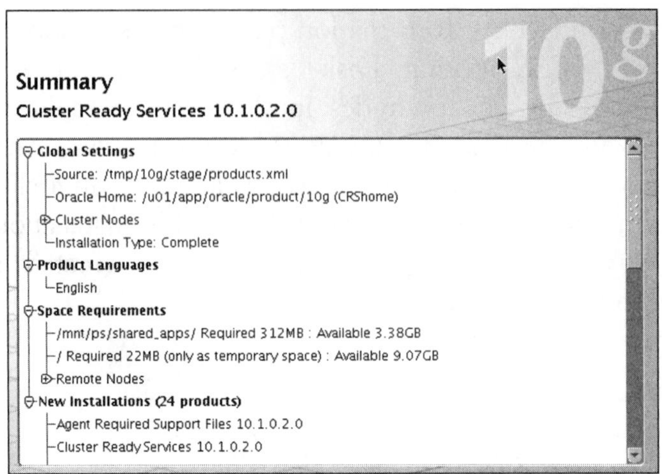

Figure 6.12: *Summary Page for CRS installation*

9. Now the installation begins. First, OUI copies software to the local node and then copies the software to the remote nodes.

10. Then at the end of copying the files, the OUI displays a dialog indicating that the *root.sh* script must be run on all the nodes as shown in Figure 6.13.

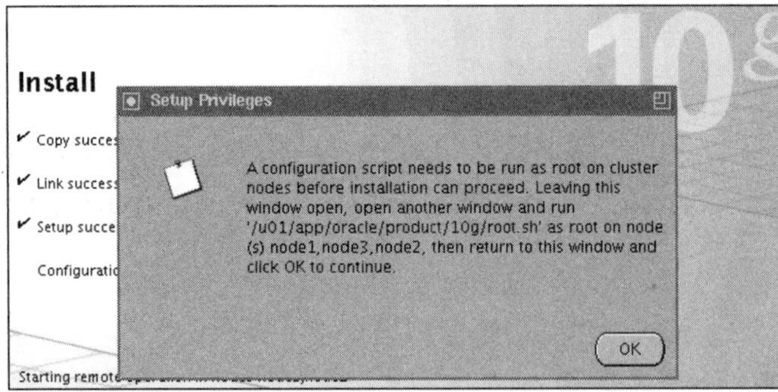

Figure 6.13: *root.sh script*

11. Figure 6.14 shows the output of the *root.sh* file. In this stage, voting disk is formatted, daemons are added to *inittab*, and CSS daemon is activated.

```
oracle@node1:/u01/app/oracle/product/10g
[root@node1 10g]# pwd
/u01/app/oracle/product/10g
[root@node1 10g]# sh ./root.sh
Checking to see if Oracle CRS stack is already up...
/etc/oracle does not exist. Creating it now.
Setting the permissions on OCR backup directory
Oracle Cluster Registry configuration upgraded successfully
WARNING: directory '/u01/app/oracle/product' is not owned by root
WARNING: directory '/u01/app/oracle' is not owned by root
WARNING: directory '/u01/app' is not owned by root
WARNING: directory '/u01' is not owned by root
assigning default hostname node1 for node 1.
assigning default hostname node2 for node 2.
assigning default hostname node3 for node 3.
Successfully accumulated necessary OCR keys.
Using ports: CSS=49895 CRS=49896 EVMC=49898 and EVMR=49897.
node <nodenumber>: <nodename> <private interconnect name> <hostname>
node 1: node1 rac1-2 node1
node 2: node2 rac2-2 node2
node 3: node3 rac3-2 node3
Creating OCR keys for user 'root', privgrp 'root'..
Operation successful.
Now formatting voting device: /mnt/ps/db/css_voting_disk
Successful in setting block0 for voting disk.
Format complete.
Adding daemons to inittab
Preparing Oracle Cluster Ready Services (CRS):
Expecting the CRS daemons to be up within 600 seconds.
CSS is active on these nodes.
        node1
CSS is inactive on these nodes.
        node2
        node3
Local node checking complete.
Run root.sh on remaining nodes to start CRS daemons.
[root@node1 10g]# █
```

Figure 6.14: *Execution of CRS root.sh*

12. Remember to run the *root.sh* scripts on each node one by one. When executing the *root.sh* on the last node, the *root.sh* script runs the following assistants without intervention:

    a. Oracle Cluster Registry Configuration Tool (*ocrconfig*). If this tool detects a 9.2.0.2 version of RAC, then the tool upgrades the 9.2.0.2 OCR block format to an Oracle Database 10g OCR block format.

b. Cluster Configuration Tool (*clscfg*) - This tool automatically configures the cluster and creates the OCR keys.

13. This completes the CRS installation.

After the CRS is successfully installed, the following services should be running:

- **oprocd** - Process monitor for the cluster. Note that this process will only appear on platforms that do not use vendor clusterware with CRS.
- **evmd** - Event manager daemon that starts the *racgevt* process to manage callouts.
- **ocssd** - Manages cluster node membership and runs as oracle user. Failure of this process results in cluster restart.
- **crsd** - Performs high availability recovery and management operations such as maintaining the OCR. Also manages application resources and runs as root user and restarts automatically upon failure.

The Installer also adds entries to the /etc/init.d as shown below. The main init scripts help to spawn processes required for cluster ready services functioning.

```
[root@node2 rc.d]# cd /etc/init.d
[root@node2 init.d]# ls -lt | head
total 384
-rwxr-xr-x    1 root     root           763 Jan 27 17:28 init.crs
-rwxr-xr-x    1 root     root          2261 Jan 27 17:28 init.crsd
-rwxr-xr-x    1 root     root          5950 Jan 27 17:28 init.cssd
-rwxr-xr-x    1 root     root          2280 Jan 27 17:28 init.evmd
```

The /etc/inittab.crs file controls and describes the INIT processes for the CRS. The details are shown next:

```
[root@node2 etc]# more /etc/inittab.crs
#
# inittab       This file describes how the INIT process should set
up
#               the system in a certain run-level.
#
```

```
# Author: Miquel van Smoorenburg, <miquels@drinkel.nl.mugnet.org>
#         Modified for RHS Linux by Marc Ewing and Donnie Barnes
#

# Default runlevel. The runlevels used by RHS are:
# 0 - halt (Do NOT set initdefault to this)
# 1 - Single user mode
# 2 - Multiuser, without NFS (The same as 3,if you do not have
networking)
#   3 - Full multiuser mode
#   4 - unused
#   5 - X11
#   6 - reboot (Do NOT set initdefault to this)
#
id:3:initdefault:

# System initialization.
si::sysinit:/etc/rc.d/rc.sysinit

l0:0:wait:/etc/rc.d/rc 0
l1:1:wait:/etc/rc.d/rc 1
l2:2:wait:/etc/rc.d/rc 2
l3:3:wait:/etc/rc.d/rc 3
l4:4:wait:/etc/rc.d/rc 4
l5:5:wait:/etc/rc.d/rc 5
l6:6:wait:/etc/rc.d/rc 6

# Things to run in every runlevel.
ud::once:/sbin/update

sm:S:wait:/sbin/sulogin

# Trap CTRL-ALT-DELETE
#ca::ctrlaltdel:/sbin/shutdown -t3 -r now

# When our UPS tells us power has failed, assume we have a few
minutes
# of power left.  Schedule a shutdown for 2 minutes from now.
# This does, of course, assume you have powerd installed and your
# UPS connected and working correctly.
pf::powerfail:/sbin/shutdown -f -h +2 "Power Failure; System
Shutting Down"

# If power was restored before the shutdown kicked in, cancel it.
pr:12345:powerokwait:/sbin/shutdown -c "Power Restored; Shutdown
Cancelled"


# Run gettys in standard runlevels
1:2345:respawn:/sbin/mingetty tty1
2:2345:respawn:/sbin/mingetty tty2
3:2345:respawn:/sbin/mingetty tty3
4:2345:respawn:/sbin/mingetty tty4
5:2345:respawn:/sbin/mingetty tty5
6:2345:respawn:/sbin/mingetty tty6

# Run xdm in runlevel 5
```

```
# xdm is now a separate service
x:5:respawn:/etc/X11/prefdm -nodaemon
S0:2345:respawn:/sbin/agetty -L rconsole 38400 dumb
h1:235:respawn:/etc/init.d/init.evmd run >/dev/null 2>&1 </dev/null
h2:235:respawn:/etc/init.d/init.cssd fatal >/dev/null 2>&1
</dev/null
h3:235:respawn:/etc/init.d/init.crsd run >/dev/null 2>&1 </dev/null
h4:235:once:/etc/init.d/init.crsd run -1 >/dev/null 2>&1 </dev/null
```

Also note that the ports used by the services are shown at the time of running *root.sh*. The ports range from 49895 to 49898, and they are used for various services.

```
Using ports: CSS=49895 CRS=49896 EVMC=49897 and EVMR=49898
```

The *netstat* command shows ports listening.

```
[root@node2 /]# netstat | grep 4989
tcp  0 0 private-link1:32813     private-link2:49897     ESTABLISHED
tcp  0 0 private-link1:49895     private-link2:32773     ESTABLISHED
tcp  0 0 private-link1:49897     private-link2:32803     ESTABLISHED
```

Thus each node in the cluster will have the CRS Home to enable the clusterware to operate on each node.

This has been a description of the CRS installation and preparation of Cluster Environment in a typical Linux environment. The next step would be to install the Oracle Database software with RAC option on the selected cluster nodes.

In case of the operating platforms where vendor supplied clusterware is installed, follow the documentation supplied by the vendor. The next couple of sections will provide brief details. These methods are very specific to a particular server and platform.

Using Sun Cluster 3.x Environment

First install the Solaris Operating System on the nodes and apply patches where required. Ensure that the recommended patches for the SPARC operating system, storage array interface firmware, and storage array drive firmware are duly applied.

The following steps explain the procedure involved:

1. Prepare Disk Partitions as required.
2. A partition named /globaldevices, with a file system of 100Mb at minimum, is required for the *scinstall* utility in order to configure the global devices.
3. Connect the node with the cluster interconnect.
4. Install the Cluster software and create a cluster configuration.

scinstall utility performs the following operations on the cluster node:

- Installs the cluster software packages.
- Disables routing on the node (touch /etc/notrouter).
- Creates an installation log (/var/cluster/logs/install).
- Reboots the node.
- Creates the Disk ID devices during the reboot.

In order for RAC to use the shared disk architecture of Sun Cluster, to share the single database among multiple instances of RAC, to access the database concurrently, and to control conflicting access to the database, the Oracle UNIX distributed lock manager (*udlm*) is needed. There is another component called the Oracle Node Monitor, referred to as ORCLUdlm package, which is usually supplied along with the Oracle software. Bboth of these packages need to be installed.

Using Veritas DBE/Advanced Cluster

VERITAS Storage Foundation for Oracle RAC provides an integrated solution that includes the VERITAS clustering, file system, and volume management technologies. The solution delivers cluster and file system supporting Oracle RAC on the Solaris and HP-UX operating systems. Storage Foundation includes the Database Edition/Advances Cluster for Oracle RAC.

The software components installed by the VERITAS Storage Foundation for Oracle RAC 4.0 installation utility, *installsfrac*, includes the following:

- VERITAS Storage Foundation for Oracle RAC 4.0
- VERITAS Cluster Server (VCS)
- VERITAS Volume Manager (VxVM)
- VERITAS Group Lock Manager
- VERITAS File System (VxFS)
- VERITAS extension for Oracle Disk Manager (ODM
- VERITAS Cluster Server enterprise agent for Oracle

Veritas Database Edition/Advanced Cluster (DBE/AC) provides a complete I/O and communications stack to install, configure, and support Oracle RAC on a Solaris-based Sun cluster. It also provides monitoring and management of instance startup and shutdown. DBE/AC provides a comprehensive cluster framework and software facility.

With the availability of Veritas DBE/AC for RAC implementation on a Sun Cluster and HP-UX cluster, the limitation to clusterware provided by Sun and HP no longer exists. The Veritas Cluster Server, supporting Oracle RAC, is pretty much an extended and enhanced version of the VCS used for database failover clusters. Administrators already familiar with the VCS for HA cluster find it easier to understand and implement. Veritas DBE/AC is a certified cluster framework that is built in with Cluster File System and it is ODM compliant.

The following topics will be examined in this section:

- Communication stacks which deal with inter-node communication
- Shared Storage Configuration, ODM, CFS, and Cluster Volume Manager
- VCS architecture framework
- IO Fencing
- Installation of Veritas software

Communication Stack

There are two components in the Veritas communication stack.

- Low Level Transport (LLT)
- Group membership services/Atomic Broadcast (GAB).

Veritas has implemented its own communication transport for the node message transfers. It is called Low Latency Transport (LLT). LLT provides kernel-to-kernel communication and monitors network connections. It is a replacement for the IP stack. LLT runs on top of the data link protocol interface (DPLI). The use of LLT rather than IP provides low latency and removes the overhead usually associated with the IP stack. When implemented, RAC IPC uses the VCSIPC shared library for inter-process communication. LLT also distributes inter-node communication across all available private interconnects, which can reach as many as 8. LLT, is also responsible for heartbeat message transfers among the nodes.

GAB is responsible for monitoring the cluster membership. As the nodes or members join and exit, the GAB framework keeps track. Cluster membership is determined by the LLT heartbeats. The GAB component handles the point-to-point message delivery and the broadcast messages for all the nodes. Atomic broadcast ensures that all systems receive all messages.

Shared Storage Configuration

Setting up volumes and making sure the cluster file system is accessible by all nodes configures the shared storage. In sum, the volumes and the CFS depend on the physical storage. The cluster volume manager manages all related objects such as physical disks (LUNS), disk groups, volumes, and file systems. Oracle uses the ODM (Oracle disk manager) interface to communicate with Veritas volumes and CFS files.

Cluster Volume Manager (CVM)

CVM is basically an extension of the widely used Veritas Volume Manager. CVM extends the functionality of the VxVM to all the nodes in the cluster. Each node sees the same state of all volume resources. It follows master/slave architecture. One node usually acts as master and others as slaves. There is only one master in a given cluster. The volume manager daemon (*vxconfigd*) maintains the configuration of the logical volumes. Each node has the *vxconfigd* daemon. Changes to a volume are propagated first to the master daemon and then the master passes it on to slave daemons. These changes happen at the kernel level. CVM does not attempt to do any locking between the nodes. That is the responsibility of the application, as in the RAC database. CVM also follows the uniform shared storage model. This means that all systems must be connected to the same disk sets for a given disk group. If a node loses contact with a specific disk, it is excluded from using the disk.

Cluster File System (CFS)

Veritas CFS has evolved from the Veritas File System (VxFS). CFS allows the same file system to be simultaneously mounted on multiple nodes in the cluster.

Once again, the CFS is designed with master/slave architecture. Though any node can initiate an operation to create, delete, or resize data, the master node carries out the actual operation. CFS caches the metadata in memory, typically in the memory buffer cache or the vnode cache. A distributed locking mechanism, called GLM, is used for metadata and cache coherency among the multiple nodes.

However, with implementation of the ODM interface, Oracle RAC accesses data files stored on CFS, bypassing the file system buffer and file system locking processes. Oracle manages its own consistency mechanism. The ODM facility is automatically invoked with RAC.

VCS Framework and Service Groups

Veritas Cluster Server (VCS) is the overall framework that controls the Oracle RAC database and other required essential resources such as shared storage and listener. VCS acts as a director of operations. All activities within Oracle RAC and its infrastructure are managed with the VCS framework.

VCS manages its resources in the form of a group. A collection of resources of different types for a given application or task is called a service group. Service groups act as containers for all the necessary components and resources of an application. They are defined and managed as a single unit. A service group definition typically consists of:

- The keyword group in the configuration file.

- Name of the service group.
- The service group's attribute values (enclosed in parentheses). VCS predefine service group attributes.
- The definition of service group resources with attributes/values.
- The dependencies between the service group resources.

In Veritas DBE/AC, two service groups are defined to support and control the RAC database. One service group deals with the volume manager resources, file system resources, listener resources, and shared Oracle Home directory. The other service group deals with the Oracle database and supports CVM and CFS resources. These two groups are specified to be parallel groups as shown in Figure 6.15. VCS does not attempt to migrate a failed service group.

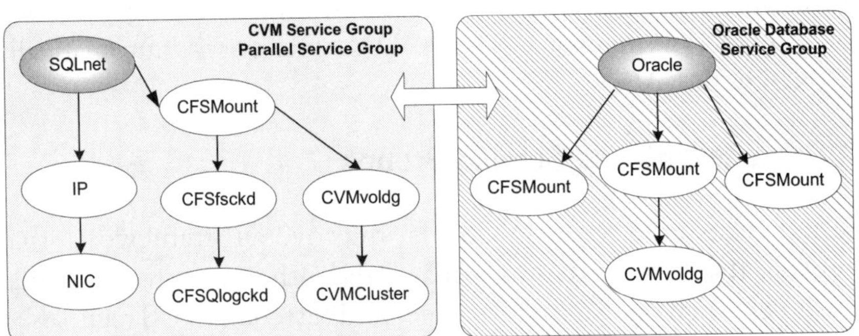

Figure 6.15: *Veritas DBE/AC Service Groups*

DBEAC provides agents to operate and control all resources. Agents are the VCS processes that bring resources online and take them offline. Resources are brought online and offline in an orderly manner based on the resource dependency. Agents also monitor resources and report. Some of the agents are specific to advance clusters including CVMCluster, CVMVoldg and CFSMount. The Agents stop and start the resources as required.

The VCS implementation for Oracle Failover clusters does not include these agents.

Using HACMP

When using the AIX 5L as the operating system, there are two combinations possible:

- Raw devices with the use of HACMP/ES CRM 4.4.x cluster OSD.
- GPFS – General Parallel File System with the use of HACMP/ES 4.4.x OSD.

The IBM High Availability Cluster Multi-Processing for AIX (HACMP) Version 4.4.x has been in use for quite sometime. HACMP is designed to detect system failures and manage failover, where necessary, to a recovery processor with a minimal loss of end-user time. HACMP 4.4.x offers improved usability, more flexible installation options, and additional hardware and software support for RS/6000 customers with mission critical applications.

We examine the RAC setup in two ways:

- Using the VSD using PSSP on RS/6000 SP systems.
- Using HACMP/ES on RS/6000 and pSeries machines.

The VSD are to be used with a SP machine running AIX 4.3.3, and PSSP 3.2. PSSP stands for IBM's Parallel System Support Programs. The HACMP/ES is used for the clusters of pSeries machines with AIX 4.3.3 and above.

What is VSD?

The IBM VSD (Virtual Shared Disk) software is a component of PSSP that allows data on disks attached to some SP nodes to be shared with other nodes using a high-speed interconnect network like SP Switch or SP Switch2. The Parallel System Support Programs (PSSP) software provides a comprehensive suite of applications for the installation, operation, management, and administration of the RS/6000 SP attached servers and Clustered Enterprise Servers (CES) from a single point of control.

The VSD is a logical volume that can be accessed both by the node to which it belongs and also by other nodes in the system. The VSD nodes that share data may reside in a single system partition. VSD software allows applications running on different nodes to have access to raw logical volumes as if they were local. I/O requests to VSD(s) are routed by the VSD device driver, which is loaded as a kernel extension on each node, thus making raw logical volumes accessible to other nodes in the system.

Depending on the VSD function, a node can be:

- VSD Server that has the local attached disks. It is able to complete I/O requests from VSD clients by using a communication network inside the system.
- A VSD Client that is a node requesting access to VSD(s).

There is another variation for VSD, which is known as Concurrent VSD. The Concurrent Virtual Shared Disk feature of PSSP allows multiple VSD servers to simultaneously access logical volumes inside a volume group using the Concurrent Logical Volume Manager (CLVM) component supplied by AIX. I/O requests from nodes that do not have locally attached disks are spread across VSD servers, thus improving raw logical volume access.

When using the Concurrent Virtual Shared Disk, recovery from node failure is much faster because the failed node is marked as unavailable to all other nodes. Its access to the physical disk is fenced, while the other nodes can continue to access the disks. Virtual Shared Disks provide access to non-local disks. They behave like raw logical volumes. They can be configured using SMIT or commands. VSD(s) are accessed through the SP Switch so the network overhead is very low.

The HACMP method may involve the use of concurrent logical volume groups. The HACMP layer includes the concurrent logical volume manager (CLVM). HACMP/ES installation has many steps, which include:

- Installing and setting up the hardware.
- Installing the AIX operating system.
- Installing the latest maintenance and required patches.
- Installing the HACMP/ES on each node and applying patches.

General Parallel File System – GPFS

With AIX 5.1 (5L), database files can also be placed on GPFS. In this case, create a GPFS capable of holding all required database files, control files, and log files. GPFS is only supported with HACMP/ES in a RAC configuration. When placing data files on GPFS, no CRM (Concurrent Resource Manager) needs to be installed.

GPFS is a clustered file system defined over multiple nodes. GPFS is a high-performance, scalable file system designed for cluster environments. It allows users shared access to files that may span multiple disk drives on multiple nodes. It offers many of the standard UNIX file system interfaces, allowing most applications to execute without modification or recompiling. UNIX file system utilities are also supported by GPFS. It allows both parallel and serial applications running on different nodes to share data spanning multiple disk drives attached to multiple nodes. See Figure 6.16.

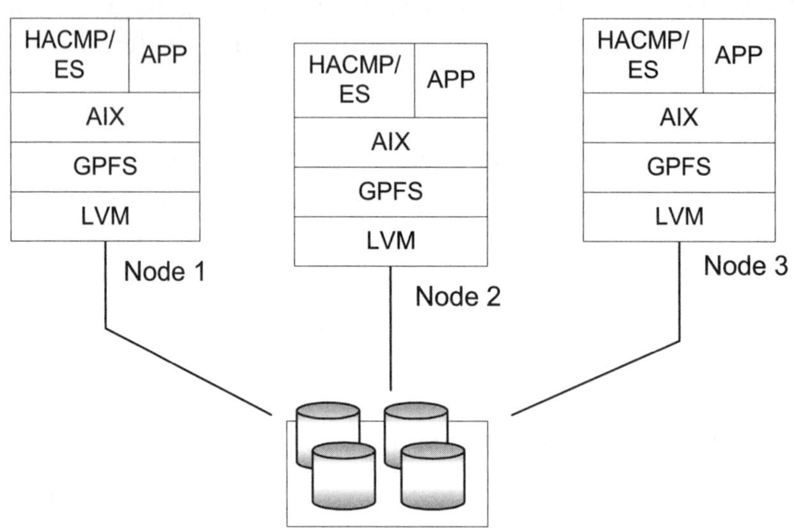

Figure 6.16: *AIX Cluster Environment*

A GPFS cluster in an HACMP environment is formed by a group of RS/6000 and IBM pSeries machines taking part in an HACMP/ES cluster. In this environment, every node in the GPFS cluster must be connected to the disks through their physical attachment so that each disk is available to all nodes for concurrent access.

GPFS operates under the HACMP/ES cluster environment. HACMP/ES provides the logical volume manager (LVM) subsystem. GPFS administrative scripts to each node in the cluster vary - on the volume groups containing the GPFS data - at proper times for file system operations. This GPFS operation is done without locking the disks that make up the volume group using the *varyonvg* command with the *-u* flag.

Disks for a GPFS file system now support both SSA and fiber channel attachment. Once the file system is created, it can be automatically mounted whenever the GPFS daemon is started.

The auto-mount feature assures that whenever the system and disks are up, the file system will be available.

The Concurrent Logical Volume Manager (CLVM) component of AIX is not required for a GPFS cluster in a HACMP environment. The GPFS kernel extension provides the interfaces to the operating system VNODE and virtual file system (VFS) interfaces for adding a file system. Structurally, applications make file system calls to the operating system, which presents them to the GPFS file system kernel extension. In this way, GPFS appears to applications as just another file system. The GPFS daemon performs all I/O and buffer management for GPFS. This includes read-ahead for sequential reads, and write-behind for all writes not specified as synchronous. All I/O is protected by token management, which ensures that the file system on multiple nodes honors the atomicity and provides data consistency for a file system. The daemon is a multi-threaded process with some threads dedicated to specific functions.

GPFS performs all file system functions, including metadata functions, on all members of the cluster both within a file and across different files in a file system. When an inoperative node is detected by group services, GPFS fences it out using environment-specific subsystems. This prevents any write operations that might interfere with recovery.

With this review of the variety of ways the cluster software is installed and configured concluded, it is time to switch gears and begin looking into Oracle RAC software installation in the next section.

Oracle RAC software Installation

The CRS services should be running, before beginning installation of the Oracle RAC Database software.

1. From the CD or from the software location, launch the *runInstaller* command.
2. When the OUI displays the Welcome page, click Next, and the OUI displays the Specify File Locations page as seen in Figure 6.17. In this example, Oracle Home has been set to /u01/app/oracle/product/10g/db_1. The Source field on the Specify File Locations page is pre-populated with the path to the file Oracle Database 10g products.xml.

Note: Do not install Oracle Database 10g with RAC software into the same home in which the CRS software is installed.

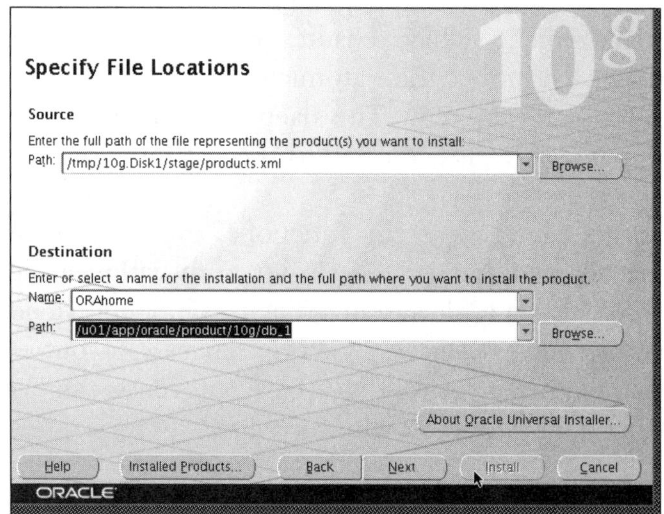

Figure 6.17: *Specify Oracle Home*

3. Next, the Specify Hardware Cluster Installation Mode page is presented. This is where an installation mode is selected. The Cluster Installation mode is selected by default when the OUI detects that the installation is being performed on a cluster. In addition, the local node is always selected for the installation. Select additional nodes that are to be part of this installation

session. In this example, three nodes in the cluster have been selected.

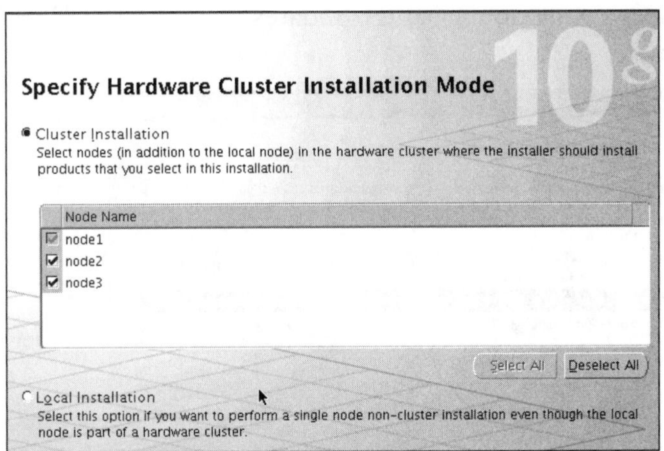

Figure 6.18: *Specify Cluster Nodes*

4. After clicking Next on the Specify Hardware Cluster Installation page, the OUI verifies that the Oracle home directory is writable on the remote nodes and that the remote nodes are operating. The OUI also re-validates user equivalence.

5. On the Install Type page, select Enterprise Edition, Standard Edition, or Custom Install type.

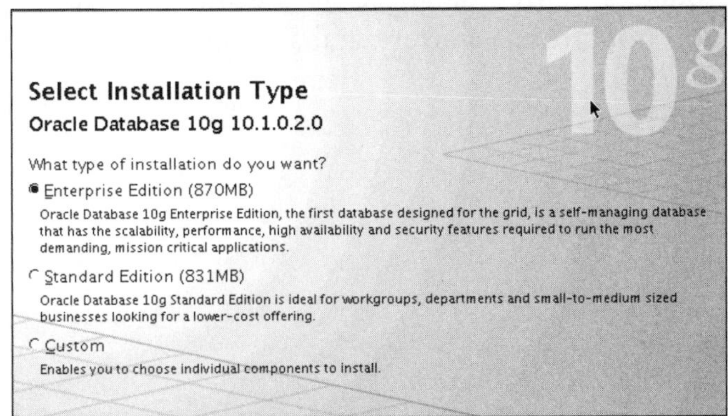

Figure 6.19: *Specify Installation Type*

6. Then the OUI displays the Prerequisite Check page. The Prerequisite Check page verifies the operating system kernel parameters or attributes and validates the ORACLE_BASE location etc.

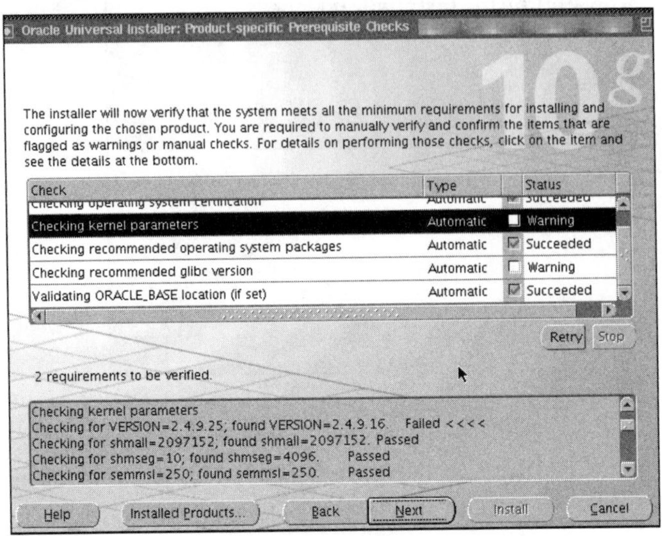

Figure 6.20: *Specify Database Configuration*

7. Next, select the Database Configuration desired. Optionally, the creation of the starter database can be skipped, as shown below in Figure 6.21. We wanted to install only the software and not build a starter database at this time, therefore we selected, 'do not create a starter database' option.

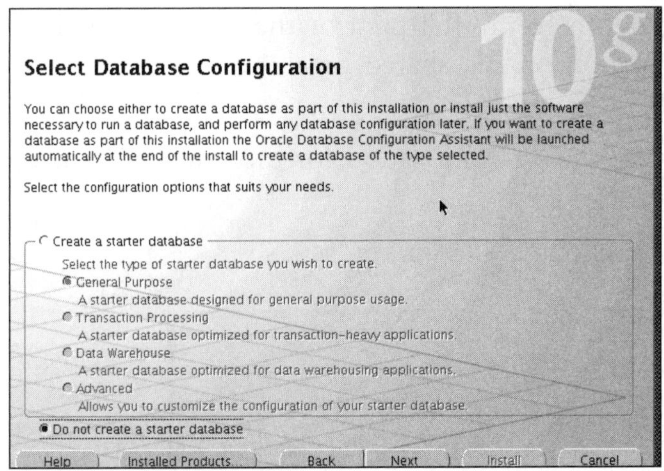

Figure 6.21: *Specify Database Configuration*

From this point, installation progress will be indicated by a progress bar.

However, if the starter database option is selected, there will be more selection pages. In the Database Configuration Options page, enter a global database name. A global database name is a name that includes the database name and database domain, such as db.us.acme.com. SID names automatically populate.

Next, OUI displays the Database Management Option for Database Control page where Grid or Local Database Control can be specified. If Grid Control is selected, Grid Management Server should be running and be accessible.

After that, OUI displays the Data Storage Option page. The following options are presented:

- Automatic Storage Management (ASM) where the disk partition locations can be specified.

- File System where the full path of the location for the data files destination on the shared or cluster file system can be specified.
- Raw devices - specify a location for the raw device mapping file.

Next, the progress bar is shown.

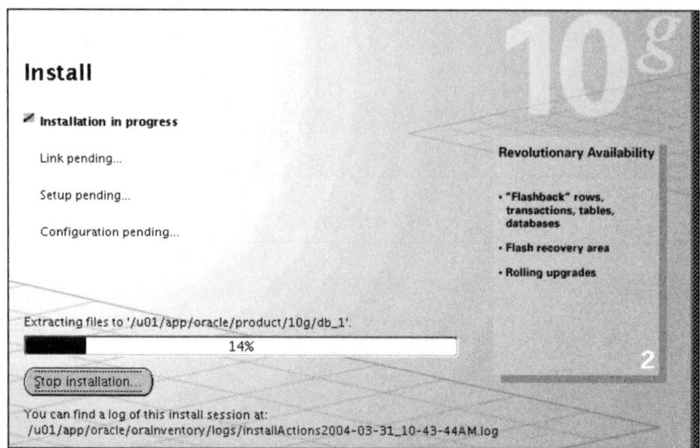

Figure 6.22: *Installation in progress*

In the end, the OUI displays a prompt to run the *root.sh* script on all the selected nodes to start the Virtual Internet Protocol Configuration Assistant (VIPCA) and display the VIPCA Welcome page. Before running *root.sh*, make sure that the display environment variables are properly set. It may be more convenient to launch the VIPCA later to formulate the appropriate services. However, note that the VIP has to be configured before starting the DBCA to create the Database.

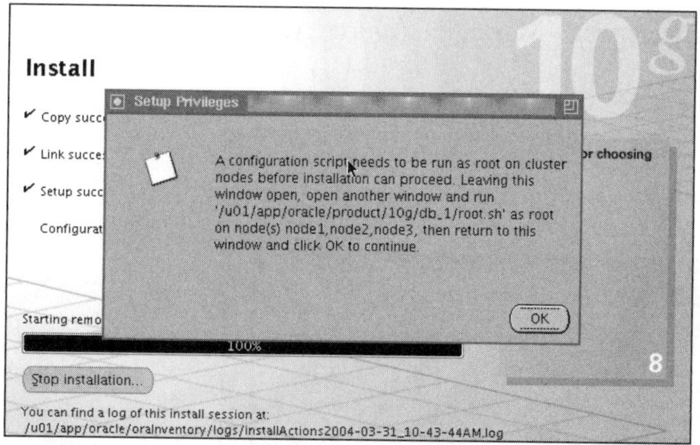

Figure 6.23: *Installation root.sh*

Virtual IP Configuration Assistant is launched by *vipca* command:

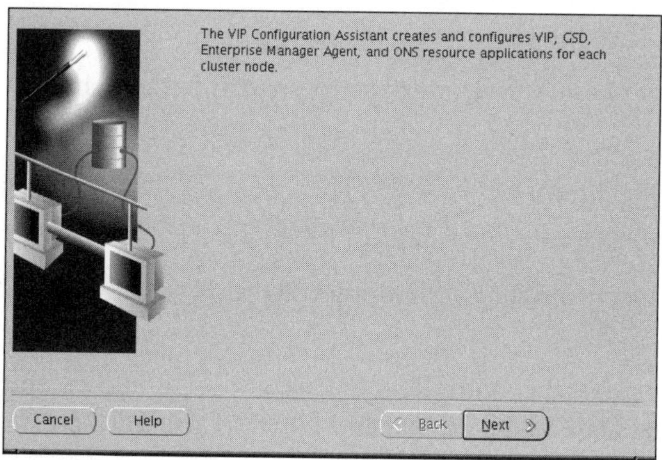

Figure 6.24: *VIP Configuration Welcome Page*

In the next page, provide the Virtual IP address, the node name, and the Virtual IP address, which will be used later by the HA services functionality. Finally, as shown the in the next figure, VIP application resources, GSD resources, ONS application resources and Enterprise Manager Agent Application resources are created.

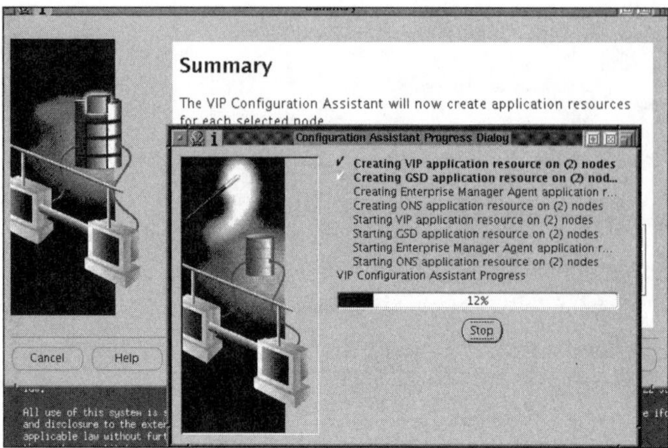

Figure 6.25: *VIP Resources Creation*

Assistants shown below (GUI interface tools) can be launched at any time.

- Net Configuration Assistant (NetCA)
- Database Configuration Assistant (DBCA)
- Virtual Internet Protocol Configuration Assistant (VIPCA)

Finally, OUI displays the completion page and also shows the port numbers associated with *isqlplus* and Ultra Search Tool etc.

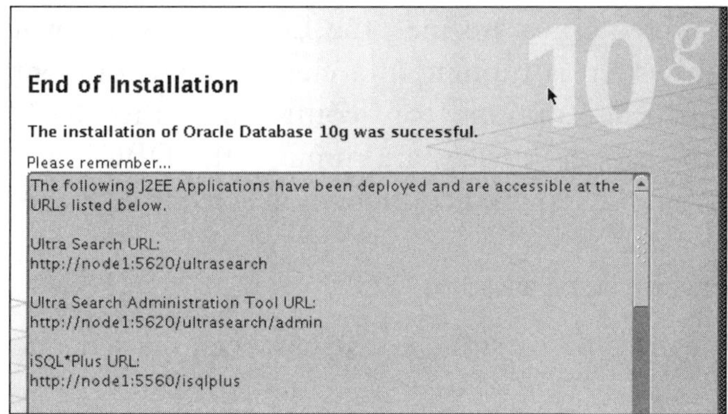

Figure 6.26: *End of Installation Page*

Next will be the creation of the Database by using the DBCA.

Oracle Database Creation

The Database Configuration Assistant (DBCA) can now be used to fully configure Real Application Clusters (RAC) environment. In order to use this new feature there are various prerequisites that must be met:

- Shared disk subsystem must in place. The details of which were covered extensively in the previous chapter. RAW partitions or Oracle Cluster File System or a certified CFS provided by the system vendor must be installed and configured. If planning to use the ASM, ASM resources (disk devices) should be available.
- Oracle Cluster Ready Services must be installed and configured. This encompasses what were formally Oracle Cluster Manager (*oracm*) and the global services daemon (GSD). In addition to GSD, the CRS starts the EVMD, CSSD, and CRSD daemons.
- The Oracle Database 10g software must be installed, as described in the previous section.

Once the above prerequisites are met, the DBCA program will recognize that the system is running in a clustered environment and will provide the options of configuring the RAC environment. If the proper services are running, the DBCA will automatically provide the required configuration screens.

The DBCA processing steps are:

1. Depending on the type of storage that has been chosen, the DBCA will:
   - If using Automatic Storage Management (ASM), then the DBCA will initialize the ASM subsystem and then start the ASM instance(s).
   - If using CFS (Cluster File System), then the DBCA will validate the data file destination to be validly shared across all the nodes that are going to be part of the cluster database.
   - If using raw devices, then the DBCA will validate the raw device tablespaces sizes and then validate their access permissions.
2. It obtains a variety of inputs from the DBA and then it creates the database.
3. It configures the Oracle network services.
4. Then, it creates and starts the high availability services.
5. Finally, it starts the listeners and database instances and then starts the high availability services.

Creating RAC Database with DBCA

Once the DBCA is invoked, the first page that the DBCA displays is the Welcome page for RAC as shown in Figure 6.27. However, the DBCA only displays this RAC specific Welcome page if it detects that the DBCA is running on a cluster node and the DBCA can communicate with Oracle Cluster Ready Services (CRS) previously installed by the OUI.

If the DBCA does not display the Welcome Page for RAC, then the DBCA was unable to detect that the clusterware (CRS) is running. If this happens, perform clusterware diagnostics by executing the *olsnodes* command. Once the DBCA RAC Welcome screen appears, create a RAC database:

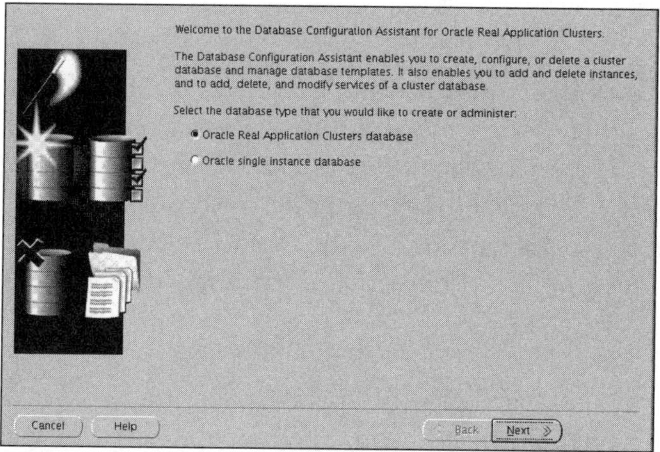

Figure 6.27: *DBCA Welcome Page for RAC*

Select the Real Application Clusters database option and click Next, and the DBCA will display the Operations page. The DBCA only enables Instance Management and Services Management if there is at least one RAC database configured on the cluster.

Next, select Create A Database and then click Next, and the DBCA will display the Node Selection page.

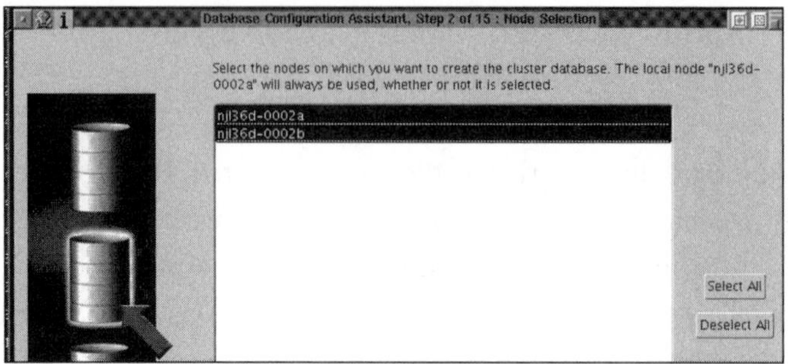

Figure 6.28: *DBCA Node Selection*

The DBCA will highlight the local node by default. The DBA must select the other nodes to configure as members of the cluster database, and then click Next. The DBCA will then display the Database Templates page. If nodes that are part of the cluster installation do not appear on the Node Selection page, perform clusterware diagnostics by executing the *olsnodes* command.

The templates on the Database Templates page are the Data Warehouse, General Purpose, and Transaction Processing preconfigured templates. These templates include data files and specially configured options for each environment. However, the New Database template does not include data files or the specially configured options. Use a template with data files to create a preconfigured database. Select a template from which to create the cluster database.

Database Configuration Assistant, Step 3 of 15 : Database Templates

Select a template from the following list to create a database:

Select	Template Name	Includes Datafiles?
	Custom Database	No
	Data Warehouse	Yes
	General Purpose	Yes
	Transaction Processing	Yes

Figure 6.29: *DBCA Database Template Selection Page*

Then click Next, and the DBCA will display the Database Identification page.

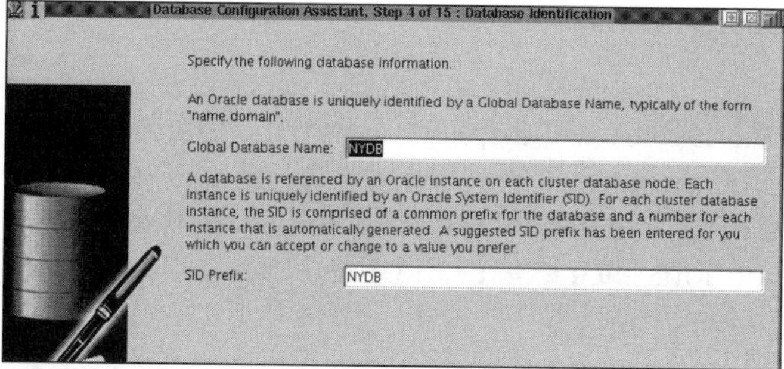

Figure 6.30: *DBCA Database Identification Page*

Then, enter the global database name and the Oracle system identifier (SID) prefix, as well as the SYS and SYSTEM user passwords, for the cluster database.

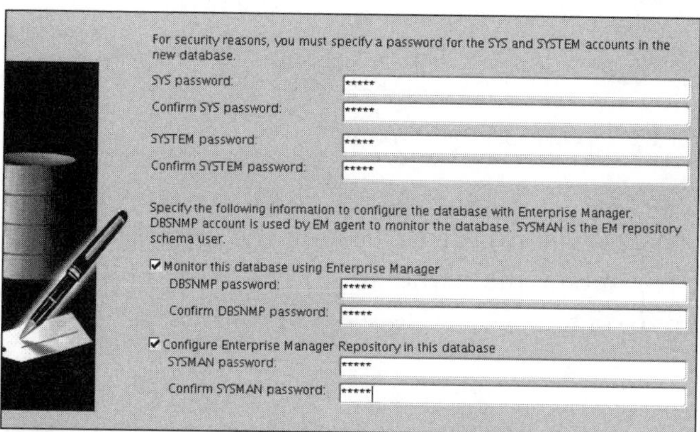

Figure 6.31: *DBCA Database Credentials Page*

Note: The global database name is limited to eight characters in length and must begin with an alphabetical character. The SID prefix must be between one and five characters in length and also begin with an alphabetical character. Allow space for as many characters as are required for the numeric designations of the instances, for example, 1-9 is one character; 10-99 would be two characters. The DBCA uses the SID prefix to generate a unique value for the oracle_sid for each instance.

Click Next, and the DBCA will display the Storage Options page. Use the Storage Options page to select a storage type for database creation. The Cluster File System option is the default. Select a storage option, click Next, and the DBCA displays the Database Components page.

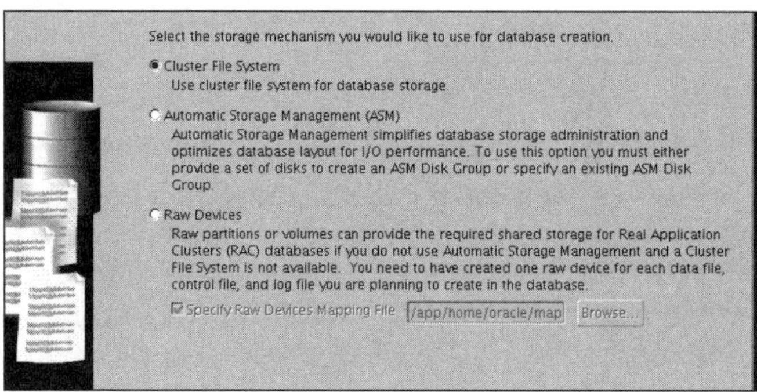

Figure 6.32: *DBCA Database Storage Options*

At this point a prompt will appear requesting the Disk Discovery String and ASM parameter file name and other ASM credentials as shown in Figure 6.33.

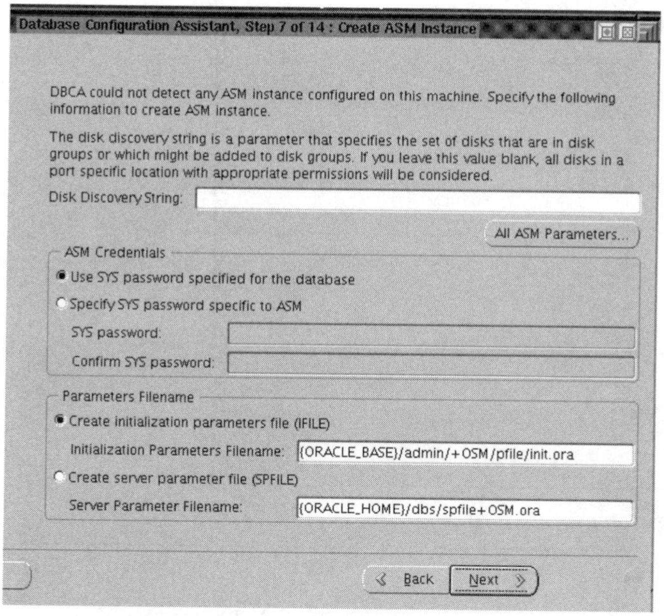

Figure 6.33: *DBCA ASM Instance Page*

From this page, select the database components that are required for the database and their respective default tablespaces, then click Next, and the DBCA will display the Connection Options page.

On this page, enter the database connection choices, then click Next, and the DBCA will display the DBCA Database Services page. In this example, a service called SALES has been created, which uses two instances with equal preference for load balancing and follows the basic TAF policy.

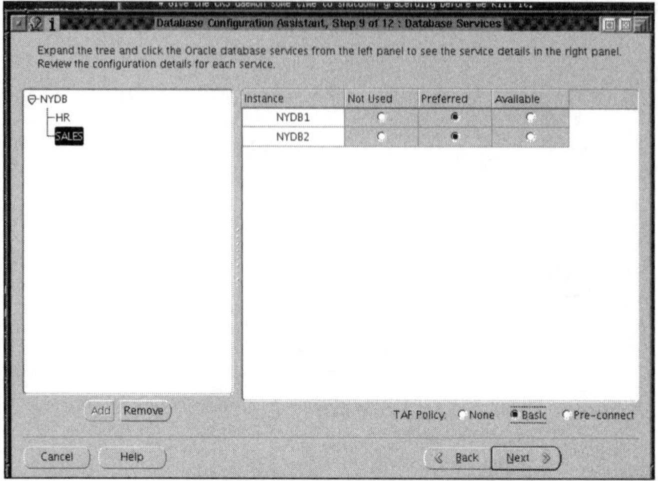

Figure 6.34: *DBCA Database Services Page*

To create the required services on the DBCA Database Services page, expand the Services tree. Oracle displays the global database name in the top left-hand corner of the page. Select the global database name and then click Add to add services to the database. Enter a service name in the Add a Service dialog and click OK.

The service name will appear under the global database name. Select the service name and the DBCA will display the service preferences for the service on the right-hand side of the DBCA Database Services page. Change the instance preference (preferred or available) and total application failover (TAF) policies for the service as needed. Repeat this procedure for each service and when configuration of the services for the database is complete, click Next. The DBCA will now display the Initialization Parameters page.

Now, select the File Locations tab on the Initialization Parameters page.

If Create server parameter file (*spfile*)is selected, then it may be necessary to modify the location for the server parameter file depending on the type of file system used as described for the following conditions:

- If using a cluster file system, or if a single-node RAC environment exists, then the server parameter file can be placed on the file system.
- If not using a cluster file system and you not creating a single-node RAC database, then a raw device name for the location of the server parameter file must be entered in the Server Parameter Filename field in the center of the Initialization Parameters page.

Next, select the Archive tab on the Initialization Parameters page to see or check the archive log destination settings.

Now, click the Advanced Parameters tab and the DBCA will display the All Initialization Parameters dialog. Carefully review the parameter settings displayed in this dialog because the DBCA will configure these settings in the server parameter file. Instance-specific parameter settings for the RAC database appear at the bottom of this dialog. The *sid* prefixes for these entries will appear in the left-hand column.

To review the instance-specific parameter settings, scroll downward using the scroll bar on the right-hand side of the dialog box.

Note: Using the DBCA you cannot specify archive log destinations for each instance in the cluster.

Use the check box in the Included (Y/N) column of the dialog to indicate whether the DBCA should place the parameter setting in the server parameter file. The DBCA will only place a parameter entry into the server parameter file if the entry displays a check mark in the Included (Y/N) column on the All Initialization Parameters dialog. Also note the following about the All Initialization Parameters dialog:

- The SID in the Instance column cannot be modified.
- Although the self-tuning parameters can be altered with this dialog, setting these parameters to inappropriate values will disable the Oracle self-tuning features.
- Instance-specific values for global parameters cannot be specified with the DBCA.

Once all entries are complete in the All Initialization Parameters dialog, click on Close. Make sure that entries for the File Locations tab and the other tabs are correct for the RAC database, and then click Next. The DBCA will display the Database Storage page.

If preconfigured database template was selected, such as the General Purpose template, then the DBCA will display the control files, datafiles, and redo logs on the Database Storage page.

Select the folder and the file name underneath the folder to edit the file name. However, if the New Database template is selected, the template is without datafiles, and the DBCA displays the control files, tablespaces, datafiles, and redo logs. To change the tablespace properties, such as the datafile or the tablespace size, click the tablespaces icon to expand the object tree and click the tablespace.

The tablespace property dialog appears on the right-hand side. Make necessary changes and click OK. Platform-specific topics for entering file names in the Database Storage page are:

- For UNIX-based platforms, if the *dbca_raw_config* environment variable is not set, then the DBCA displays default datafile names. Override values must be entered for these names to provide raw device names for each control file, datafile, and redo log group file.
- For Windows-based platforms, if the default symbolic links exist, then the DBCA replaces the default datafiles with these symbolic link names and displays them in the Storage page. If the symbolic links do not exist, then the DBCA displays the default file system datafile file names on the Storage page. In this case, replace the default datafile file names with the symbolic link names.

After completing the entries on the Database Storage page, click Next, and the DBCA displays the Creation Options page. Select one of the following database options and then click Finish.

- Create Database: This option creates the database.
- Save as a Database Template – This option creates a template that records the database structure, including the supplied inputs, initialization parameters, and so on. This template can be used later to create a database.
- Generate Database Creation Scripts – This option generates database creation scripts.

The DBCA only displays the last option if the New Database template was selected. After clicking Finish, the DBCA will display a Summary dialog. Review the Summary dialog information and click OK. To cancel database creation at this point, click on Cancel.

After completion of above steps, the DBCA:

- Creates the RAC data dictionary views
- Creates an operative RAC database

- Configures the network for the cluster database
- Starts the services if on a Windows-based platform
- Starts the listeners and database instances and then starts the high availability services

Now a new database exists. It can be accessed via Oracle SQL*Plus or other applications designed to work with an Oracle RAC database. The above method is a generic procedure that is applicable irrespective of the cluster platform.

Database Creation Manually

When the database is created manually, there is complete control over the process. Tablespaces can be added or reduced and the flow of the creation process can be managed. Here are the steps to be followed to create a Real Application Clusters database manually:

1. Make *init.ora* in the $ORACLE_HOME/dbs directory. On Windows, this file is in $ORACLE_HOME\database. To simplify, *init.ora* can be copied to *init.ora* and the file modified. Remember that the control file must be pointing to a pre-existing raw device or cluster file system location or ASM storage pool. Path names, file names, and sizes will need to be modified.

   Here are some example parameter settings for the first instance:

```
Cluster-Wide Parameters for Database "RAC":

db_block_size=8192
db_cache_size=52428800
background_dump_dest=/u01/app/oracle/product/10.0.2/rdbms/log
core_dump_dest=/u01/app/oracle/product/10.0.2/rdbms/log
user_dump_dest=/u01/app/oracle/product/10.0.2/rdbms/log
timed_statistics=TRUE
control_files=("/dev/RAC/control_01.ctl",
"/dev/RAC/control_02.ctl")
```

```
db_name=RAC
shared_pool_size=52428800
sort_area_size=524288
undo_management=AUTO
cluster_database=true
cluster_database_instances=2
remote_listener=LISTENERS_RAC

Instance Specific Parameters for Instance "RACDB1":
instance_name=RACDB1
instance_number=1
local_listener=LISTENER_RACDB1
thread=1
undo_tablespace=UNDOTBS1
```

2. Run the following *sqlplus* command to connect to the database:

```
sqlplus /nolog
connect / as sysdba
```

3. Startup the database in NOMOUNT mode:

4. Create the database. If the raw devices are in use, they must be pre-created. Path names, file names, and sizes will need to be modified as needed.

Use the following script to create the database.

```
SQL> startup nomount

Then execute this code:

CREATE DATABASE racdb
MAXINSTANCES  8
MAXLOGHISTORY 100
MAXLOGFILES   64
MAXLOGMEMBERS 6
MAXDATAFILES 100
DATAFILE
'/data/oradata/aultdb1/test/system01.dbf' SIZE 300M REUSE
AUTOEXTEND ON NEXT 10240K MAXSIZE UNLIMITED
EXTENT MANAGEMENT LOCAL
SYSAUX DATAFILE '/data/oradata/aultdb1/test/sysaux01.dbf' SIZE
200M REUSE AUTOEXTEND ON NEXT 10240K MAXSIZE UNLIMITED
DEFAULT TEMPORARY TABLESPACE TEMP TEMPFILE
'/data/oradata/aultdb1/test/temp01.dbf' SIZE 20M
REUSE AUTOEXTEND ON NEXT 640K MAXSIZE UNLIMITED
EXTENT MANAGEMENT LOCAL
UNDO TABLESPACE "UNDOTBS1" DATAFILE
'/data/oradata/aultdb1/test/undotbs01.dbf' SIZE 200M REUSE
AUTOEXTEND ON NEXT 5120K MAXSIZE UNLIMITED
```

```
CHARACTER SET WE8ISO8859P1
NATIONAL CHARACTER SET AL16UTF16
LOGFILE GROUP 1
('/data/oradata/aultdb1/test/redo01.log') SIZE 10240K,
GROUP 2 ('/data/oradata/aultdb1/test/redo02.log') SIZE 10240K,
GROUP 3 ('/data/oradata/aultdb1/test/redo03.log') SIZE 10240K
USER SYS IDENTIFIED BY "password"
USER SYSTEM IDENTIFIED BY "password";
```

5. Now, Create the USERS tablespace:

```
CREATE TABLESPACE "USERS" LOGGING DATAFILE
'/dev/RAC/users_01_125.dbf' SIZE 120M REUSE
NEXT 1280K MAXSIZE UNLIMITED EXTENT MANAGEMENT LOCAL;
```

6. Then create a temporary tablespace:

```
CREATE TEMPORARY TABLESPACE "TEMP" TEMPFILE
'/dev/RAC/temp_01_50.dbf' SIZE 40M REUSE
```

7. Now Create a 2nd UNDO tablespace for the use of second instance:

```
CREATE UNDO TABLESPACE "UNDOTBS2"
DATAFILE '/dev/RAC/undotbs_02_210.dbf' SIZE 200M
REUSE NEXT 5120K MAXSIZE UNLIMITED;
```

8. Run the necessary scripts to build views, synonyms, etc.

   The primary scripts that must be run are:

   - CATALOG.SQL--creates the views of data dictionary tables and the dynamic performance views.
   - CATPROC.SQL--establishes the usage of PL/SQL functionality and creates many of the PL/SQL Oracle-supplied packages.
   - CATCLUST.SQL--creates RAC specific views. (The CATPARR.SQL script is still provided but will not be maintained.)

9. Edit *init.ora* and set appropriate values for the 2nd instance on the 2nd Node. Names may need to be modified:

```
instance_name=RACDB2
instance_number=2
local_listener=LISTENER_RAC2
thread=2
```

10. undo_tablespace=UNDOTBS2From the first instance, run the following command:

```
alter database
add logfile thread 2
group 4 ('/dev/RAC/redo2_01_100.dbf') size 100M ,
group 5 ('/dev/RAC/redo2_02_100.dbf') size 100M ,
group 6 ('/dev/RAC/redo2_03_100.dbf') size 100M ;
```

11. Then make thread available by:

```
alter database enable public thread 2;
```

12. Start the second instance if the cluster configuration is up and running. At this point, the Oracle database is installed, patched, and running on all members of the cluster.

Notice that the SYSAUX tablespace is specified with the CREATE DATABASE command. This is demonstrated in the example database creation script.

The SYSAUX tablespace is required in all new 10g databases. Only the SYSAUX tablespace data file location is specified. Oracle specifies the remainder of the tablespace properties including:

- online
- permanent
- read write
- extent management local
- segment space management auto

If a datafile is specified for the SYSTEM tablespace, then one must be specified for the SYSAUX tablespace as well. If one is not specified, then the CREATE DATABASE command will fail. The only exception is for an Oracle Managed File system. During any update of a database to Oracle Database 10g, a SYSAUX tablespace must be created or the upgrade will fail. The SYSAUX tablespace has the same security profile as the SYSTEM tablespace. However, loss of the SYSAUX tablespace will not result in a database crash, only the functional loss of the schemas it contains.

Conclusion

In this chapter, many installation steps and configuration issues have been covered. Oracle RAC is supported on many diverse platforms and operating systems. The overall steps in creating a cluster, installing cluster software, creating necessary storage volumes, and preparing the system environment for creating the RAC database have been highlighted.

As Oracle releases new versions, and new certified vender combinations are announced, configuration and installation details may change. Current installation and configuration details are available at Oracle.

The system administrator generally handles storage configuration and operating environment preparation. If the SA and DBA team plan and act as a cohesive team, superior results can be achieved in a shorter amount of time.

Cache Fusion and Instance Recovery

CHAPTER **7**

"I think that it's an issue with Oracle RAC cache fusion."

Introduction

The topics that will be covered in this chapter include the nature, internals, and working mechanism of cache fusion technology along with the following subjects:

- Virtualization of multiple caches into a single cache.
- How the data blocks are moved across among multiple SGAs in a multi-node environment
- Synchronization of resource access.
- Resource coordination methodology.
- Re-mastering of resources in the event of unforeseen failure of any instance

A good place to start is with an overview of cache fusion.

Cache Fusion

Cache fusion is an important technology that transforms Oracle Real Application Cluster System (RAC) into a high-performance database cluster. The cache fusion method extends the scale out capabilities to applications that use Oracle RAC without requiring any additional investment in modifications to the existing applications.

A RAC system equipped with low-latency and high speed interconnect technology enables the buffer cache of each node in the cluster to fuse and form into a single virtual global cache, hence the term cache fusion. The cache fusion architecture creates a shared-cache and provides a single cache image or view to the applications. Internals are transparent to the applications.

From a functional viewpoint, an instance in a RAC system is equivalent to a single instance of Oracle. It has all the bells and whistles of a single instance, which the DBA(s) understand very well. The extension of multiple cache buffers into a single, fused global cache improves scalability, reliability, and availability.

While cache fusion provides Oracle users with an expanded database cache for queries and updates of I/O operations, the improved performance depends greatly on the efficiency of the inter-node message passing mechanism that handles the data block transfers.

Evolution of Cache Fusion

Before looking deeper into the implementation of cache fusion in Oracle 9i RAC, some time needs to be taken to look at the implementation in the 8i release. Oracle Release 8i (Oracle

Parallel Server) introduced the initial phase of cache fusion. The data blocks were transferred from the SGA of one instance to the SGA of another instance without the need to write the blocks to disk. This was aimed at reducing the ping overhead of data blocks. However, the partial implementation of cache fusion in 8i could help only in certain conditions, as indicated in Table 7.1.

REQUESTING INSTANCE	HOLDING INSTANCE	DIRTY BLOCK EXISTS IN HOLDING INSTANCE	CACHE COHERENCY METHOD
For Read	Read	Yes	Cache Fusion
For Read	Write	No	Soft Ping (read from disk)
For Read	Write	Yes	Cache Fusion
For Write	Write	Does Not matter	Ping (force disk write)

Table 7.1: *The Methods of maintaining cache coherency*

Oracle 8i (Oracle Parallel Server) had a background process called the Block Server Process (BSP), which facilitated cache fusion. BSP was responsible for transferring the required blocks directly from the owning instance to the buffer cache of the requested instance.

For read/write operations, if the block was already written to disk by the holding instance, the requested block was read from the disk. It involved a soft ping or an I/O-less ping. If the block was available on the holding instance buffer, the BSP process prepared a consistent read (CR) image of the data block. It was then sent to the requesting instance.

A write/write operation invariably involved the ping of the data block. When the ping occurred, the holding instance wrote to disk and downgraded the lock mode. Then, the requesting instance acquired the necessary lock mode and read from the disk. This frequent pinging hurt the performance of the OPS database. With the full implementation of cache fusion in release 9i, all these ping, soft ping, and false ping issues have been solved. With the RAC system release in 9i, cache fusion fully resolves write/write conflicts using the new architecture of resource coordination and global cache service.

Nature of Cache Fusion

Multi-node Oracle RAC systems are comprised of multiple instances with each instance residing on an individual node or server. Each Oracle instance in the cluster has a dedicated set of memory structures including background processes and system global areas (SGA) that exist irrespective of another node's instance. Thus, each node's instance has its local buffer cache. When applications or users connect and process their SQL operations, they primarily connect to one of the nodes. When the user processes fetch and access data blocks, the scope of such activity is confined to the SGA of the connected instance.

However, as the database is mounted with multiple instances, data blocks may exist on any of the instances or any instance may fetch the data blocks as needed by the user processes. In other words, when a user process is looking for a set of data blocks to satisfy the SQL operation requirement, the same set of blocks or some of the blocks may already be available in another node's instance. This highlights an important fact of a RAC system. As opposed to a single stand-alone Oracle instance, there are multiple server locations in a RAC system where data blocks reside. Thus, there are several cache buffers dealing with the same physical database objects.

This is where the method of cache fusion plays a key role. For all practical purposes, multiple buffer caches join and act as if they were a single entity. As shown in Figure 7.1, cache buffers from three nodes are fused together to form a single entity and share data blocks. Maintaining consistency among the cached versions of data blocks in multiple instances is called cache coherency. Cache fusion treats multiple buffer caches as one joint global cache, solving data consistency issues internally, without any impact on the application code or design.

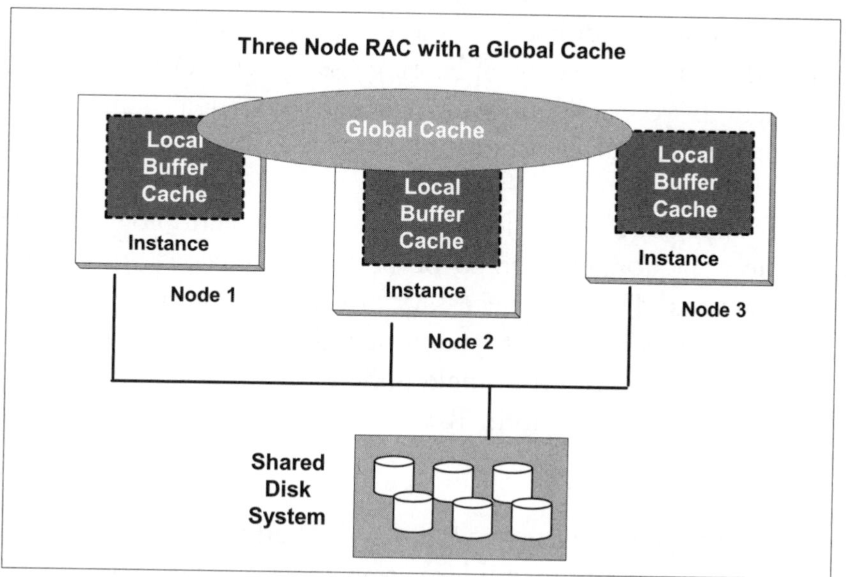

Figure 7.1: *Global Cache – Cache Fusion in a three-node cluster*

Benefits of Cache Fusion

Oracle RAC, with its multiple instances, is able to provide more resources through multiple system global areas (SGA). Cache fusion technology makes it easier to process a very high number of concurrent users and SQL operations without compromising data consistency. It adheres to Oracle's multi-version consistency model and ensures data integrity and data consistency across the instances.

Cache fusion in 9i, implemented fully, creates an environment where users are able to utilize any instance in the cluster without giving undue preference for a particular instance. There is no need for the extra effort of partitioning data access across nodes, as required in earlier versions of parallel servers. Load balancing is more effective in such an environment.

As a result, very high scalability of database performance can be achieved simply by adding nodes to the cluster. RAC also enables better database capacity planning and conserves capital investment by consolidating many databases on a single large database, thus reducing administrative overhead.

Another advantage realized with cache fusion technology is that applications no longer need to be partitioned according to data access patterns. This was necessary in earlier versions of Oracle parallel databases in order to avoid or reduce data-block pinging. A scalable application on a single-node Oracle server will be just as flexible on a multi-node RAC, even in different workload situations.

However, scalability performance may be better with a workload of minimal cross-instance block transfers (OLTP operations) compared to a workload of large cross-instance block transfers. Where there is a large cross-instance transfer of resources, there is a certain overhead due to lock conversions and block transfers from one cache to another.

The advantage of improved load balancing can be used to leverage application performance. User connections can randomly access any instance in the cluster. Depending on the node capacity, instances can be balanced effectively. Contention for server resources, such as the CPU and memory, is reduced.

Concurrency and Consistency

Database systems provide data concurrency by enabling multiple users to access the same data without compromising data consistency. Data consistency means that each user sees a consistent view of the data, including the visible changes made by the users' own transactions, as well as the transactions of other users. Oracle automatically supplies a query with read-consistent data, so that all data that the query sees comes from a single point in time (statement-level read consistency).

Optionally, Oracle can provide read consistency to all queries in a transaction (transaction-level read consistency). Oracle maintains undo records to manage such consistent views. The undo segments contain the old data values that have been changed by uncommitted or recently committed transactions.

In a RAC system, users can connect with multiple instances to run database queries. Typically, users will be connected to different nodes but access the same set of data or data blocks. This situation demands that the data consistency, formerly confined to a single instance, be effectively extended to multiple instances. Therefore, buffer cache coherence from multiple instances must be maintained.

Instances require three main types of concurrency:

- Concurrent reads on multiple instances – When users on two different instances need to read the same set of blocks.
- Concurrent reads and writes on different instances - A user intends to read a data block that was recently modified, and the read can be for the current version of the block or for a read-consistent previous version.

- Concurrent writes on different instances – When the same set of data blocks are modified by different users on different instances.

Cache Coherency

Whether the database is a single-instance stand-alone system or a multi-instance RAC system, maintaining data consistency is a fundamental requirement. If data blocks are already available in the local buffer cache, then they are immediately available for user processes. And, if they are available in another instance within the cluster, they will be transferred into the local buffer cache.

Maintaining the consistency of data blocks in the buffer caches of multiple instances is called cache coherency. The Global Cache Service (GCS), implemented by a set of Oracle processes requires an instance to acquire cluster-wide data before a block can be modified or read. In this way, cache coherency is ensured and maintained. This resource can be explained in terms of enqueue and/or lock.

GCS synchronizes global cache access, allowing only one instance at a time to modify the block. Thus, cache coherency is maintained in the RAC system by coordinating buffer caches located on separate instances. GCS ensures that the data blocks cached in different cache buffers are maintained globally. That is why some people prefer to call cache fusion a diskless cache coherency mechanism. This is true in a sense, because the previous Oracle parallel server version (OPS) utilized forced disk writes to maintain cache coherency.

Global Cache Service

GCS is the main controlling process for cache fusion. It tracks the location and status (mode and role) of the data blocks, as well as the access privileges of the various instances. GCS guarantees data integrity by employing global access levels. It maintains block modes for data blocks in the global role. It is also responsible for block transfers between instances. As shown in Figure 7.2, upon a request from an instance, GCS organizes the block shipping and the appropriate lock mode conversions. Various background processes, such as global cache service processes (LMSn) and the global enqueues service daemon (LMD), implement the global cache service.

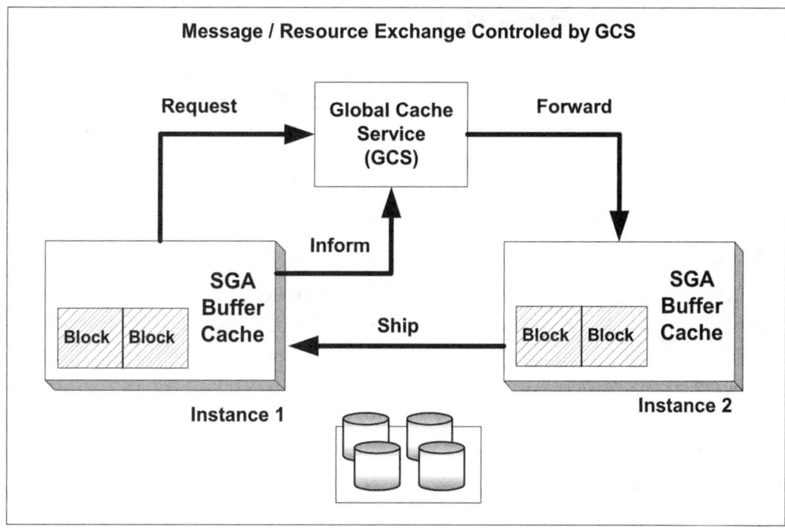

Figure 7.2: *Message/Resource Exchange controlled by GCS*

Before going further into a detailed examination of the cache fusion mechanism and how GCS operations are performed in different scenarios, the next section will take a look at and recap some basic SGA structures and locking concepts. A more detailed review of SGA structures was provided in Chapter 4.

SGA Components and Locking

The Oracle database is accessed through an instance. The combination of SGA (System Global Area) with one or more Oracle processes constitutes an instance. After the instance is started, the database is associated with it. This process is called database mounting. In the case of a RAC system, the database can be associated with multiple instances. The main purpose of the SGA is to store data in memory for quick access and for processing.

SGA – System Global Area

The instance is the structure or entity with which application users connect. The SGA is a group of shared memory structures that contain data and control information for the database instance. Oracle allocates memory for an SGA system whenever the instance is started. Multiple instances can be associated with a database in a RAC system, and each instance has its own SGA. The SGA contains five main areas.

- The fixed area.
- The variable area.
- The database buffer cache.
- The log buffer.
- The resource directory for a RAC system.

The fixed area of the SGA contains several thousand atomic variables. These are small data structures, such as latches and pointers, which refer to other areas of the SGA. The size of the fixed area is static. It also contains general information about the state of the database and the instance which the background processes need to access.

The variable part of the SGA is made up of a large pool and a shared pool. All memory in the large pool is dynamically allocated, whereas the shared pool contains both dynamically managed memory and a permanent memory. The database buffer cache is where database block copies are held for processing. All user processes concurrently connected to the instance share access to the database buffer cache. There are many groups of buffers within the SGA.

Shared Pool and Large Pool

The shared pool segment of the SGA contains three major areas: the library cache, the dictionary cache, and buffers for parallel execution messages.

Library Cache - The library cache includes the shared SQL areas, private SQL areas (in shared server), PL/SQL procedures and packages, and control structures such as library cache handles, locks, synonym translations, and dependency tracking information. It contains parse trees and execution plans for shareable SQL statements, as well as pseudo code for PL/SQL program units. All users access the shared SQL areas.

Dictionary Cache – Includes the usernames, segment information, profile data, tablespace information, and the sequence numbers. The dictionary cache also contains descriptive information or metadata about the schema objects. Oracle uses this metadata when parsing SQL cursors or during the compilation of PL/SQL programs.

The dictionary cache is also known as the row cache because it holds the data in rows instead of buffers. It also holds entire blocks of data. This helps to reduce physical access to the data dictionary tables from the system tablespace, and also enables fine-grained locking of individual data dictionary rows.

The large pool is an optional area. If the *large_pool_size* parameter is set, then the large pool is configured as a separate heap within a variable area of the SGA. The large pool is not a part of the shared pool.

Using the large pool instead of the shared pool decreases fragmentation of the shared pool. Unlike the shared pool, the large pool does not have an LRU list. Oracle does not attempt to age memory out of the large pool.

The large pool is useful to allocate large memory allocations for:

- Session memory for the shared server and the Oracle XA interface that is used where transactions interact with more than one database.
- I/O server processes.
- Oracle backup and restore operations - recovery manager can use the large pool to cache I/O buffers during backup and restore operations.
- Parallel execution message buffers, when the initialization parameter *parallel_automatic_tuning* is set to TRUE.

Redo Log Buffers

A log buffer is a circular buffer in the SGA that holds information about changes made to the database. This information is stored in the redo entries. Redo entries contain the information necessary to reconstruct or redo changes made to the database by insert, update, delete, create, alter, or drop operations. Redo entries are primarily used for database recovery as necessary.

The server processes generate redo data into the log buffer as they make changes to the data blocks in the buffer. LGWR subsequently writes entries from the redo log buffer to the online redo log.

Database Buffer Cache

The database buffer cache holds copies of data blocks read from the data files. The term data block is used to describe a block containing table data, index data, clustered data, and so on. Basically, it is a block that contains data. All user processes concurrently connected to the instance share access to the database buffer cache. The database buffer cache is logically segmented into multiple sets. This reduces contention on multiprocessor systems.

This area of the SGA contains only the buffers themselves and not their control structures. For each buffer, there is a corresponding buffer header in the variable area of the SGA.

Program Global Area (PGA)

A Program Global Area (PGA) is a memory region that contains data and control information for a server process. It is a non-shared memory region created by Oracle when a server process is started. Access to the PGA is exclusive to that server process and it is read and written only by Oracle code acting on its behalf. It contains a private SQL area and a session memory area.

A private SQL area contains data such as bind information and runtime memory structures. Each session that issues a SQL statement has a private SQL area. Session memory is the memory allocated to hold a session's variables (logon information) and other information related to the session. For a shared server, the session memory is shared and not private.

Buffer Cache Management

The database buffer cache is organized in two lists: the write list and the least-recently-used (LRU) list. The write list holds dirty buffers, which contain data that has been modified but has not yet been written to disk. The LRU list holds free buffers, pinned buffers, and dirty buffers that have not yet been moved to the write list. Free buffers do not contain any useful data and are available for use. Pinned buffers are buffers that are currently being accessed.

When an Oracle process requires data, it searches the buffer cache, finds the data blocks, and then uses the data. This is known as a cache hit. If it cannot find the data, then it must be obtained from the data file. In this case, it finds a free buffer to accommodate the data block by scanning the LRU list, starting at the least-recently-used from the end of the list. The process searches either until it finds a free buffer or until it has searched the threshold limit of buffers.

When the user process is performing a full table scan, it reads the data blocks into buffers and places them on the LRU end instead of the MRU end of the LRU list. This is because a fully scanned table is usually needed only briefly and the blocks should be moved out quickly.

What Is a Dirty Block?

Whenever a server process changes or modifies a data block, it becomes a dirty block. Once a server process makes changes to the data block, the user may commit transactions, or transactions may not be committed for quite some time. In either case, the dirty block is not immediately written back to disk.

Writing dirty blocks to disk takes place under the following two conditions:

- When a server process cannot find a clean, reusable buffer after scanning a threshold number of buffers, then the database writer process writes the dirty blocks to disk.
- When the checkpoint takes place, the database writer process writes the dirty blocks to disk.

Multi-Version Consistency Model

Oracle's multi-version consistency model architecture distinguishes between a current data block and one or more consistent read (CR) versions of the same block. It is important to understand the difference between the current block and the CR block. The current block contains changes for all the committed and yet-to-be-committed transactions. A consistent read (CR) block represents a consistent snapshot of the data from a previous point in time. Applying undo/rollback segment information produces consistent read versions. Thus, a single data block can reside in many buffer caches under shared resources with different versions.

Multi-version data blocks help to achieve read consistency. The read consistency model guarantees that the data block seen by a statement is consistent with respect to a single point in time and does not change during the statement execution. Readers of data do not wait for other writer's data or for other readers of the same data. At the same time, writers do not wait for other readers for the same data. Only writers wait for other writers if they attempt to write. As mentioned earlier, the undo (rollback) segment provides the required information to construct the read-consistent data blocks. In case of a multi-instance system, like the RAC database, the requirement for the same data block may arise from another instance. To support this type of requirement, past images of the data blocks are created within the buffer cache. Past images will be covered later in the chapter.

Process Architecture

Oracle uses several processes to execute the different parts of Oracle code and to spawn additional processes for the users. Whenever a user connects to the database, a new server process is created on behalf of the user session.

Functions of the server process include the following:

- Parse and execute SQL statements issued through the application.
- Read the necessary data blocks from the disk data files into the shared database buffers of the SGA, if the blocks are not already present in the SGA.
- Interact and return results in such a way that the application can process the information.

There are many additional processes that are automatically spawned whenever the instance starts. These processes are called background processes, and they perform the Oracle kernel functions.

Locking Mechanism

Locking is another important requirement of a multi-version consistency model. Oracle also uses a locking mechanism to control concurrent access to the data blocks. Locks help prevent destructive interaction between users accessing data blocks.

As seen earlier, when a user intends to update a data block that has already been updated by another user, but is still in an uncommitted state, the update event has to wait. Without a lock mechanism, the data integrity would have been lost in this case.

Locks also ensure that the data being viewed or updated by a user is not changed (by other users) until the user is finished using the data.

In the case of a RAC system, new and improved components or services namely, the Global Cache Service (GCS) and Global Enqueue Service (GES)) handle the lock and access management functions better than the earlier Oracle Parallel Server distributed lock manager (DLM). GES is covered in more detail later in this chapter.

RAC Components

When Oracle reads a data block into the cache, it opens a GCS resource to coordinate concurrent access by multiple instances. Oracle coordinates and converts the resource into different modes and roles, depending on the following:

- The data block accessed will be modified or read.
- A data block exists in the cache of only one instance or in multiple caches.

Thus, a resource is a concurrency control mechanism on the data blocks. It is also called a GCS resource

In a stand-alone Oracle instance, various locks are used to control data integrity and concurrency. Similarly, the multi-instance RAC architecture deals with cached data block mode roles and the controlling access levels. The cached data blocks acquire a global nature.

GCS resources comprise the concurrency control mechanism on data blocks. They include enqueues involving the transaction locks, table locks, library cache locks, and the dictionary cache locks. Global Enqueue resources are normally held for a very short time and then quickly released. For example, the TX locks are acquired whenever a transaction starts. They are released immediately after the transaction commits or rolls back. Figure 7.3 shows the main groups of resources involved in the synchronization process.

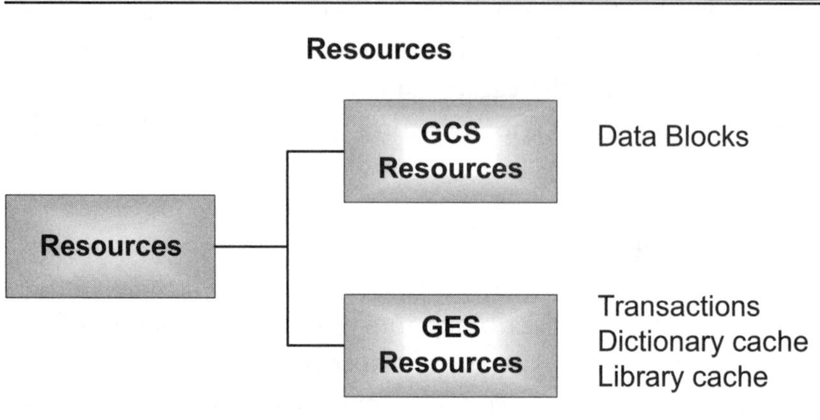

Figure 7.3: *Resources for Coordination*

Now, the three main components, the global cache service, global enqueue service, and the global resource directory, will be examined more closely.

Global Cache Service

The main function of the global cache service (GCS) is to track the status and location of the data blocks. Status is the resource role and the resource mode. The GCS is the main mechanism by which cache coherency among the multiple caches is maintained.

GCS maintains the modes for blocks in the global role and is responsible for block transfers between the instances. The LMS processes handle the GCS messages and carry out the bulk of the GCS processing. GCS resource coordination is explained in detail in later sections.

Global Enqueue Service

The global enqueue service (GES) tracks the status of all Oracle enqueuing mechanisms. This involves all non-cache fusion intra-instance operations. The GES performs concurrency control on dictionary cache locks, library cache locks, and transactions. It performs this operation for resources that are accessed by more than one instance.

Enqueues

What exactly is an enqueue? Enqueues are shared memory structures that serialize access to the database resources. For example, when a user updates a row and gets a row-level lock, a TX enqueue is created for that user. If another user subsequently attempts to update that same row, that user's session will block (wait on) the enqueue that the initial user created. They are sometimes referred to as positive waits.

Enqueues are local to one instance, if real application clusters are not enabled. When the real application cluster is enabled, the enqueues can be global to the database. Enqueues are comprised of transaction locks, DML locks, SCN locks, etc.

Enqueues are associated with a session or a transaction. They are held longer than the latches, have finer granularity, more modes than the latches, and protect more database resources. For example, when a table lock is requested, the request is assigned to an enqueue. Oracle can use enqueues in any of three modes: null (N) mode, shared (S) mode, or exclusive (X) mode.

The GES controls access to data files and control files but not for the data blocks. GES processing includes the coordination for enqueues other than the data blocks.

The resources managed by the GES include the following:

Transaction locks – It is acquired in the exclusive mode when a transaction initiates its first row level change. The lock is held until the transaction is committed or rolled back.

Library Cache locks - When a database object (such as a table, view, procedure, function, package, package body, trigger, index, cluster, or synonym) is referenced during parsing or compiling of a SQL, DML or DDL, PL/SQL, or Java statement, the process parsing or compiling the statement acquires the library cache lock in the correct mode.

Dictionary Cache Locks - Global enqueues are used in the cluster database mode. The data dictionary structure is the same for all Oracle instances in a cluster database, as it is for instances in a single-instance database. However, in real application clusters, Oracle synchronizes all the dictionary caches throughout the cluster. Real application clusters use latches to do this, just as in the case of a single-instance Oracle database.

Table locks – These are the GES locks that protect the entire table(s). A transaction acquires a table lock when a table is modified. A table lock can be held in any of several modes: null (N), row share (RS), row exclusive (RX), share lock (S), share row exclusive (SRX), or exclusive (X).

Row-Level Locks

Oracle Row-level Locks are "very subtle," in Steve Adam's words. When a transaction updates or modifies a row, its transaction identifier is recorded in the entry as a part of the transaction list. The list is located in the header of the data block itself, and the row header is modified to point to the transaction list entry.

Row-Level locks are the locks that protect selected rows. They are implicit in nature. The following statements create row-level locks:

- INSERT
- UPDATE
- DELETE
- SELECT with the FOR UPDATE clause

These row locks or row-level locks are stored in the block, and each lock refers to the global transaction lock. As in the case of a single instance Oracle, the RAC controls concurrency down to the row level. The finest lock granularity is at the row level.

However, to keep the cache coherent, access to the data blocks is controlled by the GCS. This has no effect on the row-level lock. GCS resources and row locks operate independently of the GCS. An instance can request or ship the data block to another instance in the cluster without affecting the row-level locks that are held inside the data block. The row-level lock is fully controlled by the transaction that causes the row-level lock. When the transaction commits or rolls back, the row-level lock is released. In the meantime, if another transaction intends to update the same row, it has to wait until the initial transaction commits or rolls back.

The row lock method has an important advantage in maintaining data consistency, even if there are multiple instances, as in the RAC system. The behavior of the row lock and the release is the same, whether it is a single stand-alone database or a multi-instance RAC system. During the row lock period, even if the data block gets transferred to another instance, the row lock remains intact until released.

Global Resource Directory

The GES and GCS together maintain a global resource directory (GRD) to record information about resources and enqueues. The GRD remains in the memory and is stored on all the instances. Each instance manages a portion of the directory. The distributed nature of the GRD is a key point for the fault tolerance of RAC.

The GRD is an internal database that records and stores the current status of the data blocks. Whenever a block is transferred out of a local cache to another instance's cache, the GRD is updated. The following resource information is available in GRD:

- Data Block Addresses (DBA). This is the address of the block being modified.
- Location of most current version of the data block. This exists only if multiple nodes share the data block.
- Modes of the data blocks ((N)Null, (S)Shared, (X)Exclusive).
- The Roles of the data blocks (local or global). This indicates the role in which the data block is being held by the instance.
- SCN – System Change Number.
- Image of the Data Block – it could be past image or current image. Current image represents the copy of the block held by the current instance. Past image represents the global dirty data block image maintained in the cache.

More details about the above resources are covered in later sections.

The GRD is similar to the previous version of the lock directory from a functional perspective, but it has been expanded with more components. It contains an accurate inventory of resource status and location.

RAC Processes

The following additional processes are spawned to support multi-instance coordination:

LMON - The global enqueue service monitor (LMON) monitors the entire cluster to manage global enqueues and resources. LMON manages the instance, the process expirations, and the associated recovery for the global cache service.

LMD - The global enqueue service daemon (LMD) is a lock agent process that coordinates enqueue manager service requests. The requests are for global cache service enqueues that control access to global enqueues and resources. The LMD process also handles deadlock detection and remote enqueue requests.

LMSn - (Lock Manager Server process): These global cache service processes (LMSn) are processes for the global cache service (GCS). RAC software provides up to 10 global cache service processes. The number of LMSns varies, depending on the amount of messaging traffic between nodes in the cluster.

The LMSn handles blocking interrupts from the remote instance for the global cache service resources by:

- Managing the resource requests and cross-instance call operations for the shared resources.
- Building a list of invalid lock elements and validating the lock elements during recovery.
- Handling global lock deadlock detection and monitoring lock conversion timeouts.

LCK – This process manages global enqueue requests and cross-instance broadcasts.

DIAG - Diagnosability Daemon – Monitors the health of the instance and captures the data for instance process failures.

Resource Coordination

Since the RAC system allows many users to connect and process database SQL operations concurrently, many resources, such as data blocks and enqueues, are used simultaneously. This situation demands an effective synchronization of the concurrent tasks.

Synchronization

Within the shared cache (global cache or fused cache of multiple instances), the coordination of concurrent tasks is called synchronization. Resources such as data blocks and enqueues are synchronized as nodes within a cluster as they acquire and release ownership. The synchronization provided by real application clusters maintains a cluster wide concurrency of resources, and in turn ensures the integrity of the shared data. Even though there is seamless and transparent synchronization of concurrent tasks within the shared cache, it does not come without a cost in overhead. Processing within the local buffer cache is always faster than processing blocks across instances.

The key to successful cluster database processing is to divide the tasks that require resources among the nodes, so that very little synchronization is necessary. The less synchronization necessary, the better the system's performance and scalability will be. The overhead of synchronization can be very expensive if there is excessive inter-node communication. Block access times vary, as shown in Figure 7.4. According to Oracle studies, accessing a block within the local cache is many times faster than accessing a block in a remote cache (or buffer of another instance in the cluster). At the same time, accessing a block from disk is even more expensive. A combination of local cache block access with occasional access to remote cache blocks gives good performance levels.

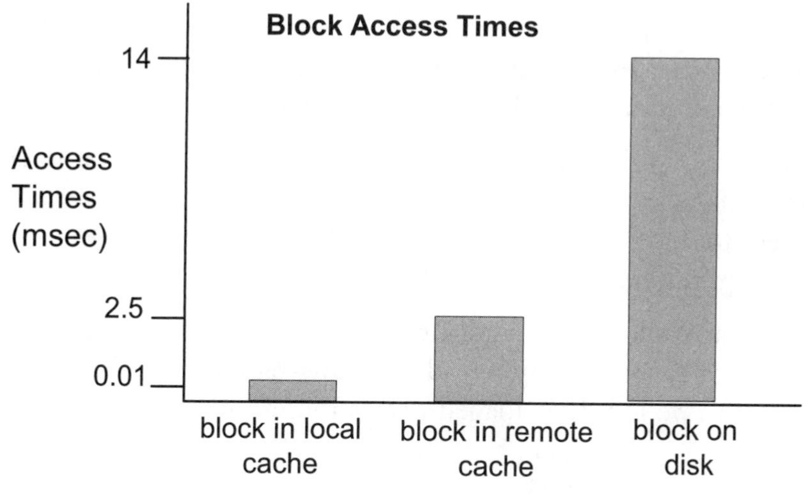

Figure 7.4: *Block Access Times*

GCS Resource Modes and Roles

Because of data block transfers among multiple instances, the same data block can exist in multiple caches. The resource mode is defined as a concurrency control that establishes global access rights for instances in a cluster. The data block (or GCS resource) can be held in different resource modes, depending on whether a resource holder intends to modify the data or read the data. The modes are as follows:

- **Null (N) mode** - Holding a resource at this level conveys that there are no access rights. Null mode is usually held as a placeholder, even if the resource is not actively used. [Steve Adams]

- **Shared (S) mode** - When a resource is held at this level, it will ensure that the data block is not modified by another session, but will allow concurrent shared access.
- **Exclusive (X) mode** - This level grants the holding process exclusive access. Other processes cannot write to the resource. It may have consistent read blocks.

The resource mode is an important mechanism to maintain data integrity and avoid data corruption issues. GCS resources are specified to have global roles or local roles. These roles are mutually exclusive.

- When a block is first read into the cache of an instance and other instances have not read the same block, then the block is said to be locally managed and is therefore assigned a local role.
- After the block has been modified by the local instance and transmitted to another instance, it is considered to be globally managed, and is therefore assigned a global role.

Basically, the concept of role supplements the access mode characteristic. A typical data block has both of these characteristics.

Concept of Past Image

The past image concept was introduced in the RAC version of Oracle 9i to maintain data integrity. In an Oracle database, a typical data block is not written to the disk immediately, even after it is dirtied. When the same dirty data block is requested by another instance for write or read purposes, an image of the block is created at the owning instance, and only that block is shipped to the requesting instance. This backup image of the block is called the past image (PI) and is kept in memory. In the event of failure, Oracle can reconstruct the current version of the block by reading PIs. It is also possible to have more than one past image in the memory depending on how many times the data block was requested in the dirty stage.

A past image copy of the data block is different from a CR block, which is needed for reconstructing a read-consistent image. A CR version of a block represents a consistent snapshot of the data at a point in time. It is constructed by applying information from the undo/rollback segments. The PI image copy helps the recovery process and aids in maintaining data integrity.

For example, suppose user A of instance 1 has updated row 2 on block 5. Later, user B of instance 2 intends to update row 6 on the same block 5. The GCS transfers block 5 from instance A to instance B. At this point, the past image (PI) for block 5 is created on instance A.

Lock Modes

From the examination of resource roles, resource modes, and past images, the next step is to consider the possible resource access modes as shown in Table 7.2.

There are 3 characters that distinguish lock or block access modes. The first letter represents the lock mode, the second character represents the lock role, and the third character (a number) indicates any past images for the lock in the local instance.

LOCK MODE	DESCRIPTION
NL0	Null Local and No past Images
SL0	Shared Local with no past image
XL0	Exclusive Local with no past image
NG0	Null Global – Instance owns current block image
SG0	Global Shared Lock – Instance owns current image
XG0	Global Exclusive Lock – Instance own current image
NG1	Global Null – Instance Owns the Past Image Block.

LOCK MODE	DESCRIPTION
SG1	Shared Global – Instance owns past Image
XG1	Global Exclusive Lock – Instance owns Past Image.

Table 7.2: *Lock Modes*

When a block is brought into the local cache of an instance, it is acquired with the local role. But, if a dirty buffer for the same data block is present in a remote instance, a past image is created in the remote instance before the data block is sent to the requesting instance's cache. Therefore, the data block resource acquires a global role.

For recovery purposes, instances that have past images will keep those past images in their buffer cache, until the master instance prompts the lock to release them. When the buffers are discarded, the instance holding the past image will write a block written redo (BWR) to the redo stream. The BWR indicates that the block has already been written to disk and is not needed for recovery by the instance. Buffers are discarded when the disk write is initiated on the master instance. The master instance is where the current status and position of the data block is maintained.

This has been a review of how a GCS resource maintains its access mode and its role. There is another feature called the buffer state, which is covered in the next section.

Block Access Modes and Buffer States

The buffer state indicates the status of a buffer in the local cache of an instance. Information about the buffer state can be seen in the dynamic performance view *v$bh*. The buffer state of a block relates to the access mode of the block. For example, if a buffer state is in exclusive current (XCUR) state, it indicates that the instance owns the resource in exclusive mode.

To see a buffer's state, query the STATUS column of the *v$bh* dynamic performance view. The *v$bh* view provides information about the block access mode and their buffer state names as follows:

- **Buffer state 'CR'** indicates that the block access mode is NULL. It means the owning instance can perform a consistent read of the block, if the instance holds an older version of the data.
- **Buffer state 'SCUR'** indicates that the block access mode is S (shared). It means the instance has shared access to the block and can only perform reads.
- **Buffer state 'XCUR'** indicates that access mode is X (exclusive). It means the instance has exclusive access to the block and can modify it.
- **Buffer state 'PI'** indicates that block access mode is NULL. It means that the instance has made changes to the block but retains copies of past images.

BLOCK ACCESS MODE	BUFFER STATE NAME	DESCRIPTION
X	XCUR	Instance has exclusive access to the block and therefore can modify the block.
S	SCUR	Instance has shared access to the block and can only perform reads.
NULL	CR	Contains an older version of the data. Can perform consistent read
--	PI	Past Image Exist (useful for recovery)

Table 7.3: *Buffer States shown in v$bh view.*

Only the SCUR and PI buffer states are real application cluster-specific. There can be only one copy of any block buffered in the XCUR state at any time. To perform modifications on a block, a process must assign an XCUR buffer state to the buffer containing the data block.

For example, if another instance requests a read access to the most current version of the same block, then Oracle changes the access mode from exclusive to shared, sends the current read version of the block to the requesting instance, and keeps a PI buffer if the buffer contained a dirty block

At this point, the first instance has the current block and the requesting instance also has the current block in shared mode. Therefore, the role of the resource becomes global. There can be multiple shared current (SCUR) versions of this block cached throughout the cluster database at any given point of time.

Cache Fusion Scenarios

The GCS plays a key role in performing the necessary block transfers. Three scenarios are presented to explain the concept of cache fusion:

- Scenario 1: Read/Read
- Scenario 2: Write/Write
- Scenario 3: Disk Write

Scenario 1: Read/Read

Figure 7.5 (a) shows Scenario 1, where a typical data block is requested from another instance where it is in shared access mode with a local role. Instance(1) desires to read a data block and it makes a request to the GCS, which keeps track of the resources, location, and status. The GCS in turn forwards the request to owning Instance(2).

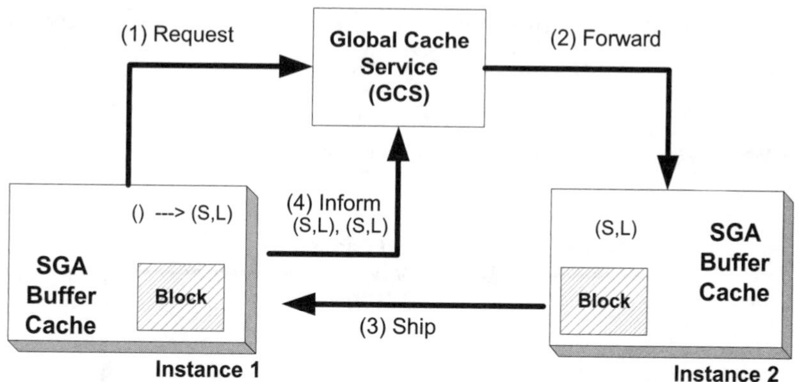

Figure 7.5(a): *Read/Read Cache Fusion – GCS processing*

The holding instance (Instance 2) transmits a copy of the block to the requesting instance (Instance 1), but keeps the resource in shared mode and also retains the local role.

Instance 2 now informs the GCS of its own resource disposition (S, L) and also that of the instance that sent the block (S, L). Thus, there is no disk read involved. The block transfer took place through the high-speed private interconnect.

Scenario 2: Write/Write

As shown in Figure 7.5(b), instance 1 intends to modify or update the data block and submits a request to GCS. The GCS transmits the request on to the holder (Instance 2).

Upon receiving the message, instance 2 sends the block to instance 1. Before sending the block, the resource is downgraded to null mode and the changed (dirty) buffer is kept as a PI. Thus, the role changes to global (G) because the block is dirty.

Along with the block, instance 2 informs the requestor that it retained a PI copy and a null resource. The same message also specifies that the requestor can take the block held in exclusive mode and with a global role (X, G).

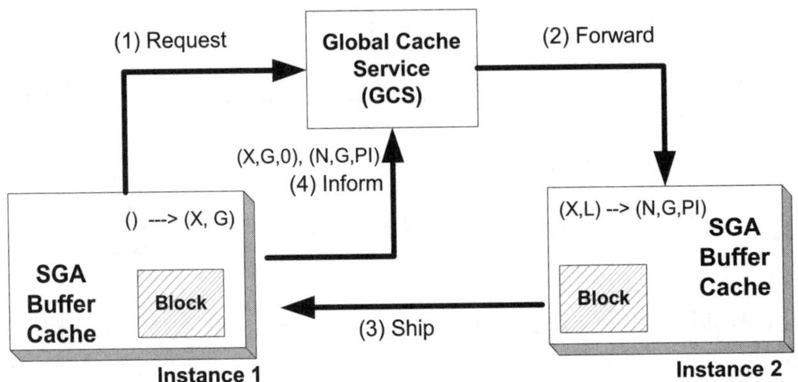

Figure 7.5 (b): *Write/Write Cache Fusion – GCS processing*

Upon receipt of the block and the resource dispositions, instance 1 informs the GCS of the mode and role (X, G). Note that the data block is not written to disk before the resource is granted to the other instance. That is, DBWR is not involved in the cache coherency scheme at this stage.

Scenario 3: Disk Write

As shown in Figure 7.5(c), instance 2 first sends a write request to the GCS. This might be due to a user-executing checkpoint on instance 2. Note that there is a past image for the block on instance 2. The GCS forwards the request to instance 1 (the current block holder). The GCS remembers that a write at the system change number (SCN) is pending and it also remembers that it has to notify the nodes that have PIs of the same block.

Instance 1 then receives the write request and writes the block to disk. Instance 1 completes the write and notifies the GCS. Instance 1 also informs the GCS that the resource role can become local because the instance has completed the write of the current block. After completion of the protocol, all PIs of the block should be discarded.

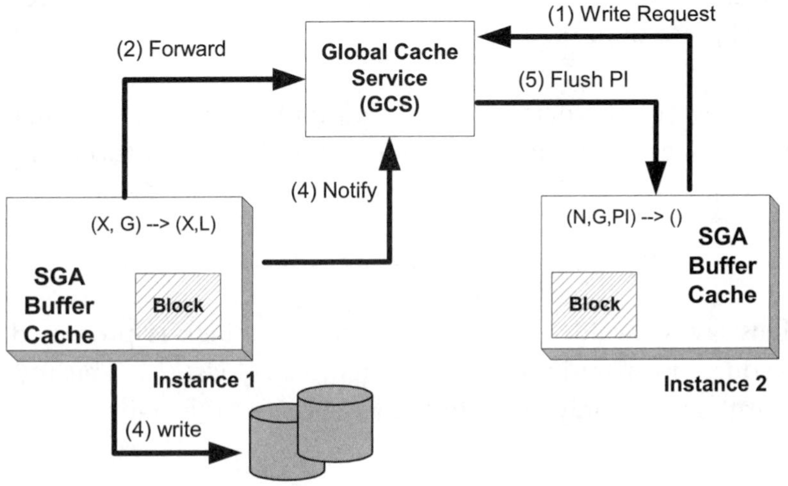

Figure 7.5 (c): *Write blocks to disk – GCS Processing*

Upon receipt of the notification, the GCS orders all PI holders to discard (or flush) their PIs. Discarding, in this case, means that upon receipt of the message the PI holder records that the current block has been written and the buffer is released. The PI is no longer needed for recovery. The buffer is essentially free and the resource previously held in null mode is closed.

Block Transfers Using Cache Fusion – Example

The following is another example of how block shipping takes place. Assume that in a 3-node RAC cluster a typical block (of table 'salesman') is brought into instance 3 by a select operation of user C. Initially, the instance acquires SL0 (shared lock with no past image) and the same Block/Lock-element undergoes many conversions, as different users at different instances handle it. The following operations show a clear movement of the blocks among the instances using cache fusion. It also shows the complexity involved. Refer to Figures 7.6 (a) and (b).

Assumption: Transactions update with commit, but there is no checkpoint until the end.

In Stage (1), the data block is read into the buffer of instance 3, and it opens with an SL0 mode (Shared Local without any past image):

```
select sales_rank from salesman where salesid = 10;
```

This gives a value of 30. Thus, the data block is protected by a resource in shared mode (S) and its role is local (L). This indicates that the block only exists in the local cache of instance 3.

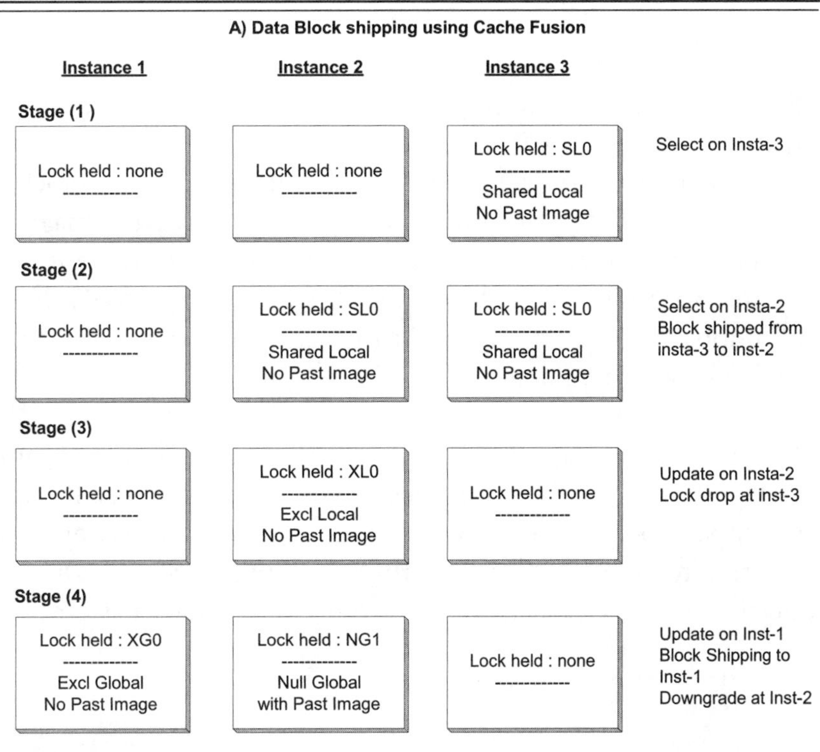

Figure 7.6 (a) *Data Block Shipping using Cache Fusion*

In Stage (2), user B issues the same select statement against the salesman table. Instance 2 will need the same block; therefore, the block is shipped from instance 3 to instance 2 via the cache fusion interconnect. There is no disk read at this time. Both instances are in shared (S) mode and the role is local (L). So far, no buffer is dirtied.

In Stage (3), user B decides to update the row and commit at instance 2. The new sales rank is 24. At this stage, instance 2 acquires XL0 (Exclusive Local) at instance 2 and the share lock is removed on instance 3.

```
Update salesman set sales_rank = 24
Where salesid = 10;
```

In Stage (4), user A decides to update on instance 1 the same row (and therefore the block) with the salesrank value of 40. It finds that the block is dirty in instance 2. Therefore, the data block is shipped to instance 1 from instance 2, however, a past image of the data block is created on instance 2 and the lock mode is also converted to Null with a global role. Instance 2 now has a NG1 (Null Global with past image). At this time, instance 1 will have exclusive lock with global role (XG0).

In Stage (5), user C executes a select on instance 3 on the same row. The data block from instance 1 being the most recent copy, it is shipped to instance 3. As a result, the lock on instance 1 is converted to shared global with past image (SG1). On the requesting instance (Instance 1), the SG0 lock resource is created.

```
Select sales_rank from salesman
Where salesid = 10;
```

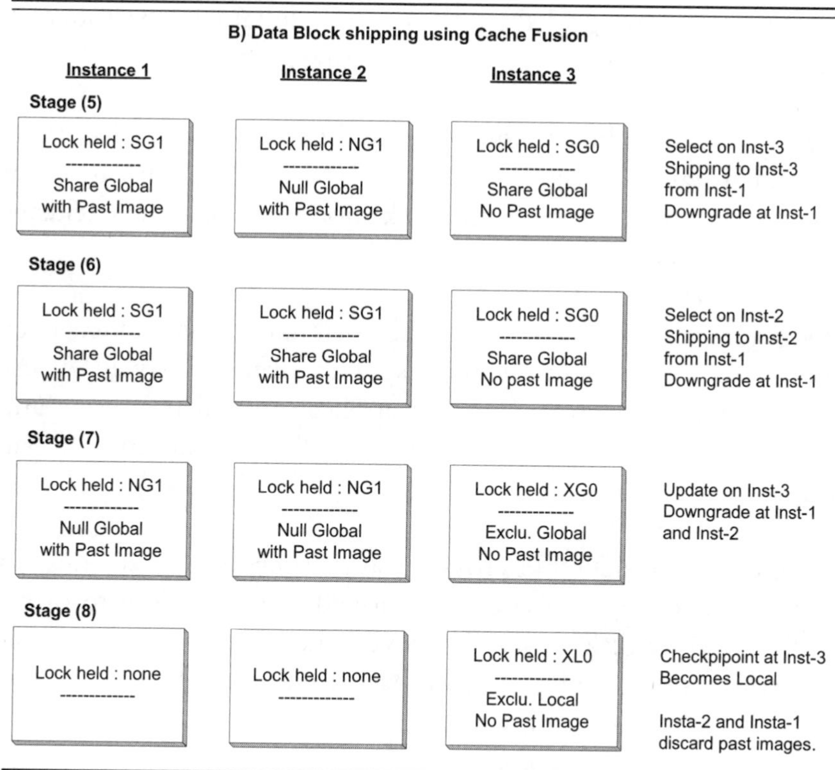

Figure 7.6 (b) *Data Block Shipping using Cache Fusion*

In Stage (6), user B issues the same select against the salesman table on instance 2. Instance 2 will request a consistent read copy of the buffer from another instance, which happens to be the current master.

Therefore, instance 1 will ship the block to instance 2, where it will be acquired with SG1. Then, at instance 1, the lock will be converted to SG1.

In Stage (7), user C on instance C updates the same row. Therefore, instance 3 acquires an exclusive lock and instances 1 and 2 will be downgraded to NG1 (Null global with past image). Instance 3 will have exclusive mode with a global role.

In Stage (8), the checkpoint is initiated and a write to disk takes place at instance 3. Instance 1 and instance 2 will discard their past images. At instance 3, the lock mode will become exclusive with a local role.

The stages above illustrate that consistency is maintained even though the same block is requested at different levels. These operations are transparent to the application. All the mode and role conversions are handled by Oracle without any human configuration.

If there are considerable cross-instance updates and queries for the same set of blocks, blocks are moved across without resorting to disk read or disk writes. However, there will be considerable lock conversions, which may be expensive, though they are less expensive than disk read/writes.

Block Access, Grants, and Interrupts

The GCS maintains the status of the resources. It also keeps an inventory of the access requests for the data blocks. After the blocks are transferred from one instance to another to meet requests, the requesting processes need to be notified that the block is actually available. Therefore, processes utilize interrupts to inform of the arrival or completion of block transfers. The GCS uses various interrupts to manage resource allocation. These interrupts are:

- **Blocking Interrupt** - When exclusive access is needed for a requestor, the GCS sends a blocking interrupt to a process that currently owns the shared resource, notifying it that a request for an exclusive resource is waiting.

- **Acquisition Interrupt** - When the requested access (e.g., exclusive) is made available after releasing an earlier access mode, an acquisition interrupt is sent to alert the process that has requested the exclusive resource. The acquisition interrupt helps to notify the requesting process.
- **Block Arrival Interrupt** - When a process requests a block from the GCS, the request is forwarded to the instance holding the block. Then the requested block is sent to the requesting process, and the process informs the GCS that it has received the block. This notification is called block arrival interrupt.

The block requests are granted for many processes at the same time, but they follow a queuing mechanism. The GCS maintains two types of queues for resource requests.

If the GCS is unable to grant a resource request immediately, then the GCS puts it in the convert queue. The GCS then tracks all waiting requests.

Once a resource is granted to the requesting process, it is kept in the granted queue. The GCS tracks resource requests in the granted queue.

Cache Fusion and Recovery

In the RAC system, whenever there is a node failure, the instance running on the failed node crashes and becomes unusable. There can be several reasons for such a failure. In this section, focus will be placed on the changes that take place in the global cache and how the recovery of the failed instance is undertaken by one of the surviving instances.

Recovery Features

Only the cache resources that reside on the failed nodes or are mastered by the GCS on the failed nodes need to be re-built or re-mastered. Rebuilt or re-master does not mean building a block; the lock ownership is merely changed and this is explained later with examples.

All resources previously mastered at the failed instance are redistributed across the remaining instances. These resources are reconstructed at their new master instance. All other resources previously mastered at surviving instances remain unaffected.

The cluster manager first detects the node and instance failure. It communicates the failure status to the GCS by way of the LMON process. At this stage, any surviving instance in the cluster initiates the recovery process.

Remember, instance recovery does not include restarting the failed instance or recovering applications that were running on that instance. Also note that, even after a node failure and instance loss, the redo log file of the failed instance is still available to the other recovering instance, since the redo log file is located on the shared cluster file system or shared raw partition. This is an important feature of the RAC system.

Because of past images, instance recovery is performed differently in the RAC implementation. The SMON process of a surviving instance performs recovery of the failed instance or thread. However, note that the foreground process performs recovery in a stand-alone instance.

Recovery Methodology and steps

Oracle performs the following steps to recover:

1. In the initial phase of recovery, GES enqueues are reconfigured and the global resource directory is frozen. All GCS resource requests and writes are temporarily halted.
2. GCS resources are reconfigured among the surviving instances. One of the surviving instances becomes the recovering instance. The SMON process of the recovering instance starts a first pass of the redo log read of the failed instance's redo thread.
3. Block resources that need to be recovered are identified and the global resource directory is reconstructed. Pending requests or writes are cancelled or replayed.
4. Resources identified in the previous log read phase are defined as recovery resources. Buffer space for recovery is allocated.
5. Assuming that there are past images of blocks to be recovered in other caches in the cluster, source buffers are requested from other instances. The resource buffers are the starting point of recovery for a particular block.
6. All resources and enqueues required for subsequent processing have been acquired and the global resource directory is now unfrozen. Any data blocks that are not in recovery can now be accessed. At this time, the system is partially available.
7. The SMON merges the redo thread order by SCN to ensure that changes are written in an orderly fashion. This process is important for multiple simultaneous failures. If multiple instances die simultaneously, neither the PI buffers nor the current buffers for a data block can be found in any surviving instance's cache. Then a log merger of the failed instances is performed.
8. Now the second pass of recovery begins and redo is applied to data files, releasing the recovery resources immediately

after block recovery, so that more and more blocks become available as cache recovery proceeds.

9. After all blocks have been recovered and recovery resources have been released, the system is available for normal use.

Figure 7.7 shows the basic steps in the recovery.

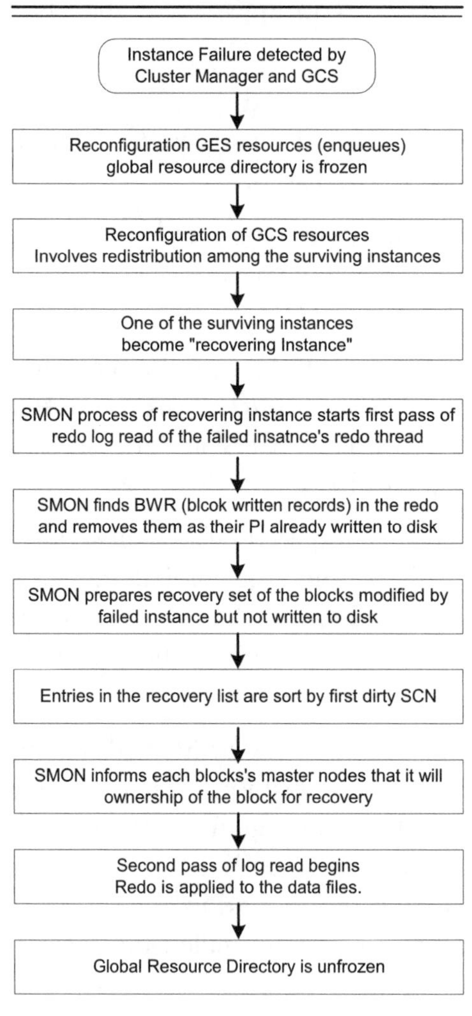

Figure 7.7: *Online Instance Recovery Steps*

Recovery Process – Re-mastering Resources

The recovery process is done in two passes. The first pass will construct recovery sets and the appropriate lock modes, after eliminating the not-needed entries like BWR. This process makes use of extra buffers in the recovering instance's cache to store the recovery list. In the second pass, the actual recovery of the blocks takes place, and redo is applied to the data files.

The following is an examination of some of these situations to facilitate understanding of how the process works.

The scenario involves a RAC with three instances (A, B, C) and instance C has failed. Instance A has taken over the role of recovering instance and instance B is an open, good instance. The situation is constructed as if the failed instance existed.

Scenario 1:

Neither the recovering instance (A) nor the open instance (B) has a lock element (or it may be in NL0 mode). This indicates that the failed instance had XL0. Therefore, SMON acquires a lock in XL0 mode, reads the block from disk, and applies redo changes. Therefore, the block is kept in the recovery set. Later, DBWR writes the recovery buffer out when recovery is completed.

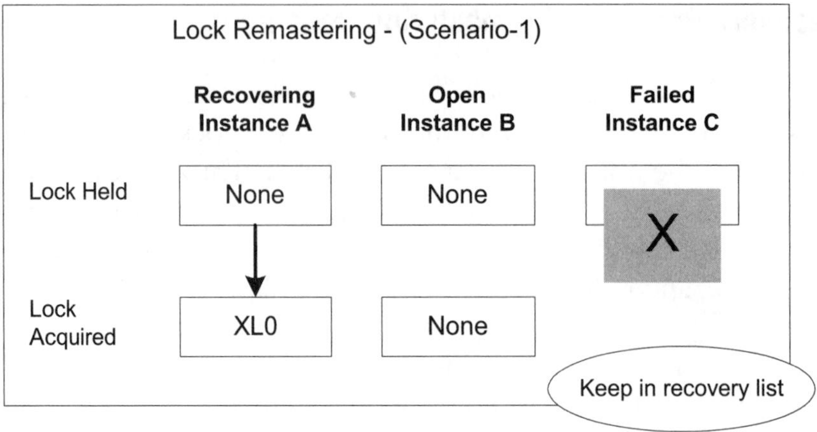

Figure 7.8: *Lock Re-Mastering – (Scenario-1)*

Scenario 2:

Instance (B) has the block buffer in either XL0 mode or SL0, but the recovering instance (A) does not have anything. Since instance (B) is holding the lock in exclusive local mode, it is more current than the redo stream. Therefore, no recovery is needed. There is also no need to write this block to disk.

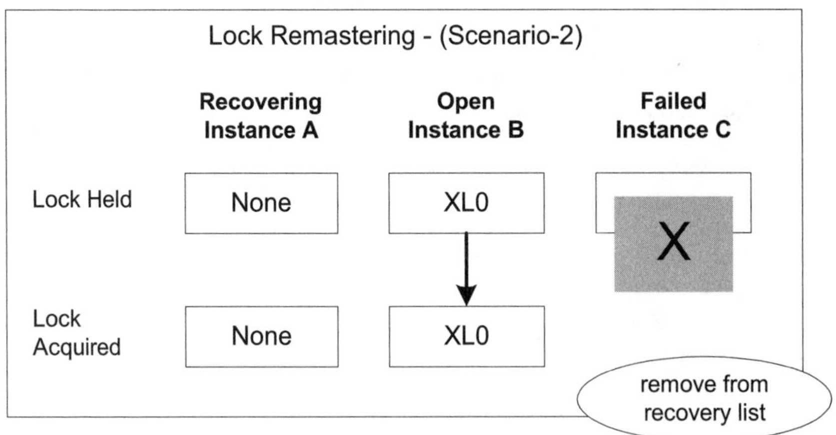

Figure 7.9: *Lock Remastering – (Scenario-2)*

Scenario 3:

Instance (B) has the block buffer in either XG# mode or SG# mode (both global), but the recovering instance (A) does not have anything. Here, the resource is in global role. Therefore, SMON initiates the write of the current block on instance (B). No recovery is needed because a current copy of the block exists in instance (B). The entry is removed from the recovery set. Write completion will release the recovery buffer and instance A acquires NG1.

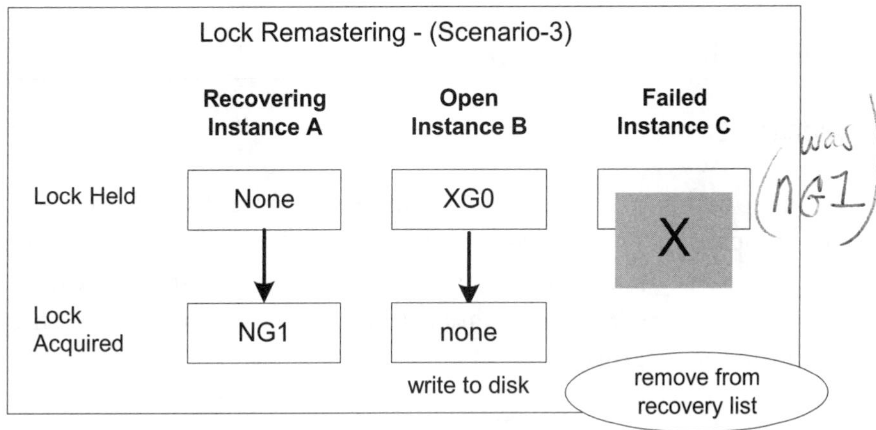

Figure 7.10: *Lock Remastering – (Scenario-3)*

Scenario 4:

The recovering instance (A) does not have anything and instance (B) has NG1 mode, which indicates the failed instance had the more current block (maybe something like XG0). Therefore, instance (A) gets a consistent-read image block based on SCN from instance B, and acquires XG0 mode. It keeps the block in the recovery list.

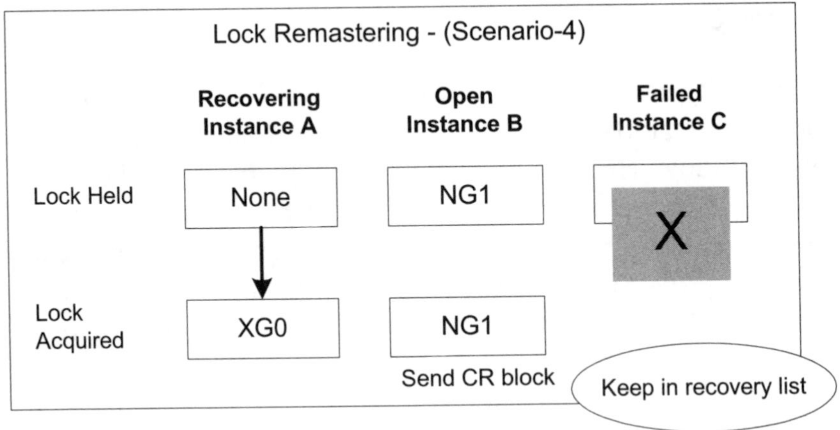

Figure 7.11: *Lock Re-Mastering – (Scenario-4)*

Scenario 5:

The recovering instance (A) has the lock element in SL0 or XL0 (both local) and other instances have no lock elements on this block. This scenario requires no recovery, as the current copy of the buffer is present in instance (A). It removes the redo entry from the recovery list.

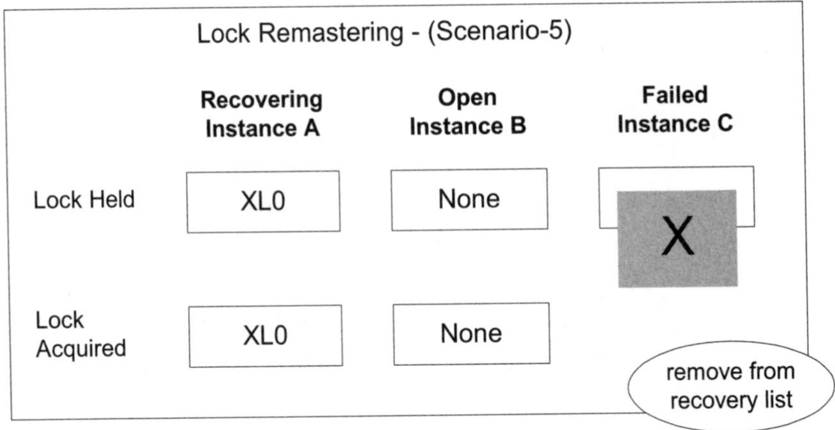

Figure 7.12: *Lock Remastering – (Scenario-5)*

Scenario 6:

The recovering instance (A) has the lock element in SG# or XG# (both Global). Since it has a global role (shared or exclusive), the status on the other open instance is immaterial. Therefore, instance (A) initiates the writing of the current block to disk. There is no recovery needed and it releases the buffer from the redo list.

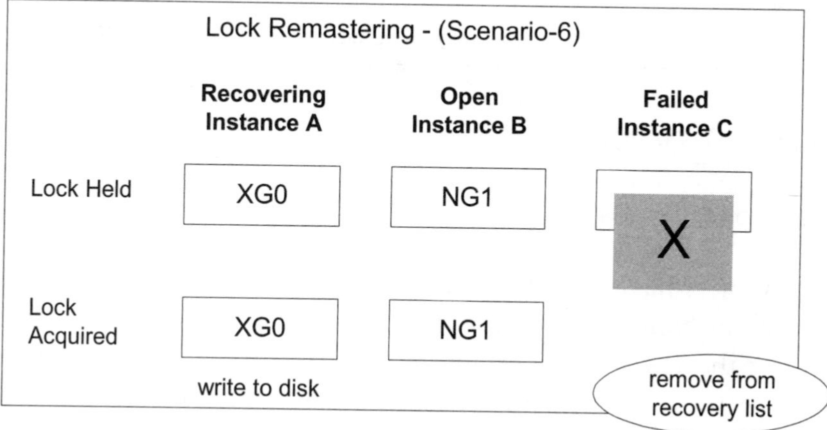

Figure 7.13: *Lock Remastering – (Scenario-6)*

Scenario 7:

Instance (A) has the lock element in NG1 and instance B has XG# or SG#. This involves writing the current block on instance (B) and no recovery is needed.

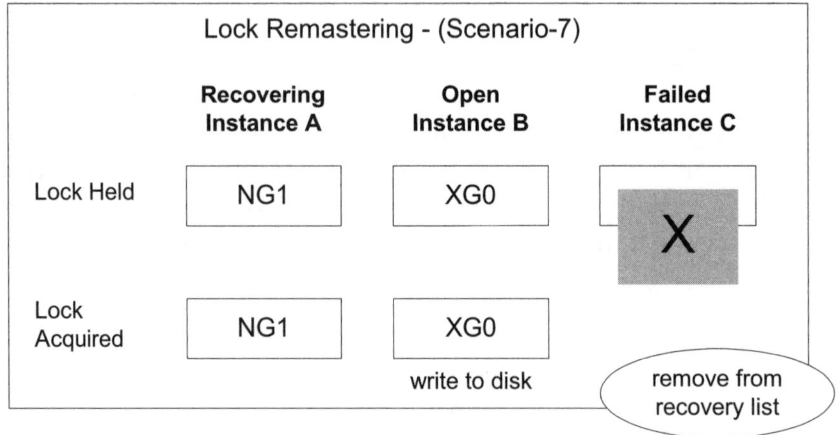

Figure 7.14: *Lock Remastering – (Scenario-7)*

Scenario 8:

Instance (A) has the lock element in NG1 and instance (B) has the lock in NG0/NG1 mode. It indicates the failed instance was holding the resource in exclusive mode. This involves getting a consistent-read copy from the highest past image, based on SCN, and applying redo changes. Instance (B) sends the CR block to instance (A). This block is kept for recovery.

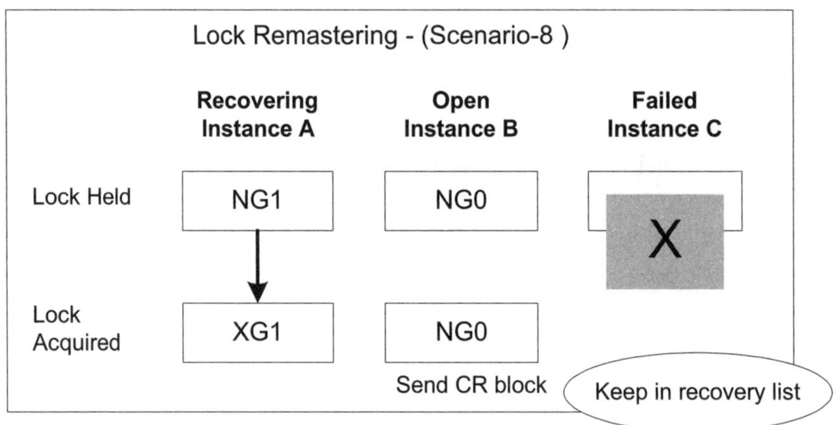

Figure 7.15: *Lock Remastering – (Scenario-8)*

Thus, after the first pass, the recovering instance will have locks on every block in the recovery list (set). Other instances will not be able to acquire these locks until the recovery operation is completed. Now the second pass begins, the redo is applied to the data files.

During instance recovery, if the recovering instance dies, a surviving instance (if one exists) will acquire instance recovery enqueue and starts recovery. If a non-recovering instance fails, SMON will abort recovery, release the IR enqueue, and the next live instance will reattempt instance recovery.

Conclusion

This chapter has explained the nature of cache fusion, resource coordination, cache-to-cache transfers, resource management, and lock conversions. It also covered instance failure and the associated re-mastering of resources by the surviving instance.

The main points of this chapter include:

- Cache fusion technology avoids expensive block pings or forced writes to disk. Data blocks are shipped across the nodes or instances by means of the interconnect technology.
- Local caches of all instances in the cluster fuse to form a global cache. Therefore, it is called cache fusion. There are additional background processes to manage the global cache service (GCS).
- Data concurrency and cache coherency are the most important requirements. The Oracle RAC system maintains cache coherency by means of global cache service processes (GCS).

- The Global Enqueue Service (GES) focuses on synchronizing the enqueues and managing transaction locks, library cache locks, and dictionary cache locks.
- GCS resources exist in different modes and different roles. The GCS manages the block transfers and resource access. Failure or loss of an instance triggers immediate instance recovery, undertaken by any of the surviving instances. This involves the reconfiguration of enqueues and GCS resources. Then, a two-pass redo log read takes place for the recovering instance.

RAC Administration

CHAPTER 8

Pay attention class! Let's review Oracle parameters.

Introduction

This chapter is devoted to the administration features that are specific to a RAC system. Even though the instances in a RAC system generally follow the same administration methods and principles as a stand-alone instance, RAC has certain unique administration issues.

Topics covered in this chapter will include parameter management, undo management, space management, handling redo threads, and data files. Additionally, some focus will be given to server control utility, the global services daemon, the Oracle Enterprise Manager, and the usage of SQL*plus utility.

A good place to start is with setting up and managing the configuration parameters that control all of the system features of the database and instances.

Parameter Management

When the Oracle server starts up, it uses a file that contains initialization parameters. These parameters specify the name of the database, the amount of memory to allocate, the names of control files, and various limits and other system parameters. In Oracle Database 10g, the initialization files can be replaced with an SPFILE, which allows many Oracle parameters to be changed dynamically.

Overview

Initialization parameters control the configuration of the database system. They are the key directives to start and manage any instance in the database. While launching the database instance, parameters are specified and they remain until the instance is shutdown. Optionally, certain parameters can be modified during the instance run time by the ALTER SYSTEM SET method, provided the instance has been started with the SPFILE method.

Before Oracle9i, Oracle instances were always started using a text file called an *init.ora*. This file is located by default in the *$ORACLE_HOME/dbs* directory. In Oracle9i, the server parameter file (SPFILE) was introduced. An SPFILE is a binary file stored on the database server. The Oracle Database 10g instance can be started using either the SPFILE or an *init.ora* file.

The SPFILE feature allows the change of parameter values dynamically. It also allows them to be set either permanently or in memory only. For Oracle Real Application Clusters (RAC), one server parameter file can be used and shared among instances.

The usage of a single copy of the SPFILE for the entire database provides administrative convenience and simplification.

Many important values are specified by the initialization parameters, some of which include:

- The Global Database Name (*db_name*)
- Control Files name and location
- Database Block Sizes
- Initialization Parameters that affect the size of the SGA
- Maximum Number of Processes
- Method of Undo Space Management
- License Parameters

RAC and Initialization Parameters

The RAC system is a multi-instance single database system, and in general each of the instances can have its own parameter values. But certain parameters are common, such as *db_name*, etc. Since the RAC system can function on nodes that utilize different resources, such as CPUs and memory, database administrators can set appropriate values for the SGA configuration. Those values need not be the same for all the nodes and its instances. At the same time, there are certain parameters that are unique to each of the cluster instances.

There are three types of initialization parameters in the Real Application Clusters environment:

- Parameters That Must Be Identical Across All Instances
- Parameters That Must Be Unique Across All Instances
- Multi-Valued Parameters

Identical Parameters (Across Instances)

These parameters are generally critical directives. Some are specified at the time of database creation, and some are specified (or modified) while the RAC system is running. They must always be common in order for the clustered instances to function.

Table 8.1 shows parameters that must be identical across all the instances. For example, since RAC is a single database with multiple instances, it must have a single parameter to show the maximum number of data files for the database. This is explained in more detail in the Oracle Database 10g Database Reference Manual. These parameters indicate the fact that there is a single database, even though access is through multiple instances. The parameters, which need to be common, are mostly database-level parameters.

PARAMETER	DESCRIPTION
active_instance_count	Designates one instance in a two-instance cluster as the primary instance, and the other as the secondary instance. This parameter has no functionality in a cluster with more than two instances.
archive_lag_target	Specifies a log switch after a user-specified time period elapses.
cluster_database	Specifies whether or not Oracle Database 10g RAC is enabled.
cluster_database_ instances	Equal to the number of instances. Oracle uses the value of this parameter to compute the default value of the *large_pool_size* parameter when the *parallel_automatic_tuning* parameter is set to true.
cluster_interconnects	Specifies the additional cluster interconnects available for use in RAC environment. Oracle uses information from this parameter to distribute traffic among the various interfaces.
compatible	This parameter specifies the release with which the Oracle server must maintain compatibility.

PARAMETER	DESCRIPTION
control_files	Specifies one or more names of control files.
db_block_size	Specifies the size (in bytes) of Oracle database blocks.
db_domain	In a distributed database system, *db_domain* specifies the logical location of the database within the network structure.
db_files	Specifies the maximum number of database files that can be opened for this database.
db_name	Specifies a database identifier. It must correspond to the name specified in the create database statement.
dml_locks (if 0, same on all)	They can be different if the *dml_locks* are positive.
gc_files_to_locks	Controls the mapping of pre-release 9.0.1 parallel cache management (PCM) locks to data files.
license_max_users	Specifies the maximum number of users you can create in the database.
max_commit_ propagation_delay	Specifies the maximum amount of time allowed until the system change number (SCN), held in the SGA of an instance, and is refreshed by the log writer process (LGWR). It determines whether the local SCN should be refreshed from the lock value when getting the snapshot SCN for a query. Units are in hundredths of seconds.
parallel_execution_ message_size	Specifies the size of messages for parallel execution (formerly referred to as parallel query, PDML, Parallel Recovery, and replication).
parallel_max_servers	Specifies the maximum number of parallel execution processes and parallel recovery processes for an instance.
remote_login_ passwordfile	Specifies whether Oracle checks for a password file and how many databases can use the password file.
row_locking	Specifies whether row locks are acquired during update operations.

PARAMETER	DESCRIPTION
spfile	The value of this parameter is the name of the current server parameter file (SPFILE) in use. This parameter can be defined in a client side PFILE to indicate the name of the server parameter file to use.
trace_enabled	Controls tracing of the execution history, or code path; Oracle Support Services uses this information for debugging. When *trace_enabled* is set to true, Oracle records information in specific files when errors occur.
undo_management	Specifies which undo space management mode the system should use. When set to AUTO, the instance starts in automatic undo management mode. In manual undo management mode, undo space is allocated externally as rollback segments.
undo_retention	Specifies (in seconds) the amount of committed undo information to retain in the database. You can use *undo_retention* to satisfy queries that require old undo information in order to rollback changes to produce older images of data blocks. You can set the value at instance startup.

Table 8.1: *Parameters that should remain identical among the instances*

Unique Parameters (across instances)

The next category of parameters uniquely identifies a particular instance. They specify the identifiers of the independent instance, and give independent characteristics to an instance. Table 8.2 shows these parameters, which need to be unique in the cluster.

PARAMETER	DESCRIPTION
instance_name	Specifies the unique name of this instance.
instance_number	Specifies a unique number that maps the instance to one free list group for each database object created with storage parameter freelist groups.
rollback_ segments	Allocates one or more rollback segments by name to this instance.

PARAMETER	DESCRIPTION
thread	Specifies the number of the redo thread to be used by an instance.
undo_tablespace	Specifies the undo tablespace to be used when an instance starts up. If this parameter is specified when the instance is in manual undo management mode, an error will occur and startup will fail.

Table 8.2: *Parameters Unique for each of the instances*

Multi-Valued Parameters

There are many parameters whose values can vary from one instance to another in the cluster. Table 8.3 shows the parameters that can have different values across the instances of the RAC system. Based on the resources available on a particular node and the tuning methodology desired for a specific instance, many of the values can be set up without affecting other instances. This gives a true independent environment for any given instance.

PARAMETER	DESCRIPTION
db_block_buffers	Specifies the number of database buffers in the buffer cache.
fast_start_io_target	Specifies the number of I/Os that should be needed during a crash or instance recovery.
fast_start_mttr_target	Specifies the number of seconds the database takes to perform crash recovery of a single instance.
ifile	Use *ifile* to embed another parameter file within the current parameter file. For example: *ifile = common.ora*
instance_groups	Lets you restrict parallel query operations to a limited number of instances.
job_queue_processes	Specifies the maximum number of processes that can be created for the execution of jobs.
license_max_sessions	Specifies the maximum number of concurrent user sessions allowed.

PARAMETER	DESCRIPTION
license_sessions_ warning	Specifies a warning limit on the number of concurrent user sessions.
log_archive_dest	Uses a text string to specify the default location and root of the disk file or tape device when archiving redo log files.
log_archive_format	Specifies the default filename format when archiving redo log files. (Oracle recommends keeping the same format on all instances.)
log_archive_start	Value of True indicates that archiving is automatic.
log_archive_trace	Controls output generated by the archive log process.
log_checkpoint_interval	Specifies the frequency of checkpoints in terms of the number of redo log file blocks that can exist between an incremental checkpoint and the last block written to the redo log. This number refers to physical operating system blocks, not database blocks.
log_checkpoint_timeout	Specifies the amount of time, in seconds, that has passed since the incremental checkpoint at the position where the last write to the redo log (sometimes called the tail of the log) occurred. This parameter also signifies that no buffer will remain dirty (in the cache) for more than integer seconds.
open_links_per_instance	Specifies the maximum number of open connections globally for each database instance that can be migrated.
parallel_instance_group	Used in conjunction with the *instance_groups* parameter, it lets you restrict parallel query operations to a limited number of instances.
parallel_min_percent	Specifies the minimum percentage of parallel execution processes (of the value of *parallel_max_servers*) required for parallel execution.
parallel_min_servers	Specifies the minimum number of parallel execution processes for the instance. This value is the number of parallel execution processes Oracle creates when the instance is started.

PARAMETER	DESCRIPTION
Processes	Specifies the maximum number of operating system user processes that can simultaneously connect to Oracle. Its value should allow for all background processes such as locks, job queue processes, and parallel execution processes.
query_rewrite_enabled	Enables or disables global query rewriting for the database.
query_rewrite_integrity	Determines the degree to which Oracle must enforce query rewriting.
session_cached_cursors	Lets you specify the number of session cursors to cache. Repeated parse calls of the same SQL statement cause the session cursor for that statement to be moved into the session cursor cache.
transactions	Specifies the maximum number of concurrent transactions.
transactions_per_ rollback_segment	Specifies the number of concurrent transactions you expect each rollback segment to have to handle.

Table 8.3: *Parameters that can vary from one instance to another instance*

By using the SET clause of the ALTER SYSTEM statement or by using the OEM (Oracle Enterprise Manager), initialization parameter values can be changed for a given instance. Many of the changes can be made effective immediately. Optionally, they can be made persistent across reboot of the instance.

ASM Related Initialization Parameters

In Oracle Database 10g some initialization parameters have been modified that control the relationship of the RAC instance with the new Oracle Database 10g Automated Storage Management interface. The modified parameters are shown in table 8.4.

PARAMETER	DESCRIPTION
db_create_file_dest	This parameter allows the specification of 10g ASM disk groups using a format similar to: +dgroup2, where dgroup2 is an existing ASM disk group mounted in the nodes ASM instance.
db_recovery_file_dest	This parameter allows the specification of ASM disk groups for recovery files location using a format similar to: +dgroup6, where dgroup6 is an existing ASM disk group mounted in the nodes ASM instance.
db_recovery_file_dest_size	This parameter specifies the size area to reserve in the *db_recovery_file_dest* specified disk group for recovery files. An example setting would be: 5G where 5 is the integer size and "G" in this setting tells Oracle this is gigabytes. The use of K and M are also allowed for kilobytes and megabytes.
db_create_online_log_ dest_n	This parameter (where "n" is replaced with 1-5) allows you to specify the disk group where redo logs will be created. For example specifying: +dgroup7, places the log files in ASM disk group dgroup7.

Table 8.4: *ASM Initialization Parameters*

By using the *db_create_file_dest* and *db_recovery_file_dest* parameters, ASM knows the disk groups on which to place the database datafiles and recovery area. This allows the DBA to simply specify *create tablespace test;* and the database and ASM will create a 100 megabyte file within the *db_create_file_dest* location, automatically striped and load balanced.

Initialization Parameters for ASM Instances

The initialization parameters in Table 8.5 relate only to an ASM instance, there will be at least one ASM instance per node in a RAC cluster. Parameters that start with ASM_ cannot be set in a normal database instance, although they will be present to the show parameter command.

PARAMETER	DESCRIPTION
instance_type	In order to set the ASM parameters, this parameter must be set to *instance_type* = ASM. **Note**: This is the only required parameter. All other parameters take suitable defaults for most environments.
db_unique_name	This parameter specifies the unique name for this group of ASM instances within the cluster or on a node. This parameter defaults to +ASM and only needs to be modified if you are trying to run multiple ASM instances on the same node.
asm_power_limit	This parameter determines the maximum power on an ASM instance for disk rebalancing operations. The default is 1, which is also the most intrusive to database operations, a higher setting makes the rebalancing operations less intrusive.
asm_diskstring	The purpose of this parameter is to limit the set of disks that Automatic Storage Management considers for discovery. If not specified the entire system is searched for compatible volumes which can lengthen startup time. The parameters default value is NULL. (This default causes ASM to find all of the disks in a platform-specific location to which it has read/write access.)

PARAMETER	DESCRIPTION
asm_diskgroups	This parameter lists the names of disk groups that will be mounted by an ASM instance at startup, or when the ALTER DISKGROUP ALL MOUNT statement is issued. The parameters default value is NULL. (If this parameter is not specified, then no disk groups are mounted.) This parameter is dynamic if you are using a server parameter file (SPFILE), however you should rarely need to alter this value. ASM automatically adds a disk group to this parameter when a disk group is successfully mounted by the ASM instance, and automatically removes a disk group that is specifically dismounted. However, if you use a traditional text initialization parameter file, remember that you need to edit the initialization parameter file to add the name of any disk group that you want automatically mounted at instance startup, and remove the name of any disk group that you no longer want mounted.

Table 8.5: *ASM Only Initialization Parameters*

Client Side Initialization Parameter File vs. Server Parameter File

By default, Oracle uses parameter settings in the server parameter file to control database resources. The traditional client side parameter file (*init.ora*) can also be used; however, Oracle recommends that the server parameter file be used because it is easier to use and manage.

The server parameter file (also called SPFILE) is in a single location where all the necessary parameters are defined and stored. The defined parameter values are applicable for all the instances in the cluster. The SPFILE permits dynamic changes without requiring the instance be brought down.

The client side parameter file can still be used to manage parameter settings in Real Application Clusters; however, administrative convenience is sacrificed and the advantage of dynamic change is lost. By default, if PFILE is not specified in the STARTUP command, Oracle will use a server parameter file.

Server Parameter File

A server parameter file is basically a repository for initialization parameters. Initialization parameters stored in an SPFILE are persistent, meaning any parameter changes made while an instance is running can persist across instance shutdown and startup. In this way, all the initialization parameters manually updated by ALTER SYSTEM SET commands become persistent. It also provides a basis for the Oracle database server to self-tune. Another advantage, particularly for multi-instance RAC systems, is that a single copy of the parameter file can be used by all instances. Even though a single file is used to specify parameters, it has different format styles to support both the common values for all instances, as well as the specific values for an individual instance.

A server parameter file is initially built from the traditional text initialization parameter file, using the *create* SPFILE statement. It is a binary file that cannot be browsed or edited with a text editor. Oracle provides other interfaces for viewing and modifying parameter settings.

At system startup, the default behavior of the STARTUP command is to read an SPFILE to obtain initialization parameter settings. If the STARTUP command doesn't have a PFILE clause, it reads the SPFILE from a location specified by the operating system. If the DBA chooses to use the traditional text initialization parameter file, the PFILE clause must be specified when issuing the STARTUP command.

Setting the Server Parameter File Values

Use the SID designator to set instance-specific parameter values in the server parameter file. For settings across the database, use an asterisk ('*'). For a specific instance, set the prefix with SID as indicated below.

```
*.OPEN_CURSORS=300 # For database-wide setting
RACDB1.OPEN_CURSORS=1500 # For RACDB1 instance
```

Note that even though *open_cursors* is set at 300 for all instances in the first entry, the value of 1500 remains in effect for the SID RACDB1.

Some initialization parameters are dynamic since they can be modified using the ALTER SESSION or ALTER SYSTEM statement while an instance is running. Use the following syntax to dynamically alter initialization parameters:

```
ALTER SESSION SET parameter_name = value
ALTER SYSTEM SET parameter_name = value [DEFERRED]
```

Use the SET clause of the ALTER SYSTEM statement to set or change initialization parameter values. Additionally, the SCOPE clause specifies the scope of a change as described below:

```
SCOPE = SPFILE
(For both static and dynamic parameters, changes are recorded in the
spfile, to be given effect in the next restart.)

SCOPE = MEMORY
(For dynamic parameters, changes are applied in memory only. No
static parameter change is allowed.)

SCOPE = BOTH
(For dynamic parameters, the change is applied in both the server
parameter file and memory. No static parameter change is allowed.)
```

For dynamic parameters, the DEFERRED keyword can also be specified. When specified, the change is effective only for future sessions. Here are some examples.

The following statement affects all instances. However, the values only affect the current instances as they are not written to the binary SPFILE.

```
ALTER SYSTEM SET OPEN_CURSORS=2000 SID='*' SCOPE=MEMORY;
```

The next statement resets the value for the instance RACDB1. At this point, the database-wide setting becomes effective for the SID with the value of RACDB1.

```
ALTER SYSTEM RESET OPEN_CURSORS SCOPE=SPFILE sid='RACDB1';
```

To reset a parameter to its default value throughout the cluster database, use the command:

```
ALTER SYSTEM RESET OPEN_CURSORS
SCOPE=SPFILE sid='*';
```

Creating a Server Parameter File

The server parameter file is initially created from a text initialization parameter file (*init.ora*). It must be created prior to its use in the STARTUP command. The create SPFILE statement is used to create a server parameter file. The following example creates a server parameter file from an initialization parameter file:

```
CREATE SPFILE FROM PFILE='/u01/oracle/product/920/dbs/initRAC1.ora';
```

Below is another example that illustrates creating a server parameter file and supplying a name:

```
CREATE SPFILE='/u01/oracle/product/920/dbs/racdb_spfile.ora'
FROM PFILE='/u01/oracle/product/920/dbs/init.ora';
```

Exporting the Server Parameter File

The server parameter file can be exported to create a traditional text initialization parameter file. This would be useful for:

- Creating backups of the server parameter file.
- For diagnostic purposes to list all of the parameter values currently used by an instance.
- Modifying the server parameter file by first exporting it, editing the output file, and then recreating it.

The following example creates a text initialization parameter file from the server parameter file. Since no paths are specified, the files will be located in $ORACLE_HOME/database or its equivalent:

```
CREATE PFILE FROM SPFILE;
```

The example below creates a text initialization parameter file from a server parameter file, where the names of the files are specified:

```
CREATE PFILE='/u01/oracle/product/920/dbs/racdb_init.ora'
FROM SPFILE='/u01/oracle/product/dbs/racdb_spfile.ora';
```

Refer to *Oracle Database 10g Database Reference* for all the parameters that can be changed with an ALTER SYSTEM command.

UNDO Management

The Oracle database uses undo segments for undo transactions. They are also used to provide read-consistent images. Traditionally, Oracle maintained rollback segments to store the undo records. Undo records are used for three main purposes. These purposes are:

- Undo records provide read consistency by maintaining the before image of the data.
- Multi-version read consistency models require that users always have access to consistent data. Even though many concurrent users access and modify the same set of data blocks, every user has to get consistent data, and data integrity has to be maintained.
- During database recovery, undo records are used to undo any uncommitted changes applied from the redo log to the data file. Data integrity is maintained even though a failure occurred during active transactions.
- When the user issues a rollback statement during an active transaction, the undo records are used to undo changes that were made to the database by the uncommitted transaction.

Oracle databases have used rollback segments for a long time. But with release 9i, a new method of undo process was introduced which stores the records in a tablespace. Tablespace-based automatic undo management avoids the tedious management of rollback segments. It is considered a good practice to use the automatic undo method for managing undo segments in Oracle Database 10g. However, the manual rollback segments can be used as well. Therefore, there are two modes of rollback or undo methods:

- **Automatic** – Automatic Undo Management (AUM) designates the rollback segments as Undo Segments.
- **Manual** – Follows the traditional method of manually creating the rollback segments.

The mode can be set at instance startup using the *undo_management* initialization parameter. In the automatic undo management system, the undo segments are internally managed by Oracle. The following initialization parameter setting causes the STARTUP command to start an instance in automatic undo management mode:

```
UNDO_MANAGEMENT = AUTO
```

An undo tablespace must be available for Oracle to store undo records. The specific tablespace is defined at startup by setting the *undo_tablespace* initialization parameter. In RAC there must be one UNDO tablespace for each instance. For example:

```
RACDB1.undo_tablespace=UNDO1TBS
RACDB2.undo_tablespace=UNDO2TBS
```

Undo Management in RAC

Oracle recommends using the automatic undo method for rollback purposes in a RAC system. Each instance in the RAC system can only use one undo tablespace at a time. In other words, instances cannot share undo tablespaces. Each instance in the cluster, being an independent transaction-processing environment, maintains its own UNDO area for undo management.

Either automatic undo management or rollback segment undo can be used to manage undo space. If the automatic rollback method will be used, set the global parameter *undo_management* to *auto* in the server parameter file, and set the *undo_tablespace* parameter to assign the undo tablespace to the instance.

The RAC system allows the creation and use of several undo tablespaces. When the instance is started, it uses the first available undo tablespace. A second instance will use another undo tablespace. Thus, each instance in a RAC system will have exclusive access to a particular undo tablespace at a given time. The undo tablespace cannot be shared among the instances at the same time. Only once an undo tablespace is released by an instance, it can be assigned to another instance. However, all instances can read blocks from any or all undo tablespaces for the purpose of constructing read-consistency images.

If the need arises, an idle undo tablespace can be utilized. This feature is useful for switching to a new undo tablespace located in a different file system, or utilizing a new undo tablespace that is larger in size.

For the purpose of executing a large batch process at night, a new undo tablespace can be utilized. This way, the instance keeps running without any down time. At the time of the switch, the instances maintain control of both the old and new undo tablespaces. The old undo tablespace is marked as pending-offline until all the transactions using it are completed.

Undo tablespaces can be dynamically redirected by executing the ALTER SYSTEM SET UNDO_TABLESPACE statement. For example, assume instances RAC1 and RAC2 are accessing undo tablespaces undotbs01 and undotbs02 respectively. Using an idle undo tablespace, undotbs03 for example, the following statement can be executed from either instance to redirect undo processing to undotbs03.

```
ALTER SYSTEM SET UNDO_TABLESPACE = undotbs3;
```

The undo tablespace is usually defined when the database is created by using the CREATE DATABASE statement as shown in the following example:

```
CREATE DATABASE racdb
.
.
UNDO TABLESPACE undotbs_01
DATAFILE '/u01/oracle/rbdb1/undo_01' SIZE 1024M;
```

The undo tablespace can also be defined after the database is created, as shown here in this example:

```
Create UNDO tablespace UNDOTBS_3
DATAFILE '/u01/oracle/rbdb1/undo_3' SIZE 512M ;
```

If an undo tablespace runs out of space, or to prevent it from doing so, add files to it or resize the existing data files. The following example adds a data file to the undo tablespace undotbs_3:

```
ALTER TABLESPACE undotbs_3
ADD DATAFILE '/u01/oracle/rbdb1/undo_31' SIZE 128M ;
```

Initialization Parameters for UNDO management

The initialization parameters shown in Table 8.6 are relevant for undo management.

PARAMETER	DESCRIPTION
undo_management	If AUTO, use automatic undo management mode. If MANUAL, use manual undo management mode.
undo_tablespace	A dynamic parameter specifying the name of an undo tablespace to use.
undo_retention	A dynamic parameter specifying the length of time to retain undo. Default is 900 seconds.
undo_suppress_errors	Set to TRUE to suppress error messages generated by manual undo SQL statements when operating in automatic undo management mode. If set to FALSE, error messages are issued. This is a dynamic parameter.

Table 8.6: *Undo Initialization Parameters*

To view the existing parameters, use the command:

```
SQL>  show parameter undo

NAME                                 TYPE        VALUE
------------------------------------ ----------- ----------
undo_management                      string      AUTO
undo_retention                       integer     900
undo_suppress_errors                 boolean     FALSE
undo_tablespace                      string      UNDOTBS1
```

UNDO Tablespace Features

Some of the general features of undo tablespaces include:

- They are locally managed with system extent allocation.
- The UNDO tablespace cannot be used for any purpose other than UNDO segments and no operations can be performed on system-generated undo segments. When trying to create a table using the following statement:

  ```
  create table salesman
  name varchar2(4), salesid number(6) )
  tablespace undo_rbs1 ;
  ```

  The following message will be generated: ORA-30022: Cannot create segments in undo tablespace
- Only one UNDO tablespace can be used at the instance level.
- UNDO segments are created automatically and are owned by PUBLIC. They are named as *_syssmun$* and are not manually manageable. The number of segments depends on the *sessions* parameter.
- When AUM is chosen, it will not be possible to manage an undo or rollback.

For example, if this statement is issued:

```
create public rollback segment rsg1 tablespace rbs1 ;
```

The following error will be generated: ORA-30019: Illegal rollback segment operation in automatic mode

- Only the undo segments of the active UNDO tablespace and the SYSTEM rollback segments are kept online.
- All the instances in RAC must run in the same undo mode (i.e. AUTO or MANUAL).

Table 8.7 shows the views that provide undo information.

VIEW	DESCRIPTION
v$undostat	Contains statistics for monitoring and tuning undo space. Use this view to help estimate the amount of undo space required for the current workload.
v$rollstat	For automatic undo management mode, information reflects behavior of the undo segments in the undo tablespace.
v$transaction	Contains undo segment information.
dba_undo_extents	Shows the commit time for each extent in the undo.

Table 8.7: *Dynamic performance views related to undo*

System Rollback Segment

The system rollback segment is shared, and is used by all instances for transactions involving system objects. Even when using the AUM method, Oracle can still use the system rollback segment. There is only one system rollback segment for the entire database. It resides in the SYSTEM tablespace.

Using Rollback Segments – Manual Method

Even though the recommended method is to use AUM, the traditional method of manually creating rollback segments is allowed. In such a case, set the initialization parameter *undo_management*=MANUAL. When operating in manual mode, each instance needs at least one rollback segment to start successfully. A rollback segment may be acquired by only one instance. Once an instance acquires a particular rollback segment, it is used exclusively by that instance. No other instance can write to it, although they can read from it for the purpose of read-consistent images.

Public and Private Rollback

Rollback segments can be either public or private. Private rollback segments are used exclusively by an instance. Public rollback segments can be acquired by any of the instances. They are exactly the same in their functionality.

A public rollback segment is created by the PUBLIC clause with the create ROLLBACK SEGMENT command. Any rollback segment created without the PUBLIC clause is considered a private rollback segment. As mentioned, public rollback segments can be acquired by any instance, while private rollback segments are acquired by a specific instance only when the rollback segment's name has been listed in the *rollback_segment* initialization parameter for the instance, as shown here:

```
ROLLBACK_SEGMENTS = (RBS10, RBS11, RBS12)
```

It is preferable to use private rollback segments and they are recommended for ease of administration. When private rollback segments are used, it is easy to determine which rollback segments are in use by which instance. This facilitates planning in advance based on the workload for a typical instance. The following example shows how to create a public rollback segment:

```
create public rollback segment rbseg1
tablespace rbs11 ;
```

Concept of Thread

In the RAC system, each instance has to have its own redo log groups. The redo log file groups of an instance are collectively called a thread, or more appropriately, a redo log thread. Each instance has its own redo thread. The redo log groups function in a true circular fashion; as one fills up, another one records the redo entries. In a stand-alone instance, there is only one thread. In a RAC system, typically there are as many threads as instances. The thread number identifies each thread. The threads may have different numbers of redo groups, but each group must have at least two members, as shown in Figure 8.1.

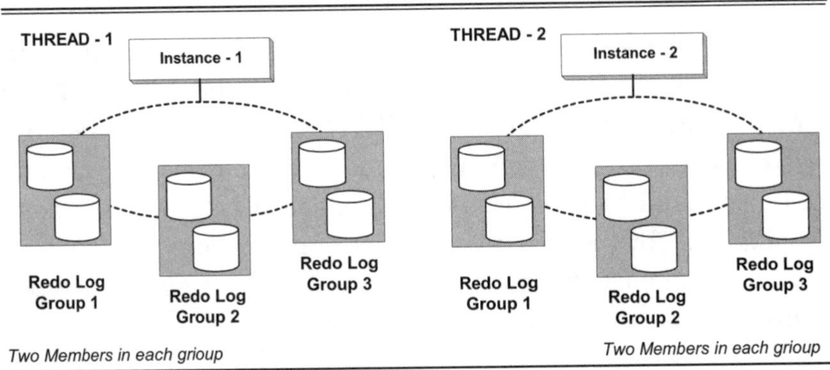

Figure 8.1: *Redo Log threads*

Online redo logs record the redo entries as transactions commit and rollback. Redo groups may optionally have additional members to provide mirroring of the redo groups.

Thread Features

Each instance must have a minimum of two redo groups, with each group having at least one member in the group. Every redo group has a group number, which is a unique number in the database. All the redo log files supporting the redo groups reside on shared storage, so that every instance in the cluster can access all the redo groups during the recovery process. As shown in Figure 8.2, all the redo groups are located on a shared storage unit.

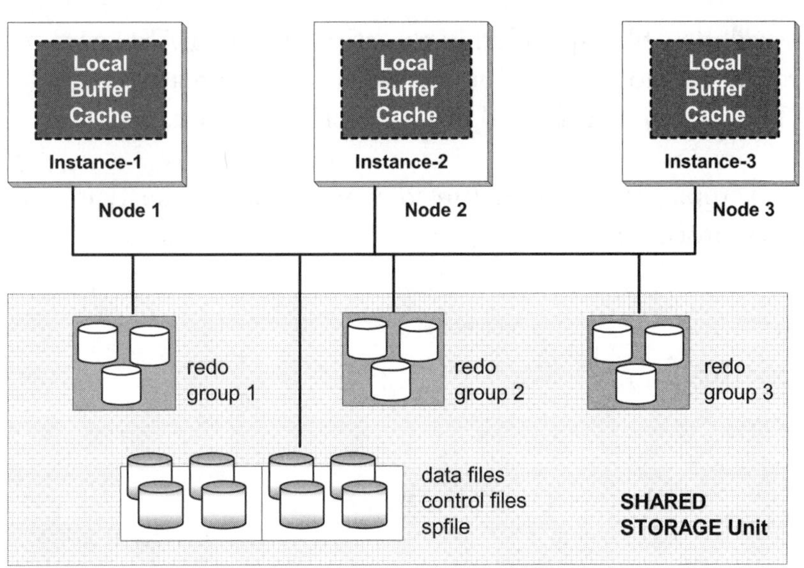

Figure 8.2: *Redo Groups on a shared storage*

Use a minimum of three or more redo groups in a thread. Keep at least two redo members for each redo group for multiplexing and protection. Multiplexing the redo members is optional but is highly recommended. Different degrees of mirroring are permitted in different threads.

The redo log thread can be public or private. When the redo thread is enabled, it can be specified as a private thread. This means it is associated with a specific instance as defined in the initialization parameter thread of the instance. Alternatively, it can be specified as public, in which case any instance can acquire it.

Redo Thread Maintenance

The redo log files specified in the create DATABASE command become thread 1. Additional threads are created using the ALTER DATABASE ADD LOGFILE command.

For example, to create a thread while creating the database (a manual process):

```
CREATE DATABASE 'RACDB'
  MAXLOGFILES 300 MAXLOGMEMBERS 6
  MAXDATAFILES 512 MAXINSTANCES 24
  MAXLOGHISTORY 1024
  DATAFILE '/u01/oracle/data/sys_racdb1' size 1024M
  LOGFILE
  GROUP 1
('u01/oracle/redo/file1a',
      'u02/oracle/redo/file1b') size 50M,
  GROUP 2
('u01/oracle/redo/file2a',
      'u02/oracle/redo/file2b') size 50M,
  GROUP 3
('u01/oracle/redo/file3a',
      'u02/oracle/redo/file3b') size 50M ;
```

To add an extra redo log thread:

```
ALTER DATABASE ADD LOGFILE THREAD 2
 GROUP 4 ('u01/oracle/redo/file4a',
         'u02/oracle/redo/file4a') size 50M,
 GROUP 5 ('u01/oracle/redo/file5a',
         'u02/oracle/redo/file5a') size 50M,
 GROUP 6 ('u01/oracle/redo/file6a',
         'u02/oracle/redo/file6a') size 50M  ;
```

A thread needs to be enabled before an instance can use it. While enabling, it can be designated as a public or a private thread. For example, to enable as a public thread:

```
ALTER DATABASE ENABLE PUBLIC THREAD 2 ;
```

To enable as a private thread:

```
ALTER DATABASE ENABLE PRIVATE THREAD 3 ;
```

When a thread is enabled as private, the *thread* parameter in the SPFILE (or *init.ora*) can be used to associate the instance with a thread. For example, instances racdb1 and racdb2 will have thread 1 and 2 respectively.

```
RACDB1.THREAD=1  # RACDB1 instance uses Thread 1
RACDB2.THREAD=2  # RACDB2 instance uses Thread 2
```

Next, here are some examples of how to drop a group or member.

For dropping an online redo log group, use the ALTER DATABASE statement with the DROP LOGFILE clause. The following statement drops redo log group number 3:

```
ALTER DATABASE DROP LOGFILE GROUP 3;
```

To drop specific inactive online redo log members, use the ALTER DATABASE statement with the DROP LOGFILE MEMBER clause. The following statement drops the redo log */u01/oracle/redo/log3c*:

```
ALTER DATABASE DROP LOGFILE
MEMBER '/u01/oracle/redo/log3c';
```

Table 8.8 shows the views that deal with online redo information.

VIEW	DESCRIPTION
v$log	Displays the redo log file information from the control file.
v$logfile	Identifies redo log groups and members and member status.
v$log_history	Contains log history information.

Table 8.8: *Dynamic performance views related to Redo-Log*

Segment Space Management

Each object in the database that occupies space is associated with a segment. A segment is a set of extents that contains all the data for a specific logical storage within a tablespace or multiple tablespaces. An extent is a storage unit composed of contiguous blocks. The free and used space in a segment can be managed in two ways:

- Manual
- Automatic

When a locally managed tablespace is created using the CREATE TABLESPACE statement, the SEGMENT SPACE MANAGEMENT clause allows the DBA to specify how free and used space within a segment is to be managed.

- The Manual Method involves managing the free space using the free lists of the data blocks. This method depends on the storage settings like *pctused, freelists,* and *freelist groups* for schema objects. Manual method is the default parameter when creating a tablespace.
- In the Automatic Method, Oracle uses bitmaps to manage the free space within segments. A bitmap, in this case, is a map that describes the status of each data block within a segment with respect to the amount of space in the block available for inserting rows. As more space becomes available or some space gets reduced in a data block, the new amount of free space is reflected in the bitmap. Automatic segment-space management is specified at the tablespace level. The Oracle database server automatically and efficiently manages free and used space within objects created in such tablespaces.

Automatic Segment Space Management

Automatic segment-space management is a simpler and more efficient way of managing space within a segment. It completely eliminates any need to specify and tune the *pctused*, *freelists*, and *freelist groups* storage parameters for schema objects created in the tablespace. If any of these attributes are specified, they are ignored.

For example, the following statement creates tablespace mytbs1 with automatic segment-space management:

```
CREATE TABLESPACE mytbs1
DATAFILE '/u01/oracle/data/mytbs01.dbf' SIZE 500M
EXTENT MANAGEMENT LOCAL
SEGMENT SPACE MANAGEMENT AUTO;
```

When an object such as a table or index is created using the locally managed tablespace, with automatic segment-space management enabled, there is no need to specify the *pctfree* or freelists.

The in-segment free/used space is tracked using bitmaps as opposed to the free lists. When the locally managed tablespace cannot be used, and therefore the automatic management space feature cannot be used, the remaining option is to depend on the traditional method of managing free lists and free lists groups. The free list method of RAC will be covered in a later part of this section.

Automatic segment-space management offers the following benefits:

- It provides administrative ease of use by avoiding the specification of storage parameters.
- It is a good method for handling objects with varying row sizes.

- It provides better run-time adjustment for variations in concurrent access and avoids tedious tuning methods.
- It provides better multi-instance behavior in terms of performance/space utilization.

However, note that this automatic feature of segment space management is available only with locally managed tablespaces and their objects. A new column called SEGMENT_SPACE_MANAGEMENT has been added to the *dba_tablespaces* view to indicate the segment space management mode used by a tablespace.

Use the Oracle procedure *dbms_space.space_usage* to provide the space usage ratio within each block in the Bitmap Managed Block (BMB) segments. It provides information regarding the number of blocks in a segment with the following range of free space.

```
0-25%   free space within a block
25-50%  free space within a block
50-75%  free space within a block
75-100% free space within a block
```

RAC Related Advantages

The performance and manageability gains provided by the automatic segment space management feature are particularly noticeable in a Real Application Cluster environment. It eliminates the need to alter the number of *freelists and freelist groups* when new instances are brought online, thereby saving the downtime associated with such table reorganizations. It also avoids the tuning effort previously required for multiple instance environments.

An Oracle internal benchmark comparing the performance of automatic and manual segment space management, conducted on a two node Real Application Cluster database by inserting about 3 million rows in a table, showed that automatic segment space management provided a 35% performance gain over an optimally tuned segment (8 freelist groups, 20 freelists) using the manual mode. For more details, refer to Oracle Metalink Note 180608.1.

Use the new *dbms_space.space_usage* procedure for reporting the space position in BMB segments. This procedure provides the space usage ratio within each block. It is preferred over the *dbms_space.free_blocks* procedure. Here is an SQL example of how to get information about the blocks:

block_count.sql

```
-- ***********************************************
-- Copyright © 2003 by Rampant TechPress
-- This script is free for non-commercial purposes
-- with no warranties.  Use at your own risk.
--
-- To license this script for a commercial purpose,
-- contact info@rampant.cc
-- ***********************************************

DECLARE
 v_unformatted_blocks number;
 v_unformatted_bytes number;
 v_fs1_blocks number;
 v_fs1_bytes number;
 v_fs2_blocks number;
 v_fs2_bytes number;
 v_fs3_blocks number;
 v_fs3_bytes number;
 v_fs4_blocks number;
 v_fs4_bytes number;
 v_full_blocks number;
 v_full_bytes number;
BEGIN
dbms_space.space_usage ('SYSTEM', 'TEST', 'TABLE',
v_unformatted_blocks, v_unformatted_bytes, v_fs1_blocks,
v_fs1_bytes, v_fs2_blocks, v_fs2_bytes, v_fs3_blocks, v_fs3_bytes,
v_fs4_blocks, v_fs4_bytes, v_full_blocks, v_full_bytes);
dbms_output.put_line('Unformatted Blocks = '||v_unformatted_blocks);
dbms_output.put_line('FS1 Blocks         = '||v_fs1_blocks);
dbms_output.put_line('FS2 Blocks         = '||v_fs2_blocks);
dbms_output.put_line('FS3 Blocks         = '||v_fs3_blocks);
dbms_output.put_line('FS4 Blocks         = '||v_fs4_blocks);
dbms_output.put_line('Full Blocks        = '||v_full_blocks);
end;
```

It yields the following output:

```
  Unformatted Blocks = 0
  FS1 Blocks         = 0
  FS2 Blocks         = 0
  FS3 Blocks         = 0
  FS4 Blocks         = 1
  Full Blocks        = 9

Where:
  FS1 means 0-25%   free space within a block
  FS2 means 25-50%  free space within a block
  FS3 means 50-75%  free space within a block
  FS4 means 75-100% free space within a block
```

Manual Space Management

In the manual method, free space within a segment is tracked by structures such as free lists and free list groups.

Within the first block of each segment, there is a segment header. The segment header contains a list of blocks with free space, called the master free list. Blocks are removed from the master free list when the free space in those blocks becomes less than that specified by the *pctfree* storage parameter. Blocks are added back to the master free list when their used space falls below the threshold specified by the *pctused* storage parameter.

The master free list is accessed and used by all the processes that insert or update an object. These processes remove and add blocks from free lists based on the space remaining after DML operations on those blocks. Simultaneous update to the free list involves writes to the segment header, and also may result in contention as shown in the Figure 8.3.

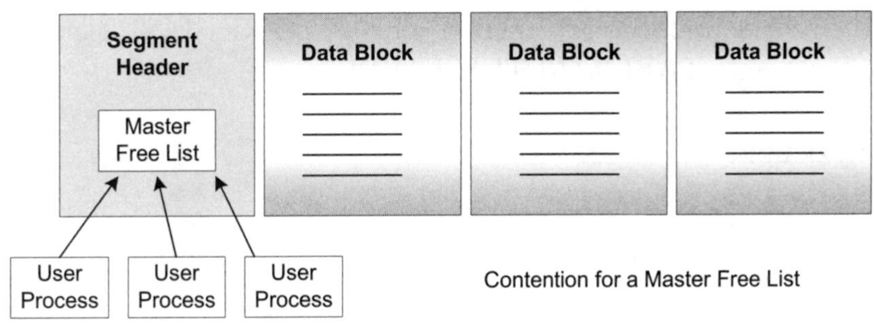

Figure 8.3: *Free List in the Segment Header*

To handle such contention situations, many free lists can be specified at the segment level. These are sometimes called process free lists. The *freelist* storage parameter indicates the number of free list sets. Each user process is assigned to one process free list. When the user process needs a block with free space, it scans its assigned process free lists. Existence of multiple process free lists improves performance for concurrent OLTP activities on the same segment and avoids segment header contention. As shown in Figure 8.4, multiple free lists help reduce contention.

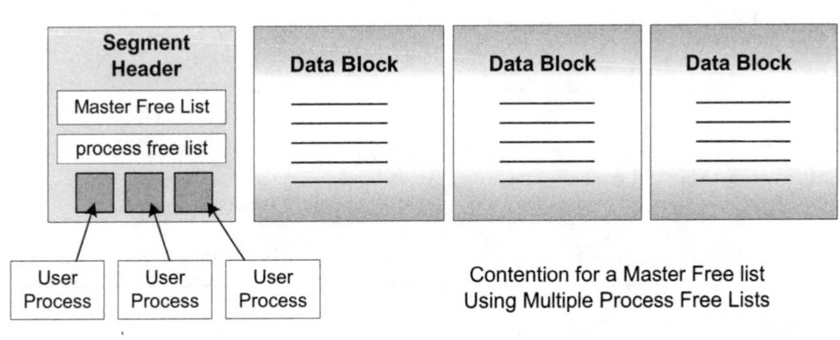

Figure 8.4: *Multiple Process Free Lists in the Segment Header*

The process free lists are created when the FREELIST clause is used in a *create* TABLE/ALTER TABLE statement.

For example:

```
CREATE TABLE salesman
( name varchar2(4), salesid number(6) )
STORAGE ( FREELISTS 6) ;
```

There is a possibility of additional overhead and contention in the RAC system since multiple instances concurrently access the segment for DML operations. To reduce such contention, create groups of free lists and assign them to the individual instances. This way, users from a particular instance are confined to free lists from a group. This is shown in Figure 8.5. The free list group is a combination of a group specific master free lists and group specific process free lists. Each free list group is stored in its own block. Instances are assigned to different free list groups, thereby reducing contention between instances.

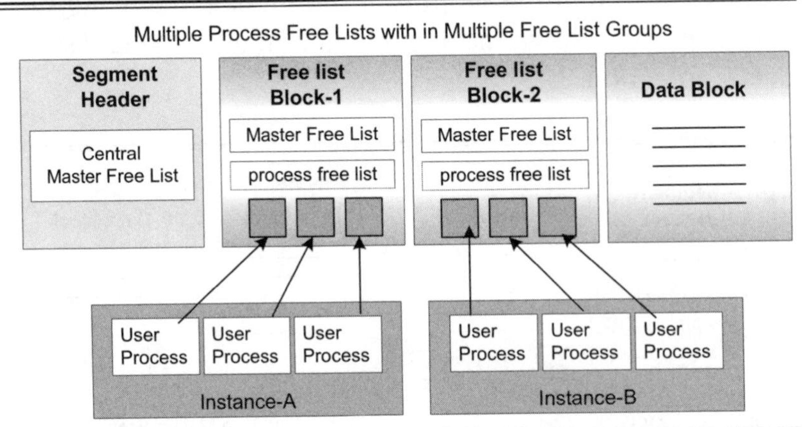

Figure 8.5: *Multiple Free List Groups in a segment header*

The process free lists are created when the freelist group clause is used in a CREATE TABLE/ALTER TABLE statement.

For example:

```
CREATE TABLE sales
( . . . )
STORAGE (INITIAL 10M NEXT 10M
MINEXTENTS 2 MAXEXTENTS 512
PCTFREE 20 PCTUSED 60 PCTINCREASE 0
FREELIST GROUP 2 FREELISTS 6 );
```

The *freelist* and *freelist group* parameters can also be specified for other objects such as indexes and clusters.

For example:

```
CREATE INDEX sales_index ( . . . )
STORAGE ( FREELIST GROUP 3 FREELISTS 4) ;
```

Storage Parameters

freelists: Specifies the number of free lists for each of the free list groups of the schema object.

freelist groups: The number of groups of free lists for the database objects being created. Oracle uses the instance number of Oracle Real Application Cluster instances to map each instance to one free list group.

Associating Instances with Free List Groups

Once the multiple freelist groups for an object in the RAC system have been assigned, the instances and user sessions can be associated with free list groups as follows:

- ***instance_number* parameter**: Various SQL clauses with the *instance_number* initialization parameter can be used to associate extents of data blocks with instances.

- **SET INSTANCE clause**: The SET INSTANCE clause of the ALTER SESSION statement can be used to ensure that a session uses the free list group associated with a particular instance, regardless of the instance to which the session is connected.

For example:

```
ALTER SESSION SET INSTANCE = inst_no
```

The ALLOCATE EXTENT clause of the ALTER TABLE or ALTER CLUSTER statement enables the pre-allocation of an extent to a table, index, or cluster using parameters that specify the extent size, data file, and group of free lists with which to associate the object. Pre-allocating and associating extents to different instances helps reduce contention during the concurrent inserts. For example:

```
ALTER TABLE SALES
ALLOCATE EXTENT (SIZE 5M INSTANCE 2);
```

Oracle Managed Files

Oracle Managed Files (OMF) directly manages file creation and deletion at the operating system level. Operations are specified in terms of database objects rather than filenames. Oracle internally uses standard file system interfaces to create and delete files as needed for the database structures such as tablespaces, online redo log files, and control files.

Administrators need to specify the file system directory to be used for a particular type of file. Thereafter, Oracle manages to create unique files when needed and also deletes files that are not needed. The advantages include:

- No need to bother about the file names and storage requirements. Oracle provides a unique file name.

- Eliminates the need for the DBA to directly manage OS files.
- Allows operations to be specified in terms of objects and not files.
- Reduces the chance of overwriting a file. Avoids accidental corruption of data files.
- Reduces wasted disk space consumed by obsolete files. When a tablespace is dropped, the relevant files are automatically removed at the host level.

The following initialization parameters specify the file location:

- ***db_create_file_dest:*** Defines the location of the default file system directory where Oracle creates data files or temp files when no file specification is given in the object creation statement.
- ***db_create_online_log_dest_n*:** Defines the location of the default file system directory for online redo log files and control files when no file specification is given in the creation statement. This initialization parameter can be used multiple times where *n* specifies a multiplexed copy of the online redo log or control file.

Note that the file system directory specified by either of these parameters must already exist. Oracle does not create it. The directory must also have permissions to allow Oracle to create the files in it. The default location is used whenever a location is not explicitly specified for the operation of creating a file. Oracle creates the filename, and a file thus created is an Oracle-managed file. The following example sets */u01/oracle/data/applic* as the default directory to use when creating Oracle-managed files:

```
DB_CREATE_FILE_DEST = '/u01/oracle/data/applic'
```

By default, this location would be applicable for data files, temp files, Online redo log files, and control files. However, the *db_create_online_log_dest_n* initialization parameter can be included in the initialization parameter file to identify the default location for the database server to create online redoes log files and control files. For example:

```
DB_CREATE_ONLINE_LOG_DEST_1 = '/u03/oracle/redo/applic'
DB_CREATE_ONLINE_LOG_DEST_2 = '/u04/oracle/redo/applic'
```

Also, the DB_CREATE location can also be changed with the ALTER SYSTEM command.

For example, the following commands change the OMF directory location to '*/u05/oracle/data/applic*', and creates a new tablespace.

```
ALTER SYSTEM SET
DB_CREATE_FILE_DEST = '/u05/oracle/data/applic' ;

CREATE TABLESPACE tbs_1; # creates def.size of 100MB
CREATE TABLESPACE tbs_3
DATAFILE AUTOEXTEND ON MAXSIZE 800M;
```

For more details, refer to the chapter on *Using Oracle Managed Files* in the Oracle 10g Database Administrator's Guide.

With RAC systems, the OMF facility can only be used if the cluster system is using the cluster file system. The availability of the cluster file system with a set of mounted file systems, allows a directory to be set up for OMF files. The DBCA also supports Oracle Managed Files for operating systems that support a cluster file system.

Oracle Disk Manager

Oracle Disk Manager (ODM) is a disk management interface defined by Oracle to enhance file management and disk I/O performance. Implementation of an ODM interface in a file system or a logical volume manager (LVM) provides many benefits including simplified file administration, improved file integrity, and reduced system overhead. It is completely transparent from an application/DBA perspective. It is an improvement over standard UNIX I/O.

ODM eliminates file descriptors, which simplifies the operating system kernel configuration and saves operating system resources. Other ODM capabilities include special locking modes that prevent errors and the ability to pass usage hints, such as Oracle file type information and I/O priorities for third party application integration. It manages all I/O type files on both system files and raw partitions with one system call, which is not possible with native operating system calls.

Some of the visible advantages include:

- Files being created/initialized are not visible until they are committed.
- Files must be identified or opened with a common key and cannot be removed if they are in use.
- Works with regular files and raw volumes.

Oracle Database 10g automatically takes advantage of the ODM interface when the underlying file system or logical volume manager becomes ODM enabled. A file is considered an ODM file if it is in a file system that supports the ODM interface. ODM is also compatible with the new Oracle Real Application Clusters.

Many of the file system/volume manager vendors have incorporated the ODM interface. Well known examples include, Veritas Database Edition (Advanced Cluster for Oracle Database 10g RAC) and Polyserve Matrix Server for Oracle 10g RAC. Several ODM semantics have been included in the DAFS v1.0 Protocol Specifications offered by Network Appliances.

Oracle 10g Automated Storage Management

Automated Storage Management (ASM) divides files into 1 MB extents and spreads the extents for each file evenly across all of the disks in a disk group. ASM does not use a mathematical function to track the placement of each extent; it uses pointers to record extent location. This allows ASM to move individual extents of a file when the disk group configuration changes without having to move all extents to adhere to a formula based on the number of disks.

As stated above, for normal datafiles, ASM uses 1 megabyte extents. For log files that require low latency, ASM provides fine-grained (128k) striping to allow larger I/Os to be split and processed in parallel by multiple disks. The DBA decides at creation time whether or not to use fine-grained striping. File-type specific templates in the disk group determine the default behavior.

Automatic Storage Management's native mirroring mechanism is an option that can be set when creating a disk group. The redundancy protection for that group can be specified and, if the DBA prefers to use an external mirroring system or has no need for fault-tolerance, the DBA can set the redundancy to *external*, in which case ASM will not mirror at all. Unless otherwise specified, redundancy defaults to *normal*, in which case ASM mirrors each 1 MB extent.

For the highest level of fault tolerance, *high redundancy* can be specified, which provides three-way mirroring.

Server Control Utility

To manage the RAC database and its instances, Oracle provided a utility called the Server Control Utility (SRVCTL) in version 9i.

This replaced the earlier utility *opsctl* which was used in the parallel server.

The Server Control Utility is a single point of control between the Oracle Intelligent agent and each node in the RAC system. The SRVCTL communicates with the global daemon service (GSD) and resides on each of the nodes. The SRVCTL gathers information from the database and instances and acts as an intermediary between nodes and the Oracle Intelligent agent.

When using the SRVCTL to perform configuration operations on a cluster, the SRVCTL stores configuration data in the Server Management (SRVM) configuration repository. The SRVM includes all the components of Enterprise Manager such as the Intelligent Agent, the Server Control Utility (SRVCTL), and the Global Services Daemon. Thus, the SRVCTL is one of the SRVM Instance Management Utilities. The SRVCTL uses SQL*Plus internally to perform stop and start activities on each node.

For the SRVCTL to function, the Global Services Daemon (GSD) should be running on the node. The SRVCTL performs mainly two types of administrative tasks: Cluster Database Tasks and Cluster Database Configuration Tasks.

SRVCTL Cluster Database tasks include:

- Starts and stops cluster databases.
- Starts and stops cluster database instances.
- Starts and stops listeners associated with a cluster database instance.
- Obtains the status of a cluster database instance.
- Obtains the status of listeners associated with a cluster database.

- Start and stop ASM instances.
- Manage disk groups in an ASM instance.
- SRVCTL Cluster Database Configuration tasks include:
- Adds and deletes cluster database configuration information.
- Adds an instance to, or deletes an instance from a cluster database.
- Renames an instance name within a cluster database configuration.
- Moves instances in a cluster database configuration.
- Sets and unsets the environment variable for an instance in a cluster database configuration.
- Sets and unsets the environment variable for an entire cluster in a cluster database configuration.

To manage the RAC environment, first build a configuration profile and optionally save it. The configuration can be built by commands such as *add* and *setenv*. It is a good practice to build configuration profiles and export them to ASCII files.

SRVCTL syntax has the following components:

```
> srvctl verb noun options
```

Where:

srvctl is the SRVCTL command.

verb is an action word such as start, stop, or remove.

noun is an object upon which SRVCTL performs the action verb, such as a database or instance. Alternatively, abbreviations can be used, which in this case are *db* and *inst* respectively.

options extends the use of preceding verb-noun combinations.

To see the online command syntax and options for each SRVCTL command, enter:

```
> srvctl verb noun -h
```

Table 8.9 shows the common SRVCTL verbs.

VERB	DESCRIPTION
add	Add a database or instance.
config	Lists the configuration for the database or instance.
Getenv	Lists the environment variables in the SRVM configuration.
Modify	Modifies the instance configuration.
remove	Removes the database or instance.
Setenv	Sets the environment variable in the SRVM configuration.
Start	Starts the database or instance.
Status	Status of the database or instance.
Stop	Stops the database or instance.
Unsetenv	Sets the environment variable in the SRVM configuration to unspecified.

Table 8.9: *Common SRVCTL verbs*

Table 8.10 shows the common *srvctl* nouns.

NOUN	ABBREVIATION	DESCRIPTION
database	db	Operation refers to objects for the database.
asm	asm	To add, configure, enable, start, obtain the status of, stop, disable, and remove ASM instances.
instance	Inst	Operation refers to objects for the instances.
nodeapps	no abbreviation	To add, configure, modify, manage environment variables for, start, obtain the status of, stop, and remove node applications.
Service	serv	To add, configure, modify, manage environment variables for, enable, start, obtain the status of, relocate, disable, stop, and remove services from your cluster database.

Table 8.10: *Common SRVCTL nouns*

Table 8.11 shows the common *srvctl* command options.

OPTION	MEANING
-d	Database name
-h	Print Usage
-i	Comma-separated list of instance names
-n	Node names or comma-separated node list

Table 8.11: *Common SRVCTL command options*

Some commonly used commands will be examined next.

srvctl add

This command adds configuration information for the database or for named instances. Command specific actions for add command:

```
-n Node name that will support an instance.
-o $ORACLE_HOME to locate lsnrctl (node option) and oracle binaries
(other options)
-s SPFILE name
-m Database domain name, in the form "us.domain.com"
```

For example, to add a new database:

```
> srvctl add database -d racdb -o /app/oracle/product/920
```

To add named instances to a database:

```
> srvctl add instance -d racdb -i rac1 -n mynode1
> srvctl add instance -d racdb -i rac2 -n mynode2
> srvctl add instance -d racdb -i rac3 -n mynode3
```

srvctl config

This command displays a list of configured databases. The syntax is:

```
srvctl config database -d database_name
```

For example, to display configured databases:

```
> srvctl  config database -d RACDB
```

```
Gives the output:
```

```
mynode1 RACDB1 /app/oracle/product/dbms/920
mynode2 RACDB2 /app/oracle/product/dbms/920
```

srvctl getenv

This command displays values for the environment from the SRVM configuration file. The syntax is:

```
> srvctl getenv database -d database_name [-t name]

> srvctl getenv instance -d database_name
  -i instance_name [-t name]
```

For example, to list all environment variables for a database:

```
> srvctl getenv database -d racdb
```

srvctl setenv

This command sets values for the environment in the SRVM configuration file. The syntax is:

```
> srvctl setenv database -d database_name
  -t name=value [,name=value,…]

srvctl setenv instance -d database_name
   [-i instance_name] -t name=value [,name=value,…]
```

For example, to set list all environment variables for a database:

```
> srvctl setenv database -d mydb -t LANG=en
```

srvctl start

This command starts the database, all or named instances, and all listeners associated with the database. The syntax is:

```
> srvctl start database -d database_name
  [-o start_options]  [-c connect_string]

> srvctl start instance -d database_name -i instance_name
  [,insta_name-list] [-o start_options] [-c connect_string]
```

Command-Specific Options for *srvctl* start

-o Options passed directly to startup command in SQL*Plus including PFILE.

-**c** Connect string for connecting to the Oracle instance using SQL*Plus.

For example, to start the database and all enabled instances:

```
> srvctl start database -d mydb
```

To start specified instances:

```
> srvctl start instance -d racdb -i racdb1, racdb3
```

srvctl status

This command displays the status of the database and instance. The syntax is:

```
> srvctl status database -d database_name

> srvctl status instance -d database_name
-i instance_name [,instance_name-list]
```

For example, to get the current status of two instances:

```
> srvctl  status instance -d RAC -i racdb1, racdb2
```

Gives the output:

```
Instance RACDB1 is running on node mynode1
Instance RACDB2 is not running on node mynode1
```

srvctl stop

This command stops the database and all or named instances. The syntax is:

```
> srvctl stop database -d database_name
  [-o stop_options] [-c connect_string]

> srvctl stop instance -d database_name
  -i instance_name [,instance_name_list]
  [-o stop_options][-c connect_string]
```

For example, to stop the database all instances:

```
> srvctl stop database -d RACDB
```

To stop named instances:

```
> srvctl stop instance -d RACDB -i racdb1
```

Use the *srvconfig* command to export/import the SRVM configuration information. The following is an example of how to export the contents of the configuration information to the text file:

```
> srvconfig -exp file_name
```

To import the configuration information from the text file named to the configuration repository for the RAC, use the command:

```
> srvconfig -imp file_name
```

Using the Oracle Interface Configuration Tool

Next, the use of the Oracle Database 10g Oracle Interface Configuration (OIFCFG) utility and RAC will be explored. The OIFCFG utility is used to define Network Interfaces. The OIFCFG command-line tool is used in both single-instance Oracle databases and in RAC database environments:

- Allocate and de-allocate network interfaces to components
- Direct components to use specific network interfaces
- Retrieve component configuration information

Here are some of the uses of OIFCFG.

Defining Network Interfaces with OIFCFG

A network interface is uniquely identified using these three components:

- An interface name
- An interface subnet address
- An interface type

The interface type is based on the purpose for which the network interface is configured. The OIFCFG supported interface types are:

- **Public**—Any interface that is used for communication with components external to RAC instances, such as Oracle Net and Virtual Internet Protocol (VIP) addresses
- **Cluster interconnect**—A private interface used for the cluster interconnect to provide inter-instance or Cache Fusion communication
- **Storage**—Usually a disk interface used for high-speed file I/O

Network interfaces are stored as one of two possible types:

- global interface
- node-specific interface

An interface should be stored as a global interface when all the nodes of a specific RAC cluster have the same interface connected to the same subnet. An interface is stored as a node-specific interface when any of the nodes in the cluster utilize a different set of interfaces and subnets. If an interface is configured as both a global and a node-specific interface by mistake or design, it will default to the node-specific definition.

A network interface specification is in the form of:

```
<interface_name>/<subnet>:<interface_type>.
```

For example, the following identifies eth0 as a cluster interconnect located at the address 1.1.1.1:

```
eth0/1.1.1.1:cluster_interconnect
```

OIFCFG Syntax and Commands

As with many of the other Oracle command line tools, use the oifcfg -help command to display online help for OIFCFG. For example:

```
<add output>
```

The elements of OIFCFG commands, some of which are optional, are:

- *nodename* is the name of the host, as known to the network
- *if_name* is the name by which the interface is known in the node in which it resides
- *subnet* is the subnet address of the interface, usually its IP address

- *if_type* is the type of interface: one of the values of: *public*, *cluster_interconnect*, or *storage*

Use the *iflist* option with the OIFCFG utility to list the interface names and the subnets of all the interfaces available on the local node, for example:

```
oifcfg iflist
eth0 1.1.1.1
eth0 1.1.1.2
```

Use the getif option to retrieve specific OIFCFG information:

```
oifcfg getif [ [-global | -node <nodename>] [-if
<if_name>[/<subnet>]] [-type <if_type>] ]
```

Use the setif keyword to store a new interface. For example, to store the interface hme0, with the subnet 187.188.130.0, as a global interface to be used as an interconnect for all the RAC instances in the cluster, use the command:

```
oifcfg setif -global hme0/187.188.130.0:cluster_interconnect
```

For a cluster interconnect that exists between only two nodes, for example aultlinux1 and aultlinux2, the eth1 interface could be created with the following commands, assuming 1.1.1.1 and 1.1.1.2 are the subnet addresses for the interconnect on aultlinux1 and aultlinux2:

```
oifcfg setif -node aultlinux1 eth1/1.1.1.1:cluster_interconnect
oifcfg setif -node aultlinux2 eth1/1.1.1.2:cluster_interconnect
```

Use the OIFCFG *delif* command to delete the stored configuration for global or node-specific interfaces. A specific node-specific or global interface can be deleted by supplying the interface name, with an optional subnet, on the command line. Without the *-node* or *-global* options, the *delif* keyword deletes either the given interface or all the global and node-specific interfaces on all the nodes in the cluster, so be careful with this command. For example, the following command deletes the global interface named gif1 for the subnet 207.122.63.66:

```
oifcfg delif -global gif1/207.122.63.66
```

On the other hand, the next command deletes all the global interfaces stored with the OIFCFG utility:

```
oifcfg delif -global
```

The next section is an examination of the cluster registry and its management in Oracle Database 10g.

The Oracle Cluster Registry in RAC

The purpose of the Oracle Cluster Registry (OCR) is to hold cluster and database configuration information for RAC and Cluster Ready Services (CRS) such as the cluster node list, and cluster database instance to node mapping, and CRS application resource profiles.

There are two methods of copying OCR content and using the content for recovery. The first method uses automatically generated physical OCR file copies and the second method uses manually created logical OCR export files.

Management of the Oracle Cluster Registry Backup Files in Real Application Clusters

The CRS are managed by a CRS instance. There will be one CRS instance for each node in a RAC cluster. In a cluster, CRS instance automatically creates an OCR backup every four hours. At any one time, the last three backup copies are automatically retained. The CRS instance also creates and retains an OCR backup for each *full day* and at the end of each *week*. The backup frequencies or the number of files that Oracle will retain cannot be customized as they are completely controlled by the CRS instance.

Because of the importance of OCR information, the *ocrconfig* tool should be used to make daily copies of the automatically generated backup files.

To make a backup, use the *ocrconfig* tool with the showbackup option to identify the backup files, and then copy each file to a location that is redundant to the location of the original OCR backup file. This ensures that there are at least two copies of each OCR backup file.

Oracle also recommends that the OCR location reside on RAID arrays. If possible, use a backup location that is shared by all nodes in the cluster. The default target location of each OCR backup file is as follows where <cluster name> is the name assigned to the cluster when CRS was installed:

```
<CRS Home>/cdata/<cluster name>
```

This location can be changed by using the following syntax:

```
ocrconfig -backuploc <directory name>
```

Restoration of the OCR File from the Automatically Generated OCR Backups

Before attempting to resolve any configuration-related problems, retry the application that failed. If the problem continues, then use one of the following platform-specific procedures to restore the OCR configuration.

Procedure for Restoring the Oracle Cluster Registry on UNIX-Based Systems

1. Stop the following OCR daemons: CSSD, CRSD, EVMD, and the EVM logger. On Linux the init.crs script located in the /etc/init.d directory is used to stop these daemons, for example:

   ```
   [root@aultlinux1 init.d]#/etc/init.d/init.crs stop
   ```

2. Shut down all the nodes in the cluster and restart from one node in single-user mode.
3. Identify the recent backups using the *ocrconfig -showbackup* command.
4. Execute the restore by applying an OCR backup file identified in Step 3 with the *ocrconfig -restore <file name>* command.
5. Restart the CRS, CSS, and EVM daemons and resume operations in cluster mode. The daemons can be restarted using the same script as in step one only use the start option:

   ```
   [root@aultlinux1 init.d]#/etc/init.d/init.crs start
   ```

Procedure for Restoring the Oracle Cluster Registry on Windows-Based Systems

1. Shut down all but one node in th RAC database.
2. Disable the following OCR clients and stop them using the Service Control Panel:
   - OracleClusterVolumeService,
   - OracleCSService,
   - OracleCRService, and the
   - OracleEVMService.
3. Identify the recent backups using the *ocrconfig -showbackup* command.

4. Execute the restore by applying an OCR backup file identified in Step 3 with the *ocrconfig -restore <file name>* command.
5. Start all the services that were stopped in step 2. Restart all the instances and resume operations in cluster mode.

Importing the Oracle Cluster Registry with OCR Exports

To ensure the OCR files are recoverable, in addition to using the automatically created OCR backup files, export the OCR contents before and after making significant configuration changes. This is done by using the *ocrconfig -export* command. This will enable the restoration of the OCR if the configuration changes cause errors. For example, if there are unresolvable configuration problems, or if the clusterware will not restart after making changes, restore the configuration using one of the following platform-specific procedures. The configuration cannot be restored from an automatically created OCR backup file using the -import option. Instead, the -restore option must be used.

Importing Oracle Cluster Registry Content on UNIX-Based Systems

1. Shut down all of the nodes in the cluster and restart one of them in single-user mode.
2. Import a valid OCR export file using the *ocrconfig -import* command from any node.
3. Restart all the nodes in the cluster in multi-user mode.

To avoid stopping the entire cluster, this alternate method can be used:

1. Update the inittab entries on all the nodes and remove the CRS-specific entries. Retain a copy of the original inittab file.

2. Run the */etc/init.d/init.crs stop* command on all the nodes.
3. Import the valid OCR export file using the *ocrconfig -import* command from any cluster node.
4. Restore the original inittab file on all nodes.
5. Run the */etc/init.d/init.crs start* command on all nodes.
6. Run the */etc/init q* command.

Importing Oracle Cluster Registry Content on Windows-Based Systems

1. Stop the following OCR clients using the Service Control Panel:
   - OracleClusterVolumeService,
   - OracleCMService,
   - OracleEVMService,
   - OracleCSService, and the
   - OracleCRService.
2. Import a valid OCR export file using the *ocrconfig -import* command from one of the cluster nodes.
3. Restart all of the affected services on all cluster nodes.

The *ocrconfig* Tool Command Syntax and Options

Execute OCR commands from a user with administrative privileges on UNIX-based platforms or from a user with Administrator privileges on Windows-based systems. The OCR command syntax is as follows:

```
ocrconfig -<option>
```

OPTION	PURPOSE
-export	To export the contents of the OCR into a target file.
-import	To import OCR contents from a previously exported OCR file.
-restore	To restore the OCR from an automatically created OCR backup file.

Table 8.12: *Common OCR command options*

To export the OCR contents to a binary file, for example, use the *ocrconfig* command with the following syntax where *file_name* is the file to which the OCR contents are to be exported:

```
ocrconfig -export file_name
```

The export file is not editable. If OCR clients such as the clusterware are running when an export is attempted, then Oracle will report an error.

Implementing the Oracle Hardware Assisted Resilient Data (HARD) Initiative for the OCR

The purpose of the Oracle Hardware Assisted Resilient Data (HARD) initiative is to prevent data corruptions before they can occur. When HARD is enabled, the OCR writes what are known as HARD-compatible blocks.

While data corruptions are rare, they can have a catastrophic effect on a database, and by extension, on the business it supports. By providing Oracle's data validation algorithms to disk manufacturers and having these algorithms at work inside storage devices, Oracle, with disk vendor support, will prevent corrupted data from being written to the database files on permanent storage. This type of end-to-end high-level software to low-level hardware validation is currently a unique capability provided only by Oracle and its storage partners. Oracle program algorithms validate and add protection information to the database blocks and once passed to the disk, the protection information is validated by the HARD compliant storage device. In this manner, HARD prevents corruptions from being introduced into the I/O path between the database and storage and therefore eliminates a large percentage of failures that the database industry has previously not been able to prevent. While RAID, in its many flavors (0, 1, 1+0, 5) has gained a wide following with system operators by ensuring the physical protection of data, the HARD algorithm implementation takes data protection to the next level by going beyond protecting physical bits, to protecting business data.

The HARD algorithms were first made available in the Oracle9i Database and have been extended into the Oracle Database 10g. The validation in Oracle Database 10g is more comprehensive and all file types and blocks are inoculated by HARD including database files, online logs, archive logs and backups. In addition the use of ASM enables HARD without having to use raw disk devices. With the cooperation of hardware vendors HARD support is being offered in conjunction with many of the major storage arrays.

The classes of data corruptions that Oracle addresses with HARD include:

- Writes of physically and logically corrupt blocks
- Writes of blocks to incorrect locations
- Erroneous writes by programs other than Oracle to Oracle data
- Partially written blocks
- Lost writes

- Corrupted third party backups

The HARD initiative includes several algorithms that will be embedded in Oracle storage partner's storage devices to prevent all these classes of corruptions. These algorithms will be rolled out in stages by Oracle's storage partners over time.

The following companies have joined the HARD initiative as of this writing:

- EMC
- Compaq
- Fujitsu
- Hewlett Packard
- Hitachi
- NEC
- Network Appliance
- Sun Microsystems
- VERITAS
- IDC

HARD Validated Products

HARD Test Kit Version 2.2 for Oracle9i Release 2

Validation Description	Hitachi SANRISE 9900V/Lightning 9900V (DB Validator)	HP Surestore xp1024	NEC iStorage Disk Array	Sun StorEdge 9900
Checks for writes of corrupted datafile blocks. This includes the checksum value as well as validation of selected fields in the block.	4 (out of 5 possible checks)	4 (out of 5 possible checks)	5 (out of 5 possible checks)	4 (out of 5 possible checks)
Checks for writes of corrupted redo log blocks. This includes the checksum value as well as validation of selected fields in the block.	3 (out of 4 possible checks)	3 (out of 4 possible checks)	4 (out of 4 possible checks)	3 (out of 4 possible checks)
Checks for writes of corrupted controlfile blocks. This includes the checksum value as well as validation of selected fields in the block.	4 (out of 5 possible checks)	4 (out of 5 possible checks)	5 (out of 5 possible checks)	4 (out of 5 possible checks)

Validation Description	Hitachi SANRISE 9900V/Lightning 9900V (DB Validator)	HP Surestore xp1024	NEC iStorage Disk Array	Sun StorEdge 9900
Check for writes of Oracle data that is not a multiple of Oracle blocksize for target device.	Yes	Yes	Yes	Yes

HARD Test Kit Version 2.1 for Oracle8i and Oracle9i Release 1

Validation Description	Hitachi SANRISE 9900V/Lightning 9900V (DB Validator)	HP Surestore xp1024	Sun StorEdge 9900
Checks for writes of corrupted datafile blocks. This includes the checksum value as well as validation of selected fields in the block.	4 (out of 5 possible checks)	4 (out of 5 possible checks)	4 (out of 5 possible checks)
Checks for writes of corrupted controlfile blocks. This includes the checksum value as well as validation of selected fields in the block.	4 (out of 5 possible checks)	4 (out of 5 possible checks)	4 (out of 5 possible checks)

Validation Description	Hitachi SANRISE 9900V/Lightning 9900V (DB Validator)	HP Surestore xp1024	Sun StorEdge 9900
Check for writes of Oracle data that is not a multiple of Oracle blocksize for target device.	Yes	Yes	Yes

HARD Test Kit Version 1 for Oracle8i

Validation Description	EMC Symmetrix (Double Checksum)
Checks the checksum value of an Oracle data block on write.	Yes

Upgrading and Downgrading the OCR in RAC

When CRS is installed, Oracle automatically executes the *ocrconfig –upgrade* command. To downgrade, follow the downgrade instructions for each CRS component and also downgrade the OCR using the *ocrconfig -downgrade* command.

Cluster Database Configuration Import and Export with SRVCONFIG

Use SRVCONFIG utility to import and export SRVM cluster database configuration information to and from the OCR. For example, the following command exports the configuration information to a text file (replace the file_name.txt with the desired file name):

```
srvconfig -exp file_name.txt
```

While the following command would be used to *import* the configuration information from a text file into the OCR:

```
srvconfig -imp file_name.txt
```

OPTION	PURPOSE
-backuploc	To change OCR backup file location. For this entry, use a full path that is accessible by all nodes.
-showbackup	To display the location, timestamp, and the node name of origin for the last three automatically created backup files.
-upgrade	To upgrade the OCR to a later version.
-downgrade	To downgrade the OCR to an earlier version.
-help	To display help for the ocrconfig commands.

Table 8.13: *Common SRVCONFIG command options*

GSD daemon

The GSD daemon has been replaced with the CRS in Oracle Database 10g.

Using SQL*Plus

SQL*plus can also be used to administer the RAC system. It uses SQL statements to perform necessary tasks. Prior to executing SQL*plus commands, ensure that the cluster manager is running and the nodes are valid.

Starting the database in Cluster mode

After ensuring that the cluster nodes are valid, the cluster manager component is running, and the shared storage is accessible, start the database on one of the nodes through SQL*plus.

On a UNIX Platform:

```
sqlplus /nolog
connect sys/<password> as sysdba
startup PFILE=init$ORACLE_sid.ora
```

On a Windows Platform:

Ensure that the *OracleServicesid* service is running. If not, start at the DOS command prompt:

```
> net start OracleServicewsid
```

Then:

```
sqlplus /nolog
connect sys/<password> as sysdba
startup PFILE=%ORACLE_HOME%\database\initsid.ora
```

The first instance in cluster mode determines the values of the global parameters for the other instances that may join later. When second and subsequent instances join the cluster, Oracle compares the values of any global parameters in its parameter file with those already in use. An instance cannot join the database unless it has the comparable values for its global parameters.

To launch the subsequent instances on other nodes, use the same startup commands shown above with SQL*plus. Since the first instance is already running, the subsequent instances join the clustered database.

Administering ASM Instances with SRVCTL in RAC

Automated Storage Management (ASM) in Oracle Database 10g allows the use of Oracle centric disk management for Oracle related files. The ASM uses an Oracle instance to provide an interface into a set of raw volumes which Oracle then administers as a disk group.

The Server Control Utility (SRVCTL) can be used to add, remove, enable, and disable an ASM instance. The following are some quick examples of managing the ASM environment with SRVCTL.

Use the following syntax to add configuration information about an existing ASM instance:

```
srvctl add asm -n <node_name> -i <asm_instance_name> -o
<oracle_home>
```

Use the following syntax to remove an ASM instance:

```
srvctl remove asm -n <node_name> [-i <asm_instance_name>]
```

Use the following syntax to enable an ASM instance:

```
srvctl enable asm -n <node_name> [-i <asm_instance_name>]
```

Use the following syntax to disable an ASM instance:

```
srvctl disable asm -n <node_name> [-i <asm_instance_name>]
```

Use SRVCTL to start, stop, and obtain the status of an ASM instance as in the following examples.

Use the following syntax to start an ASM instance:

```
srvctl start asm -n <node_name> [-i <asm_instance_name>] [-o
<start_options]
```

Use the following syntax to stop an ASM instance:

Note: For all of the SRVCTL commands in this section for which the -i option is not required, if an instance name is not specified, then the command applies to all the ASM instances on the node.

```
srvctl stop asm -n <node_name> [-i <asm_instance_name>] [-o
<stop_options]
```

Use the following syntax to configure an ASM instance:

```
srvctl config asm -n <node_name>
```

Use the following syntax to obtain the status of an ASM instance:

```
srvctl status asm -n <node_name>
```

Using Enterprise Manager

This section will explain the administration of RAC system using Enterprise Manager (EM). The EM, either with the help of a management server or as a stand-alone component, can manage the complete RAC system environment. The OEM tool is completely cluster-aware. When connecting to a RAC system after discovery by a management server, it would enable the management of the RAC system, the database, and its instances as a single system.

The EM management server can be located on any of the machines in the network and the EM component/console can be launched from any of the machines in the network. When connecting to the RAC system by using the management server, there are additional facilities such as the event manager and job scheduler to manage, compared to the stand-alone EM component.

The Enterprise Manager Console provides a central point of control for the Oracle environment. Use the EM to discover the nodes on which the cluster database resides. Once discovery is completed, all of the databases and their instances and listeners that are associated with the nodes discovered by Oracle Enterprise Manager can be administered.

The EM enables the DBA to start, stop, and monitor databases, instances, and their listeners, as well as to schedule jobs or register events. These tasks can be performed simultaneously on multiple cluster databases. The Console can also be used to manage schemas, security, and cluster database storage features. Figure 8.6 shows the relation of all the components.

Following are the general requirements to manage the RAC system using the OEM tool.

- Oracle Intelligent Agent on each node.
- Global Service Daemon (GSD) on each node.
- The Management Server.
- EM Console on the requesting client machine.

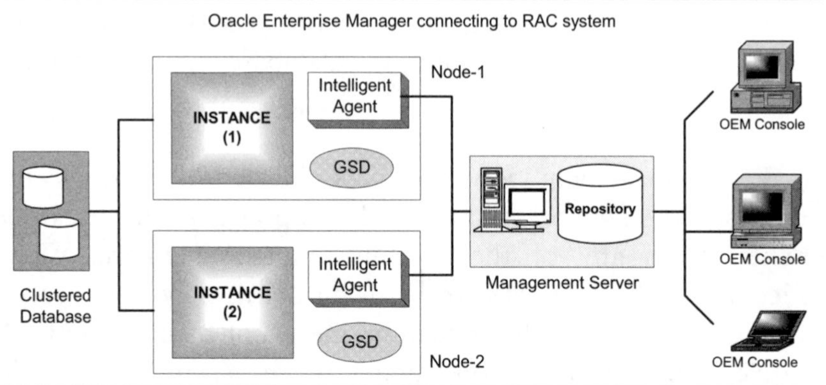

Figure 8.6: *Managing Cluster with Oracle Enterprise Manager*

For more details, please refer to the chapter *Administering RAC with EM* in the Oracle manual *Oracle 10g RAC Administration.*

Configuration of OEM with RAC

To manage the RAC system with the help of the OEM console and the management server requires a certain amount of discipline at the RAC nodes and instances. The steps to configure such requirements will be covered briefly with the help of an example.

This example assumes a cluster with two node clusters, with node names RAC1 and RAC2.

```
db_name=V920  # database name
service_name=V920
db_domain=acme.com
Instance on host RAC1 : V9201
Instance on host RAC2 : V9202
```

Configuration Steps

Ensure that the */var/opt/oracle/oratab* file exists and it has an entry for the database (not for the instance) on each of the nodes.

```
V920:/u01/app/oracle/product/920:N
```

Check that both nodes are properly configured. The command *lsnodes* gives the node name on each of the nodes.

```
Command> lsnodes -l -n
```

Ensure that the global service daemon is running on each of the nodes.

Configure the *listener.ora* file using port 1545 (as an example) on both the nodes.

```
LISTENER_N1 =
(DESCRIPTION =
(ADDRESS = (PROTOCOL = TCP)(HOST = RAC1)
(PORT = 1545)) )
SID_LIST_LISTENER_N1 =
(SID_LIST =
(SID_DESC =
(ORACLE_HOME = /uo1/app/oracle/product/920)
(SID_NAME = V9201) ))
```

Since the listener is not running on the default port of 1521, the *local_listener* parameter in the *init.ora* of the instances will need to be set so that dynamic service registration will work properly.

```
local_listener = "(address=(port=1545)(protocol=tcp)(host=rac1))"
```

On the second node change the references of listener_N1 to listener_N2 and change the host=rac1 to host=rac2.

Configure *tnsnames.ora* on all nodes.

An example of the *tnsnames.ora* file is shown below.

```
V10g.ACME.COM=
(DESCRIPTION=
(LOAD_BALANCE=ON) (FAILOVER=ON)
(ADDRESS_LIST=
(ADDRESS=(PROTOCOL=TCP)(HOST=RAC1.ACME.COM)
(PORT=1545))
(ADDRESS=(PROTOCOL=TCP)(HOST=RAC2.ACME.COM)
(PORT=1545)) )
(CONNECT_DATA=
(SERVICE_NAME=V10g.ACME.COM) ))

V10g1.ACME.COM=
(DESCRIPTION=
(ADDRESS=(PROTOCOL=TCP)(HOST=RAC1.ACME.COM)
(PORT=1545))
(CONNECT_DATA=
(SERVICE_NAME=V10g.ACME.COM)
(INSTANCE_NAME=V10g1) ) )

V10g2.ACME.COM=
(DESCRIPTION=
(ADDRESS=(PROTOCOL=TCP)(HOST=RAC2.ACME.COM)
(PORT=1545))
(CONNECT_DATA=
(SERVICE_NAME=V10g.ACME.COM)
(INSTANCE_NAME=V10g2) ) )
```

Note that the intelligent agent on the node will use the *tnsnames.ora* file. The *service_names* parameter is the combination of the *init.ora* parameters <service_names>.<db_domain> with the dot "." separating the two values. The *tnsnames.ora* file is the same on all nodes, except the order of the addresses in the *address_list* section of the V10g.acme.com alias is different.

Test SQL*Net connections - if the *listener.ora* file, *local_listener* parameter, *tnsnames.ora* file, and the *sqlnet.ora* file are properly configured it should be possible to successfully connect to the V10g, V10g1, and V10g2 aliases from all nodes.

From the first node test the following connections:

```
> sqlplus system/manager@v10g
> sqlplus system/manager@v10g1
```

From the second node test the following connections:

```
> sqlplus system/manager@v10g
> sqlplus system/manager@v10g2
```

Start the intelligent agent on both nodes. To start, use the command *agentctl start*.

Check the *$ORACLE_HOME/network/agents/services.ora* file for correct discovery. The contents of this file help to understand the correctness of the configuration. If any problems are noticed, set a higher trace level and check the message.

To set up trace level 16, add the following line in the *$ORACLE_HOME/network/admin/snmp_rw.ora* file:

```
DBSNMP.TRACE_LEVEL=16
```

From the Enterprise Manager Console, discover the nodes *rac1* and *rac2*. This will create one entry as V10g.acme.com under the Databases folder with a subfolder called Instances. The Instances folder will contain a subfolder named Cluster Database Instances. Within this folder, the two instances V10g1.acme.com and V10g2.acme.com should be visible.

An important point to note is that in the case where ORACLE_HOME is shared by multiple RAC nodes (Cluster File system implementations or NFS situations), it is not possible to start the Intelligent Agent on both nodes simultaneously, since the *$ORACLE_HOME/network/agent/*.q* files would be overwritten each time the agent is started.

Therefore, Oracle recommends three options to avoid this. Follow one of these options to handle the shared Oracle Home situation.

Install the Intelligent Agent for each node in its own Oracle Home location, distinct from the shared Oracle home location. Copy or link the *tnsnames.ora* and *listener.ora* to the Intelligent Agent's Oracle home location from the shared Oracle home. Then, start the Intelligent Agent using Intelligent Agent's Oracle home.

For RAC systems like HP TruCluster and PolyServe Matrix Server-based Linux RAC, it is possible to use the Context Dependent Symbolic Link (CDSL) facility to separate the *$ORACLE_HOME/network* directory from the shared Oracle Home installation without having to physically install the Intelligent Agent on each node in the cluster. This employs using a specific keyword in the filename (or a symbolic link) that distinguishes the name of the current member node of the cluster.

Beginning with version 9.2.x, the Intelligent Agent can store the binary state files (*.q) into an alternate directory rather than use the hard-coded *$ORACLE_HOME/network/agent* directory. This functionality is very similar to the CDSL method listed in option 2 above.

To force the agent to read and write the binary state files to/from an alternate location, the environment variable *ora_oemagent_dir* must be set prior to starting the agent. For example, the following would force the agent to read and write its state files to the */usr/oracle/agent* directory:

```
export ORA_OEMAGENT_DIR=/usr/oracle/agent
agentctl start
```

For more details and updates, please refer to the Oracle Metalink Note (158295.1).

Conclusion

In this chapter some of the RAC-specific administrative features have been examined. The main points of the chapter include:

- Parameter Management involves maintaining either the server side SPFILE or client side *init_sid.ora* files. The SPFILE method is recommended and is a better method, because it allows the initialization parameters to be changed dynamically. Beginning with Release 9i, Oracle permits many more parameters to be changed dynamically.
- There are basically three types of initialization parameters for RAC systems. They are: 1) Parameters whose values have to be unique among the instances. 2) Parameters whose values have to be common among the instances. 3) Parameters that can take different values in different instances.
- The Automatic Segment Space Management method takes care of segment space management internally. It employs bit-mapped blocks (BMB) and keeps track of the used and free space. Auto method can be specified at the tablespace level. Optionally, the old method that uses Free List and Free List groups can still be used.
- Auto Undo Management simplifies the rollback or undo segment management. When auto undo management is chosen, required undo segments are automatically created.
- ASM – Automatic Storage Management is used to manage disk resources.

- Oifcfg is used to manage network resources.
- Ocrconfig is used to configure and maintain the cluster register.
- The new oracle HARD initiative is used for preventing data corruptions.
- The Server Control Utility (SRVCTL) interfaces with the CRS service to control the configuration and stop/start operations of the cluster databases.
- In a traditional way, SQL*plus and Oracle Enterprise Manager can still be used to manage the general administration of RAC system.

Reference Sources

Oracle Disk Manager - Oracle White Paper April, 2001

Oracle 10g RAC Administration

Oracle 10g RAC Configuration and Deployment

Oracle 10g Administration Guide

Oracle 10g Database Reference

HARD White papers and announcements from www.oracle.com

Managing RAC Using Oracle Grid Control

CHAPTER

"I'm holding out for a senior DBA position and I come with a Grid Control."

Introduction

If it is not already obvious, 10g is the Grid release of Oracle. What exactly is a grid, and how does it apply to Oracle Database 10g RAC? A grid is a loosely coupled group of computers which are used to solve a common problem An example of a grid at its most basic level is the Search for ExtraTerrestial Intelligence (SETI) grid which uses a screen saver motif to get people all over the USA and the World to process single data chunks from the SETI radio telescopes. Each person on the SETI grid receives a chunk of data, when their computer goes into screen saver, rather than just display some interesting graphics or the latest failure from American Idol, it shows the data graphically and processes it. When it finishes processing, it sends the results back to SETI and gets another chunk. If the system discovers the first intelligent signal from outer space, they guarantee the user a footnote in the history books. Oracle Database 10g is a bit more complex in its use of grid technology than this.

Figure 9.1 shows how Oracle Database 10g utilizes grid technology. Essentially Oracle's grid depends on agents and remote access via *ssh* and other connection protocols. Each server, whether it is RAC or single instance type of Oracle has a Grid agent. The Grid agent reads the configuration files and provides this data back to the Grid repository. The Grid control is a set of web pages that allow access to all facets of the Oracle databases. From Grid control, the DBA can startup, shutdown, monitor, tune, perform import, export and backup and recovery. In addition, the DBA can manage patches and configure service groups as well as specify service level agreement parameters. Grid provisioning can also automatically move applications onto and off of nodes to provide application level load balancing for clusters.

RAC is required by GRID in order to allow the auto provisioning and load balancing to occur.

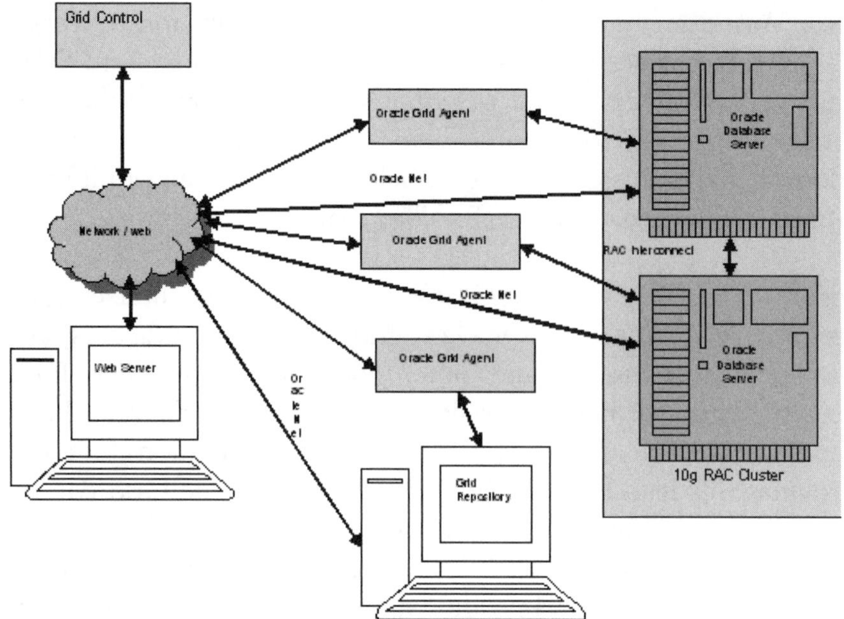

Figure 9.1: *Pictorial Representation of Oracle Grid Control*

Establishing Preferred Credentials in Grid Control

Just like in its predecessor Oracle Enterprise Manager, a set of preferred credentials is established at both the database and server level for each server and database to be managed. This preferred credential entry screen is shown in Figure 9.2. The preferred credentials are used to establish the active connections to the servers and databases to actually perform the required actions.

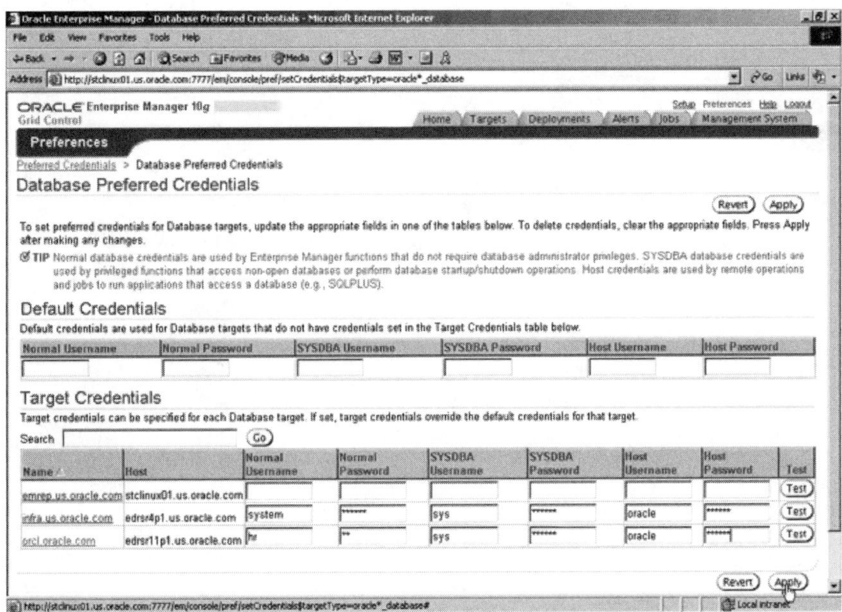

Figure 9.2: *Example Preferred Credential Entry Screen*

Monitoring RAC with Grid Control

To use the Grid Control to monitor RAC, all that is needed is the login user and password established when the Grid Control was installed and a valid web browser such as Internet Explorer, Netscape or Mozilla. The address of the Grid Control portal is entered, and the main Grid Control login screen is invoked as shown in Figure 9.3.

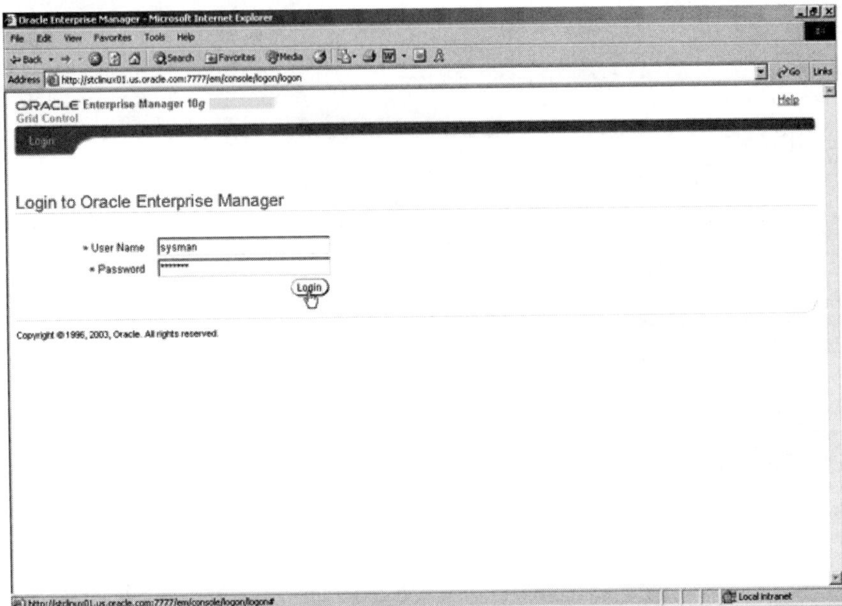

Figure 9.3: *Grid Control Login aka Enterprise Manager*

The standard address for invoking Grid Control is:

```
http://<server>.com:7777/em/console/logon/logon
```

The port 7777 is the standard port although there are also secured versions of the screen which use https and port 7779.

Once successfully logged on to Grid Control, the top level Grid control screen is displayed. This top level screen is shown in Figure 9.4.

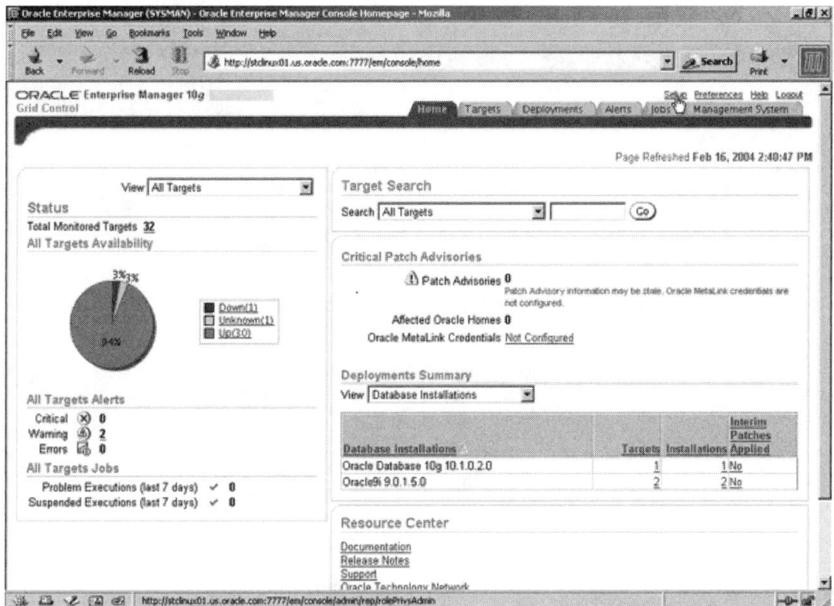

Figure 9.4: *Grid Control (Top level Enterprise Manager)*

From the top level screen, the mouse can be used to click on various controls, specifically under Targets, to get to the cluster database screen. The cluster database screen will be used whenever a target is selected that is part of a RAC installation. The RAC cluster screen shows all instances, their status and any alerts that pertain to the currently selected cluster database. This screen is shown in Figure 9.5.

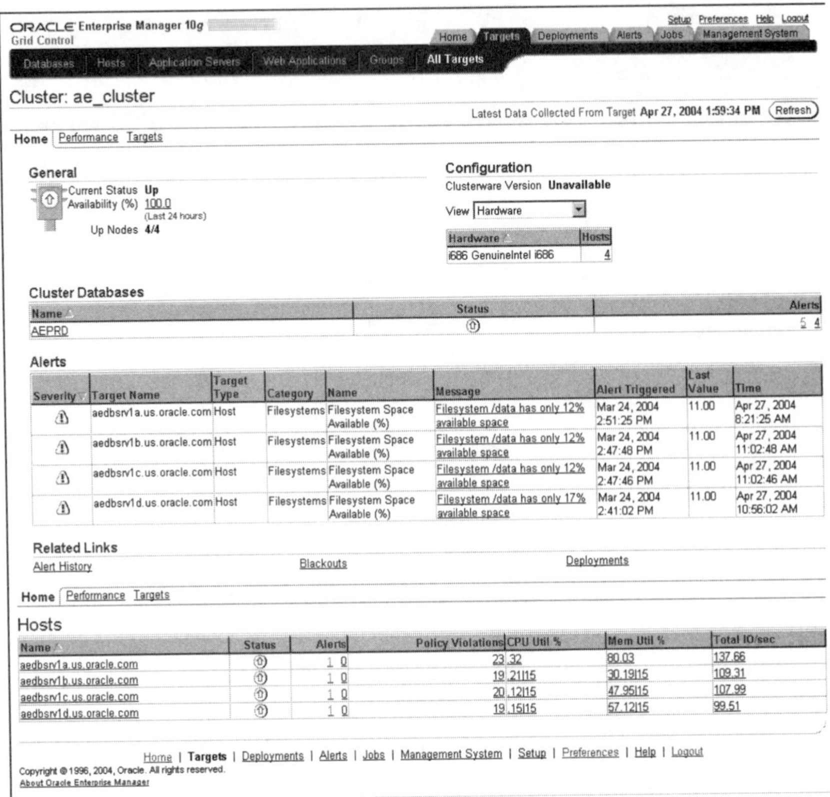

Figure 9.5: *Grid Cluster Monitor Screen*

This screen contains a great deal of information. Each underlined item provides drill down capability to more and more detailed information. Notice there are the Home, Performance and Targets subscreens available from this top level screen along with the usual Alert History, Blackouts which is the time when monitoring is specifically turned off, and Deployments screens. The Performance screen gives cluster specific performance metrics. The Performance Screen is shown in Figure 9.6.

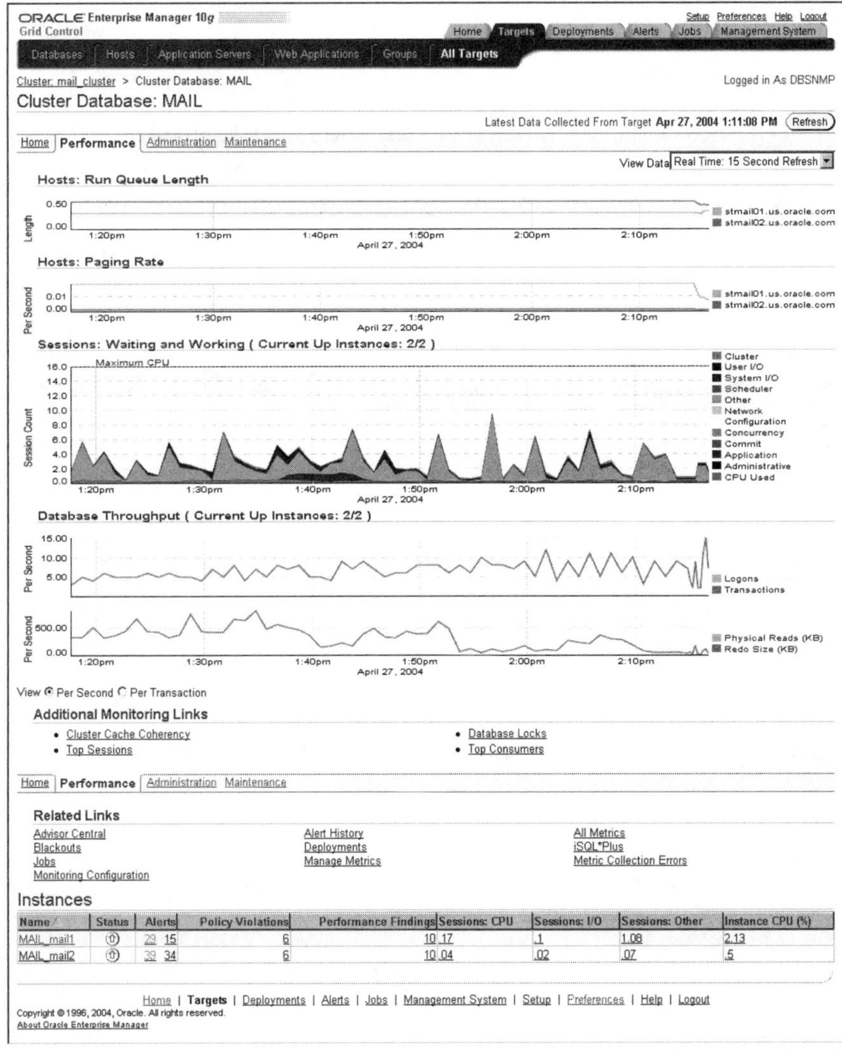

Figure 9.6: *Cluster Database Top Level Performance Screen*

From the Cluster Performance Screen, there are four additional performance related screens for drilling down:

- Cluster Cache Coherency
- Top Sessions

- Database Locks
- Top Consumers

The Top Sessions, Database Locks and Top Consumers pages are the standard Oracle Grid Control or Enterprise Manager performance screens. The only one specifically dealing with RAC is the Cluster Cache Coherency page, which is shown in Figure 9.7.

Figure 9.7: *Cluster Database Cache Coherency Screen*

The Cache Coherency Screen provides detailed information about the performance of the RAC environment. This data is updated in real time with a normal update frequency of every 15 seconds. This screen provides drill downs into the standard Top Sessions and Database Locks screens.

Creating RAC Related Jobs Using Grid Control

Another valuable capability of the Grid Control system is the ability to specify jobs to be run against databases, servers or groups of related resources known as services. Figure 9.8 shows an example Job Specification screen from Grid Control.

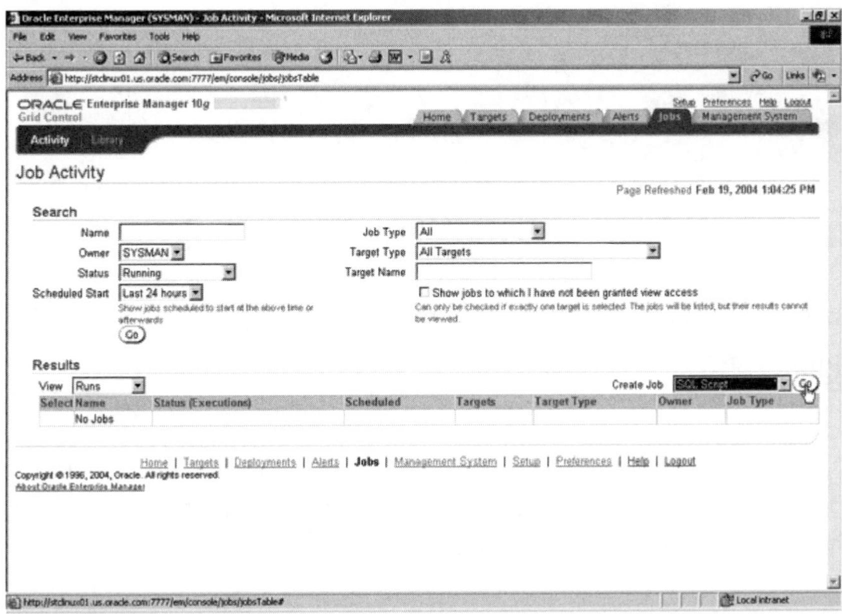

Figure 9.8: *Grid Control Job Screen*

This screen specifies the desire to create a SQL Script job. The types of jobs that can be created include shell script, OS command, Backup and Recovery and several others. The job is created using the Job Specification screens, the first of which, Target Selection, is shown in Figure 9.9.

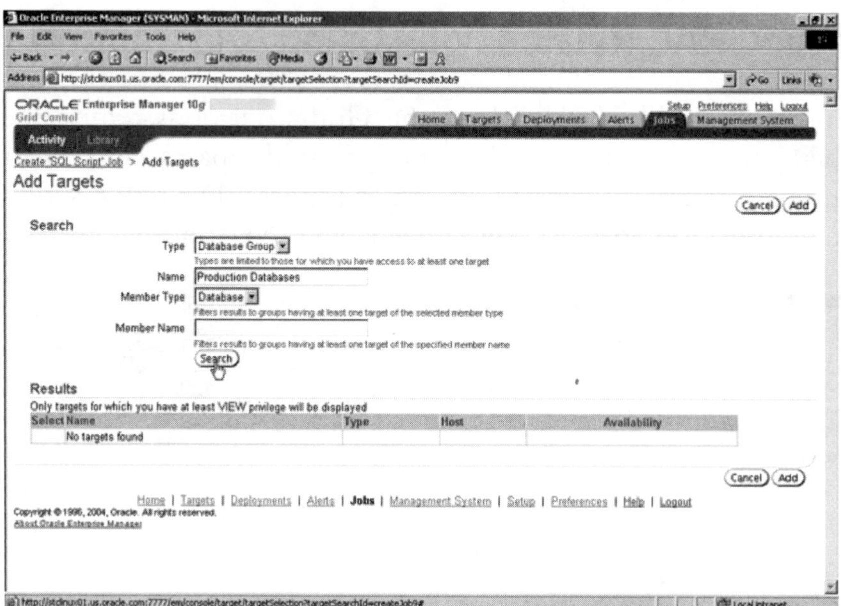

Figure 9.9: *Target Selection Screen*

Once targets are selected, the Create Script Job Screen to actually specify the SQL Script for this example is next. Figure 9.10 shows the Create Job Script screen.

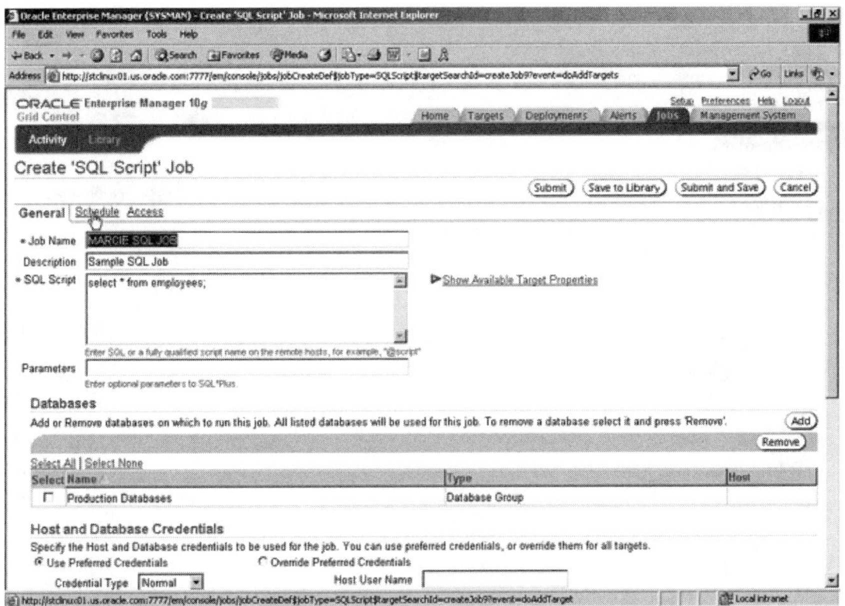

Figure 9.10: *Create SQL Script Job Page*

Once SQL is entered, the Scheduling screen, shown in Figure 9.11, is next.

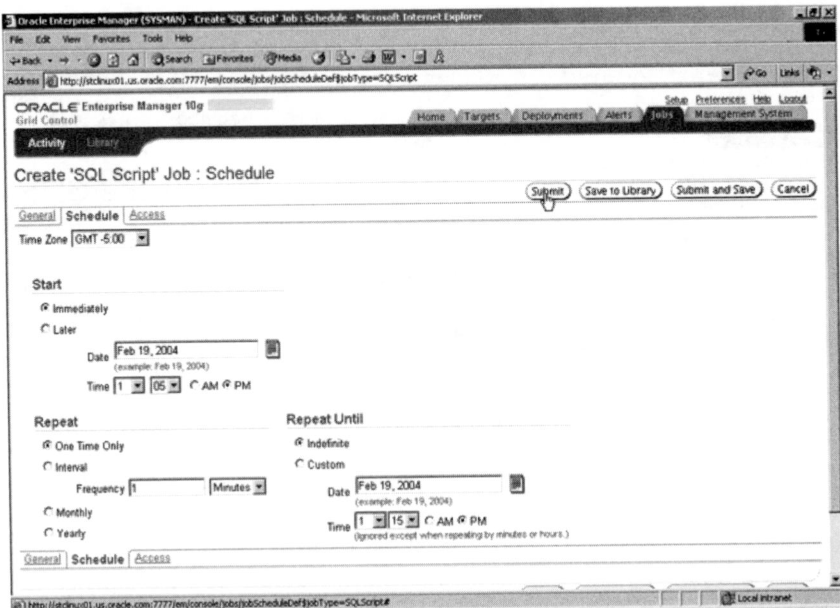

Figure 9.11: *Job Scheduling screen.*

Once the execution schedule has been established, the results of the creation of the job can be observed by getting a successful configuration message in the Job Main Screen as shown in Figure 9.12.

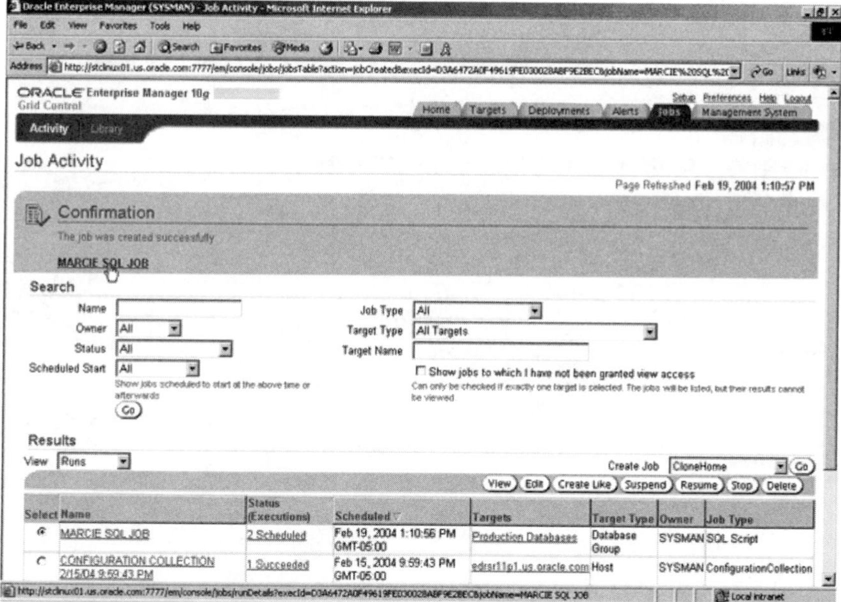

Figure 9.12: *Successful Job Creation Message.*

Once the job has been successfully created, it can be monitored for successful execution using the Job Run screen shown in Figure 9.12.

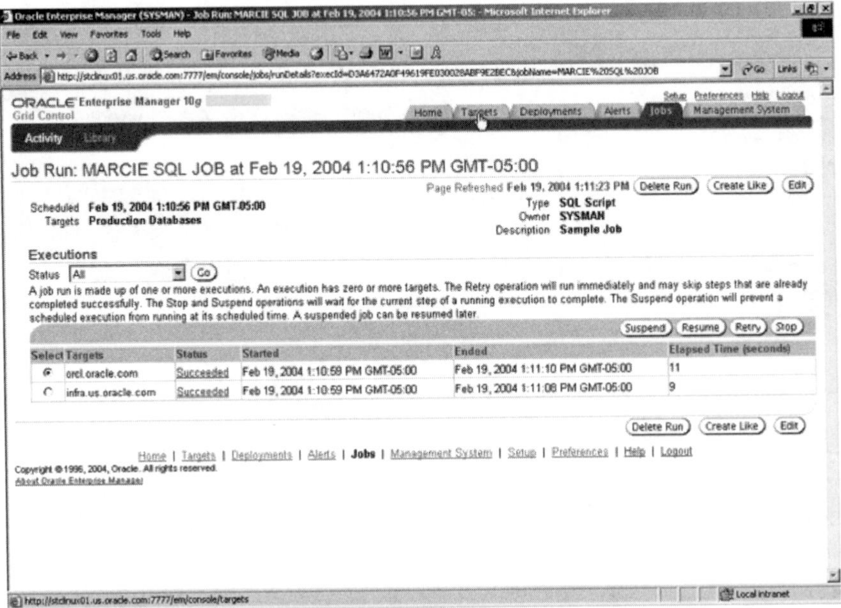

Figure 9.13: *Job Run Screen*

Conclusion

This chapter has examined how RAC and GRID in the Oracle 10g Database are related. For the advanced levels of GRID, such as provisioning and reapportionment, it is now apparent that RAC will be required.

The various areas of the GRID control that allow the monitoring and maintenance of RAC have also been reviewed.

Oracle Failover with TAF

CHAPTER 10

What could happen without TAF!

This chapter will cover the concept and practice of total application failover (TAF) in an Oracle Database 10g RAC environment. TAF is a multileveled application feature in Oracle Database 10g. TAF supports everything from simple connection failover to nearly transparent statement and application failover. The following sections provide a more detailed overview of TAF.

Overview of Transparent Application Failover

The TAF function is controlled by processes external to the Oracle Database 10g RAC cluster control. The cluster failover types and methods can be unique for each Oracle Net client. Under more complex environments, application code may have to be altered or modified to fully support TAF, using Oracle OCI calls. In its most basic form, TAF supports:

- **Active Transactions:** Any active, non-committed transaction (INSERT, UPDATE, or DELETE) is rolled back at the time of failure, because TAF cannot preserve active transactions after failover. The application will receive an error message until a rollback command is submitted.
- **Client-Server Database Connections:** TAF automatically reestablishes the client-server database connection using the same connect string or an alternate connect string specified when configuring TAF in the *tnsnames* file.
- **Executed Commands:** If a command was committed at the time of the connection failure and the command changed the state of the database, TAF will not reissue the command. If, by mistake, TAF reconnects in response to a command that may have changed the database, TAF issues an error message to the application.
- **Open Cursors Used for Fetching:** TAF enables applications that began fetching rows from a cursor before the failover event to refetch the rows after failover. This type of failover is called select failover. TAF accomplishes this by re-executing the cursor select statement using the same working set, effectively retrieving the rows again. TAF verifies that the discarded rows are those that were returned initially, or it returns an error message to the application.
- **Server side Program Variables:** Server side program variables, such as PL/SQL package states, are lost during failures. TAF cannot recover them. Making a call from the failover OCI callback functions to the server-side processes can initialize them.
- **Users' Database Sessions:** TAF logs the users in with the same user IDs that were in use prior to failure. If multiple

users were using the connection, TAF automatically logs them in as they attempt to process database commands. Unfortunately, TAF cannot automatically restore non-persistent session properties. These properties can, however, be restored by invoking an OCI callback function that notifies the calling transaction of the switchover and requests the non-persistent session properties.

In a nutshell, the above means that at the time of failover, in-progress queries are reissued and processed from the beginning. Rows already fetched are discarded. All of this discarding of rows and re-fetching can delay the completion of the original transaction. However, TAF can also be configured to issue two connections at a time, one to the main instance and one to the standby instance. This speeds the processing by eliminating the reconnection penalty. DDL operations are not reissued. Committed transactions are not reissued.

Uncommitted INSERT, UPDATE and DELETE commands are rolled back and must be resubmitted after reconnection. Again, use of the OCI packages should be utilized to have the DML operations reissued.

The Oracle Net process carries out TAF functionality. The failover is configured in the *tnsnames* file. The TAF settings are placed in the net service name area, within the *connect_data* section of the *tnsnames*, using the *failover_mode* and *instance_role* parameters.

failover_mode	Subparameter Description
BACKUP	Used to set a different net service name for backup instance connections. A backup should be specified when using preconnect to pre-establish connections.

failover_mode	Subparameter Description
TYPE	Used to specify the type of connection failover. There are three types of Oracle Net failover functionality available to Oracle Call Interface (OCI) applications: ▪ **session**: Used to set to failover the session. When a user's connection is lost, a new session is automatically created for the user on the backup. This type of failover will not recover selects. ▪ **select**: Used to enable users with open cursors (selects) to continue fetching on them after failure. It should be noted that this mode involves some overhead on the client side during normal select operations. ▪ **none**: This setting is the default. With none, no failover functionality is provided. If the goal is to prevent failover, use the none setting.
METHOD	This is used to determine how failover occurs from the primary node to the backup node: ▪ **basic**: Set this mode to establish connections only at failover time. Since no preconnection is done, basic requires virtually no work on the backup server until failover occurs. ▪ **preconnect**: Set this mode to pre-established connections to a backup server. The preconnect setting provides for faster failover but does require that the backup instance be capable of supporting all connections from all supported instances.
RETRIES	This sets the number of times that the server will attempt to connect after a failover. With DELAY specified but RETRIES not specified, RETRIES will default to five retry attempts.
DELAY	This specifies the number of seconds between connection attempts. When RETRIES is specified and DELAY is not, DELAY defaults to one second.

Table 10.1: *fail_over Mode Options*

Setting *load_balance*=YES instructs Net to progress through the list of listener addresses in a random sequence, balancing the load on the various listeners. When set to OFF, *load_balance* instructs Net to try the addresses sequentially until one succeeds. This parameter must be correctly coded in the net service name or connect descriptor. By default, this parameter is set to ON for *description_list*. Load balancing can be specified for an *address_list*, associated with a set of addresses or set descriptions. If *address_list* is used, the *load_balance*=YES should be within the (*address_list*=) portion. If *address_list* is not used, the *load_balance*=YES should be within the DESCRIPTION clause.

failover=ON is the default for *address_list*, *description_list* and the set of description; therefore, it does not have to be specified. This only applies for connect time failover not transparent application failover (TAF).

The *failover_mode* parameter must be included in the *connect_data* portion of a *net_service_name*. There is no BACKUP=failover in *failover_mode*=. This implies (*failover_mode*=(TYPE=SELECT) (METHOD=BASIC) (BACKUP=failover)), meaning whenever failover occurs, the connected session will failover to the *net_service_name* failover again. A backup should be specified when using PRECONNECT to pre-establish connections.

If it is desired to have remote instances registered with the listener, even if the listener is using port 1521, *local_listener* still needs to be in the *init.ora* file. Otherwise, with *remote_listener*="<*remote_listener*>" alone, the remote instances will not be registered with the listener, and there will be no server-side listener connection load balancing. This is due to bug 2194549 that is fixed in 10g.

If the configuration is not using the default port 1521, the *local_listener* parameter in the initialization file is required. If the hostname output is the interconnect IP address as opposed to the public Ethernet IP address, the PMON process will register the service and instance with the hostname's listener. In this case, the *local_listener* parameter should be set to instruct the PMON to register the service and instance with the public Ethernet IP address listener.

The following script demonstrates the initialization parameters that would be set for the example server setup. Both nodes' *init.ora* file would have the following parameters:

```
ault1.local_listener="LISTENER_ault1"
ault2.local_listener="LISTENER_ault2"
db_name='ault'
ault1.instance_name='ault1'
ault2.instance_name='ault2'
remote_listener='LISTENERS_AULT'
```

The TAF parameters must be manually added to the *tnsnames* file, since the network configuration assistant (NETCA) cannot configure them. Once configured, Oracle Net will failover the connection, transparently to the user in many cases, with the exceptions noted in the list of failover objects above.

In order to configure TAF, the static service information must be removed in the *<sid>_list_<listener_name>* entry from the *listener.ora*, allowing the instance to self-register. This is known as Dynamic Service Registration and has been available since Oracle8i. In addition, the *global_dbname* parameter must be removed from the *tnsnames* file or TAF will be disabled.

Load Balancing

Oracle10g provides virtually the same listener connection load balancing feature is provided as was available in 9i. This feature is utilized to increase connection performance through the balancing, almost like the time share networks of the past, the active connections between multiple user defined dispatchers and instances. When utilizing load balancing in a single-instance environment, the listener process selects the dispatcher to handle the incoming client requests based on its percent busy. When moving into an Oracle Real Application Clusters environment, this connection load balancing process also provides the capability to spread the number of active connections using a pseudo-round-robin methodology between the instances in the RAC cluster based on entries in the *tnsnames* file.

Dynamic service registration (DSR) allows a listener to always know of all instances, and when multi-threaded server (MTS) is utilized, the listener is also always aware of the database dispatcher processes, no matter where they are running. Oracle uses the following criteria when deciding which dispatcher to utilize:

- The least loaded node
- The least loaded instance
- The least loaded dispatcher for that instance

If, on the other hand, a dedicated server configuration is being utilized, the listener uses this reduced set of criteria. OF course, dispatchers need not be considered if they are not being used:

- The least loaded node
- The least loaded instance

In Oracle versions lower than 9.0.1.3, for dedicated connections, the server side load balancing will route most connections to one node. This is due to bug 2134254. The workaround is to add *dispatchers="(pro=ipc)(dis=0)"* in the *init.ora* file.

The following script includes an example *listener.ora.* This script shows how easy the setup of the listener file can be.

```
LISTENER =
  (DESCRIPTION_LIST =
    (DESCRIPTION =
      (ADDRESS_LIST =
        (ADDRESS = (PROTOCOL = IPC)(KEY = EXTPROC))
      )
      (ADDRESS_LIST =
       (ADDRESS = (PROTOCOL = TCP)(HOST = aultlinux1)(PORT = 1521))
      )
    )
  )

SID_LIST_LISTENER =
  (SID_LIST =
    (SID_DESC =
      (SID_NAME = PLSExtProc)
      (ORACLE_HOME = /u01/oracle/product/9.2.0)
      (PROGRAM = extproc)
    )
    (SID_DESC =
      (ORACLE_HOME = /u01/oracle/product/9.2.0)
      (SID_NAME = ault1)
    )
  )
```

Example TAF Configurations

The next few sections will provide example TAF configurations:

- Connect-Time Failover with Client Load Balancing
- Retry of connections
- Pre-established failover connections
- TAF with Connect-Time Failover and Client Load Balancing

To implement TAF with connect-time failover and client load balancing for multiple addresses, the *tnsnames.ora* files should be configured similar to the script shown below, in which Oracle Net connects randomly to one of the protocol addresses on *aultlinux1* or *aultlinux2*. If the instance were to fail after the connection, the TAF application fails over to the other node's listener, reissuing any SELECT statements in flight.

```
ault=
 (DESCRIPTION=
  (LOAD_BALANCE=on)
```

```
    (FAILOVER=on)
    (ADDRESS=
         (PROTOCOL=tcp)
         (HOST=aultlinux1)
         (PORT=1521))
    (ADDRESS=
         (PROTOCOL=tcp)
         (HOST=aultlinux2)
         (PORT=1521))
    (CONNECT_DATA=
       (SERVICE_NAME=ault)
       (FAILOVER_MODE=
         (TYPE=select)
         (METHOD=basic))))
```

Configuring TAF to Retry a Connection

With a proper configuration, TAF will automatically retry connecting if the first connection attempt fails. The *tnsnames.ora* file is configured with the retries and delay parameters. In the script below, Oracle Net tries to reconnect to the listener on the *aultlinux1* server. If the failover connection fails, Oracle Net waits ten seconds before trying to reconnect again. Using this *tnsnames.ora* file, Oracle Net attempts to reconnect up to ten times.

```
ault=
 (DESCRIPTION=
  (ADDRESS=
       (PROTOCOL=tcp)
       (HOST=aultlinux1)
       (PORT=1521))
  (CONNECT_DATA=
     (SERVICE_NAME=ault)
     (FAILOVER_MODE=
       (TYPE=select)
       (METHOD=basic)
       (RETRIES=10)
       (DELAY=10))))
```

Configuring TAF for Pre-Establishing Connections

TAF can be configured to create pre-established connections to a second instance. The initial and backup connections are explicitly specified. In the following example script, clients that use net service name *ault1* to connect to the listener on *aultlinux1* are also preconnected to *aultlinux2*. If the *aultlinux1* fails after the connection, Oracle Net automatically fails over to *aultlinux2*, reissuing any SELECT statements in progress. In this reciprocal setup, Oracle Net preconnects to *aultlinux1* for those clients that use *ault2* to connect to the listener on *aultlinux2*.

```
ault1 =
 (DESCRIPTION=
  (ADDRESS=
       (PROTOCOL=tcp)
       (HOST=aultlinux1)
       (PORT=1521))
  (CONNECT_DATA=
     (SERVICE_NAME=ault)
     (INSTANCE_NAME=ault1)
     (FAILOVER_MODE=
       (BACKUP=ault2)
       (TYPE=select)
       (METHOD=preconnect))))
ault2=
 (DESCRIPTION=
  (ADDRESS=
       (PROTOCOL=tcp)
       (HOST=ault2)
       (PORT=1521))
  (CONNECT_DATA=
     (SERVICE_NAME=ault)
     (INSTANCE_NAME=ault2)
     (FAILOVER_MODE=
       (BACKUP=ault1)
       (TYPE=select)
       (METHOD=preconnect))))
```

Verifying TAF Configurations

The *v$session* view contains the *failover_type*, *failover_method*, and *failed_over* columns. These columns are used to monitor connected clients and the TAF status. An example select against this view is shown below:

```
SELECT MACHINE, FAILOVER_TYPE, FAILOVER_METHOD, FAILED_OVER,
COUNT(*)
FROM V$SESSION
GROUP BY MACHINE, FAILOVER_TYPE, FAILOVER_METHOD, FAILED_OVER;
```

The output before failover of the *aultlinux1* server resembles the following:

```
MACHINE              FAILOVER_TYPE FAILOVER_M FAI   COUNT(*)
-------------------- ------------- ---------- --- ----------
aultlinux1           NONE          NONE       NO          11
aultlinux2           select        PRECONNECT NO           1
```

The output after a failover from the *aultlinux1* server is:

```
MACHINE              FAILOVER_TYPE FAILOVER_M FAI   COUNT(*)
-------------------- ------------- ---------- --- ----------
aultlinux2           NONE          NONE       NO          10
aultlinux2           select        PRECONNECT YES          1
```

Using Instance Role for Configuring the Primary and Secondary Instance

The parameter *instance_role*, is optional and when used is placed in the *connect_data* section of the instance connect descriptor. It specifies a connection to the primary or secondary instance of Oracle Database 10g Real Application Clusters and Oracle Database 10g Real Application Clusters Guard configurations. The concept of the primary and secondary instance will be covered elsewhere in this book.

The *instance_role* parameter is used to explicitly connect to a primary or secondary instance. Of course, since it should be obvious that the default is the primary instance, TAF should only be used to preconnect only to a secondary instance.

instance_role can have the following values:

- **primary:** Specifies to make this connection to the primary instance
- **secondary:** Specifies to make this connection to the secondary instance

- **any:** Allows a user connection to whichever instance has the lowest load, regardless of whether the instance has a primary or secondary role

A useful package is called *dbms_libcache.*. This package is used to transfer information in the library cache of the primary instance to the library cache of the secondary instance, which is also referred to as warming the library cache.

Connection to Instance Role Type

In the script below, the net service name *ault_primary* allows users to connect to the designated primary instance, and net second service name, *ault_secondary* allows user connection to the designated secondary instance.

```
ault_primary=
 (DESCRIPTION=
  (ADDRESS=
       (PROTOCOL=tcp)
       (HOST=aultlinux1)
       (PORT=1521))
  (ADDRESS=
       (PROTOCOL=tcp)
       (HOST=aultlinux2)
       (PORT=1521))
  (CONNECT_DATA=
     (SERVICE_NAME=ault)
     (INSTANCE_ROLE=primary)))
ault_secondary=
 (DESCRIPTION=
  (ADDRESS=
       (PROTOCOL=tcp)
       (HOST=aultlinux1)
       (PORT=1521))
  (ADDRESS=
       (PROTOCOL=tcp)
       (HOST=aultlinux2)
       (PORT=1521))
  (CONNECT_DATA=
     (SERVICE_NAME=ault)
     (INSTANCE_ROLE=secondary)))
```

Establishing a Connection to a Specific Instance

There are times when the Oracle Enterprise Manager (OEM) and other system management products need to connect to a specific instance, regardless of their role, to perform administrative tasks. For specific instance connections, (*instance_name=instance_name*) and (*instance_role*=any) would be configured to connect to a specific instance regardless of its primary or secondary role.

In the following script, the net service name *ault1* allows user connections to the instance on *aultlinux1*, and *ault2* allows user connections to the instance on *aultlinux2*. The setting *(SERVER=dedicated)* is used when the goal is to force a dedicated server connection even when shared server (MTS) is being used.

```
ault1=
 (DESCRIPTION=
  (ADDRESS=
       (PROTOCOL=tcp)
       (HOST=aultlinux1)
       (PORT=1521))
  (CONNECT_DATA=
     (SERVICE_NAME=ault)
     (INSTANCE_ROLE=any)
     (INSTANCE_NAME=ault1)
     (SERVER=dedicated)))
ault2=
 (DESCRIPTION=
  (ADDRESS=
       (PROTOCOL=tcp)
       (HOST=aultlinux2)
       (PORT=1521))
  (CONNECT_DATA=
     (SERVICE_NAME=ault)
     (INSTANCE_ROLE=any)
     (INSTANCE_NAME=ault2)
     (SERVER=dedicated)))
```

Using BACKUP with TAF Pre-Establishing a Connection

When Transparent Application Failover (TAF) is utilized, it is easy to specify a backup connection to the secondary instance.

When this is done, the initial and backup connections must be explicitly specified. In the next example, Oracle Net connects to the listener on *aultlinux1* and preconnects to *aultlinux2*, the secondary instance. If *aultlinux1* fails after the connection, the TAF application fails over to *aultlinux2*, the secondary instance, automatically preserving any SELECT statements in progress due to the *(TYPE=select)* setting. The following script shows an example of this configuration.

```
Ault1=
 (DESCRIPTION=
  (ADDRESS=
       (PROTOCOL=tcp)
       (HOST=aultlinux1)
       (PORT=1521))
  (CONNECT_DATA=
     (SERVICE_NAME=ault)
     (INSTANCE_ROLE=primary)
     (FAILOVER_MODE=
       (BACKUP=ault2)
       (TYPE=select)
       (METHOD=preconnect))))
ault2=
 (DESCRIPTION=
  (ADDRESS=
       (PROTOCOL=tcp)
       (HOST=aultlinux2)
       (PORT=1521))
  (CONNECT_DATA=
     (SERVICE_NAME=ault)
     (INSTANCE_ROLE=secondary)))
```

Using OCI Driver

Since the RAC system is a multi-instance single database, whenever one of the instances has failed, all the client connections to the failed instance receive error. They can, however, reconnect to the surviving instance on a different node. Applications can also use a callback function through an OCI call to notify clients or users of the failover or control and mask the failover behavior.

TAF enables the application to automatically reconnect to the database if the database instance to which the connection is made goes down. After the reconfiguration of the failed instance is completed, and when the database is available, the user session is re-authenticated and the open cursors are either re-executed (*failover_mode*=SESSION) or can continue fetching (*failover_mode*=SELECT). When TAF is utilized, a new connection to the database is automatically obtained by Oracle. This allows users to continue working as if the original connection had never failed.

TAF functionality is achieved through the use of the Oracle provided client side network libraries, the Oracle call interface (OCI). The client needs to use the Oracle Net OCI libraries to take advantage of TAF. With OCI callback functions, OCI API applications can monitor the failure status of the Oracle Instance.

There are seven possible failover events in the OCI API that can be captured in the application code. They are

- *FO_BEGIN = 1* is used to indicate that a lost connection has been detected during and a fail over is starting.
- *FO_END = 2* is used to indicate that a successful fail over occurred.
- *FO_ABORT = 3* is used to indicate that a fail over was not successful and there is no retry option.
- *FO_REAUTH = 4* is used to indicate that a users handle has been re-authenticated.
- *FO_ERROR = 5* is used to indicate that a fail over was temporarily unsuccessful. This gives the application the opportunity to fail gracefully or to retry fail over. This retry is usually done by issuing a SLEEP() and then retry by returning the value *FO_RETRY*

- *FO_RETRY = 6* is used to tell OCI to retry failover
- *FO_EVENT_UNKNOWN = 7* is used to indicate a bad failover event

To implement TAF in Real Application Clusters, Client Applications need to use the JDBC OCI instead of PL/SQL packages. While RAC supports both thin JDBC and JDBC OCI, TAF is only supported with JDBC OCI.

Oracle TechNet can provide a sample as how to use the TAF using OCI driver. The link is:

```
http://otn.oracle.com/sample_code/tech/java/sqlj_jdbc/files/10g_jdbc
/OCIdriverTAFSample/OCIdriverTAFSample.java.html
```

Conclusion

This chapter has covered the basics of total application failover (TAF) and RAC. Information has also been provided for several failover and load balancing configurations for the *tnsnames.ora* file, as well as the basic *listener.ora* setup required for TAF.

When configuring TAF, it is advisable to move from the simple to the complex and test at each step. Several of the references give good examples for further configurations and testing.

References

Metalink Note:226880.1: *Configuration of Load Balancing and Transparent Application Failover*

Metalink Note:200543.1: *RMAN: Load Balancing and Failover not Supported in RAC Environment*

Metalink Doc ID: 158295.1: *How to Configure EM with 19i Real Application Clusters (RAC)*

Metalink Doc ID: 214070.996: *Client Failover(DML) in RAC environment*

Metalink Doc ID: 151243.995: Re: Problem Configuring listener.ora and tnsnames.ora for Transparent Application Failure

Oracle High Availability Architecture and Best Practices 10g, Release 1 (10.1), Part No. B10726-01, December 2003

Application Deployment

CHAPTER

Excuse me, how does that apply to RAC databases?

This chapter addresses application deployment in an Oracle RAC database environment. The suitability of a RAC database for various types of applications that can take advantage of greater computing power for multi-instance RAC databases will also be covered.

Overview

The RAC database provides the breakthrough technology of cache fusion, which simplifies application deployment issues. Before cache fusion had been fully implemented, many of the applications had to selectively access the multiple instances in a way that would not result in update contentions, thereby minimizing pings and false pings. With the full implementation of cache fusion, many types of applications are able to connect and use the multiple RAC instances, while avoiding the performance issues that result from cross instance updates. There are two broad types of data access methodologies.

- **OLTP:** Traditionally, online transaction processing users (OLTP users) access the database resources or data blocks randomly. The transaction life, or access duration, is usually very short. With this method, there is limited conflict or contention with the data sets.
- **DSS:** Decision support systems (DSS) and data warehousing (DW) applications focus more on analysis of the data and the creation of various reports. A data warehouse is a relational database that is designed for analysis rather than transaction processing. A data warehouse usually contains historical data that is derived from transaction data, as well as from other sources. The warehouse separates the analysis workload from transaction workloads and consolidates data from several sources.

Using tools such as online analytical processing (OLAP) extraction engines or other statistical tools, large data sets are processed. With this method, for any given query, a large number of data blocks are read and analyzed. Performance is a crucial factor with this type of access.

The OLTP and DW databases have traditionally been separated into different servers and instances. The data warehouse is updated or refreshed by loading data from the OLTP on an appropriate schedule. Data warehouses typically use an extract, transport, transform, and load (ETL) process, which involves complex and time consuming steps, such as data exports and network copies. The mixed OLTP and DW databases often used to compete for resources resulting in update contentions. This created performance issues.

With multiple instances, the RAC database is in a perfect position to segregate the activity on different nodes while still maintaining single database storage. This not only results in better performance levels for both types of data activities, OLTP and DSS, but also gives administrative flexibility and cost savings.

Database Consolidation

Many enterprises are showing keen interest in data or database consolidation. For example, dozens of instances residing on several hosts or servers are merged into a large database. With a powerful server platform, abundant memory, and ample processor resources, it is common to establish a very large database (VLDB) that can accumulate terabytes of data.

Even in a packaged application environment, as in SAP, there is a tendency towards consolidating the databases to provide lower cost and better administrative flexibility. A good example is the new approach taken by the SAP application suite that is called Multiple Components in One Database (MCOD).

MCOD is a new installation feature for mySAP.com components. It provides the capability of installing several components independently in one single database. Each mySAP.com component connects the database with one single database user.

Oracle VLDB has proven to be a good cost saving solution. It employs dynamic parallel processing techniques in accessing data sets and table partitions. Even from the administrative point of view, it makes more sense for management to have a smaller number of large databases than vice versa. This approach provides:

- Reduced TCO in terms of licensing, staffing, and consulting fees.
- Improved availability with the focus on fewer databases.
- Higher security.

- Centralized backup and archive.

RAC with Grid is an ideal solution to take advantage of these developments. RAC supports VLDB databases for data consolidation and large data warehousing databases.

E-business Applications

E-business applications are becoming a dominant category considering the steep growth of the use of Internet in commercial, retail, and entertainment businesses. E-business activity brought many challenging demands to IT management. The wide adoption of e-business as a way of commerce by the common public has resulted in a huge accumulation of data at these enterprises. Supporting these applications 24/7 has become the most important feature. It is common for thousands of concurrent users to access an e-business application and the associated database system.

As a result, the workload pattern has become almost unpredictable. There may be sudden spurts of commerce activity at any time. The days are gone when database systems were shutdown during the night and weekends for backups and other maintenance activities.

RAC databases, with the built-in multiple instance nodes and pay as you grow approach, are a good solution for meeting all these challenging developments.

The next section will cover the suitability of RAC databases for application deployment.

RAC Suitability

In a typical 2-tier or 3-tier application deployment, the back end tier consists of the database component, with the middle tier accessing the backend database resources. There are hardly any applications that do not depend on database resources. Whether it is a web-based e-commerce application, or an in-house client server application, or packaged applications like ERM and CRM, they all need database resources to store, retrieve, and update.

The Oracle RAC GRID enabled database is a very well positioned back end database that provides a scalable and highly available data storage platform. With its increased robustness and higher computing power, it provides a reliable back end database engine for mission critical applications needing higher throughput and shorter response times. Multi-instances and multiple nodes make it an enhanced and powerful database platform. Most applications can use this multi-node clustered database without any code modification. As a result, the acceptability of multi-instance RAC databases is very high among existing and stand-alone Oracle database users.

Advantages of the RAC Database

As enterprises rely more on organized data and databases, an explosion of data accumulation has occurred in the recent past. This trend will continue as information and data processing is the key to many business operations and business decisions. None of the day-to-day business operations can run without the use of database resources. Dependence on the database is total. As a result, the stress on scalability and performance of database system software is greater than ever. The major benefits of the RAC database system are scalability and high availability.

Scalability

In a dedicated server environment, every connected client is associated with a server process that consumes memory resources and contributes to context switching overhead in a production environment. However, the TP monitors and MTS, now called shared server, features of the Oracle database have been used to reduce the numbers of processes on the server and better utilize these resources. To solve the resource crunch, the RAC database provides additional memory resources as more nodes are added to the clustered database system.

A RAC database system provides excellent scalability options for the users. As the need arises, users can expand or add the number of nodes in the cluster. This enhances the total database engine computing power when the need for high performance arises. With the additional nodes and instances in the database cluster, the system is able to accommodate demands.

Cache fusion technology provides transparency in the way the data blocks are accessed and the results are composed to meet the needs of the SQL query.

Horizontal scalability is generally easy to achieve with the addition of extra nodes at the operating system and at the physical cluster level. Once the cluster is physically expanded, it is relatively easy for the Oracle instance to be created and added into the RAC database system.

Addition of another instance creates the opportunity to support a large number of concurrent users. Any instance introduced into the RAC system opens up new memory buffers and permits more user connections without affecting the performance of the other instances.

In the past, the only way to scale the database server was to scale up by replacing a small system with a larger system. Oracle9i/10G RAC provides another option: the addition of more small systems, also known as scale out. In a typical SMP server, a limit is reached in the number of CPUs and memory buffers. With the addition of extra nodes and instances, the total number of processors in the clusters can be enhanced. For complex database queries, it now becomes possible to achieve higher parallelism, spanning across the multiple nodes. In other words, a higher degree of parallelism for queries can be realized.

If a lot of processing is going on in one of the instances, the applications accessing the database through that instance can be shifted to another instance. Thus, the processing or activity can be dispersed.

Unpredictable Loads

With the increase of internet-based business operations and around the clock commercial activities, IT and data resources are always online. The Internet has made all the difference in the way the database is used and accessed. One can never know when the sudden increase in access levels will occur. The traditional 9 to 5 type of database access is a thing of the past.

Case Study #1

EA.com is one of the most frequently visited and largest sites on the Internet. This site offers the popular Sims Online. Sims Online is a virtual world built from the imaginations of thousands of players. The Internet allows the users to play simultaneously.

Sims Online is an artificial online world where many people treat the Sims as if they were real. The player can be him or herself, or whoever they want to be. In this world, the players have their own piece of land to do with it as they please. The player can create a house, coffee bar, dance club, museum, or whatever else inspires their imagination. Neighborhoods around the player can be explored and other real Sims can be met along the way. The player can develop a network of real Sims friends to enhance power, wealth, reputation and social standing.

Sims Online is a massive online world that can be accessed at any time. Interaction with the world is through one Sim that is developed over time. Everything that is bought, built or created will still be there when the player returns. This massive online environment requires a powerful database infrastructure to store profiles, game play statistics, player attributes and interactions. To manage this level of complexity, Electronic Arts uses Oracle 9i RAC database technology.

EA.com uses the RAC solution to improve and manage stability, scalability and availability. The popularity, and hence the economic feasibility of the project, depends on the subscribers playing each other. How they play, behave, move and react is hard to anticipate because there is no order and no uniformity. To support such complexity, the database has to scale. When more Sims enter an already crowded room, it causes a ripple effect and causes more data to be stored and processed. The status of the entire simulated world and all of its occupants are stored in Oracle Real Application Clusters.

Oracle RAC is able to meet the challenges of an unpredictable load. An important feature of the RAC database is that it is always online and available. Even if one or two nodes and their instances fail, the RAC database is available and accessible through the surviving nodes. When the load increases at sustained levels, additional nodes or instances can easily be added. Effectively, it is able to enhance and scale without totally re-engineering the backend database. When Sims Online was launched, it had 1.5 TB of data. EA expects to increase it to eight TB as the popularity grows.

This case study is based on the article, 'Foundation for New World' by David Baum and Ed Baum in Oracle Magazine – March/April 2003.

Case Study #2

In another example, the Rapid Rewards Program by Southwest Airlines is supported by an Oracle RAC database. The Rewards program enrolls members into the instance and keeps track of rewards based on the interactions.

There are multiple channels for the customer to view and update their position. For example, information is continuously updated and accessed at the gates with a card swipe, by phone contact, by name and phone searches, via the reservation system, and through airport kiosks.

This kind of high exposure, with critical sources of information, has to be maintained 24/7. At the same time, it has to provide scalability as the program becomes more popular. With requirements such as client side transparency and sub-second response times to view and update data, Oracle RAC is a good choice. The RAC system, by providing multiple instances, is able to set up separate access regions for different input points; therefore, contention for resources is minimized.

High Availability

With multiple instances, the RAC system gives a near zero failure environment. Even when one or more nodes fail in the cluster, for whatever reason, as long there is one instance running, the database resources are provided.

With the help of the transparent application failover (TAF) configuration, operations are transferred automatically to the surviving instance.

Application Deployment Issues

There are many applications that are designed in such a way that the user connections or application instances act on different sets of data blocks. This kind of situation provides good scalability. There is minimum contention for the data blocks. At the same time, many of the applications need 24/7 support.

The following section will show how each of the categories that use the RAC database uses the architectural advantage.

OLTP Applications Using Exclusive or Specific Data

In this type of application, the RAC system gives almost linear scalability. Instead of using a stand-alone database with limited resources, the RAC database provides more than one database instance, allowing applications to connect to any of the instances. For example, a bank branch is accessing the central database system. Any particular branch usually inserts or updates only the data pertaining to it. It rarely needs to access another branch's data. This kind of arrangement allows a set of branches to be grouped by region or load, say, on instance one. Another group of branches accesses instance two, and so on. Since the data blocks of one branch are rarely spread across multiple instances, scalability is almost linear, with nearly zero cross instance transfers.

Departmental Applications

Extending the analogy explained above, assume that there are many functional entities or departments accessing a common RAC database system. For example, human resources, sales, distribution, manufacturing, and finance all access the same database system. Each of these functional units has a set of data. It is very rare that the data pertaining to one department is needed for another department.

In this case, access can easily be vertically partitioned. For example, sales and distribution can access through instance one, human resources and finance can access through instance two, and manufacturing can access through instance three. All these applications modify different sets of tables. Conflicts and cross instance block transfers are minimized.

Data Warehousing Applications

DW applications involve large and complex queries against a huge database. Data warehouses are designed to accommodate ad hoc queries. It might not be possible to anticipate the workload of a data warehouse in advance, so a data warehouse should be optimized to perform well for a wide variety of possible query operations.

DW is updated on a regular basis by the ETL process, which is run nightly or weekly, using bulk data modification techniques. ETL stands for extraction, transformation, and loading. The end users of a data warehouse do not directly update the data warehouse. During the data loading, SQL queries accessing the data may experience poor response times owing to low memory resources.

Compared to a typical OLTP operation, which accesses only a handful of records, a typical data warehouse query scans thousands or millions of rows or data blocks. For example, a DW query may be asking to find the total sales for all customers last month or analyze the stock price of the airline industry during the current year.

To meet these kinds of challenges, parallel processing is an apt solution. Oracle's parallel execution feature uses multiple processes to execute SQL statements on one or more CPUs. Parallel execution is available on both single instance and Real Application Clusters databases.

Real Application Clusters takes full advantage of parallel execution by distributing parallel processing to all the nodes in the cluster. The number of processes that can participate in parallel operations depends on the degree of parallelism (DOP) assigned to each table or index.

Since the RAC solution provides multiple instances, the instance that uses SQL queries can effectively be separated from the instance that is specialized for data loading and ETL processing.

Applications Requiring HA

Many mission critical applications, like brokerage trading systems, airline traffic movement, credit card sales, online shopping, and retail banking, etc., cannot afford to have any downtime. All these applications are heavily dependent on the database systems.

The RAC database provides an ideal solution to withstand node or host failures. With multiple nodes, redundancy is built into the database system.

Large Batch Jobs

Many applications require large batch jobs to make changes or to update the database system. These batch jobs usually run during the off-peak hours. Many of these jobs are run to upload data feeds into the database, and also to extract data as required for internal or external business users.

The RAC system, by providing multiple instances, allows a specific instance to be allotted to do batch jobs, without affecting the performance levels of the other instances.

Using Parallel Instance Groups

Besides the physical connection to a specific instance, there is another interesting facility that allows control over which instances allocate parallel execution server processes with instance groups. Each active instance can be assigned to at least one or more instance service groups. By activating a particular service group of instances, the instances that spawn parallel processes can be dynamically controlled.

Instance group membership can be established on an instance-by-instance basis by setting the *instance_groups* initialization parameter to a name representing one or more instance groups. For example, on an 8-node system owned by both marketing and HR departments, half the nodes can be assigned to one department and the other half to the other one. Either the old method of instance group assignment or the new 10g service assignments can be used.

To do this using groups, nodes 1-4 are assigned to the marketing department using the following parameter syntax in the initialization parameter file:

```
sid[1-4].INSTANCE_GROUPS=marketing
```

Nodes 5-8 are then assigned to HR using the following syntax in the parameter file:

```
sid[5-8].INSTANCE_GROUPS=HR
```

The nodes owned by HR are activated to spawn a parallel execution server process by entering the following:

```
ALTER SESSION SET PARALLEL_INSTANCE_GROUP = 'HR';
```

In response, Oracle allocates parallel execution server processes to nodes 5-8. The default value for *parallel_instance_group* is all active instances.

Services in Oracle Database 10g

Oracle Database 10g allows the user to define RAC instances as services. The services can then be individually managed and controlled. Applications are defined as a service, and the RAC instances are then assigned to the individual services. This allows the application to show affinity for a node or set of nodes.

The use of services allows for the replacement of the primary/secondary metaphor from 9i RAC with one in 10g where the primary database becomes the preferred instance while the secondary instance becomes an available instance.

The *srvctl* utility is used to configure the services in a RAC grid configuration. For example:

```
srvctl add database -d v10g -o $ORACLE_HOME -s
$ORACLE_HOME/dbs/v10g_spfile
srvctl add instance -d v10g -I v10g1 -n aultlinux1
srvctl add instance -d v10g -I v10g2 -n aultlinux2
srvctl add instance -d v10g -I v10g3 -n aultlinux3
srvctl add instance -d v10g -I v10g4 -n aultlinux4
srvctl add service -d v10g -s CRM -r V10g1,v10g2 -a v10g3,v10g4
srvctl add service -d v10g -s AR -r v10g3,v10g4 -a v10g1,v10g2
```

This would add the *v10g* database and its four instances, *v10g1, v10g2, v10g3,* and *v10g4,* create two services, CRM and AR, where the CRM service uses instances *v10g1* and *v10g2* as its preferred instances with *v10g3* and *v10g4* as its available instances. Service AR uses the reverse of these assignments.

The *v$active_services* view provides the information on what services are currently running.

Once configured, the service name can be used to define TAF and load balance configurations to allow user connections to be sent to the proper instances.

RAC Grid Suitability for Packaged Applications

Many applications such as ERP, CRM, Supply Chain, and SAS are bought ready made off-the-shelf from the vendors and then customized to the unique needs of the specific enterprise. Invariably, these packaged applications rely on a relational database system to store the control data and transactional data. Control data includes the application suite, metadata, etc. These packaged applications generally provide a certified version of the database to use. Generally, revision or release of package applications and the database systems do not coincide.

To illustrate the point, whenever Oracle releases a new version with advanced features and enhancements, the package application vendor takes their own time to implement the new Oracle version. Applications tend to lag the database in releasing a matching product that leverages the new features of the database technology.

For example, after the 10g RAC database was released, many of the packaged application vendors are attempting to leverage the multi-instance RAC Grid database system. With built-in advantages like scalability, high availability, and enhanced parallelism, RAC is a suitable complement to the ERP, CRM applications. There is an opportunity for most of the packaged applications to utilize the RAC features.

Applications like SAP, Oracle e-Business Suite, Siebel, and Peoplesoft are making serious attempts to use the Oracle RAC database as a backend layer. Some have formally certified and others are in the evaluation stage.

In the next section, the focus is on the opportunity or suitability for some selected ERP applications.

SAP and Real Application Clusters

SAP R/3 and mySAP ERP offer companies a comprehensive solution for managing financials, human resources, analytics, operations, and corporate services. It is a huge collection of software modules. The database is a vital component in the whole architecture of the SAP ERP system.

The database stores almost everything needed for the functionality of the SAP system. Data pieces such as program source code, screen text, menu details, customer information, parameter definitions, statistical information, and transactional data are stored in the database. Data is classified in three broad types: master data; control data; and transaction data.

The architecture of a SAP system involves multiple SAN instances. The SAN instance is an administrative entity that consists of several processes such as message, gateway, update, enquire, and dialog processes. A SAP instance can be a central instance with message, gateway, update, and enqueue processes, or it can be a dialog instance with dialog and background processes. All instances connect to the database. The SAP instance is basically implemented as an application server. A typical SAP installation will have many application servers accessing the Oracle database.

Oracle RAC provides a good opportunity for separating the database processing activity into different Oracle instances. As shown in Figure 11.1, in a three-tier SAP R/3 environment, a specific set of application servers can be configured to access one instance, and another set of application servers can be configured to access and update the second instance. The RAC system provides excellent scalability. As the SAP installation grows in terms of application servers, the Oracle RAC can grow in the number of nodes/instances to meet demands.

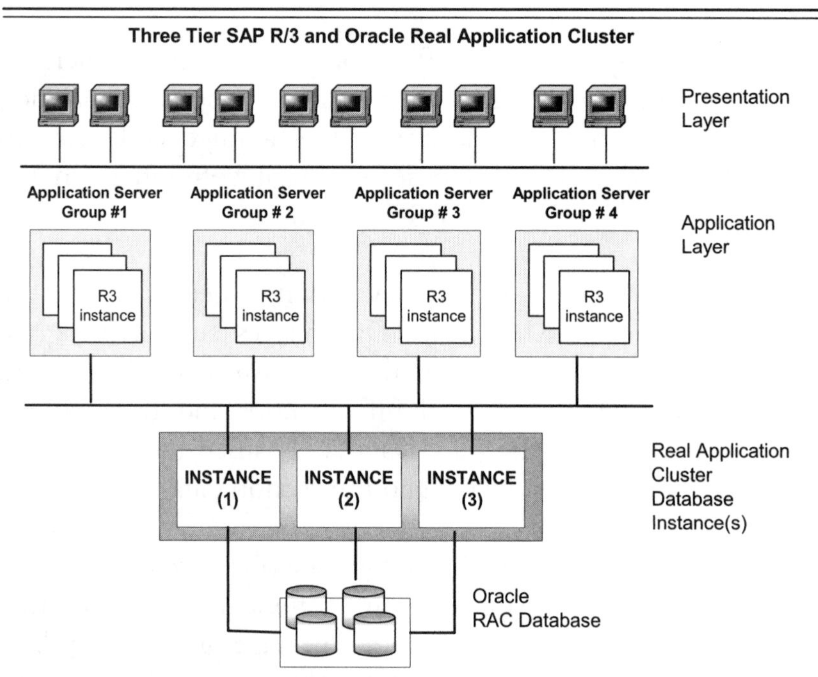

Figure 11.1: *SAP R/3 system using the Oracle RAC database*

At the same time, the Oracle RAC provides high availability by absorbing the failed instance's application server connections. Failure of any of the cluster nodes is of no consequence to the SAP application servers, as they can move over and connect to the surviving database instances.

There are hundreds of objects and sometimes these objects are created when the system is in use. It would be practically impossible to deal with the raw partitions. It is recommended that a RAC database supporting SAP applications be based on a cluster file system or ASM. This gives much flexibility in managing the data files and tablespaces.

Status of Oracle RAC/SAP Certification

Oracle and SAP have conducted many certification tests on selected platforms. Tests have shown a viable combination of RAC with the SAP system. One such test was done using the SAP R/3 4.6D and Oracle 9i RAC on a HP Tru64 UNIX Cluster. Many customers have implemented SAP with an Oracle RAC database. Readers are urged to check with the SAP vendor for the current status.

Also see the website for certification status:

```
http://www.oracle.com/features/ow/index.html?0626_ow_saprac.html
```

SAP's MCOD

mySAP architecture requires more and more databases for the different modules. At the same time, the SAP modules in a mySAP.com environment are not independent, e.g. SAP SD, SAP CRM, and BW interact and share data. To guarantee the required consistency within all these databases, SAP has developed a new method or strategy of Multiple Components in One Database (MCOD). MCOD is a new feature in the installation process for mySAP.com components. It provides the capability of installing several components independently into one single database.

As shown in Figure 11.2, the data needs are consolidated into one large database system, aided by the RAC system.

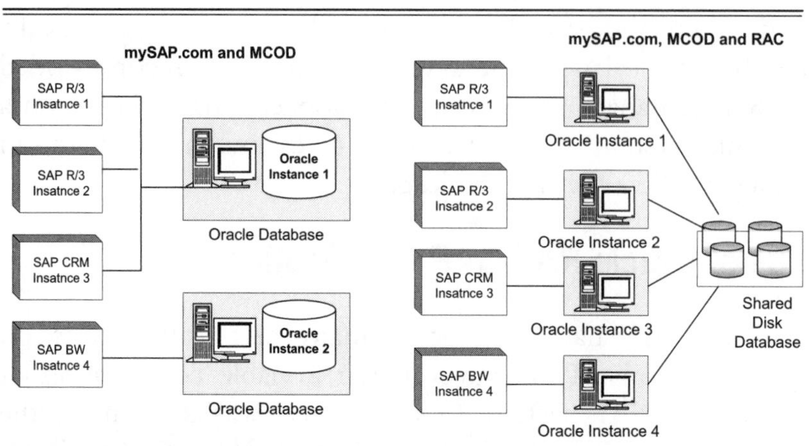

Figure 11.2: *mySAP , MCOD and Oracle RAC Database*

With Oracle 10g RAC, nodes can be optimally customized for dedicated workloads such as CRM, HR, SD, and retail. By utilizing different database instances for these functional modules and batch-centric modules, they can be fine tuned without affecting each other.

By having a single database, administrative flexibility and cost savings are achievable. Running all the related SAP modules in only one database guarantees the consistency and availability of current data. However, as all the eggs are kept in one basket, it becomes much more important to protect the MCOD database for high availability and also to provide acceptable levels of performance. The Oracle RAC database system meets these challenges very well.

Performance Considerations

Some database systems require different parameterization, depending on the transactional behavior of the application. For these database systems, a separate installation of OLTP and OLAP systems is necessary. With the implementation of RAC-based multiple instances, a specific instance can be assigned to a specific SAP module, and it can have its own set of parameters or customization.

Siebel and RAC

The Siebel eBusiness application suite is another important packaged application supporting business operations. Siebel eBusiness application suite provides an integrated set of solutions for sales, marketing, customer service, and partner organization.

Siebel suite is developed on multi-tier models with application clients, application servers, and backend database layers. As shown in Figure 11.3, the client interacts with the middle tier and the middle tier accesses the database. The business logic is in the middle tier, also known as the Siebel application server. The business logic is encapsulated in one or more server components. These server components provide services to both the interactive and the batch operations. Typically, the following components make up the middle tier: the object manager, assignment manager, enterprise integration manager (EIM), and WorkFlow, etc.

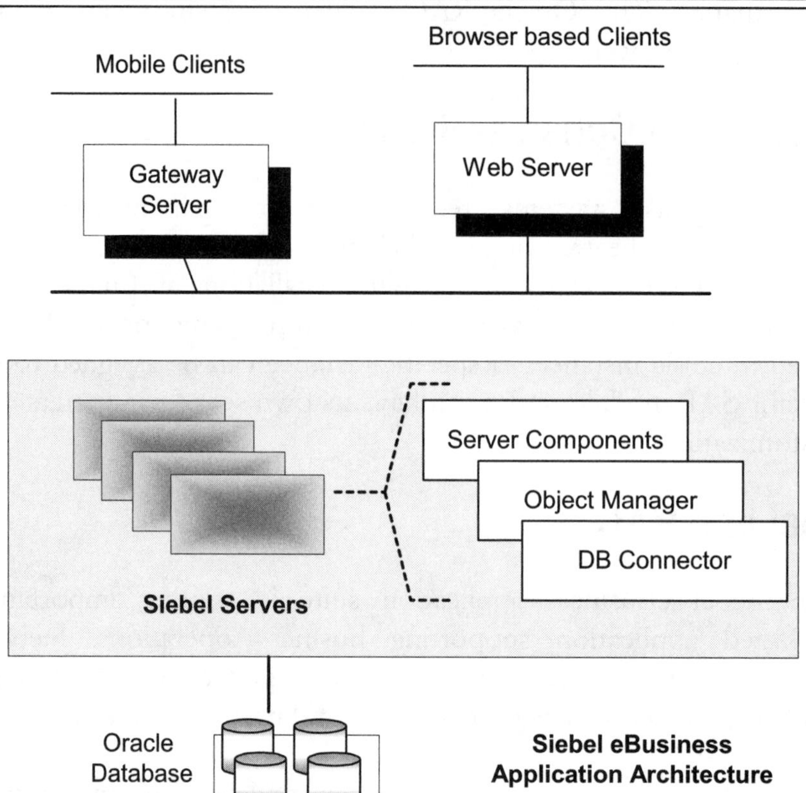

Figure 11.3: *Siebel Architecture*

The Oracle database has been an important backend database choice for many Siebel customers. With a heavy reliance on the database system by Siebel servers, any malfunction in the database layer cripples the entire application framework. Any database component can become a single point failure for the whole Siebel suite. Therefore, a clustered database such as a RAC database, provides true high availability and scalability. When one of the nodes fails along with the database instance, the other surviving instances can still provide the database resources.

Siebel can also leverage the RAC database's ability to provide scalability. As the number of users increases, Siebel Servers can be added to support and maintain performance levels. At the same time, database access increases. The Oracle database server can provide the same type of growth. As the need arises, additional nodes can be added to support the extra workloads.

Another important feature of RAC is the ability to use a selective database instance for a specific group of application servers. This allows the more critical application needs to be prioritized and a specific database instance to be assigned to avoid conflicts and contention.

At the time of writing, tests are being conducted to certify the Siebel backend database with the Oracle RAC system. The reader is urged to consult with Siebel to enquire about the certification status.

Oracle eBusiness Suite

The Oracle eBusiness suite, formerly known as Oracle Applications, is a collection of integrated software applications that provide a complete business solution. It consists of many products or modules, supporting a variety of business functions. Some of these product families are: financials, supply chain, human resource management (HRMS), manufacturing, projects, and public sector and customer relationship management (CRM).

Oracle eBusiness suite is implemented in three-tier architecture. These tiers are:

- Desktop tier or Presentation layer: Comprised of a Web browser and Oracle initiator.

- Application tier: The middle tier consists of a Web server, forms server, concurrent processing server, report server, administration server, and optionally, the discoverer server.
- Backend database tier: The Oracle database server, a single stand-alone or a clustered Oracle 10g RAC.

As shown in Figure 11.4, the database layer in the Release 11i technology stack occupies a pivotal role in providing transactional and control data for the entire suite of applications.

The database provides key functionality by storing data, and is heavily used by all the modules. It is common for all necessary functional data storage to take place there.

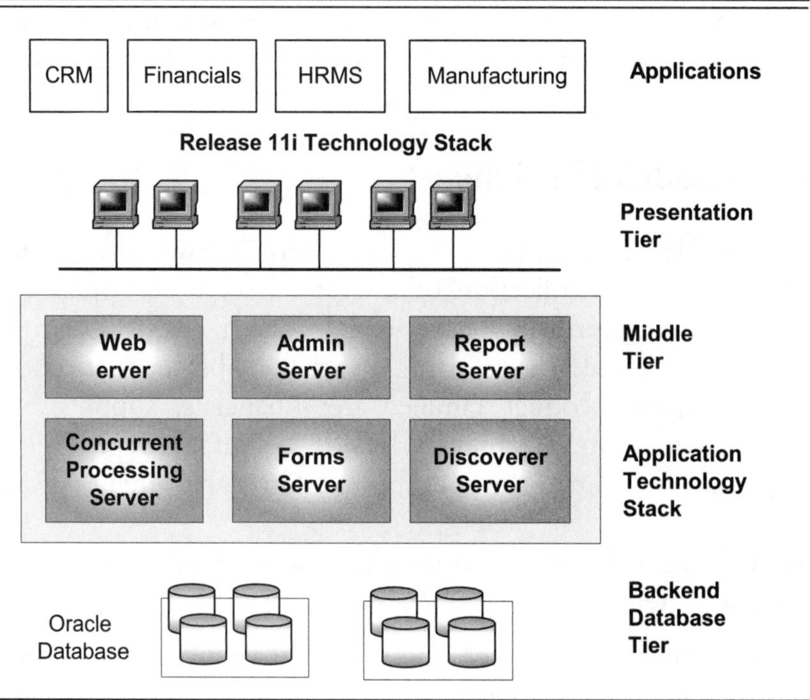

Figure 11.4: *Oracle Applications Architecture and Technology stack*

The critical demands placed on the application suite for running the business operations, handling increased workloads, and maintaining adequate performance levels have become a real challenge. Keeping the eBusiness suite database online 24/7 is mandatory in order to maintain the enterprise operation. To improve overall performance, the time taken for batch jobs and provide fast online response times, the middle tier is usually expanded with additional application servers. This approach generally causes another bottleneck in the database layer.

The Oracle Database 10g RAC database is a good solution to meet these challenges. With the availability of multiple database instances, it becomes possible to service a specific group of application servers with a specific database instance, and so on. This is done while still maintaining a single database. Database resource consumption by different functional units is effectively separated.

The architecture of multiple application servers in the technology stack can take advantage of multiple Oracle database instances to work in different computing environments. By grouping the application servers for database access, scalability and high availability is achieved. The recent release of the Oracle eBusiness 11i suite (11.5.x) is certified with the Oracle RAC database system.

An example will help to explain a typical Oracle eBusiness suite. As shown in Figure 11.5, the middle tier is deployed with many application servers. They are grouped into the form server, HRMS server, portal, iExpense, and concurrent manager server. All the middle tier servers exhibit a particular personality in terms of their functionality. By providing the RAC database system as a backend, application servers get many choices. Based on functionality, the application servers can be configured to access and update a particular database instance.

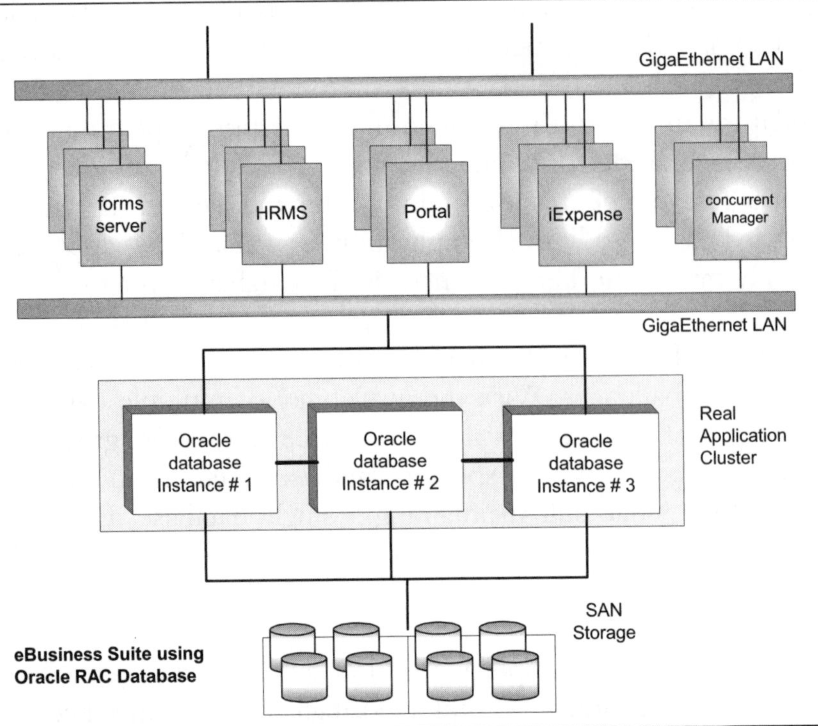

Figure 11.5: *Oracle eBusiness suite using Oracle RAC database*

For instance, form servers can connect to instance-1. HRMS and the portal connect to instance-2, and iExpense and concurrent managers connect to instance-3. This method uses all the instances in a partitioned way. This utilizes the instances uniformly and avoids hot spots. At the same time, with the help of the TAF configuration, high availability of the database server is achieved.

As the business grows and concurrent users increase, middle tier application servers can be added. Database instances can also be added to the existing RAC cluster to meet the additional workload.

Middleware Software

With the growth of internet-based business operations, the web is the primary place of user interaction. Most applications are coded in java or other languages and are usually deployed through middleware application, or java servers such as WebLogic, WebSphere, or Oracle Applications Server. Java is also used in many of the stand-alone applications. In this section, the issues surrounding JDBC connectivity to a typical Oracle RAC database are examined.

JDBC Connectivity

JDBC is a database access protocol that enables the DBA to connect to a database and prepare and execute SQL statements against the database. Core Java class libraries provide only one JDBC API. JDBC is designed, however, to allow vendors to supply drivers that offer the necessary specialization for a particular database.

Oracle delivers the three distinct JDBC drivers: JDBC Thin Driver; JDBC OCI Driver; and JDBC Server-side Internal Driver (KPRB driver).

JDBC Thin Driver

The Oracle JDBC Thin driver is classified as a 100% pure Java, Type IV driver. This means that it is used primarily for Oracle JDBC applets, but it can, of course, be used for other applications as well. Since the driver is written entirely in Java, it is platform independent. No additional Oracle software is required on the client side. Thin driver communication with the server via TTC, a special protocol developed by Oracle Corporation to access the Oracle Database.

The JDBC Thin driver gives the user process a direct connection to Oracle by implementing a form of TCP/IP imitating Oracle Net and TTC on top of Java sockets. These protocols are both lightweight versions of their server counterparts. A limitation is that the Oracle Net protocol runs only over a TCP/IP type connection.

tnsnames entries are not used to identify services since the JDBC Thin driver can only be used in applets that do not depend on an Oracle client installation, therefore one of the following must be done:

- Explicitly define the host name, TCP/IP port, and Oracle SID of the database to which the connection is desired.
- Use a keyword-value pair list.

For example, the following string should be used if the database is to connect on the host *aultlinux2*, which utilizes a TCP/IP listener on port 1521, for the database system identifier (SID) *ault1*. Using the user *appowner* with the password of *f514*:

```
Connection conn = DriverManager.getConnection
("jdbc:oracle:thin:@aultlinux2:1521:ault1", "appowner", "f514");
```

As stated above, the database can alternatively be specified with an Oracle Net keyword-value pair. This may be less readable than the explicit definition, but it has the strength of also working with other JDBC drivers.

```
Connection conn = DriverManager.getConnection
("jdbc:oracle:thin:@(description=(address=(host=aullinux2)
(protocol=tcp)(port=1521))(connect_data=(INSTANCE_NAME=ault1)))",
"appowner", "f514");
```

If it is not possible to use a *tnsnames* entry, then it is not possible to take advantage of the transparent application failover (TAF) facility to provide virtually uninterrupted access the Oracle RAC database. The good news is that the JDBC OCI driver will allow the full utilization of the functionality of TAF.

JDBC Oracle Call Interface Driver

There is also the Type II JDBC OCI driver for use with Oracle-based client-server Java applications. The disadvantage to this driver is that it requires an Oracle client installation, so it is not suitable for applets.

The advantage to this Type II JDBC OCI driver is that it accesses Oracle-specific, non-Java, native code libraries on either the client or middle tier, thus providing a more complete set of functions, and better performance.

Another advantage in the use of the JDBC OCI driver is that it allows the *tnsnames* entries to be utilized. Therefore, it can be used with the full capabilities of the Oracle TAF configuration including automatic failover, connection failover and load balancing.

When the JDBC OCI driver is used, the database is specified using an Oracle Net keyword-value pair, this keyword pair replaces the *tnsnames* entry. The following is the example from before, but in the JDBC OCI keyword-value format:

```
Connection conn = DriverManager.getConnection
(jdbc:oracle:oci:@ault1","appowner","f514");
```

JDBC Server-Side Internal Driver

On the server side, the Oracle JDBC internal driver will support any Java code that can run inside an Oracle database. Examples include Java stored procedures or Enterprise JavaBeans. The Java Virtual Machine (JVM) can communicate directly with the SQL engine using this driver.

The middleware software layers now handle connectivity to the backend Oracle database. The following section will show how some of the popular application servers handle database connectivity and utilize the RAC database.

WebLogic and RAC Database

WebLogic is a popular java application server that codes and deploys web applications. WebLogic supports connectivity to the Oracle database through JDBC drivers. Code that opens a connection to a database can be inserted into web pages or applications in the presentation or business layer. Thick clients, such as standalone Java applications, can connect to remote databases with RMI. Thin clients can embed database connection code in servlets and JSP tags. Both EJB session beans and entity beans can also use JDBC to connect to the Oracle database.

WebLogic has an advanced feature called connection pooling that opens a specified number of connections upon startup.

Connecting to a database using a WebLogic Server in a two-tier configuration involves creating a java.util.Properties object describing the connection. This object contains name-value pairs containing information such as user name, password, database name, server name, and port number.

For example:

```
Properties props = new Properties();
props.put("user", "appowner");
props.put("password", "f514");
props.put("server", "ault1");
```

The server name, *ault1* in the preceding example, refers to an entry in the *tnsnames.ora* file, which is located in the Oracle client installation. The server name defines host names and other information about an Oracle database instance. Once the *tnsnames.ora* entry is in use, the TAF facility suitable for the Oracle RAC database can be used.

A WebLogic connection pool consists of a group of JDBC connections that are created when the connection pool is registered. This is done either by starting up the WebLogic Server or by assigning the connection pool to a target server or cluster. Connection pools use type 2 or type 4 JDBC drivers to create physical database connections. An application borrows a connection from the pool, uses it, and then returns it to the pool by closing it.

MultiPool is a group of connection pools. MultiPool helps in:

- **Load Balancing:** Pools in WebLogic are accessed using a standard round-robin method. When moving to a new connection, the WebLogic Server will select a connection based on the next connection pool in the specified order.
- **High Availability:** Connection pools are listed in the order that determines when connection pool switching occurs. The WebLogic Server provisions database connections from starting with the first connection pool on the list. If for some reason that connection pool fails, it uses the others specified in order.

As shown in Figure 11.6, there are two connection pools. Each of the connection pools can be configured to access a particular database instance of the Oracle RAC.

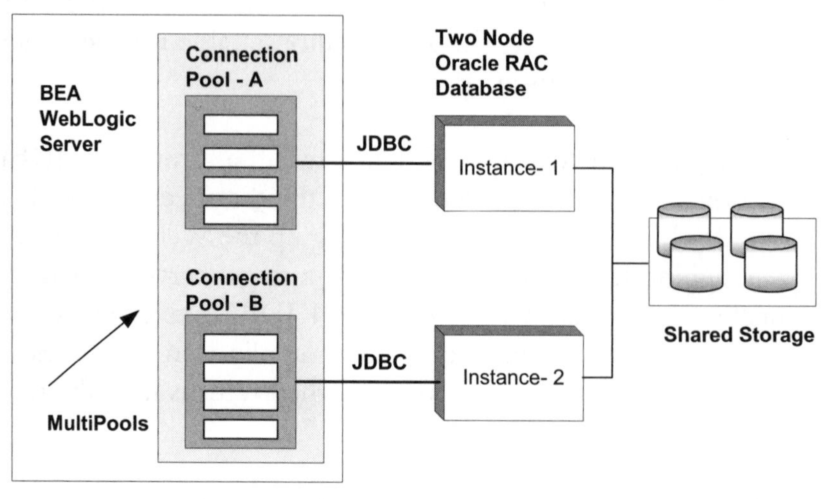

Figure 11.6: *WebLogic with JDBC MultiPool Architecture*

All of the connections in a given connection pool are identical, but the connections within a multipool can vary. These pools can be configured to access different instances of the same database, as with the Oracle RAC. In this way, the instances are effectively used and the database resources are load balanced.

This feature is particularly useful even if the JDBC thin driver is used. When a type 2 JDBC driver or WebLogic jDriver for Oracle is used, the *tnsnames.ora* connect string entry can be specified. The TNS entry can be based on a TAF configuration so that load balancing and failover features can be defined.

Conclusion

This chapter has provided an examination of various application deployments in the Oracle RAC database environment. The suitability of RAC was discussed for applications developed in-house and packaged ERP/CRM applications.

The packaged applications, like SAP, Oracle eBusiness Suite, and Siebel, can take advantage of the existence of a multi-instance database environment, so as to provide high availability and scalability to the applications. Some of the applications are already certified to use the Oracle RAC and others are in the process of being tested for certification.

Both the OLTP and the DW applications can access the consolidated RAC databases concurrently without experiencing performance issues. Because of multiple instances in a RAC database, the contention for database resources is kept low.

References

Configuring SAP R/3 4.6D for Use with Oracle Real Application Clusters - Oracle White Paper - February 2003

Oracle Java Developer's Guide 10g Release 1 (10.1), Part No. B12021-01

Oracle9i RAC for SAP Customers - Presentation by Thomas Baus

Multiple Components in One Database - (MCOD) Presentation by Georg Leffers

BEA WebLogic Server and WebLogic Express Administration Guide

Supporting Siebel eBusiness Suites in an Oracle High Availability and Scalability Environment - James Qiu, Jianwen Lai, Anda Zhao - Oracle World Presentation

Oracle Real Application Clusters Deployment and Performance Guide 10g Release 1 (10.1) Part No. B10768-01

RAC Design Considerations

CHAPTER 12

Introduction

This chapter focuses on the issues that must be considered when designing for RAC. The reasons for utilizing RAC must be well understood before a proper implementation can be achieved.

Essentially, there are only a couple of reasons to use RAC. RAC spreads the load across multiple servers, provides high availability, and allows larger SGA sizes than can be accommodated by a single Oracle10g instance, on Windows2000 or Linux implementations, for example.

The most stringent design requirements come from the implementation of high availability. A high availability RAC design must have no single point of failure, a transparent application failover, and reliability, even in the face of disaster at the primary site. A high availability design requires attention to equipment, software, and the network. This three-tier approach can be quite daunting to design.

The following sections provide a look into two key design considerations. The first is the design of the equipment needed to support a high availability (HA) RAC configuration. Next, the methods of configuring RAC instances in a RAC cluster to meet performance and HA requirements must also be considered.

Designing Equipment for Real Application Clusters

The most important design feature of the equipment used in HA RAC clusters is a layout that eliminates any single point of failure. The diagram in Figure 12.1 provides an opportunity to look at some design features and their impact on the potential success of HA RAC clusters in the environment.

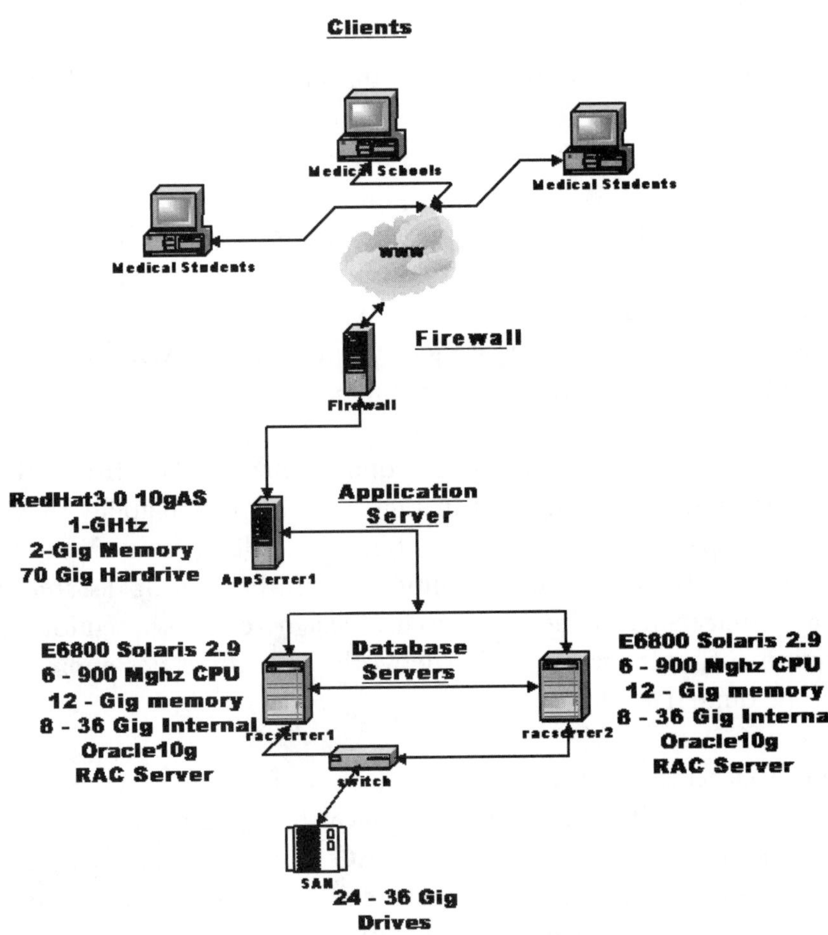

Figure 12.1: *Non-Redundant Configuration*

Figure 12.1 shows a typical RAC configuration. However, this configuration, other than the RAC cluster itself, has no redundancy and many single points of failure. The single points of failure are:

- Firewall
- Application Server
- Fabric Switch
- SAN array

A failure of any one of these single points will result in system unavailability, no matter how well the RAC cluster itself is laid out, designed and tuned.

It is critical to ensure that there is no single point of failure in a high availability configuration. Figure 12.2 illustrates exactly what eliminating single points of failure means.

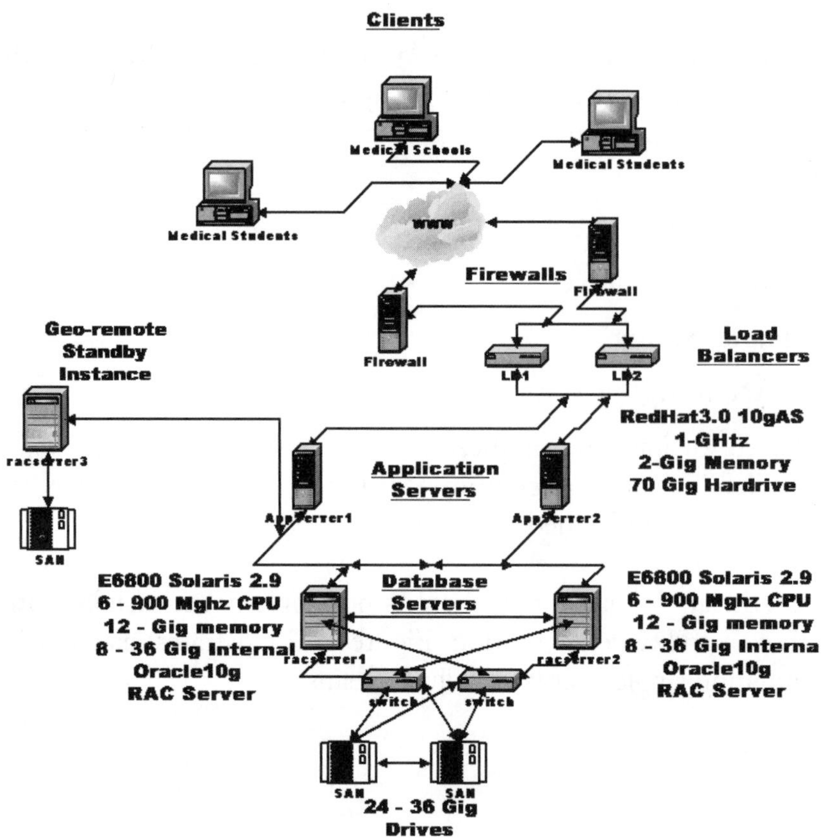

Figure 12.2: *Example of a Redundant RAC Configuration*

The system shown in Figure 12.2 has had the following redundancies added:

- A second firewall with an independent connection to the web.
- A second application server.
- A second fabric switch with redundant pathways.
- A second SAN array.
- A set of load balancers.

- A geo-remote RAC Guard configuration.

Now, the single points of failure in Figure 12.1 have been eliminated. A third server has also been added, as well as a SAN array in a geographically remote location. This third server and SAN ensure that not even a disaster at the primary location will bring the application down. The application server and firewall for this third server are not shown and may not be required if the firewalls and application servers are in a different location from the database servers.

For highly active websites, the application servers may include web caches as well as OC4J servers. The servers that run OC4J are the building blocks of the application tier and provide the application service to the clients. OC4J is J2EE compliant and includes:

- A JSP translator.
- A servlet container.
- An EJB container.
- Several other Java specifications.

OC4J clustering connects servers that run individual containers so that they act in tandem. This provides more availability and scalability than a single Oracle instance can provide. Additional OC4J instances can be added or removed transparently to increase scalability or do system maintenance. The OC4J cluster at the primary site has identical hardware, OS, application server software, and application-specific software to the secondary site. They are configured similarly in all respects.

By having Oracle10gAS Web Cache Cluster and load balancers in front of the OC4J clusters, performance, scalability, and availability of a web site are increased. Web Cache eliminates the need to repeatedly process requests on the application web server by storing frequently accessed URLs in memory. Multiple instances of Web Cache can be configured to run as members of a cache cluster. This provides:

- Higher scalability of the website by allowing more content to be cached and more client connections.
- Higher availability by detecting failures and failing over of caches.

Because each OC4J instance and cache cluster member is redundant on multiple sets of machines, problems and outages within a site are transparent to the client. The OPMN monitoring infrastructure ensures nearly uninterrupted availability of an application's services by automatically detecting and restarting failed components of the application tier or the Web Cache.

In Figure 12.2, the use of a RAC server platform capable of CPU partitioning is shown. This means that multiple CPUs, in systems like the E6800 from SUN, can be separated into virtual servers that act like independent servers. This partitions malfunctioning CPUs or memory, which is on the CPU cards in the E6800, and the rest of the server continues to work.

In addition, the SAN, perhaps a SUN T3, Hitachi or EMC Clariion or Symmetrix, can be configured using redundant disk configurations such as RAID-1, RAID5, or a combination, sometimes called plaid, of RAID1 and RAID5 that virtually eliminate downtime from the loss of a single disk. It should be stressed that application performance can suffer horribly from a disk failure during either a disk rebuild with installed spares or a rebuild of the information using parity information from the other disks in a RAID5 set.

What Are the Effects of Component Failure?

This section will provide a quick look at the effects of component failure.

Failure of the Internet or Intranet

While not a component that a DBA usually has control over, failure of the Internet connection, usually due to the provider having a failure, means no one outside the company can access the application. Failure of the intranet or internal networks means no one inside the company can access the application. These components, usually comprised of multiple components, should also have built in redundancy.

Failure of the Firewall

The firewall acts as the gatekeeper between the company's assets and the rest of the world. If the database is strictly internal with no connection to the web, a firewall is not needed. If there is only one firewall, a failure will prevent anyone outside the firewall, such as the rest of the universe, from contacting the database. Internal users, those inside the firewall, may still have access and some limited processing can occur.

Failure of the Application Server

The application server usually serves the web pages, reports, forms, or other interfaces to the users of the system. If there is only a single application server and it goes down, even if the database is fully functional, there is no application to run against it. A failed application server without redundancy means no one can use the database, even if all other components are still functional. This also applies to single web cache servers or OC4J servers.

Failure of the Database Server

The failure of the database server is the one failure that is taken care of in a normal RAC configuration. Failure of a single database server leads to failover of the connections to the surviving node. While not a critical failure that will result in loss of the system, a single server failure means a reduction in performance and capacity. Of course, a catastrophic failure of both servers will result in total loss of service.

The servers will have disk controllers or interfaces that connect through the switches to the SAN arrays. These controllers or interfaces should also be made redundant and have multiple channels per controller or interface. In addition, multiple network interface cards (NICs) should also be redundant, with at least a single spare to take the place of either the network connection card or the cluster interconnect should a failure occur.

Failure of the Fabric Switch

The fabric switch allows multiple hosts to access the SAN array. Failure of the fabric switch or other interconnect equipment can result in loss of performance or total loss of the application. If the SAN cannot be accessed, the database will crash and no one will be able to access it, even if all other equipment is functional.

SAN Failure

SAN failure can come in many forms. Catastrophic failure will, of course, result in total loss of the database. Failure of a single drive, if there is no hot spare or if the hot spare has been utilized, will result in severe performance degradation, by as much as 400-1000 percent, in a RAID5 situation where the data on the failed drive has to be rebuilt on the fly from parity information stored on the other drives in the RAID5 set. Even if there is an available hot spare, it still takes time to rebuild this hot spare from the parity data on the other drives. During this rebuild, performance will suffer.

Usually, SANs are configured with disk trays or bricks of a specific number of drives. This is usually comprised of eight active and a single spare in each tray or brick. A single tray becomes an array, in the case of a RAID0+1 setup, the array will be striped across the eight drives and would be mirrored to another tray in the array. Failure of a RAID0+1 drive has little effect on performance, as its mirror drive takes over while the hot spare is rebuilt on an "on available" basis. In a RAID5 array, the eight drives are usually set up in a 7+1 configuration, meaning seven drives in a stripe set and one parity drive.

When a drive fails, there must be an immediate spare available to replace it, even if the hot spare is available. If the hot spare has already activated and a second drive is lost, the entire array is in jeopardy. Most of these arrays use hot pluggable drives, meaning they can, in time of failure, be replaced with the system running.

NICs and HBAs

While not shown in the diagram, every component requires a connection to the others. This connection is usually via a network interface card (NIC) or host bus adapter (HBA) interface. These NIC or HBA interfaces should be the fastest possible, especially in the case of the cluster interconnect and disk connect. Failed NIC interfaces result in the loss of that component, unless a second NIC card is immediately failed over to. A failure of the HBA results in loss of connection to the disk array. At a minimum, a spare NIC and HBA for each and every component must be available. Wherever possible, use interchangeable NIC and HBA interfaces.

Provide Redundancy at Each Level

It is easy to see that redundancy at the hardware level is vital. At each level of the hardware layout an alternate access path must be available. Duplicating all equipment and configuring the automatic failover capabilities of the hardware reduce the chances of failure to virtually nil. It is also critical to have spares on hand for non-redundant equipment such as NIC and HBA cards and interface cables.

By providing the required levels of redundancy, the system becomes highly available. Once there is an HA configuration, it is up to the manager to plan any software or application upgrades to further reduce application downtime. In Oracle Database 10g using grid control, rolling upgrades are supported, further increasing reliability. At the SAN level, appropriate duplication software such as Veritas must be used to ensure the SAN arrays are kept synchronous. Oracle Database 10g allows for use of the Oracle Automatic Storage Management or ASM. ASM allows for automated striping, backup and database flashback capability.

Designing for High Performance

Designing for high performance means that every tier of the design must eliminate contention for resources. If there is no contention, each process gets the resources it needs to perform optimally. Resources fall into multiple categories: physical, as in disk and network; and internal, such as CPU speed and memory capacity. Designing for performance means utilizing these resources properly and not relying on memory or disk resources to make up for poor application design.

As with normal databases, the application design will drive performance. The finest equipment will not make up for a poor application design. In the days of Oracle Parallel Server (OPS),

Oracle recommended partitioning the application data and the servers to make OPS perform. Now, Oracle salesmen insist that any application can be run with RAC, with no need for changes.

To add capacity, the solution is to just add a server and bingo, more capacity is provided and more users, no matter what they do with the application, can connect. This all sounds wonderful until the manual, Oracle9i Real Application Clusters Deployment and Performance, Release 1 (9.0.1)", Part No. A96598-01, Chapter 3, Scaling Applications for Real Application Clusters, and Chapter 4, Scaling Applications for Real Application Clusters, is consulted. There, Oracle recommends partitioning both the application data and the users to optimize performance. This unfortunate fact is omitted from the 9.2 and 10g versions of the manual which seems to indicate the automated tuning features of 9.2 and 10g relieve the DBA of this arduous task.

Of course, the difference is that now partitioning is based on reducing intra-node block pinging between instances over the cluster interconnects, instead of reducing disk pinging. At most, a factor of 40 improvements can be expected for the same application running on a RAC server versus an OPS-based server. Once the various system latencies are added, the speed difference between memory operations and disk operations falls to approximately a factor of 40 between a disk ping and an intra-node memory ping. The speed is dependent upon the speed of the interconnect. Still, a factor of 4000% (40) is nothing to sneeze at.

Designing applications for better performance on RAC involves:

- Assigning transactions with similar data access characteristics to specific nodes.
- Creating data objects with parameters that enable more efficient access when globally shared.

- Automating free space allocation and de-allocation through the use of locally managed tablespaces.
- Automating block management through local freelist management.
- Using sequences properly by using sequence ranging triggers for each instance.
- Optimizing all SQL in the application.
- Understanding the workload on the system and planning the application to properly utilize resources.

These factors should be considered for proper application design one-by-one in order to see how they can be utilized to make RAC applications perform optimally.

Compartmenting Transactions to Specific Nodes

One obvious method of reducing pings between instances is to isolate the transactions that use a specific data set to a specific server in the RAC cluster. For example, in a multiuse instance that contains multiple applications, isolate each application's user logins to a specific node. For example, sales users use the sales node, accounting uses the accounting node, and so on. In the case of a node failure, the users switch to one of the other nodes.

This compartmenting of transactions is difficult to implement for a large, multiuse RAC database where many different groups of users use each of the applications on the RAC cluster. In the case of a multi-use instance that is used by almost all corporate users, other techniques must be employed to optimize performance.

Creating Efficient RAC Data Objects

The creation of efficient RAC data objects entails using storage wisely in accordance with good RAC practices. Some of the good

RAC practices, to put it quite frankly, waste disk and memory space to improve data sharing and dispersal characteristics.

An example of an efficient RAC object is one that is used by only a single instance at a time. To achieve this singularity of use, the rows-per-block (RPB) of the data object must be reduced. By reducing the RPB, the chances that multiple instances in the RAC cluster will require data in the same block are decreased. The following are several techniques that can be used to reduce the RPB in a RAC data object:

- Use a smaller block size for objects that will be used across several instances.
- Adjust *pctfree* to restrict the RPB since a higher *pctfree* will reduce the RPB.
- Use data fillers, for example, CHAR data types can be used to artificially extend the size of a data row, thus reducing RPB.

Other techniques to improve the efficiency of data objects include:

- Use as few indexes as possible to optimize data retrieval from the RAC data objects. Index node contention is the largest source of intra-node block pings, or as Oracle calls them, intra-instance block transfers. Index maintenance causes a great deal of intra-node pinging.
- Use automated freelist management.
- For high insert objects, pre-allocate extents to avoid dynamic space management. Assign allocated extents to specific instances. This avoids intra-instance block transfers during insert activity from multiple nodes. For example:

```
ALTER TABLE ad_proofs
ALLOCATE EXTENT ( SIZE 200K
DATAFILE '/usr/u01/oradata/addb/ad_file3.dbf'
INSTANCE 2);
```

- Use locally managed tablespaces to avoid *uet$* and *fet$* block pinging between instances.
- Use reverse-key indexes for indexes that may become right-hand indexes due to high insert rates. This removes the capability to use index scans. Use only when required.
- Design indexes such that the clustering factor is as close to the number of used blocks as is possible. Testing various column orders in concatenated indexes does this. In single column indexes required for SQL optimization, consider re-ordering the table in index order to reduce clustering factor. This technique can result in hot blocks and is the reverse of the previous suggestion to use reverse-key indexes, which actually increases the clustering factor.

This may seem perplexing, since some of the suggestions are contradictory. The correct approach depends on the specific tuning situation. In a situation where hot blocking is occurring in that multiple instances want the same index block because all of the current data entries are indexed there, randomizing the index nodes will reduce the possibility of intra-node index block pinging.

This is demonstrated in Figure 12.3 below. In the case where the data referenced in a single index block is needed by a single instance, the number of data blocks required is reduced by concentrating the data into as small a number of data and index nodes as possible. This reduces the intra-node pinging of data blocks. This is demonstrated in Figure 12.4. So in the first case shown in Figure 12.3, intra-node index block pinging is reduced, and in the second shown in Figure 12.4, the intra-node pinging of data blocks is reduced. The appropriate technique will have to be determined for each tuning situation.

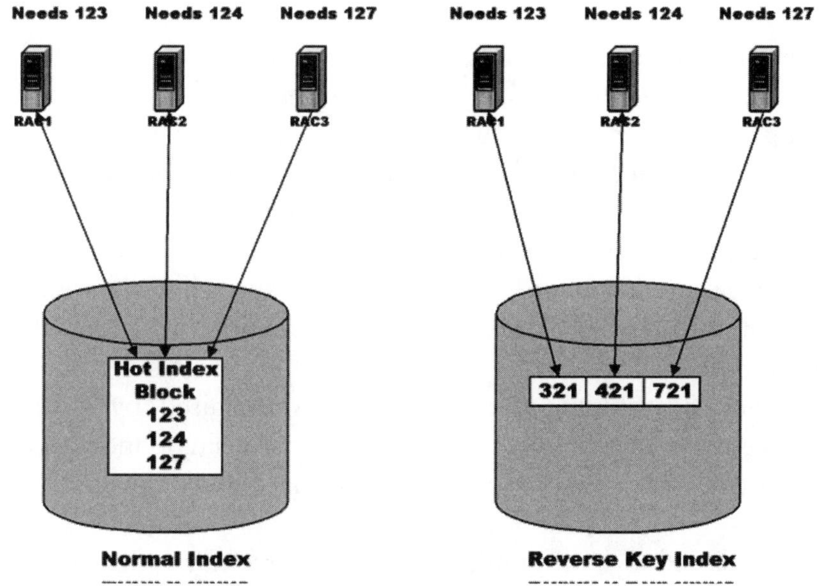

Figure 12.3: *Example of a Reverse Key Index*

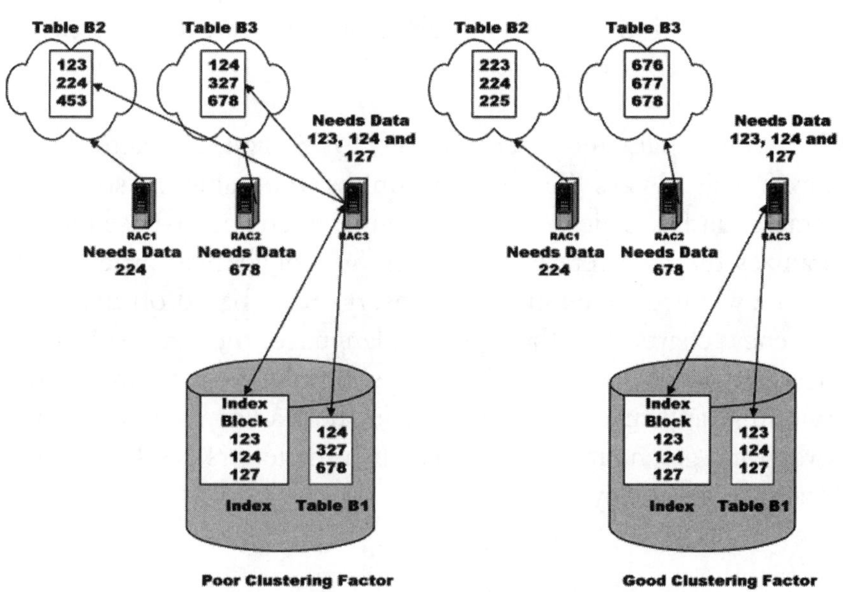

Figure 12.4: *Clustering Factor Affects*

Figure 12.3 illustrates that a hot index block, such as an index containing sequential data, by date or number, that is required by multiple nodes, increases the intra-node index block pinging, as the nodes transfer the index block to perform data lookups.

This demonstrates the effects of a poor clustering factor when the data in a table is poorly ordered, thus spreading data blocks containing index-sequential data across multiple instances. This random scattering of data into data blocks results in the possibility of multiple data blocks being required by a single instance to satisfy a range type query against a single index node. The result is the false pinging of data blocks between instances.

Neither situation is desirable. Use the reverse-key index method when multiple instances will require access to current data referenced in ascending numeric key or date key indexes. Use method two when data is usually accessed by an index range scan for specific periods from the individual instances. Method two is also good for concatenated indexes.

What about character-based indexes? By design, character-based indexes will always be random unless the table is sorted in character index order. This is because a character-based index organizes the data reference pointers in alphabetical order, while the data will usually be in natural insert order, based on the mean frequency charts for the specific language the database uses. Character-based indexes will always be skewed towards those letters that appear most frequently in the leading portions of the words for a given language. In English the letters N, R, S, L, and T lead the frequency charts.

Proper Sequence Usage

If not used properly, sequences can be a major headache in RAC. Generally speaking, sequences should be either CACHED or ORDERED, but not both. The preferred sequence is a CACHED, non-ordered sequence. If the ordering of sequences is forced, performance in a RAC environment will suffer unless ordering the sequence to a single node in the RAC cluster isolates insert activity.

Another method to optimize the use of sequences is to use a staggered sequence insert trigger. A staggered sequence insert trigger is a specific constant added to the sequence value based on the instance number. This isolates each set of inserts and prevents inadvertent attempts to use the same sequence number. An example of a staggered sequence insert trigger is shown in the following script:

```
CREATE TRIGGER insert_EMP_PK
 BEFORE insert ON EMP
 FOR EACH ROW
DECLARE
 INST_ID NUMBER;
 SEQ_NUM NUMBER;
 INST_SEQ_ID NUMBER;
BEGIN
 select
    INSTANCE_NUMBER INTO INST_ID
  FROM
    V$INSTANCE;
  select
    EMP_ID_SEQ.NEXTVAL INTO SEQ_NUM
  FROM
    DUAL;
  INST_SEQ_ID:=(INST_ID-1)*100000 + SEQ_NUM;
  :NEW.EMP_ID:=INST_SEQ_ID;
END;.
```

A staggered sequence trigger will insert the values into indexes such that each instance's values are staggered to prevent index node intra-node transfers. The formula to allow this is:

```
index key = (instance_number -1)* 100000+ Sequence number
```

Generally, sequences can be cached with cache values as high as 200 in RAC. This is much higher than for a regular Oracle instance. If there is insufficient caching, contention can result and will show up as an increase in service times. If there are performance problems due to sequences, the *row cache locks* statistics in the *v$system_event* view should be examined to determine whether the problem is due to the use of Oracle sequences. This is discussed in the following points:

- A problem with sequences is indicated in a *v$system_event* as an extended average wait time for *row cache locks* in the range of a few hundred milliseconds. The proportion of time waiting for *row cache locks* to the total time waiting for non-idle events will be relatively high.

- In the *v$rowcache* view, for the *dc_sequences* parameter, the ratio of *dlm_conflicts* to *dlm_requests* will be high. If this ratio exceeds 10 to 15% and the *row cache lock* wait time is a significant portion of the total wait time, it is likely that the service time deterioration is due to insufficiently cached sequences. For example:

  ```
  SQL> col parameter format a15

  SQL> select parameter, dlm_conflicts, dlm_requests,
  dlm_conflicts/dlm_requests ratio
     2 from v$rowcache
     3 where dlm_requests>0;

  PARAMETER         DLM_CONFLICTS   DLM_REQUESTS          RATIO
  --------------- -------------- --------------    -----------
  dc_sequences                  0              2              0
  ```

In some applications, the sequence numbers used must be sequential. An example would be the line numbers for a purchase order or perhaps check numbers for an automatic check printer. In this case, a sequence table may have to be used to store the highest sequence number. The value is read from the sequence table, increased by one, and then updated. While all of this occurs, the row for the sequence being used is locked, thus no one else can use it. If this type of logic must be used, the table should be placed in a tablespace with a 2048 block size and the *pctfree* should be set high enough that only one row per block is allowed. This will reduce the chances of intra-instance pinging, assuming there is more than one sequence stored in the table.

Tablespace Design in Real Application Clusters

The goal in tablespace design is to group database objects according to their data access distribution patterns. The dependency analysis and transaction profiles of the database must be considered, and then tablespaces are divided into containers for the following objects:

- Frequently and randomly modified tables and indexes belonging to particular functional areas.
- Frequently and randomly modified tables and indexes with a lower probability of having affinity to any functional area.
- Tables and indexes that are mostly READ or READ-ONLY and infrequently modified.

The following criteria must also be considered for separating database objects into tablespaces:

- Tables should be separated from indexes.
- Assign READ-ONLY tables to READ-ONLY tablespaces.
- Group smaller reference tables in the same tablespace.

Using this strategy to group objects into tablespaces will improve the performance of Oracle's dynamic resource mastering. Oracle's dynamic resource remastering by datafiles algorithm re-distributes GCS resources to the instance where they are needed most. This remastering strategy is designed to improve resource operation's efficiency. Oracle remasters cache blocks to the instance with which the cache blocks are most closely associated based on historical access patterns. As a result, resource operations, after remastering, require minimal communication with remote instances through the GES and GCS.

Extent Management and Locally Managed Tablespaces

Allocating and de-allocating extents are expensive operations that should be minimized. Most of these operations in Real Application Clusters require inter-instance coordination. A high rate of extent management operations can adversely affect performance in Real Application Clusters environments more than in single instance environments. This is especially true for dictionary-managed tablespaces.

Identifying Extent Management Issues

If the *row cache lock* event is a significant contributor to the non-idle wait time in *v$system_event*, there is contention in the data dictionary cache. Extent allocation and de-allocation operations could cause this. *v$rowcache* provides data dictionary cache information for *dc_used_extents* and *dc_free_extents*. This is particularly true when the values for *dlm_conflicts* for those parameters increase significantly over time. This means that excessive extent management activity is occurring.

Minimizing Extent Management Operations

Proper storage parameter configuration for tables, indexes, temporary segments, and rollback segments decreases extent allocation and de-allocation frequency. This is accomplished using the *initial*, *next*, *pctincrease*, *minextents*, and *optimal* parameters.

Using Locally Managed Tablespaces

Extent allocation and de-allocation overhead can be greatly reduced if locally managed tablespaces are used. For optimal performance and the most efficient use of space, segments in locally managed tablespaces should ideally have similar space allocation characteristics. This enables the tablespace to be created with the proper uniform extent size that corresponds to the ideal extent size increment calculated for the segments.

For example, tables with relatively high insert rates can be placed in a tablespace with a 10MB *uniform extent size*. On the other hand, small tables with limited DML activity can be placed in a tablespace with a 100K *uniform extent size*. For an existing system, where tablespaces are not organized by segment size, this type of configuration can require significant reorganization efforts with limited benefits. For that reason, compromise by making most of the tablespaces locally managed, with AUTOALLOCATE instead of UNIFORM extent allocation.

Minimizing Table Locks to Optimize Performance

For RAC, table locks are coordinated through global inter-instance communication. Due to the fact that properly designed applications do not need to lock entire tables, table locks can be disabled to improve locking efficiency with minimal adverse side effects. Essentially, there are two methods for disabling table locks:

- Disabling table locks for individual tables.
- Setting *dml_locks* to zero.

The following sections will examine these methods.

Disabling Table Locks for Individual Tables

To prevent users from acquiring individual table locks, the following statement can be used:

```
ALTER TABLE table_name DISABLE TABLE LOCK
```

When users attempt to lock tables with disabled locks, they will receive an error. To re-enable table locking after a transaction, the following statement can be used:

```
ALTER TABLE table_name ENABLE TABLE LOCK
```

Using this syntax forces all currently executing transactions to commit before enabling the table lock. The statement does not wait for new transactions to start after issuing the ENABLE statement. The disadvantage to this statement is that it must be executed for all tables that may experience improper locking.

To determine whether a table in the schema has its table lock enabled or disabled, the *table_lock* column in the *user_tables* data dictionary table should be queried. If SELECT privilege is on *dba_tables*, the table lock state of other user's tables can be queried as well. The *all_tables* views can be used to see the locking state of tables for which a user has been granted SELECT privileges.

Setting *dml_locks* to Zero

Using the *dml_locks* initialization parameter, table locks can be set for an entire instance. This will disable the DROP TABLE, CREATE INDEX and LOCK TABLE commands. If these commands are not needed, *dml_locks* should be set to zero to minimize lock conversions and achieve maximum performance. DDL statements cannot be executed against tables with disabled locks.

SQL*Loader checks the flag to ensure that there is not a non-parallel direct load running against the same table. The use of direct load forces Oracle to create new extents for each session.

If *dml_locks* are set to zero on one instance, it must be set it to zero on all instances. If non-zero values are used with the *dml_locks* parameter, the values need not be identical on all instances.

Performance for Object Creation in Real Application Clusters

In any Oracle database, DDL statements should be used for maintenance tasks, not during normal system operations. For example, global temporary tables or PL/SQL tables should be used rather than permanent tables for reports. If this guideline is followed, in most systems, the frequency of DDL statements should be low.

If the application has to create objects frequently, performance degradation to the RAC environment will occur. This is due to the fact that object creation requires inter-instance coordination. A large ratio of *dlm_conflicts* to *dlm_requests* on the *dc_object_ids* row cache in *v$rowcache,* the same SELECT as was used for sequences will work here as well, along with excessive wait times for the *row cache lock* event in *v$system_event,* is indicative that multiple instances in the cluster are issuing excessive amounts of concurrent DDL statements.

About the only method to improve object creation performance in these situations is to set event 10297 so that it caches *object_id* values. This will improve concurrent object creation by eliminating the recursive DDL and some of the intra-instance pinging. To set event 10297, the following line can be added to the initialization parameter file:

```
event="10297 trace name context forever, level 1"
```

If the additional level argument is set to one, the caching behavior is automatically adjustable internally. Otherwise, the level can be set to the desired cache size.

Conclusion

Cache fusion in Oracle10g RAC introduces an improved diskless algorithm that handles cache coherency more efficiently than Oracle's earlier disk-ping-based architectures. This enables simpler database designs to be implemented while achieving optimal performance. However, great care must be taken to select the fastest interface and network components to get optimal performance from the cluster interconnect in order to realize the true benefits of Oracle's improvements.

Designing for true high availability starts with redundant hardware. If there are multiple single-points of failure, the finest RAC implementation in the known Universe will do little to achieve high availability.

The response time and throughput requirements placed on the system by service-level agreements and customer/client expectations ultimately determine whether a data and functional partitioning strategy should be implemented and how stringent the strategy must be. The response time and throughput needs for the application also determine how much effort needs to be invested to achieve an optimal database design.

To determine how to allocate work to particular instances, start with a careful analysis of the system's workload. This analysis must consider:

- System resource consumption by functional area.
- Data access distributions by functional area.
- Functional dependencies between application software components.

Proper implementation of a strategy that considers these points will make the system more robust and scalable.

The old 80/20 rule applies here; 80% or more of the overhead results from 20% or less of the workload. If the 20% is fixed by observing some simple guidelines, tangible benefits can be achieved with minimal effort. Workload problems can be corrected by implementing any or all of the following:

- Use Oracle automated free list management, or define free list groups for partitioned, as well as non-partitioned, data that is frequently modified.
- Use read-only tablespaces wherever data remains constant.
- Use locally managed tablespaces to reduce extent management costs.
- Use Oracle sequences to generate unique numbers and set the CACHE parameter to a high value, if needed.
- Use sequence staggering to help prevent index block contention.
- If possible, reduce concurrent changes to index blocks. However, if index key values are not modified by multiple instances, or if the modification rate is not excessive, the overhead may be acceptable. In extreme cases, techniques like physical table partitioning can be applied.

References

Metalink Note: 226880.1: *Configuration of Load Balancing and Transparent Application Failover*

OOW 2003 Presentation 32035: *Oracle 9i RAC: A Case Study, Steve Teeters, Science Applications International Corporation, Bobby Hampton, Science Applications International Corporation*

OOW 2003 Presentation 32949: *Oracle 9i Real Application Clusters Helping Southwest Airlines Take Off, Kerry Schwab. Director IT, Southwest Airlines*

OOW 2003 Presentation 33433: Oracle RAC and Linux in the real enterprise, Mark Clark, Director, Merrill Lynch Europe PLC, Global Database Technologies

SEOUC 2003 Presentation: *A Bare Bones RAC Installation, Michael R. Ault, Senior Technical Management Consultant, TUSC Inc - The Oracle Experts*

UKOUG 2001 Presentation: *Advantages of Oracle9i Real Application Clusters, Michael R. Ault, Senior Technical Management Consultant, TUSC Inc - The Oracle Experts.*

Oracle Real Application Clusters Deployment and Performance Guide 10g Release 1 (10.1), Part Number B10768-01

Oracle Real Application Clusters Administrator's Guide 10g Release 1 (10.1) Part Number B10765-01

Oracle Real Application Clusters Installation and Configuration Guide 10g Release 1 (10.1) for AIX-Based Systems, hp HP-UX PA-RISC (64-

bit), hp Tru64 UNIX, Linux, Solaris Operating System (SPARC 64-bit) Part No. B10766-01

OOW 2003 Presentation 32539: Maximum Availability Architecture Oracle's Recipe For Building An Unbreakable System, Ashish Prabhu, Douglas Utzig

High Availability Systems Group, Server Technologies, Oracle Corporation

OOW 2003 Presentation 32630: *Real-World Performance of Oracle9i Release 2, Andrew Holdsworth, Director of Real World Performance, Server Technologies, Oracle Corporation.*

Building Highly Available Database Servers Using Oracle Real Application Clusters, An Oracle White Paper, May, 2002

Oracle RAC Backup and Recovery

CHAPTER 13

Backup and Recovery

The backup and recovery of Oracle Database 10g RAC databases may at first seem unnecessary. That is until one remembers that RAC can handle failure at the instance level, but it cannot handle failure at the disk, or more commonly, the user level.

Essentially, there are two types of recovery with which the DBA needs to be concerned. These recovery types are:

- **Physical recovery:** results from a physical insult such as a hardware failure or other disaster.
- **Instance recovery:** caused by the janitor unplugging the server to plug in his vacuum cleaner.

The following section will provide a look at these in more detail.

Overview of RAC Backup and Recovery

Believe it or not, other than a few quirks which will be covered in detail, RAC backup and recovery is identical to almost all other Oracle database backup and recovery operations. At the basic level, after all, it is only a single Oracle Database 10g database being backed up.

In most cases, an instance failure will be recovered by other RAC instances. Special cases of instance failure will be covered at the end of this chapter.

The quirks come into play when dealing with a RAC database that uses archive logging. Archive logging introduces an added layer of complexity, due to the requirement that all archive logs from all instances in the RAC environment must be backed up. Luckily, Oracle Database 10g allows the database to archive log to more than one destination, and with a little ingenuity on the DBA's part, all archive logs can be available for recovery at all times.

Oracle Database 10g RAC offers a multitude of backup possibilities:

- Export
- Cold backup using scripts
- Hot backup using scripts
- RMAN backup with a catalog
- RMAN backup without a catalog
- The use of third party tools to perform backup and restore operations

As detailed in the following sections, each of these options has its good and bad qualities.

Export

A database export is a logical copy of the structure and data contained in an Oracle database. Archive log information cannot be applied against a database recovered using the import of an export file. This means that an export is a point-in-time copy of a database. In this way, an export is like a cold backup of a database that is not in ARCHIVELOG mode.

Exports are useful in that they allow easy restoration of tables and other structures, instead of having to bring back entire tablespaces, as would be required with most other forms of backup and recovery. The import process can also be used to rebuild tables and indexes into more optimal configurations or to place data into new locations. Another benefit is that exports are capable of being copied across platforms. For example, an export from a WIN2K server can be copied to a Solaris server and applied there.

The drawbacks to exports are that they take a great deal of time to generate depending on database size. They can only be performed against a running database, and they take a long time to recover, again based on database size. In some versions of Oracle, there are also file size limitations.

Cold Backup Using Scripts

Cold backup using scripts can backup an Oracle Database 10g RAC database whether it is in ARCHIVELOG mode or not. A cold backup means that the database is shutdown, and all files are backed up via a manually created script.

Generally speaking, the DBA can always recover from a cold backup unless something happens to the backup media or files. However, unless the database is in ARCHIVELOG mode, a cold backup is a point-in-time backup. If a database is archive logging, which means that all filled redo logs are copied to an archive log before being reused, the cold backup can be restored to the server and archive logs applied to make the database as nearly current as possible.

The drawbacks to cold backups are that the database must be shutdown in order to perform a cold backup, a cold backup can take a long period of time depending on database size, and the

DBA has to manually maintain the backup scripts. Another problem is that cold backup on raw partitions on UNIX or Linux involves the command dd. Cold backup, by its very nature, defeats the purpose of a high availability 24x7 RAC database solution.

Hot Backup Using Scripts

A hot backup is taken while the database is operating. A special command places the database's tablespaces into BACKUP mode, which copies live files. Once the copy operation in a hot backup is complete, the datafiles are taken out of BACKUP mode.

In order to use hot backup, the database must be in ARCHIVELOG mode. Once the datafiles are copied, the archive logs that were generated while the datafiles were in BACKUP mode are also copied to the backup location. The datafile backups and the archive logs are then used to recover the database to the exact state it was in at the end of the backup.

Once the backup is complete, any subsequent archive logs can be applied in order to recover to any point in time between the backup and the last available archive log.

As mentioned, the database is active and in use during a hot backup. This allows a 24X7 shop to operate without having to shut down to backup the database.

Drawbacks of the hot backup include:

- Database performance can degrade during the backup.
- All archive logs generated during the backup process must be captured.
- The scripting for a hot backup can be quite complex.

A Few Words on Using Manual Scripts

Manual scripts should be generated using SQL and PL/SQL routines against the data dictionary of an operating database. This allows the addition of a tablespace or a change in an archive log destination to be automatically engineered into the script. Most attempts to manually maintain backup scripts ultimately end in disaster, as a DBA misses a new tablespace or other structural element and thus, it is not backed up.

In RAC, the *gv$* and *dba_* series of views should be used to create dynamically generated cold and hot backup scripts. Examples of hot and cold backup script generators are available on the Rampant website, using the username and password provided with this book. These scripts have been tested under WIN2K and UNIX environments, but they should be thoroughly tested on the DBA's own system before they are fully relied upon.

Recovery Manager (RMAN)

Oracle RMAN provides the DBA with a comprehensive backup environment. Using RMAN, a DBA can perform a multitude of backup types. The abilities of RMAN depend entirely on whether a backup catalog is being used or not. A backup catalog is a set of tables stored in an Oracle database that track backup sets, pieces, and databases. If a catalog is not available, RMAN stores the backup data in the control file of the instance against which it is performing the backup.

RMAN also allows a block level backup, where only the changed blocks of a tablespace get backed up. For large databases, the space savings in using a block level backup can be enormous.

RMAN is also critical to Automatic Storage Management (ASM). Since ASM is critical to GRID operations, RMAN is then critical for GRID based systems. In ASM, RMAN is responsible for tracking the ASM filenames and for performing the deletion of obsolete ASM files. ASM files cannot, however, be accessed through normal operating system interfaces; therefore, RMAN is the preferred means of copying ASM files. It is also possible to use FTP through XDB, but generally, RMAN will be less complex. It is important to learn to use RMAN first because RMAN is the only method for performing backups of a database containing ASM files.

During conversion to ASM, RMAN is used for moving databases or files into ASM storage.

Using RMAN with the Oracle Enterprise Manager (OEM) allows for the scheduling of backup jobs with automated notification capabilities. Using OEM requires that Oracle Intelligent Agents be running on all RAC nodes. The configuration of Oracle Intelligent Agents can sometimes be complex, and the DBA needs to be careful in the setup of the OEM agents in a RAC environment. Later sections will provide a look at various RMAN scenarios in detail.

Third Party Solutions

Many providers of SAN and NAS storage also provide backup capabilities with their hardware. Complete backups of databases can be maintained with no impact on database operations with the use of shadow volumes or the Third Mirrors, EMC's Business Continuance Volumes (BCV). Recovery using third party solutions can also be incredibly fast, as these solutions often either mirror the entire database to a second location or provide only for backup of changed blocks.

Backup of RAC Databases

The two major backup modes are cold, where the database is shutdown, and hot, where the database is open and in use. An Oracle DBA can use either of these modes to backup a RAC database. However, the main reason for utilizing Oracle RAC is to provide uninterrupted service to the customer base, so it makes little sense to use a cold backup with RAC because it requires the shutdown of all instances that are using the Oracle database.

The DBA must also ensure that all archive log files from all instances are gathered into the backup set. If even a single archive log is missed, the integrity of the backup is placed in serious question.

Using RMAN for Backups

The DBA should seriously consider using RMAN for all RAC backups. By following a few simple requirements, a RAC instance can be backed up with little or no human intervention. If GRID and ASM storage are used for storage, RMAN must be for backups.

The RMAN process can only attach to a single RAC instance at any one point in time. The RMAN connection is called a utility connection because it does not perform any of the backup or restore operations itself. The connection is only an information gathering tool for RMAN.

Creating a Recovery Catalog

RMAN can be used either with or without a recovery catalog. A recovery catalog is a schema stored in a database that tracks backups and stores scripts for use in RMAN backup and recovery situations. Generally, an experienced DBA would suggest that the Enterprise Manager instance schema and RMAN catalog schema be placed in the same utility database on a server separate from the main servers. The RMAN schema generally only requires 15 megabyte per year per database backed up.

The RMAN schema owner is created in the RMAN database using the following steps:

1. Start SQL*Plus and connect as a user with administrator privileges to the database containing the recovery catalog. For example, enter:

   ```
   CONNECT SYS/oracle@catdb AS SYSDBA
   ```

2. Create a user and schema for the recovery catalog. For example, enter:

   ```
   CREATE USER rman IDENTIFIED BY cat
     TEMPORARY TABLESPACE temp
     DEFAULT TABLESPACE tools
     QUOTA UNLIMITED ON tools;
   ```

3. Grant the *recovery_catalog_owner* role to the user. This role provides all of the privileges required to maintain and query the recovery catalog:

   ```
   SQL> GRANT RECOVERY_CATALOG_OWNER TO rman;
   ```

Once the owner user is created, the RMAN recovery catalog schema can be added:

1. Connect to the database that contains the catalog owner. For example, using the RMAN user from the above example, enter the following from the operating system command line. The use of the CATALOG keyword tells Oracle this database contains the repository:

   ```
   % rman CATALOG rman/cat@catdb
   ```

2. It is also possible to connect from the RMAN utility prompt:

   ```
   % rman
   RMAN> CONNECT CATALOG rman/cat@catdb
   ```

3. Now, the CREATE CATALOG command can be run to create the catalog. The creation of the catalog may take several minutes. If the catalog tablespace is this user's default tablespace, the command would look like the following:

```
CREATE CATALOG;
```

While the RMAN catalog can be created and used from either a 9i or 10g database, the Enterprise Manager Grid Control database must be a 9i database. This is true at least for release 1, although this may change with future releases.

Each database that the catalog will track must be registered.

Registering a Database with RMAN

The following process can be used to register a database with RMAN:

1. Make sure the recovery catalog database is open.
2. Connect RMAN to both the target database and recovery catalog database. For example, with a catalog database of RMANDB and user RMAN, owner of the catalog schema, and the target database, AULT1, which is the database to be backed up, database user SYS would issue:

```
% rman TARGET sys/oracle@ault1 CATALOG rman/cat@rmandb
```

3. Once connected, if the target database is not mounted, it should be opened or mounted:

```
RMAN> STARTUP;
--or--
RMAN> STARTUP MOUNT;
```

4. If this target database has not been registered, it should be registered it in the connected recovery catalog:

```
RMAN> REGISTER DATABASE;
```

The database can now be operated on using the RMAN utility.

Example RMAN Operations

The following is an example of the command line connection to a RAC environment, assuming the RAC instances are AULT1 and AULT2:

```
$ rman TARGET SYS/kr87m@ault2 CATALOG rman/cat@rmandb
```

The connection string, in this case AULT2, can only apply to a single instance, so the entry in the *tnsnames.ora* for the AULT2 connection would be:

```
ault2 =
  (DESCRIPTION =
    (ADDRESS_LIST =
    (LOAD_BALANCE = OFF)
    (FAILOVER = ON)
      (ADDRESS = (PROTOCOL = TCP)(HOST = aultlinux2)(PORT = 1521))
    )
    (CONNECT_DATA =
      (SERVICE_NAME = ault)
      (INSTANCE_NAME = ault2)
    )
```

If the instances use archive logs, RAC requires that a channel connection be specified for each instance that will resolve to only one instance. For example, using the AULT1 and AULT2 instances from the previous example:

```
CONFIGURE DEFAULT DEVICE TYPE TO sbt;
CONFIGURE DEVICE TYPE TO sbt PARALLELISM 2;
CONFIGURE CHANNEL 1 DEVICE TYPE sbt CONNECT = 'SYS/kr87m@ault1';
CONFIGURE CHANNEL 2 DEVICE TYPE sbt CONNECT = 'SYS/kr87m@ault2';
```

This configuration only has to be specified once for a RAC environment. It should be changed only if nodes are added or removed from the RAC configuration. For this reason, it is known as a persistent configuration, and it need never be changed for the life of the RAC system. This configuration requires that each of the specified nodes be open, the database is operational, or closed, the database shutdown. If one specified instance is not in the same state as the others, the backup will fail.

RMAN is also aware of the node affinity of the various database files. The node with the greatest access will be used to backup those datafiles that the instance has greatest affinity for. Node affinity can, however, be overridden with manual commands, as follows:

```
BACKUP
     #Channel 1 gets datafiles 1,2,3
     (DATAFILE 1,2,3 CHANNEL ORA_SBT_TAPE_1)
     #Channel 2 gets datafiles 4,5,6,7
     (DATAFILE 4,5,6,7 CHANNEL ORA_SBT_TAPE2)
```

The nodes chosen to backup an Oracle RAC cluster must have the ability to see all of the files that require backup. For example:

```
BACKUP DATABASE PLUS ARCHIVELOG;
```

The specified nodes must have access to all archive logs generated by all instances. This could entail some special considerations when configuring the Oracle RAC environment.

The essential steps for using RMAN in Oracle RAC are:

- Configure the snapshot control file location.
- Configure the control file autobackup feature.
- Configure the archiving scheme.
- Change the archivemode of the database, although this is optional.
- Monitor the archiver process.

The following section will show how the snapshot control file location is configured.

Snapshot Control File Location

Identical copies of the control file must be maintained on every node that participates in the RAC backup process. Therefore, each node must have an identical directory location to store a snapshot of the current control file, taken at the time of the backup. This directory location is referred to as the snapshot control file location. Issuing the following command shows the default snapshot control file location:

```
SHOW SNAPSHOT CONTROLFILE NAME;
```

To change the default location to */u02/backup/ault_rac/snap_ault.cf*, the command would be:

```
CONFIGURE SNAPSHOT CONTROLFILE NAME TO
'/u02/backup/ault_rac/snap_ault.cf'
```

The control file is only specified for a single location, which requires each node to have a */u02/backup/ault_rac* directory in the configuration. Like the channel specifications shown in the previous section, the control file is a persistent global specification.

The control file can be backed up automatically during each backup operation with the command:

```
CONFIGURE CONTROLFILE AUTOBACKUP ON;
```

This automatic control file backup is a persistent setting and need never be specified again. By using the automatic control file backup, RMAN can restore the control file even after loss of the recovery catalog and the current control files.

Archive Logs and RAC Backup Using RMAN

Archive logging, while vital to the backup of any Oracle database, causes special problems when backing up a RAC database. All archived logs, no matter which instance has generated them, must be backed up in order to recover using the backup.

The configuration for archive logs must be carefully set up. For example, if AULT1 instance archives a log file to the location:

```
/u01/backups/archives/ault_rac/ault_log_1_1234.log,
```

Then, a duplicate file must be placed on any node that performs backup operations in a directory with the same name. Only one node performs backup operations in a RAC environment. That node must have access to all archived logs.

The parameter *log_archive_format*, must be specified identically on all nodes and should include the instance number and redo log thread number.

The configuration of archive log locations depends on the type of file systems used in the RAC environment. The file systems available for RAC are:

- OCFS based file systems
- RAW (non-CFS file systems)
- ASM managed disk groups (10g)

An OCFS or ASM based file system allows any node to read the archive logs from any other node. In fact, all logs can be placed in a centralized area. This is the preferred setup for Oracle RAC. If node AULT1 writes a log to */u01/backup/archives/ault_rac*, any other RAC instance in an OCFS setup could see the log. This is demonstrated in Figure 13.1.

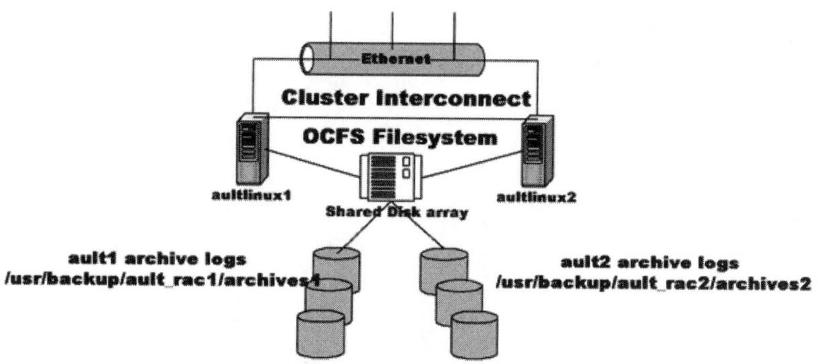

Figure 13.1: *Example OCFS Archive Log Layout*

In a RAW file system, the shared drives are configured into raw partitions. Only a single file can be written to a specific raw device, thus raw devices must not be used for archive logs. This means that for a raw configuration, the archive logs are written to server-local disks that are not shared. Unless special configuration options such as NFS are used, no instance can see the archive logs for any other in a raw environment. This is demonstrated in Figure 13.2. The following section will present a technique for overcoming this problem in a raw file system environment.

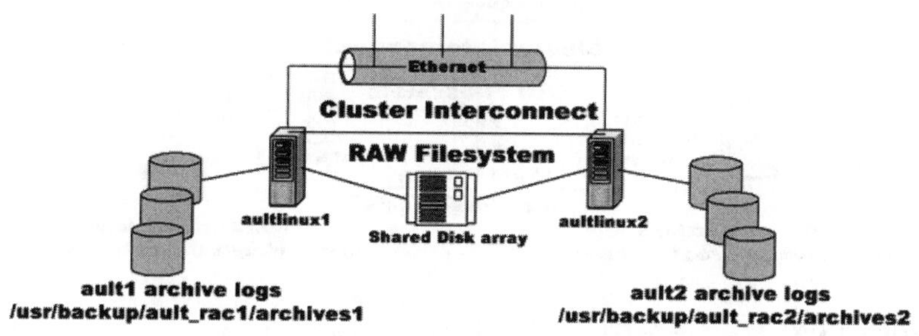

Figure 13.2: *Example RAW Archive Log Layout*

In order to make the archive log files visible to the other nodes, the directories must be named according to which node they service. In the AULT1, AULT2 configuration, this would be:

On node AULTLINUX1:

```
/usr/backup/ault_rac1/archives1
```

On node AULTLINUX2:

```
/usr/backp/ault_rac2/archives2
```

To make the archive logs available, the */usr/backup//ault_rac2/archives2* directory should be NFS-mounted to the AULTLINUX1 node, and the */usr/backup/ault_rac1/archives1* directory NFS-mounted to the AULTLINUX2 node. To make things even easier, a periodic job could be scheduled to copy the archive log files from the NFS mounts into the local archive destination. By copying the archive logs from the NFS-mounted directories into the local archive log location, the DBA can be sure that even if the NFS mount is lost, the database will be recoverable. This setup is illustrated in Figure 13.3.

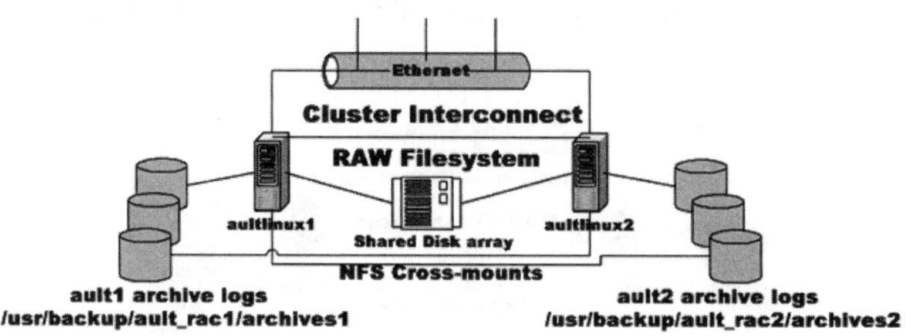

Figure 13.3: *Example Use of NFS Mounting*

An UNIX utility, known as fuser, verifies if a file is open or closed. If an archive log is being written, UNIX will allow it to be copied, deleted, or have just about anything else done to it. Therefore, using fuser before copying an archive file will ensure all files are complete and usable for recovery. Any script written on a UNIX or Linux box for copying archive logs should use fuser to verify that a log is not being written before attempting to copy it.

About the only advantage of the raw configuration is the ability to parallel the archive log portion of the backup, if multiple tapes, one on each node, are used.

If only a single tape drive is available, the NFS mount scheme must be used. If the NFS mount is lost along with archive logs, the database may not be fully recoverable.

The initialization parameters should be set similar to:

```
ault1.LOG_ARCHIVE_DEST_1="LOCATION=/u01/backup/ault_rac1"
ault2.LOG_ARCHIVE_DEST_1="LOCATION=/u01/backup/ault_rac2"
```

By using the NFS mount scheme, either node can backup the archive logs in the other. On Linux, an explanation of the process to set up an NFS-mounted drive follows.

Configure the services such that the NFS services are running:

```
NFS
NFSLOCK
NETFS
```

Figure 13.4 shows the Service Configuration GUI with these services checked.

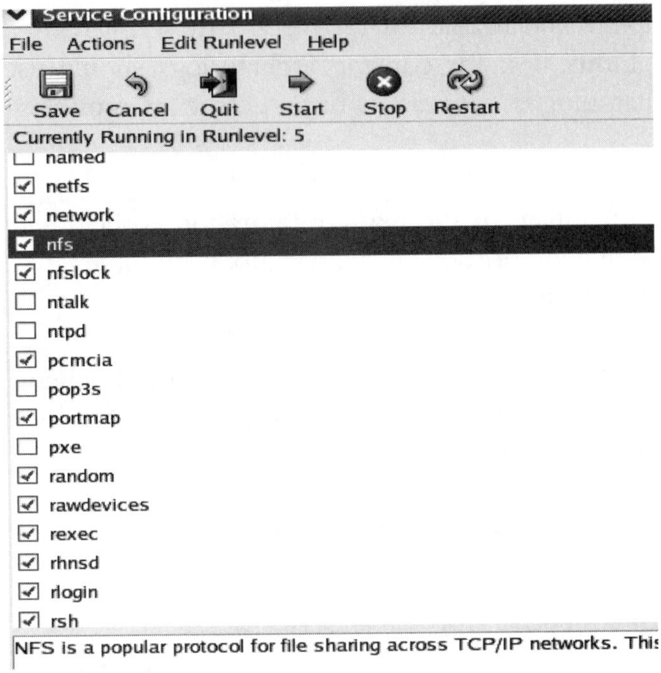

Figure 13.4: *Service Configuration Screen with NFS services selected.*

The NFS server must be configured on each node. Figure 13.5 shows the NFS Server GUI configuration screen for Linux.

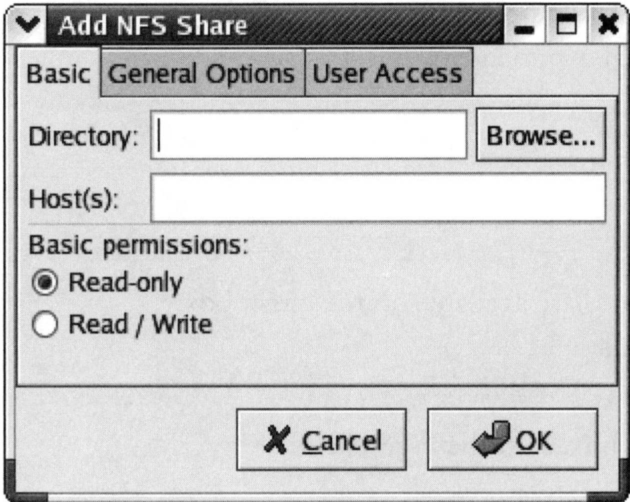

Figure 13.5: *Example NFS Configuration Screen*

The root user performs the configuration for NFS mounts as follows.

1. On each RAC node, create the mount point directory exactly as it appears on each remote node. For example, for the server AULTLINUX2, the command to create the mount directory for the archive directory on AULTLINUX 1 would be:

```
$ mkdir /usr/backup/ault_rac1/archives1
```

2. On each RAC node, the MOUNT command would be used to mount the NFS drive(s) from the other nodes. This is done using the mount directory created in the previous step. The example setup would be:

```
$ mount aultlinux1:/usr/backup/ault_rac2/archives2
/usr/backup/ault_rac2/archives2
```

Once the directories are cross-mounted, the process can then continue.

The configuration of NFS mount points on Solaris 9 would be done using manual commands:

1. Start the NFS server:

```
# /etc/init.d/nfs.server start
```

2. Set up the shares:

```
# share -F nfs -o rw=v10gsolaris2 /usr/backup/ault_rac1/archives1
```

3. Verify the shares are available on the target box:

```
# dfshares -F nfs v10gsolaris1
RESOURCE SERVER          ACCESS          TRANSPORT
V10gsolaris1:/usr/backup/ault_rac1/archives1  v10gsolaris1-
```

4. On the target box, start the NFS client:

```
# /etc/init.d/nfs.client start
```

5. On the target box, create the required mount directory:

```
# mkdir /usr/backup/ault_rac1/archives1
```

6. On the target, mount the shared directory:

```
# mount -F nfs -o rw v10gsolaris1:/usr/backup/ault_rac1/archives1
```

Make sure the mount directory is created with the owner and group that will have access to the cross-mounted directory tree.

In Windows2000, the drives are shared across the network to achieve the same functionality.

The *log_archive_format* parameter determines the format of the archive logs that have been generated. It must be the same on all clustered nodes. The format strings allowed for *log_archive_format* are:

```
%T -- Thread number, left-zero-padded so LOG_ARCHIVE_FORMAT =
ault_%T would be ault_0001

%t -- Thread number, non-left-zero-padded so LOG_ARCHIVE_FORMAT =
ault_%t would be ault_1

%S -- Log sequence number, left-zero-padded, so LOG_ARCHIVE_FORMAT =
ault_%S would be ault_0000000001
```

```
%s -- Log sequence number, non-left-zero_padded, so
LOG_ARCHIVE_FORMAT = ault_%s would be ault_1.
```

The format strings can be combined to show both thread and sequence number. The *%T* or *%t* parameters are required for RAC archive logs.

In order to perform a complete recovery, a database, whether it is a normal database or a RAC database, must use archive logging. In order to turn on archive logging in RAC, the following procedure should be used:

1. Shut down all instances associated with the RAC database.
2. Choose one instance in the RAC cluster. In its unique initialization parameter file set the *cluster_database* parameter to false. If a server parameter file is being used, <sid.> should be appended to the parameter.
3. In the instance parameter file, the *log_archive_dest_n*, *log_archive_format* and *log_archive_start* parameters should be set for the example instances:

   ```
   v10g2.LOG_ARCHIVE_DEST_2 = "LOCATION=/u01/backup/ault_rac2
   MANDATORY"
   LOG_ARCHIVE_FORMAT = ault_%T_%s
   LOG_ARCHIVE_START = TRUE
   ```

4. Start the instance.

   ```
   $ sqlplus /nolog
   SQL> connect / as sysdba

   Connected to an idle instance

   SQL> startup

   <normal startup messages>
   ```

5. Execute the following command from the SQL*PLUS session:

   ```
   SQL> alter database archivelog;

   Command executed.
   ```

6. Shut down the instance.
7. Edit the instance initialization parameter file or server parameter file to reset *cluster_database* to TRUE.
8. Restart the instances.

Deletion of Backed-up Archive Logs

After a successful backup, the archive logs should be deleted. RMAN can automate the deletion of archive logs. It is suggested that only the logs that have actually been backed up be deleted. To achieve the deletion of backed up archive logs, the BACKUP command is issued with either the DELETE INPUT or DELETE ALL INPUT clause following the ARCHIVELOG portion of the command.

The command to delete just the archive logs that have been backed up for instance v10g1 would be:

```
BACKUP DATABASE PLUS ARCHIVELOG delete INPUT;
```

The command used to delete all of the archive logs at the archive log destination would be:

```
BACKUP DATABASE PLUS ARCHIVELOG delete ALL INPUT;
```

To be absolutely sure that only backed up archive logs are deleted, use the DELETE command with a MAINTENANCE connection in RMAN. For the example with instances v10g1 and v10g2:

```
ALLOCATE CHANNEL FOR MAINTENANCE DEVICE TYPE DISK CONNECT
'SYS/kr87m@ault1';
DELETE ARCHIVELOG LIKE '%arc_dest_1%'
BACKED UP 1 TIMES TO DEVICE TYPE sbt;
RELEASE CHANNEL;

ALLOCATE CHANNEL FOR MAINTENANCE DEVICE TYPE DISK CONNECT
'SYS/kr87m@ault1';
DELETE ARCHIVELOG LIKE  '%arc_dest_1%'
```

```
BACKED UP 1 TIMES TO DEVICE TYPE sbt;
RELEASE CHANNEL;
```

The BACKED UP 1 TIMES clause appears in the above commands. This tells RMAN not to delete the archive logs unless it has a record of them being backed up at least once. The *$arch_dest_1%* token tells what logs to remove and translates into the value specified for *log_archive_dest_1* for the instance specified in the connection alias, such as: @AULT1.

RMAN is capable of autolocating files it needs to backup. RMAN, through the database synchronization and resync processes, is aware of which files it needs to backup for each node. RMAN can only backup the files it has autolocated for each node on that node.

During recovery, autolocation means that only the files backed up from a specific node will be written to that node.

Backup Procedures for RMAN and RAC

Various aspects of the backup procedures using RMAN have been presented thus far. In this section, they will be tied into a coherent set of backup procedures. Essentially, RMAN scripts will be used to perform a cluster file system backup with a single drive, a raw file system backup with multiple drives, and a raw file system backup with a single drive.

CFS Single Tape Drive Backup

Perhaps the simplest RAC backup is the CFS backup using a single tape drive. Basically, one backup device and one channel are configured, and the backup command is ready to be issued. After connecting to both the RMAN catalog database and the target database, the following RMAN commands would be issued:

```
CONFIGURE DEVICE TYPE sbt PARALLELISM 1;
CONFIGURE DEFAULT DEVICE TYPE TO sbt;
BACKUP DATABASE PLUS ARCHVIELOG delete INPUT;
```

The backup set of commands is simple in a CFS single tape drive backup because all nodes can see all drives in the CFS array, which allows any node to backup the entire instance.

CFS Multiple Tape Drive Backup

If the RAC setup includes a tape drive on each node or the backup is to a disk on each node, the backup can be parallel, which will make it go faster, utilizing the entire available instance for the backup operation. For the example 2-node RAC setup, after connecting to the RMAN catalog and the target instance, these commands would be issued:

```
CONFIGURE DEVICE TYPE sbt PARALLELISM 2;
CONFIGURE DEFAULT DEVICE TYPE sbt;
CONFIGURE CHANNEL 1 DEVICE TYPE sbt CONNECT 'SYS/kr87m@ault1';
CONFIGURE CHANNEL 2 DEVICE TYPE sbt CONNECT 'SYS/kr87m@ault2';
```

If a device type of DISK is in use, substitute DISK for SBT and specify the path to the backup directory as a part of the CHANNEL configuration. For example:

```
CONFIGURE CHANNEL 1 TYPE disk FORMAT
'/u01/backup/ault_rac1/b_%u_%p_%c' CONNECT 'sys/kr87m@ault1';
```

This configuration need only be specified once unless something happens to the RMAN catalog. Once the configuration is set, the command to perform the backup is fairly simple:

```
BACKUP DATABASE PLUS ARCHIVELOG delete INPUT;
```

There is also provision for a control file backup:

```
BACKUP DATABASE INCLUDE CURRENT CONTROLFILE PLUS ARCHIVE LOG delete
INPUT;
```

RMAN Backup: Raw File Systems To a Single Tape Drive

The major problem with RAW file system setups is that each node only sees the archive logs it has produced. In order for the node to see the other archive logs from the other nodes, the archive log directories must be NFS-mounted to the backup node. The NFS mounts must be read/write in order to specify DELETE ALL INPUT or DELETE ALL.

The script to perform the backup of a RAW file system would resemble:

```
CONFIGURE DEVICE TYPE sbt PARALLELISM 1;
CONFIGURE DEFAULT DEVICE TYPE TO sbt;
BACKUP DATABASE PLUS ARCHIVELOG delete INPUT;
```

The above commands will only work if the backup node has read/write access to the archive log directories for all nodes in the RAC database cluster.

RMAN Backup: Raw File Systems to Multiple Tape Drives

The script to perform this backup would resemble:

```
CONFIGURE DEVICE TYPE sbt PARALLELISM 2;
CONFIGURE DEFAULT DEVICE TYPE TO sbt;
CONFIGURE CHANNEL 1 DEVICE TYPE sbt CONNECT 'SYS/kr87m@ault1';
CONFIGURE CHANNEL 2 DEVICE TYPE sbt CONNECT 'SYS/kr87m@ault2';
```

If a device type of DISK is in use, substitute DISK for SBT and specify the path to the backup directory as a part of the CHANNEL configuration. For example:

```
CONFIGURE CHANNEL 1 DEVICE TYPE disk FORMAT
'/u01/backup/v10g_rac1/b_%u_%p_%c' CONNECT 'sys/kr87m@v10g1';
```

As mentioned, this configuration only has to be specified once, unless something happens to the RMAN catalog. Once the configuration is set, the command to perform the backup is fairly simple:

```
BACKUP DATABASE PLUS ARCHIVELOG delete INPUT;
```

There is also provision for a control file backup.

```
BACKUP DATABASE INCLUDE CURRENT CONTROLFILE PLUS ARCHIVELOG delete
INPUT;
```

The DELETE INPUT clause was used in this case. This is because the process performing the backup is local to each node and has read/write access to the archive log directory.

Example Configuration and Backup Using Grid Control/EM and RMAN

This section will show actual screen shots of the configuration and execution of a backup. This example uses a SUN environment using The Grid Control (EM) interface for RMAN.

First, the Schedule Backup: Strategy screen is called from the Maintenance section of Grid Control. Figure 13.6 shows the Grid Control Job Strategy screen.

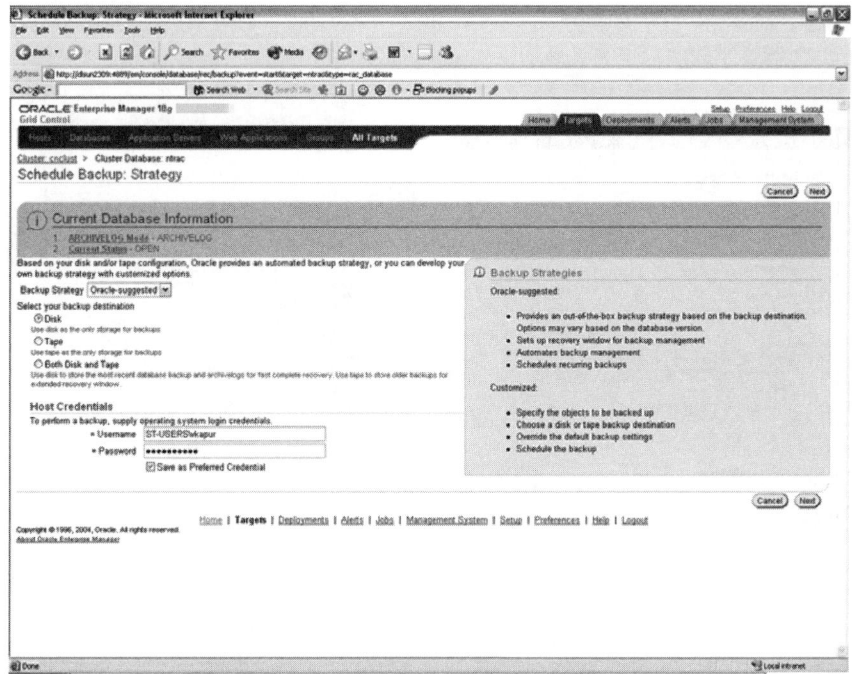

Figure 13.6: *Grid/EM Schedule Backup: Strategy*

The selection of the Backup Strategy list box offers the choice of Oracle suggested methodology or custom methodology. Figure 13.7 shows the use of the customized screen. On the custom screen, pick lists are used to customize the backup.

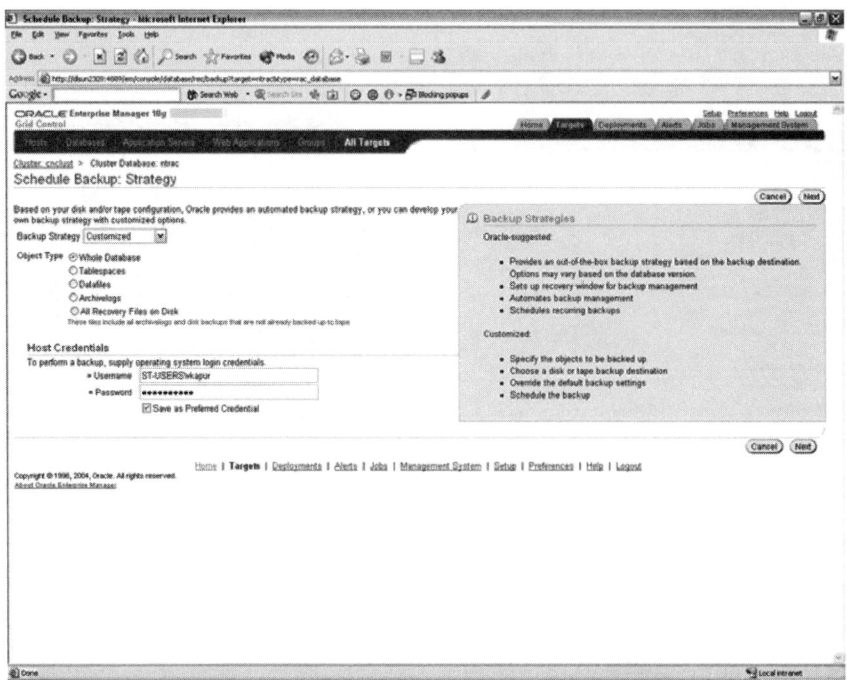

Figure 13.7: *Grid/EM Screen for Customized Backup*

Once the user decides whether to use Oracle suggested or customized backup, the Next button is used to advance to the next window. The Grid/EM interface will then show a summary of the script used for backup and allows it to be approved. This is shown in Figure 13.8.

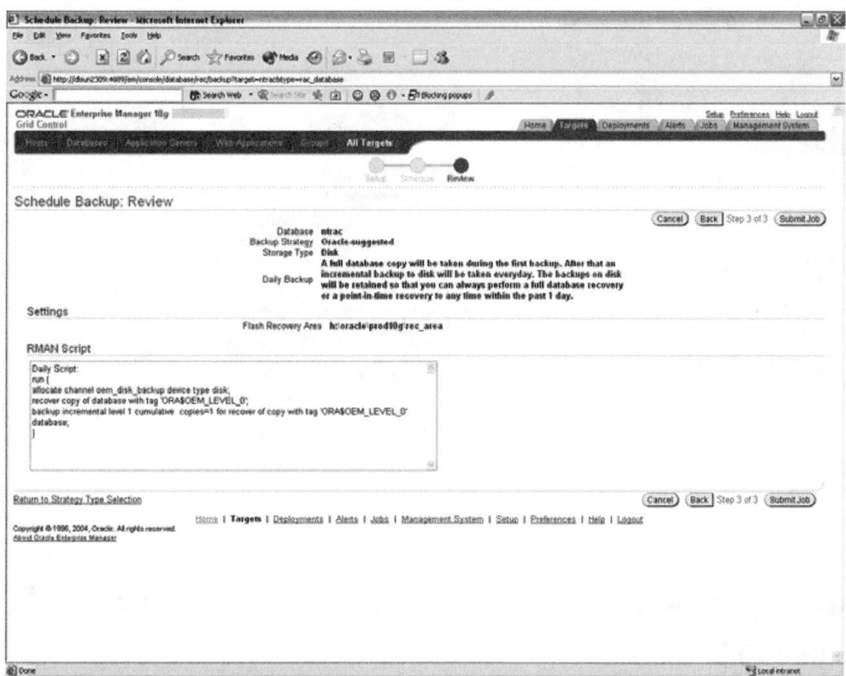

Figure 13.8: *Grid/EM Schedule Backup: Review Screen*

Once the RMAN script has been reviewed, the job is submitted using the Submit Job button. The status of the job can be monitored using the Grid/EM Job Status screen from the Jobs tab. The Job Status screen is shown in Figure 13.9.

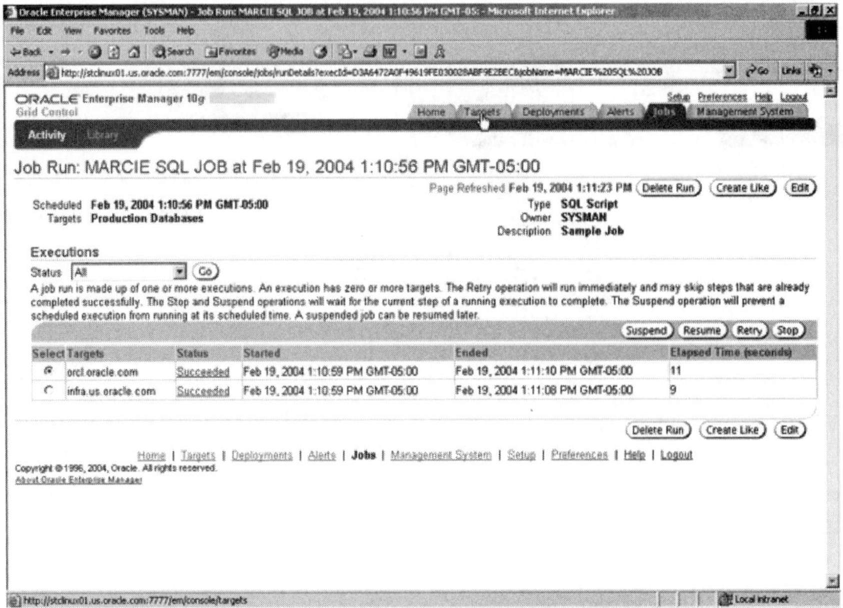

Figure 13.9: *Grid/EM Job Status Screen*

The screen in Figure 13.9 shows the status of all jobs, not just the backup job. The example above shows the results of a SQL job run. By clicking on the various steps of the job process, any output generated can be displayed.

Recovery in the RAC Environment

There are basically two types of failure in a RAC environment: instance and media. Instance failure involves the loss of one or more RAC instances, whether due to node failure or connectivity failure. Media failure involves the loss of one or more of the disk assets used to store the database files themselves.

If a RAC database undergoes instance failure, the first node still available that detects the failed instance or instances will perform instance recovery on all failed instances using the failed instances redo logs and the SMON process of the surviving instance. The redo logs for all RAC instances are located either on an OCFS shared disk asset or on a RAW file system that is visible to all the other RAC instances. This allows any other node to recover for a failed RAC node in the event of instance failure.

Recovery using redo logs allows committed transactions to be completed. Non-committed transactions are rolled back and their resources released.

There are experts with over a dozen years of working with Oracle databases that have yet to see an instance failure result in a non-recoverable situation with an Oracle database. Generally speaking, an instance failure in RAC or in normal Oracle requires no active participation from the DBA other than to restart the failed instance when the node becomes available once again.

If, for some reason, the recovering instance cannot see all of the datafiles accessed by the failed instance, an error will be written to the alert log. To verify that all datafiles are available, the ALTER SYSTEM CHECK DATAFILES command can be used to validate proper access.

Instance recovery involves nine distinct steps. The Oracle manual only lists eight, but in this case, the actual instance failure has been included:

1. Normal RAC operation, all nodes are available.
2. One or more RAC instances fail.
3. Node failure is detected.
4. Global Cache Service (GCS) reconfigures to distribute resource management to the surviving instances.

5. The SMON process in the instance that first discovers the failed instance(s) reads the failed instance(s) redo logs to determine which blocks have to be recovered.
6. SMON issues requests for all of the blocks it needs to recover. Once all blocks are made available to the SMON process doing the recovery, all other database blocks are available for normal processing.
7. Oracle performs roll forward recovery against the blocks, applying all redo log recorded transactions.
8. Once redo transactions are applied, all undo records are applied, which eliminates non-committed transactions.
9. Database is now fully available to surviving nodes.

Instance recovery is automatic, and other than the performance hit to surviving instances and the disconnection of users who were using the failed instance, recovery is invisible to the other instances. If RAC failover and transparent application failover (TAF) technologies are properly utilized, the only users that should see a problem are those with in-flight transactions. The following listing shows what the other instance sees in its alert log during a reconfiguration.

```
Sat Feb 15 16:39:09 2003
Reconfiguration started
List of nodes: 0,
 Global Resource Directory frozen
one node partition
 Communication channels reestablished
 Master broadcasted resource hash value bitmaps
 Non-local Process blocks cleaned out
 Resources and enqueues cleaned out
 Resources remastered 1977
 2381 GCS shadows traversed, 1 cancelled, 13 closed
 1026 GCS resources traversed, 0 cancelled
 3264 GCS resources on freelist, 4287 on array, 4287 allocated
 set master node info
 Submitted all remote-enqueue requests
 Update rdomain variables
 Dwn-cvts replayed, VALBLKs dubious
 All grantable enqueues granted
 2381 GCS shadows traversed, 0 replayed, 13 unopened
 Submitted all GCS remote-cache requests
```

```
 0 write requests issued in 2368 GCS resources
 2 PIs marked suspect, 0 flush PI msgs
Sat Feb 15 16:39:10 2003
Reconfiguration complete
 Post SMON to start 1st pass IR
Sat Feb 15 16:39:10 2003
Instance recovery: looking for dead threads
Sat Feb 15 16:39:10 2003
Beginning instance recovery of 1 threads
Sat Feb 15 16:39:10 2003
Started first pass scan
Sat Feb 15 16:39:11 2003
Completed first pass scan
 208 redo blocks read, 6 data blocks need recovery
Sat Feb 15 16:39:11 2003
Started recovery at
 Thread 2: logseq 26, block 14, scn 0.0
Recovery of Online Redo Log: Thread 2 Group 4 Seq 26 Reading mem 0
  Mem# 0 errs 0: /oracle/oradata/ault_rac/ault_rac_raw_rdo_2_2.log
Recovery of Online Redo Log: Thread 2 Group 3 Seq 27 Reading mem 0
  Mem# 0 errs 0: /oracle/oradata/ault_rac/ault_rac_raw_rdo_2_1.log
Sat Feb 15 16:39:12 2003
Completed redo application
Sat Feb 15 16:39:12 2003
Ended recovery at
 Thread 2: logseq 27, block 185, scn 0.5479311
 6 data blocks read, 8 data blocks written, 208 redo blocks read
Ending instance recovery of 1 threads
SMON: about to recover undo segment 11
SMON: mark undo segment 11 as available
```

One word of caution, during testing for this listing, an instance could not be brought back up after failure, a rare occurrence. A kill -9 was done on the SMON process on AULTLINUX1, within the Linux/RAC/RAW environment. AULTLINUX2 continued to operate and recovered the failed instance; however, an attempted restart of the instance on AULTLINUX1 yielded a Linux Error: 24: Too Many Files Open error. This was actually caused by something blocking the SPFILE link. Once the instance was pointed towards the proper SPFILE location during startup, it restarted with no problems.

Media Recovery in RAC Instances

Media recovery is only required if a physical insult occurs to the database files, preventing proper access to Oracle data or transaction files. The presentation of RMAN in the backup section of this chapter has been intended to instruct the DBA to copy Oracle files, making recovery possible if a physical insult occurs.

If the Oracle database uses self-created scripts for backup, self-generating recovery scripts may be beneficial as well. An example is available on the Rampant website, using the username and password provided with this book. Generating a recovery script and storing it with the backup set assures an easily performed recovery.

Generally, it is wisest to use RMAN or a third party tool to perform backups in complex environments. Any backup and recovery process must be thoroughly tested. An untested backup and recovery plan is no plan at all. The steps for media recovery depend on what files are lost. However, RMAN simplifies this, since it will recover files up to a complete database, if need be.

Once a failed file is detected, RMAN, a third party program, or the DBA's own scripts and procedures are used to bring the affected file or files back from the backup media. From ARCHIVELOG mode, apply the archived logs to bring the database to a fully recovered state. If archive logs are not used, the loss of any datafile means the database must be fully recovered to the point in time of the last backup.

The node that performs recovery must be able to access all files that need to be recovered. This means that the recovery node must be able to access the online redo logs, datafiles, rollback tablespaces, and all archived redo logs from all database instances. This requirement to see all archive logs may require that the NFS mount strategy be implemented.

Using RMAN to Recover a RAC Environment

As in backup, there are two environments that must be considered when performing a RAC recovery, these are:

- Recovery in an OCFS environment
- Recovery in a RAW filesystem environment

In an OCFS environment, all nodes can see all files. This ability of OCFS greatly simplifies the recovery process. The recovery process using OCFS does not require NFS-mounting or elaborate archive log copying schemes. For example, in the sample environment using RAC nodes AULTLINUX1 and AULTLINUX2, which support instances AULT1 and AULT2, the commands for an OCFS-based recovery could be as simple as:

```
CONFIGURE DEVICE TYPE sbt PARALLELISM 1;
CONFIGURE DEFAULT DEVICE TYPE TO sbt;
RESTORE DATABASE;
RECOVER DATABASE;
```

If more than one tape device is available, the parallelism of the recovery can be increased, thus reducing recovery time. For example:

```
CONFIGURE DEVICE TYPE sbt PARALLELISM 2;
CONFIGURE DEFAULT DEVICE TYPE TO sbt;
CONFIGURE CHANNEL 1 DEVICE TYPE sbt CONNECT 'SYS/kr87m@ault1';
CONFIGRE CHANNEL 2 DEVICE TYPE sbt CONNECT 'SYS/kr87m@ault2';
RESTORE DATABASE;
RECOVER DATABASE;
```

Since Oracle RMAN uses autolocation, the channel connected to each node restores the files backed up by that node. Remember, the configure commands only have to be issued once.

Recovery in a Raw File System Environment

The use of a clustered file system is highly recommended because it is easier to manage, backup, and restore. In a RAW file system, the archive logs from each of the nodes are not available to any of the other nodes for recovery, unless some form of log copy procedure, scripted and run through a system-scheduling program, is employed, or all of the other node's archive log locations are NFS-mounted to the node performing the recovery operation.

If the NFS mounting scheme is used and one or more nodes are not available, only an incomplete recovery can be performed, up to the first unavailable archive log. Even in a NFS scheme, it is suggested that some form of log copy script be used to allow the unavailable node's logs to be available for recovery. The frequency of log copying should be based on the required concurrency of the database. If the DBA can only afford to lose 15 minutes worth of data, they had better have all archive logs available up to the last fifteen minute interval before the media failure.

Using RMAN, a recovery using a single tape looks identical to a single tape recovery in the OCFS environment:

```
CONFIGURE DEVICE TYPE sbt PARALLELISM 1;
CONFIGURE DEFAULT DEVICE TYPE TO sbt;
RESTORE DATABASE;
RECOVER DATABASE;
```

However, this assumes all of the archived redo logs are available. If all of the logs are not available, a RMAN script similar to the following would be used to recover until the first unavailable log is encountered. In the example log, sequence 2245 in thread two is the first unavailable log.

```
RUN
{
    SET UNTIL LOG SEQUENCE 2245 THREAD 2'
    RESTORE DATABASE;
    RECOVER DATABASE;
}

ALTER DATABASE OPEN RESETLOGS;
```

The ALTER command is used to open the database. The RESETLOGS option resets the archive log sequences and renders previous archive logs unusable for most recovery scenarios.

Parallel Recovery

Recovery with Oracle Database 10g RAC is automatically parallel for these three stages of recovery:

- Restoration of data files.
- Application of incremental backups.
- Application of redo logs.

The number of channels configured for a RAC database in RMAN determines the degree of parallelism for data file restoration. In the previous example configuration, two streams could have been involved in restoring data files since two channels were configured. The degree of parallelism for restoration of incremental backups is also dependent on the number of configured channels.

Redo logs are applied by RMAN using the degree of parallelism specified in the initialization parameter *recovery_parallelism*.

In Oracle Database 10g, there is no server manager program, so all DBA functions are done through SQL*PLUS. Using manual recovery methods such as SQL*PLUS, values can be specified for *recovery_parallelism*, since it is a dynamic parameter. However, it cannot exceed the setting for *parallel_max_servers*. Using the

DEGREE option for the RECOVER command, the degree of parallelism can also be controlled for other recovery operations.

Standby Databases in RAC Configuration

The Oracle Database 10g Dataguard feature has revolutionized the standby database concept. It allows Oracle10g to have both physical and logical standby databases, for either normal instances or RAC instances.

In the case of a normal instance, Oracle executes processes on the main node that handle the copying of archive logs to the standby server for physical standby. It also executes processes that read the changes from the redo logs and apply them as SQL statements, in the case of logical standby.

There are two types of standby databases supported for RAC. A standby database can be created on a single node or on a clustered node system. In Oracle10g, the DataGuard Manager does support RAC; however, if its use is desired, the Dataguard configuration must be set up manually.

Setting up a Standby Database for a RAC Cluster to a Single-Instance (One Node)

Creating a standby database on a single instance is exactly like a normal standby database creation. The steps to create a physical standby database for a RAC environment are similar to those employed for a regular instance:

1. Take a full backup, either hot or cold, of the Oracle Database 10g RAC database. As an alternative, the files can be placed in backup mode and transferred using FTP if the database is smaller than 10 Gigabytes.

2. Create a standby control file from any instance in the RAC system:

```
ALTER DATABASE create STANDBY CONTROLFILE AS <path>;
```

3. Restore the database to the standby node and place the standby control file in the appropriate location.

4. Copy any required archive logs to the new node.

5. Configure the *log_archive_dest_n* parameter for the RAC instance to the proper standby configuration.

6. Metalink NOTE:180031.1: *Creating a Data Guard Configuration* can be used for appropriate network settings, such as *tnsnames.ora* and *listener.ora.*

7. Configure the log transport services. Setting up the *log_archive_dest_n* parameter on all primary instances does this. All instances must archive the logs to the service of the single node standby system. The standby system creates a pool of archive logs, and on the basis of the SCN, it can determine which archive log from which thread is the next one to apply. So the next free *log_archive_dest_n* parameter must be set to the standby service. The other settings, such as which process to use for transfer or type of transfer (SYNC or ASYNC), depend on the preferred Protection Mode. The Metalink NOTE:68537.1: *init.ora* Parameter *log_archive_dest_n* Reference Note can provide additional information.

8. Now perform startup mount on the standby database and set it to the RECOVER mode.

Configuration When the Standby Database is Also a Cluster (RAC) System

The standby system may also be created in a second RAC environment. This provides more confidence, scalability, and performance. If two identical systems can be utilized, there should be no performance and availability degradation in the case of switchover or failover. Normally, there is the same number of instances or nodes on the standby system as on the primary system; however, this is not required.

Essentially, the process is the same as with a normal standby database creation. Full backup is taken from the primary database, and the standby control file is created from any of the instances. Next, the standby system is prepared for the database by creating the RAW devices if OCFS is not being used, creating the logical links, configuring the hardware and installing the Oracle software on each node. At this point, the backup of the primary instance can be restored, including the newly created standby control file. Next, the appropriate parameters are set in the PFILE or SPFILE for each instance correctly. Follow the process from the preceding section, Setting Up a Standby Database For a RAC Cluster To a Single-Instance (One Node) and also configure the network parameters, such as *tnsnames.ora* and *listener.ora,* corresponding to the system's particular requirements and settings.

The greatest difference between the multi-node and single node system is that with the multi-node setup, there are now multiple standby instances and only one of them can perform the recovery.

Every primary instance transports its archive logs to a corresponding standby instance. The standby instance receiving the logs now transfers them to the instance performing the recovery. This is configured by the *log_archive_dest_n* parameter. It is also suggested that all standby redo logs be copied on the standby database for each standby instance. For clarification, consider the following example:

There is a primary RAC database with two nodes and two instances: AULT1 and AULT2). There is a standby RAC environment with two nodes and two instances: AULT3 and AULT4. The normal primary RAC database has archive log mode enabled. Each primary instance archives its redo logs on a formatted partition of the shared disk if a cluster file system (CFS) is supported for the platform used. Otherwise, the archive logs are stored on each node's private disk area. Different formats must be used for naming the archive logs to prevent overwriting. At the very least, the *%t* in *log_archive_format* should be used to prevent overwriting. The *%t* represents the thread number where the log comes from.

Thus, the following settings:

Instance AULT1:

```
LOG_ARCHIVE_DEST_1=(location=/usr/backup/ault_rac1/archives1)
LOG_ARCHIVE_FORMAT=arc_%s_%t
```

Instance AULT2:

```
LOG_ARCHIVE_DEST_1=(location=/usr/backup/ault_rac2/archives2)
LOG_ARCHIVE_FORMAT=arc_%s_%t
```

Next, the log transport for each primary RAC instance is added to the corresponding standby RAC instance. As standby redo logs have already been created with maximum performance as the goal, these are the settings:

Instance AULT1:

```
LOG_ARCHIVE_DEST_1=(location=/usr/backup/ault_rac1/archives1)
LOG_ARCHIVE_DEST_2=(SERVICE=ault3 LGWR ...)
LOG_ARCHIVE_FORMAT=arc_%s_%t
```

Instance AULT2:

```
LOG_ARCHIVE_DEST_1=(location=/usr/backup/ault_rac2/archives2)
LOG_ARCHIVE_DEST_2=(SERVICE=ault4 LGWR ...)
LOG_ARCHIVE_FORMAT=arc_%s_%t
```

Now, instance AULT4 is designated as the recovering instance. It can be either AULT3 or AULT4. This means that the archive logs from the instance AULT3 have to be transferred to instance AULT4. Instance AULT4 is also performing the archiving to disk process. Again, this is on the shared disk that is available for both standby instances. The resulting settings for instance AULT3 and AULT4 are:

Instance AULT3:

```
LOG_ARCHIVE_DEST_1=(SERVICE=ault4 ARCH SYNC)
```

Instance AULT4:

```
LOG_ARCHIVE_DEST_1=(location=/usr/backup/ault_rac4/archives4)
```

Once this is complete, the STARTUP NOMOUNT and ALTER DATABASE MOUNT standby database commands can be issued for all instances and the recovering instance can be put into recovery mode.

Log Shipping When the Standby Database is a Single Node System

If the RAC standby configuration is on a single node system, the prerequisites are the same. The difference is that all instances from the primary database have to ship their archive logs to one single system. Due to the SCNs in the archive logs, the managed recovery process (MRP) on the standby database determines the correct order in which to apply the archive logs from the different threads on the standby database. The primary instances in this example are instances AULT1 and AULT2. The single node standby instance is AULT3. This results in the following settings for *log_archive_dest*:

Instance AULT1 and AULT2:

Instance AULT1:

```
LOG_ARCHIVE_DEST_1=(location=/usr/backup/ault_rac1/archives1)
LOG_ARCHIVE_DEST_2=(SERVICE=ault3 LGWR ...)
```

Instance AULT2:

```
LOG_ARCHIVE_DEST_1=(location=/usr/backup/ault_rac2/archives2)
LOG_ARCHIVE_DEST_2=(SERVICE=ault3 LGWR ...)
```

Different standby redo log threads must also be created on the standby database. Instance AULT3 now receives all the logs and applies them to the standby database.

Instance AULT3:

```
LOG_ARCHIVE_DEST_1=(location=/usr/backup/ault_rac3/archives3)
```

Cross Instance Archival

In addition to the parameters shown above, cross instance archival can be configured. This means archive logs can be shipped from one primary RAC instance to another primary RAC instance. This could be helpful in case of gap resolution, if one instance loses network connectivity or archive logs are deleted by default.

To enable cross instance archival, one free *log_archive_dest_n* parameter is configured for shipping to another primary instance. For cross-instance archival, only the archive process is supported and can be used. If the earlier example were used, the result would be:

Instance AULT1:

```
LOG_ARCHIVE_DEST_1=(location=/usr/backup/ault_rac1/archives1)
LOG_ARCHIVE_DEST_2=(SERVICE=ault3 LGWR ...)
LOG_ARCHIVE_DEST_3=(SERVICE=ault2 ARCH ...)
LOG_ARCHIVE_FORMAT=arc_%s_%t
```

If cross instance archival is also used on instance AULT2:

```
LOG_ARCHIVE_DEST_1=(location=/usr/backup/ault_rac2/archives2)
LOG_ARCHIVE_DEST_2=(SERVICE=ault3 LGWR ...)
LOG_ARCHIVE_DEST_3=(SERVICE=ault1 ARCH ...)
LOG_ARCHIVE_FORMAT=arc_%s_%t
```

Archive Log Gap Resolution and FAL

There are two modes of gap resolution:

- The automatic one, which is controlled by the archiver and is turned on automatically. The automatic gap resolution works proactively and will produce some network overhead.
- The Fetch Archive Log (FAL) method, which requests certain logs as required from the remote systems. On the receiving instance, one or more FAL Server is published from which it receives its archive logs. On the sending instance, one or more FAL Client is published, which receive archive logs from a specified instance. The publishing is done by the initialization parameters *fal_server* and *fal_client.*

FAL is not supported for logical standby databases. A typical configuration using the current example RAC could be:

Instance AULT1 and AULT2:

```
FAL_CLIENT=ault3
```

Instance AULT3 and AULT4:

```
FAL_SERVER=ault1,ault2
```

When cross instance archival is configured, instance AULT3 will now receive missing archive logs from instance AULT2, and instance AULT4 from instance AULT1.

Conclusion

Although RAC configurations can be complex, the backup and recovery of RAC need not be a nightmare. Using RMAN, the configuration, backup, and recovery in RAC environments is greatly simplified. Log transport in RAC can be configured to easily support standby or Data Guard.

References

Metalink NOTE:180031.1: *Creating a Data Guard Configuration*

Metalink NOTE:68537.1: *Init.ora Parameter "LOG_ARCHIVE_DEST_n"*

Metalink NOTE:150584.1: *Data Guard 9i Setup with Guaranteed Protection Mode*

Oracle Database 10g Data Guard Concepts and Administration, Release 1 (10.1) B10823-01

Oracle Database 10g Database Reference, Release 1(10.1), B10755-01

Oracle Database 10g SQL Reference, Release 1 (10.1), B10759-01

Oracle Database 10g Real Application Clusters Administrator's Guide, Release 1 (10.1), B10765-01

MetaLink NOTE: 203326.1: *Data Guard 9i Log Transportation on RAC*

Metalink Note: 186592.1: *Backing Up Archivelogs in a RAC Cluster*

Metalink Note: 145178.1: *RAMN9i: Automatic Channel Allocation and Configuration*

Metalink Note: 150584.1: *Data Guard 9i Setup with Guaranteed Protection Mode*

Oracle Database Recovery Manager Reference 10g Release 1 (10.1), Part No. B10770-01, December 2003

Performance Monitoring & Tuning

CHAPTER 14

The focus of this chapter is on RAC tuning issues. Tuning a RAC database is very similar to tuning a non-RAC database; however, there are some major differences that will be covered.

This chapter will also cover the views used to monitor the RAC environment. Finally, the Oracle Enterprise Manager features that automate some of the DBA's RAC monitoring tasks will be introduced.

Analysis of Performance Issues

The analysis of performance issues in RAC involves several key areas:

- Normal database tuning and monitoring.
- Monitoring RAC cluster interconnect performance.
- Monitoring workloads.
- Monitoring RAC-specific contention.

Normal database monitoring is covered thoroughly in any number of other texts. Thus, aspects of database tuning such as SQL tuning or standard SGA and internals tuning are not covered in this text other than the required extensions to normal database monitoring.

Monitoring RAC Cluster Interconnect Performance

The most important aspects of RAC tuning are the monitoring and tuning of the global services directory processes. The processes in the Global Service Daemon (GSD) communicate through the cluster interconnects. If the cluster interconnects do not perform properly, the entire RAC structure will suffer no matter how well everything else is tuned. The major processes of concern are the Global Enqueue Services (GES) and Global Cache Services (GCS) processes.

The level of cluster interconnect performance can be determined by monitoring GCS waits that show how well data is being transferred. The waits that need to be monitored are shown in *v$session_wait*, *v$obj_stats*, and *v$enqueues_stats*. The major waits to be concerned with for RAC are:

- *global cache busy*
- *buffer busy global cache*
- *buffer busy global cr*

In later versions of Oracle, the global cache is shortened to just *gc*. To find the values for these waits, the *gv$session_wait* view is used to identify objects that have performance issues. The *gv$session_wait* view contents are shown in the following results:

```
Description of GV$SESSION_WAIT
 Name                                      Null?    Type
 ----------------------------------------- -------- -------------
 INST_ID                                            NUMBER
 SID                                                NUMBER
 SEQ#                                               NUMBER
 EVENT                                              VARCHAR2(64)
 P1TEXT                                             VARCHAR2(64)
 P1                                                 NUMBER
 P1RAW                                              RAW(4)
 P2TEXT                                             VARCHAR2(64)
 P2                                                 NUMBER
 P2RAW                                              RAW(4)
 P3TEXT                                             VARCHAR2(64)
 P3                                                 NUMBER
```

```
P3RAW                                                      RAW(4)
WAIT_CLASS#                                                NUMBER
WAIT_CLASS                                                 VARCHAR2(64)
WAIT_TIME                                                  NUMBER
SECONDS_IN_WAIT                                            NUMBER
STATE                                                      VARCHAR2(19)
```

New in 10g is the *wait_class* column which is used to restrict returned values based on 12 basic wait classes, one of which is the *cluster wait class.*

The following wait events indicate that the remotely cached blocks were shipped to the local instance without having been busy, pinned or requiring a log flush and can safely be ignored:

- *gc current block 2-way*
- *gc current block 3-way*
- *gc cr block 2-way*
- *gc cr block 3-way*

However, the object level statistics for *gc current blocks received* and *gc cr blocks received* enable the rapid identification of the indexes and tables which are shared by the active instances.

The columns *p1* and *p2* identify the file and block number of any object experiencing the above waits for the events, as shown in the following queries:

```
SELECT
  INST_ID,
  EVENT,
  P1 FILE_NUMBER,
  P2 BLOCK_NUMBER,
  WAIT_TIME
FROM
  GV$SESSION_WAIT
WHERE
  EVENT IN ('buffer busy global cr', 'global cache busy',
            'buffer busy global cache');
```

The output from this query should resemble the following:

```
INST_ID EVENT                       FILE_NUMBER BLOCK_NUMBER  WAIT_TIME
------- ----------------------- ----------- ------------ ----------
      1 global cache busy                 9          150 0
      2 global cache busy                 9          150 0
```

In order to find the object that corresponds to a particular file and block, the following query can be issued for the first combination on the above list:

```
SELECT
  OWNER,
  SEGMENT_NAME,
  SEGMENT_TYPE
FROM
  DBA_EXTENTS
WHERE
  FILE_ID = 9
  AND 150 BETWEEN BLOCK_ID AND BLOCK_ID+BLOCKS-1;
```

In this example, there is no need to worry about the instance as this SELECT is issued from within the cluster because they all see the same tables, indexes and objects.

The output will be similar to:

```
OWNER      SEGMENT_NAME                  SEGMENT_TYPE
---------- ----------------------------- ---------------
SYSTEM     MOD_TEST_IND                  INDEX
```

Once the objects causing the contention are determined, they should be modified by:

- Reducing the rows per block.
- Adjusting the block size.
- Modifying *initrans* and *freelists*.

All of these object modifications reduce the chances of application contention for the blocks in the object. *Index leaf* blocks are usually the most contended objects in the RAC environment; therefore, using a smaller block size for index objects can decrease intra-instance contention for *index leaf* blocks.

Contention in blocks can be measured by using the *block transfer time*. To determine *block transfer time*, examine the statistics *global cache cr block receive time* and *global cache cr blocks received*. The time is determined by calculating the ratio of *global cache cr block receive* time to *global cache cr blocks received*. The values for these statistics are taken from the *gv$sysstat* view shown below:

```
Description of GV$SYSSTAT
 Name                                      Null?    Type
 ----------------------------------------- -------- -------------
 INST_ID                                            NUMBER
 STATISTIC#                                         NUMBER
 NAME                                               VARCHAR2(64)
 CLASS                                              NUMBER
 VALUE                                              NUMBER
 HASH                                               NUMBER
```

The following script shows this calculation.

```
column "AVG RECEIVE TIME (ms)" format 9999999.9
col inst_id for 9999
prompt GCS CR BLOCKS
select b1.inst_id, b2.value "RECEIVED",
b1.value "RECEIVE TIME",
((b1.value / b2.value) * 10) "AVG RECEIVE TIME (ms)"
from gv$sysstat b1, gv$sysstat b2
where b1.name = 'global cache cr block receive time' and
b2.name = 'global cache cr blocks received' and b1.inst_id =
b2.inst_id

INST_ID   RECEIVED RECEIVE TIME AVG RECEIVE TIME (ms)
------- ---------- ------------ ---------------------
      1       2791         3287                  14.8
      2       3760         7482                  19.9
```

If the transfer time is too high, or if one of the nodes in the cluster shows excessive transfer times, the cluster interconnects should be checked using system level commands to verify that they are functioning correctly. In the above SELECT result, instance two exhibits an average receive time that is 69% higher than instance one.

Another useful SELECT for determining latency measures the overall latency, including that for queue, build, flush and send time. These statistics are also found in the *gv$sysstat* view. The SELECT is shown below:

```
SELECT
   a.inst_id "Instance",
   (a.value+b.value+c.value)/d.value "LMS Service Time"
FROM
  GV$SYSSTAT A,
  GV$SYSSTAT B,
  GV$SYSSTAT C,
  GV$SYSSTAT D
WHERE
  A.name = 'global cache cr block build time' AND
  B.name = 'global cache cr block flush time' AND
  C.name = 'global cache cr block send time' AND
  D.name = 'global cache cr blocks served' AND
  B.inst_id=A.inst_id AND
  C.inst_id=A.inst_id AND
  D.inst_id=A.inst_id
ORDER BY
  a.inst_id;

 Instance LMS Service Time
--------- ----------------
        1       1.07933923
        2       .636687318
```

Why does instance two show a lower service time than instance one? The node containing instance two is the slower node, while the node containing instance one serves blocks faster. The reason is that the slower node two serves blocks to node one, so node one shows a slower service time even though it is a faster node! Be aware of this in a two node cluster. Where there are multiple nodes, the service times should average out. If not, the aberrant node is probably troubled.

The following code can be used to examine the individual components of the service time to determine the source of the problem:

```
SELECT
   A.inst_id "Instance",
   (A.value/D.value) "Consistent Read Build",
   (B.value/D.value) "Log Flush Wait",
   (C.value/D.value) "Send Time"
FROM
  GV$SYSSTAT A,
  GV$SYSSTAT B,
  GV$SYSSTAT C,
  GV$SYSSTAT D
WHERE
  A.name = 'global cache cr block build time' AND
  B.name = 'global cache cr block flush time' AND
  C.name = 'global cache cr block send time' AND
  D.name = 'global cache cr blocks served' AND
  B.inst_id=a.inst_id AND
  C.inst_id=a.inst_id AND
  D.inst_id=a.inst_id
ORDER BY
  A.inst_id;

 Instance Consistent Read Build Log Flush Wait  Send Time
--------- --------------------- -------------- ----------
        1             .00737234     1.05059755  .02203942
        2             .04645529      .51214820  .07844674
```

If problems are detected, operating system specific commands should be used to pinpoint the node having difficulties. For example, in the SUN Solaris environment, commands such as the following can be used:

```
netstat -l
netstat -s
sar -c
sar -q
vmstat
```

These commands are used to monitor the cluster interconnects for:

- A large number of processes in the run queue waiting for CPU or scheduling delays.
- Platform specific operating system parameter settings that affect IPC buffering or process scheduling.
- Slow, busy or faulty interconnects. In these cases, look for dropped packets, retransmits, or cyclic redundancy check

(CRC) errors. Ensure that the network is private and that inter-instance traffic is not routed through a public network.

The DBA will be interested in the waits and statistics for tuning shown in Table 14.1.

Statistic or Wait	Description	Source
buffer busy global cache	A wait event that is signaled when a process waits for a block to be available because another process is already obtaining a resource for this block.	*gv$system_event, gv$session_wait*
buffer busy waits	A wait event that is signaled when a process cannot get a buffer due to another process using the buffer at that point in time.	*gv$system_event, gv$session_wait*
cache convert waits	A statistic showing the total number of waits for all up-convert operations, these are: *global cache null to S*, *global cache null to X*, and *global cache S to X*.	*gv$sysstat*
cache open waits	A statistic that shows the total number of waits for *global cache open S* and *global cache open X*.	*gv$sysstat*
consistent gets	The consistent gets statistic shows the number of buffers obtained in consistent read (CR) mode.	*gv$sysstat*
cr request retry	A statistic that quantifies when Oracle resubmits a consistent read request due to detecting that the holding instance is no longer available.	*gv$sysstat*
db block changes	The number of current buffers that where obtained in exclusive mode for DML.	*gv$sysstat*
db block gets	The number of current buffers that were obtained for a read.	gv$sysstat

Statistic or Wait	Description	Source
DBWR cross-instance writes	These are also forced writes and show the number of writes that an instance had to perform to disk in order to make a previously exclusively held block available for another instance. Generally, DBWR cross-instance writes are eliminated due to Cache Fusion unless a value greater than 0 (zero) is set for the *gc_files_to_locks* parameter.	gv$sysstat
global cache bg acks	This wait event can only occur during the startup or shutdown of an instance as the LMS process completes its operations.	*gv$system_event, gv$session_wait*
global cache busy	This is a wait event that accumulates when a session has waits for an ongoing operation on the resource to complete.	*gv$system_event, gv$session_wait*
global cache cr cancel wait	This is a wait event that accumulates when a session waits for the completion of an AST for a canceled block access request. The canceling of the request is part of the Cache Fusion Write Protocol.	*gv$system_event, gv$session_wait*
global cache converts	This is a statistic that shows the resource converts for buffer cache blocks. Whenever GCS resources are converted from NULL to SHARED, NULL to EXCLUSIVE or SHARED to EXCLUSIVE this statistic is incremented.	*gv$sysstat*
global cache convert time	This statistics shows the accumulated time for global conversions on GCS resources for all sessions.	*gv$sysstat*
global cache convert timeouts	Whenever a resource operation times out this statistic is incremented.	*gv$sysstat*
global cache cr block flush time	This statistic shows the time waited for a log flush whenever a CR request is served. This is part of the serve time.	*gv$sysstat*

Statistic or Wait	Description	Source
global cache cr blocks received	If a process requests a consistent read for a data block that is not in its local cache it has to send a request to another instance, this statistic is incremented once the buffer has been received.	*gv$sysstat*
global cache cr block receive time	This statistic records the accumulated round trip time for all requests for consistent read blocks.	*gv$sysstat*
global cache cr blocks served	This statistic shows the number of requests for a consistent read block served by LMS. This statistic is incremented by Oracle when the block is sent.	*gv$sysstat*
global cache cr block build time	This statistic shows the accumulated time that the LMS process needs to create a consistent read block on the holding instance	*gv$sysstat*
global cache cr block send time	This statistic shows the time needed by LMS to begin a send of a consistent read block. For send time, timing does not stop until send has completed. Only the time it takes to initiate the send is measured; the time elapsed before the block arrives at the requesting instance is not included.	*gv$sysstat*
global cache cr cancel wait	This is a wait event that happens when a session waits for a canceled CR request to complete its acquisition interrupt. The process of canceling the CR request is part of the Cache Fusion Write Protocol.	*gv$system_event, gv$session_wait*

Statistic or Wait	Description	Source
global cache cr request	This is a wait event that happens because a process is made to wait for a pending CR request to complete. The process must wait for either shared access to a block to be granted before it can read the block from disk, or it waits for the LMS of the holding instance to send the block.	*gv$system_event, gv$session_wait*
global cache current block flush time	This is a statistic that shows the time it takes to flush the changes from a block to disk before the block can be shipped to the requesting instance.	*gv$sysstat*
global cache current block pin time	This is a statistic that shows the time it takes to pin a current block before shipping it to a requesting instance. The pinning of a block prevents further changes to the block while it is prepared to be shipped.	*gv$sysstat*
global cache current blocks received	This is a statistic that shows the number of current blocks received over the interconnect from the holding instance.	*gv$sysstat*
global cache current block receive time	This is a statistic that shows the current blocks accumulated round trip time for all requests.	*gv$sysstat*
global cache current block send time	This is a statistic that shows the time it takes to send the current block over the interconnect to the requesting instance.	*gv$sysstat*
global cache current blocks served	This is a statistic that shows the number of current blocks shipped over the interconnect to the requesting instance.	*gv$sysstat*
global cache freelist wait	This is a statistic that shows Oracle must wait after it detects that the local element free list is empty.	*gv$sysstat*

Statistic or Wait	Description	Source
global cache freelist waits	This is a statistic that shows the number of times that the resource element free list was found empty by Oracle.	*gv$sysstat*
global cache gets	This is a statistic that shows the number of buffer gets that caused the opening of a new GCS resource.	*gv$sysstat*
global cache get time	This is a statistic that shows the accumulated time for all sessions that was needed to open a GCS resource for a local buffer.	*gv$sysstat*
global cache null to S	A wait event that occurs whenever a session has to wait for a resource conversion to complete.	*gv$system_event, gv$session_wait*
global cache null to X	This is a wait event that occurs whenever a session has to wait for this type of resource conversion to complete.	*gv$system_event, gv$session_wait*
global cache open S	This is a wait event that occurs when a session has to wait for receiving permission for shared access to the requested resource.	*gv$system_event, gv$session_wait*
global cache open X	This is a wait event that occurs when a session has to wait for receiving exclusive access to the requested resource.	*gv$system_event, gv$session_wait*
global cache S to X	This is a wait event that occurs whenever a session has to wait for this type of resource conversion to complete.	*gv$system_event, gv$session_wait*
global cache pending ast	This is a wait event that can occur when a process waits for an acquisition interrupt before Oracle closes a resource element.	*gv$system_event, gv$session_wait*

Statistic or Wait	Description	Source
global cache pred cancel wait	This is a wait event that occurs when a session must wait for the acquisition interrupt to complete for a canceled predecessor read request. The canceling of a predecessor read request is a part of the Cache Fusion Write Protocol.	*gv$system_event, gv$session_wait*
global cache retry prepare	This is a wait event that occurs whenever Oracle cannot ignore or skip a failure to prepare a buffer for a consistent read or Cache Fusion request.	*gv$system_event, gv$session_wait*
global lock async converts	This is a statistic showing the number of resource converts from an incompatible mode.	*gv$sysstat*
global lock sync gets	This is a statistic showing the number of synchronous GCS resources that Oracle must open. These sync gets are usually for GES resources. Library cache resources are one example.	*gv$sysstat*
global lock async gets	This is a statistic showing the number of Ansynchronous GES resources that Oracle must open. Normally, *async gets* include the number of *global cache gets* and are only used for GES resources.	*gv$sysstat*
global lock get time	This is a statistic that shows the accumulated open time for all GES resources.	*gv$sysstat*
global lock sync converts	This statistic shows the number of GES resources that Oracle converted from an incompatible mode. Usually *sync converts* occur for GES resources only.	*gv$sysstat*
global lock convert time	This is a statistic that shows the accumulated *global lock sync converts* and *global lock async converts* time.	*gv$sysstat*

Statistic or Wait	Description	Source
lock buffers for read	This is a statistic that shows the number of NULL to SHARED up converts.	*gv$sysstat*
lock gets per transaction	This is a statistic that shows the number of *global lock sync gets* and *global lock async gets per transaction.*	*gv$sysstat*
lock converts per transaction	This is a statistic that shows the number of *global local sync converts* and *global lock async converts per transaction.*	*gv$sysstat*
messages flow controlled	This shows the number of messages that are intended to be sent directly but that were instead queued and delivered later by LMD/LMS.	*gv$dml_misc*
messages received	This statistics shows the number of messages received by the LMD process.	*gv$dml_misc*
messages sent directly	This statistic shows the number of messages sent directly by Oracle processes.	*gv$dml_misc*
messages sent indirectly	This statistics shows the number of explicitly queued messages.	*gv$dml_misc*
physical reads	This is a statistic that shows the total number of disk reads performed because a request for a data block could not be satisfied from a local cache.	*gv$sysstat*
physical writes	This statistics shows the number of write I/Os performed by the DBWNn processes. This number includes the number of DBWR cross instance writes (forced writes) in Oracle Database 10g when *gc_files_to_locks* is set. Setting *gc_files_to_locks* for a particular datafile will enable the use of the old ping protocol and will not leverage the Cache Fusion architecture.	*gv$sysstat*

Statistic or Wait	Description	Source
remote instance undo block writes	This is a statistic that shows the number of undo blocks written to disk by DBWn due to a forced write.	*gv$sysstat*
remote instance undo header writes	This is a statistic that shows the number of rollback segment header blocks written to disk by DBWn due to a forced write.	*gv$sysstat*

Table 14.1: *Waits and Statistics for RAC Monitoring from Oracle RAC Manual Glossary*

Oracle has provided the *racdiag.sql* script that can help troubleshoot RAC slowdowns; however, it has limited applicability to RAC system tuning. It is suggested that STATSPACK be used, combined with the selects provided in this chapter for RAC tuning.

racdiag.sql is available at metalink.oracle.com.

The *class* column in the *gv$sysstat* view indicates the type of statistic. Oracle RAC related statistics are in classes eight, 32, and 40.

Undesirable Global Cache Statistics

The following are undesirable statistics or statistics for which the values should always be as near to zero as possible:

- *global cache blocks lost*: This statistic shows block losses during transfers. High values indicate network problems. The use of an unreliable IPC protocol such as UDP may result in the value for *global cache blocks lost* being non-zero. When this occurs, take the ratio of *global cache blocks lost* divided by *global cache current blocks served* plus *global cache cr blocks served*. This ratio should be as small as possible. Many times, a non-zero value for *global cache blocks lost* does not indicate a problem because Oracle will retry the block transfer operation until it is successful.

- *global cache blocks corrupt*: This statistic shows if any blocks were corrupted during transfers. If high values are returned for this statistic, there is probably an IPC, network, or hardware problem.

An example SELECT to determine if further examination is needed would be:

```
SELECT
      A.VALUE "GC BLOCKS LOST 1",
      B.VALUE "GC BLOCKS CORRUPT 1",
      C.VALUE "GC BLOCKS LOST 2",
      D.VALUE "GC BLOCKS CORRUPT 2"
FROM GV$SYSSTAT A, GV$SYSSTAT B, GV$SYSSTAT C, GV$SYSSTAT D
WHERE A.INST_ID=1 AND A.NAME='gc blocks lost'
  AND B.INST_ID=1 AND B.NAME='gc blocks corrupt'
  AND C.INST_ID=2 AND C.NAME='gc blocks lost'
  AND D.INST_ID=2 AND D.NAME='gc blocks corrupt';
```

A sample result from the above select should look like the following:

```
GC BLOCKS LOST 1 GC BLOCKS CORRUPT 1 GC BLOCKS LOST 2 GC BLOCKS CORRUPT 2
---------------- ------------------- ---------------- -------------------
               0                   0              652                   0
```

In this result, instance 2 is showing some problems with lost blocks, so it might be useful to look at the ratio described above:

```
SELECT A.INST_ID "INSTANCE", A.VALUE "GC BLOCKS LOST",
B.VALUE "GC CUR BLOCKS SERVED",
C.VALUE "GC CR BLOCKS SERVED",
A.VALUE/(B.VALUE+C.VALUE) RATIO
FROM GV$SYSSTAT A, GV$SYSSTAT B, GV$SYSSTAT C
WHERE A.NAME='gc blocks lost' AND
      B.NAME='gc current blocks served' AND
      C.NAME='gc cr blocks served' and
      B.INST_ID=a.inst_id AND
      C.INST_ID = a.inst_id;

  Instance gc blocks lost gc cur blocks served gc cr blocks served      RATIO
---------- -------------- -------------------- ------------------- ----------
         1              0                 3923                2734          0
         2            652                 3008                4380 .088251218
```

The question now becomes, how small is "as small as possible"? In this example, database instance one takes 22 seconds to perform a series of tests and instance two takes 25 minutes.

Investigation showed that the TCP receive and send buffers on instance two were set at 64K. Since this is an 8k-block size instance with a *db_file_multiblock_read_count* of 16, this was causing excessive network traffic because the system was using full table scans resulting in a read of 128K. In addition, the actual TCP buffer area was set to a small number. Setting these values for the TCP receive and send buffers is an operating specific operation. DBA's should talk this over with the system operator or check out:

```
http://www.psc.edu/networking/perf_tune.html
```

The following section covers example commands for various operating systems.

DEC Alpha (Digital UNIX)

```
$ dbx -k /vmunix
(dbx) assign sb_max = (u_long) 524288
(dbx) patch sb_max = (u_long) 524288
```

The first command changes the value for the operating system and the second patches the value into the kernel so it will not be lost at the next reboot. *mbclusters* can be modified to at least 832, and the kernel variables *tcp_sendspace* and *tcp_recvspace* cam also be modified in this manner. Under version 4.0, use the *sysconfig -r inet <variable> <value>* command to do this type of modification.

HPUX (11)

Use the *ndd* command to view and modify the various TCP variables. Use the *ndd -h <parm_name>* to get the method for changing the values.

AIX

Use the "no" command.

Linux

To check the values you CAT the contents of the various */proc/sys/net* files:

```
$cat /proc/sys/net/core/rmem_default
```

The values of interest are:

```
rmem_default
rmem_max
wmem_default
wmem_max
tcp_rmem
tcp_wmem
```

The value under Linux can be set by echoing the proper values into the files in */proc/sys/net*. Some example values that have been found to be beneficial are:

```
echo '100 5000 640 2560 150 30000 5000 1884 2'>/proc/sys/vm/bdflush
hdparm -m16 -c1 -d1 -a8 /dev/hda
hdparm -m16 -c1 -d1 -a8 /dev/hdb
echo '131071'>/proc/sys/net/core/rmem_default
echo '262143'>/proc/sys/net/core/rmem_max
echo '131071'>/proc/sys/net/core/wmem_default
echo '262143'>/proc/sys/net/core/wmem_max
echo '4096 65536 4194304'>/proc/sys/net/ipv4/tcp_wmem
echo '4096 87380 4194304'>/proc/sys/net/ipv4/tcp_rmem
```

The call to */proc/sys/vm/bdflush* actually improves memory handling. The two *hdparm* commands improve IDE disk performances. The most interesting ones here are the ones echoing values into */proc/sys/net/core* and */proc/sys/net/ipv4* subdirectory files.

SUN (2.x)

SUN uses the ndd command:

```
$ndd -set /dev/tcp tcp_max_buff xxx
$ndd -set /dev/tcp tcp_xmit_hiwat xxx
$ndd -set /dev/tcp tcp_recv_hiwat xxx
```

Windows NT/2000

Use the various settings in the registry under the key:

```
HKEY_LOCAL_MACHINE\SYSTEM\CurrentControlSet\Services\Tcpip\Parameters
```

Additional detailed notes are available at:

```
http://rdweb.cns.vt.edu/public/notes/win2k-tcpip.htm
```

After increasing both the buffer size and buffer space for the TCP area, the following results were obtained with the query above after the same series of tests were repeated:

```
  INSTANCE GC BLOCKS LOST GC CUR BLOCKS SERVED GC CR BLOCKS SERVED      RATIO
---------- -------------- -------------------- ------------------- ----------
         1              0                 3892                3642          0
         2              0                 3048                2627          0
```

By correcting the TCP issue, performance increased such that the tests now required only three minutes 20 seconds to complete on the poor performing node. This provides an 800% improvement at a minimum recalling that the poor node is a single CPU using an old technology motherboard and bus structures.

Monitoring *current* Blocks

In addition to *cr blocks*, RAC performance is also a concern when processing *current mode blocks*. *Current mode blocks* suffer from latency as well as build and wait time concerns similar to *cr blocks*.

The average latency for a *current mode block* is calculated with the SELECT:

```
column "AVG RECEIVE TIME (ms)" format 9999999.9
col inst_id for 9999
prompt GCS CURRENT BLOCKS
select b1.inst_id, b2.value "RECEIVED",
b1.value "RECEIVE TIME",
((b1.value / b2.value) * 10) "AVG RECEIVE TIME (ms)"
from gv$sysstat b1, gv$sysstat b2
where b1.name = 'gc current block receive time' and
b2.name = 'gc current blocks received' and b1.inst_id = b2.inst_id;

INST_ID   RECEIVED RECEIVE TIME AVG RECEIVE TIME (ms)
------ ---------- ------------ ---------------------
     1      22694        68999                  30.4
     2      23931        42090                  17.6
```

The service time for receiving a current block is calculated in a similar fashion to the value for a *cr block*, except there is a pin time instead of a build time:

```
SELECT
   a.inst_id "Instance",
   (a.value+b.value+c.value)/d.value "Current Blk Service Time"
FROM
  GV$SYSSTAT A,
  GV$SYSSTAT B,
  GV$SYSSTAT C,
  GV$SYSSTAT D
WHERE
  A.name = 'gc current block pin time' AND
  B.name = 'gc current block flush time' AND
  C.name = 'gc current block send time' AND
  D.name = 'gc current blocks served' AND
  B.inst_id=A.inst_id AND
  C.inst_id=A.inst_id AND
  D.inst_id=A.inst_id
ORDER BY
  a.inst_id;

 Instance Current Blk Service Time
--------- ------------------------
        1               1.18461603
        2               1.63126376
```

Instance two is requiring more time to service current blocks. How is the source of the problem determined? The overall service time can be decomposed to determine where the area of concern lies:

```
SELECT
   A.inst_id "Instance",
   (A.value/D.value) "Current Block Pin",
   (B.value/D.value) "Log Flush Wait",
   (C.value/D.value) "Send Time"
FROM
  GV$SYSSTAT A,
  GV$SYSSTAT B,
  GV$SYSSTAT C,
  GV$SYSSTAT D
WHERE
  A.name = 'gc current block build time' AND
  B.name = 'gc current block flush time' AND
  C.name = 'gc current block send time' AND
  D.name = 'gc current blocks served' AND
  B.inst_id=a.inst_id AND
  C.inst_id=a.inst_id AND
  D.inst_id=a.inst_id
ORDER BY
  A.inst_id;

 Instance Current Block Pin Log Flush Wait  Send Time
--------- ----------------- -------------- ----------
        1         .69366887     .472058762 .018196236
        2        1.07740715     .480549199 .072346418
```

In this case, most of the time difference comes from the pin time for the current block in instance two. High pin times could indicate problems at the I/O interface level.

A final set of statistics deals with the *average global cache convert time* and the *average global cache get times.* The following SELECT can be used to get this information from the RAC database:

```
select
  a.inst_id "Instance",
  a.value/b.value "Avg Cache Conv. Time",
  c.value/d.value "Avg Cache Get Time",
  e.value "GC Convert Timeouts"
from
   GV$SYSSTAT A,
   GV$SYSSTAT B,
   GV$SYSSTAT C,
   GV$SYSSTAT D,
   GV$SYSSTAT E
where
```

```
  a.name='gc convert time' and
  b.name='gc converts' and
  c.name='gc get time' and
  d.name='gc gets' and
  e.name='gc convert timeouts' and
  b.inst_id=a.inst_id and
  c.inst_id=a.inst_id and
  d.inst_id=a.inst_id and
  e.inst_id=a.inst_id
order by
  a.inst_id;

 Instance Avg Cache Conv. Time Avg Cache Get Time GC Convert Timeouts
--------- ------------------- ------------------ -------------------
        1          1.85812072         .981296356                   0
        2          1.65947528         .627444273                   0
```

For this database, instance one has the highest convert and get times, as expected, since it is converting and getting from instance two, which is the slow instance. None of the times are excessive, >10-20 ms.

Some things to consider about these values are:

- High convert times indicate excessive global concurrency requirements. In other words, the instances are swapping a lot of blocks over the interconnect.
- Large values or rapid increases in the gets, converts, or average times indicate GCS contention.
- Latencies for resource operations may be high due to excessive system loads.
- The *gv$system_event* view can be used to review the *time_waited* statistics for various GCS events if the get or convert times become significant. STATSPACK is good for this.
- Values other than zero for the GC converts timeouts indicate system contention or congestion. Timeouts should not occur and indicate a serious performance problem.

Additional Wait Events of Concern

Most of the events reported in the dynamic performance views or in a STATSPACK report that show a high total time are actually normal. However, if monitored response times increase and the STATSPACK report shows a high proportion of wait time for cluster accesses, the cause of these waits needs to be determined. STATSPACK reports provide a breakdown of the wait events, with the five highest values sorted by percentages. The following specific RAC-related events should be monitored:

- *global cache open s*: A block was selected.
- *global cache open x*: A block was selected for IUD.
- *global cache null to s*: A block was transferred for SELECT.
- *global cache null to x*: A block was transferred for IUD.
- *global cache cr request*: A block was requested transferred for consistent read purposes.
- Global Cache Service Utilization for Logical Reads.

The following sections will provide more information on these events to help show why they are important to monitor.

The *global cache open s* and *global cache open x* Events

The initial access of a particular data block by an instance generates these events. The duration of the wait should be short, and the completion of the wait is most likely followed by a read from disk. This wait is a result of the blocks that are being requested and not being cached in any instance in the cluster database. This necessitates a disk read.

When these events are associated with high totals or high per-transaction wait times, it is likely that data blocks are not cached in the local instance and that the blocks cannot be obtained from another instance, which results in a disk read. At the same time, suboptimal *buffer cache hit ratios* may also be observed. Unfortunately, other than preloading heavily used tables into the buffer caches, there is little that can be done about this type of wait event.

The *global cache null to s* and *global cache null to x* Events

These events are generated by inter-instance block ping across the network. Inter-instance block ping is when two instances exchange the same block back and forth. Processes waiting for *global cache null to s* events are waiting for a block to be transferred from the instance that last changed it. When one instance repeatedly requests cached data blocks from the other RAC instances, these events consume a greater proportion of the total wait time. The only method for reducing these events is to reduce the number of rows per block to eliminate the need for block swapping between two instances in the RAC cluster.

The *global cache cr request* Event

This event is generated when an instance has requested a consistent read data block and the block to be transferred had not arrived at the requesting instance. Other than examining the cluster interconnects for possible problems, there is nothing that can be done about this event other than to modify objects to reduce the possibility of contention.

Global Cache Service Times

When global cache waits constitute a large proportion of the wait time, as listed on the first page of the STATSPACK or AWRRPT report, and if response time or throughput does not conform to service level requirements, the Global Cache Service workload characteristics on the cluster statistics page of the STATSPACK or AWRRPT reports should be examined. The STATSPACK or AWRRPT reports should be taken during heavy RAC workloads.

If the STATSPACK report shows that the average GCS time per request is high, it is the result of one of the following:

- Contention for blocks.
- System loads.
- Network issues.

The operating system logs and operating system statistics are used to indicate whether a network link is congested. A network link can be congested if:

- Packets are being routed through the public network instead of the private interconnect.
- The sizes of the run queues are increasing.

If CPU usage is maxed out and processes are queuing for the CPU, the priority of the GCS processes (LMSn) can be raised over other processes to lower GCS times. The load on the server can also be alleviated by reducing the number of processes on the database server, increasing capacity by adding CPUs to the server, or adding nodes to the cluster database.

New 10g RAC Waits

This section covers the most important Oracle Database 10g wait events to be aware of when analyzing performance reports. When user response times increase and a high proportion of time waited is due to the *global cache* (*gc*), the cause must be determined and corrected.

It is best to start with an ADDM report if that option has been purchased. This will analyze the routinely collected performance statistics with respect to their impact pinpoint the objects and

SQL contributing most to the time waited. After that, the analysis can move on to the more detailed reports produced by the AWR and STATSPACK utilities.

The most important wait events for RAC fall into four main categories, arranged alphabetically these are:

- Block-oriented waits:
  - *gc current block 2-way*
  - *gc current block 3-way*
  - *gc cr block 2-way*
  - *gc cr block 3-way*
- Contention-oriented waits:
  - *gc current block busy*
  - *gc cr block busy*
  - *gc current buffer busy*
- **Load-oriented waits:**
  - *gc current block congested*
  - *gc cr block congested*
- **Message-oriented waits:**
  - *gc current grant 2-way*
  - *gc cr grant 2-way*

Block Oriented Wait Events

As their names imply, these block related wait events are the result of some combination of message and transfer event. Whether the wait occurred between a resource master and a requesting node as a single message and block transfer or was the result of a message passed from a node several times removed from the resource master causing two messages and a block transfer, the result is the same. A wait event of some duration occurred.

These wait events consist of several components:

- Physical network latency
- Request processing time
- Requesting process sleep time

By looking at the total and average wait times associated with these events, the DBA can be alerted when performance is being affected in a negative manner, such as when average times increase beyond statistical norms, something is wrong and needs investigation. Usually, the impact of interconnect malfunctions or load issues or the interactions of nodes against hot blocks are the culprit when these waits become significant.

Message Related Wait Events

The wait events dealing with messages usually indicate that the block requested was not present in any of the caches for the various nodes. This results in the need to issue a global grant and allow the requesting instance to read the block from disk in order to modify it. When messaging events result in high waits, it is usually due to frequently accessed SQL causing disk IO, due to cache areas being too small, in the event of *cr* grants, or the instances are inserting a lot of new records requiring format of disk blocks, if current grants are the cause.

Contention-Oriented Wait Events

Contention-oriented wait events are caused by:

- Waits for blocks pinned by other nodes
- Waits for changes to be flushed to disk

- Waits due to high concurrency for block access
- Intra-node cache-fusion contention

If high service times are experienced in the global cache, this type of wait can get worse. In general, this type of wait results from multiple nodes requiring read or write of the same block of data or index entries.

Load-Oriented Wait Events

These types of waits indicate that delays have occurred within the global cache services (GCS). Load-oriented events are usually caused by high loads on the nodes and their CPUs. This type of event is solved by:

- Increasing the available CPUs
- Load balancing
- Offloading processing until a lower load is available
- Adding a new node

For load-oriented events, the time is the total time for the round-trip, beginning when the request is made and ending when the block is received.

The following section will cover the STATSPACK report sections that are useful when dealing with RAC. The report is only in relation to the node/instance on which it was run. To compare other instances, the *statspack.snap* procedure and *spreport.sql* report script can be run on each node/instance that is to be monitored.

RAC and STATSPACK

The following is a STATSPACK report for the troubled instance. The sections covered will be those that involve RAC statistics. The first section deals with the top five timed events:

```
Top 5 Timed Events
~~~~~~~~~~~~~~~~~~                                                    % Total
Event                                              Waits    Time (s) Ela Time
-------------------------------------------- ------------ ----------- --------
global cache cr request                              820         154    72.50
CPU time                                                          54    25.34
global cache null to x                               478           1      .52
control file sequential read                         600           1      .52
control file parallel write                          141           1      .28
          -------------------------------------------------------------
```

Observe the events in the report that are taking a majority of the *% total elapsed time* column that are greater than or near the *%total ela time* value for *cpu time*. The *cpu time* statistic should be the predominant event as it denotes processing time. If *cpu time* is not the predominant event, the events that exceed *cpu time's* share of the total elapsed time need to be investigated. In the above report section, *global cache cr request* events are dominating the report. This indicates that transfer times are excessive from the other instances in the cluster to this instance. The excessive transfer times could be due to network problems or buffer cache sizing issues. After making the network changes and adding an index, the STATSPACK wait report for instance one looks like:

```
Top 5 Timed Events
~~~~~~~~~~~~~~~~~~                                                    % Total
Event                                              Waits    Time (s) Ela Time
-------------------------------------------- ------------ ----------- --------
CPU time                                                          99    64.87
global cache null to x                             1,655          28    18.43
enqueue                                               46           8     5.12
global cache busy                                    104           7     4.73
DFS lock handle                                       38           2     1.64
```

The number one wait is now *cpu time*, followed by *global cache null to x*, which indicates the major wait has been shifted from intra-cache to I/O-based as *global cache null to x* indicates a read from disk.

The next report in the STATSPACK listing shows the workload characteristics for the instance for which the report was generated:

```
Cluster Statistics for DB: MIKE  Instance: mike2  Snaps: 25 -26

Global Cache Service - Workload Characteristics
-----------------------------------------------
Ave global cache get time (ms):                          3.1
Ave global cache convert time (ms):                      3.2

Ave build time for CR block (ms):                        0.2
Ave flush time for CR block (ms):                        0.0
Ave send time for CR block (ms):                         1.0
Ave time to process CR block request (ms):               1.3
Ave receive time for CR block (ms):                     17.2

Ave pin time for current block (ms):                     0.2
Ave flush time for current block (ms):                   0.0
Ave send time for current block (ms):                    0.9
Ave time to process current block request (ms):          1.1
Ave receive time for current block (ms):                 3.1

Global cache hit ratio:                                  1.7
Ratio of current block defers:                           0.0
% of messages sent for buffer gets:                      1.4
% of remote buffer gets:                                 1.1
Ratio of I/O for coherence:                              8.7
Ratio of local vs remote work:                           0.6
Ratio of fusion vs physical writes:                      1.0
```

In the above report, the statistics in relation to the other instances in the cluster should be examined. The possible causes of any statistics that are not in line with the other cluster instances should be investigated. By making the network changes and index changes stated before, the workload was increased by a factor of greater than three, and the response time was still less than in the original STATSPACK. The following is the same section from the STATSPACK report taken after the network changes. Almost all statistics show an increase:

```
Cluster Statistics for DB: MIKE  Instance: mike2  Snaps: 105 -106

Global Cache Service - Workload Characteristics
-----------------------------------------------
Ave global cache get time (ms):                          8.2
```

```
Ave global cache convert time (ms):                      16.5

Ave build time for CR block (ms):                         1.5
Ave flush time for CR block (ms):                         6.0
Ave send time for CR block (ms):                          0.9
Ave time to process CR block request (ms):                8.5
Ave receive time for CR block (ms):                      18.3

Ave pin time for current block (ms):                     13.7
Ave flush time for current block (ms):                    3.9
Ave send time for current block (ms):                     0.8
Ave time to process current block request (ms):          18.4
Ave receive time for current block (ms):                 17.4

Global cache hit ratio:                                   2.5
Ratio of current block defers:                            0.2
% of messages sent for buffer gets:                       2.2
% of remote buffer gets:                                  1.6
Ratio of I/O for coherence:                               2.8
Ratio of local vs remote work:                            0.5
Ratio of fusion vs physical writes:                       0.0
```

The next report shows the global enqueue service statistics. The global enqueue services (GES) control the inter-instance locks in Oracle Database 10g RAC. These times should all be in the less than 15 millisecond range and the ratio should be near one. If they are not, it shows possible network or memory problems. Application locking issues can also cause this and the enqueue report, which is shown later in the STATSPACK listing, should be consulted to further diagnose the possible problems:

```
Global Enqueue Service Statistics
---------------------------------
Ave global lock get time (ms):                            0.9
Ave global lock convert time (ms):                        1.3
Ratio of global lock gets vs global lock releases:        1.1
```

The next STATSPACK report deals with GCS and GES messaging. Queue times greater than 20-30 ms should be considered excessive and should be watched:

```
GCS and GES Messaging statistics
--------------------------------
Ave message sent queue time (ms):                         1.8
Ave message sent queue time on ksxp (ms):                 2.6
Ave message received queue time (ms):                     1.2
Ave GCS message process time (ms):                        1.2
```

```
Ave GES message process time (ms):                              0.2
% of direct sent messages:                                     58.4
% of indirect sent messages:                                    4.9
% of flow controlled messages:                                 36.7
-------------------------------------------------------------
```

The next section of the STATSPACK report also deals with the global enqueue services statistics. Blocked converts are one thing to look for. There are several in this report example. Blocked converts means the instance requested a block from another instance and for one reason or another was unable to obtain the conversion of the block. This can indicate that users are going after the same records, and it may be desirable to prevent that from occurring.

Blocked converts can also indicate insufficient freelists. This should not be the issue if Oracle Database 10g bitmap freelists are used. Block contention can be reduced through *freelists, ini_trans*, and limiting rows per block to avoid conversions being blocked.

If there are excessive message processing times, thought should be given to tuning the network to increase bandwidth, or perhaps upgrading the NIC's to faster, high bandwidth versions.

```
GES Statistics for DB: MIKE  Instance: mike2  Snaps: 25 -26

Statistic                                   Total   per Second    per Trans
--------------------------------- ---------------- ------------ ------------
dynamically allocated gcs resourc               0          0.0          0.0
dynamically allocated gcs shadows               0          0.0          0.0
flow control messages received                  0          0.0          0.0
flow control messages sent                      0          0.0          0.0
gcs ast xid                                     0          0.0          0.0
gcs blocked converts                          904          2.1        150.7
gcs blocked cr converts                     1,284          2.9        214.0
gcs compatible basts                            0          0.0          0.0
gcs compatible cr basts (global)                0          0.0          0.0
gcs compatible cr basts (local)                75          0.2         12.5
gcs cr basts to PIs                             0          0.0          0.0
gcs cr serve without current lock               0          0.0          0.0
gcs error msgs                                  0          0.0          0.0
gcs flush pi msgs                              21          0.0          3.5
gcs forward cr to pinged instance               0          0.0          0.0
gcs immediate (compatible) conver               4          0.0          0.7
gcs immediate (null) converts                  79          0.2         13.2
gcs immediate cr (compatible) con               4          0.0          0.7
gcs immediate cr (null) converts                3          0.0          0.5
gcs msgs process time(ms)                   3,193          7.3        532.2
gcs msgs received                           2,586          5.9        431.0
gcs out-of-order msgs                           0          0.0          0.0
```

```
gcs pings refused                               0          0.0          0.0
gcs queued converts                             0          0.0          0.0
gcs recovery claim msgs                         0          0.0          0.0
gcs refuse xid                                  0          0.0          0.0
gcs retry convert request                       0          0.0          0.0
gcs side channel msgs actual                   65          0.1         10.8
gcs side channel msgs logical               1,383          3.2        230.5
gcs write notification msgs                     0          0.0          0.0
gcs write request msgs                          0          0.0          0.0
gcs writes refused                              0          0.0          0.0
ges msgs process time(ms)                     136          0.3         22.7
ges msgs received                             578          1.3         96.3
implicit batch messages received               90          0.2         15.0
implicit batch messages sent                   12          0.0          2.0
lmd msg send time(ms)                          55          0.1          9.2
lms(s) msg send time(ms)                        8          0.0          1.3
messages flow controlled                      806          1.8        134.3
messages received actual                    1,980          4.5        330.0
messages received logical                   3,164          7.3        527.3
messages sent directly                      1,281          2.9        213.5
messages sent indirectly                      108          0.2         18.0
msgs causing lmd to send msgs                 231          0.5         38.5
msgs causing lms(s) to send msgs               97          0.2         16.2
msgs received queue time (ms)               3,842          8.8        640.3
msgs received queued                        3,164          7.3        527.3
msgs sent queue time (ms)                     202          0.5         33.7
msgs sent queue time on ksxp (ms)           4,337          9.9        722.8
msgs sent queued                              111          0.3         18.5
msgs sent queued on ksxp                    1,658          3.8        276.3
process batch messages received               269          0.6         44.8
process batch messages sent                   191          0.4         31.8
          -------------------------------------------------------------
```

The next section of the report deals with waits. Waits are a key tuning indicator. The predominant wait is for *global cache cr request*, which was caused by the network not being tuned properly, as already mentioned. The second highest wait is the *global cache null to x*, which, if severe, indicates problems with the I/O subsystem. In this case, the total time waited was one second or less, hardly a concern when compared with the 154 second wait on *global cache cr request*. The waits with the highest total time should be tuned first. Waits such as SQL*Net waits and any having to do with *smon*, *pmon*, or *wakeup* timers can be safely ignored in most situations.

```
Wait Events for DB: MIKE  Instance: mike2  Snaps: 25 -26
-> s  - second
-> cs - centisecond -     100th of a second
-> ms - millisecond -    1000th of a second
-> us - microsecond - 1000000th of a second
-> ordered by wait time desc, waits desc (idle events last)

Avg
                                                       Total Wait   wait    Waits
Event                               Waits   Timeouts   Time (s)    (ms)     /txn
---------------------------- ------------ ---------- ---------- ------ --------
global cache cr request               820        113        154    188    136.7
global cache null to x                478          1          1      2     79.7
control file sequential read          600          0          1      2    100.0
control file parallel write           141          0          1      4     23.5
enqueue                                29          0          1     18      4.8
```

```
library cache lock                      215          0          0       2      35.8
db file sequential read                  28          0          0       7       4.7
LGWR wait for redo copy                  31         16          0       4       5.2
ksxr poll remote instances              697        465          0       0     116.2
global cache open x                      48          0          0       2       8.0
CGS wait for IPC msg                    899        899          0       0     149.8
log file parallel write                 698        697          0       0     116.3
latch free                               24          0          0       2       4.0
global cache s to x                      41          0          0       1       6.8
log file sync                             3          0          0      13       0.5
DFS lock handle                          30          0          0       1       5.0
global cache open s                      16          0          0       1       2.7
global cache null to s                    9          0          0       1       1.5
library cache pin                       133          0          0       0      22.2
KJC: Wait for msg sends to c             17          0          0       0       2.8
db file parallel write                   19          0          0       0       3.2
cr request retry                         27         27          0       0       4.5
gcs remote message                   10,765      9,354        840      78   1,794.2
virtual circuit status                   15         15        440   29307       2.5
ges remote message                    9,262      8,501        421      45   1,543.7
wakeup time manager                      14         14        408   29135       2.3
SQL*Net message from client           4,040          0        216      53     673.3
SQL*Net message to client             4,040          0          0       0     673.3
          -------------------------------------------------------------
```

The next report deals with enqueues. These are the normal system enqueues. The non-RAC related ones have been removed from this listing. Enqueues are high level locks used to protect memory areas. When the report is reviewed, the enqueues with the highest totals should be of the most interest. In the following report, all of the enqueues of concern are again dealing with message times and cache block transfers. These types of enqueues again point to network tuning.

```
Enqueue activity for DB: MIKE  Instance: mike2  Snaps: 25 -26
-> Enqueue stats gathered prior to 10g should not be compared with 10g data
-> ordered by Wait Time desc, Waits desc

Instance Activity Stats for DB: MIKE  Instance: mike2  Snaps: 25 -26

Statistic                                      Total     per Second    per Trans
--------------------------------- ------------------ -------------- ------------
gcs messages sent                              1,570            3.6        261.7
ges messages sent                                805            1.9        134.2
global cache blocks lost                          88            0.2         14.7
global cache convert time                        171            0.4         28.5
global cache converts                            528            1.2         88.0
global cache cr block build time                  28            0.1          4.7
global cache cr block flush time                   2            0.0          0.3
global cache cr block receive tim              1,158            2.7        193.0
global cache cr block send time                  117            0.3         19.5
global cache cr blocks received                  674            1.6        112.3
global cache cr blocks served                  1,147            2.6        191.2
global cache current block pin ti                 12            0.0          2.0
global cache current block receiv                170            0.4         28.3
global cache current block send t                 57            0.1          9.5
global cache current blocks recei                541            1.2         90.2
global cache current blocks serve                653            1.5        108.8
global cache defers                                0            0.0          0.0
global cache get time                             57            0.1          9.5
global cache gets                                183            0.4         30.5
global cache skip prepare failure                 37            0.1          6.2
global lock async converts                         0            0.0          0.0
global lock async gets                           197            0.5         32.8
```

```
global lock convert time                           4            0.0          0.7
global lock get time                             290            0.7         48.3
global lock releases                           3,064            7.0        510.7
global lock sync converts                         30            0.1          5.0
global lock sync gets                          3,120            7.2        520.0
```

The next three reports deal with latches. Latches are low level lock structures that protect memory areas. There is usually no concern with latches unless high sleeps or misses are observed. Generally, adjusting internal parameters or tuning SQL code tunes latches. An example would be adjusting the *_kgl** parameters to tune the library related or shared pool locks. Sometimes, increasing the shared pool size can also help to relieve latch issues. For some latches, the number of latches available are derived from the size of the shared pool and the settings for related initialization parameters.

```
Latch Activity for DB: MIKE  Instance: mike2  Snaps: 25 -26
->"Get Requests", "Pct Get Miss" and "Avg Slps/Miss" are statistics for
  willing-to-wait latch get requests
->"NoWait Requests", "Pct NoWait Miss" are for no-wait latch get requests
->"Pct Misses" for both should be very close to 0.0

                                           Pct    Avg   Wait                 Pct
                                    Get    Get   Slps   Time       NoWait NoWait
Latch                          Requests   Miss  /Miss    (s)     Requests   Miss
------------------------ -------------- ------ ------ ------ ------------ ------
KCL bast context freelis          1,150    0.0             0            0
KCL freelist parent latc            713    0.0             0            0
KCL gc element parent la          8,399    0.0             0          166    0.0
KCL name table parent la          1,780    0.0             0          144    0.0
KJC message pool free li            655    0.0             0          194    0.0
KJCT flow control latch           2,238    0.0    1.0      0           91    0.0
gcs opaque info freelist          1,922    0.0             0            0
gcs resource freelist                77    0.0             0            0
gcs resource hash                 5,719    0.0    1.0      0            0
gcs shadows freelist                681    0.0             0            0
ges caches resource list          3,518    0.0             0        2,130    0.0
ges deadlock list                   411    0.0             0            0
ges domain table                  4,206    0.0             0            0
ges enqueue table freeli          6,271    0.0             0            0
ges group parent                  4,238    0.0             0            0
ges group table                   6,409    0.0             0            0
ges process hash list               207    0.0             0            0
ges process parent latch         18,354    0.0    1.0      0            0
ges process table freeli              4    0.0             0            0
ges resource hash list           10,294    0.1    1.0      0        1,248    0.0
ges resource table freel          5,703    0.0             0            0
ges timeout list                     72    0.0             0            0

Latch Sleep breakdown for DB: MIKE  Instance: mike2  Snaps: 25 -26
-> ordered by misses desc

                                      Get                            Spin &
Latch Name                       Requests      Misses      Sleeps Sleeps 1->4
-------------------------- -------------- ----------- ----------- ------------
ges resource hash list             10,294          13          13 0/13/0/0/0
redo allocation                    41,394           4           4 0/4/0/0/0
KJCT flow control latch             2,238           1           1 0/1/0/0/0
cache buffers lru chain             3,055           1           1 0/1/0/0/0
gcs resource hash                   5,719           1           1 0/1/0/0/0
ges process parent latch           18,354           1           1 0/1/0/0/0
          -------------------------------------------------------------
Latch Miss Sources for DB: MIKE  Instance: mike2  Snaps: 25 -26
```

```
-> only latches with sleeps are shown
-> ordered by name, sleeps desc

                                                           NoWait              Waiter
Latch Name               Where                             Misses     Sleeps   Sleeps
------------------------ -------------------------- ------- ---------- --------
KJCT flow control latch  kjcts_sedeqv: dequeue a ve         0          1        0
cache buffers lru chain  kcbzgb: wait                       0          1        1
gcs resource hash        kjbmpconvert                       0          1        1
ges resource hash list   kjrmas1: lookup master nod         0         13        0
redo allocation          kcrfwr                             0          4        2
          -------------------------------------------------------------
```

The next report deals with the data dictionary cache area of the shared pool. If there are no conflicts or releases, the *dc* caches are sized correctly. The dictionary cache area is sized by properly sizing the shared pool.

```
Dictionary Cache Stats for DB: MIKE  Instance: mike2  Snaps: 25 -26
                                      GES          GES          GES
Cache                             Requests    Conflicts     Releases
------------------------- ------------ ------------ ------------
dc_global_oids                       0            0            0
dc_object_ids                       22            0            0
dc_objects                          97            0            0
dc_profiles                          0            0            0
dc_rollback_segments                 0            0            0
dc_segments                          3            0            0
dc_tablespace_quotas                 2            0            0
dc_tablespaces                       0            0            0
dc_user_grants                       0            0            0
dc_usernames                         0            0            0
dc_users                             0            0            0
-------------------------------------------------------------
```

The next report gives a breakdown of enqueues by type of enqueue. This enqueue type report will help isolate the cause of enqueue problems. The types of enqueue are shown in Table 14.2

Type	Description
BL	Buffer Cache Management
CF	Controlfile Transaction
CI	Cross-instance Call Invocation
CU	Bind Enqueue
DF	Datafile
DL	Direct Loader Index Creation
DM	Database Mount
DR	Distributed Recovery
DX	Distributed TX

Type	Description
FS	File Set
IN	Instance Number
IR	Instance Recovery
IS	Instance State
IV	Library Cache Invalidation
JQ	Job Queue
KK	Redo Log "Kick"
L[A-P]	Library Cache Lock
MR	Media Recovery
N[A-Z]	Library Cache Pin
PF	Password File
PI	Parallel Slaves
PR	Process Startup
PS	Parallel Slave Synchronization
Q[A-Z]	Row Cache
RT	Redo Thread
SC	System Commit Number
SM	SMON
SQ	Sequence Number Enqueue
SR	Synchronized Replication
SS	Sort Segment
ST	Space Management Transaction
SV	Sequence Number Value
TA	Transaction Recovery
TM	DML Enqueue
TS	Temporary Segment (also TableSpace)
TT	Temporary Table
TX	Transaction
UL	User-defined Locks
UN	User Name
US	Undo Segment: Serialization
WL	Being Written Redo Log
XA	Instance Attribute Lock
XI	Instance Registration Lock

Table 14.2: *List of Enqueues*

In the report, the majority enqueue is the TM or DML related enqueue. However, its average wait time is only 2.43 milliseconds. The transaction recovery (TA) enqueue has a whopping 497 millisecond wait time. This high value was driven by several rollbacks in the test procedure. Once the enqueue causing the problems are determined, standard tuning techniques can be used to resolve them.

```
Enqueue activity for DB: MIKE  Instance: mike2  Snaps: 25 -26
-> Enqueue stats gathered prior to 10g should not be compared with 10g data
-> ordered by Wait Time desc, Waits desc

                                                          Avg Wt         Wait
Eq     Requests     Succ Gets Failed Gets       Waits   Time (ms)      Time (s)
-- ------------ ------------ ----------- ----------- ------------- ------------
TA            1            1           0           1        497.00            0
TM        1,582        1,582           0          14          2.43            0
HW           13           13           0           5          2.60            0
FB            4            4           0           4          3.00            0
TT            3            3           0           3          2.33            0
          -------------------------------------------------------------
```

The final report section to be reviewed is the library cache report dealing with the GES. GES invalid requests and GES invalidations could indicate insufficient sizing of the shared pool, resulting in GES contention.

```
Library Cache Activity for DB: MIKE  Instance: mike2  Snaps: 25 -26
->"Pct Misses"  should be very low

                     GES Lock      GES Pin      GES Pin   GES Inval GES Invali-
Namespace            Requests     Requests     Releases    Requests     dations
--------------- ------------ ------------ ------------ ----------- -----------
BODY                       1            0            0           0           0
CLUSTER                    4            0            0           0           0
INDEX                     84            0            0           0           0
SQL AREA                   0            0            0           0           0
TABLE/PROCEDURE          617          192            0          77           0
TRIGGER                    0            0            0           0           0
          -------------------------------------------------------------
```

This section on the STATSPACK reports has only covered the reports that dealt with the RAC environment. This does not mean that the rest of the report can be ignored. The sections on SQL use are critical in light of the need to find the code that may actually be causing the problems. The other waits, latches, enqueues, and statistics that deal with the mundane parts of the

Oracle environment are also important to review, monitor, and tune.

GCS Monitoring

The use of the GCS relative to the number of buffer cache reads, or logical reads can be estimated by dividing the sum of GCS requests (*global cache gets* + *global cache converts* + *global cache cr blocks received* + *global cache current blocks received*) by the number of logical reads (*consistent gets* + *db block gets*) for a given statistics collection interval. A global cache service request is made in Oracle when a user attempts to access a buffer cache to read or modify a data block and the block is not in the local cache. A remote cache read, disk read or change access privileges is the inevitable result. These are logical read related. Logical reads form a superset of the global cache service operations. The calculation for *global cache hit ratio* since instance startup is:

```
SELECT
  a.inst_id "Instance",
  (A.VALUE+B.VALUE+C.VALUE+D.VALUE)/(E.VALUE+F.VALUE) "GLOBAL CACHE
HIT RATIO"
FROM
  GV$SYSSTAT A,
  GV$SYSSTAT B,
  GV$SYSSTAT C,
  GV$SYSSTAT D,
  GV$SYSSTAT E,
  GV$SYSSTAT F
WHERE
  A.NAME='gc gets'
  AND B.NAME='gc converts'
  AND C.NAME='gc cr blocks received'
  AND D.NAME='gc current blocks received'
  AND E.NAME='consistent gets'
  AND F.NAME='db block gets'
  AND B.INST_ID=A.INST_ID
  AND C.INST_ID=A.INST_ID
  AND D.INST_ID=A.INST_ID
  AND E.INST_ID=A.INST_ID
  AND F.INST_ID=A.INST_ID;

  Instance GLOBAL CACHE HIT RATIO
---------- ----------------------
         1             .02403656
         2            .014798887
```

The instance with the best access to the drives, or the faster I/O path, will likely have the best *cache hit ratio*. This is due to the way Oracle's RAC caching algorithm works as it may decide that the cost of doing a local read is higher than reading into the other cache and siphoning it across the cluster interconnect. In formula form:

```
(gc gets + gc converts + gc cr blocks received +
gc current blocks received) / (consistent gets + db block gets)
```

Blocks frequently requested by local and remote users will be very hot. If a block is hot, its transfer is delayed for a few milliseconds to allow the local users to complete their work. The following ratio provides a rough estimate of how prevalent this is:

```
SELECT
  A.INST_ID "Instance",
  A.VALUE/B.VALUE "BLOCK TRANSFER RATIO"
FROM
  GV$SYSSTAT A, GV$SYSSTAT B
WHERE
  A.NAME='gc defers'
  AND B.NAME='gc current blocks served'
  AND B.INST_ID=A.INST_ID;

  Instance BLOCK TRANSFER RATIO
---------- --------------------
         1           .052600105
         2           .078004479
```

If the above SELECT generates a ratio of more than 0.3, a fairly hot data set is indicated. If this is the case, blocks involved in busy waits should be analyzed. The following columns should be queried to find the blocks involved in busy waits:

- *name*
- *kind*
- *forced_reads*
- *forced_writes*

For example:

```
col instance format 99999999
col name format a20
col kind format a10
set lines 80 pages 55
Select
INST_ID "Instance",
NAME,
KIND,
sum(FORCED_READS) "Forced Reads",
sum(FORCED_WRITES) "Forced Writes"
FROM GV$CACHE_TRANSFER
WHERE owner#!=0
GROUP BY INST_ID,NAME,KIND
ORDER BY 1,4 desc,2
/

Instance NAME                 KIND       Forced Reads Forced Writes
--------- -------------------- ---------- ------------ -------------
        1 MOD_TEST_IND         INDEX               308             0
        1 TEST2                TABLE                64             0
        1 AQ$_QUEUE_TABLES     TABLE                 5             0
        2 TEST2                TABLE               473             0
        2 MOD_TEST_IND         INDEX               221             0
        2 AQ$_QUEUE_TABLES     TABLE                 2             0
```

These values come from the *gv$cache_transfer* view. Alternatively, the *cr_requests* and *current_requests* columns in *gv$cr_block_server* can be examined. Also, the values shown for the *global cache busy*, *buffer busy global cache*, and *buffer busy global cr* statistics from the *gv$sysstat* view should be examined.

```
SELECT
  INST_ID,
  sum(CR_REQUESTS) "CR Requests",
  sum(CURRENT_REQUESTS) "Current Requests"
FROM
  GV$CR_BLOCK_SERVER
GROUP BY
  INST_ID;

   INST_ID CR Requests Current Requests
---------- ----------- ----------------
         1       28940             2244
         2       31699              837

SELECT
  inst_id "Instance",
  event "Wait Event",
  total_waits,
```

```
  time_waited
FROM
  GV$SYSTEM_EVENT
WHERE
      event in (
       'global cache busy',
       'buffer busy global cache',
       'buffer busy global CR')
ORDER BY
  INST_ID;
```

```
 Instance Wait Event                 TOTAL_WAITS TIME_WAITED
--------- ------------------------ ----------- -----------
        1 buffer busy global CR              1           0
        1 global cache busy               1073        7171
        2 global cache busy                973        7524
```

If a problem is discovered, the object causing the problem should be identified along with the instance that is accessing the object, and how the object is being accessed. If necessary, the contention can be alleviated by:

- Reducing hot spots by spreading the accesses to index blocks or data blocks.
- Using Oracle hash or range partitions wherever applicable, just as it would be done in single instance Oracle databases.
- Reducing concurrency on the object by implementing load balancing or resource management. For example, decrease the rate of modifications to that object by using fewer database processes.

In RAC, as in a single instance Oracle database, blocks are only written to disk for aging, cache replacement, or checkpoints. When a data block is replaced from the cache due to aging or when a checkpoint occurs and the block was previously changed in another instance but not written to disk, Oracle sends a message to notify the other instance that Oracle will perform a fusion write to move the data block to disk.

These fusion writes are monitored with the following ratio. It reveals the proportion of writes that Oracle manages.

```
SELECT
 a.inst_id "Instance",
 A.VALUE/B.VALUE "Cache Fusion Writes Ratio"
FROM
  GV$SYSSTAT A,
  GV$SYSSTAT B
WHERE
      a.name='DBWR fusion writes'
  AND b.name='physical writes'
  AND b.inst_id=a.inst_id
ORDER BY
  A.INST_ID;

Instance Cache Fusion Writes Ratio
--------- -------------------------
        1                .216290958
        2                .131862042
```

The larger this ratio is, the higher the number of written blocks that have been copied with their previous changes between the RAC instances. A large ratio is the result of:

- Insufficiently sized caches.
- Insufficient checkpoints.
- Large numbers of buffers written due to cache replacement or checkpointing.

For example, 0.21 means that 21% of the buffers written to disk were globally dirty. A fusion write does not involve an additional write to disk. A fusion write does require messaging to arrange the transfer with the other instances. This indicates that fusion writes are in fact a subset of all the instance's physical writes.

Use of the *cache_transfer* Views

The *v$cache_transfer* and *v$file_cache_transfer* views are used to examine RAC statistics. The types of blocks that use the cluster interconnects in a RAC environment are monitored with the *v$* cache transfer series of views:

- *v$cache_transfer:* This view shows the types and classes of blocks that Oracle transfers over the cluster interconnect on a per-object basis. The *forced_reads* and *forced_writes* columns can be used to determine the types of objects the RAC instances are sharing. Values in the *forced_writes* column show how often a certain block type is transferred out of a local buffer cache due to the current version being requested by another instance. The following columns are the same for all of the views.
- *v$class_cache_transfer:* -- This view can be used to identify the class of blocks that experience cache transfers. *v$class_cache_transfer* has a *class* column showing the class of a block; therefore, this view can be used to assess block transfers per class of object.
- *v$file_cache_transfer:* This view can be used to monitor the blocks transferred per file. The *file_number* column identifies the datafile that contained the blocks transferred.
- *v$temp_cache_transfer:* -- This view can be used to monitor the transfer of temporary tablespace blocks. The view contains a *file_number* column that is used to track, by the tempfile file number, the number of blocks transferred. This view has the same structure as the *v$temp_cache_transfer* view.

The contents of the *v$cache_transfer* view are shown below.

```
Description of the V$CACHE_TRANSFER view


Name                       Type
-----------------------    --------------
FILE#                      NUMBER
BLOCK#                     NUMBER
CLASS#                     NUMBER
STATUS                     VARCHAR2(5)
XNC                        NUMBER
FORCED_READS               NUMBER
FORCED_WRITES              NUMBER
NAME                       VARCHAR2(30)
PARTITION_NAME             VARCHAR2(30)
```

```
KIND                        VARCHAR2(15)
OWNER#                      NUMBER
GC_ELEMENT_ADDR             RAW(4)
GC_ELEMENT_NAME             NUMBER
```

The *v$cache_transfer* view shows the types and classes of blocks that Oracle transfers over the cluster interconnect on a per-object basis. The *forced_reads* and *forced_writes* columns are used to determine which types of objects the RAC instances are sharing.

The *v$file_cache_transfer* view is used to identify files that have experienced cache transfers. For example, while *v$cache_transfer* has a *name* column showing the name of an object, the *v$file_cache_transfer* view has the *file_number* column to show the file numbers of the datafiles that are the source of blocks transferred; therefore, this view can be used to assess block transfers per file. The *v$file_cache_transfer* view contents are shown below:

```
Description of the V$FILE_CACHE_TRANSFER View
 Name                                 Type
 ------------------------------------ ----------
 FILE_NUMBER                          NUMBER
 X_2_NULL                             NUMBER
 X_2_NULL_FORCED_WRITE                NUMBER
 X_2_NULL_FORCED_STALE                NUMBER
 X_2_S                                NUMBER
 X_2_S_FORCED_WRITE                   NUMBER
 S_2_NULL                             NUMBER
 S_2_NULL_FORCED_STALE                NUMBER
 RBR                                  NUMBER
 RBR_FORCED_WRITE                     NUMBER
 RBR_FORCED_STALE                     NUMBER
 NULL_2_X                             NUMBER
 S_2_X                                NUMBER
 NULL_2_S                             NUMBER
 CR_TRANSFERS                         NUMBER
 CUR_TRANSFERS                        NUMBER
```

Even though the shared disk architecture virtually eliminates forced disk writes, the *v$cache_transfer* and *v$file_cache_transfer* views may still show the number of block mode conversions per block class or object. Values in the *forced_writes* column, however, will be zero.

Monitoring the GES Processes

The monitoring of the global enqueue services (GES) process is performed using the *gv$enqueue_stat* view. The contents of the *gv$enqueue_stat* view are shown below:

```
Description of the view GV$ENQUEUE_STAT

Name                              Type
--------------------------------- ----------
INST_ID                           NUMBER
EQ_TYPE                           VARCHAR2(2)
TOTAL_REQ#                        NUMBER
TOTAL_WAIT#                       NUMBER
SUCC_REQ#                         NUMBER
FAILED_REQ#                       NUMBER
CUM_WAIT_TIME                     NUMBER
```

An example SELECT to retrieve all of the enqueues with *total_wait* number greater than zero would be:

```
select
   *
from
   gv$enqueue_stat
where
   total_wait#>0
order by
   inst_id,
cum_wait_time desc;

   INST_ID EQ TOTAL_REQ# TOTAL_WAIT#  SUCC_REQ# FAILED_REQ# CUM_WAIT_TIME
---------- -- ---------- ----------- ---------- ----------- -------------
         1 TX      31928          26      31928           0        293303
         1 PS        995         571        994           1         55658
         1 TA       1067         874       1067           0         10466
         1 TD        974         974        974           0          2980
         1 DR        176         176        176           0           406
         1 US        190         189        190           0           404
         1 PI         47          27         47           0           104
         1 CF     499314          23     499314           0            47
         1 TM      41928           8      41928           0            35
         1 MR         93          13         93           0            21
         1 HW        637           6        637           0             8
         1 XR          4           2          4           0             5
         1 DM          4           2          4           0             4
         1 SR          1           1          1           0             3
         1 SW          3           1          3           0             3
         1 TS          2           1          2           0             3
         2 TA       1064        1015       1064           0        437648
         2 PS       2208         325       1597         611        104273
         2 TX     440843          18     440843           0         62787
         2 US        197          41        197           0          8551
         2 IR        193          29        193           0          4593
```

```
2 TT       4393        131      4393         0        3363
2 CF     507497        540    507497         0        1726
2 TM    1104694        101   1104694         0         766
2 DM          5          2         5         0         483
2 HW        444         41       444         0         108
2 PI         90         18        90         0          81
2 DL         32         18        32         0          55
2 DR        176         23       176         0          52
2 RT          4          4         3         1          12
2 FB         10          2        10         0           6
2 IA          1          1         1         0           4
2 PG          1          1         1         0           3
2 TS          4          1         4         0           3
```

According to Oracle, the enqueues of interest, as shown in the *eq_type* column of the *gv$enqueue_stat* view in the RAC environment are:

- SQ Enqueue: This indicates that there is contention for sequences. In almost all cases, executing an ALTER SEQUENCE command can increase the cache size of sequences used by the application. When creating sequences for a RAC environment, DBAs should use the NOORDER keyword to avoid an additional cause of SQ enqueue contention that is forced ordering of queued sequence values.
- TX Enqueue: This is usually an application related issue pertaining to row locking. Real Application Clusters processing can magnify the effect of TX enqueue waits. Performance bottlenecks can also appear on leaf blocks of right growing indexes as TX enqueue waits while the index block splits are occuring. TX enqueue performance issues can be resolved by setting the value of the *initrans* parameter for a TABLE or INDEX to be equal to the number of CPUs per node multiplied by the number of nodes in the cluster multiplied by 0.75. Another technique is to determine the number of simultaneous accesses for DML for the objects experiencing TX enqueues, and setting *initrans* to that value. Oracle Corporation recommends avoiding setting this parameter greater than 100. Another parameter that can reduce TX enqueues is *maxtrans*. *maxtrans* determines the maximum number of transactions that can access a block.

maxtrans will default to 255 and it is a good practice to reset this to less than 100.

PS (Parallel Slave Synchronization) and TA (Transaction Recovery) enqueues also seem to have some importance in the environment. Therefore, start with a wide sweep and then focus on the waits that are causing performance issues in the environment.

There are other interesting views that provide information on tuning that the DBA in a RAC environment should be aware of, for example:

- *gv$segment_statistics:* Provides statistics such as *buffer busy waits* on a per segment basis. This allows tracking of exactly which segments, indexes or tables, are causing the *buffer busy waits* or other statistics to increment. To select against the *gv$segment_statistics* view, the user will want to SELECT for a specific statistic name where the value is greater than a predetermined limit. The contents of *gv$segment_statistics* are shown below:

```
Description of gv$segment_statistics
 Name                                      Null?    Type
 ----------------------------------------- -------- ------------
 INST_ID                                            NUMBER
 OWNER                                              VARCHAR2(30)
 OBJECT_NAME                                        VARCHAR2(30)
 SUBOBJECT_NAME                                     VARCHAR2(30)
 TABLESPACE_NAME                                    VARCHAR2(30)
 TS#                                                NUMBER
 OBJ#                                               NUMBER
 DATAOBJ#                                           NUMBER
 OBJECT_TYPE                                        VARCHAR2(18)
 STATISTIC_NAME                                     VARCHAR2(64)
 STATISTIC#                                         NUMBER
 VALUE                                              NUMBER
```

Another useful view shows which file IDs which have been remastered, which happens when they are transferred from one instance to another, this view is called *gv$gcspfmaster_info* and its contents are shown below:

```
Description of gv$gcspfmaster_info
 Name                                      Null?    Type
 ----------------------------------------- -------- -------
 INST_ID                                            NUMBER
 FILE_ID                                            NUMBER
 CURRENT_MASTER                                     NUMBER
 PREVIOUS_MASTER                                    NUMBER
 REMASTER_CNT                                       NUMBER
```

The *file_id* column corresponds to the data file ID. The current and previous masters refer to the instances that are either the current or previous master of the specified file. A view related to the *gv$gcspfmaster_info* view is the *gv$gchvmaster_info* view which shows the same information but for the PCM hash value IDs for specific resources that have been remastered. This views contents are shown below:

```
Description of gv$gcshvmaster_info
Name                                      Null?    Type
----------------------------------------- -------- -------
INST_ID                                            NUMBER
HV_ID                                              NUMBER
CURRENT_MASTER                                     NUMBER
PREVIOUS_MASTER                                    NUMBER
REMASTER_CNT                                       NUMBER
```

To select against these views, it may be desirable to restrict on the *remaster_cnt* value being greater than a predetermined limit.

The *gv$sqlarea* view has also been enhanced in Oracle Database 10g RAC. The column *cluster_wait_time* in *gv$sqlarea* represents the wait time incurred by individual SQL statements for global cache events and will identify the SQL which may need to be tuned based on its contribution to RAC contention.

Monitoring and Tuning using OEM

The first part of this chapter covered the manual aspects of RAC tuning, showing techniques and providing scripts to obtain the needed information from the various underlying Oracle views.

This section will cover the tools provided by Oracle in the Oracle Enterprise manager (OEM) Performance Monitor. In order to use OEM to monitor a RAC environment, the following must be in place:

- OEM installed.
- OEM repository.
- Oracle Intelligent Agents running.

Normally, if the standard installation is used, OEM will be installed as a matter of course. If possible, the OEM and its repository should be set up on a separate system, such as a small Windows-based server. At the least, a small repository database should be created on one of the RAC servers. This can be used for the RMAN repository as well. The OEM client software can be installed on any desktop as long as that desktop has SQL*Net connectivity to the OEM repository.

The most difficult part of the setup for OEM is probably getting the intelligent agents to work properly with the RAC environment.

Configuring the Oracle Intelligent Agent with RAC

In order to be sure that the agent is installed properly in Oracle Database 10g, the following Metalink documents should be reviewed:

- EM 10g Database Control Release Notes 10.1.0.2.0 Note: 266770.1
- EM 10g GRID Control Release Notes 10.1.0.2.0 Note: 266769.1
- How to Log and Trace the EM 10g Management Agents Note: 229624.1

- How To Install The Downloadable Central Management Agent in EM 10g Grid Control Note: 235287.1

The nodes and databases must be properly discovered and viewable from the OEM webpage before they can be monitored.

Using EM in Oracle Database 10g

In 10g, Oracle is moving to the web based interface for EM and will soon deprecate the Java based version. Monitoring and management functions should be migrated into the HTML Web based version of EM as soon as possible. The following sections will provide a quick look at the screens in the new HTML version that the DBA should be using for RAC monitoring and management.

The Cluster Performance Page

In the HTML based web version of the EM, the Cluster Performance Page is used to display the usage statistics for all RAC hosts or for individual RAC hosts. This information allows you to add, suspend, or redistribute resources as the need arises. Figure 14.1 shows this page.

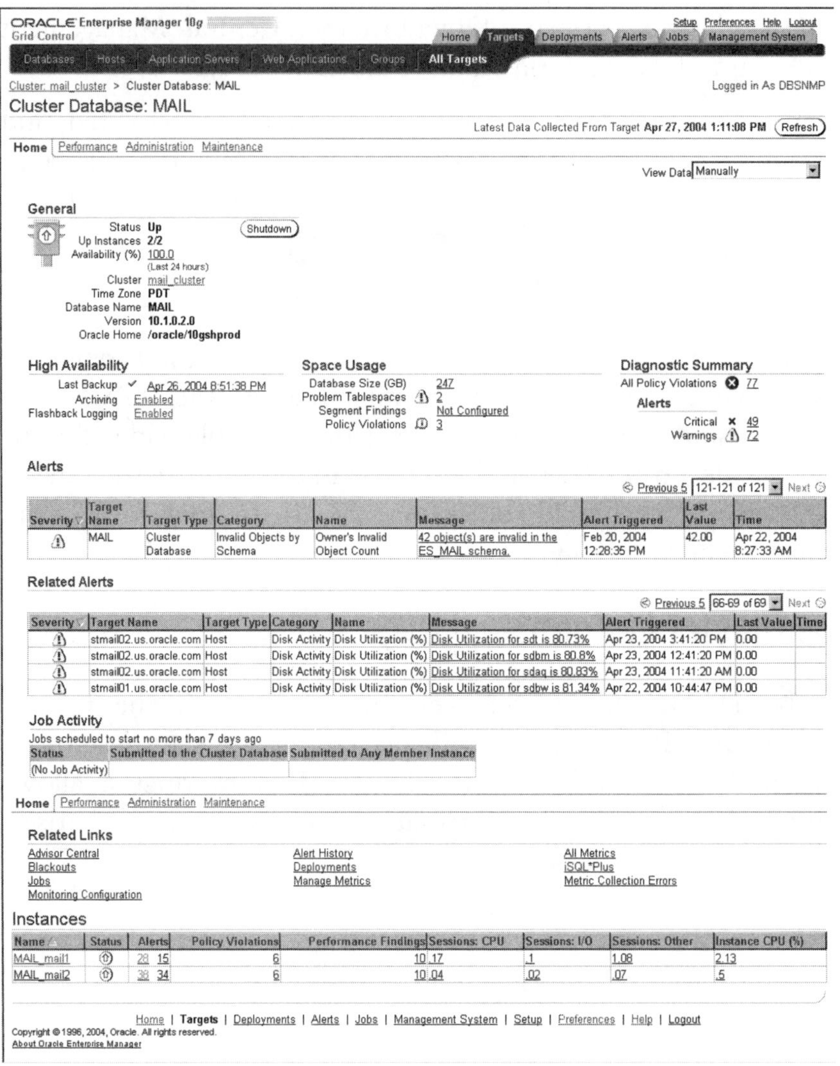

Figure 14.1: *Example Cluster Performance Page*

The Cluster Database Performance Page

The Oracle Database 10g EM Cluster Database Performance Page displays statistics via charts that show run queue length, paging rate, service time, and the database throughput for each

RAC host or RAC instance. The page is also used to access the detailed information for the Wait Class Page for Service Time and the Top Sessions Page for Database Throughput. Figure 14.2 shows an example of this page.

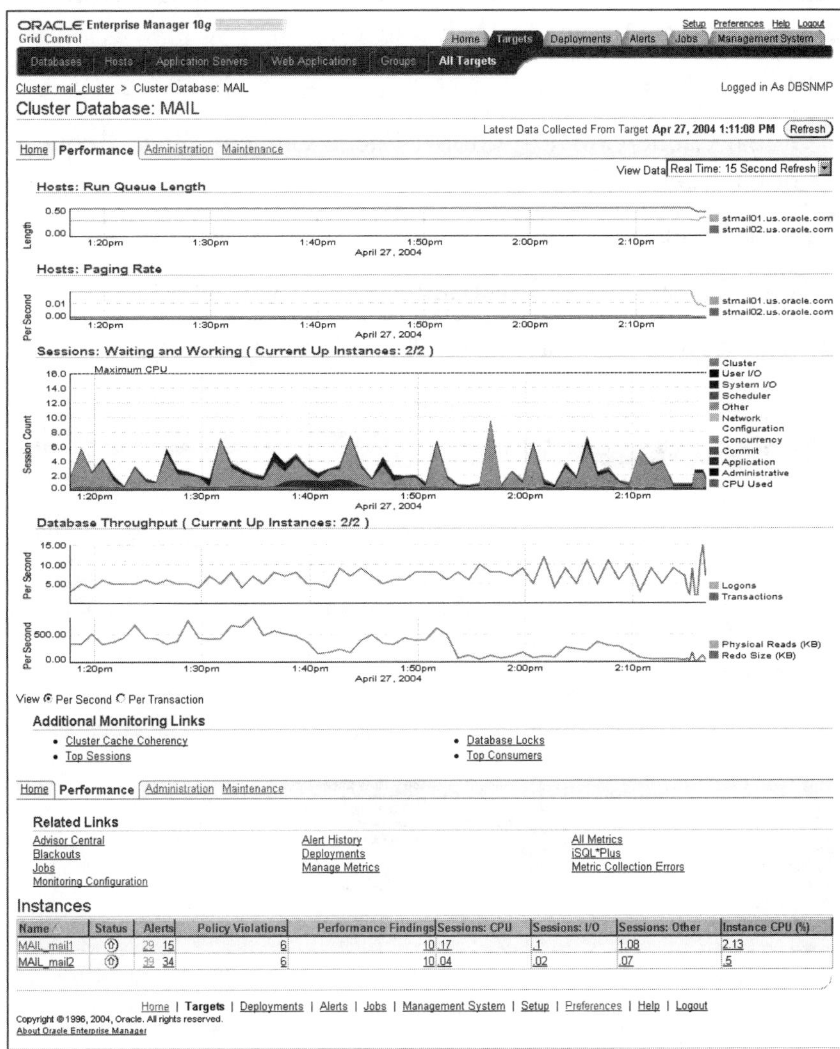

Figure 14.2: *Example Cluster Database Performance Page*

The Cluster Cache Coherency Instances Page

The Cluster Cache Coherency Instances Page is used to provide real-time monitoring of global cache statistics. The Cluster Cache Coherency Instances Page will display tables of metrics from the following groups for all cluster instances:

- Block Access Statistics
- Global Cache Convert, Global Cache Current Block Request, Global Cache CR
- Block Request
- Top 5 Library Cache Lock and Top 5 Row Cache Lock

Figure 14.3 shows the Cluster Cache Coherency Page:

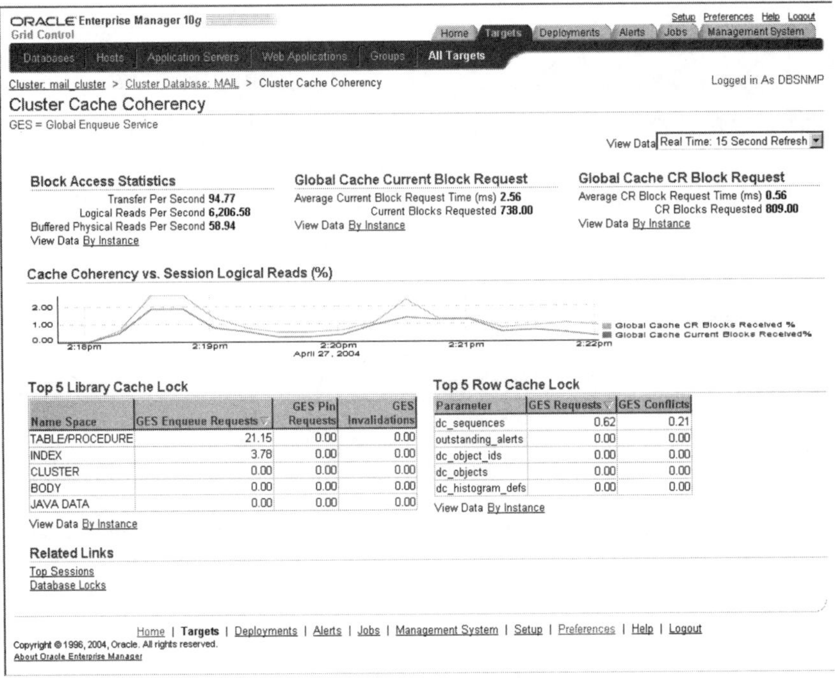

Figure 14.3: *Example Cluster Cache Coherency Page*

While the Enterprise Manager monitors events at the database and instance levels and any available node can monitor database events, only one node at a time monitors the entire database while each node monitors events for its local instances.

By using the various screens and reports in OEM Performance Manager for RAC, the status of virtually any section of the RAC environment can be seen. The screens and reports provide suggestions to correct problems as they occur.

Other Items to Monitor for RAC

In RAC, it is important to remember that multiple nodes are accessing the same database files. If the DBA only monitors from a single instance using the *v$* views, the effects from the other nodes will not be visible. The *gv$* views must be used to examine data from all nodes in order to get a complete picture of the RAC environment's performance.

An excellent example of this is the monitoring of file IO rates and file IO timing:

```
rem NAME: fileio.sql
rem
rem FUNCTION: Reports on the file io status of all of the
rem FUNCTION: datafiles in the database.

rem HISTORY:
rem WHO             WHAT            WHEN
rem Mike Ault               Created         1/5/2003
rem
column sum_io1 new_value st1 noprint
column sum_io2 new_value st2 noprint
column sum_io new_value divide_by noprint
column Percent format 999.999 heading 'Percent|Of IO'
column brratio format 999.99 heading 'Block|Read|Ratio'
column bwratio format 999.99 heading 'Block|Write|Ratio'
column phyrds heading 'Physical | Reads'
column phywrts heading 'Physical | Writes'
column phyblkrd heading 'Physical|Block|Reads'
column phyblkwrt heading 'Physical|Block|Writes'
column name format a45 heading 'File|Name'
column file# format 9999 heading 'File'
```

```
column dt new_value today noprint
select to_char(sysdate,'ddmonyyyyhh24miss') dt from dual;
set feedback off verify off lines 132 pages 60 sqlbl on trims on
rem
select
     nvl(sum(a.phyrds+a.phywrts),0) sum_io1
from
     sys.gv_$filestat a;
select nvl(sum(b.phyrds+b.phywrts),0) sum_io2
from
         sys.gv_$tempstat b;
select &st1+&st2 sum_io from dual;
rem
@title132 'File IO Statistics Report'
spool rep_out\&db\rac_fileio&&today
select
     a.inst_id, a.file#,b.name, a.phyrds, a.phywrts,
     (100*(a.phyrds+a.phywrts)/&divide_by) Percent,
     a.phyblkrd, a.phyblkwrt, (a.phyblkrd/greatest(a.phyrds,1))
brratio,
      (a.phyblkwrt/greatest(a.phywrts,1)) bwratio
from
     sys.gv_$filestat a, sys.gv_$dbfile b
where
     a.inst_id=b.inst_id and
     a.file#=b.file#
union
select
     c.inst_id,c.file#,d.name, c.phyrds, c.phywrts,
     (100*(c.phyrds+c.phywrts)/&divide_by) Percent,
     c.phyblkrd, c.phyblkwrt,(c.phyblkrd/greatest(c.phyrds,1))
brratio,
      (c.phyblkwrt/greatest(c.phywrts,1)) bwratio
from
     sys.gv_$tempstat c, sys.gv_$tempfile d
where
        c.inst_id=d.inst_id and
     c.file#=d.file#
order by
     1,2
/
spool off
pause Press enter to continue
set feedback on verify on lines 80 pages 22
clear columns
ttitle off
```

The output from the above script looks like the following:

```
Date: 01/22/04
Page:   1
Time: 01:38 PM                                           File IO Statistics Report
TSTDBMRA
                                                           tstdb database
```

```
Physical   Physical   Block   Block
                File                                          Physical   Physical
Percent      Block      Block     Read    Write
   INST_ID  File Name                                             Reads     Writes    Of
IO      Reads      Writes   Ratio   Ratio
---------- ----- -------------------------------------------- ---------- ---------- ------
-- ---------- ---------- ------- -------
         2     1 /od04_01/oradata/tstdb/system01.dbf                1731       2540
.009      2717       2540    1.57    1.00
         2     1 /od04_01/oradata/tstdb/temp01.dbf                195386     135805
.723    1688145    1724988    8.64   12.70
         2     2 /od04_01/oradata/tstdb/undotbs01.dbf                524        523
.002       524        523    1.00    1.00
         2     3 /od04_01/oradata/tstdb/drsys01.dbf                  524        523
.002       524        523    1.00    1.00
         2     4 /od04_01/oradata/tstdb/indx01.dbf                   524        523
.002       524        523    1.00    1.00
         2     5 /od04_01/oradata/tstdb/tools01.dbf                  524        523
.002       524        523    1.00    1.00
         2     6 /od04_01/oradata/tstdb/undotbs02.dbf                545      23867
.053       545      23867    1.00    1.00
         2     7 /od04_01/oradata/tstdb/undotbs03.dbf                524        523
.002       524        523    1.00    1.00
         2     8 /od04_01/oradata/tstdb/users01.dbf                  524        523
.002       524        523    1.00    1.00
         2     9 /od04_01/oradata/tstdb/xdb01.dbf                    530        523
.002       545        523    1.03    1.00
         2    10 /od04_01/oradata/tstdb/tstdb_globald01.dbf            525        523
.002       525        523    1.00    1.00
         2    11 /od04_01/oradata/tstdb/tstdb_globalx01.dbf            525        523
.002       525        523    1.00    1.00
         2    12 /od04_01/oradata/tstdb/tstdb_reportd01.dbf            524        523
.002       524        523    1.00    1.00
         2    13 /od04_01/oradata/tstdb/tstdb_reportx01.dbf            524        523
.002       524        523    1.00    1.00
         2    14 /od04_01/oradata/tstdb/nomadd01.dbf                 524        523
.002       524        523    1.00    1.00
         2    15 /od04_01/oradata/tstdb/TA1d01.dbf                   524        523
.002       524        523    1.00    1.00
         2    16 /od04_01/oradata/tstdb/TA1x01.dbf                   524        523
.002       524        523    1.00    1.00
         2    17 /od04_01/oradata/tstdb/SRCd01.dbf                131430        523
.288    3762539        523   28.63    1.00
         2    18 /od04_01/oradata/tstdb/SRCx01.dbf                  5410        523
.013      5410        523    1.00    1.00
         2    19 /od04_01/oradata/tstdb/REEd01.dbf                   524        523
.002       524        523    1.00    1.00
         2    20 /od04_01/oradata/tstdb/REEx01.dbf                   524        523
.002       524        523    1.00    1.00
         2    21 /od04_01/oradata/tstdb/CRWd01.dbf                   524        523
.002       524        523    1.00    1.00
         2    22 /od04_01/oradata/tstdb/CRWx01.dbf                   524        523
.002       524        523    1.00    1.00
         2    23 /od04_02/oradata/tstdb/LWEd01.dbf                   519        519
.002       519        519    1.00    1.00
         2    24 /od04_02/oradata/tstdb/LWEx01.dbf                   519        519
.002       519        519    1.00    1.00
         2    25 /od04_01/oradata/tstdb/perfstat01.dbf               110        110
.000       110        110    1.00    1.00
         3     1 /od04_01/oradata/tstdb/system01.dbf             5870952      43328
12.920     5879481      43328    1.00    1.00
         3     1 /od04_01/oradata/tstdb/temp01.dbf               2459053    1219824
8.036   22005243   15402399    8.95   12.63
         3     2 /od04_01/oradata/tstdb/undotbs01.dbf              62411        601
.138     62411        601    1.00    1.00
         3     3 /od04_01/oradata/tstdb/drsys01.dbf               475816        601
1.041     475816        601    1.00    1.00
         3     4 /od04_01/oradata/tstdb/indx01.dbf                   604        601
.003       604        601    1.00    1.00
         3     5 /od04_01/oradata/tstdb/tools01.dbf                  835        643
.003      1553        643    1.86    1.00
         3     6 /od04_01/oradata/tstdb/undotbs02.dbf                608        707
.003       608        707    1.00    1.00
         3     7 /od04_01/oradata/tstdb/undotbs03.dbf              88095     547959
1.389      88095     547959    1.00    1.00
```

```
         3     8 /od04_01/oradata/tstdb/users01.dbf                     3907        4289
.018       6098      5497     1.56     1.28
         3     9 /od04_01/oradata/tstdb/xdb01.dbf                    4370138         601
9.548    4370317         601     1.00     1.00
         3    10 /od04_01/oradata/tstdb/tstdb_globald01.dbf           1547848       29866
3.446    1941544       29866     1.25     1.00
         3    11 /od04_01/oradata/tstdb/tstdb_globalx01.dbf           4353943        6356
9.525    4354433        6357     1.00     1.00
         3    12 /od04_01/oradata/tstdb/tstdb_reportd01.dbf               604         601
.003       604         601     1.00     1.00
         3    13 /od04_01/oradata/tstdb/tstdb_reportx01.dbf               604         601
.003       604         601     1.00     1.00
         3    14 /od04_01/oradata/tstdb/nomadd01.dbf                  288384         601
.631     288384         601     1.00     1.00
         3    15 /od04_01/oradata/tstdb/TA1d01.dbf                    338417         601
.741     338417         601     1.00     1.00
         3    16 /od04_01/oradata/tstdb/TA1x01.dbf                    963876         601
2.107     963876         601     1.00     1.00
         3    17 /od04_01/oradata/tstdb/SRCd01.dbf                   3075710      936826
8.765    9782425      971945     3.18     1.04
         3    18 /od04_01/oradata/tstdb/SRCx01.dbf                   1315213       94012
3.078    1550400      275893     1.18     2.93
         3    19 /od04_01/oradata/tstdb/REEd01.dbf                   1191132         601
2.603    1191132         601     1.00     1.00
         3    20 /od04_01/oradata/tstdb/REEx01.dbf                   3109339         601
6.794    3109339         601     1.00     1.00
         3    21 /od04_01/oradata/tstdb/CRWd01.dbf                       604         601
.003       604         601     1.00     1.00
         3    22 /od04_01/oradata/tstdb/CRWx01.dbf                       604         601
.003       604         601     1.00     1.00
         3    23 /od04_02/oradata/tstdb/LWEd01.dbf                   7042322     3913365
23.933   88147193     4346731    12.52     1.11
         3    24 /od04_02/oradata/tstdb/LWEx01.dbf                   1381676      508355
4.129    2064523     1265528     1.49     2.49
         3    25 /od04_01/oradata/tstdb/perfstat01.dbf                   647        1845
.005       672        1845     1.04     1.00
```

The I/O balance is off between the two instances, two and three. If only instance two or only instance three were researched, the possible I/O problem would not have been evident.

Another I/O related statistic is the I/O timing. I/O timing would show if there are latency problems between the nodes. The following code shows an example file I/O timing report for RAC:

```
rem Purpose: Calculate IO timing values for datafiles
col inst_id format 9999999 heading 'Instance'
col name format a50 heading 'File Name'
set lines 132 pages 45
start title132 'IO Timing Analysis'
spool rep_out\&db\rac_io_time
select  f.inst_id,f.FILE#
,d.name,PHYRDS,PHYWRTS,READTIM/PHYRDS,WRITETIM/PHYWRTS
from gv$filestat f, gv$datafile d
where   f.inst_id=d.inst_id and
        f.file#=d.file#
order by readtim/phyrds desc
/
```

```
spool off
ttitle off
clear col
```

An example output from the report above is shown below.

```
Date: 02/02/04
Page:   1
Time: 08:59 AM                              IO Timing Analysis
PERFSTAT
                                                 tstdb database

Instance FILE# File Name                                 PHYRDS PHYWRTS READTIM/PHYRDS
WRITETIM/PHYWRTS
-------- ----- ----------------------------------------  ------- ------- -------------- --
       2    10 /od04_01/oradata/tstdb/tstdb_global01.dbf     592      11           21.8
0
       1    10 /od04_01/oradata/tstdb/tstdb_global01.dbf     632      21           20.4
0
       2    23 /od04_02/oradata/tstdb/LWEd01.dbf          100027    4023           5.94
.177479493
       1    17 /od04_01/oradata/tstdb/SRCd01.dbf           77626       6           3.61
0
       2    24 /od04_02/oradata/tstdb/LWEx01.dbf            1801     341           1.61
.263929619
       3    10 /od04_01/oradata/tstdb/tstdb_global01.dbf  299320    6370           1.58
.195918367
       3    23 /od04_02/oradata/tstdb/LWEd01.dbf          294166   31246           1.44
1.53120399
       1    18 /od04_01/oradata/tstdb/SRCx01.dbf            1879       6           1.43
0
       3    24 /od04_02/oradata/tstdb/LWEx01.dbf          196574   35080           1.30
1.57374572
       2    17 /od04_01/oradata/tstdb/SRCd01.dbf           58099      61           1.16
0
       3     1 /od04_01/oradata/tstdb/system01.dbf        688550    2071           1.10
.125060357
       3    18 /od04_01/oradata/tstdb/SRCx01.dbf          186020       4           1.09
0
       3    17 /od04_01/oradata/tstdb/SRCd01.dbf          504230      36           1.06
1.02777778
       1    24 /od04_02/oradata/tstdb/LWEx01.dbf               8       6           .875
.333333333
       1    11 /od04_01/oradata/tstdb/tstdb_globalx01.dbf     45      10     .755555556
0
       1    23 /od04_02/oradata/tstdb/LWEd01.dbf              79      17     .683544304
.529411765
       3     7 /od04_01/oradata/tstdb/undotbs03.dbf           60   15243     .583333333
.460145641
       1     2 /od04_01/oradata/tstdb/undotbs01.dbf           29    2453     .551724138
.043212393
       2     6 /od04_01/oradata/tstdb/undotbs02.dbf           33    2501     .515151515
.019992003
       2    11 /od04_01/oradata/tstdb/tstdb_globalx01.dbf     65      12     .461538462
0
       1     7 /od04_01/oradata/tstdb/undotbs03.dbf            7       6     .428571429
0
       1    16 /od04_01/oradata/tstdb/TA1x01.dbf               7       6     .428571429
0
       1     1 /od04_01/oradata/tstdb/system01.dbf          1416     248     .399717514
.008064516
       2     1 /od04_01/oradata/tstdb/system01.dbf          2357     366     .391599491
.013661202
       2    25 /od04_01/oradata/tstdb/perfstat01.dbf         198       6     .328282828
0
       3     5 /od04_01/oradata/tstdb/tools01.dbf            174       8     .293103448
0
       1     6 /od04_01/oradata/tstdb/undotbs02.dbf            7       6     .285714286
0
       1    15 /od04_01/oradata/tstdb/TA1d01.dbf               7       6     .285714286
0
```

```
         1     13 /od04_01/oradata/tstdb/tstdb_reportx01.dbf       7         6       .285714286
0
         3      4 /od04_01/oradata/tstdb/indx01.dbf                7         4       .285714286
0
         2      5 /od04_01/oradata/tstdb/tools01.dbf               7         6       .285714286
0
         2      3 /od04_01/oradata/tstdb/drsys01.dbf               7         6       .285714286
0
         1     20 /od04_01/oradata/tstdb/REEx01.dbf                7         6       .285714286
0
         3      6 /od04_01/oradata/tstdb/undotbs02.dbf             5        18               .2
0
         3      8 /od04_01/oradata/tstdb/users01.dbf            6731         4       .199227455
0
         3     14 /od04_01/oradata/tstdb/nomadd01.dbf          24614       192       .188835622
.588541667
         3     25 /od04_01/oradata/tstdb/perfstat01.dbf        56010         4       .185841814
0
         3      3 /od04_01/oradata/tstdb/drsys01.dbf           51063         4       .181422948
0
         2     18 /od04_01/oradata/tstdb/SRCx01.dbf             3562         6       .179955081
0
         3     11 /od04_01/oradata/tstdb/tstdb_globalx01.dbf  468503        81       .179932679
.074074074
         3      2 /od04_01/oradata/tstdb/undotbs01.dbf             6        10       .166666667
0
         3      9 /od04_01/oradata/tstdb/xdb01.dbf            475840         4       .147650471
0
         1      4 /od04_01/oradata/tstdb/indx01.dbf                7         6       .142857143
0
         1      9 /od04_01/oradata/tstdb/xdb01.dbf                 7         6       .142857143
0
         1     14 /od04_01/oradata/tstdb/nomadd01.dbf              7         6       .142857143
0
         1     12 /od04_01/oradata/tstdb/tstdb_reportd01.dbf       7         6       .142857143
0
         1     21 /od04_01/oradata/tstdb/CRWd01.dbf                7         6       .142857143
0
         2      4 /od04_01/oradata/tstdb/indx01.dbf                7         6       .142857143
0
         3     22 /od04_01/oradata/tstdb/CRWx01.dbf                7         4       .142857143
0
         2     21 /od04_01/oradata/tstdb/CRWd01.dbf                7         6       .142857143
0
         2     20 /od04_01/oradata/tstdb/REEx01.dbf                7         6       .142857143
0
         2     15 /od04_01/oradata/tstdb/TA1d01.dbf                7         6       .142857143
0
         2     12 /od04_01/oradata/tstdb/tstdb_reportd01.dbf       7         6       .142857143
0
         2      9 /od04_01/oradata/tstdb/xdb01.dbf                 7         6       .142857143
0
         2      8 /od04_01/oradata/tstdb/users01.dbf               7         6       .142857143
0
         2      2 /od04_01/oradata/tstdb/undotbs01.dbf             7         6       .142857143
0
         1     25 /od04_01/oradata/tstdb/perfstat01.dbf            7         6       .142857143
0
         3     19 /od04_01/oradata/tstdb/REEd01.dbf           109796         4       .133611425
0
         3     15 /od04_01/oradata/tstdb/TA1d01.dbf            40327         4       .132839041
0
         3     20 /od04_01/oradata/tstdb/REEx01.dbf           333992         4       .121095715
0
         3     16 /od04_01/oradata/tstdb/TA1x01.dbf           103495         4       .120218368
0
```

At this point, it is still important to look for unbalanced timings between the instances.

The final example will look at system events. The following code shows the report script.

```
col event format a30 heading 'Event Name'
col waits format 999,999,999 heading 'Total|Waits'
col average_wait format 999,999,999 heading 'Average|Waits'
col time_waited format 999,999,999 heading 'Time Waited'
col total_time new_value divide_by noprint
col value new_value val noprint
col percent format 999.990 heading 'Percent|Of|Non-Idle Waits'
col duration new_value millisec noprint
col p_of_total heading 'Percent|of Total|Uptime' format 999.9999
set lines 132 feedback off verify off pages 50
 select to_number(sysdate-startup_time)*86400*1000 duration from
v$instance;
select
sum(time_waited) total_time
from gv$system_event
where total_waits-total_timeouts>0
     and event not like 'SQL*Net%'
     and event not like 'smon%'
     and event not like 'pmon%'
     and event not like 'rdbms%'
         and event not like 'PX%'
         and event not like 'sbt%'
         and event not in ('gcs remote message','ges remote message',
                           'virtual circuit status','dispatcher
timer') ;
select max(value) value from gv$sysstat where name ='CPU used when
call started';
@title132 'RAC System Events Percent'
break on report
compute sum of time_waited on report
spool rep_out/&db/rac_sys_events
select    inst_id,
          name event,
          0 waits,
   0 average_wait,
   value time_waited,
   value/(&&divide_by+&&val)*100 Percent,
   value/&&millisec*100 p_of_total
from gv$sysstat
where name ='CPU used when call started'
union
select inst_id,
       event,
       total_waits-total_timeouts waits,
       time_waited/(total_waits-total_timeouts) average_wait,
       time_waited,
       time_waited/(&&divide_by+&&val)*100 Percent,
       time_waited/&&millisec*100 P_of_total
from gv$system_event
where total_waits-total_timeouts>0
     and event not like 'SQL*Net%'
     and event not like 'smon%'
```

```
    and event not like 'pmon%'
    and event not like 'rdbms%'
        and event not like 'PX%'
        and event not like 'sbt%'
        and event not in ('gcs remote message','ges remote message',
                          'virtual circuit status','dispatcher
timer')
        and time_waited>0
order by inst_id,percent desc
/
spool off
clear columns
ttitle off
clear computes
clear breaks
```

Example results from the script above are shown below.

```
Date: 02/02/04
Page:   1
Time: 01:51 PM                    RAC System Events Percent
TSTDBMRA
                                          tstdb database


Percent   Percent
                                           Total      Average
Of  of Total
   INST_ID Event Name                      Waits        Waits  Time Waited Non-Idle
Waits    Uptime
---------- ----------------------------- ------------ ------------ ------------ ----------
---- ---------
         1 io done                        222,168            2      532,399
7.930     .1285
         1 CPU used when call started           0            0      360,648
5.372     .0870
         1 imm op                             168        1,812      304,377
4.533     .0735
         1 control file parallel write    134,810            1      160,829
2.395     .0388
         1 control file sequential read   748,737            0      106,655
1.589     .0257
         1 i/o slave wait                 377,955            0       99,104
1.476     .0239
         1 enqueue                        574,470            0       56,854
.847      .0137
         1 IPC send completion sync         6,328            7       44,580
.664      .0108
         1 wait for master scn            272,879            0       25,184
.375      .0061
         1 DFS lock handle                 65,619            0       18,470
.275      .0045
         1 library cache pin                2,027            8       16,750
.249      .0040
         1 db file sequential read         56,356            0       10,377
.155      .0025
         1 name-service call wait             190           49        9,280
.138      .0022
         1 direct path read               119,524            0        9,210
.137      .0022
         1 log file parallel write         68,692            0        7,989
.119      .0019
         1 global cache cr request         71,664            0        7,130
.106      .0017
         1 process startup                    145           35        5,112
.076      .0012
```

```
        1 async disk IO                     497,496          0        3,636
.054    .0009
        1 db file scattered read              3,749          0        1,738
.026    .0004
        1 switch logfile command                 17         82        1,399
.021    .0003
        2 CPU used when call started              0          0      625,945
9.323    .1511
        2 control file parallel write       134,052          1      155,664
2.318    .0376
        2 enqueue                         1,146,971          0      149,334
2.224    .0360
        2 control file sequential read      736,589          0       89,883
1.339    .0217
        2 wait for master scn               274,211          0       24,081
.359    .0058
        2 global cache cr request           308,585          0       21,361
.318    .0052
        2 DFS lock handle                    70,138          0       16,284
.243    .0039
        2 db file sequential read            78,344          0       16,000
.238    .0039
        2 log file parallel write            70,637          0        9,560
.142    .0023
        2 db file scattered read             50,454          0        8,247
.123    .0020
        2 IPC send completion sync           59,587          0        5,567
.083    .0013
        2 name-service call wait                 97         53        5,116
.076    .0012
        2 direct path read                   67,032          0        4,462
.066    .0011
        2 process startup                        68         43        2,904
.043    .0007
        2 CGS wait for IPC msg                4,344          0        1,632
.024    .0004
        2 library cache pin                   3,939          0        1,384
.021    .0003
        2 db file parallel read               3,664          0          789
.012    .0002
        2 log file sequential read               71         11          757
.011    .0002
        2 row cache lock                      8,193          0          649
.010    .0002
        3 CPU used when call started              0          0    3,171,613
47.238   .7655
        3 db file sequential read         3,838,010          0      571,051
8.505    .1378
        3 global cache cr request         2,670,668          0      388,165
5.781    .0937
        3 control file parallel write       134,107          1      177,376
2.642    .0428
        3 library cache pin                  11,677         12      142,391
2.121    .0344
        3 control file sequential read      979,741          0      122,439
1.824    .0296
        3 IPC send completion sync            2,378         20       47,029
.700    .0114
        3 db file scattered read            123,285          0       27,301
.407    .0066
        3 global cache busy                     257        105       27,044
.403    .0065
        3 direct path read                  135,560          0       23,154
.345    .0056
        3 DFS lock handle                    75,839          0       18,137
.270    .0044
        3 name-service call wait                197         49        9,683
.144    .0023
        3 log file parallel write            84,689          0        9,356
.139    .0023
        3 latch free                          1,983          4        7,881
.117    .0019
        3 process startup                       127         48        6,037
.090    .0015
        3 global cache s to x                26,158          0        3,521
.052    .0008
```

```
          3 global cache open x                          20,776           0          3,452
.051      .0008
          3 row cache lock                               28,131           0          2,916
.043      .0007
          3 log file sequential read                        654           4          2,541
.038      .0006
          3 pipe get                                        125          19          2,420
.036      .0006
                                                                              ------------
sum                                                                              7,700,701
```

The above example has been reduced to 20 events per node to make displaying the report easier. Node three is using more CPU cycles than the other nodes and is also using more *db file reads* and more *global cache cr request* waits. At this point, node three should be reviewed for bad SQL.

Conclusion

Quite a bit of territory has been covered on RAC tuning in this chapter. The following are a few general guidelines:

- The cluster interconnect network should be tuned to get an optimal transfer rate and buffering.
- RAC objects should be tuned for:
  - *initrans.*
  - Freelists.
  - Rows per block (pctfree).
- Freelists and *init_trans* should be used whenever possible.
- Larger shared pools should be used rather than those used with normal Oracle, to allow for the Global Directory.
- Cache transfer speeds and intra-instance pings should be monitored to determine latencies.
- Holistic monitoring should be performed at all times

Using these guidelines, and the scripts and techniques covered in this chapter, the RAC environment can be made to perform optimally.

References

Oracle Real Application Clusters Administrator's Guide 10g, Release 1 (10.1), Part No. B10765-01, December 2003

Oracle Real Application Clusters Deployment and Performance Guide 10g, Release 1 (10.1), Part No. B10768-01, December 2003

RAC Migration Topics

CHAPTER 15

This chapter will cover migration related topics such as the conversion to RAC from a single instance database and configuring virtual IPs for RAC environments, which are required for Oracle10g.

Migration to RAC Databases

In this section, we discuss the procedure to migrate from a standalone non-RAC database to a RAC database with multiple instances. There are many special requirements to migrate the current non-RAC database to a RAC database. We will examine these requirements and also discuss the appropriate environmental changes.

When is RAC Not a Migration Option?

Conversion to RAC may not benefit the system if:

- A supported configuration of a cluster file system or shared disks is not in use. This can be determined via the Metalink site.
- The application was specifically designed to not use cluster database processing. For example, if it was designed to always use a majority of data for all users.

What Will Be Covered in this Chapter?

Various combinations like migrating from a lower version of Oracle to Oracle 10g and then to a RAC environment will be covered. In addition, in place migration where existing standalone Oracle Database 10g infrastructure is upgraded to a certified cluster environment will be included as has creating a new cluster environment and moving the data while converting from HA cluster environment to a RAC parallel database environment.

RAC Migration Overview

With the advances in RAC technology in Oracle 10g RAC cluster databases utilizing Grid technology, there is increased interest among many Oracle database customers in using the new features and converting their existing Oracle database to an Oracle RAC database. The current standalone database may be in one of any number of conditions. For example, the database may be in 10g stand-alone, it may be in the 9i version, or it might even still be in lower releases. At the same time, the server environment may not be from the Oracle certified hardware list. Based on these various factors, the DBA needs to develop an appropriate migration plan.

From an application point of view, there may be certain additional requirements and modifications needed to access the RAC database. Once the database is migrated to a RAC database, the client applications can either use load balancing via Oracle*Net configurations or access a specific database instance of the RAC database. In case of packaged applications that with this upgrade will just begin accessing the RAC database, appropriate configuration changes have to be performed. For example, in the Oracle eBusiness suite, cookies have to be set up in order to use RAC. In the SAP infrastructure, it may be necessary to replace the SAP software library, *dboraslib*,' with the latest RAC supported version.

Migration Methodology

There are many types of migration paths. Figure 15.1 shows the two main paths.

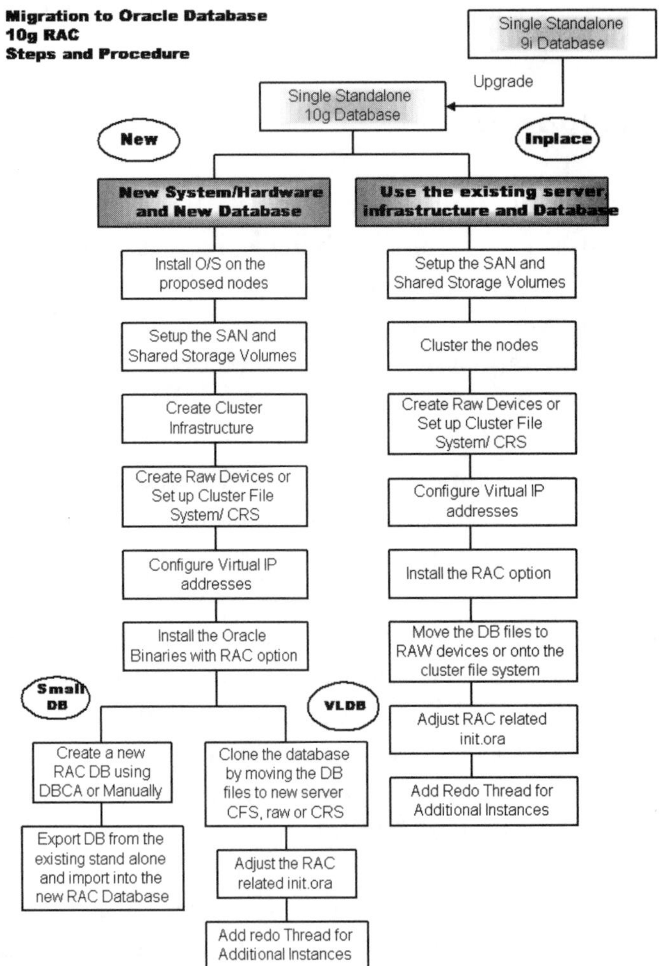

Figure 15.1: *Main procedures to migrate to Oracle Database 10g RAC*

The first procedure involves the use of the existing hardware infrastructure. To use existing hardware, additional servers nodes would be added to the environment and form the cluster. Obviously the availability of Shared Storage is an important piece of the RAC architecture, since without it utilization of RAC is not possible.

Requirements for Conversion

The system must meet the following hardware and software requirements to convert to RAC:

- Be able to run a cluster file system
- Have the required additional license(s) for Oracle Database 10g Enterprise Edition with RAC.
- Have at least two network interface cards of at least 100 mbit/sec, the preference is a Gigabyte or better, communication speed. One for the public and virtual private interface and the other for the RAC cluster interconnect.
- Have shared disk storage

The conversion from a single instance to clustered configuration will be covered first.

Conversion from Single Instance to Cluster-Enabled System Administrative Concerns

Before beginning the conversion to RAC, the following administrative considerations should be addressed:

- Make sure there are adequate backup procedures before converting from a single instance Oracle database to RAC. This may involve the use of RMAN, transportable tablespaces or the RMAN CONVERT utility.

- The additional archiving considerations that apply in RAC environments must be considered. For example, the archive file format requires a thread number. This is done automatically for DBCA created RAC instances. In addition, the archived logs from all instances of a RAC database are required for media recovery. This means that if information is archived to a file and a cluster file system is not in used, a method of accessing the archive logs from all nodes on which the cluster database has instances, such as NFS, is required where file systems are not shared.

All right, the following section provides more information on the actual conversion procedure from single instance to RAC on Oracle Database 10g.

Converting from Single Instance to 10g RAC

It is strongly recommended that the Database Configuration Assistant (DBCA) be used to convert from single instance Oracle to 10g RAC. Oracle has added many new features such as CRS, Virtual IP management, and GRID control which can make the conversion difficult. Use of the DBCA utility provides the following benefits:

- Automation of the configuration of the control file attributes
- Creation of the needed undo tablespaces and the redo logs
- Makes the initialization parameter file entries for cluster-enabled environments.
- Configuration of the Oracle Net Services
- Configuration of the Cluster Ready Services (CRS) resources
- Configuration of the EM (Grid control) and SRVCTL to allow for RAC database management

This section will describe the following procedures:

- Conversion of a single instance on a Non-Clustered system to Oracle Database 10g with RAC
- Conversion of a single instance on a Cluster to Oracle Database 10g RAC

Single Instance on a Non-Clustered System to Oracle Database 10g with RAC

Conversion from a single instance, non-clustered database to a clustered RAC system involves the following procedures, performed in the order given:

- Backup the original single instance database.
- Perform the required pre-installation steps
- Set up the cluster environment
- Copy the preconfigured database image into the cluster
- Install the Oracle Database 10g RAC software

The following sections will detail each of these procedures.

Duplication of the Original Single Instance Database

The Database Configuration Assistant (DBCA) should be used to create a preconfigured image of the single instance database. This is accomplished by invoking the DBCA from the bin directory under *oracle_home* and following the menu path as follows: Welcome Manage Templates → Create a database template [select From an existing database (structure as well as data)] → Database Name [select the database name] → Template Name [enter template name, use database name as the default, and description and template datafile location] → Finish.

The DBCA will then generate two files:

- The database structure file (*template_name.dbc*)
- The database preconfigured image file (*template_name.dfb*)

By default, these files are generated on UNIX in the *oracle_home/assistants/dbca/templates* directory and in the *%oracle_home%\assistants\dbca\templates* directory on Windows - based systems.

Perform the Pre-Installation Steps

The pre-installation steps as documented in *Software Installation, Database Creation and Configuration,* in a previous chapter of this book should be followed. For example, on UNIX-based systems, this includes creating the Oracle user account and the DBA group on all nodes, setting up oracle user equivalence with *rsh* and *rlogin* using *rhost* and *hosts.equiv* files, set the *dbca_raw_config* environment variable, if raw files are used, and so on. Shared storage can then be set up by referring to the *Preparing Shared Storage* section in an earlier chapter of this book.

Vendor manuals should be used to setup the shared disk array, RAID, and other shared disk requirements.

Setting Up the Cluster

If vendor supplied clusterware is in use, the vendor's documentation on how to form a cluster with the required number of nodes should be followed. Once all of the nodes in the cluster have been configured, either with or without vendor clusterware, CRS must be installed by referring to the procedures in *Software Installation, Database Creation and Configuration*, from an earlier chapter in this book. This process depend on the operating system.

Move the Preconfigured Database Image to the Install Target

This involves copying the database structure file and the database preconfigured image file that was created with the DBCA in the previous section. The database structure file is copied to a holding location on the node in the cluster from which the DBCA will run to create the RAC database physical files.

Install the Oracle Database 10g RAC Software

The following procedure is followed to install the RAC software:

1. Run the Oracle Universal Installer (OUI) to perform an Oracle installation for the Oracle 10g Database software with RAC. If the CRS has not been installed, the RAC option will not be available

2. Select Cluster Installation Mode on the Specify Hardware Cluster Installation page of the Oracle Universal Installer (OUI) and select the nodes to utilize for the RAC database.

3. On the OUI Database Configuration Types page, select Advanced install. After installation of the Oracle software, the OUI automatically runs the post installation configuration tools such as the Network Configuration Assistant (NetCA) and the DBCA.

4. From the DBCA Template Selection screen, select the template that was copied to the temporary location in the previous section. Utilize the browse option to select the temporary location where the template files are located.

5. If raw storage is to be utilized, then on the DBCA File Locations Tab on the Initialization Parameters page, if the *dbca_raw_config* environment variable has not been set up, replace the data files, control files, log files and so on, with

the corresponding raw device files. Replace default database files with raw devices on the Storage page as well.

6. Once the RAC database is created, the DBCA utility displays the Password Management page. Use this page to change the passwords for privileged database users who have the SYSDBA and SYSOPER roles. Once the DBCA finishes, the conversion process is complete.

This method works because the template creation makes a compressed copy of the database datafiles. Transactions on the source database should not be allowed at this point or the RAC instances will not be in sync.

Creating a Single Instance on a Cluster to Oracle Database 10g RAC

There are three possible scenarios where a single instance database can exist on a cluster machine, they are:

- The Oracle home where the database is running is cluster installed.
- The Oracle home where the database is running is cluster installed, but the RAC feature is disabled.
- The Oracle home where the database is running is not cluster installed.

If the above situations exist, the following sections should be used to convert the single instance database on a clustered machine into a RAC instance for all three of these scenarios.

The Instance Is On a Cluster and Running From a Cluster Enabled Oracle Home

The next procedure is used for conversion of a single instance database on a cluster running from a cluster installed Oracle home into a RAC enabled instance.

1. Use the DBCA to create a preconfigured image of the single instance database as was previously documented and shut down the single instance database.
2. To add other nodes to the cluster, add and connect these nodes to the cluster as described earlier. Verify that all of the nodes added to the cluster can access the shared storage.

To verify that the installation is configured correctly, perform the following steps:

1. Verify that the new cluster nodes can access the private interconnect. The interconnects must be properly configured before these procedures can be completed.
2. When a cluster file system is not used, determine the location where the cluster software was installed on the existing nodes. Verify that there is at least 250MB of free space on the same location on each of the new nodes in which to install the Cluster Ready Services software. In addition, make sure there is enough free space, about two Gigabytes, on each new node to install the Oracle binaries.
3. Ensure that user equivalence is established on the new nodes by executing the following platform-specific commands:
   - For UNIX/Linux-based systems: Verify user equivalence to and from an existing node to the new nodes using *rsh* or *ssh*. Verify it in both directions.
   - For Windows-based systems: Make sure that the following command can be executed from each of the existing

nodes of the cluster where the *host_name* specified is the public network name of the new node:

```
NET USE \\host_name\C$
```

If the proper administrative privileges on each node are set, the operating system responds with:

```
Command completed successfully.
```

After the above procedures are complete, the new nodes are connected to the cluster and configured with the required software to make them visible to the clusterware. The new nodes are configured as members of the cluster by extending the cluster software to the new nodes as described next.

Extending Clusterware and Oracle Software to New Nodes

The next sections describe how to add new nodes to the clusterware and to the Oracle database software layers. The topics covered will be:

- Adding Nodes at the Vendor Clusterware Layer in UNIX
- Adding Nodes at the Oracle Clusterware Layer in UNIX and Windows

Adding Nodes at the Vendor Clusterware Layer in UNIX/Linux

In UNIX/Linux-based systems using non-Oracle supplied clusterware, new nodes are added at the clusterware layer by using the vendor supplied clusterware documentation. When systems use shared storage for the CRS home, it is important to make sure that the existing clusterware is accessible by the new nodes. Test that prove that the new nodes can be brought online as part of the existing cluster should be conducted. The next section will cover adding the nodes at the clusterware layer.

All platforms require the following steps. The OUI requires access to the private interconnect which has already been verified:

1. Using one of the existing nodes, go to the *<CRS home>/OUI/bin* directory on UNIX/Linux-based systems or to the *<CRS home>\oui\bin* directory on Windows-based systems. The *addnode* script, which is *addNode.sh* on UNIX/Linux and *addNode.bat* on Windows, is used to start the OUI.

2. The OUI is started in the add node mode and the OUI Welcome screen appears. Click on the Next button, and the Specify Cluster Nodes for Node Addition screen will appear.

3. On the Specify Cluster Nodes for Node Addition screen, the upper table shows the existing nodes associated with the CRS home from which the OUI was launched, and the lower table is used to enter the public and private node names of the new nodes.

4. When vendor supplied clusterware is used, the public node names automatically appear in the lower table. Click Next and the OUI verifies connectivity on the existing nodes and on the new nodes. The verifications performed by the OUI include:

   - That the nodes are up
   - That the nodes are accessible by way of the network
   - That the user has WRITE permission to create the CRS home on the new nodes
   - That the user has write permission to the OUI inventory in the *oraInventory* directory on UNIX/Linux or *Inventory* directory on Windows

5. When the OUI detects that the new nodes do not have an inventory location:
   - On UNIX/Linux platforms, the OUI displays a dialog asking the user to run the *oraInstRoot.sh* script on the new nodes
   - On Windows platforms, the OUI automatically updates the inventory location in the proper Registry key with no special script required.

When any verifications fail, the OUI will re-display the Specify Cluster Nodes for Node Addition screen with the Status column in both upper and lower tables indicating the errors that occurred. The errors should be corrected or if correction is not possible, deselect the nodes that have errors and proceed. However, if the errors are on existing nodes, they cannot be deselected; the errors must be corrected if nodes are already part of the CRS cluster before node addition can proceed. When all the checks succeed, the OUI Node Addition Summary screen will be displayed.

It is a good practice to install CRS on every node in the cluster that has vendor clusterware installed. The Node Addition Summary screen displays information about the products that are installed in the CRS home that is being extending to the new nodes. The information shown is:

- The source directory for the add node process, which should be the CRS home.
- The private node names or interconnects that were entered for the new nodes.
- The new nodes that where entered.
- The required space and the available space on the new nodes.
- The installed products listing the products that are installed in the existing CRS home.

If everything is satisfactory, click Next and the OUI displays the Cluster Node Addition Progress screen.

The purpose of the Cluster Node Addition Progress screen is to show the status of the cluster node addition process. The table shown on this screen displays two columns showing the phase of the node addition process and the phase's status according to the following platform specific content:

For UNIX/Linux-based systems this screen shows four OUI phases:

- Instantiate Root Scripts: This phase instantiates *rootaddnode.sh* with the public and private node names that were entered on the Cluster Node Addition page.
- Copy the CRS Home to the New Nodes: This phase copies the CRS home to the new nodes unless this is not required because the CRS home is on a cluster file system.
- Run *rootaddnode.sh* and *root.sh:* This phase displays a dialog prompting the DBA to run *rootaddnode.sh* on the local node from which the OUI is running. The system then prompts the DBA to run *root.sh* on the new nodes.
- Save Cluster Inventory:This phase updates the node list associated with the CRS home and its inventory.

For Windows-based systems, this screen shows only three OUI phases:

- Copy CRS Home to New Nodes: Copies the CRS home to the new nodes unless this is not required because the CRS home is on the Oracle Cluster File System.
- Performs Oracle Home Setup: Updating the Registry entries for the new nodes, creating the services, and creating folder entries.

- Save Cluster Inventory: Updates the node list associated with the CRS home and its inventory.

For all platforms, the Cluster Node Addition Progress page's Status column displays one of three possible modes:

- IN PROGRESS: while the phase is in progress
- SUSPENDED: when the phase is pending execution,
- SUCCEEDED: after the phase completes.

Once completion is reached, click Exit to end the OUI session. After the OUI displays the End of Node Addition screen, click on Exit to end the OUI session.

Adding Nodes at the Oracle Clusterware Layer in UNIX/Linux and Windows

1. For Windows-based systems, the command line (Start → run → cmd) uses the following command to determine the node names and node numbers that are currently in use:

```
<CRS home>\bin\olsnodes- n
```

2. Next, the *crssetup.exe* command is used with the next available node names and node numbers to add the CRS data for the new nodes. The following syntax is used for *crssetup.exe* where *n* is the first new node number, *<noden>* through *<noden+i>* is a list of the nodes that are being added, *<nodei-number>* through *<noden+i-number>* represent the node numbers assigned to the new nodes where the number is the last node assigned prior to the crssetup.exe execution, and *<pnn>* through *<pnn+i>* is the list of private networks for the new nodes:

```
<CRS home>\bin\crssetup.exe
-nn <noden>,<noden-number>,<noden+1>,<noden+1-
number>,...<noden+i>,<noden+i-number>
-pn <pnn>,<noden-number>,<pnn+1>,<noden+1-
number>,...<pnoden+i>,<noden+i-number>
```

3. The values entered are the private network names or IP addresses that were entered in the above procedure in the Specify Cluster Nodes for Node Addition screen. For example:

```
crssetup.exe -nn node4,4,node5,5 -pn node4_pvt,4,node5_pvt,5
```

4. On Windows, UNIX and Linux platforms, execute the *racgons* utility from the bin subdirectory of the CRS home to configure the Oracle Notification Services (ONS) port number as follows:

```
racgons <noden>:4948 <noden+1>:4948 ... <noden+i>:4948
```

Once the nodes have been added at the Oracle clusterware layer, the CRS home has been successfully extended from the existing CRS home to the new nodes.

Transferring *oracle_home* to Other Nodes

To add nodes to the Oracle RAC database later, the existing *oracle_home* will have to be transferred. To do this, the OUI should be run in ADD NODE mode to configure the new nodes. If there are multiple Oracle homes and the DBA wants to add them to the other nodes, the following steps should be performed for each Oracle home to which the new nodes should be transferred:

1. On the existing main node, from the *$oracle_home/oui/bin* directory on UNIX-based systems, *%oracle_home%\OUI\bin* on Windows run either the *addNode.sh* or *addnode.bat* script. This starts OUI in the add node mode, which displays the OUI Welcome screen.

2. Using the mouse click the Next button on the Welcome screen and the OUI displays the Specify Cluster Nodes for Node Addition screen.

3. From the Specify Cluster Nodes for Node Addition screen, use the top table showing the existing nodes associated with the Oracle home from which the OUI was launched to determine existing nodes. At the bottom of the page, there is a node selection table showing the nodes that are available for addition. Using the mouse, select the nodes to be added and then click on the Next button.

4. The OUI now verifies proper connectivity and performs availability checks on both the existing nodes and on the nodes to be added. The following list are examples of what items are verified:

   - The nodes are active
   - The nodes are network enabled
   - The installing user has the proper permissions to create the Oracle home on the new nodes
   - The installing user has write permission to the OUI inventory in the *oraInventory* directory on UNIX or the *Inventory* directory on Windows on the existing nodes and on the new nodes

5. When the new nodes do not have an inventory set up, depending on the system, one of the following will occur:

   - For UNIX-based systems, the OUI displays a dialog asking that the *oraInstRoot.sh* script be run on the new nodes.
   - For Windows-based systems, the Registry is automatically updated with the inventory location by the OUI

   If any of the other checks fail, the node that has the error should be deselected or the error fixed in order to proceed. Nodes that are already a part of the cluster cannot be deselected. The problems on the existing nodes must be corrected before proceeding with node addition. Once all of the checks are successful, the OUI displays the Node Addition Summary screen.

The following information about the products that are installed in the Oracle home that are going to extend to the new nodes is listed on the Node Addition Summary screen:

- The Oracle home that is the source for the add node process
- The existing node and new node information
- The new nodes that have been selected
- For new nodes, the required and available space
- The listing of all the products that are already installed in the existing Oracle home

6. Click the Finish button, and the OUI will display the Cluster Node Addition Progress screen.

   The status of the cluster node addition process is shown on the Cluster Node Addition Progress screen. The table on this page shows two columns profiling the addition phases:

   - The node addition phase progress
   - The phase's status according to the following platform-specific content:

   On Linux or UNIX-based systems, the Cluster Node Addition Progress page shows four distinct OUI phases:

   - Instantiation of the Root Scripts: This phase instantiates the *root.sh* script in the new Oracle home by copying it from the local node
   - Copying of the Oracle Home to the New Nodes: This phase copies the rest of the entire Oracle home from the source node to the new nodes, unless the Oracle home is on a cluster file system

- Running of the *root.sh*: Displays the dialog about running the *root.sh* script from the root user on the new nodes
- Saving of the Cluster Inventory: Update of the node list associated with the Oracle home and its inventory

While on Windows-based systems, the Cluster Node Addition Progress will show the following three OUI phases:

- Copying of the Oracle Home To New Nodes: Copies the entire Oracle home to the new nodes unless the Oracle home is already on a cluster file system
- Perform the Oracle Home Setup: Update of the Registry entries for the new nodes, creation of the needed services, and creation of the needed folder entries
- Saving Cluster Inventory: The update of the node list associated with the Oracle home and its inventory

For all of the platforms, the Cluster Node Addition Progress screen's Status column displays one of three status messages:

- SUCCEEDED when the phase completes
- IN PROGRESS when the phase is active
- SUSPENDED when the phase is awaiting execution

7. When the OUI displays the End of Node Addition screen, click on the Exit button to end the OUI session.
8. For UNIX/Linux-based systems only, the *root.sh* script will be run next.
9. Next, the *vipca* utility must be run from the bin subdirectory of the Oracle home using the *-nodelist* option identifying the complete set of nodes that are now part of the RAC database beginning with *Node1* and ending with <*NodeN*> using the following syntax:

```
vipca -nodelist Node1,Node2,Node3,...<NodeN>
```

When the private interconnect interface names on the new nodes are not the same as the interconnect names on the existing nodes, the private interconnect must be configured for the new nodes. This is done by executing the Oracle Interface Configuration (OIFCFG) utility with the SETIF option. The OIFCFG executable is run from the bin directory of the hosts Oracle home. The command is executed using the following syntax where <*subnet*> is used the subnet for the private interconnect for the RAC databases to which nodes are added:

```
oifcfg setif <interface-name>/<subnet>:<cluster_interconnect|public>
```

```
For example:
```

```
oifcfg setif eth0/162.178.26.0:cluster_interconnect
```

Once the procedures in the previous section are complete, the new nodes are defined at the cluster database layer. The new database instances can now be added to the new nodes as described next.

Adding Instances to Nodes

The following steps can be followed to add instances to nodes:

1. From any of the newly added and configured nodes, the additional nodes listener processes are configured using the Network Configuration Assistant (NETCA) utility. Choose the same port number and protocol used on the existing nodes. If the NETCA utility shows the existing node on the node list page, there is no need to select this node because it already has a listener configured on it.
2. Once the listeners are up, convert the database to RAC starting up the instances on the other nodes using one of the following procedures:
   - Automated Conversion Procedure

- Manual Conversion Procedure

Automated Conversion Procedure

If a duplicate of the single instance database was created as described in the section *Duplication of the Original Single Instance Database*, the DBCA is used to complete the conversion to a multi-instance RAC database.

1. Start by executing the DBCA utility from the primary or initial node. On the node selection screen, select the names of the nodes that to be included as part of the cluster database. On the Template Selection screen, select the preconfigured template, which is the single instance duplicate, that was created earlier. Enter the database name for the RAC database and respond to the remaining DBCA prompts.
2. Enter the name of the raw device for the SPFILE on the Initialization Parameters screen to use raw devices for the cluster database files. On the Storage page, if a RAW file mapping file has not been specified, the default database file names should be replaced with the raw devices for the control files, redo logs, and datafiles to create the cluster database. Click the Finish button and create the database.
3. Once DBCA completes the conversion to the RAC database, the Password Management screen is displayed. It is a requirement that the passwords for database users who have SYSDBA and SYSOPER roles be changed. Once the conversion process is complete, DBCA will exit.

Manual Conversion Procedure

If DBCA was not used to create a duplicate image of the single instance database, the following steps are performed complete the manual conversion to RAC:

1. For each new node, create an Optimal Flexible Architecture (OFA) directory structure to support the Oracle system. This structure should be the same on all of the nodes.
2. If there is a need to convert the single instance database files from a regular cooked file system to RAW devices, on UNIX/Linux copy the database datafiles, control files, redo logs, and server parameter file into corresponding raw devices using the DD command, or use the OCOPY command on Windows-based systems. If no conversion is required, continue on to the next step.
3. Use the ALTER DATABASE BACKUP CONTROLFILE TO TRACE command to create a control file recreation script in the location specified by the *user_dump_dest* initialization parameter.
4. Edit the control file recreation script with the REUSE keyword, a specification for *maxinstances* with the Oracle suggested setting being 32, *maxlogfiles* and such for a RAC database.
5. Recreate the control files by executing the script as explained in the script header.
6. If the single instance database is using an SPFILE parameter file, a temporary PFILE must be created from the SPFILE using the following SQL statement:

```
CREATE PFILE='pfile_name' from spfile='spfile_name'

(the file names should be full path names)
```

7. Shut down the database instance.
8. Edit the temporary parameter file and set the *cluster_database* parameter to TRUE, and set the *instance_number* parameter to a unique value for each instance, using the *sid.parameter*=value syntax.

9. At this point, the size of the SGA must be adjusted to avoid swapping and paging when converting to RAC. RAC requires around 350 bytes for each buffer to accommodate the Global Cache Service (GCS). Therefore, if there are 15,250 buffers, RAC requires about 350*15,250 bytes or about 5 MB more memory. Change the size of the SGA by changing the *db_cache_size* and *db_nk_cache_size* parameters accordingly.

10. Once the PFILE has been edited, use it to start up the database instance.

11. Once the instance is started, create an undo tablespace for each additional instance using the CREATE UNDO TABLESPACE SQL statement. If RAW devices are in used, then ensure that the datafile for the undo tablespace is on a RAW device.

12. Create a new redo thread that has at least two redo logs for each additional instance. If RAW devices are being used, ensure that the new redo log files are also on RAW devices. Enable the new redo threads by using the ALTER DATABASE SQL statement.

13. Shutdown the database instance using either a shutdown normal or shutdown immediate command.

14. Copy the Oracle password file from the source node to the corresponding location on the additional RAC cluster nodes. Make sure that the *oracle_sid* name is replaced in each password file name appropriately for each additional instance.

15. Edit the PFILE and add the *remote_listener=listeners_db_name* and *sid.local_listener=listener_sid* parameters.

16. Configure the net service entries for the database and instances and address entries for the *local_listener* for each instance and *remote_listener* in the *tnsnames.ora* file and copy it to all nodes.

17. Create an SPFILE from the PFILE using the command:

    ```
    CREATE SPFILE='Spfile_name' from pfile='pfile_name'
    ```

    ```
    (the file names should be full path names)
    ```

18. If a cluster file system is not in use, ensure that the SPFILE is on a RAW device.

19. Create a *$oracle_home/dbs/initsid.ora* file on UNIX-based systems or a *%oracle_home%\database\initsid.ora* file on Windows-based systems that contains the following entry:

    ```
    spfile='spfile_path_name'
    ```

    where *spfile_path_name* is the complete path name of the SPFILE.

20. Add the configuration for the RAC database and its instance-to-node mapping using SRVCTL

21. Start the RAC database using SRVCTL

Once the database has been started with SRVCTL, the conversion process is complete, and the following SQL statement can be used to see the status of all the instances in the converted RAC database:

```
select * from v$active_instances
```

Conversion of a Single Instance on a Cluster Running from a RAC-Disabled Oracle Home

On UNIX/Linux-based systems, where relink of the Oracle executables is possible, having a single instance running from a RAC-disabled Oracle home installation is possible, if improbable, if a one-node cluster with RAC installation was performed but later the RAC feature was disabled by unlinking it from the Oracle binary before creating the single instance database. An alternative method is to select the local, non-cluster option on the Node Selection screen in OUI to create a non-RAC-enabled single instance home on a cluster. The following technique can be used to convert this special type of single instance database into a RAC database:

1. On the cluster node where the single instance database is running, create a duplicate template of the database as described in previous sections using DBCA.
2. Change the working directory to the *lib* subdirectory in the *rdbms* directory under the Oracle home.
3. Relink the Oracle binary through use of the following commands:

```
make -f ins_rdbms.mk rac_on
make -f ins_rdbms.mk ioracle
```

At this point, the normal conversion procedure for a RAC enabled Oracle home can be used.

Conversion of a Single Instance on a Cluster Running from Non-Cluster Installed Oracle Home

This situation is only possible if the Local Installation option was specified on the OUI Specify Hardware Cluster Installation screen during an Oracle Database 10g installation.

To covert this type database to a RAC database, perform the procedures described under these previous sections:

- Duplicate the Original Single instance Database
- Perform the Pre-Installation Steps
- Setting up the Cluster
- Install Oracle Database 10g Software with RAC. In this step, make sure that a new Oracle home other than the one from which the single instance database was running is selected.

Required Post-Conversion Steps

After completing the conversion, the following items should be reviewed as covered in other chapters of this book:

- Use of load balancing and TAF
- Considering the use of locally managed tablespaces instead of dictionary managed tablespaces to reduce contention and manage sequences
- Properly configuring an interconnect for using automatic segment space management and for using SRVCTL to administer multiple instances
- Sizing of database buffer cache and shared pool: Database buffer cache and shared pool capacity requirements in RAC are greater than those in single instance Oracle databases. Therefore, increase the size of the buffer cache by at least 10% and the size of the shared pool by at least 15%.
- If ASM is used for the file systems, use RMAN for backup.

Moving HA Cluster to a RAC Cluster

Many enterprises currently have the High Availability (HA) clusters in their data centers. For example, a system may have a two node VCS based failover cluster. It is an Oracle single instance that is a part of one of the VCS Service groups. This section will briefly examine the issues and procedures involved in moving a HA based Oracle instance to multi-node RAC parallel database.

Procedure to Move the VCS to Veritas DBE/AC RAC

For this section, assume that there is a HA cluster, or so called Failover Cluster, supporting Oracle 9i Standalone Database. The single instance is implemented with VCS cluster framework. This is currently in an Active/Passive configuration.

To take advantage of the multi-node, scalable architecture of the parallel database, which is a 10g RAC, it must be migrated to the Oracle Database 10g RAC using the Veritas DBE/Advance Cluster software.

The following procedure can be used to undertake such migration.

A look at the current environment shows that there are two servers currently supporting a two-node HA cluster. All the Oracle Database Files are already on shared storage volumes. The database files are file system based files. Optionally, they may have been using the Quick I/O facility.

Migration Features

If the necessary hardware in terms of nodes, interconnect, and storage arrays, etc. is already available, the same infrastructure will be used.

9i-RAC implementation with Veritas Advance Cluster requires that the shared storage support the SCSI-3 PR. In this case, it would be important to ensure that the supporting storage array is used.

The utility *vxfentsthdw* can be used to verify that shared storage arrays support SCSI-3 persistent reservations and I/O fencing. The utility can be used to test one disk at a time, a set of disks specified in a file, or a disk group.

For Release 3.5 MP1 of DBE/AC for Oracle9i RAC, disk groups created on shared volumes are not automatically configured with

I/O fencing enabled. To enable I/O fencing, the shared disk group must be deported and then imported.

If the current database files are using the Veritas Quick I/O feature, they should be converted to regular VxFS files before installing VERITAS DBE/AC for Oracle9i RAC, which uses the ODM (Oracle Disk Manager) interface for high performance file access.

Remove the earlier version VCS software and install patches and the new DBE/AC packages. Follow the Veritas documentation to configure the CVM, CFS, and VCS with default service groups. Start the cluster and keep it running.

Ensure that DB files are moved to the CFS based file system. Then, perform the same changes at the database level as explained in the previous section to move DB files into a RAC database. These steps convert the single instance Oracle into a multi-node RAC database.

Packaged Applications

When the Oracle database supporting vendor supplied packaged applications is migrated or converted to a multi-node RAC database, there are specific ways these applications can utilize the features of the RAC database. With the multiple instances providing more scalability and high availability at the database level, the applications need to make use of such features. The following sections will provide a brief look at the discipline followed in an application client environment.

In Case of SAP Applications

The server side and client side configuration changes may include:

Verification Process

Before the database files are transferred to the target system, verify that the Oracle database on the existing system is in the right condition for the upgrade. Specifically for this task, SAP provides two specific SQL scripts to perform some checks in advance of the Oracle Database 10g database upgrade. The scripts are called *checks.sql* and *premig.sql* and they can be found on the first RDBMS CD from SAP for Oracle Database 10g Release 10.1.

Upgrade SAP Software and Tools

For the correct use of transparent application failover, the SAP software library *dboraslib* must be replaced by a new version. This library is located in the directory */usr/sap/<SID>/exe/run* together with all other executables for a specific SAP R/3 system. The new version of the library is compiled using the OCI 8 call interface to access the database, whereas the original version up to SAP R/3 4.6D was compiled and shipped using OCI 7 call semantics.

The new *dboraslib* must be requested from SAP directly. It is not currently part of any shipping CD set for release 4.6D. Additionally, it is not available on SAP´s service market place or through OCS.

The library must be replaced on all SAP R/3 application servers. Additional SAP R/3 application servers outside of the database cluster configuration may possibly use a different operating system.

The Oracle client software for Oracle9i must also be installed on every additional SAP R/3 application server. The Oracle software version used to build the shared library, *dboraslib,* and the installed Oracle client version must match.

BRTOOLS

BRTOOLS is the name for the suite of programs and utilities from SAP to administer the Oracle database perform backup and recovery, as well as many other reorganization tasks.

For an Oracle Database 10g RAC configuration, replace these tools with the latest version shipped by SAP. The latest version is available on SAP´s service market place or through OCS.

Along with all the other executables for a SAP installation, BRTOOLS are located in the directory */usr/sap/<SID>/exe/run.* BRTOOLS consist of the following set of files:

- SAPDBA
- BRCONNECT
- BRRESTORE
- BRBACKUP
- BRARCHIVE

For more details, Oracle white paper *Configuring SAP R3 4.6D for use with Oracle Database 10g RAC* is an excellent reference.

In Case of Oracle eBusiness Suite

When the Oracle Single Instance supporting the Oracle eBusiness suite is converted and migrated to a RAC database, there are certain considerations to take into account so as to better utilize the RAC database. They are as follows:

- **Step-1:** Configure the *tnsnames.ora* file. Change the *tnsnames.ora* files on the middle tier systems, i.e. database clients, to reflect the RAC environment. For a 2-node cluster system, two separate TNS aliases should be defined. The *load_balance* option in the *tnsnames.ora* should not be used as it will result in application errors.

- **Step-2:** Configure Self-Service for RAC: The self-service infrastructure (ICX), by default, uses the database instance name as part of the cookie name if the administrator has not explicitly set the cookie name. In the RAC environment, the database instance name can change based on which instance the users are connected. Hence, the cookie name (*session_cookie_name*) should be explicitly set to a constant value in the *icx_parameters* table. Update the *icx_parameters* table from the Apps schema using the following example.

```
SQL> update ICX_PARAMETERS
set SESSION_COOKIE_NAME='PRODRAC1';
```

  In the example above, the cookie name is set to *prodrac1*.

- **Step-3:** Start up the Application servers: These would include the Forms servers, Report Server, Apache (JServ and Mod PL/SQL), and Concurrent Manager, etc.

- **Step-4:** Application Partitioning: In order to direct a certain class of users to a particular instance in the RAC cluster, the Oracle Applications profile option Database Instance, i.e. *instance_path,* can be used to bind users with a particular responsibility to a particular instance. For example, Purchasing Forms users can be bound to instance A, and Order Management Forms users to instance B using the Database Instance profile option.

Oracle eBusiness lets users specify or define Oracle Application Object Library profiles with a variety of options. Profile Database Instance allows different responsibilities and users to connect to different nodes of the RAC database sever. The internal name for this profile option is *instance_path*.

Configuring Virtual IPs for 10g RAC

In order to install or upgrade to Oracle Database 10g RAC, the use of a virtual IP address to mask the individual IPO addresses of the clustered nodes is required. The virtual IP addresses are used to simplify failover and are automatically managed by CRS.

To create a Virtual IP (VIP) address, the Virtual IP Configuration Assistant (VIPCA) is called from the *root.sh* script of a RAC install, which then configures the virtual IP addresses for each node specified during the installation process. In order to be able to run VIPCA, there must be unused public IP addresses available for each node that has been configured in the */etc/hosts* file.

This means that when installing 10g RAC, at least three network interfaces are required for each node in the RAC cluster, these are:

- Public Interface: Used for normal network communications to the node
- Virtual (Public) Interface: Used for failover and RAC management
- Private Interface: Used as the cluster interconnect

The Oracle 10g RAC installation guide states the following requirements for installing RAC:

- External shared disks.
- One private internet protocol (IP) address for each node to serve as the private cluster interconnect. This IP address must be separate from the public network, and it must have the same interface name on every node that is part of the cluster. This requires its own high speed network interface card (NIC).

- One public IP address for each node to use for its Virtual IP address for client connections and for connection failover. This IP address is in addition to the operating system managed public host IP address that is already assigned to the node by the operating system. This public Virtual IP must be associated with the same interface name on every node that is a part of the cluster. The IP addresses that are used for all of the nodes that are part of a cluster must be from the same subnet. The host names for the VIP addresses must be registered with the domain name server (DNS). The Virtual IP address should not be in use at the time of the installation because this is a Virtual IP address that Oracle manages internally to the RAC processes. This virtual IP address does not require a separate NIC.
- Redundant switches as a standard configuration for all cluster sizes; however, they will not be checked for.

In order to verify that each node meets the network requirements, you should follow these steps:

1. Verify the presence of or install a minimum of two NICs for the public and private networks and configure them with either public or private IP addresses.
2. Use OS utilities to register the host names and IP addresses for the public network interfaces in DNS.
3. For each node in the cluster, register the virtual host name and IP address in DNS.
4. Edit the */etc/hosts file* on UNIX or Linux, and add the private, public, and virtual interfaces.

The following is an example on a two-node Linux system:

```
[aultlinux1]/etc> more /etc/hosts
# Do not remove the following line, or various programs
# that require network functionality will fail.
138.1.137.45    aultlinux1.acme.com   aultlinux1
138.1.137.46    aultlinux2.acme.com   aultlinux2
```

```
192.168.0.10    int-aultlinux1.acme.com       int-aultlinux1
192.168.0.20    int-aultlinux2.acme.com       int-aultlinux2
138.1.137.25    aultlinux1-v.acme.com aultlinux1-v
138.1.137.26    aultlinux2-v.acme.com aultlinux2-v
127.0.0.1       aultlinux1 localhost.localdomain   localhost
```

In this example, the *int-** addresses are private and the **-v* addresses are for the virtual IP's.

To identify the interface name and associated IP address for every network adapter, the following command can be entered:

```
# /sbin/ifconfig -a
...or /usr/bin/netstat -in on HP-UX
...or ipconfig on Windows
```

The virtual IP's do not have to be added to IFCONFIG. This is because the VIPCA takes care of it.

At this point, if everything is properly configured, it should be possible to ping the public IP names from any of the machines on the network. For example:

```
[aultlinux2]/home/oracle>ping aultlinux1
    Pinging aultlinux1.acme.com [138.1.137.45] with 32 bytes
    Reply from 138.1.137.45: bytes=32 time<10ms TTL=255
    Reply from 138.1.137.45: bytes=32 time<10ms TTL=255
```

At this point, it should also be possible to do an NSLOOKUP on the virtual IP names:

```
[aultlinux2]/home/oracle>nslookup aultlinux1-v
```

Once the DBA can ping and do NSLOOKUP on various addresses, the system is ready to install CRS and RAC as long as the shared disks are configured and ready!

At the end of the RAC installation, the user will be prompted to run *root.sh*. When *root.sh* runs, it automatically invokes the

VIPCA. When this happens, the following steps should be followed:

1. The VIPCA welcome page will be displayed first. Review the information on the VIPCA Welcome page. Click Next, and the VIPCA will display the Public Network Interfaces page.

2. On the Public Network Interfaces page, determine the network interface cards (NICs) to which the public VIP addresses should be assigned. Click Next, and the VIPCA will display the IP Address page.

3. On the IP Address page, an unused or unassigned public virtual IP address should be assigned for each node displayed and click Next. The VIPCA will display a Summary page. Review the information on the summary page and click Finish. A progress dialog will appear while the VIPCA configures the virtual IP addresses for the network interfaces that were specified. The VIPCA creates and starts the VIPs, GSD, and the Oracle notification Service (ONS) node applications. When the configuration is complete, click OK and the VIPCA will show the session results. Review the information displayed on the Configuration Results page, and click Exit to exit the VIPCA.

4. Repeat the *root.sh* procedure on all nodes that are part of this installation.

5. The VIPCA will not run again on the remote node because the remote node is already configured.

If the VIP's are not set up correctly, the VIPCA will fail with the error CRS-215 Could not start resource for the VIP resource and any resources that depend on the CRS resource such as GSD and ONS.

After VIPCA has been successfully run, the VIP addresses will be visible in IFCONFIG or NETSTAT-IN on HP-UX. The following is an example of a VIP IFCONFIG output:

```
 eth0:1    Link encap:Ethernet  HWaddr 00:91:26:BD:D6:9E
          inet addr:172.1.137.27  Bcast:172.1.255.255
Mask:255.255.0.0
          UP BROADCAST RUNNING MULTICAST  MTU:1500  Metric:1
          Interrupt:11 Base address:0x9000
```

The information is also available via CRS. Go to the *crs_home/bin* directory or its equivalent on the current system and run the command CRS_STAT. The following is an example of the VIP resource information from CRS_STAT:

```
NAME=ora.aultlinux1.vip
TYPE=application
TARGET=ONLINE
STATE=ONLINE on aultlinux1

NAME=ora.aultlinux2.vip
TYPE=application
TARGET=ONLINE
STATE=ONLINE on aultlinux2
```

This output shows that both of the *aultlinux* cluster VIP's are online and are assigned to their proper nodes. In the event of a failover scenario, one or more VIP's will be moved to another node. This VIP movement is automatically managed by the CRS processes.

When there is a need to change VIP's to a different address, remove the node level applications and recreate them using SRVCTL, for example:

```
srvctl stop nodeapps
srvctl remove nodeapps
srvctl add nodeapps
```

What If There are Issues with VIP

If there are issues with the VIP setup, review the following files or use the following commands:

- IFCONFIG-A for output from each node
- NSLOOKUP <Virtual Host Name> for each virtual host name
- */etc/hosts* file from each node
- output of *$ora_crs_home/bin/crs_stat*
- output of SRVCTL START NODEAPPS -N <node name> on the node having the issue

In light of the information presented in previous sections, review the output of the above files and commands and correct as needed.

Conclusion

This chapter has examined the various migration scenarios. Enterprises have started realizing the scalability and high availability features of a RAC. However, enterprises will have to face the challenge of migrating the existing single instance standalone Oracle database to a multi-node RAC database.

Broadly, there are two ways of migrating. One is converting an existing sever into a cluster node and then adding additional nodes into the clusters. Another approach is to create a new cluster environment by using a new set of servers as cluster nodes. In this case, the data has to be moved either by export/import method or by the database cloning method.

Information was also provided in this chapter on specific application or client related configuration and issues related to the use of the RAC database.

References

White Paper – Oracle Corporation *Migrating your eBusiness Suite Single Instance to Real Application Clusters* – Ahmed Alomari

Oracle white paper *Configuring SAP R3 4.6D for use with Oracle RAC*

Oracle Real Application Clusters Installation and Configuration Guide 10g Release 1 (10.1) for AIX-Based Systems, hp HP-UX PA-RISC (64-bit), hp Tru64 UNIX, Linux, Solaris Operating System (SPARC 64-bit), and Windows (32-bit) Platforms, Part No. B10766-02

Oracle Metalink Note:264847.1, *How to Configure Virtual IPs for 10g RAC*

Oracle RAC and Parallel Processing

CHAPTER 16

This chapter will examine concepts and examples of parallel processing. The Oracle implementation of parallel query and DML execution is designed to provide faster, more efficient query results.

Even though Oracle RAC is a scalable and multi-node parallel database, each node in the cluster has its own multiple processors that act as a parallel processing entity. Each node is typically a SMP server that can parallelize many tasks. The parallel execution process is not exclusive to Oracle Database 10g RAC but is an integral part of the Oracle processing architecture.

Overview

Parallel processing is a vital part of any high performance computing model. It involves the utilization of large amounts of computing resources to complete a complex task or problem. The resources specific to parallel processing are CPU and memory. Originally confined to use in scientific applications, parallel processing has quickly made inroads into commercial and business applications that need high performance computing facilities like data mining, decision support, and risk management applications.

Parallel execution or processing involves the division of a task into several smaller tasks and making the system work on each of these smaller tasks in parallel. In simple terms, if multiple processors engage a computing task, it is generally executed faster. Parallel processing thereby improves response time and increases throughput by utilizing all of the available computing resources. Parallel execution helps systems scale performance by making optimal use of the hardware resources. In a parallel processing system, multiple processes may reside on a single computer or may be spread across several computers or nodes, as in an Oracle10g RAC cluster.

Some basic requirements for achieving parallel execution and better performance are:

- Computer system/servers with built in multiple processors and better message facilitation among processors.
- Operating system capable of managing the multiple processors.
- Clustered nodes with application software, such as Oracle RAC, that can parallel across the nodes.

There are many distinct benefits and advantages of utilizing parallel execution, such as:

- Better response times: As the computing tasks are engaged by a group of processors, the tasks are completed in a smaller amount of time.
- Higher Throughput: Parallel processing results in faster execution of tasks, increasing throughput. A large number of tasks can be performed in a given unit of time.
- Better Price/Performance: It is usually more expensive to make one very fast single CPU instead of using several slower ones.

Types of Parallelism

There are many types of parallelism. Some of the types are as follows:

- **Pipeline Parallelism:** In this type of processing, long sequences of operations, or tasks, are parallel, but there are also overlapping sequential processes during which no parallel tasks are possible. The relational model fits into this model very well. The output of some relational operators becomes the input for other operators; therefore, some waiting time is involved. There is a considerable amount of time saved in the completion of a task through the proper use of pipeline parallelism.
- **Independent or Natural Parallelism:** - In this type of parallelism, the tasks do not depend on other tasks. As a result, total execution time is considerably reduced. Sometimes this type is called "embarrassingly parallel."
- **Inter-query and Intra-query Parallelism:** - Transactions are independent. No transaction requires the output of another transaction to complete. Many CPUs can be kept busy by assigning each task or query to a separate CPU. This type of parallelism, utilizing many separate, independent queries at the same time, is called *inter-query parallelism.* This is a natural solution for OLTP-type operations. Even some small DSS operations work this way. Hence, the greater the number of CPUs available on a database server, the better the performance will be, in most situations. To speed up the execution of a single large and complex query, this model decomposes it into smaller problems. It then executes these smaller tasks concurrently by assigning them separate CPUs. This type of parallelism is a natural solution for DSS-type operations where a single transaction analyzes, computes, and updates thousands of database blocks.

Parallelism in Oracle Relational Database

An Oracle relational database system is designed to take advantage of the parallel architecture. The database is a multi-process system as set up in UNIX systems and is a multi-threaded application in the Windows architecture. In general, the databases are accessed by a large number of concurrent users or connections. Many of these users, with their own data and instructions, take advantage of the multi-processor availability to perform database processing. Also, a single user task, such as a SQL query, can be paralleled to achieve higher speed and throughput by using multiple processors.

The relational model consists of structured tables with rows and columns. Usually, the SQL query aims at extracting or updating target data, which is a set of rows and columns based on a given condition. Typically, any SQL database operation gets divided into multiple database sub-operations such as SELECTION, JOIN, GROUP, SORT, PROJECTION, etc. Thus, the sub-operations become excellent candidates for simultaneous or parallel execution. This makes the RDBMS system ideal for the implementation of parallel processing software.

Databases have a component called the query optimizer that selects a sequence of inputs, joins, and scans to produce the desired output table or data set. The query optimizer is aware of the underlying hardware architecture and finds a suitable parallel execution path. Hence, from the database perspective, parallel execution is useful for many types of operations that access significant amounts of data.

Generally, parallel execution improves performance for:

- Queries.
- Creation of large indexes.
- Bulk INSERTs, UPDATEs, and DELETEs.
- Aggregations and copying.

The Oracle database application can take advantage of the underlying parallel computer architecture to process the SQL statements that are created at the basic user or client initiated interfaces. SQL statements are processed in parallel whenever possible by Oracle. Oracle adapts very well to the available number of multiple processors, whether they are SMP, NUMA, or MPP architecture. The Oracle Database 10g RAC architecture takes advantage of the existence of multiple nodes, and therefore multiple SMP entities, in the cluster to provide high performance computing. It has the added advantage of engaging processors from all nodes in the cluster for a given query.

To achieve better parallelism in Oracle, it is essential to have sufficient I/O bandwidth and additional or sporadically used CPUs. Also, adequate memory to support additional memory-intensive processes, such as sorts, hashing, and I/O buffers is required.

Parallel Execution Mechanism

A SQL statement is executed in parallel using multiple parallel processes. The user process acts as the parallel execution coordinator (PEC), and it dispatches the statement to several parallel execution servers and coordinates the end results. The results from all of the server processes are sent back to the user. The basic unit of work in parallelism is called a granule. Oracle divides the operation being paralleled, such as a table scan, table update, or index creation, into granules. Parallel processes execute the operation one granule at a time.

Granules for Parallelism

There are two types of granules: block ranges and partition ranges:

- Block Range Granules: These are the ranges of physical blocks from a table. Block range granules are the basic unit of most parallel operations. The size of the object table and the degree of parallelism (DOP) determine the size of the granule at runtime. Block range granules do not depend on static pre-allocation of tables or indexes. During the computation of the granules, Oracle takes the DOP into account and tries to assign granules from different data files to each of the parallel execution servers, avoiding contention whenever possible. Thus, the tables involved in the query are divided dynamically into granules and a single parallel execution server reads each granule. PEC manages this process.

- Partition Granules: A query server process works on an entire partition or sub-partition of a table or index. Partition granules are the basic unit of parallel index range scans and of parallel operations that modify multiple partitions of a partitioned table or index. These operations include parallel update, parallel delete, parallel creation of partitioned indexes, and parallel creation of partitioned tables. This is collectively known as parallel data manipulation language or PDML.

Parallel Execution Servers

There are two types of distinct processes: the PE Coordinator and the PE Servers. Together, they perform the parallel execution process. In a parallel operation, the SQL statement from the user becomes the coordinator and spawns execution servers. The SQL statement's foreground process becomes a PEC. The PEC obtains as many parallel execution servers as needed, determined by the DOP, from the server pool or creates new parallel execution servers as needed. Multiple memory buffers facilitate asynchronous communication among the parallel execution servers. Figure 16.1 shows a typical PE process.

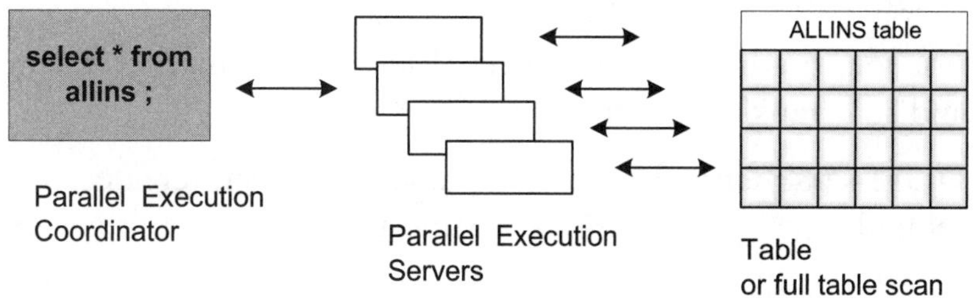

Figure 16.1: *Parallel Execution Mechanism*

The number of PE Servers is configured by the following initialization parameters.

- *parallel_max_servers:* This is the maximum number of parallel servers allowed in the instance.
- *parallel_min_servers:* This parameter specifies the number of parallel execution servers that Oracle creates at instance startup. This is zero by default in a normal database but is set to five for a RAC database created by DBCA.

Adequate care should be taken when setting the parameter *parallel_max_servers.* When there are too many query server processes, memory contention (paging), I/O contention or excessive context switching will occur. This often results in poorer performance and less throughput than if parallel operations were not attempted at all!

In RAC, *parallel_min_servers* is set to five to allow for selections against the GV series of internal views, any selects against the GV views is performed in parallel.

Parallel execution can be used for any of the following:

- For access methods like table scans, full index scans and partitioned index range scans.
- For join methods such as nested loops, sort merges, hashes, and star transformations.
- DDL statements like create table as select, create index, rebuild index, rebuild index partition, and move split coalesce partition.
- DML Statements like inserts as select, updates, deletes, and merges.
- Miscellaneous SQL Operations like group by, not in, select distinct, union, union all, cube, and rollup, as well as aggregate and table functions.
- For others, including parallel recovery, parallel propagation or replication, and parallel load, which is through the SQL*Loader utility.

Degree of Parallelism (DOP)

Before the database operations that can be paralleled are covered in more detail, it is important to understand the concept of degree of parallelism (DOP). The DOP is a key derivative that controls the parallelism process. The degree of parallelism represents the number of parallel execution servers associated with a single operation. The whole design, implementation, and tuning of parallel execution is aimed at achieving higher DOP. The higher a DOP that can be achieved for a given SQL statement, the faster the SQL statement is completed as long as resources are not over utilized. DOP directly applies only to intra-operation parallelism within an instance. If inter-instance parallelism is possible, the total number of parallel execution servers for a statement can be twice the specified DOP.

There are two major steps in parallel processing:

- Decide to use Parallel processing
- Determine or Work out DOP

These steps are different for queries, DDL operations, and DML operations.

Figure 16.2 shows how the degree of parallelism is determined.

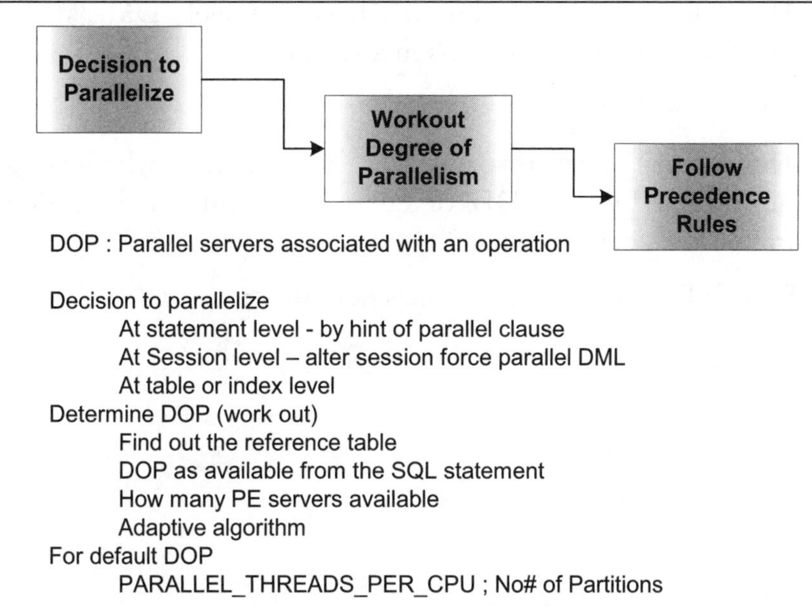

Decision to Parallelize
Workout Degree of Parallelism
Follow Precedence Rules
DOP : Parallel servers associated with an operation
Decision to parallelize
At statement level - by hint of parallel clause
At Session level – alter session force parallel DML
At table or index level
Determine DOP (work out)
Find out the reference table
DOP as available from the SQL statement
How many PE servers available
Adaptive algorithm
For default DOP
PARALLEL_THREADS_PER_CPU ; No# of Partitions

Figure 16.2: *Determination of DOP*

Once the decision to parallel is made, the directive to the statement or query session is set up.

1. Specify at the statement level, with HINTS and with the PARALLEL clause. For Example, to parallel with a DOP of four:

```
SELECT /*+ PARALLEL (allinsured, 4) */ COUNT(*) FROM allinsured ;
```

Assuming that table ALLINSURED is partitioned, an update is paralleled with a DOP of three in the next example:

```
UPDATE /*+ PARALLEL(allinsured,3) */ allinsured SET prem = prem *
1.25 ;
```

2. Specify at the session level by issuing the ALTER SESSION FORCE PARALLEL statement. For Example:

```
ALTER SESSION FORCE PARALLEL DML;
```

This allows the session to have parallel DML(s) for subsequent insert operations in a session.

```
Syntax: ALTER Session Force PARALLEL DML | DDL | QUERY
```

Thus, the parallel parameter determines whether all subsequent DML, DDL, or query statements in the session will be considered for parallel execution.

3. Specify DEGREE in the table's definition:

Example:

```
CREATE TABLE salesman
(name          varchar2(20) ,
 sales_id      number(4) ,
 join_dt       date)
 PARALLEL (DEGREE 4); -- sets default DOP

-- OR --

ALTER TABLE allinsured PARALLEL 4;
```

The above example sets the DOP to four on a table.

The *user_tables*, *alltables* or *dba_tables* views can be queried to see the DOP settings for tables.

4. Specify at the index level in the index's definition:

```
CREATE INDEX PLAN_AI ON allinsured (plan_id)
TABLESPACE savelog unrecoverable PARALLEL (DEGREE 4);

ALTER INDEX cust_indx PARALLEL 4;
Above exmaple sets the DOP to 4 on index
```

Query the *user_indexes*, *all_indexes* or *dba_indexes* views to understand the DOP settings for indexes.

There is an additional requirement that the objects of DML operations, such as UPDATE, DELETE, and MERGE must be partitioned.

Once the decision is made to utilize parallel processing according to the directives above, the DOP is determined for operation. There are a few more stages to determine the final degree of parallelism.

First, the optimizer finds the reference table and uses the following guidelines.

The parallel query looks at each table and index in the portion of the query being paralleled to determine which reference table it is. The query picks up the table or index with the largest DOP.

- For parallel DML, INSERT, UPDATE, MERGE, and DELETE, the table being modified by an INSERT, UPDATE or DELETE operation is the reference object that determines the DOP. If the statement includes a subquery, the subquery's DOP will be the same as the DOP for the DML operation.
- For parallel DDL, the reference object is the table, index or partition being created, rebuilt, split or moved that is used to determine the DOP. If the DDL statement uses a subquery, the subquery's DOP will be the same as that of the DDL operation

In the second stage, the optimizer picks up the DOP value as it is specified in the statement. When a DOP is not specified in a hint or within the definition of a table or index, the default DOP is used. The default degree of parallelism is determined by the initialization parameters. The DOP is equal to the number of

CPUs available on all participating instances, times the value of the *parallel_threads_per_cpu* initialization parameter. The default value of this parameter is two.

Another factor to note is that, while determining the DOP, if the value is supplied by multiple methods, it follows certain precedence rules. Usually the precedence order is: hint → parallel declaration specification of target table.

In the third stage, the actual number of parallel execution servers or DOP used depends upon how many processes are available in the parallel execution server pool.

Another factor that plays a role is the initialization parameter *parallel_adaptive_multi_user*. When this is set to TRUE, it enables an adaptive algorithm that automatically reduces the requested degree of parallelism, based on the system load at query startup time. Thus, the effective degree of parallelism is based on the default degree of parallelism, or the degree from the table or hints, divided by a reduction factor.

The following section will provide a look at the specific types of database operations, including parallel query, parallel DML, parallel DDL, etc. and some relevant examples.

Parallel Query: SELECT

Queries and sub-queries can be paralleled in SELECT statements. The query portions of DDL statements and DML statements, such as INSERT, UPDATE and DELETE, can also be paralleled. However, the query portion of a DDL or DML statement cannot be paralleled if it references a remote object.

A SELECT statement can be paralleled only if the following conditions are satisfied.

The query includes a parallel hint specification, *parallel* or *parallel_index*, or the schema objects referred to in the query have a parallel declaration associated with them.

- At least one of the tables specified in the query requires a full table scan or an index range scan spanning multiple partitions.
- *parallel_index* is effective only on partitioned indexes and only when the range scans are being performed.
- Also, it may be noted that queries cannot be paralleled if there is a nested table involved.

If a table has both a parallel hint specification in the query and a parallel declaration in its table specification, the hint specification takes precedence over the parallel declaration specification. Also, note that the parallel hint is used only for operations on a table and the *parallel_index* hint parallels an index range scan of a partitioned index.

As discussed in an earlier section, the DOP can be specified within a table or index definition by using one of the following statements: CREATE TABLE, ALTER TABLE, CREATE INDEX or ALTER INDEX.

Parallel DML: UPDATE, MERGE, DELETE

UPDATEs, MERGEs and DELETEs can only be paralleled on partitioned tables.

To specify parallel directives, follow one of the following methods:

- ALTER SESSION FORCE PARALLEL DML
- Use an UPDATE, MERGE or DELETE parallel hint in the statement.

- Use a parallel clause in the definition of the table or reference object being updated or deleted.

The precedence rule in this category of operations is: Hint → Session → Parallel declaration specification of target table.

If the statement contains sub-queries or updatable views, they may have their own separate parallel hints or clauses. Remember, these parallel directives do not affect decisions to parallelize the UPDATE, MERGE or DELETE activities.

Once it is decided to use parallel processing, the maximum DOP that can be achieved in DELETE, MERGE and UPDATE is equal to the number of partitions or sub-partitions, in the case of composite sub-partitions, in the table. Multiple partitions can be updated, merged into or deleted from by a single parallel execution, but each partition can only be updated or deleted by one parallel execution server at a time. Each parallel process transaction is a result of a different parallel execution server. Therefore, parallel DML requires multiple undo segments for performance.

However, there are some restrictions, quoting the Oracle documentation for accuracy, as shown below:

- A transaction can contain multiple parallel DML statements that modify different tables, but after a parallel DML statement modifies a table, no subsequent serial or parallel statement (DML or query) can access the same table again in that transaction.

- Parallel DML operations cannot be done on tables with triggers. Relevant triggers must be disabled in order to parallel DML on the table.

- A transaction involved in a parallel DML operation cannot be or become a distributed transaction.

- Clustered tables are not supported.

Parallel DML: INSERT .... SELECT

An INSERT … SELECT statement parallels its INSERT and SELECT operations independently, except for the DOP. The INSERT operation will be paralleled if at least one of the following is true:

- The parallel hint is used in the INSERT in the DML statement.
- The table being inserted into was specified with a parallel declaration specification.
- The session is under the affect of an ALTER SESSION FORCE PARALLEL DML statement.

The select statement follows its own set of rules, as specified in the query section. Only one parallel directive is picked for deciding the DOP of the whole statement. Then the chosen DOP is applied to both the SELECT and INSERT operations using the precedence rule: Insert Hint directive → Session → Parallel declaration specification of the inserting table → Maximum query directive.

Parallel DDL Statements

DDL operations can be paralleled if a parallel clause or declaration is specified in the syntax. The parallel DDL statements for non-partitioned tables and indexes are:

```
CREATE INDEX
CREATE TABLE ... AS select
ALTER INDEX ... REBUILD
```

The parallel DDL statements for partitioned tables and indexes are:

```
CREATE INDEX
CREATE TABLE ... AS select
ALTER TABLE ... MOVE PARTITION
ALTER TABLE ... SPLIT PARTITION
ALTER TABLE ... COALESCE PARTITION
ALTER INDEX ... REBUILD PARTITION
ALTER INDEX ... SPLIT PARTITION
```

The ALTER SESSION FORCE PARALLEL DDL statement can be used to override the parallel clauses of subsequent DDL statements in a session. The DOP is determined by the specification in the parallel clause, unless an ALTER SESSION FORCE PARALLEL DDL statement overrides it. A rebuild of a partitioned index is never paralleled.

When indexes and tables are created in parallel, each parallel execution server allocates a new extent and fills the extent with the table or index data. Hence, if an index is created with a DOP of four, the index will have at least four extents initially. The parallel allocation of extents is the same for indexes are built in parallel or partitions are being moved, split, or rebuilt in parallel. While serial operations only require that the schema object has at least one extent, parallel creations initially require that tables or indexes have at least as many extents as there are parallel execution servers creating the schema object. After creation, the extents may be coalesced, but there must be a plan for the additional space that may be required for the initial multiple extents caused by parallel DDL operations.

Rules for Paralleling Create Table as Select (CTAS)

CTAS is a very widely used and useful operation while dealing with the reorganization of large tables. The CTAS statement contains two parts: a CREATE part (DDL) and a SELECT part (query). Oracle can parallellize both parts of the statement. The CREATE part of the CTAS must follow the same rules as apply to other DDL operations. The following conditions must be satisfied if the query part of a CTAS statement is to be parallellized:

- The query includes a parallel hint specification, the CREATE part of the statement has a parallel clause, or objects referred to in the query have a parallel declaration.
- At least one of the tables specified in the query requires a full table scan or an index range scan spanning multiple partitions.

The DOP for the query part of CTAS is then determined as follows:

- The query part of the CTAS uses the settings specified in the parallel clause of the CREATE part.
- When the parallel clause is not specified, the default DOP will be the number of CPUs.
- When the CREATE is done as a serial operation, the DOP is determined by the query settings.

The CREATE operation of CTAS can be paralleled only by a parallel clause or an ALTER SESSION FORCE PARALLEL DDL statement. The DOP for the CREATE operation, and for the SELECT operation if it is paralleled, is specified by the parallel clause of the CREATE statement, unless it is overridden by an ALTER SESSION FORCE PARALLEL DDL statement.

SQL*LOADER: Parallel Load

Placing large data loads into database tables often involves considerable time. However, with the help of concurrent or parallel loading, the whole loading process can be accomplished faster.

Using Concurrent Conventional Path Loads

For loading, multiple load sessions executing concurrently on a multiple-CPU system are used. The input data files are split into separate files on logical record boundaries and are then loaded each such input data file with a conventional path load session.

This is faster than a single conventional load on a multiple-CPU system, but it is probably not as fast as a direct load. Also, triggers are executed, integrity constraints are applied to the loaded rows, and indexes are maintained using the standard DML execution logic.

Parallel Direct Path Load

SQL*Loader permits multiple, concurrent sessions to perform a direct path load into the same table or into the same partition of a partitioned table. Multiple SQL*Loader sessions improve the performance of a direct path load, given the available resources on the system. Parallel data loading is enabled by setting both the direct and the parallel parameters to TRUE. However, there are some restrictions to parallel direct load. They are:

- Referential integrity and CHECK constraints must be disabled.
- Triggers must be disabled.
- Rows can only be appended. REPLACE, TRUNCATE and INSERT cannot be used.
- Indexes are not maintained during a parallel direct path load. Any table indexes must be created manually or dropped and recreated manually after the load completes.

The following commands invoke three direct path SQL*Loader load sessions on the same table. These are in separate server sessions:

```
Session 1:
>sqlldr USERID=nyora/frodo CONTROL=pload1.ctl DIRECT=TRUE
PARALLEL=true
Session 2:
>sqlldr USERID=nyora/frodo CONTROL=pload2.ctl DIRECT=TRUE
PARALLEL=true
```

```
Session 3:
>sqlldr USERID=nyora/frodo CONTROL=pload3.ctl DIRECT=TRUE
PARALLEL=true
```

Other Parallel Operations

The following are some of the other miscellaneous parallel execution opportunities.

DBWR and LGWR

Using multiple DBWRs parallels the writing of buffers. Therefore, multiple DBWR processes should deliver more throughput than one DBWR process with the same number of I/O slaves. Since the mirroring of redo log files on separate disks, does not slow LGWR considerably, LGWR writes to each disk in parallel and waits until each part of the parallel write is complete.

Parallel Recovery

Recovery performed in parallel can speed up the crash, instance, and media recovery considerably. During a parallel recovery process, the SMON background process reads the redo-log files sequentially, and the redo-blocks are then distributed evenly to all recovery processes to be read into the buffer cache. The parallel slave processes apply the changes to data files. If the data files involved in the recovery are many, the parallel process really helps.

To specify the number of concurrent recovery processes for instance or crash recover use the *recovery_parallelism* initialization parameter to specifies the number of concurrent recovery processes. This parameter has no affect on media recovery. To parallelize media recovery, use the parallel clause in the RECOVER DATABASE statement.

The SQL*Plus *recovery_parallelism* command specifies parallel media recovery. The default is NOPARALLEL.

Example:

```
SQL>RECOVER PARALLEL integer;
SQL>RECOVER TABLESPACE myTBS, yourTBS PARALLEL (degree 4);
SQL>RECOVER DATAFILE '/u01/orodata/NYORA/sales1.dbf' PARALLEL
(DEGREE 3);
SQL>RECOVER DATABASE PARALLEL ; -- default DOP is used.
```

For media recovery, Oracle uses a division of labor approach to allocate different processes to different data blocks while rolling forward, thereby making the procedure more efficient. For example, if parallel recovery is performed with parallel four, and only one data file is recovered, four spawned processes read blocks from the data file and apply records instead of only one process.

Using Fast-Start Parallel Rollback

During an instance recovery process, Oracle rolls back uncommitted transactions. Oracle can use fast-start parallel rollback to increase the efficiency of this recovery phase.

When using fast-start parallel rollback, the background process SMON is used as a coordinator and rolls back sets of transactions in parallel, using multiple server processes. Setting the initialization parameter *fast_start_parallel_rollback* controls the number of processes involved in transaction recovery. Values can be set FALSE, LOW, or HIGH.

Fast-start parallel rollback is mainly useful when a system has transactions that run for a long time before committing, especially parallel INSERT, UPDATE, and DELETE operations. SMON decides when to begin parallel rollback and then distributes the task among several parallel processes. Each if these processes execute one transaction, but they are all done in parallel.

Replication: Parallel Propagation

When parallel propagation is utilized, replicated transactions are propagated using multiple, parallel streams giving higher throughput. Oracle automatically orders the execution of dependent transactions to preserve data integrity when necessary. The parallelism parameter should be set to a minimum of one, but usually higher, in the *dbms_defer_sys.schedule_push* procedure in order to configure a scheduled link with parallel propagation. As an alternative, the replication management tool should be used to set the parallel propagation processes control setting to one or higher in the Edit Push Schedule dialog box.

Oracle RAC and Inter-Instance parallelism

Oracle RAC is a multi-instance single database with a shared storage. Besides providing a very good, high availability solution, RAC gives load balancing capabilities and a high performance environment. With RAC, it is possible for an intra-parallel operation to utilize the processors across the nodes which gives an additional degree of parallelism while executing in parallel. For instance, in a two node RAC cluster, a parallel query can be set up with PARALLEL HINT to utilize the CPUs from the both instances.

```
SELECT /*+ FULL(nydata) PARALLEL(nydata, 3,2) / count(*) FROM
nysales;
```

In this example, the DOP is three and uses two instances. It is executed with a total of six processes, three on each instance.

Initialization Parameters at a Glance

Shown below are the parameters that play a role in setting and performing the PE process.

- *prallel_max_servers*: This parameter specifies the maximum number of parallel execution processes and parallel recovery processes for an instance.
- *parallel_min_servers*: This parameter is used at startup to specify for a single instance, the number of processes to be started for parallel operations.
- *large_pool_size* or *shared_pool_size*: When *parallel_automatic_tuning* is FALSE, Oracle will allocate the query server processes from the shared pool. In this case, tune the shared pool, otherwise size the large pool properly.
- *parallel_min_percent*: Use this parameter to allow users to wait on an acceptable DOP. Setting this parameter causes Oracle to return an error if the requested DOP cannot be satisfied at a given time. The Oracle recommended value for this parameter is 0 (zero).
- *cluster_database_instances*: This parameter is used to specify the number of instances configured in a RAC environment. This value is used by Oracle to compute values for *large_pool_size* when *parallel_automatic_tuning* is set to TRUE.
- *parallel_execution_message_size*: This specifies the upper limit for the size of parallel execution messages. The default will be specific to the operating system. The default value should be adequate for most applications. The max recommended value for this parameter is four KB. Oracle sets this based on *parallel_automatic_tuning*. If this is TRUE, the default size is four KB. When *parallel_automatic_tuning* is set to FALSE, the setting will be slightly greater than two KB.

- *parallel_adaptive_multi_user*: When this parameter is set to TRUE, it causes Oracle to use an adaptive algorithm which automatically adjusts the requested DOP based on the system load.
- *parallel_automatic_tuning*: Setting this to TRUE allows Oracle to determine the default values for parameters that control parallel execution.
- *parallel_broadcast_enabled*: When this is set to TRUE, the rows of the small tables involved in parallel operations are broadcast to each slave.

Monitoring and Diagnosing the Parallel Execution

There are quite a number of dynamic performance tables/views, which helps monitor the PE process. After a query or DML operation is run, the *v$px_process*, *v$sesstat*, *v$pq_slave*, *v$pq_sesstat*, and *v$pq_sysstat* views can be used to see the number of server processes used and other information for the session and system.

Conclusion

All nodes in the Oracle RAC are capable of paralleling SQL operations. Parallel execution is not exclusive to Oracle RAC, and it can be achieved in a stand-alone single instance database. Parallelism of SQL operations is accomplished with the help of SQL statement hints, table declaration clauses or session settings.

The degree of parallelism determines the number of parallel execution servers that are used to execute a SQL operation. Many types of SQL operations with examples that use parallel execution have been presented in this chapter.

References

Madhu Tumma - IOUG - Live 2002 San Diego, Presentation *PARALLEL EXECUTION IN ORACLE 9i*

Oracle Manual - *Data Warehousing Guide Release 1* (10.1)

Oracle Manual - *Oracle9i Database Concepts - Release 1* (10.1)

Michael Ault - *Oracle Administration and Management*, 2000, Wiley and Sons

Oracle's Grid Integration

CHAPTER

"Ms. Jones, should I wait till you integrate Oracle and Grid?"

Introduction

This chapter will cover Oracle's database technologies and utilities that integrate the database with Grid Architecture and provide extensions to the grid framework. Oracle's Grid Architecture deals with large numbers of computing resources such as the servers, storage units and client connections. There are various demand and supply situations in terms of resource consumption. Oracle's focus is on providing the database processing power to the ultimate consumers. It is usually a service based architecture where a service is demanded by the consumers. As the demand for database processing service grows, the automatic provisioning of additional servers and database computing entities takes care of the demand and supply.

Oracle also provides a sophisticated work load management, which makes it possible for the users or applications to share database resources. Based on the work load pattern changes, the automatic shifting of resources from less priority activities to the more important user needs takes place. When needed, DBA's can also provision more servers to the application to handle increased load.

Exploring Grid Technology

In 10g database release, Oracle provides many technology differentiators and also grid technology enablers. Some of these are new additions and some are enhancements. To name a few, data pump utilities is an addition in 10g release and cross-platform transportable tablespace is an enhancement. Automatic Storage management is another notable addition in 10g release.

The Database Processing is a key component in any Grid Framework. At the same time, data movement, data loading and data sharing among the databases and non-database computing areas, is a key prerequisite for the Data Grid implementation. The Oracle Storage Management is an important component in dealing with resource provision. ASM makes the adjustment of disk resources quite transparent.

Many of the well-known and minor features of the Oracle database product are enhanced with a view to participate actively in the Grid Architecture. For Example, the easier data transfers using data pump, Oracle data files transfers among different operating systems, quicker and easier software installation, new replication and messaging methods using the Streams technology etc., are the new features Oracle has emphasized.

Grid Control is well designed to manage besides the databases, the web applications, the application servers and hosts of different operating systems. Grid control provides a bird's eye view of all resources for easier management.

Oracle 10g database has many new and innovative features to facilitate the setting up of multiple databases in a clustered environment and non-clustered grid environment. It has the advantage of leveraging the underlying grid infrastructure components and manages them efficiently. The grid components such as low cost servers or blades, powerful interconnect and storage arrays are well utilized by the Oracle 10g database.

Grid Enabling Components

Oracle 10g Database comes equipped with many grid-enabling technologies. The following sections will introduce some of these technologies.

Automatic Storage Management (ASM)

ASM simplifies and manages the storage requirements needed to support the database. It provides data provisioning methods. As the demand for data arises, new disk devices can be added dynamically. Within a specific disk group, Oracle automatically allocates the storage, creates and deletes the data files as needed for the database. The detection of hot spots and I/O balancing functions are managed by the ASM methodology, thereby lessening the manual intervention by DBA and SA. ASM also offers the benefit of the RAID and logical volume functionality where applicable.

Oracle is capable of reassigning disks from one node to another and from one cluster to another. Oracle can also balance the IO activity from multiple databases across all of the devices in disk group. It can also implement striping and mirroring methodology to improve the IO performance. Storage can be assigned when needed and can be removed when it is not needed. This gives a true grid friendly functionality.

Portable Clusterware

As previously noted in this text, the Cluster software is the software stack that defines, configures and manages the cluster members or the cluster nodes. Cluster software, sometimes called the cluster manager, keeps track of the health of the nodes and communicates with the cluster database system. In order to provide a uniform cluster software stack across many operating systems and platforms, Oracle has introduced Portable Clusterware to support the Oracle Real Application Cluster.

By supplying uniform, standard and integrated cluster software, cluster vendor imposed limitations such as number of nodes and using a particular type of interconnect technology etc., are avoided. Now Oracle RAC implementations will have a common look and feel even if they are implemented on different operating systems and different server hardware. In the Grid Environment, where the RAC database systems become a key component, Portable Clusterware adds to the functionality and eases management issues.

Support for Infiniband Interconnect

With the support and availability of Infiniband for Oracle database and Oracle RAC Clusters, client to server, server to server, and server to storage communication achieves higher throughput and reduces bottlenecks.

Oracle Database Resonance

Resources are dynamically expanded when needed and are shrunk when not needed or when priority tasks need them. Database Resonance is the provisioning utility for the Oracle RAC.

Through the database resonance utility, it becomes possible for the administrators to define and configure the policy-based CPU provisioning in terms of nodes) and capacity on demand with automatic load balancing

DBA's can define the services-level policies based on CPU utilization or service response times and also set up priority of each database. Oracle automatically starts and stops the additional instances to meet service-level policies.

It is estimated that this module or utility will be available in 10.2g database release.

Oracle Job Scheduler

This new tool allows the creation of jobs and schedules, which enables the assignment of the jobs with the appropriate schedules. Oracle scheduler provides many advanced capabilities to schedule and perform business and IT tasks in the enterprise grid.

Jobs can be grouped in job classes and a suitable priority can be assigned to these groups, which affect all the jobs under a group. Using the Oracle Resource Manager, the resource plans can be defined and assigned to the job classes. More details about the scheduler utility and the role it plays in the grid architecture will be examined further.

Oracle Database Resource Manager

Resource Manager provisions resources to database users or services within an Oracle database. It allows the DBA's to limit the database resources allocated to grid users, applications or services. Wise use of resource manager can ensure that each grid user, grid application or service gets its fair share of the available computing resources. While this utility is available in previous releases of the database, it is now strengthened with additional features.

Data Provisioning and Sharing in the Grid Framework

In a multiple database scenario in the grid architecture, it may be necessary to move the data from one database to another more often than not. In case where all the database or data resources cannot be consolidated or pooled, one last resort approach would be active data sharing by moving data from an over utilized database to underutilized database. Sometimes the target database may be put to use for a particular purpose or particular department or particular region. At the same time, it may be necessary to move data to non-database platforms with the help of heterogeneous gateways.

In order to achieve most optimum and efficient data transfers, Oracle provides many new features like Oracle Streams, Transportable Tablespaces, Oracle Data pump, distributed SQL support, distributed transactions and gateways. These Grid Enabling and Data Sharing topics will be covered next.

Transportable and Big Tablespace

When it is not feasible to consolidate the database resources, database systems tend to grow in different geographical locations and in different departments and often in different operating systems or platforms. In such cases, the feature of Oracle Transportable Tablespace offers an efficient way of sharing large subsets of data and then sharing the processing on this data on different hardware resources. This also is a key requirement for effective grid-enabling architecture.

Transportable Tablespace gives the grid users a very fast and efficient mechanism to move large data from one database system to another. Another feature that is particularly useful for large enterprises is the facility of mounting read-only tablespace by two or more databases.

With 10g release, it becomes possible to move the transportable tablespace across different platforms or operating systems. Another new feature is the provision of big tablespaces, which support ultra-large tablespaces to store the objects.

New Cross-Platform Transportable Tablespace

A transportable tablespace allows the quick movements of a subset of an Oracle database from one Oracle database to another. However, in the previous release of Oracle server, it was only possible to move a tablespace across Oracle databases within the same platform. Oracle 10g is going one step further by allowing the movement of tablespace across different platforms. This feature becomes particularly significant in the Grid framework where many different operating systems coexist and conduct data movements and data sharing.

The limitation requiring transportable tablespaces to be transferred to the same operating system has been removed. However, to transport tablespaces across different platforms, both the source and target databases must be at least on Oracle Database 10g, be on at least version 10.0.1, and have the *compatible* initialization parameter set to 10.0. Using the new cross-platform transportable tablespace method to move data is more efficient than the traditional method of export and import.

Oracle Database 10g supports many platforms for transportable tablespace. A new data dictionary view, *v$transportable_platform*, lists all the supported platforms, along with platform ID and endian format.

The *v$database* data dictionary view also adds two columns, platform ID and platform name:

```
SQL> select name, platform_id,platform_name from v$database;

NAME       PLATFORM_ID      PLATFORM_NAME
-------    -----------      -----------------------
GRID                 2      Solaris[tm] OE (64-bit)
```

For example, it is not necessary to convert the data file to transport a tablespace from an AIX-based platform to a Sun platform, since both platforms use a big endian. However, to transport a tablespace from a Sun Platform (big endian) to a Linux Platform (little endian), the CONVERT command in the RMAN utility should be used to convert the byte ordering. This can be done on either the source platform or the target platform.

Determine Platform Endianness

To transport a tablespace from one platform to another, datafiles on different platforms must be in the same endian format, byte ordering. The pattern for byte ordering in native types is called endianness. There are only two main patterns, big endian and little endian. Big endian means the most significant byte comes first, and little endian means the least significant byte comes first. If the source platform and the target platform are of different endianness, an additional step must be taken on either the source or target platform to convert the tablespace being transported to the target format. If they are of the same endianness, no conversion is necessary and tablespaces can be transported as if they were on the same platform.

However, there are certain restrictions in using the transportable tablespace:

- The source and target database must use the same character set and national character set.
- A tablespace cannot be transported to a target database in which a tablespace with the same name already exists. However, the tablespace to be transported or the destination tablespace can be renamed before the transport operation. Renaming a tablespace is a new feature in 10g.
- The set should be self-containing

Transporting Tablespaces between Databases: A General Procedure

Perform the following steps to move or copy a set of tablespaces.

1. Pick a self-contained set of tablespaces. Verify this using the *dbms_tts.transport_set_check* package.
2. Next, generate a transportable tablespace set, using the Export utility.
3. A transportable tablespace set consists of the set of datafiles for the set of tablespaces being transported and an Export file containing metadata information for the set of tablespace and corresponding data files.
4. Transporting a tablespace set to a platform different from the source platform will require connection to the Recovery Manager (RMAN) and invoking the CONVERT command. An alternative is to do the conversion on the target platform after the tablespace datafiles have been transported.
5. Next, the tablespace datafile set is transported. Copy the datafiles and the export file containing the metadata to the target database. This can be accomplished using any facility for copying flat files, such as the operating system copy utility, ftp, or publishing on CDs or DVDs.

6. The final step is to plug in the tablespace. Use the Import utility to plug the set of tablespaces metadata, and hence the tablespaces themselves, into the target database.
7. If these tablespaces are being transported to a different platform, the Recovery Manager CONVERT command can be used to perform the conversion.

Note: As an alternative to conversion before transport, the CONVERT command can be used for the conversion on the target platform after the tablespace set has been transported.

The RMAN CONVERT Clause

The purpose of the CONVERT clause is to convert the format of a transport set from one platform to another to allow a quick transport of a tablespace across different platforms. Content providers can now publish structured data as transportable tablespaces and distribute it to customers who can quickly integrate this data into Oracle, regardless of their current platform within compatibility limits.

Data from a large data warehouse server can be distributed to data marts on smaller computers, such as Windows 2000 workstations.

Example uses of the command are:

```
CONVERT Clause Syntax:

CONVERT [TABLESPACE 'tablespace_name'[,]| DATAFILE 'filename'[,]]
convert_optionList ;

convert_optionList::=

[[FROM|TO] PLATFORM [=] {identifier|quoted_string}]|
[FORMAT [=] formatSpec]|
[DB_FILE_NAME_CONVERT [=] ( 'string_pattern'[,])]|
[PARALLELISM [=] integer]]
```

Keywords and Parameters

```
TABLESPACE tablespace_name
```

The TABLESPACE keyword specifies the name of a tablespace in the source database to be transported to the destination database on a different platform. CONVERT TABLESPACE can only be used when connected to the source database, not from the destination database. This is because, until the tablespace transport has been completed, the destination database has no way of recognizing the tablespace name for use with the CONVERT TABLESPACE statement.

```
DATAFILE datafile_name
```

This specifies the name of a to-be-converted data file that is to be transported into the destination database.

If the decision is made to convert at the destination database instead of at the source, CONVERT DATAFILE must be used instead of CONVERT TABLESPACE, and each data file that is being converted must be named. This is because the files have not yet been imported into the destination database, so RMAN does not yet know which files belong to the tablespace being converted.

To convert a single data file at a time, the DATAFILE argument can be used in place of the TABLESPACE argument on the source platform, though it is more convenient to use the TABLESPACE argument and do all data files at one time for a specific tablespace.

```
FROM PLATFORM = platform_name
```

This parameter specifies the name of the source platform as it is displayed in a select from the *v$transportable_platform.platform_name* column.

```
TO PLATFORM = platform_name
```

This parameter specifies the name of the destination platform as displayed in a select from the *v$transportable_platform.platform_name* column.

```
FORMAT formatSpec
```

This parameter specifies the name template for the output files.

```
DB_FILE_NAME_CONVERT='string_pattern'
```

This parameter accepts filename pairs where the first name in the pair is the converted filename, performs the required substitutions, and places the converted files in the new location after the substitution. As many pairs of replacement strings as required can be specified. Single or double quotation marks can be used around the entries.

Restrictions and Usage Notes

- The read-only tablespaces can be transported across the platforms.
- Both source and destination databases must be running Oracle Database 10g with the initialization parameter *compatible* set to 10.0 or higher.
- A tablespace must have been made read-write at least once in Oracle Database 10g before it can be transported to any other platform. Therefore, any read-only tablespaces or currently existing transported tablespaces that exist from a version prior to Oracle Database Oracle10g must be made read-write

first on the platform where they were created, before they can be transported to a different platform.

- RMAN cannot process user data types that require endian conversions. If it is necessary to transport objects built on underlying types that store data in a platform-specific format, such as endian, then Oracle's Data Pump feature should be used.

- Query the view *v$transportable_platform* to determine the platforms supported by the RMAN CONVERT command. Cross-platform tablespace transport is only supported when both the source and destination platforms are contained in this view. In Oracle Database 10g, the CONVERT command is only required when transporting between platforms for which the value in *v$transportable_platform.endian_format* is different. If the *endian_format* column is the same, the files can simply be copied from the source to the destination machine, no conversion is required.

- If conversion is needed, the CONVERT command must be run either on the source host, using CONVERT TO and identifying the destination platform, or on the destination host, where the FROM parameter is not needed because the source platform is noted in the datafile, and where the TO parameter is not needed because conversion will default to the platform RMAN is running on. CONVERT does not convert the datafiles in-place; instead, it creates an output file that is readable on the specified platform.

The following are the supported data types for the CONVERT command:

- VARCHAR2
- CHAR
- NUMBER
- DATE

- TIMESTAMP
- TIMESTAMP WITH TIME ZONE
- TIMESTAMP WITH LOCAL TIME ZONE
- INTERVAL YEAR MONTH
- INTERVAL DAT TO SECOND
- BFILE
- LONG
- ROWID
- RAW
- BLOB
- LONG RAW
- UROWID
- NVARCHAR2
- Native numbers
- CLOB
- Media Types (ORDSYS.ORDAudio, ORDSYS.ORDImage, RDSYS.ORDVideo)

In releases prior to Oracle Database 10g, Oracle created CLOBs in a variable-width character set and stored them in an endian-dependent format. The CONVERT command will not perform conversions on these CLOBs. Instead, RMAN will capture the endian format of each LOB column and propagate it to the target database. Subsequent reads of this data by the SQL layer will interpret the data correctly, based on either of the endian formats, then write it out in an endian-independent way if the tablespace is writeable. If new CLOBs are created in an Oracle Database 10g or later release, RMAN creates the CLOB in character set AL16UTF16, which is platform independent.

Convert Datafiles using RMAN

A simple example:

```
RMAN> CONVERT TABLESPACE 'USERS'
      TO PLATFORM = 'Linux IA (32-bit)'
      DB_FILE_NAME_CONVERT = '/u02/oradata/grid/users01.dbf',
      '/dba/recovery_area/transport_linux'
```

Example: Source Platform Tablespace Conversion

Suppose there is a need to transport tablespaces RESEARCH, datafiles */oracle/oradata/rec/frec01.dbf* and */oracle/oradata/rec/rec02.dbf* and PL, datafiles */oracle/oradata/rec/project01.dbf* and */oracle/oradata/rec/project02.dbf*, from a source database running on a Linux host to a destination database running on a Windows NT 4.0 server. The plan is to store the converted datafiles in the temporary directory *tmp/oracle/transport_windows/* on the source host.

The example assumes that the following steps have been carried out in preparation for the tablespace transport:

- The tablespaces to be transported have been set to be read-only.
- Oracle's name for the destination platform is known.
- Oracle's internal name for the target platform will be needed. This name will be used as a parameter to the CONVERT command. To get the platform name, use SQL*Plus to query the view *v$transportable_platform*:

```
SQL> SELECT PLATFORM_ID, PLATFORM_NAME, ENDIAN_FORMAT
 2 FROM V$TRANSPORTABLE_PLATFORM;

PLATFORM_ID PLATFORM_NAME                  ENDIAN_FORMAT
----------- ------------------------------ --------------
          1 Solaris[tm] OE (32-bit)        Big
          2 Solaris[tm] OE (64-bit)        Big
          3 HP-UX (64-bit)                 Big
          4 HP-UX IA (64-bit)              Big
          5 HP Tru64 UNIX                  Little
```

```
 6 AIX-Based Systems (64-bit)     Big
 7 Microsoft Windows NT           Little
10 Linux IA (32-bit)              Little
11 Linux IA (64-bit)              Little
```

To restrict the results to a single platform type, simply add a WHERE clause such as:

```
WHERE UPPER(PLATFORM_NAME) LIKE '%WINDOWS%';
```

The results show that the *platform_name* for Windows NT is Microsoft *Windows NT*.

Now, RMAN would be used to convert the datafiles to be transported to the destination host's Linux format on the source host. The FORMAT argument controls the name and location of the converted datafiles.

```
% rman TARGET /
RMAN> CONVERT TABLESPACE research
2> TO PLATFORM 'Microsoft Windows NT'
3> FORMAT='/tmp/oracle/transport_windows/%U';

Starting backup at 09-SEP-03
using target database controlfile instead of recovery catalog
allocated channel: ORA_DISK_1
channel ORA_DISK_1: sid=37 devtype=DISK
RMAN-00571:
===========================================================
RMAN-00569: ========= ERROR MESSAGE STACK FOLLOWS =========
RMAN-00571:
===========================================================
RMAN-03002: failure of backup command at 09/09/2003 13:22:57
RMAN-06598: conversion between platforms 'Linux IA (32-bit)' and
'Microsoft Windows NT' is not needed
```

So, why is it saying no conversion is required? In the listing of platforms, the endian setting for both Linux and NT is Little; this means their files are compatible. If a SUN platform had been specified instead, the results would have looked like the following:

```
RMAN> CONVERT TABLESPACE research
2> TO PLATFORM 'Solaris[tm] OE (64-bit)'
```

```
3> FORMAT = '/tmp/oracle/transport_sun/%U';

Starting backup at 09-SEP-03
using target database controlfile instead of recovery catalog
allocated channel: ORA_DISK_1
channel ORA_DISK_1: sid=37 devtype=DISK
channel ORA_DISK_1: starting datafile conversion
input datafile fno=00004
name=/usr/oracle/product/10.1/oradata/aultdb1/research01.dbf
converted datafile=/tmp/oracle/transport_windows/data_D-AULTDB1_I-
1051447236_TS-RESEARCH_FNO-4_02f0td2t
channel ORA_DISK_1: datafile conversion complete, elapsed time:
00:00:04
channel ORA_DISK_1: starting datafile conversion
input datafile fno=00005
name=/usr/oracle/product/10.1/oradata/aultdb1/research01.dbf
converted datafile=/tmp/oracle/transport_windows/data_D-AULTDB1_I-
1051447236_TS-RESEARCH_FNO-5_03f0td31
channel ORA_DISK_1: datafile conversion complete, elapsed time:
00:00:04
Finished backup at 09-SEP-03
```

The result will be a set of converted datafiles with data in the right endian order for the specified platform that will be located in the directory specified by the FORMAT clause. From this point, the same procedure is followed as for a normal tablespace transport.

The Export utility is used to create the file of metadata information. The metadata information file should be moved from its location and the converted datafiles from */tmp/oracle/transport_linux/* to their respective target directories on the destination host if it has not already been done, then plug the tablespace(s) into the new database with the Import utility.

Example: Converting Tablespaces on the Target Platform

Suppose there is a need to transport tablespaces RESEARCH, datafiles */oracle/oradata/rec/rec01.dbf* and */oracle/oradata/rec/rec02.dbf*, and PL, datafiles */oracle/oradata/pl/proj01.dbf* and */oracle/oradata/pl/proj02.dbf*, from a source database running on a Sun Solaris host to a destination database running on a Linux PC host. The plan is to perform conversion on the target host. The unconverted datafiles will be temporarily stored in the directory */tmp/oracle/transport_solaris/* on the target host. When the datafiles are plugged into Oracle, they will be stored in */oradata/oracle/rec/*.

The example assumes that the following steps have been carried out in preparation for the tablespace transport:

The source tablespaces to be transported are set to be read-only, the Export utility has been used to create the metadata information file, which is named research.dchmp, the research.dmp and the unconverted tablespace datafiles to be transported have been gathered and copied to the destination host, to the */tmp/oracle/transport_solaris/* directory.

The subdirectory structure from the files original location has been preserved, that is, the datafiles are stored as:

/tmp/oracle/transport_solaris/rec/research01.dbf
/tmp/oracle/transport_solaris/rec/research02.dbf
/tmp/oracle/transport_solaris/pl/proj01.dbf
/tmp/oracle/transport_solarisr/pl/proj02.dbf

Now RMAN's CONVERT command can be used to convert the datafiles to be transported into the destination host's format and deposit the results in */oracle/oradata/rec.*

The following should be noted:

- Datafiles must be identified by their names, not by their tablespace name. The local instance has no way of knowing the desired tablespace datafile names until the tablespace is plugged in.
- The FORMAT argument controls the naming and location of the converted datafiles.

- The source or destination platform cannot be specified by the user. RMAN determines the source platform by examining the datafile, and the target platform defaults to the platform of the host running the RMAN conversion.

```
% rman TARGET /
RMAN> CONVERT DATAFILE='/tmp/oracle/transport_solaris/*'
DB_FILE_NAME_CONVERT=
'/tmp/oracle/transport_solaris/research',
'/oracle/oradata/rec/research',
'/tmp/oracle/transport_solaris/pl','/oracle/oradata/pl'
```

The result is a set of converted datafiles in the */oracle/oradata/rec/* and */oracle/oradata/pl* directories, named thus:

/oracle/oradata/rec/research01.dbf
/oracle/oradata/rec/research02.dbf
/oracle/oradata/pl/proj01.dbf
/oracle/oradata/pl/proj02.dbf

Now follow the usual method for tablespace transport. Use Import to plug the converted tablespaces metadata into the new database, and as a final step, make the tablespaces read-write if needed.

Bigfile Tablespace Overview

A bigfile tablespace (BFT) is a tablespace containing a single file that can have a very large size. The traditional tablespace is referred to as a smallfile tablespace (SFT). A SFT contains multiple, relatively small files. The BFT has the following characteristics:

- An Oracle database can contain both bigfile and smallfile tablespaces.
- System default is to create the traditional SFT.
- The SYSTEM and SYSAUX tablespaces are always created using the system default type.

- BFT's are supported only for locally managed tablespaces with automatic segment-space management. There are two exceptions when BFT segments are manually managed: Locally managed undo tablespace and Temporary tablespace

BFT's are intended to be used with Automated Storage Management (ASM) or other logical volume managers that support RAID. However, it can also be used without ASM.

BFT Benefits

BFT has the following benefits:

- It simplifies large, database tablespace management by reducing the number of datafiles needed.
- It simplifies datafile management with Oracle-managed files and ASM by eliminating the need for adding new datafiles and dealing with multiple files.
- It allows the creation of a BFT of up to eight exabytes in size, and significantly increases the storage capacity of an Oracle database.
- It follows the concept that a tablespace and a datafile are logically equivalent.

rowids of Rows that belong to BFTs do not contain the relative file number.

- SFT has a four piece format: OOOOOOFFFBBBBBBRRR, in which:
    - OOOOOO is the data object number of the segment.
    - FFF is the tablespace-relative datafile number of the datafile that contains the row.
    - BBBBBB is the data block that contains the row.
    - RRR is the slot number identifying the row inside a particular block.

BFT ROWID Format

In a BFT, there is only one file that always has a relative file number of 1024. A BFT has a three piece format, OOOOOOLLLLLLLLLRRR, in which LLLLLLLLL is used to denote the block number. The concatenation of FFF and BBBBBB makes the encoded block number.

For BFTs, the only supported way of getting components of extended rowids is to use the *dbms_rowid* package.

The following is an example on how to use the *dbms_rowid* package to retrieve rowid information:

```
select dbms_rowid.rowid_relative_fno(rowid, 'BIGFILE')
       bigfile_rowid,
       dbms_rowid.rowid_relative_fno(rowid, 'SMALLFILE')
       smallfile_rowid,
       first_name, last_name
FROM   hr.employees where  rownum < 3;

BIGFILE_ROWID SMALLFILE_ROWID FIRST_NAME           LAST_NAME
------------- --------------- -------------------- -------------
         1024               4 Mike                 Ault
         1024               4 Madhu                Tumma
```

Data Dictionary Views Enhancement

A new column is added to both *dba_tablespaces* and *v$tablespace* views to indicate whether a particular tablespace is bigfile or smallfile:

```
SQL> select name, bigfile
     from v$tablespace;

NAME                           BIGFILE
------------------------------ -------
SYSTEM                         NO
UNDOTBS01                      NO
SYSAUX                         NO
TEMP                           NO
EXAMPLE                        NO
USERS                          NO
BIG_TBS                        YES
```

```
SQL> select tablespace_name,bigfile
     from   dba_tablespaces;

TABLESPACE_NAME                BIGFILE
------------------------------ ---------
SYSTEM                         SMALLFILE
UNDOTBS01                      SMALLFILE
SYSAUX                         SMALLFILE
TEMP                           SMALLFILE
EXAMPLE                        SMALLFILE
USERS                          SMALLFILE
BIG_TBS01                      BIGFILE
```

Examples

The following creates a database with default bigfile tablespace:

```
CREATE DATABASE GRID
SET DEFAULT BIGFILE TABLESPACE
DATAFILE '/u02/oradata/grid/system01.dbf' SIZE 500 M,
SYSAUX DATA FILE '/u02/oradata/grid/sysaux01.dbf' SIZE 500 M
DEFAULT TEMPORARY TABLESPACE tbs01
TEMPFILE '/u02/oradata/grid/temp01.dbf' SIZE 1024 M
UNDO TABLESPACE undo01
DATAFILE '/u02/oradata/grid/undo01.dbf' SIZE 1024 M;
```

The following shows how to move data between smallfile and bigfile tablespaces:

```
ALTER TABLE employee MOVE TABLESPACE bigfile_tbs;
```

The following shows how to create a BFT and change its size:

```
CREATE BIGFILE TABLESPACE user_tbs
DATAFILE '/u02/oradata/grid/user_tbs01.dbf' SIZE 1024 M;

ALTER TABLESPACE user_tbs RESIZE 10G;
```

In the previous release of Oracle server, K and M were used to specify storage size. In this DDL statement, a user can specify size in gigabytes and terabytes using G and T respectively.

The following example uses DBVERIFY utility with bigfile. With SFT, multiple instances of DBVERIFY can be run in parallel on multiple datafiles to speed up integrity checking for a tablespace. Integrity checking parallelism can be achieved with BFTs by starting multiple instances of DBVERIFY on parts of the single big file.

```
$dbv FILE=bigfile01.dbf  START=1 END=10000
$dbv FILE=bigfile01.dbf  START=10001

Note: START = Start Block; END = End Block
```

Data Pump Utilities

Data Pump is a new utility in Oracle 10g that enables very high-speed metadata and data loading and unloading from one database to another. The Data Pump Export and Import utilities are restartable and expdp and impdp have a similar look and feel to the original Export and Import utilities, exp and imp. However, they use a new mechanism that provides a dramatic increase in performance as well as new features and functions.

Data Pump Overview

The Oracle Data Pump utility – API is implemented through a PL/SQL package, *dbms_datapump*. The Data Pump makes use of the direct path load and the external table mechanisms for data movement.

The Major functional components of Data Pump are as follows:

- *dbms_datapump*: This package embodies the API for high-speed export and import utilities for bulk data and metadata movement.
- Direct Path API: This supports a stream interface in addition to its existing column array interface. Row data is read or written to dump file sets as a Direct Path API stream. The Direct Path API also minimizes data conversion and parsing at both unload and load time.

- *dbms_metadata*: This package is used by worker process for all metadata, database object definitions, loading and unloading. The metadata is extracted and written to the dump file set as XML documents rather than as SQL Data Definition Language (DDL) in the original export utility. The XML format brings great flexibility when creating the DDL during import time. For example, the DBA can easily change an object's ownership and default tablespace during an import operation. However, the XML format takes up more dump file space than DDL.

- External Table API: The Data Pump uses Direct Path API to load and unload when a table's structure allows it. However, when Direct Path API cannot be used, the Data Pump uses External Table API to move data. Oracle External Table API has two access drivers. The *oracle_loader* access driver provides external tables read-only access to SQL Loader compatible files. The *oracle_datapump* driver also provides external tables write and read access to data file set.

The Direct Path API is much faster than the External Table API. However, Direct Path does not support the following structures for loading and unloading data:

- Partitioned tables on which global index exists during a single-partition load.

- LOB column for which domain index exists.

- Clustered tables.

- Tables with active triggers.

- Tables with fine-grained access control enabled in insert and select modes.

- Table that contains BFILE or opaque type columns.

- Structures on which a referential integrity constraint is present.

- Table that contains VARRAY columns with an embedded opaque type.

The Figure 17.1 shows a broad outline of the utilities and components of Data Pump.

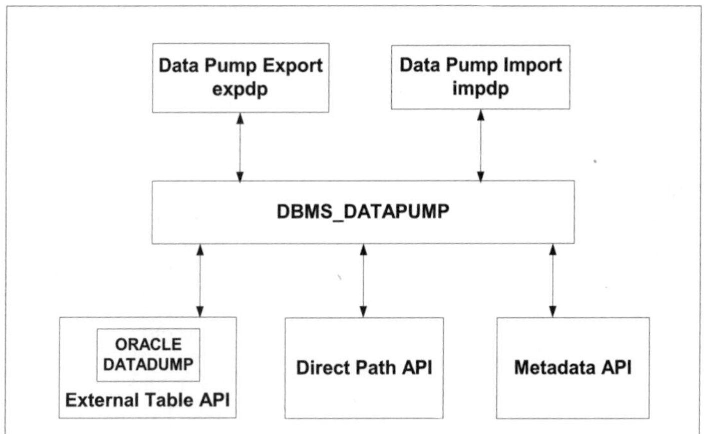

Figure 17.1: *Data Pump General Architecture*

The Master Table

At the heart of the Data Pump operation is the Master Table. This table is created at the beginning of a Data Pump operation and is dropped at the end of the successful completion of a Data Pump operation. The Master Table can also be dropped if the job is killed using the *kill_job* interactive command. If a job is stopped using the *stop_job* interactive command or if the job is terminated unexpectedly, the Master Table will be retained. The *keep_master* parameter can be set to Y to retain the Master Table at the end of a successful job for debugging purposes. The name of the Master Table is the same as the Data Pump job name and has the following columns:

```
SQL> desc SYS_ESTIMATE_SCHEMA_01
 Name                                      Null?    Type
 ----------------------------------------- -------- ----------------
 PROCESS_ORDER                                      NUMBER
```

```
DUPLICATE                                          NUMBER
DUMP_FILEID                                        NUMBER
DUMP_POSITION                                      NUMBER
DUMP_LENGTH                                        NUMBER
DUMP_ALLOCATION                                    NUMBER
COMPLETED_ROWS                                     NUMBER
ERROR_COUNT                                        NUMBER
ELAPSED_TIME                                       NUMBER
OBJECT_TYPE_PATH                                   VARCHAR2(200)
OBJECT_PATH_SEQNO                                  NUMBER
OBJECT_TYPE                                        VARCHAR2(30)
IN_PROGRESS                                        CHAR(1)
OBJECT_NAME                                        VARCHAR2(500)
OBJECT_SCHEMA                                      VARCHAR2(30)
PARTITION_NAME                                     VARCHAR2(30)
FLAGS                                              NUMBER
COMPLETION_TIME                                    DATE
OBJECT_TABLESPACE                                  VARCHAR2(30)
SIZE_ESTIMATE                                      NUMBER
OBJECT_ROW                                         NUMBER
PROCESSING_STATE                                   CHAR(1)
PROCESSING_STATUS                                  CHAR(1)
BASE_OBJECT_TYPE                                   VARCHAR2(30)
BASE_OBJECT_NAME                                   VARCHAR2(30)
BASE_OBJECT_SCHEMA                                 VARCHAR2(30)
PARALLELIZATION                                    NUMBER
UNLOAD_METHOD                                      NUMBER
GRANULES                                           NUMBER
SCN                                                NUMBER
DOMAIN_INDEX                                       VARCHAR2(30)
DOMAIN_INDEX_SCHEMA                                VARCHAR2(30)
GRANTOR                                            VARCHAR2(30)
NAME                                               VARCHAR2(30)
VALUE_T                                            VARCHAR2(4000)
VALUE_N                                            NUMBER
IS_DEFAULT                                         NUMBER
FILE_TYPE                                          NUMBER
USER_DIRECTORY                                     VARCHAR2(4000)
USER_FILE_NAME                                     VARCHAR2(4000)
FILE_NAME                                          VARCHAR2(4000)
EXTEND_SIZE                                        NUMBER
FILE_MAX_SIZE                                      NUMBER
EXTEND_ACTIVE                                      NUMBER
OVERFLOW_TO                                        NUMBER
PROCESS_NAME                                       VARCHAR2(30)
LAST_UPDATE                                        DATE
WORK_ITEM                                          VARCHAR2(30)
NON_TRANSACTIONAL                                  CHAR(1)
OBJECT_NUMBER                                      NUMBER
COMPLETED_BYTES                                    NUMBER
TOTAL_BYTES                                        NUMBER
METADATA_IO                                        NUMBER
DATA_IO                                            NUMBER
CUMULATIVE_TIME                                    NUMBER
OLD_VALUE                                          VARCHAR2(4000)
SEED                                               NUMBER
LAST_FILE                                          NUMBER
```

```
USER_NAME                                          VARCHAR2(30)
OPERATION                                          VARCHAR2(30)
JOB_MODE                                           VARCHAR2(30)
VERSION                                            NUMBER
DB_VERSION                                         VARCHAR2(30)
STATE                                              VARCHAR2(30)
PHASE                                              NUMBER
GUID                                               RAW(16)
START_TIME                                         DATE
BLOCK_SIZE                                         NUMBER
METADATA_BUFFER_SIZE                               NUMBER
DATA_BUFFER_SIZE                                   NUMBER
DEGREE                                             NUMBER
LANGUAGE                                           VARCHAR2(30)
PLATFORM                                           VARCHAR2(100)
ABORT_STEP                                         NUMBER
INSTANCE                                           VARCHAR2(16)
```

The Master Table is used to track the detailed progress information of a Data Pump job:

- The current set of dump files.
- The current state of every object exported or imported and their locations in the dump file set.
- The job's user-supplied parameters.
- The status of every worker process.
- The state of current job status and restart information.

The Master Table is created in the schema of the current user running the Pump Dump export or import, and it keeps tracks of lots of detailed information. As a result, this table can take up a significant amount of storage space.

> Tip: If an export or an import job is running on a database with a large number of database objects, make sure the schema user has sufficient tablespace quota.

The Master Table is the key to Data Pump's restart capability in the event of a planned or unplanned job stoppage.

Process Architecture

Data Pump has many processes through which the entire data load and unload methodology is conducted. Figure 17.2 shows all components and their interrelation.

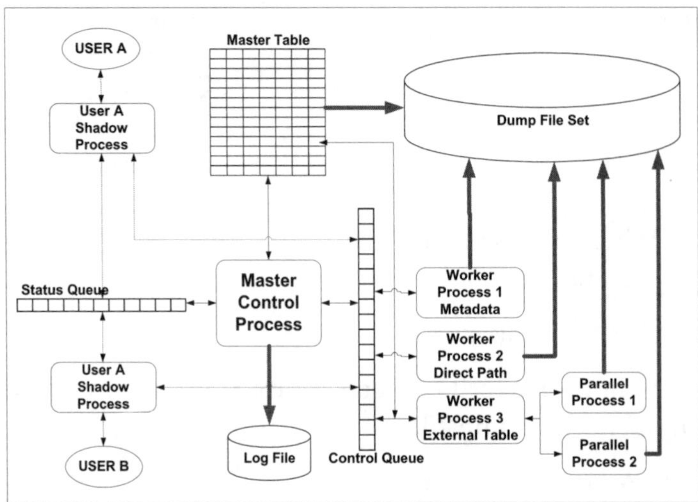

Figure 17.2: *Process architecture*

The following is a listing of some of the most important components:

- **Client Process**: This process, impdp or expdp, makes calls to the Data Pump API. After a Data Pump job is established, the client process is not required to keep the job running. Multiple clients can attach and detach from a job for the purpose of monitoring and control.
- **Shadow Process**: This is a foreground process that resides on the database server. This process is created when a client logs into the Oracle server. The shadow process creates a job, which primarily consists of creating the Master Table, creating the queues in Advanced Queues (AQ) used for

communication among the various processes, and creating the master control process. Once a job is running, the shadow process' main job is to check the job status for the client process. If the client process detaches, the shadow process goes away; however, the remaining Data Pump job processes are still active. Another client process can create a new shadow process and attach to the existing job.

- **Master Control Process**: This process controls the execution and sequencing of a Data Pump job. It mainly sits in a work dispatch loop during a job's execution and stays until the job is successfully completed. The master process has two main functions: to divide the loading and unloading of data and metadata tasks and handle the worker processes; and to manage the information in the Master Table and record job activities in the log file. The master control process maintains job state, job description, restart, and dump file set information in the Master Table.

- **Worker Process**: This process handles the request assigned by the master control process. The worker process is responsible for loading and unloading data and metadata. The number of worker processes needed can be defined by assigning a number to the parallel parameter. The worker process maintains the object rows and their current status, such as pending, completed, or failed, in the Master Table and maintains information about on what type of object, such as tables, indexes, or views, work is being done. This process can be used to stop or restart a job.

- **Parallel Query Process**: This process is used when the Data Pump chooses External Table API as the data access method for loading and unloading data. The worker process that uses the External Table API creates multiple parallel query processes for data movement, with the worker process acting as the query coordinator.

Advanced Queuing (AQ) Queue in the Data Pump

The Oracle Data Pump also features two AQ queues:

- **Status Queue**: The master control process writes to the status queue. This queue is mainly used for shadow processes to receive work in progress and error messages queued by the master control process.
- **Control Queue**: This queue enables communication among the various processes. All API commands, work requests, responses, file requests, and log messages are processed on this queue.

Data Pump Data Directory View

The following shows the data dictionary views related to the data pump.

- *dba_datapump_jobs* summarizes all active Data Pump jobs on the system.
- *user_datapump_job* summarizes the current user's active Data Pump jobs.
- *dba_datapump_sessions* displays all sessions currently attached to Data Pump jobs.
- *v$session_longops* displays each active Data Pump job and its progress.

Data Pump Export

Table 17.1 lists the new Data Pump export utility's commands and its comparable command in the original export utility.

DATA PUMP EXPORT	ORIGINAL EXPORT
ATTACH	
CONTENT=ALL	ROWS=Y

DATA PUMP EXPORT	ORIGINAL EXPORT
CONTENT=METADATA_ONLY	ROWS=N
CONTENT=DATA_ONLY	
DIRECTORY	
DUMPFILE	FILE
ESTIMATE	
ESTIMATE_ONLY	
EXCLUDE and INCLUDE	GRANTS, INDEXES, TRIGGERS, CONSTRAINTS
FILESIZE	FILESIZE
FLASHBACK_SCN	FLASHBACK_SCN, CONSISTENT OBJECT_CONSISTENT
FLASHBACK_TIME	FLASHBACK_TIME, CONSISTENT OBJECT_CONSISTENT
FULL	FULL
HELP	HELP
JOB_NAME	
KEEP_MASTER	
LOGFILE	LOG
NETWORK_LINK	
NOLOGFILE	
PARALLEL	
PARFILE	PARFILE
QUERY	
SCHEMAS	OWNER
STATUS	FEEDBACK
TABLES	TABLES
TABLESPACE	TABLESPACE
TRANSPORT_TABLESPACES	TRANSPORT_TABLESPACES
TRANSPORT_FULL_CHECK	TTS_FULL_CHECK
VERSION	

Table 17.1: *Datapump and Original Export Commands*

The following are descriptions of some of the new commands in Data Pump export:

- **ATTACH:** This attaches the client session to an existing export job and automatically places the user in an interactive-command mode. A job name does not have to be specified if there is only one running job associated with the schema. In order to attach a job other than one belonging to the user, the *exp_full_database* role must be granted.

The following is an example of how to use Oracle ATTACH during an export job:

```
$ expdp oracle/password attach

Export: Release 10.1.0.0.0 - 64bit Beta on Sun Sep 21 18:02:15
2003

(c) Copyright 2002 Oracle Corporation. All rights reserved.

Connected to: Oracle10i Enterprise Edition Release 10.1.0.0.0 -
64bit Beta
With the Partitioning, OLAP and Oracle Data Mining options

Job: SYS_ESTIMATE_SCHEMA_01
  Owner: ORACLE
  Operation: ESTIMATE
  Creator Privs: FALSE
  GUID: C7E1A01B0E3F2229E03400000E25041D
  Start Time: Sunday, 21 September, 2003 6:01
  Mode: SCHEMA
  Instance: grid
  MaxDegree: 1
  EXPORT Job Parameters:

Job: SYS_ESTIMATE_SCHEMA_01
  Operation: ESTIMATE
  Mode: SCHEMA
  State: COMPLETING
  Percent Done: 100
  Degree: 1
  Job Error Count: 0

Worker 1 Status:
  State: WORK WAITING
```

- **CONTENT:** This specifies what export unloads. The default value is ALL, which is equivalent to the old export utility's ROWS=Y. This option allows unloading of both data and metadata. If the option is set to METADATA, which is equivalent to ROWS=N in the old export utility, only object definitions will be exported. Now, *data_only* can be used to specify to unload table row data only without unloading database object definitions.

- **DIRECTORY:** Unlike the previous export utility, a default database directory in which to place dump file set and log file must be specified before performing any export or import operation. Failure to create a directory before performing an export will result in an error as shown below:

```
$ /dba/oracle/admin/grid/pfile :) expdp

Export: Release 10.1.0.0.0 - 64bit Beta on Sun Sep 14 17:09:00
2003

(c) Copyright 2002 Oracle Corporation. All rights reserved.

Username: oracle
Password:

Connected to: Oracle10i Enterprise Edition Release 10.1.0.0.0 -
64bit Beta
With the Partitioning, OLAP and Oracle Data Mining options
ORA-39002: invalid operation
ORA-39070: Unable to open the log file.
ORA-39087: directory name DPUMP_DIR is invalid
```

The following steps must be taken to prepare the directory:

```
Grant "create any directory" privilege to  the export/import
administrator.
SQL> grant create any directory to dliu;

Grant succeeded.

Create a directory for dump file set and log file.
SQL> create directory dpump_dir as '/dba/export/grid';

Directory created.
```

- **ESTIMATE:** This specifies whether or not export should estimate how much disk space the export job consumes in bytes. The estimated size is displayed in the log file and on the client's output screen. The estimate is only for table row data; it does not include metadata.

Valid values for this parameter are:

- **BLOCKS:** The estimate is calculated by multiplying the number of database blocks used by the target objects by the appropriate block size. This is the default value.
- **SAMPLING:** The estimate is calculated by sampling a fixed number of rows per table.
- **STATISTICS:** The estimate is calculated by using each table's statistics from the most recent analysis.
- When *estimate_only*=Y, the export estimates the space that would be consumed, but no data is actually exported. The default value is N. The following is an example of an export using estimate_only=Y:

```
$ expdp oracle/passwd estimate_only=y

Export: Release 10.1.0.0.0 - 64bit Beta on Sun Sep 21
18:00:59 2003

(c) Copyright 2002 Oracle Corporation. All rights reserved.

Connected to: Oracle10i Enterprise Edition Release 10.1.0.0.0
- 64bit Beta
With the Partitioning, OLAP and Oracle Data Mining options
Starting "ORACLE"."SYS_ESTIMATE_SCHEMA_01":   estimate_only=y
Estimate in progress using BLOCKS method...
Processing object type SCHEMA_EXPORT/TABLE/TABLE_DATA
.  estimated "ORACLE"."PLAN_TABLE"                        64 KB
.  estimated "ORACLE"."TEST"                              64 KB
Total estimation using BLOCKS method: 128 KB
Job "ORACLE"."SYS_ESTIMATE_SCHEMA_01" successfully completed
```

- **EXCLUDE:** This allows fine-grained specification of objects and object types that are to be excluded from the export operation. The default value is NONE. The *exclude* and *include* parameters are mutually exclusive.

  The following are some examples of how to use the exclude option:

  - **EXCLUDE=CONSTRAINT** will exclude all (non-referential) constraints except for NOT NULL constraints.

- **EXCLUDE=GRANT** will exclude object grants on all object types and system privilege grants.
- **EXCLUDE=USER** will exclude only the definitions of users, not the objects contained within the user's schemas.
- **EXCLUDE=SCHEMA:"='HR'"** will exclude a specific user HR and all of the HR schema's objects.
- **EXCLUDE=PACKAGE, FUNCTION, PROCEDURE** will exclude all packages, functions, and procedures associated with this export.

- *flashback_scn*: This specifies the system change number (SCN) that the export uses to enable the Flashback utility. The export operation is performed with data that is consistent as of this SCN.
- *flashback_time*: This will use a SCN that is most closely matched to the specified time to enable the Flashback utility. The export operation is performed with data that is consistent as of this SCN.
- *include:* This allows the fine-grained specification of objects and object types that are to be included in the export operation. The *include* and *exclude* parameter are mutually exclusive.

TIP: Either INCLUDE or EXCLUDE can be used with CONTENT=DATA_ONLY, which implies access to table rows only.

The following is an example of a parameter file for an export operation that only includes views and procedures for schemas HR and OE:

```
SCHEMAS=HR, OE
INCLUDE=VIEWS
INCLUDE=PROCEDURE
```

- *job_name*: This is used to identify the export job in subsequent actions such as when the ATTACH parameter is used to attach a job. There is a previous example for ATTACH. The job name can be up to 30 characters. In the default system-generated name, *SYS_<operation>_<mode>_NN, <operation>* is the type of export operations, such as EXPORT, EXTIMATE, and so on, <mode> can be FULL, SCHEMAS, TABLESPACES, *transport_tablespaces* or TABLES, and NN is a two-digit monotonically increasing integer start at 01.

  Here are two examples of system generated job names:

  - SYS_EXPORT_SCHEMA_01
  - SYS_ESTIMATE_FULL_02

- *keep_master*: A Master Table is created at the beginning of an export operation. At successful completion of the export job, this table is written to the dump file set and then dropped. If *keep_master*=Y, the Master Table will not be dropped at the end of the job. This is useful for debugging purposes.

- *network_link*: When this parameter is set to Y, it enables a network export via a valid database link. The data moves from a remote database to a dump file set.

- *nologfile*: When this parameter is set to Y, no log file will be written out. The default is N.

- *parallel*: This parameter specifies the maximum number of threads of active execution servers operating on behalf of the export job. The default value is 1. This execution set is comprised of a combination of worker processes and parallel slave processes. The Master Control process and worker processes acting as query coordinators in parallel query operations do not count towards this total.

Tip: The value specified for parallel should be at least as large as the number of output files specified with the *dumpfile* parameter.

- *schemas*: This parameter defaults to the current user's schema. If a user has the *exp_full_database* privilege, a list of schemas can be specified for an export.
- *status* – This parameter specifies how frequently detailed progress information should be written to the client's output terminal (the default value is 0). You can also use status in interactive mode to check the status of a job, as follows:

```
Export> status

Job: SYS_ESTIMATE_SCHEMA_01
  Operation: ESTIMATE
  Mode: SCHEMA
  State: COMPLETING
  Percent Done: 100
  Degree: 1
  Job Error Count: 0

Worker 1 Status:
  State: WORK WAITING
```

- *transport_full_check*: When it is set to Y, this parameter verifies that there are no dependencies between those objects inside the transportable set and those outside the transportable set. The default value is N.
- *version*: This specifies the version of Oracle database to which only compatible database objects are to be exported.

Data Pump Import

The following Table 17.2 lists the new Data Pump import utility's commands and its comparable command in the original import utility.

DATA PUMP IMPORT	ORIGINAL IMPORT
ATTACH	
CONTENT=ALL	ROWS=Y
CONTENT=METADATA_ONLY	ROWS=N
CONTENT=DATA_ONLY	
DIRECTORY	
DUMPFILE	FILE

DATA PUMP IMPORT	ORIGINAL IMPORT
ESTIMATE	
EXCLUDE and INCLUDE	GRANTS, INDEXES, TRIGGERS, CONSTRAINTS
FLASHBACK_SCN	
FLASHBACK_TIME	
FULL	FULL
HELP	HELP
JOB_NAME	
KEEP_MASTER	
LOGFILE	LOG
NETWORK_LINK	
NOLOGFILE	
PARALLEL	
PARFILE	PARFILE
QUERY	
REMAP_DATAFILE	
REMAP_SCHEMA	TOUSER
REMAP_TABLESPACE	
REUSE_DATAFILES	DESTROY
SCHEMAS	FROMUSER
SKIP_UNUSABLE_INDEXES	SKIP_UNUSABLE_INDEXES
SQLFILE	INDEXFILE, SHOW
STATUS	FEEDBACK
TABLES	TABLES
TABLE_EXISTS_ACTION	IGNORE
TABLESPACE	TABLESPACE
TRANSPORT_DATAFILES	DATAFILE
TRANSPORT_TABLESPACES	TRANSPORT_TABLESPACES
TRANSPORT_FULL_CHECK	TTS_FULL_CHECK
VERSION	

Table 17.2: *Datapump and Original Import Commands*

New Parameters for Data Pump Import

The following are descriptions of some of the new commands in Data Pump import:

- *flashback_scn*: This specifies the system change number (SCN) that import uses to enable the Flashback utility. The import operation is performed with data that is consistent as of this SCN. This parameter is only relevant when importing through a database link.
- *flashback_time*: This will use a SCN that is most closely matched to the specified time to enable the Flashback utility. The import operation is performed with data that is consistent as of this SCN. This parameter is only relevant when importing through a database link.
- *query*: This allows the filtering of data that is imported by applying a query to SELECT statements executed on the source system.
- *network_link*: This specifies a database link to the source database and enables import's network mode. This parameter is required if any of the following parameters are specified:
  - *flashback_scn*
  - *flashback_time*
  - *estimate*
  - *transport_tablespace*
  - *query*
- *remap_datafile*: This changes the name of the source datafile to the target datafile name in all DDL statements in which the source datafile is referenced. This is useful when performing database migration to another system with different file naming conventions.

- *remap_schema*: This replaces the FROMUSER and TOUSER parameters in the original import utility, and loads all objects from the source schema into the destination schema (the default for this parameter is NONE).

- *remap_tablespace*: It re-maps all objects selected for import with persistent data in the source tablespace to be created in the destination tablespace on the target system. This is very useful when the DBA wants to change the default tablespace for a user.

- *reuse_datafiles*: If the datafile specified in the CREATE TABLESPACE statement already exists and the value of this parameter is set to N, which is the default, an error message is issued. However, the import job will continue. If the value is set to Y, a warning message is issued and the existing datafile is reinitialized. However, this may result in a loss of data.

- *schemas*: This specifies a list of schemas to import. The schemas themselves are first created, including system and object grants, password history, and so on. Then all objects contained within the schemas are imported. Non-privileged users can specify only their own schemas and no information about the schema definition is imported.

- *sqlfile*: This specifies a file that will capture all the SQL DDL that the Import utility will be executing based on other parameters. The SQL statement is not executed, and the target database remains unchanged. The new SQL file can first be edited with modifications and then run on the target database. This is similar to the method used in the original export and import utilities in which export is run with ROWS=N and then import is run with SHOW=Y.

- *table_exists_action*: This instructs the import utility on what to do if the table it is trying to import already exists. This parameter is similar to the IGNORE parameter in the original import utility, yet it has more options as follows:

- **SKIP:** This leaves the table unchanged and moves on to the next table. SKIP is the default value.
- **APPEND:** This appends new rows from the source to the existing table.
- **TRUNCATE:** This deletes existing rows and then loads the row from the source.
- **REPLACE:** This drops the existing table, creates the new table according to the source table definition, then loads the source data.

When using APPEND or TRUNCATE, checks are made to ensure that rows from the source are compatible with the existing table prior to performing any action.

Original Import Utility Parameter

Some of the parameters in the original import utility are no longer needed because the new Data Pump import utility takes care of them automatically. Those parameters are: *buffer, charset, commit, compile , filesize, recordlength, resumable , resumable_name, resumable_timeout, statistics, toid_novalidate, tts_owners, userid, volsize.*

The following examples illustrate how the import can be accomplished now:

Example 1: Import User into a Different Schema

```
impdp system/manager \
SCHEMAS=usr01 \
REMAP_SCHEMA=usr01:usr02 \
DUMPFILE=dpump_dir:usr01.dmp \
EXCLUDE=index, materialized_view \
TABLE_EXISTS_ACTION=replace \
logfile=dpump_dir:impusr.log
```

Example 2: Import with Data Option

```
impdp system/manager \
TABLES=hr.jobs,hr.job_history \
CONTENT=data_only \
DUMPFILE= dpump_dir:table.dmp \
NOLOGFILE=y
```

New Scheduler Utilities

Oracle 10g provides a new package, *dbms_scheduler*, which has a number of functions and procedures. Collectively, these functions are called the Scheduler. The Scheduler provides rich functionality to meet the needs of complex enterprise scheduling in a grid environment. It helps database administrators and application developers simplify their management tasks.

Scheduler Components

The Scheduler has the following components:

- **Schedule**: This specifies when and how many times a job is executed.
- **Program**: This is a collection of metadata about what is run by the schedule. A program can be a PL/SQL procedure, an executable C program, a Shell script, or a java application, and so on. A list of arguments can be specified for a program.
- **Job**: This specifies what program needs to execute and at what time or schedule. A job class defines a category of jobs that share common resource usage requirements and other characteristics.
- **Window**: A window is represented by an interval of time with a well defined beginning and end. It is used to activate different resource plans at different times. A window group represents a list of windows.

Create, Enable, Disable, and Drop a Program

The *dbms_scheduler.create_program* procedure can be used to create a program. As mentioned previously, a program is a collection of metadata about what is to be run by the Scheduler. To create a program using *dbms_scheduler* is really just to register a program with the Scheduler.

The syntax for creating a program using the Scheduler is as follows:

```
DBMS_SCHEDULER.CREATE_PROGRAM
(
 Program_name              in varchar2,
 Program_type              in varchar2,
 Program_action            in varchar2,
 Number_of_auguments       in pls_integer default 0,
 Enable                    in Boolean default false,
 Comments                  invarchar2 default null
);
```

The *program_type* parameter includes the following values:

- *plsql_block*
- *stored_procedure*
- *executable*

To create a program in the user's own schema, the CREATE JOB privilege must be assigned. To create a program in another user's schema, the CREATE ANY JOB privilege must be assigned. When a program is created, it is created in a disabled state by default; a job cannot execute a program until the program is enabled.

The following is an example of creating a program to check database user sessions:

```
BEGIN
DBMS_SCHEDULER.CREATE_PROGRAM
(
```

```
 program_name   => `CHECK_USER`,
 program_action => `/dba/scripts/ckuser.sh`,
 program_type   => `EXECUTABLE`
);
END;
/
```

This program can be enabled as follows:

```
execute DBMS_SCHEDULER.ENABLE (`check_user`);
```

This program can be disabled as follows:

```
execute DBMS_SCHEDULER.DISABLE ('check_user');
```

In addition, this program can be dropped as follows. If force is set to TRUE, all jobs referencing the program are disabled before dropping the program:

```
BEGIN
DBMS_SCHEDULER.DROP_PROGRAM
(
 program_name => 'check_user',
 force        =>  FALSE
);
END;
/
```

Create and Drop a Schedule

The *create_schedule* procedure can be used to create a schedule for the job by using the following syntax:

```
DBMS_SCHEDULER.CREATE_SCHEDULE
(
 schedule_name      in varchar2,
 start_date         in timestamp with timezone default null,
 repeat_interval    in varchar2,
 end_date           in timestamp with timezone default null,
 comments           in varchar2 default null
);
```

In this procedure, *start_date* specifies the date on which the schedule becomes active, and *end_date* specifies that the schedule becomes inactive after the specified date. *repeat_interval* is an expression using either the calendar syntax or PL/SQL syntax, which tells how often a job should be repeated.

The *repeat_interval* calendaring expression has three parts.

The Frequency clause is made of the following elements

- YEARLY
- MONTHLY
- WEEKLY
- DAILY
- HOURLY
- MINUTELY
- SECONDLY

The repeat interval range is from 1 to 99.

The other Frequency clause is made of the following elements:

- BYMONTH
- BYWEEKNO
- BYYEARDAY
- BYMONTHDAY
- BYDAY
- BYHOUR
- BYMINUTE
- BYSECOND

The following are some examples of the use of calendaring expressions:

Every March and June of the year:

```
REPEAT_INTERVAL=> `FREQ=YEARLY; BYMONTH=3,6`
```

Every 20th day of the month:

```
REPEAT_INTERVAL=> `FREQ=MONTHLY; BYMONTHDAY=20`
```

Every Sunday of the week:

```
REPEAT_INTERVAL=> `FREQ=WEEKLY; BYDAY=SUN`
```

Every 60 days:

```
REPEAT_INTERVAL=> `FREQ=DAILY; INTERVAL=60`
```

Every 6 hours:

```
REPEAT_INTERVAL=> `FREQ=HOURLY; INTERVAL=6`
```

Every 10 minutes:

```
REPEAT_INTERVAL=> `FREQ=MINUTELY;INTERVAL=10`
```

Every 30 seconds:

```
REPEAT_INTERVAL=> `FREQ=SECONDLY;INTERVAL=30`
```

The following are some examples of using PL/SQL expressions:

```
REPEAT_INTERVAL=> `SYSDATE -1`
REPERT_INTERVAL=> `SYSDATE + 36/24`
```

The following steps are used to create a schedule:

```
BEGIN
DBMS_SCHEDULER.CREATE_SCHEDULE
(
 schedule_name      => `HOURLY_SCHEDULE`,
 start_date         => `TRUNC(SYSDATE)+23/24`
 repeat_interval    => `FREQ=HOURLY; INTERVAL=1`
);
END;
/
```

A schedule can be dropped by performing the following steps:

```
BEGIN
DBMS_SCHEDULER.DROP_SCHEDULE
(
 schedule_name      => `HOURLY_SCHEDULE`,
```

```
 force               =>  FALSE
);
END;
/
```

Create, Run, Stop, Copy, and Drop a Job

Like Program, when a Job is created, it is disabled by default. A Job must be specifically enabled so it will become active and scheduled.

A job can be created with the following four formats:

- With Program, With Schedule
- With Program, Without Schedule
- Without Program, With Schedule
- Without Program, Without Schedule

Example 1:

The following can be used to create a job using a predefined Program and Schedule:

```
BEGIN
DBMS_SCHEDULER.CREATE_JOB
(
 job_name           => `BACKUP_JOB_01`,
 program_name       => `BACKUP_PROGRAM`,
 schedule_name      => `BACKUP_SCHEDULE`);
END;
/
```

Example 2:

The following can be used to create a job using a predefined Program without a predefined Schedule:

```
BEGIN
DBMS_SCHEDULER.CREATE_JOB
(
 job_name           => `BACKUP_JOB_02`,
 program_name       => `BACKUP_PROGRAM`,
```

```
 start_date          => `TRUNC(SYSDATE)+23/24`,
 repeat_interval     => `FREQ=WEEKLY; BYDAY=SUN` );
END;
/
```

Example 3:

The following can be used to create a job using a predefined Schedule without a predefined Program:

```
BEGIN
DBMS_SCHEDULER.CREATE_JOB
(
 job_name            => `BACKUP_JOB_03`,
 schedule_name       => `BACKUP_SCHEDULE`,
 job_type            => `EXECUTABLE`,
 job_action          => `/dba/scripts/weekly_backup.sh`
);
END;
/
```

Example 4:

The following can be used to create a job without a predefined Program and Schedule:

```
BEGIN
DBMS_SCHEDULER.CREATE_JOB
(
 job_name            => `BACKUP_JOB_04`,
 job_type            => `EXECUTABLE`,
 job_action          => `/dba/scripts/weekly_backup.sh`,
 start_date          => `TRUNC(SYSDATE)+23/24`
 repeat_interval     => `FREQ=WEEKLY; BYDAY=SUN`
);
END;
/
```

The following is the syntax to run, stop, copy, and drop a job:

```
DBMS_SCHEDULER.RUN_JOB
(  job_name          in varchar2 );
DBMS_SCHEDULER.STOP_JOB
( job_name           in varchar2,
 force               in Boolean default false );
```

The *copy_job* procedure copies all attributes of an existing job to a new job.

```
DBMS_SCHEDULER.COPY_JOB
(
 old_job            in varchar2,
 new_job            in varchar2);

DBMS_SCHEDULER.DROP_JOB
(
 job_name           in varchar2,
 force              in Boolean default false
);
```

Create Job Class

A Job Class defines a category of jobs that share common resource usage requirements. A Job Class is associated with two attributes: the resource consumer group, which defines a set of user sessions that have common resource processing requirements; and a database service name, which defines the instance to which the job class belongs. Each job belongs to a single job class at any given time. By associating a Job with a Job Class, the amount of resources a Job can use during its execution can be managed.

The syntax to create a Job Class is:

```
DBMS_SCHEDULER.CREATE_JOB_CLASS
(
 job_class_name             in varchar2,
 resource_consumer_group    in varchar2 default null,
 service                    in varchar2 default null,
 log_purge_policy           in varchar2 default null,
 comments                   in varchar2 default null
);
```

By default, the Scheduler log table entries are not purged. The *log_purge_policy* defines the policy for purging the log table entries.

Data Dictionary Views

The following SQL script provides a list of data dictionary views used to monitor the Scheduler's activities:

```
SQL> select table_name, comments
  2 from   dict
  3 where table_name like 'DBA%SCHEDULER%'
  4 order by table_name;
```

Oracle Streams

In a Grid Environment, different sets of user applications access a variety of the databases, sometimes located locally and sometimes situated at a remote location. Instead of going for remote database access, processing of the same data at a locally situated database server makes much more sense in terms of logistics and performance. Instead of accessing or sharing a remote database, maintenance of a local data copy becomes more desirable. Oracle Streams helps to replicate or to duplicate the databases to different locations.

Oracle Streams provides a comprehensive and integrated framework for data and information sharing. It combines the replication of data, messaging queues, event management, data loading and notification mechanism into one integrated product and methodology. Oracle Streams helps in setting up and synchronizing multiple data sources within the grid environment very efficiently. The data movements can be real time or scheduled as needed. The changes are captured by way of redo log hot mining and then are propagated to the destination database. Oracle Streams is a key component in creating and maintaining multiple data sources with in the grid.

Streams Overview

Oracle Streams is an enabling technology for data sharing. Data sharing among the different databases and among different application environments is a very common practice. A variety of measures, such as data replication, data loading, data movement to heterogeneous database environments and message routing, involve some sort of data sharing. Even building the summarized data, such as data warehousing, is another form of data sharing.

Oracle Streams is a method to control and conduct the data flow. It is a vital component in maintaining the Grid Framework.

Typically, the changes in a database are captured by the Capture Process and are then routed or propagated to a destination database. At the destination database, the Apply Process applies the changes. The method of Streams can also create or capture events and then stage and send the events to different destinations. Figure 17.3 shows a typical data flow.

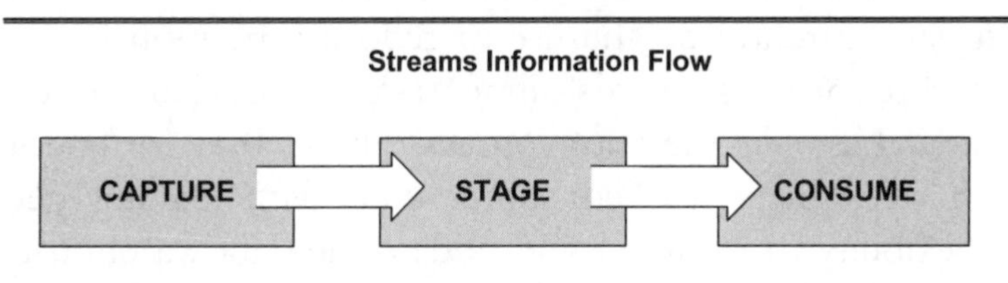

Figure 17.3: Streams Data Flow

Thus, the Streams Methodology allows users to enqueue messages, propagate messages to subscribing queues, and dequeue messages. When the Streams method is utilized for data replication, it captures the DML and DDL changes made to the database objects and then replicates those changes to one or more destination databases, the so called consumers or subscribers.

When applied to the event management and notification mechanism, the Streams Methodology provides a powerful communication infrastructure. Applications can enqueue an event explicitly or a database event can be captured implicitly. Such events, being dequeued at a destination environment, may very well serve as a notification mechanism. For instance, events pushed to a queue may be dequeued by a messaging application and then used to generate e-mail notification or a wireless message, based on the type of event content.

Maintaining a data warehouse involves periodic data refreshing and summarizing or analyzing loads of data. Operational data is fed into a data warehouse by a typical Extract, Transform, and Load (ETL) mechanism.

Streams-based feed mechanisms can capture the necessary data changes from the operational database and send it to the destination data warehouse. The use of redo information by the Streams capture process avoids unnecessary overhead on the production database. As the apply process allows transformation or selection of data at the consumer end, data loading gets additional flexibility to reformat and update the data warehouses with the received information.

Another allied utility is data protection. Streams-based data movement can easily feed a remote database with change information from the production database in order to audit all sorts of changes.

The facility of Streams was introduced in Oracle Database 9i release 9.2, and now in Oracle Database 10g, it has been measurably enhanced. The following section will examine these improvements and the new features in detail.

Managing Grid Using Grid Control (OEM)

Grid Control is utility that manages, monitors many diverse resources with in the enterprise grid. Such resources include, Database Systems, Hosts (blades/servers), application servers, web applications and storage devices. It is also extensible, so that extra components that are not supported out of the box can be added. From a single place, Grid control allows the comparison of performance levels of various comparable resources.

Grid Control can do the day-to-day management or administration on all these controlled resources. As the performance metrics are analyzed in a certain time frames, the inter-relations between the related resources can be easily understood, which leads to better problem solutions. More details on using the Grid Control Utility in the chapter in this book on Using Grid Control Utility.

Oracle Resource Manager

Database Resource Manager (DRM) provides the resource management facilities. In a database instance, which is highly active and concurrently accessed by large numbers of users, control of suitable resource allocation is essential. In the absence of a better resource control, some critical and high priority sessions or tasks may not get required resources in time. Oracle DRM is a framework that provides a mechanism to control the resource allocation.

The DRM helps to allocate a percentage of CPU time to different users, user groups, and applications. It can limit the parallelism of operation by allowing other competing processes to get their share of resources. It also can create resource pools, such as the undo pool and the active session pool that help control the execution resource availability for a group of sessions.

Components of DRM

There are three main components with which the DBA can define and manage resource allocation. They are:

- Resource Consumer Group: These are the named entities, which are groups of users or sessions combined together, based on their processing and resource needs.
- Resource Plan: Contains the directives that specify how the resources are allocated to the resource consumer groups.
- Resource Plan Directive: These are used to associate resource consumer groups with particular resource plans and allocate resources among the resource consumer groups.

The Oracle package *dbms_resource_manager* is used to create and maintain the resource plans and manage the resource consumer groups.

Resource and Plan Directives

The resource plan can be a single-level resource plan or it can be a multi-level resource plan. In a single-level resource plan, the resources are allocated among the associated resource groups. For example, the *policy_rec* plan allocates CPU resources among the three consumer groups viz., claims, sales, and legal. The resource group claims gets 55% of CPU time, sales gets 25%, and legal receives 20% of CPU time.

In a multi-level resource plan, sub-plans represent a hierarchy of plans and their associated resource groups. The *policy_rec* provides for two sub-plans, sales and claims, and one resource group named legal. The claims sub-plan allocates 60% of CPU time to the resource group called LIFE and 40% to the group called AUTO. The sales sub-plan allocates 70% of CPU time to the resource group called NEWSALES and 30% to the group called MARKET.

The resource plan directives specify how the resources are allocated to resource consumer groups. There are many resources involved in the database activity, which can be controlled by DRM. The resources include CPU availability for the competing resource groups, the number of simultaneous active sessions allowed within a consumer group, the degree of parallelism, the execution time limit, and the undo pool.

Procedure to implement and manage

To administer the DRM, Oracle has provided many procedures available through the package *dbms_resource_manager*. This section gives a brief overview of the steps involved in implementing the database resource management.

To create a simple single-level resource plan with specified allocation methods, use *create_simple_plan* will typically be used and resource groups assigned.

In order to create a complex or multi-level plan, the following stages will be implemented.

- Create a Pending Area for creating plan schemas. The procedure *create_pending_area* will be used.
- Create Resource Plans using the procedure *create_plan*.
- Create Consumer Resource Groups using the procedure *create_consumer_group*.
- Specify the Resource Plan directives using the procedure *create_plan_directive*.

Once the resource plans and resource consumer groups are defined and validated, they are submitted to make them active.

Before using the DRM facility, resource groups have to be assigned to the users or schemas. In earlier versions, until the 9i release, the consumer resource groups were manually assigned users. It was also possible to switch a user session to another resource group by using the procedures available in the *dbms_resource_manager* package.

These procedures are as follows:

- The user's initial consumer group is automatically set to *default_consumer_group* when the user is created.
- The *set_initial_consumer_group* procedure can be used to switch to a specific consumer group.
- The *switch_current_consumer_group* can be used to change the current resource consumer group of a user's current session.
- The procedure *switch_consummer_group_for_sess* causes the specified session to immediately be moved into the specified resource consumer group.
- *switch_consumer_group_for_user* can be used to change the resource consumer group for all sessions with a given user name.

Now, with the release of 10g, there are more options for assigning the resource groups to the sessions automatically. With the new features available in 10g, it now becomes possible to configure DRM to automatically assign the consumer groups to sessions. Creating mappings between the session attributes and consumer groups does this. It is also possible to prioritize these mappings and create precedence in the event of conflicts.

There are basically two types of session attributes that control the assignment of the resource group: login attributes and run-time attributes. The login attributes are evaluated at the time of session login, based on their appropriate resource group as assigned to the session. A session that is already up and running can be assigned to a different resource consumer group. Both these changes take place automatically. This provision of automatic mapping provides better control of resource usage and changes can be effected without the intervention of the administrators. It becomes possible to embed the directives in the application code itself. Based on the application needs, type of client program, operating system user level, and the client machine, the resource groups can be assigned and re-assigned.

There is a new procedure called *set_group_mapping* within the *dbms_resource_manager* that helps to map the session attributes to a consumer group. These attributes are of two types: login attributes and runtime attributes.

Conclusion

This chapter has examined the features and technologies Oracle is implementing in order to enable the Grid Architecture. 10g Database with its due emphasis on Grid Integration, has built in many new features.

Oracle has introduced many data movement utilities data pump and also introduced the enterprise grade job scheduler. With these utilities, data sharing becomes very flexible and easy. Data Sharing among many diversified systems within a Grid Environment is a very vital function. Oracle Streams and Transportable Tablespace are very useful tools for the data grid realization.

The Grid Utility is another important introduction to manage the Grid Resources.

Index

C

D

E

F

G

H

I

N

O

P

T

U

V

W

About Mike Ault

Mike Ault is one of the leading names in Oracle technology. The author of more than 20 Oracle books and hundreds of articles in national publications, Mike Ault has five Oracle Masters Certificates and was the first popular Oracle author with his landmark book "Oracle7 Administration and Management". Mike also wrote several of the "Exam Cram" books, and enjoys a reputation as a leading author and Oracle consultant.

Mike started working with computers in 1979 right out of a stint in the Nuclear Navy. He began working with Oracle in 1990 and has since become a World Renowned Oracle expert. Mike is currently a Senior Technical Management Consultant and has two wonderful daughters. Mike is kept out of trouble by his wife of 29 years, Susan.

About Madhu Tumma

Madhu Tumma has been working as a Software Developer, IT Manager, Database Administrator, and Technical Consultant for about 18 years. He has worked on a wide variety of projects and environments ranging from mainframe, client-server, eBusiness to managed services. He has provided consultancy to a variety of clients on database clusters, business continuity and high availability solutions. His experience ranges across multiple relational database systems. Madhu is a frequent speaker at Oracle World and IOUG where he presents many technical papers. Madhu has a Master's Degree in Science and attended a Business Management graduate program. He lives in New Jersey with his wife Hema and two children Sandi and Sudeep.